at Global Knowledge Certification Press

MCSD CERTIFICATION REQUIREMENTS

CORE EXAMS (3 REQUIRED)

SOLUTION ARCHITECTURE (REQUIRED):

Exam 70-100: Analyzing Requirements and Defining Solution Architectures

DESKTOP APPLICATIONS DEVELOPMENT (1 REQUIRED):

Exam 70-016*: Designing and Implementing Desktop Applications with Microsoft® Visual C++® 6.0

Exam 70-156*: Designing and Implementing Desktop Applications with Microsoft® Visual FoxPro® 6.0

Exam 70-176*: Designing and Implementing Desktop Applications with Microsoft® Visual Basic® 6.0

DISTRIBUTED APPLICATIONS DEVELOPMENT (1 REQUIRED):

Exam 70-015*: Designing and Implementing Distributed Applications with Microsoft® Visual C++® 6.0

Exam 70-155*: Designing and Implementing Distributed Applications with Microsoft® Visual FoxPro® 6.0

Exam 70-175*: Designing and Implementing Distributed Applications with Microsoft® Visual Basic® 6.0

ELECTIVE EXAMS (1 REQUIRED):

Exam 70-015*: Designing and Implementing Distributed Applications with Microsoft® Visual C++® 6.0

Exam 70-016*: Designing and Implementing Desktop Applications with Microsoft® Visual C++® 6.0

Exam 70-019: Designing and Implementing Data Warehouses with Microsoft® SQL Server™ 7.0

Exam 70-024: Developing Applications with C++ Using the Microsoft® Foundation Class Library

Exam 70-025: Implementing OLE in Microsoft® Foundation Class Applications

Exam 70-027: Implementing a Database Design on Microsoft® SQL Server™ 6.5

Exam 70-029: Designing and Implementing Databases with Microsoft® SQL Server™ 7.0

Exam 70-055: Designing and Implementing Web Sites with Microsoft® FrontPage® 98

Exam 70-057: Designing and Implementing Commerce Solutions with Microsoft® Site Server 3.0, Commerce Edition

Exam 70-069: Application Development with Microsoft® Access for Windows® 95 and the Microsoft® Access Developer's Toolkit

Exam 70-091: Designing and Implementing Solutions with Microsoft® Office 2000 and Microsoft® Visual Basic® for Applications

Exam 70-152: Designing and Implementing Web Solutions with Microsoft® V

Exam 70-175*: Designing and Implementing Distributed Applications with M

Exam 70-176*: Designing and Implementing Desktop Applications with Micr

★ These core exams may be used as electives, but only count once towards c

MICROSOFT CERTIFIED SOLUTION DEVELOPER

MCSD Visual C++

Distributed Applications

Study Guide

(Exam 70-015)

Syngress Media, Inc.

Osborne/McGraw-Hill

Berkeley New York St. Louis San Francisco Auckland Bogotá Hamburg London Madrid Mexico City
Milan Montreal New Delhi Panama City Paris São Paulo Singapore Sydney Tokyo Toronto

Osborne/McGraw-Hill
2600 Tenth Street
Berkeley, California 94710
U.S.A.

For information on translations or book distributors outside the U.S.A., or to arrange bulk purchase discounts for sales promotions, premiums, or fund-raisers, please contact Osborne/**McGraw-Hill** at the above address.

MCSD Visual C++ Distributed Applications Study Guide (Exam 70-015)

1234567890 DOC DOC 019876543210

Book p/n 0-07-212135-1   and   CD p/n 0-07-212136-X
parts of
ISBN 0-07-212137-8

Publisher	Project Editors	Indexer
Brandon A. Nordin	Julie Smalley	Valerie Robbins
	Janet Walden	
Associate Publisher and		**Computer Designers**
Editor-in-Chief	**Acquisitions Coordinator**	Jani Beckwith
Scott Rogers	Tara Davis	Gary Corrigan
		Elizabeth Jang
Acquisitions Editor	**Series Editor**	Dick Schwartz
Gareth Hancock	Michael Erickson	
		Illustrators
Associate Acquisitions	**Technical Editor**	Robert Hansen
Editor	Lauri Bryant	Brian Wells
Timothy Green		Beth Young
	Copy Editor	
Editorial Management	Lynette Crane	**Series Design**
Syngress Media, Inc.		Roberta Steele
	Proofreader	
	Pat Mannion	

This book was composed with Corel Ventura.

FOREWORD

From Global Knowledge

At Global Knowledge we strive to support the multiplicity of learning styles required by our students to achieve success as technical professionals. In this series of books, it is our intention to offer the reader a valuable tool for successful completion of the MCSD Certification Exams.

As the world's largest IT training company, Global Knowledge is uniquely positioned to offer these books. The expertise gained each year from providing instructor-led training to hundreds of thousands of students worldwide has been captured in book form to enhance your learning experience. We hope that the quality of these books demonstrates our commitment to your lifelong learning success. Whether you choose to learn through the written word, computer-based training, Web delivery, or instructor-led training, Global Knowledge is committed to providing you the very best in each of those categories. For those of you who know Global Knowledge, or those of you who have just found us for the first time, our goal is to be your lifelong competency partner.

Thank you for the opportunity to serve you. We look forward to serving your needs again in the future.

Warmest regards,

Duncan Anderson

Duncan Anderson
President and Chief Executive Officer, Global Knowledge

The Global Knowledge Advantage

Global Knowledge has a global delivery system for its products and services. The company has 28 subsidiaries, and offers its programs through a total of 60+ locations. No other vendor can provide consistent services across a geographic area this large. Global Knowledge is the largest independent information technology education provider, offering programs on a variety of platforms. This enables our multi-platform and multi-national customers to obtain all of their programs from a single vendor. The company has developed the unique CompetusTM Framework software tool and methodology which can quickly reconfigure courseware to the proficiency level of a student on an interactive basis. Combined with self-paced and on-line programs, this technology can reduce the time required for training by prescribing content in only the deficient skills areas. The company has fully automated every aspect of the education process, from registration and follow-up, to "just-in-time" production of courseware. Global Knowledge, through its Enterprise Services Consultancy, can customize programs and products to suit the needs of an individual customer.

Global Knowledge Classroom Education Programs

The backbone of our delivery options is classroom-based education. Our modern, well-equipped facilities staffed with the finest instructors offer programs in a wide variety of information technology topics, many of which lead to professional certifications.

Custom Learning Solutions

This delivery option has been created for companies and governments that value customized learning solutions. For them, our consultancy-based approach of developing targeted education solutions is most effective at helping them meet specific objectives.

Self-Paced and Multimedia Products

This delivery option offers self-paced program titles in interactive CD-ROM, videotape and audio tape programs. In addition, we offer custom development of interactive multimedia courseware to customers and partners. Call us at 1 (888) 427-4228.

Electronic Delivery of Training

Our network-based training service delivers efficient competency-based, interactive training via the World Wide Web and organizational intranets. This leading-edge delivery option provides a custom learning path and "just-in-time" training for maximum convenience to students.

ARG

American Research Group (ARG), a wholly-owned subsidiary of Global Knowledge, one of the largest worldwide training partners of Cisco Systems, offers a wide range of internetworking, LAN/WAN, Nortel Networks, FORE Systems, IBM, and UNIX courses. ARG offers hands on network training in both instructor-led classes and self-paced PC-based training.

Global Knowledge Courses Available

Network Fundamentals

- Understanding Computer Networks
- Telecommunications Fundamentals I
- Telecommunications Fundamentals II
- Understanding Networking Fundamentals
- Implementing Computer Telephony Integration
- Introduction to Voice Over IP
- Introduction to Wide Area Networking
- Cabling Voice and Data Networks
- Introduction to LAN/WAN protocols
- Virtual Private Networks
- ATM Essentials

Network Security & Management

- Troubleshooting TCP/IP Networks
- Network Management
- Network Troubleshooting
- IP Address Management
- Network Security Administration
- Web Security
- Implementing UNIX Security
- Managing Cisco Network Security
- Windows NT 4.0 Security

IT Professional Skills

- Project Management for IT Professionals
- Advanced Project Management for IT Professionals
- Survival Skills for the New IT Manager
- Making IT Teams Work

LAN/WAN Internetworking

- Frame Relay Internetworking
- Implementing T1/T3 Services
- Understanding Digital Subscriber Line (xDSL)
- Internetworking with Routers and Switches
- Advanced Routing and Switching
- Multi-Layer Switching and Wire-Speed Routing
- Internetworking with TCP/IP
- ATM Internetworking
- OSPF Design and Configuration
- Border Gateway Protocol (BGP) Configuration

Authorized Vendor Training

Cisco Systems

- Introduction to Cisco Router Configuration
- Advanced Cisco Router Configuration
- Installation and Maintenance of Cisco Routers
- Cisco Internetwork Troubleshooting
- Cisco Internetwork Design
- Cisco Routers and LAN Switches
- Catalyst 5000 Series Configuration
- Cisco LAN Switch Configuration
- Managing Cisco Switched Internetworks
- Configuring, Monitoring, and Troubleshooting Dial-Up Services
- Cisco AS5200 Installation and Configuration
- Cisco Campus ATM Solutions

Bay Networks

- Bay Networks Accelerated Router Configuration
- Bay Networks Advanced IP Routing
- Bay Networks Hub Connectivity
- Bay Networks Accelar 1xxx Installation and Basic Configuration
- Bay Networks Centillion Switching

FORE Systems

- FORE ATM Enterprise Core Products
- FORE ATM Enterprise Edge Products
- FORE ATM Theory
- FORE LAN Certification

Operating Systems & Programming

Microsoft

- Introduction to Windows NT
- Microsoft Networking Essentials
- Windows NT 4.0 Workstation
- Windows NT 4.0 Server
- Advanced Windows NT 4.0 Server
- Windows NT Networking with TCP/IP
- Introduction to Microsoft Web Tools
- Windows NT Troubleshooting
- Windows Registry Configuration

UNIX

- UNIX Level I
- UNIX Level II
- Essentials of UNIX and NT Integration

Programming

- Introduction to JavaScript
- Java Programming
- PERL Programming
- Advanced PERL with CGI for the Web

Web Site Management & Development

- Building a Web Site
- Web Site Management and Performance
- Web Development Fundamentals

High Speed Networking

- Essentials of Wide Area Networking
- Integrating ISDN
- Fiber Optic Network Design
- Fiber Optic Network Installation
- Migrating to High Performance Ethernet

DIGITAL UNIX

- UNIX Utilities and Commands
- DIGITAL UNIX v4.0 System Administration
- DIGITAL UNIX v4.0 (TCP/IP) Network Management
- AdvFS, LSM, and RAID Configuration and Management
- DIGITAL UNIX TruCluster Software Configuration and Management
- UNIX Shell Programming Featuring Kornshell
- DIGITAL UNIX v4.0 Security Management
- DIGITAL UNIX v4.0 Performance Management
- DIGITAL UNIX v4.0 Intervals Overview

DIGITAL OpenVMS

- OpenVMS Skills for Users
- OpenVMS System and Network Node Management I
- OpenVMS System and Network Node Management II
- OpenVMS System and Network Node Management III
- OpenVMS System and Network Node Operations
- OpenVMS for Programmers
- OpenVMS System Troubleshooting for Systems Managers
- Configuring and Managing Complex VMScluster Systems
- Utilizing OpenVMS Features from C
- OpenVMS Performance Management
- Managing DEC TCP/IP Services for OpenVMS
- Programming in C

Hardware Courses

- AlphaServer 1000/1000A Installation, Configuration and Maintenance
- AlphaServer 2100 Server Maintenance
- AlphaServer 4100, Troubleshooting Techniques and Problem Solving

About Syngress Media

Syngress Media creates books and software for Information Technology professionals seeking skill enhancement and career advancement. Its products are designed to comply with vendor and industry standard course curricula, and are optimized for certification exam preparation. Visit the Syngress Web site at www.syngress.com.

Contributors

Cameron Wakefield is a MCSD, MCPS, and a Senior Software Engineer. He has passed 10 Microsoft Certification exams. He works at Computer Science Innovations, Inc. (http://www.csihq.com) in Melbourne, FL, where he develops custom software solutions ranging from Satellite Communications to insurance rating software. His development work spans a broad spectrum including Visual C++, Visual Basic, COM, ADO, ASP, Delphi, CORBA, UNIX, and others. He does some work through his own business developing software for a Brazillian Hematology company and developing web sites. He also teaches Microsoft Certification courses for Herzing College (AATP) where he teaches in the MCSE and MCSD programs. His formal education was in Computer Science with a minor in Math at Rollins College. He lives in Cocoa, Florida with his wife Lorraine and daughter Rachel. He also plays racquetball competitively in central Florida. He can be contacted at cwakefield@csihq.com.

Derrick Woo (MCSD, MCSE, MCP+Internet, CCNA, A+) is a networking and solution development specialist. He is currently the technical director of ecandy.com, where he is architecting and designing the specifications for their e-business solution. Prior to ecandy.com, Derrick was the Chief Technology Officer of LA.com/Hawaii.com. LA.com and Hawaii.com are portal sites that cater to both locals and tourists. He founded Obelisk Software, worked as a network engineer at IBM, consulted for numerous Southern California firms, and was part of the support team for the world's largest fully switched Ethernet network. He works primarily with Windows NT and BackOffice solutions. In his spare time (if he has any), he enjoys investing, online chatting, weight training, and of course writing.

Michael Cross (MCSE, MCPS, MCP+Internet) is a computer programmer and network support specialist. He works as an instructor at private colleges, teaching courses in hardware, software, programming, and networking. He is the owner of KnightWare, a company that provides consulting, programming, network support, Web page design, computer training, and various other services. In his spare time, he has been a freelance writer for several years, in genres of fiction and non-fiction. He currently lives in London, Ontario.

Jason Miller (MCSD) is an MFC specialist with many years of experience with various programming languages. He worked mainly as a consultant in the past on various consumer software products, and is now in a permanent position with Qualcomm Inc. in sunny Southern California. Currently he is learning the wonders of various multimedia compression and transmission protocols, such as G.72x compression codecs and the H.323 protocol. When he has spare time he uses it to keep in shape, watch the Patriots, and travel.

Audrea Elliott (MCSD, MCP, MBA) has been an IT professional since 1978 and now works for Compuware in Madison, Wisconsin. She has in-depth experience in the design and implementation of client/server technologies and object-oriented technologies. She has worked in many IT roles, including programmer, network administrator, IT Manager, and Business Area Analyst. She is also certified in Function Point counting. A single parent, Audrea's hobby is dreaming of the day she has the time to have a hobby. She lives with her son surrounded by cornfields in a picturesque small town just south of Madison. Audrea may be reached at aelliott@inwave.com.

Adrian Logue (MCSD, MCP). With many years of experience in software development, Adrian has provided programming and consultancy services for several of the Asia-Pacific region's largest IT organizations. Working as a development consultant in Sydney, Australia, he is responsible for the design, development, and project management of n-tier Internet and intranet solutions for large scale e-commerce and knowledge management projects. In his spare time Adrian enjoys reading, golf, and cricket.

Mick Porter is an MCP working as a Development Consultant in Sydney, Australia. Mick has developed successful Web sites such as www.sportodds.com.au, and also specialises in several other Microsoft technologies such as custom extensions for Outlook, and helpdesk systems integrating with SMS. If you want to contact Mick regarding consulting services you can find him at porter@pragma.com.au.

Series Editor

Michael Erickson (MCSD, MCT) consults on development projects using various Microsoft technologies. He has over 10 years experience in software development. He has been a contributing author and technical reviewer on several books. He also trains on various Microsoft development technologies including Visual C++, Visual Basic, and SQL Server. He graduated from Weber State University in 1989 and he currently lives near Salt Lake City, Utah with his wife Sharon and their two children, Thomas and Breanne.

Technical Editor

Lauri M. Bryant (MCT, MCSD, NCI) is the principal owner of LM Bryant and Associates, a small consulting firm located in Chicago Illinois. Her firm focuses on providing support and training for Microsoft's visual tools. She has been programming for the past 15 years. Lauri's training career began 10 years ago providing end-user training for the Fortune 100. Five years ago she became certified to deliver Microsoft training. Lauri attended Rutgers University and has a background in English and graphical design.

From the Classroom Sidebars

Michael Lane Thomas (MCP, MCP+Internet, MCSE, MCSE+Internet, MCT, MCSD, MCDBA, MCP+SB, MSS, A+) is a computer industry consultant and technical trainer, who also spends his free time writing and speaking. He has spoken publicly on some of the hottest technologies to hit the industry, such as XML, SQL, and Y2K issues, and has been heard at Microsoft-sponsored national technical conferences, special interest groups, and on Kansas City's airwaves on 980KMBZ radio.

Michael teaches Microsoft Official Curriculum (MOC) courses, ranging from BackOffice products such as Proxy, SQL Server, and IIS, to development technologies such as Visual InterDev, Visual Basic, COM, and Visual Studio. Michael is certified to teach over 40 Microsoft courses, with more on the horizon, but he prefers to focus on the most recent development courses because "that's where the fun stuff is!"

When not writing, Michael spends his time consulting and training, although he prefers the challenge of designing, building, and developing complex intranet, three-tier Web applications, and advanced Web-based solutions using the full range of available Microsoft technologies. Michael is currently waiting on beta scores for the SQL 7.0 Administration and Implementation exams to secure his MCDBA charter certification, to go with status as a charter MCSE+I and MCP+SB professional. With the Visual Basic 6 Distributed exam safely under wraps, Michael has confirmed successfully passing 30 Micosoft exams.

After graduating from the University of Kansas with a B.A. and B.S. in Mathematics, Michael has continued his traditional academic pursuits with a slow but steady climb towards his M.S. in Engineering Management from the University of Kansas. Michael is a former contributor and technical editor for the *Microsoft Certified Professional* magazine, and author, contributor, and/or technical editor for a dozen books to date. Michael can be reached at michael@thefastlane.com.

Acknowledgments

We would like to thank the following people:

- Richard Kristof of Global Knowledge for championing the series and providing access to some great people and information.

- All the incredibly hard-working folks at Osborne/McGraw-Hill: Brandon Nordin, Scott Rogers, and Gareth Hancock for their help in launching a great series and being solid team players. In addition, Tara Davis and Janet Walden for their help in fine-tuning the book.

- Becky Kirsininkas and Karen Croner at Microsoft Corp., for being patient and diligent in answering all of our questions.

CONTENTS

PREFACE

This book's primary objective is to help you prepare for and pass the required MCSD exam so you can begin to reap the career benefits of certification. We believe that the only way to do this is to help you increase your knowledge and build your skills. After completing this book, you should feel confident that you have thoroughly reviewed all of the objectives that Microsoft has established for the exam.

In This Book

This book is organized around the actual structure of the Microsoft exam administered at Sylvan Testing Centers. Microsoft has let us know all the topics we need to cover for the exam. We've followed their list carefully, so you can be assured you're not missing anything.

In Every Chapter

We've created a set of chapter components that call your attention to important items, reinforce important points, and provide helpful exam-taking hints. Take a look at what you'll find in every chapter:

- Every chapter begins with the **Certification Objectives**—what you need to know in order to pass the section on the exam dealing with the chapter topic. The Certification Objectives headings identify the objectives within the chapter, so you'll always know an objective when you see it!

- Exam Watch notes call attention to information about, and potential pitfalls in, the exam. These helpful hints are written by MCSDs who have taken the exams and received their certification—who better to tell you what to worry about? They know what you're about to experience!

- **On the Job** notes point out procedures and techniques important for coding actual applications for employers or contract jobs.

EXERCISE

- **Certification Exercises** are interspersed throughout the chapters. These are step-by-step exercises that mirror vendor-recommended labs. They help you master skills that are likely to be an area of focus on the exam.

Don't just read through the exercises; they are hands-on practice that you should be comfortable completing. Learning by doing is an effective way to increase your competency with a product.

■ **From the Classroom** sidebars describe the issues that come up most often in the training classroom setting. These sidebars give you a valuable perspective into certification- and product-related topics. They point out common mistakes and address questions from actual classroom discussions.

■ **Q & A** sections lay out problems and solutions in a quick-read format. For example:

QUESTIONS AND ANSWERS

A user wishes to save a file to a pre-existing filename.	Inform the user that the file exists and prompt them as to whether they wish to overwrite the file.
A CFile object throws an exception during construction.	Ensure that the program cannot go on to attempt to use that object.

■ The **Certification Summary** is a succinct review of the chapter and a restatement of salient points regarding the exam.

■ The **Two-Minute Drill** at the end of every chapter is a checklist of the main points of the chapter. It can be used for last-minute review.

■ The **Self Test** offers questions similar to those found on the certification exams, including multiple choice and fill-in-the-blank. The answers to these questions, as well as explanations of the answers, can be found at the end of each chapter. By taking the Self Test after completing each chapter, you'll reinforce what you've learned from that chapter, while becoming familiar with the structure of the exam questions.

Some Pointers

Once you've finished reading this book, set aside some time to do a thorough review. You might want to return to the book several times and make use of all the methods it offers for reviewing the material:

1. *Re-read all the Two-Minute Drills,* or have someone quiz you. You also can use the drills as a way to do a quick cram before the exam.

2. *Re-read all the Exam Watch notes.* Remember that these are written by MCSDs who have taken the exam and passed. They know what you should expect—and what you should be careful about.

3. *Review all the Q & A scenarios* for quick problem solving.

4. *Re-take the Self Tests.* Taking the tests right after you've read the chapter is a good idea, because it helps reinforce what you've just learned. However, it's an even better idea to go back later and do all the questions in the book in one sitting. Pretend you're taking the exam. (For this reason, you should mark your answers on a separate piece of paper when you answer the questions the first time.)

5. *Complete the exercises.* Did you do the exercises when you read through each chapter? If not, do them! These exercises are designed to cover exam topics, and there's no better way to get to know this material than by practicing.

6. *Check out the web site.* Global Knowledge Network invites you to become an active member of the Access Global Web site. This site is an online mall and information repository that you'll find invaluable. You can access many types of products to assist you in your preparation for the exams, and you'll be able to participate in forums, online discussions, and threaded discussions. No other book brings you unlimited access to such a resource. You'll find more information about this site in Appendix B.

A Brief History of MCSD Certification

Although the MCSD certification for software developers was introduced in the same year as the MCSE certification for system engineers, there are currently many more MCSEs than MCSDs. There are several reasons for this discrepancy:

- The MCSE was immediately understood as being similar to the Novell's CNE (Certified Network Engineer), but there was no popular credential competing with the MCSD.

- The learning curve has traditionally been steeper for system engineers than it has been for software developers, and the consequences of error are usually much more severe. (A software developer who has an off day might end up working late every day the next week, but a system engineer who has an off day might end up working at Burger King.) Consequently, there has been more demand from companies for a network certification, and more willingness to invest in employees receiving the appropriate training.

■ The MCSD was considered by some to be more difficult than the MCSE. Although the MCSE required passing six tests (as opposed to the four required for the MCSD), there was significant overlap in the content covered on the MCSE tests. By contrast, the content learned for one MCSD test was of little value on other MCSD tests.

■ While a network engineer would encounter most of the MCSE test concepts in their day-to-day work, even an experienced developer would have to deal with new material when preparing for a MCSD test. For example, on the original WOSSA 2 Exam, a level of understanding of ODBC was required that far exceeded the needs of almost all developers.

■ Finally, while MCSE study resources were plentiful, there were few classes and fewer books covering the MCSD curriculum.

However, the popularity of the MCSD is starting to reach a critical mass. As the number of organizations dependent on custom-developed Microsoft applications increases, so does the desire of these organizations to objectively measure the skills of developers, and the willingness of these organizations to use these certifications as a factor in determining compensation. According to *Microsoft Certified Professional* magazine, developers with the MCSD certification reported a median salary of $73,600, while those holding only the MCP certification reported a median salary of $49,700. (More information is available by viewing the magazine's Web site at http://www.mcpmag.com/members/99jul/fea1main.asp.)

To Microsoft's credit, they have continually surveyed developers and employees and used this feedback to align their certification tracks with market needs. In June 1998, Microsoft revamped the MCSD program, providing new requirements and tests required to achieve this status. However, they did not discontinue the existing path, which leaves developers with the challenge of determining which to pursue.

Original and New MCSD Tracks

The primary difference between the original and the new MCSD tracks is the emphasis on architecture. The new track reduces the number of generalized architecture tests, but requires at least one test that covers distributed application development. A test-by-test comparison of the exams required is presented in Table P-1.

Note that the Microsoft Windows Architecture exams were introduced to replace the original Windows Operating System and Services Architecture exams used for MCSD certification. Microsoft has already retired these, so they are excluded from Table P-1.

TABLE P-1			
Test-by-Test Comparison of Original and New MCSD Tracks	**Test**	**Original Track Requirements**	**New Track Requirements**
	1	Core: Microsoft Windows Architecture 1 (70-160).	Core: Analyzing Requirements and Defining Solutions Architectures (70-100).
	2	Core: Microsoft Windows Architecture 2 (70-161).	Core: Desktop Application Development in VC++ 6 (70-016), VB 6 (70-176), FoxPro (70-156) , or J++.
	3	Elective: One elective from Table P-2.	Core: Distributed Application Development in VC++ 6 (70-015), VB 6 (70-175), FoxPro (70-155), or J++.
	4	Elective: One elective from Table P-2.	Elective: One elective from Table P-2.

- Tests 3 and 4 must cover different Microsoft products. For example, you cannot use Programming with Microsoft Visual Basic 4.0 for Test 3 and Developing Applications with Microsoft Visual Basic 5.0 for Test 4.
- Although the test choices for Test 2 and Test 3 are available as electives, the same test cannot be used to fill both a core and an elective test requirement.

Tests Available for MCSD Certification

As of this writing, there are 27 exams that can be used to achieve the MCSD certification (although some of these will be retired soon). These tests are listed in Table P-2, sorted by the subject they cover.

TABLE P-2		Tests Available for MCSD Certification		
Subject	**Test Number**	**Full Test Name**	**Original**	**New**
Architecture	70-160*	Microsoft Windows Architecture I	C	
Architecture	70-161*	Microsoft Windows Architecture II	C	
Architecture	70-100	Analyzing Requirements and Defining Solution Architectures		C
Visual Basic	70-065*	Programming with Microsoft Visual Basic 4.0	E	E
Visual Basic	70-165	Developing Applications with Microsoft Visual Basic 5.0	E	E
Visual Basic	70-176	Designing and Implementing Desktop Applications with Microsoft Visual Basic 6.0	E	C,E
Visual Basic	70-175	Designing and Implementing Distributed Applications with Microsoft Visual Basic 6.0	E	C,E
FoxPro	70-054*	Programming in Microsoft Visual FoxPro 3.0 for Windows	E	
FoxPro	70-156	Designing and Implementing Desktop Applications with Microsoft Visual FoxPro	E	C
FoxPro	70-155	Designing and Implementing Distributed Applications with Microsoft Visual FoxPro	E	C
C++	70-024	Developing Applications with C++ Using the Microsoft Foundation Class Library	E	E
C++	70-025	Implementing OLE in Microsoft Foundation Class Applications	E	E
C++	70-016	Designing and Implementing Desktop Applications with Microsoft Visual C++ 6.0	E	C, E
C++	70-015	Designing and Implementing Distributed Applications with Microsoft Visual C++ 6.0	E	C, E
J++	(none)	Designing and Implementing Desktop Applications with Microsoft Visual J++	E	C
J++	(none)	Designing and Implementing Distributed Applications with Microsoft Visual J++	E	C
Access	70-051*	Microsoft Access 2.0 for Windows-Application Development	E	

TABLE P-2		Tests Available for MCSD Certification *(continued)*		
Subject	**Test Number**	**Full Test Name**	**Original**	**New**
Access	70-069	Microsoft Access for Windows 95 and the Microsoft Access Developer's Toolkit	E	E
Access	(none)	Designing and Implementing Database Design on Microsoft Access	E	E
Office	70-052*	Developing Applications with Microsoft Excel 5.0 Using Visual Basic for Applications	E	
Office	70-091	Designing and Implementing Solutions with Microsoft Office 2000 and Microsoft Visual Basic for Applications	E	E
SQL Server	70-021*	Microsoft SQL Server 4.2 Database Implementation	E	E
SQL Server	70-027	Implementing a Database Design on Microsoft SQL Server 6.5	E	E
SQL Server	70-029	Designing and Implementing Databases with Microsoft SQL Server 7.0	E	E
Internet	70-055	Designing and Implementing Web Sites with Microsoft FrontPage 98	E	E
Internet	70-152	Designing and Implementing Web Solutions with Microsoft Visual InterDev 6.0	E	E
Internet	70-057	Designing and Implementing Commerce Solutions with Microsoft Site Server 3.0, Commerce Edition	E	E

- An "E" means that a test can be used as an elective; a "C" means that a test can be used as a core requirement. "Original" refers to the Original MCSD track; "New" refers to the New MCSD track.

- Exams without a number are not yet available.

- Test numbers with an asterisk are scheduled to be retired or have been retired by Microsoft. (Note that after Microsoft retires an exam, it usually remains valid for certification status, but only for a limited time. See http://www.microsoft.com/mcp/examinfo/retired.htm for the latest information on retired exams.)

- Note that this test list is adapted from the content available at http://www.microsoft.com/mcp/certstep/mcsd.htm. This content frequently changes, so it would be wise to check this site before finalizing your study plans.

Choosing a Track

So which track should you choose? Good question! Although Microsoft is obviously providing more support for the New track, there are legitimate reasons for considering both options. Some of these reasons are described below.

Advantages of the Original Track

- You may already be part way there. If you already have the Windows Architecture 1 or 2, you should pursue the Original track. These tests are of no value in the New track (both tests were retired by Microsoft on September 30, 1999, but if you have already passed them they will remain valid until October 1, 2000). Similarly, if you have already passed an exam such as Access 2 or FoxPro 3, that is a valid elective for the Original track but not for the New track (though both of these exams will be retired as of this writing).

- *You cover more architecture.* The system architecture exams are excellent overviews to client/server development. The Original track consists of two architecture tests, but the New track has only one.

- *You don't have to use the most recent versions of the tools.* If your current job responsibilities make it unlikely that you will be working with the newest versions of C++, Visual Basic, FoxPro, or J++, you should pursue the Original track. The New track requires that you pass two tests on one of these four environments, and it seems very unlikely that these tests will be adapted to support prior versions. In other words, if you are an expert in VB version 5 but won't have an opportunity to significantly use VB version 6 for at least a year, it will be very difficult for you to use the New track.

- *You can start now.* As of this writing, some of the tests used for the New track (for example, Desktop and Distribution for FoxPro and J++) haven't even been released in beta yet.

Advantages of the New Track

■ *Your credentials will last longer.* The Architecture 1 and 2 exams required for the original track will be retired more quickly than any of the New track core exams. However, this may not be as much of a disadvantage as it may seem. Remember, all of the exams you take will be retired within a few years. The certification process is designed not just to determine which developers have achieved a base level of competency, but to identify which developers are doing the best job of keeping their skills current.

■ *You can become more of a specialist in your chosen tool.* Arguably, because the New track offers more exams for each product, the Original track encourages product breadth while the New track encourages depth. Therefore, if you're selling yourself as a specialist, the New track may be an advantage. (Specialists often earn higher salaries, though sometimes generalists have steadier employment.)

■ *You'll be more closely aligned with Microsoft's strategies.* If you are just beginning to consider certification and haven't already invested time pursuing the Original track, you should probably pursue the New track. The changes made by Microsoft are a result of their research into the needs of the marketplace, and it couldn't hurt for you to leverage their investment. In addition, if Microsoft revises the MCSD requirements again, the transition would probably be easiest for those who used the New track.

■ *You'll be "New and Improved!"*

Of course, the best choice may be not to choose at all, at least not yet. As the tables in this chapter have shown, many of the exams are applicable to both tracks. For example, the Designing and Implementing Desktop Applications with Microsoft Visual Basic 6.0 Exam counts not only as a core requirement for the New track, but also as an elective for either track. You do not need to declare to Microsoft which track you are pursuing, so you can delay that decision until after you have passed your first test.

And with this book at your side, you're well on your way to doing just that.

The CD-ROM Resource

This book comes with a CD-ROM that contains test preparation software, and provides you with another method for studying for the exam. You will find more information on the testing software in Appendix A.

INTRODUCTION

How to Take a Microsoft Certification Examination

Good News and Bad News

If you are new to Microsoft certification, we have some good news and some bad news. The good news, of course, is that Microsoft certification is one of the most valuable credentials you can earn. It sets you apart from the crowd and marks you as a valuable asset to your employer. You will gain the respect of your peers, and Microsoft certification can have a wonderful effect on your income.

The bad news is that Microsoft certification tests are not easy. You may think you will read through some study material, memorize a few facts, and pass the Microsoft examinations. After all, these certification exams are just computer-based, multiple-choice tests, so they must be easy. If you believe this, you are wrong. Unlike many "multiple guess" tests you have been exposed to in school, the questions on Microsoft certification exams go beyond simple factual knowledge.

The purpose of this introduction is to teach you how to take a Microsoft certification exam. To be successful, you need to know something about the purpose and structure of these tests. We will also look at the latest innovations in Microsoft testing. Using simulations and adaptive testing, Microsoft is enhancing both the validity and security of the certification process. These factors have some important effects on how you should prepare for an exam, as well as your approach to each question during the test.

We will begin by looking at the purpose, focus, and structure of Microsoft certification tests, and examine the effect these factors have on the kinds of questions you will face on your certification exams. We will define the structure of exam questions, and investigate some common formats. Next, we will present a strategy for answering these questions. Finally, we will give some specific guidelines on what you should do on the day of your test.

Why Vendor Certification?

The Microsoft Certified Professional program, like the certification programs from Lotus, Novell, Oracle, and other software vendors, is maintained for the ultimate purpose of increasing the corporation's profits. A successful vendor certification program accomplishes this goal by helping to create a pool of experts in a company's software, and by "branding" these experts so that companies using the software can identify them.

We know that vendor certification has become increasingly popular in the last few years because it helps employers find qualified workers, and because it helps software vendors like Microsoft sell their products. But why should you be interested in vendor certification rather than a more traditional approach like a college or professional degree in computer science? A college education is a broadening and enriching experience, but a degree in computer science does not prepare students for most jobs in the IT industry.

A common truism in our business states, "If you are out of the IT industry for three years and want to return, you have to start over." The problem, of course, is *timeliness*; if a first-year student learns about a specific computer program, it probably will no longer be in wide use when he or she graduates. Although some colleges are trying to integrate Microsoft certification into their curriculum, the problem is not really a flaw in higher education, but a characteristic of the IT industry. Computer software is changing so rapidly that a four-year college just can't keep up.

A marked characteristic of the Microsoft certification program is an emphasis on performing specific job tasks rather than merely gathering knowledge. It may come as a shock, but most potential employers do not care how much you know about the theory of operating systems, testing, or software design. As one IT manager put it, "I don't really care what my employees know about the theory of our network. We don't need someone to sit at a desk and think about it. We need people who can actually do something to make it work better."

You should not think that this attitude is some kind of anti-intellectual revolt against book learning. Knowledge is a necessary prerequisite, but it is not enough. More than one company has hired a computer science graduate as a network administrator only to learn that the new employee has no idea how to add users, assign permissions, or perform the other everyday tasks necessary to maintain a network. This brings us to the second major characteristic of Microsoft certification that affects the questions you must be prepared to answer. In addition to timeliness, Microsoft certification is also job task–oriented.

The timeliness of Microsoft's certification program is obvious, and is inherent in the fact that you will be tested on current versions of software in wide use today. The job-task orientation of Microsoft certification is almost as obvious, but testing real-world job skills using a computer-based test is not easy.

Computerized Testing

Considering the popularity of Microsoft certification, and the fact that certification candidates are spread around the world, the only practical way to administer tests for the certification program is through Sylvan Prometric testing centers. Sylvan Prometric provides proctored testing services for Microsoft, Oracle, Novell, Lotus, and the A+ computer technician certification. Although the IT industry accounts for much of Sylvan's revenue, the company provides services for a number of other businesses and organizations, such as FAA preflight pilot tests. In fact, most companies that need secure test delivery over a wide geographic area use the services of Sylvan Prometric. In addition to delivery, Sylvan Prometric also scores the tests and provides statistical feedback on the performance of each test question to the companies and organizations that use their services.

Typically, several hundred questions are developed for a new Microsoft certification examination. The questions are first reviewed by a number of subject-matter experts for technical accuracy, and then are presented in a beta test. The beta test may last for several hours, due to the large number of questions. After a few weeks, Microsoft Certification uses the statistical feedback from Sylvan to check the performance of the beta questions.

Questions are discarded if most test takers get them right (too easy) or wrong (too difficult), and a number of other statistical measures are taken of each question. Although the scope of our discussion precludes a rigorous treatment of question analysis, you should be aware that Microsoft and other vendors spend a great deal of time and effort making sure their exam questions are valid. In addition to the obvious desire for quality, the fairness of a vendor's certification program must be legally defensible.

The questions that survive statistical analysis form the pool of questions for the final certification exam.

Test Structure

The kind of test we are most familiar with is known as a *form* test. For Microsoft certification, a form usually consists of 50–70 questions and takes 60–120 minutes to complete. If there are 240 questions in the final pool for an examination, then four forms can be created. Thus, candidates who retake the test probably will not see the same questions.

Other variations are possible. From the same pool of 240 questions, five forms can be created, each containing 40 unique questions (200 questions) and 20 questions selected at random from the remaining 40.

The questions in a Microsoft form test are equally weighted. This means they all count the same when the test is scored. A useful characteristic of a form test is that you can mark a question you have doubts about as you take the test. Assuming you have time left when you finish all the questions, you can return and spend more time on the questions you have marked as doubtful.

Microsoft may soon implement *adaptive* testing. To use this interactive technique, a form test is first created and administered to several thousand certification candidates. The statistics generated are used to assign a weight, or difficulty level, for each question. For example, the questions in a form might be divided into levels one through five, with level-one questions being the easiest and level-five questions the hardest.

When an adaptive test begins, the candidate is first given a level-three question. If it is answered correctly, a question from the next higher level is presented, and an incorrect response results in a question from the next lower level. When 15–20 questions have been answered in this manner, the scoring algorithm is able to predict, with a high degree of statistical certainty, whether the candidate would pass or fail if all the questions in the form were answered. When the required degree of certainty is attained, the test ends and the candidate receives a pass/fail grade.

Adaptive testing has some definite advantages for everyone involved in the certification process. Adaptive tests allow Sylvan Prometric to deliver more tests with the same resources, as certification candidates often are in and out in 30 minutes or less. For Microsoft, adaptive testing means that fewer test questions are exposed to each candidate, and this can enhance the security, and therefore the validity, of certification tests.

One problem you may have with adaptive testing is that you are not allowed to mark and revisit questions. Since the adaptive algorithm is interactive, and all questions but the first are selected on the basis of your response to the previous question, it is not possible to skip a particular question or change an answer.

Question *seeding* is another technique where a select group of questions, called seed questions, are changed on a periodic basis. This decreases the chance that the individuals taking the exam will inadvertently share questions with others. It also allows updates to be made to the exam as technology changes.

Question Types

Computerized test questions can be presented in a number of ways. Some of the possible formats are used on Microsoft certification examinations, and some are not.

True/False

We are all familiar with true/false questions, but because of the inherent 50 percent chance of guessing the correct answer, you will not see questions of this type on Microsoft certification exams.

Multiple Choice

The majority of Microsoft certification questions are in the multiple-choice format, with either a single correct answer or multiple correct answers. One interesting variation on multiple-choice questions with multiple correct answers is whether the candidate is told how many answers are correct.

Example:

Which of the following two controls can be used on an MDI form? (Choose two.)

Or

Which of the following controls can be used on a MDI form? (Choose all that apply.)

You may see both variations on Microsoft certification examinations, but the trend seems to be toward the first type, where candidates are told explicitly how many answers are correct. Questions of the "choose all that apply" variety are more difficult, and can be merely confusing.

Graphical Questions

One or more graphical elements are sometimes used as exhibits to help present or clarify an exam question. These elements may take the form of a database diagram, flow charts, or screenshots from the software on which you are being tested. It is often easier to present the concepts required for a complex performance-based scenario with a graphic than with words.

Test questions known as *hotspots* actually incorporate graphics as part of the answer. These questions ask the certification candidate to click on a location or graphical element to answer the question. For example, you might be shown the diagram of a three-tiered application and asked to click on a tier described by the question. The answer is correct if the candidate clicks within the hotspot that defines the correct location.

Free Response Questions

Another kind of question you sometimes see on Microsoft certification exams requires a *free response* or type-in answer. An example of this type of question might present a complex code sample including loops and error trapping and ask the candidate to calculate and enter the final value of a variable.

Knowledge-Based and Performance-Based Questions

Microsoft Certification develops a blueprint for each Microsoft certification exam with input from subject-matter experts. This blueprint defines the content areas and objectives for each test, and each test question is created to test a specific objective. The basic information from the exam blueprint can be found on Microsoft's Web site in the Exam Prep Guide for each test.

A demo exam is available for download at http://www.microsoft.com/mcp/articles/tesinn.htm. You can also find out the latest information about exam 70-015 at http://www.microsoft.com/Mcp/exam/stat/SP70-015.htm. This is the 70-015 Web site that lists all of the knowledge objectives covered in the exam. It is always a good idea to review this material before you take an exam.

Psychometricians (psychologists who specialize in designing and analyzing tests) categorize test questions as knowledge-based or performance-based. As the names imply, knowledge-based questions are designed to test knowledge, while performance-based questions are designed to test performance.

Some objectives demand a knowledge-based question. For example, objectives that use verbs like *list* and *identify* tend to test only what you know, not what you can do.

Example:

Objective: Identify the ADO Cursor Types that support read and write operations.

Which two of the following ADO Cursor Types support write access? (Choose two.)

A. adOpenStatic

B. adOpenDynamic

C. adOpenForwardOnly

D. adOpenKeyset

Correct answers: B and D

Other objectives use action verbs like *connect, configure,* and *troubleshoot* to define job tasks. These objectives can often be tested with either a knowledge-based question or a performance-based question.

Example:

Objective: Connect to a data source appropriately using ADO Cursor Type properties.

Knowledge-based question:

What is the correct Cursor Type to allow users to view new records created by other users?

A. adOpenStatic

B. adOpenDynamic

C. adOpenForwardOnly

D. adOpenKeyset

Correct answer: B

Performance-based question:

Your company supports several travel agents using a common data store, and each agent must be able to see the reservations taken by all other agents. What is the best application development strategy to allow users to see records modified and created by other users?

A. Use an adOpenKeyset Cursor Type to create the record set, and keep the same Recordset object open continuously.

B. Use an adOpenDynamic Cursor Type to create the record set, and keep the same Recordset object open continuously.

C. Use an adOpenStatic Cursor Type to create the record set, but destroy and create the Recordset object after every data update.

D. Use an adOpenForwardOnly Cursor Type to create the record set, but destroy and create the Recordset object after every data update.

Correct answer: B

Even in this simple example, the superiority of the performance-based question is obvious. Whereas the knowledge-based question asks for a single fact, the performance-based question presents a real-life situation and requires that you make a decision based on this scenario. Thus, performance-based questions give more bang (validity) for the test author's buck (individual question).

70-015 Designing and Implementing Distributed Applications with Microsoft® Visual C++ 6.0

At the time of this writing, the Beta Exam was being evaluated. It is important that you watch the Microsoft Web site for late-breaking news on this exam. Again, the URL is http://www.microsoft.com/Mcp/exam/stat/SP70-015.htm.

As with the other exams in this series, there may be 60 to 70 questions and approximately 120 minutes will be allowed to finish the exam. As you can see by the demo exam at the Microsoft site listed earlier, there could be a scenario followed by questions. For each type of question, there will be a button to click for instructions on completing the question. Following a case study, expect to see not only multiple choice but all forms of questions. There may be a group of five different case studies followed by anywhere from three to eight questions. The answers to these questions would be based on the information presented by that case study and would be unrelated to the other case studies. As you are answering the questions, if you are not clear on a point from the text, you may return to the case study to review it. If any multiple-choice questions were to follow the group of case-study questions, they would be unrelated to any of the previous case studies.

Testing Job Performance

We have said that Microsoft certification focuses on timeliness and the ability to perform job tasks. We have also introduced the concept of performance-based questions, but even performance-based, multiple-choice questions do not really measure performance. Another strategy is needed to test job skills.

Given unlimited resources, it is not difficult to test job skills. In an ideal world, Microsoft would fly MCP candidates to Redmond, place them in a controlled environment with a team of experts, and ask them to design, author, debug, and revise a Windows application. In a few days at most, the experts could reach a valid decision as to whether each candidate should be granted MCSD status. Needless to say, this is not likely to happen.

Closer to reality, another way to test performance is by using the actual software, and creating a testing program to present tasks and automatically grade a candidate's performance when the tasks are completed. This *cooperative* approach would be practical in some testing situations, but the same test that is presented to MCP candidates in Boston must also be available in Bahrain and Botswana. Many Sylvan Prometric testing locations around the world cannot run 32-bit applications, much less provide the complex networked solutions required by cooperative testing applications.

The most workable solution for measuring performance in today's testing environment is a *simulation* program. When the program is launched during a test, the candidate sees a simulation of the actual software that looks, and behaves, just like the real thing. When the testing software presents a task, the simulation program is launched and the candidate performs the required task. The testing software then grades the candidate's performance on the required task and moves to the next question. In this way, a 16-bit simulation program can mimic the look and feel of 32-bit operating systems, a complicated network, or even the entire Internet.

Microsoft has introduced simulation questions on the certification exam for Internet Information Server version 4. Simulation questions provide many advantages over other testing methodologies, and simulations are expected to become increasingly important in the Microsoft Certification Program. For example, studies have shown that there is a high correlation between the ability to perform simulated tasks on a computer-based test and the ability to perform the actual job tasks. Thus, simulations enhance the validity of the certification process.

Another benefit of simulations is in the area of test security. It is just not possible to cheat on a simulation question. In fact, you will be told exactly what tasks you are expected to perform on the test.

Study Strategies

There are appropriate ways to study for the different types of questions you will see on a Microsoft certification examination.

Knowledge-Based Questions

Knowledge-based questions require that you memorize facts. There are hundreds of facts inherent in each content area of every Microsoft certification exam. There are several keys to memorizing facts:

- *Repetition* The more times your brain is exposed to a fact, the more likely you are to remember it.

- *Association* Connecting facts within a logical framework makes them easier to remember.

- *Motor Association* It is often easier to remember something if you write it down or perform some other physical act, like clicking a practice test answer.

We have said that the emphasis of Microsoft certification is job performance, and that there are very few knowledge-based questions on Microsoft certification exams. Why should you waste a lot of time learning filenames, property values, and other minutiae? Read on.

Performance-Based Questions

Most of the questions you will face on a Microsoft certification exam are performance-based scenario questions. We have discussed the superiority of these questions over simple knowledge-based questions, but you should remember that the job task–orientation of Microsoft certification extends the knowledge you need to pass the exams; it does *not* replace this knowledge. Therefore, the first step in preparing for scenario questions is to absorb as many facts relating to the exam content areas as you can. In other words, go back to the previous section and follow the steps to prepare for an exam composed of knowledge-based questions.

The second step is to familiarize yourself with the format of the questions you are likely to see on the exam. You can do this by answering the questions in this study guide, by using Microsoft assessment tests, or by using practice tests. The day of your test is not the time to be surprised by the convoluted construction of Microsoft exam questions.

For example, one of Microsoft's favorite formats of late takes the following form:

- *Scenario:* You have an application with . . .

- *Primary Objective:* You want to . . .

- *Secondary Objective:* You also want to . . .

- *Proposed Solution:* Do this . . .

What does the proposed solution accomplish?

A. Satisfies the primary and the secondary objective

B. Satisfies the primary but not the secondary objective

C. Satisfies the secondary but not the primary objective

D. Satisfies neither the primary nor the secondary objective

This kind of question, with some variation, is seen on many Microsoft certification examinations.

At best, these performance-based scenario questions really do test certification candidates at a higher cognitive level than knowledge-based questions. At worst, these questions can test your reading comprehension and test-taking ability rather than your ability to use Microsoft products.

Be sure to get in the habit of reading the question carefully to determine what is being asked.

The third step in preparing for Microsoft scenario questions is to adopt the following attitude: Multiple-choice questions aren't really performance-based. It is all a cruel lie. These scenario questions are just knowledge-based questions with a little story wrapped around them.

To answer a scenario question, you have to sift through the story to the underlying facts of the situation, and apply your knowledge to determine the correct answer. This may sound silly at first, but the process we go through in solving real-life problems is quite similar. The key concept is that every scenario question (and every real-life problem) has a fact at its center, and if we can identify that fact, we can answer the question.

Simulations

Simulation questions really do measure your ability to perform job tasks. You *must* be able to perform the specified tasks. There are two ways to prepare for simulation questions:

- Get experience with the actual software. If you have the resources, this is a great way to prepare for simulation questions.

- Use official Microsoft practice tests. Practice tests are available that provide practice with the same simulation engine used on Microsoft certification exams. This approach has the added advantage of grading your efforts.

Signing Up

Signing up to take a Microsoft certification examination is easy. Sylvan operators in each country can schedule tests at any testing center. There are, however, a few things you should know:

- If you call Sylvan during a busy time period, get a cup of coffee first, because you may be in for a long wait. Sylvan does an excellent job, but everyone in the world seems to want to sign up for a test on Monday morning.

- An alternative to speaking with a human is to register using the Sylvan Prometric Web site at http://www.2test.com. You may also register online at http://www.microsoft.com/Train_Cert/mcp/certstep/examreg.htm.

- You will need your Social Security number or some other unique identifier to sign up for a Sylvan test, so have it ready.

- Pay for your test by credit card, if at all possible. This makes registration easier, and you can even schedule tests for the same day you call, if space is available at your local testing center.

- Know the number and title of the test you want to take before you call. This is not essential, and the Sylvan operators will help you if they can. However, having this information in advance speeds up the registration process and reduces the risk that you will accidentally register for the wrong test.

- If you need to reschedule your exam, you must call 24 hours ahead of the exam appointment and you may reschedule for the time and place of your choice.

Non-Disclosure Agreement

In exactly the same form as the Microsoft software installation process, you must agree to a non-disclosure statement. Clicking on the "I agree" option button signifies your signature and allows the test software to proceed. If you click on the other button indicating that you do not agree, the exam ends and you forfeit your exam fee. The new non-disclosure statement may be found at http://www.microsoft.com/mcp/articles/nda.htm.

Retake Policy

If the unthinkable were to happen—it happens to the best of us—and you do not pass the exam, the old policy was that you could retake the exam as many times it took to pass. That is all in the past. Now, if you do not pass after the second try, you must wait two weeks before trying again. Do you know how much information you can forget in two weeks?

Taking the Test

Teachers may have told you not to cram for exams, because it does no good. However, if you are faced with a knowledge-based test requiring only that you regurgitate facts, cramming can mean the difference between passing and failing. This is not the case with Microsoft certification exams. If you don't know it the night before, don't bother to stay up and cram.

Instead, create a schedule and stick to it. Follow these guidelines on the day of your exam:

1. Get a good night's sleep. The scenario questions you will face on a Microsoft certification examination require a clear head.

2. Remember to take two forms of identification—at least one with a picture. A driver's license with your picture, and Social Security or credit cards are acceptable.

3. Leave home in time to arrive at your testing center a few minutes early. It is not a good idea to feel rushed as you begin your exam.

4. Do not spend too much time on any one question. If you are taking a form test, take your best guess and mark the question so you can come back to it if you have time. You cannot mark and revisit questions on an adaptive test, so you must do your best on each question as you go.

5. If you do not know the answer to a question, try to eliminate the obviously wrong answers and guess from the rest. If you can eliminate two out of four options, you have a 50 percent chance of guessing the correct answer.

6. For scenario questions, follow the steps outlined earlier. Read the question carefully and try to identify the facts at the center of the story.

Finally, I would advise anyone attempting to earn Microsoft MCSD certification to adopt a philosophical attitude. Even if you are the kind of person who never fails a test, you are likely to fail at least one Microsoft certification test somewhere along the way. Do not get discouraged. If Microsoft certification were easy to obtain, more people would have it, and it would not be so respected and valuable to your future in the IT industry.

MICROSOFT CERTIFIED SOLUTION DEVELOPER

1

The Development Environment

CERTIFICATION OBJECTIVES

Too do any job properly, you need the right tools. That's the purpose of this chapter. Before you can use Visual C++ 6.0 to develop distributed applications, you need to set up your development environment. This means installing Visual C++ and tools that will work with the applications you create. In this chapter, we'll discuss the requirements needed for these programs and how to install and configure them.

We'll also discuss an important, and often overlooked aspect of development: source code control. If you're new to developing software, source code is the programming code that you write to make your application perform various actions. Source code control enables you to store, track changes, and retrieve previous versions of your code.

CERTIFICATION OBJECTIVE 1.01

Installing the Visual C++ Development Tools

The first steps to using Visual C++ 6.0 are acquiring it, knowing what tools are available, and what those tools are for. The first of these steps may seem simple at face value, until you realize that Visual C++ 6.0 is available for purchase as its own package or as part of the Visual Studio suite of products. Beyond this, Visual C++ 6.0 is also available in three different editions:

- **Standard** Includes the basic products and tools for creating applications. This edition also includes tutorials and samples, and is often the best choice for programmers who are just learning how to program with Visual C++

- **Professional** Includes products and tools for creating applications, and is geared toward developers of desktop applications

- **Enterprise** Includes the same products and tools as the Professional edition, but has additional features geared toward the development of distributed applications

Although Visual C++ 6.0 is available in each of these editions, Visual Studio is only available as Professional or Enterprise. Which package and edition of Visual C++ 6.0 or Visual Studio you use largely depends on individual needs and resources.

Although it's cheaper to purchase Visual C++ 6.0 on its own, Visual Studio comes with significantly more development tools. Purchasing Visual Studio costs less than if you purchased each development tool separately. In other words, you get more for your dollar, if more is what you're actually looking for.

Visual Studio is a suite of products used for developing and managing applications, components, and data access. It provides you with a wider scope of options than Visual C++ alone, because it contains more than just Visual C++ 6.0. Regardless of whether you use the Professional or Enterprise edition of Visual Studio, you receive the following:

- **Visual Basic 6.0** Development system based on the BASIC programming language

- **Visual C++ 6.0** Development system based on the C++ programming language

- **Visual J++ 6.0** Development system based on the Java programming language

- **Visual FoxPro 6.0** Development system used for creating databases and database applications

- **Visual InterDev 6.0** Development system used for creating Web applications

Although each of these is available for purchase separately, you can get them in one package with Visual Studio. If you purchase the Professional edition of Visual Studio (VS), then each of the development systems included are Professional edition as well. Similarly, the Enterprise edition includes the Enterprise editions of these systems. Therefore, if you have the VS Professional edition, then you get the Professional edition of Visual C++

6.0. If you have the Enterprise edition of VS, then you would be using the Enterprise edition of Visual C++ 6.0.

In addition to these development systems, you also receive the MSDN (Microsoft Developer Network) Library, Single Edition. This is an information resource that can help you when you need answers fast. It includes a knowledge base of information, sample code, product documentation, software developer's kit (SDK) documentation, technical documents, and examples.

The Enterprise edition of Visual Studio also includes Visual SourceSafe. Visual SourceSafe (VSS) is used for version control of source code. As we'll see in Chapter 2, this allows you to store your source code to a database, enabling you to restore and use previous versions of your source code. This is useful for organizing the source code of multiple developers as well as that of the individual developer. If an improper or incorrect change is made to source code, or you simply want to revert to the code you used earlier, you can restore that code from the VSS database to which it was saved.

Microsoft BackOffice Server 4.5, Developer Edition is also included with the Enterprise edition. BackOffice Server is made up of several pieces of server software, including Microsoft SQL Server, Microsoft SNA Server, Microsoft Exchange Server, Microsoft Site Server, and Microsoft System Management Server. However, if you're thinking of using this version of BackOffice Server for anything other than development, you may want to think twice. The Developer Edition of BackOffice Server is only licensed to support ten concurrent connections. This means only ten people can use this software at any given time.

As Table 1-1 shows, Visual Studio also includes a number of additional tools for application design, performance analysis, component management, and designing SQL Server and Oracle databases. Most of these are only available with the Enterprise edition, but some are also included in the Professional edition. Application Performance Explorer is a tool used for testing SQL Server queries and data connections. Visual Modeler is used for the design of three-tier distributed applications. Visual Component Manager (which is also available with the Professional edition) allows you to manage components, by enabling you to organize, find, and insert components into development projects. Visual Studio Analyzer is a tool

Visual Studio Feature	Professional Edition	Enterprise Edition
Visual Basic 6.0	X	X
Visual C++ 6.0	X	X
Visual J++ 6.0	X	X
Visual FoxPro 6.0	X	X
Visual InterDev 6.0	X	X
Visual SourceSafe 6.0		X
Microsoft Developer Network (MSDN) Library, Single Edition	X	X
Windows NT Option Pack	X	X
Microsoft BackOffice Server 4.5, Developer Edition		X
Visual Component Manager	X	X
Microsoft Repository		X
Visual Modeler		X
Application Performance Explorer		X
Visual Studio Analyzer		X

used in analyzing distributed applications created with Visual Studio. Each of these tools can enhance development of distributed and desktop applications.

As part of Visual Studio, or on its own, Visual C++ 6.0 includes a number of features that can be used for creating desktop and distributed applications. Unlike Visual Studio, you don't get all of the development systems, such as Visual Basic or Visual J++, when acquiring Visual C++ on its own, but you do get the Visual C++ 6.0 development system and a considerable number of the tools included with Visual Studio. As we'll see, the components included in the Visual C++ package are beneficial to the creation of distributed applications.

Although Visual C++ 6.0 is available in Professional and Enterprise editions through Visual Studio, it is also available as a Standard edition when Visual C++ 6.0 is purchased on its own. The Standard edition includes the bare bones tools for developing applications, and is useful for new programmers who wish to learn Visual C++. For this reason, previous versions of the Standard edition were called "learning" editions. New to this edition are tutorials that aren't available with any of the other editions. These step-by-step instructions teach you how to program applications using Visual C++, and are set up so that no previous knowledge of C++ is required.

Aside from these tutorials, each of the features included in the Standard edition are also available in the Professional and Enterprise editions of Visual C++ 6.0. As Table 1-2 shows, the Standard edition has many of the features included in the Professional Edition, and the Enterprise edition has all of the features of the Professional edition plus a few more. This allows you to pick the edition that best suits your needs as a developer.

Requirements

Before actually installing Visual C++ 6.0—or any software for that matter—you should determine if the computer meets the minimal system requirements. System requirements are the minimal software and hardware needed by the program to work properly. This includes such elements of your system as the operating system used, free hard disk space, processor, RAM, and so forth. If your computer doesn't meet the requirements of the Visual C++ 6.0 edition being installed, then the installation will fail or Visual C++ 6.0 won't function as expected.

exam
⚙️atch

Although minimum installation requirements aren't a specific objective of the exam, it is an important part of installing Visual C++ 6.0 development tools, which subsequently is an objective. Many installation problems are due to the fact that the system fails to meet the minimal requirements of the software you're attempting to install. This results in the installation failing completely, or the components that are installed failing to function as they should. Before taking the exam, make sure you understand the minimal requirements for each edition of Visual C++ 6.0, on both Windows 9x and Windows NT. This will help you analyze problems being discussed in exam questions, and determine why a certain installation is failing.

| TABLE 1-2 | Visual C++ 6.0 Features by Edition | | | |

Feature	Description	Standard	Professional	Enterprise
Tutorials	New tutorials to learn Visual C++ 6.0	X		
Samples	Samples of source code, used for assistance in creating applications	X	X	X
Microsoft Foundation Class (MFC) Library	The classes, global functions, global variables, and macros used in programming Visual C++ 6.0 applications	X	X	X
C\C++ Run-time Libraries	Routines used in creating Visual C++ 6.0 applications	X	X	X
Active Template Library (ATL)	Used in creating server-side components and ActiveX Controls	X	X	X
Internet Support	Controls, APIs, and classes used for integrating applications with the Internet. This includes Internet Explorer 4.0 common controls, Internet Server Application Program Interface (ISAPI) extensions, Dynamic Hypertext Markup Language (DHTML), Chttp* MFC classes	X	X	X
ActiveX Controls and Document support	Ready to use, prebuilt ActiveX Controls that can be added to your project. In addition there is the new ability to create composite controls, and you can have your applications act as active document containers	X	X	X

TABLE 1-2	Visual C++ 6.0 Features by Edition *(continued)*			
Feature	**Description**	**Standard**	**Professional**	**Enterprise**
Component and Object Gallery	Storehouse of code that can be prebuilt components, ActiveX Controls, or user defined components	X	X	X
Component Object Model (COM) support	Support for the Component Object Model, inclusive to compiler COM support	X	X	X
Visual Database Tools	Full versions of these tools are only available in the Enterprise version. Read-only version available in the Professional and Standard versions	X	X	X
Static linkage to MFC	Enables you to resolve MFC references at link time rather than run-time		X	X
Code Optimization	Enables smaller, faster executables (EXEs) and dynamic-link libraries (DLLs)		X	X
Source Code Profiler	Enables you to analyze code to determine which parts could use performance modifications		X	X
Data-bound controls	RemoteData, DBGrid, DBCombo, and DBList controls for data access		X	X
Custom AppWizard	Enables you to create an AppWizard to create projects and custom starter files		X	X
InstallShield	Packages applications you create for easy installation		X	X

TABLE 1-2	Visual C++ 6.0 Features by Edition *(continued)*			
Feature	**Description**	**Standard**	**Professional**	**Enterprise**
Cluster Resource Wizard	Used to generate projects for implementation of a Clustering Service resource type		X	X
Visual SourceSafe	Used for version control of source code			X
MFC Data binding	Ability to do simple and complex data binding to any ActiveX data control			X
Remote Automation	Used for creating and running Automation programs			X
Microsoft Transaction Server (called Component Services in Windows 2000)	Transaction processing server application. This is available for free as part of the NT Option Pack			X
Microsoft SQL Server 6.5, Developer Edition	Database server application			X
SQL Editor and Debugger	Integrated SQL Editor (for writing and editing SQL statements) and debugger (for finding bugs in SQL statements)			X
Internet Information Services	Web Server Application. This is available for free as part of the NT Option Pack			X

As we learned earlier in this chapter, Visual C++ 6.0 comes in different editions, which include different features. The Professional edition includes more tools than the Standard edition, and the Enterprise edition includes more than each of these other editions. As such, with each higher edition used, more hard disk space needs to be used, and in most cases, a faster processor is needed. As Table 1-3 shows, different amounts of free disk space are required in each edition to accommodate the installation of different features. Without checking the minimal requirements before installing, you may waste time and money on an edition of Visual C++ that doesn't work on your system.

In addition to Visual C++ 6.0 itself, the different editions include various products. As Table 1-4 shows, each edition comes with extra software that can be used when developing Visual C++ 6.0 applications. Because each of these takes up its own space on your hard disk, it's important that you take these requirements into account when determining if your system meets the minimal requirements of installing a particular edition.

TABLE 1-3		Minimum Requirements for Installing Visual C++ 6.0	
Requirement	**Standard Edition**	**Professional Edition**	**Enterprise Edition**
Operating System	Windows 95 or later, or Windows NT 4.0 or later (with Service Pack 3 installed)	Windows 95 or later, or Windows NT 4.0 or later (with Service Pack 3 installed)	Windows 95 or later, or Windows NT 4.0 or later (with Service Pack 3 installed)
Processor	486/66 MHz or higher, with Pentium 90 or higher processor recommended	Pentium class processor, with Pentium 90 or higher recommended	Pentium class processor, with Pentium 90 or higher recommended
Random Access Memory (RAM)	24MB with 32MB recommended	24MB with 32MB recommended	24MB with 32MB recommended
Free Disk Space	Typical: 225MB Full: 305MB	Typical: 290MB Full: 375MB	Typical: 305MB Full: 405MB
Other Requirements	CD-ROM, mouse, VGA Monitor (SVGA recommended), Microsoft Internet Explorer 4.01 Service Pack 1	CD-ROM, mouse, VGA Monitor (SVGA recommended), Microsoft Internet Explorer 4.01 Service Pack 1	CD-ROM, mouse, VGA Monitor (SVGA recommended), Microsoft Internet Explorer 4.01 Service Pack 1

		Professional	
Product	**Standard Edition**	**Edition**	**Enterprise Edition**
Internet Explorer	Hard disk space: Typical: 43MB Full: 59MB	Hard disk space: Typical: 43MB Full: 59MB	Hard disk space: Typical: 43MB Full: 59MB
MSDN	Hard disk space: Typical: 57MB Full: 493MB	Hard disk space: Typical: 57MB Full: 493MB	Hard disk space: Typical: 57MB Full: 493MB
Windows NT Option Pack	Not Included with this edition	Hard disk space: Windows 9x: 20MB Windows NT: 200MB	Hard disk space: Windows 9x: 20MB Windows NT: 200MB
Microsoft SQL Server 6.5	Not Included with this edition	Not Included with this edition	Windows NT (won't run on Windows 9x) Hard disk space: Typical: 80MB Full: 95MB
Microsoft SNA Server 4.0	Not included with this edition	Not included with this edition	Windows NT (won't run on Windows 9x) Hard disk space: Typical: 50MB Full: 100+MB

TABLE 1-4   Additional Requirements for Products included with Visual C++ 6.0

Installing Visual C++ Development Tools through Visual Studio

In many ways, there is little difference between installing Visual C++ 6.0 on Windows 95, Windows 98, Windows NT Workstation, and Windows NT Server. There are no separate installation programs for the different platforms, and screens that appear during the installation process appear the same. What is different is that certain tools can't be installed on every platform, and certain additional measures must be taken when installing on or from Windows NT systems.

Windows NT has higher security than Windows 9x, and Windows NT networks use permissions to dictate what applications can be used by users, and which folders on a Windows NT system's hard disk can be accessed. On Windows NT Workstations, these permissions are set with the User

Manager program. On Windows NT Server, these permissions are set with User Manager for Domains. Each of these programs is used to administer accounts on Windows NT systems and networks. A major difference between these two programs is that User Manager for Windows NT Workstation can't administer and set permissions for domain user and administrator accounts. It can, however, set permissions for local users and groups. Which of these you use has a great deal to do with how your network is set up, and should generally be discussed with your network administrator.

The reason that permissions are so important is because they control access to files and folders. This means that if your account doesn't have access to a CD-ROM from which you want to install Visual C++ 6.0, you won't be able to access the installation files. If you're installing from a distribution server, which has all the installation files stored on that server's hard disk, you will also need adequate permissions to install from that server's folder. In addition, you'll need proper permissions to use the files after they've been installed. Otherwise, you won't be able to start and use Visual C++ 6.0 after installation is complete.

If you're installing Visual C++ 6.0 or Visual Studio on a "clean machine" (that is, a computer that has just had the operating system installed), you will need to install Internet Explorer 4.01 (IE4) or later. This is used to display HTML help files, and interfaces used by some components of Visual Studio. IE4 is included on the installation disk. Once you've installed this and rebooted, you will also need to install Service Pack 3 (SP3) or later on your Windows NT machine. SP3 is also included on the installation disk, or can be downloaded for free from Microsoft's Web site. Once you've installed and rebooted, you will have met the software requirements for installing Visual C++ 6.0 and Visual Studio 6.0.

Once you've ensured that you have the proper permissions to install Visual C++ 6.0, and that your computer meets the minimal requirements, you're ready to begin the installation process. Like many of the products available from Microsoft, a wizard is used to aid you through this procedure. A wizard is a program that takes you step-by-step through a task, with each screen showing a step in completing that task. In the case of the setup wizard on the Visual C++ or Visual Studio installation disc, this would be the task of installing Visual C++ 6.0.

The setup wizard can be started in one of two ways. When you insert your installation CD-ROM into your computer's CD-ROM drive, the wizard will start automatically. If for some reason it doesn't, or if you're installing over the network, you can start the wizard by opening the SETUP.EXE file. From the Windows Start menu, you select Run and then type the path to the SETUP.EXE file. You can also use Windows NT Explorer (on Windows NT machines) or Windows Explorer (on systems running Windows 9*x*) to browse your local machine or network for the folder or CD-ROM containing the installation files. After you double-click this file, the setup wizard will start, and a welcome screen will appear.

The welcome screen outlines the purpose of the wizard, and how it will walk you through the process of installing Visual Studio. On this screen, you'll also notice a View Readme button, which is used to load a Hypertext Markup Language (HTML) file into your Internet browser. HTML files are documents used on the Internet as Web pages, and may contain graphics and hyperlinks. By clicking the underlined text or a graphic serving as a hyperlink, you can view other information. This document contains the latest information on your particular version of Visual Studio or Visual C++, inclusive to installation, known issues, and so forth. If you don't wish to read this file, simply click the Next button on this screen of the wizard to continue with the installation.

The next screen that appears is the End User License Agreement screen, which outlines the agreement between you and Microsoft on how the product(s) that you're installing can be used. You have two options on this screen: I Accept the Agreement and I Don't Accept the Agreement. Until you accept the agreement, you can't proceed with the installation. The Next button on the screen is disabled. It appears grayed out, and nothing will happen when you click it. If you choose not to accept the agreement, then the Back button will also be disabled, allowing you to either choose to accept or Exit the installation. Once you accept the agreement, all the buttons become enabled, and you can continue with the installation by clicking Next.

The screen that follows is where you prove that you have a legal copy of Visual Studio. The Product Number and User ID screen has several fields that require input. The first of these is the product's ID number, which is also referred to as a *CD Key*. The number you enter here can be found on the back of your installation CD-ROM's jewel case (the case the CD-ROM came in), or in your product documentation. The number must be entered exactly, or installation will fail. The other two fields are where you enter your name and your company's name. This will be filled out for you with information that the wizard acquires from the Windows Registry. Ensure that this information is correct, then click Next to continue.

What appears next depends on whether or not you have previous versions of the products installed on your computer. If you have previous versions of products that are included with Visual Studio (inclusive to Visual C++ 5.0, Visual Basic, and so forth), the Uninstall Visual Studio 97 screen will appear. Each of the previous versions currently installed on your system will have check boxes beside them that are selected. This indicates that you want to uninstall the previous version, and replace it with the new version of the product. However, you are able to have previous versions of Visual C++ running on the same machine as the new version that you're installing. If you wish to keep a previous version, simply clear the check box beside that product's name. Following this, click Next to continue with the installation process. If you don't have previous versions on your system, this screen won't appear.

The next screen that you'll see offers you three choices for installing Visual Studio products. These options are:

- **Custom**   Allows you to define which products and server tools you'd like to install on the workstation

- **Products**   Allows you to install preconfigured versions of Visual C++, Visual Basic, Visual FoxPro, Visual InterDev, and Visual SourceSafe

- **Server Tools**   Allows you to skip over installing the workstation products of the Products option, and only install server applications

The first of these options is used if you want to install both server tools and Visual Studio products. The second option installs only the products, whereas the third installs just the server tools. Although we'll discuss each of these options individually, you should realize that you can go back and add additional products and tools later. This is something we'll see later in this chapter, when we install Visual SourceSafe.

Regardless of the type of installation you choose, the next screen will ask you to specify where files used by multiple programs in Visual Studio should be stored. A default path is entered in the field on this screen, but you can change the path to the common folder you'd like to use by typing a new path or by clicking the Browse button. When you click the Browse button, a dialog box will appear that allows you to browse your local hard drives and the network. This enables you to specify an existing folder to store common files in. After selecting a folder and clicking OK on this dialog box, the new path will appear in the previously mentioned field. Regardless of how or where you want to store these files, you should be aware that Visual Studio requires a minimum of 50MB for the common folder. You should ensure that any local hard disk or network drive that you designate as the common folder meets this requirement. You should also keep in mind that if you choose a network drive for the common folder, and the network goes down, Visual C++ and other products in the Visual Studio suite won't function properly (if at all). Although each workstation will have more free disk space if you use a common folder on a server, this shouldn't be done if network failures are common in your organization.

If you select Product as your installation type, the next screen you'll see is the one shown in Figure 1-1. This lists each of the workstation products discussed earlier in this chapter, which you can install by selecting the check box beside the product's name. If a check box is selected, the product beside it will be installed. Otherwise, it won't be installed at this time, and if you wish to install additional products later, you'll have to re-run the setup wizard. After selecting the products you wish to install, click the Next button to continue with the installation process.

Whether you've chosen Products or Custom as your installation type, the screens that follow from this point on are the same. The only difference is the order in which they appear. When you select Custom as your installation type, clicking Next brings you to a Welcome screen for

Select the products that you wish to install from the Visual Studio Individual Tools Setup screen

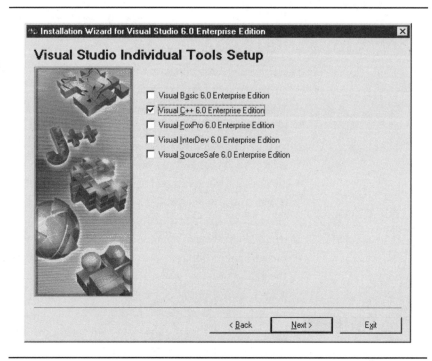

installing Visual Studio. If you choose Products, then this screen appears after clicking Next from the Individual Tools Setup screen discussed in the previous paragraph. Clicking the Continue button on this screen moves you to the next step in installing Visual C++.

The screen that appears next provides you with a product ID number. This number is made up of digits added by the setup wizard to the product registration number (CD Key) you entered earlier in the installation process. It's important that you write this number down, and keep it in a safe place, as Microsoft may request it if you call their technical support team for assistance. After installation, you can read this number by clicking About in the Help menu of Visual C++ and other Visual Studio products. However, even though you can access this number after installation from the Help menu, this will be worthless if the installation doesn't complete or if you can't open Visual C++ once it's installed. Once you've documented the product ID number, click the OK button to continue.

When you first see the Custom screen after choosing the Products installation type, you may think that you've done something wrong. This screen—shown in Figure 1-2—is the same one that appears when choosing the Custom installation type. However, there is a difference in what's selected on this screen, depending on the type of installation you've chosen. When the Custom installation type is selected, most of the options shown in the listing at the left of this screen are selected. You can then cancel the selected products and tools by clicking a check box, and removing the check mark. If there is no check mark, the product or tool to the right of the check box won't install. If you reach this screen by choosing the Products installation type, then only the options for the individual tools you've chosen will be selected. For example, if you select only Visual C++ 6.0 to be installed, then the Custom screen will have the options associated with that product selected. This not only includes Visual C++ 6.0, but ActiveX and Data Access components, various tools, and Visual SourceSafe. These are preconfigured to be selected as they all relate to that specific product.

FIGURE 1-2

You can install all or part of a component using the Custom installation

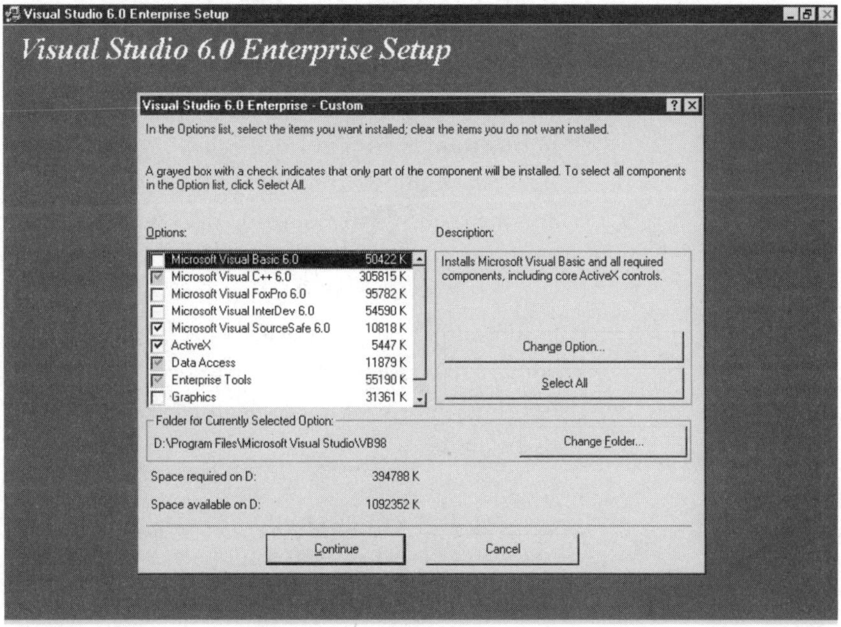

To the right of the Options listing, you'll see two buttons. The first of these is the Change Option button. When an option is selected (as shown by the highlight in the Options listing), the Change Option button becomes enabled. This lets you know that there are options within this particular option that you can add or remove. Clicking Change Option opens that particular option allowing you to view these other options. You can almost think of it as opening a folder on your hard disk to view the files within. The second button is Select All. When you click this button, each of the options shown in the Options listing will be selected (that is, their check boxes will be selected) automatically. This is useful if there are a number of items you want to install, but don't want to click each check box individually.

Below these buttons and the Options listing, you'll see the default folder where a particular option will be installed. You can change where each product will be installed by clicking the Change Folder button, which displays a dialog box. This dialog box allows you to type the path to another folder on your local or network drive. You can also browse your computer or network for an existing folder. If you type the path of a folder that doesn't exist, and click OK on the dialog box, the wizard will prompt you that the folder doesn't exist and ask if it should be created.

The Change Folder button is often used in conjunction with the information that's displayed below it on the Custom screen. There are two lines below this button that show the space available on a particular drive, and how much space is required. If the amount required exceeds the amount available, you should specify a new folder on a drive with adequate space. If you don't do this, when you click Next, the wizard will check to ensure enough space is available to install, and display a screen indicating which drives don't have enough free space. This screen will allow you to return to the Custom screen, and then pick a new folder and different drive to install to.

After using the Custom screen to select or accept options to install, clicking the Continue button will cause the setup wizard to check available space and determine any components that are already installed. For example, if it finds a previous or current version of Visual SourceSafe on your computer, it will prompt you to decide whether the new installation of Visual SourceSafe should replace it. The setup wizard will then begin copying files from the installation CD-ROM to your hard disk. As Visual C++ 6.0 is an enormous program, and there are a number of other tools and components to install, this may take a few minutes to complete. It will then proceed to modify system settings and environment variables necessary to run Visual C++ and the other options selected earlier. When this is finished, you'll be prompted to restart your computer.

After the computer has restarted and reloaded Windows, a screen will automatically appear and offer you the chance to install the Microsoft Developer Network (MSDN) Library. This is a collection of documentation and samples for the Visual Studio suite of products. If you're installing from Visual Studio, MSDN is included. Although this was the most recent version of MSDN when Visual Studio was released, you can also order a subscription to MSDN through Microsoft's Web site (http://msdn.microsoft.com). To install MSDN, ensure that the Install MSDN check box on this screen is selected, insert the MSDN CD-ROM, and click Next.

A welcome screen will appear for installing MSDN on your hard disk. Clicking Continue will show the screen we discussed earlier, which displayed the product ID. Although it appears to be identical, this is a different product ID number. For reasons discussed earlier, you should write this number down before clicking OK to continue.

A dialog box will appear with two buttons used to show your agreement to using the MSDN library. Clicking I Decline will cancel installation of MSDN. Clicking I Agree will allow you to proceed with installation of the MSDN Library.

This will bring you to a screen that allows you to select the type of installation for MSDN. There are three different types of installation, which are as follows:

- **Typical**   Installs commonly used components of MSDN
- **Custom**   Allows you to install only the components you select
- **Full**   Installs the entire MSDN Library to your hard disk

In most cases, Typical installation is what you'd choose. This installation takes up a maximum of 60MB of hard disk space, as opposed to the 800MB used by Full installation. As you choose only the components you want installed with Custom, the amount of disk space required depends on the components you've decided to install. If you have significant disk space available, it may be worthwhile to perform a full install of MSDN. This will provide you with better search capabilities when using the library.

After clicking Typical or Full, the setup wizard will check the hard disk where MSDN will be installed to ensure there is enough hard disk space. It will then begin copying the necessary files onto your hard disk, until finally displaying a message box that informs you whether the installation succeeded or failed.

If you decide to perform a Custom installation of MSDN, the next screen you see will be a listing of documentation and samples that can be installed onto your hard disk. This includes information on Visual C++, as well as items related to other products in the Visual Studio suite. It's advisable that you install items related to the programs you're using, as these will provide you with important information and online assistance. Once you've selected the items to install, clicking Next will begin the transfer of files from the CD-ROM to your hard disk. A message box will then display whether the installation succeeded or failed, and indicate the end of this portion of the installation process.

Once you've installed MSDN, you're ready for the final step in the installation process. This is deciding whether to install InstallShield. As we saw earlier in this chapter, InstallShield is a program used when setting up installation packages for programs created with Visual C++ 6.0. This appears in a Client Tools listing on the Other Client Tools screen that appears next. By selecting InstallShield from this listing, the Install button on this screen becomes enabled. You can then click this button, and InstallShield will begin its own installation process on your computer.

A welcome screen will appear for the InstallShield installation wizard, and by clicking Next you're brought to the InstallShield Software License Agreement screen. By clicking the Yes button on this screen, you can proceed with the installation. Otherwise, your only other choices are to click Back to move to the preceding screen, or No to cancel the installation.

The next screen will display your name and company name, which is already filled in from information in the Windows Registry. Ensure that this information is correct, as you won't be able to change it later. Following this, click Next to continue.

The Choose Destination Location screen allows you to specify where InstallShield will be installed. You can either accept the default installation folder, or click Browse to open a new dialog box. This dialog box enables you to specify a different directory to install to. As with the Browse dialog box that we saw earlier, you can type a path where InstallShield will be installed, or use the dialog box to browse your local computer or network drive. If you type a path to a folder that doesn't exist, you'll be prompted as to whether the wizard should create this directory.

When you click Next from the Choose Destination Location, you will be asked to specify how InstallShield should be installed. There are three setup types to choose from:

- **Typical**   Installs the most commonly used options. This is the option used by most users of InstallShield

- **Compact**   Installs the minimal options for using InstallShield. This should be used if you have limited disk space

- **Custom**   Enables you to specify which options you'd like to install

Selecting either Typical or Compact will take you to a screen informing you that you're ready to begin installing, and tells you what the Installation Wizard will do next. We'll discuss this in the paragraphs that follow. Clicking Next will begin copying the necessary files to your hard disk. However, if you select Custom, you will have a few more choices to make.

Clicking Custom from the Setup Type screen brings up a new screen where you can choose which options will be installed on your computer. There are three options on this screen:

- **Program Files**   Application files necessary to use InstallShield
- **Help Files**   Documentation files that provide online assistance
- **Templates**   Samples that can be used with InstallShield

A check box appears before each of these options, and clearing a check box will mean that particular option won't be installed. If a check box is selected, then that option will be installed.

Clicking Next brings up the previously mentioned screen that informs you that installation is ready to begin, and tells you what will take place next. This screen informs you that a shortcut to InstallShield will be added to the Start menu, and that it also will be accessible from the Tools menu of Visual C++. Clicking Next will begin installation of files on the installation CD-ROM, based on the options you choose earlier.

The final screen in the installation process includes an option to view a README file associated with InstallShield. To view this file, leave the check box selected. Otherwise, click the check box to clear the check mark. Click Finish.

After installation of InstallShield has completed, the installation process shifts from client tools to server tools. It is here that you can select individual server tools from a listing of server components. This is the same screen that appears if you selected Server Tools as the installation type mentioned early in the installation process. We'll discuss these tools, and aspects related to their installation, in later sections. Once you've selected a component from the Server Components listing (by clicking the name of the component to install), the Install button becomes enabled. Clicking the Install button invokes an installation wizard for the component selected.

After you've installed the individual server tools, by following the on-screen instructions of each individual setup wizard, you can then click the Next button and go to the final screen of the installation process. A check box appears on this screen indicating whether you would next like to register Visual Studio online. If you have a modem and Internet access, clicking the Finish button will take you to a Web site where you can register Visual Studio. If you don't have these requirements, then click the check box to clear the checkmark. Finally, click Finish to complete the installation.

DCOM Utilities for Windows 95

Except where mentioned earlier in this chapter, most of the Distributed Component Object Model (DCOM) utilities that come with Visual C++

6.0 and Visual Studio will work on Windows 95/98 systems. There is no difference in the functionality of these utilities, regardless of whether they are running on a Windows NT or Windows 9*x* computer. If you're installing on any of these systems, you will still be able to use these tools and utilities.

The exception to this is the Windows NT Option Pack. The NT Option Pack is included with both the Professional and Enterprise editions of Visual Studio. If you're installing this on Windows NT systems (that is, Windows NT Server or Windows NT Workstation), the option pack includes DCOM-based server programs such as Microsoft Transaction Server 2.0 and Internet Information Services 4.0. On Windows 9*x* systems, the options in the NT Option Pack are more limited. Installing the option pack on Windows 95 or Windows 98 will install the Personal Web Server.

Personal Web Server is a program that allows workstations to share information and files over a local intranet. With this, you can create Web pages, so that other users on the network can view them. It is included with Visual C++ and Visual Studio for the development of Internet and intranet applications. Once you've created such an application with Visual C++ 6.0, you can add it to a Web page, and test its functionality over the network.

| EXERCISE 1-1 |

Installing Visual C++ Development Tools

1. Insert your Visual Studio installation CD-ROM into your CD-ROM drive. The setup wizard should start immediately. If it doesn't appear after a minute or more, open Windows Explorer (or NT Explorer if you're using Windows NT), and select your CD-ROM drive to browse. Double-click the SETUP.EXE file in the root directory.

2. When the welcome screen appears, click the Next button.

3. The End User License Agreement screen will appear next. Select the I Accept the Agreement option if you wish to continue with the setup. Click Next.

4. When the Product Number and User ID screen appears, enter your product ID number (CD-Key). Ensure that your name and company's name are correct, then click Next.

5. If you have previous versions of Visual C++ or other Visual Studio products installed on your computer, a screen will appear asking if you want these previous versions removed and replaced with new versions that you're installing. If you clear the check boxes beside the products you wish to keep, those products won't be uninstalled. Click Next to continue.

6. Select the Products option, then click Next.

7. The screen that appears asks you to specify a folder that will be used for files commonly used by multiple products. Accept the path entered in the field provided, or enter the path to where you'd like common files to be stored. Click Next.

8. When the installation welcome screen appears, click Continue.

9. Write down the product ID number on a piece of paper, and keep it in a safe place for future use. Click OK to continue.

10. The next screen that will appear is the Custom screen. Here you can specify which products and tools will be installed. Select the Visual SourceSafe check box, to clear the check mark. We will be installing Visual SourceSafe in the next chapter. Accept the remaining preconfigured options selected in the listing, and click the Continue button.

11. After the setup wizard finishes copying files and making modifications to your system settings, you'll be prompted to restart the computer. Click the Restart Computer button on this message box to continue.

12. When your computer restarts and reloads Windows, a new screen will appear asking if you want to install MSDN. Insert the MSDN CD-ROM into your CD-ROM drive. Ensure that the Install MSDN check box is selected, and then click Next.

13. When the MSDN welcome screen appears, click Continue.

14. Another product ID screen will appear, displaying the product ID number for MSDN. Document this number, and then click OK.

15. When the End User License Agreement for MSDN appears, click the button labeled I Agree to continue with the installation.

16. When the MSDN Installation screen appears, click Typical. MSDN will then proceed to install its files onto your hard disk. When it has finished this, click OK on the message box that appears telling you whether your installation was successful or not.

17. Select InstallShield from the listing of Client Tools shown on the Other Client Tools screen that appears, then click the Install button.

18. When the InstallShield welcome screen appears, click Next.

19. To continue with the installation process of InstallShield, click the Yes button on the InstallShield Software License Agreement screen that appears.

20. Accept the default folder where InstallShield will be installed, or click Browse to specify a new target directory. Click Next to continue.

21. Click Typical to install InstallShield with the most commonly used features.

22. Click Next to begin the installation. Files will then begin to be transferred to your hard disk, and InstallShield will be installed.

23. When the files have completed being copied to your hard disk, a final screen for this portion of the installation will appear. If you wish to read the README file associated with InstallShield, leave the Yes, I Want to View the Readme File checked. Otherwise, click the check box beside this option to clear the check mark. Click Finish to complete the InstallShield's installation.

24. From the Server Setups screen, select the components you wish to install. If you're installing onto a Windows NT computer, install each of these components (as Microsoft recommends). If you're installing onto a Windows 9x computer, install the server tools in the order given in the section of this chapter that discusses the installation of server tools. Follow the on-screen instructions for any server tools installed, then click Next from the Server Setups screen to continue.

25. The final screen of the installation process appears. This screen has a check box to indicate whether you would like to register Visual Studio online. If you have a modem and Internet access, clicking the Finish button will connect you to a Web site. If you don't have a modem and Internet access, select the check box to clear the check mark. Click Finish to complete the installation.

Service Packs

Service packs can be installed to resolve issues associated with a particular product. These issues may be legal (as was the case with Visual J++), bug fixes, or other problems that weren't realized or couldn't be fixed when the product was initially released. After software has been installed, you can install the service pack. This will install updated files that deal with those problems.

exam
Watch

Don't expect to see much—if anything—regarding the service packs on your exam. The vast majority of questions that could appear on your exam were written before the service packs became available. Despite this, you should be aware of service packs, and install them to avoid problems that could result after installation. The reason the service packs exist is to upgrade problematic files.

In the case of Visual Studio's Service Pack 3, numerous issues are dealt with. One in particular is a bug in Visual C++ that can cause memory problems and crash third-party software. This bug appears in all editions of Visual C++ and Visual Studio. To deal with this problem, Service Pack 3 replaces a file associated with the heap manager (MSVCRT.DLL). Other upgraded files dealing with Visual C++ and other products are also included in the service pack.

Because the service pack upgrades files on your system that may be used by applications you create with Visual C++, it's important to install the service pack as soon as possible. This will ensure that any programs you create with Visual C++ 6.0 will have the latest files included with them, and keep users of your applications from encountering problems. As we'll see later in this book, such files may be included with applications you create and distribute.

Although there are three Visual Studio service packs at the time of this writing (that is, Service Pack 1, Service Pack 2, and Service Pack 3), you don't need to install all of them. Not only does Service Pack 3 resolve all of the issues taken care of in Service Packs 1 and 2, but it addresses additional problems that were solved after the initial release of Visual Studio and the first two service packs. As they deal with known issues resolved since your installation CD-ROM's release onto the market, you won't find the service pack on this CD-ROM. You need to obtain it from Microsoft. This can be done by contacting them directly, or by visiting the Visual Studio Web site at http://msdn.microsoft.com/vstudio/sp/default.asp. In using this URL, keep in mind that such addresses change often. If you have a problem, go to Microsoft's main URL (http://www.microsoft.com) and search for the service pack. As we'll see in the exercise that follows, it is from here that you'll be able to download the latest service pack.

When installing Service Pack 3, you should first shut down any Visual Studio products you're using. If, for example, Visual C++ were open, problems could arise when the service pack overwrites files associated with that program. Once the service pack has finished installing, you can then restart any of the Visual Studio products you were using.

Unfortunately, because the service pack overwrites files associated with Visual Studio products, there is no way to uninstall just the service pack. If there was, files would then be missing for products in the Visual Studio suite, and those products would be unable to function properly. As such, you would need to uninstall the actual product to get rid of the changes made by the service pack. For example, to get rid of the MSVCRT.DLL upgrade for Visual C++, you would need to uninstall Visual C++. Upon reinstalling Visual C++, any changes made by the service pack for Visual C++ 6.0 would be gone.

EXERCISE 1-2

Obtaining and Installing the Visual Studio Service Pack

1. Open Microsoft Internet Explorer by double-clicking the shortcut on your desktop. After connecting to the Internet, enter the URL **http://msdn.microsoft.com/vstudio/sp/default.asp** in the address bar. If you have trouble connecting, go to the MSDN Web site (http://msdn.microsoft.com), then click the link on this page for the latest service pack.

2. Click the hyperlink for the Full install of the service pack.

3. Click each link for a service pack file from *one* download site. For example, at the time of this writing, the latest service pack is Service Pack 3. This means you would download each of the following from one location: VS6SP3_1.EXE, VS6SP3_2.EXE, VS6SP3_3.EXE, and VS6SP3_4.EXE. For each file's hyperlink, select Save This Program to Disk when prompted to download the software, then click OK. Following this, select a directory on your hard disk to download the files to.

4. After download has completed, run each of the files that you downloaded. You can do this by either entering the path and filename of each downloaded file, or by using Windows Explorer. You can start Windows Explorer (or NT Explorer if you're using a Windows NT system) from the Programs folder of the Start menu. Use the browser to go to the directory in which you saved these files, and double-click each of the downloaded files. The contents of each of these files will expand upon being opened.

5. Run the SETUP.EXE program that has been expanded from the downloaded files.

6. When the End User License Agreement screen appears, click I Accept to install the service pack.

CERTIFICATION OBJECTIVE 1.02

Installing and Configuring Server Services

There are a number of different server services included with Visual Studio and Visual C++ 6.0 that can be set up to assist you in developing distributed applications. What services can be installed, however, depends on the operating system you're using. Because Windows NT Server is more powerful than Windows NT Workstation, and Windows NT Workstation is more powerful than Windows 95/98, the services you can install depend on the power of the operating system.

Many of the server services available can be installed through the Server Setups screen of the Visual Studio setup program. You can start the Visual Studio setup the same way you did when installing Visual C++ 6.0. After Visual C++ 6.0 has been installed, the Installation Wizard will automatically detect that components of Visual Studio have already been installed on the computer. Upon starting this setup program, the screen shown in Figure 1-3 will be displayed. From here, you can add and remove workstation tools and components, InstallShield, or the MSDN Library. You can also add server applications and tools used for distributed application development.

The Installation Wizard recognizes that other Visual Studio products have been installed

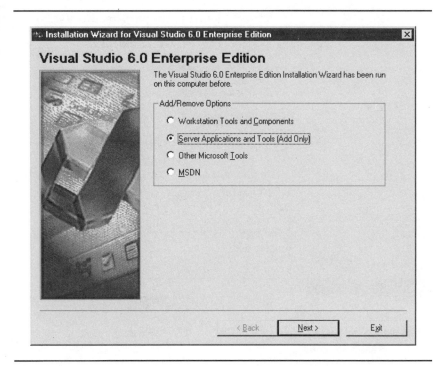

By selecting the Server Applications and Tools (Add Only) option and clicking Next, you are brought to the Server Setups screen shown in Figure 1-4. This screen shows a listing of server components that can be installed on the particular computer you are using. By selecting a component from the listing and clicking the Install button, any installation wizard associated with that component will start. You then follow the instructions on each screen of the wizard. As mentioned, some components will not work on less powerful computers or are geared toward certain operating systems. As such, what you see on the Server Setups screen will depend on the operating system that your computer is using.

If you're installing the server tools on a Windows 9x system, there is a large listing of components that can be installed. However, Windows 95 and Windows 98 require some of these server applications to be installed before others, if your installation is to succeed. The order is as follows:

1. NT Option Pack (for Windows 9*x*)

2. FrontPage 98 Server Extensions

3. Data Access Components 2.0

4. Visual InterDev Server Components

5. Application Performance Explorer

6. Visual Studio Analyzer

The remaining two components, Visual SourceSafe Server and Visual FoxPro Server Samples, can be installed in any order. This is because they don't rely on any of the other components to be installed beforehand. Later in this chapter, we'll discuss installing Visual SourceSafe Server in greater detail.

FIGURE 1-4

Choose the server tools to install from the Server Setups screen, as seen on a Windows 9x computer

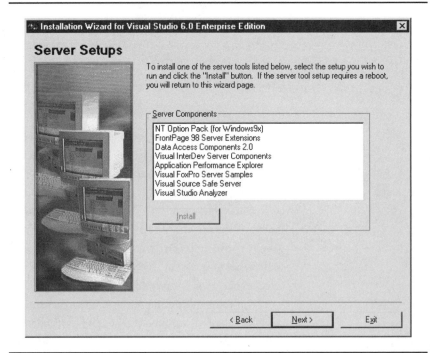

exam
ⓦatch

An easy way to remember the order in which server tools should be installed on a Windows 9x system is with the following sentence: "On Fun Days, I Am Awesome." The first letter of each word represents one of the tools: Option pack, FrontPage extensions, Data access, InterDev components, Application performance explorer, and (Visual Studio) Analyzer. At the very least, this will help you remember the order until you get into the exam, and can jot it down on paper.

If you're installing these server tools on Windows NT Workstation, it may seem that there are considerably fewer options to install. The components appearing on the Server Setups screen will consist of:

- Launch BackOffice Installation Wizard
- Visual SourceSafe Server

This doesn't mean that there are fewer components to install on an NT Workstation than on a Windows 9*x* machine. The BackOffice Installation Wizard installs the same components that are installed when Server Setups is run on a Windows 9*x* machine, plus a number of others. These include:

- Windows NT Option Pack
- SQL Server 6.5 Developers Edition
- Fox ISAPI Samples and Extensions
- SQL Server Debugging Service
- Remote Machine Debugging
- Visual Studio Analyzer
- Application Performance Explorer
- Visual InterDev Server Components
- FrontPage Server Extensions
- Posting Acceptor
- MS Data Access Components
- Microsoft SNA Server

Microsoft recommends that all of the tools appearing under Server Setups be installed on Windows NT machines. Each of these tools can be used for developing applications with Visual C++ 6.0. If you're installing these programs on a Windows NT system, then the order in which you install these products is up to you.

Microsoft Transaction Server (MTS)

Microsoft Transaction Server (MTS) is a transaction processing system that can be used to simplify your work in developing components. A transaction is a set of actions, or processing steps, that's treated as a single unit of work. You've probably heard the word *transaction* in the context of banking. For example, you might go to an ATM machine to withdraw some cash. After entering the amount to withdraw from your account, the program in the bank machine checks to see if there's enough money in your account. If there isn't, the program responds with an Insufficient Funds message. If there is enough money, it adjusts the account balance, gives you your money, and returns your bankcard. This is a transaction, which is treated as a single action (a withdrawal) even though it requires many processing steps.

Transactions provide protection from system failures or concurrent updates because transactions have four basic properties:

- **Atomicity**   Is an "all or nothing" feature of transactions. Either all of the steps in a transaction succeed or nothing happens. If any of the processing steps in a transaction fail, the transaction is aborted and the data is rolled back to its previous state.

- **Consistency**   Means that when the data is modified, it matches the state that is expected. When business rules in your application modify data, it is important that the data is correctly modified.

- **Isolation**   Is used to keep transactions from seeing the partial or uncommitted results of the other transactions. In other words, when two or more transactions are occurring on the same data, isolation makes it appear that only one transaction is running at a time.

■ **Durability**   Refers to a transaction's ability to survive failures. When an update is committed to data, it must be able to survive such things as communication failures, process failures, and server failures.

exam
ⓦatch

An easy way to remember the properties of a transaction is to think of the acronym ACID. Each letter represents a different property of the transaction: Atomicity, Consistency, Isolation, and Durability.

For the developer, using transactions ensures that all of the steps in a procedure succeed before changes are committed to data. By creating components that run on MTS, you are able to focus on developing the components without worrying about complex server issues. These components are created in Visual C++ 6.0, and then added to packages that are installed and run on MTS.

Although MTS is available for Windows 9*x*, Windows NT Workstation, and Windows NT Server, the capabilities of MTS on each of these platforms are quite different. Also, the version of MTS offered in the NT Option Pack is meant for developing packages, and is limited in its abilities to administer installations of MTS on other computers. In a later section of this chapter, we'll discuss these limitations and the features of MTS in greater detail.

Before installing MTS on your computer, you will need to ensure that DCOM is enabled. If you're using a version of Windows NT earlier than version 4.0, or don't have DCOM enabled on a computer running Windows 95 or Windows 98, the following message will appear when you try to install MTS: "Setup library mtssetup.dll could not be loaded or the function MTSSetupProc could not be found."

To enable DCOM (or to ensure that it's already enabled) follow the steps in the following exercise.

EXERCISE 1-3

Enabling DCOM on a Windows 9x Machine

1. Open the Network applet from Control Panel. When the Network applet opens, click the Access Control tab and ensure that you have the User-Level Access Control option selected. If this option isn't selected, select it and then click OK to exit the Network applet. If you've changed to user-level access control, you'll be prompted to restart your computer. Restart it, and continue to the next step upon re-entering Windows.

2. From the Windows Start menu, click Run. When the Run dialog box appears, type **DCOMCNFG** and then click OK. This starts the Distributed COM Configuration Properties.

3. Click the Default Properties tab, and ensure that the Enable Distributed COM on This Computer check box is selected. If it isn't, then click this check box to enable DCOM. Click OK to save your settings. DCOM is now enabled on your machine.

SQL

Microsoft SQL Server 6.5, Developer Edition is a fully functional version of SQL Server. This is a database server that runs on Windows NT systems. SQL (pronounced sequel) stands for Structured Query Language, which is a language that's used for communicating with databases. Using SQL, you can create queries that will return the information you need to applications that you create with Visual C++ 6.0.

Microsoft SQL Server 6.5, Developer Edition is installed through the BackOffice Installation Wizard on Windows NT. When installed, you can then design, develop, and test Visual C++ programs that work in conjunction with SQL Server. Because it is a Developer edition, you're limited to ten concurrent connections. SQL Server won't run on a Windows 9x system, and is only used on Windows NT.

MSMQ

Microsoft Message Queue (MSMQ) is another program that can aid in the development of distributed applications. The client portion of MSMQ is available for installation on Windows NT Workstation and Windows 9x systems. However, the MSMQ server can only be installed on Windows NT Server, and is included with Windows NT Server 4.0 and later as part of the NT Option Pack.

The concept of message queuing is similar to when you leave a telephone message on an answering machine. Just as you can communicate directly with someone or leave a message, a computer can send messages directly or have them queued. When one computer communicates directly with another, synchronous communication or message passing occurs. The problem with message passing is that if both devices (sender and receiver) aren't online, then messages can't be sent or received.

Message queuing sidesteps the problem, because any data sent from one computer to another goes directly into a message queue. Message queuing is also known as asynchronous communication. When a message is sent from a computer, it goes into a message queue. This message store is located on a server, where the message resides until the computer is ready to receive the data. Because the communication is indirect, the receiving computer doesn't have to be online or connected to the network when the message is sent. If the receiving computer is online when the message is sent, the sending computer's message still goes into the message store, but it is automatically sent from there to the receiving computer.

exam
ⓌatcH

Remember that asynchronous communication is message queuing whereas synchronous communication is message passing. You should also know what each does. Message queuing and asynchronous communication, and message passing and synchronous communication, are terms that can be used interchangeably, and may appear as such in some questions on the exam.

When you create applications that communicate with one another through message queues, you are working with something called Message Orientated Middleware, or MOM. Message Queue Services is an example of this kind of middleware. MSMQ provides guaranteed delivery, ensuring that all messages will eventually make it to their proper destination. It allows applications to communicate across heterogeneous networks, and provides efficient routing, security, and priority-based, reliable messaging. Best of all, it is connectionless, meaning that applications don't need to maintain sessions to communicate. Messages from sending computers are stored until the receiving computer is ready to read the message from the queue.

For developers, asynchronous communication is effective for distributed applications for a number of reasons. Because messages are stored in a queue rather than directly sent to another application, the sending application doesn't need to wait for a response. When a message is sent using synchronous communication, an application sends a message and then must wait for a response from the receiving computer. This response lets the sender know that the message was received properly. With asynchronous communication, the sender can perform other work while waiting for a response to a request. This type of communication is also useful when responses aren't required, and it is unnecessary to wait for the receiving computer to process a request. Because synchronous communication requires a connection, communication will fail if a receiving computer isn't available on the network.

<table>
<tr><td>EXERCISE 1-4</td></tr>
</table>

Installing NT Option Pack on Windows 9x Systems

1. Insert the Visual Studio installation CD-ROM into your CD-ROM drive.

2. With Windows Explorer, select the CD-ROM drive and double-click the SETUP.EXE program.

3. Select the Server Applications and Tools (Add only) option, and click Next.

4. Select NT Option Pack from the listing of components, and then click the Install button.

5. When prompted, insert the second Visual Studio installation CD-ROM, then click OK.

6. A welcome screen will appear for Personal Web Server. Click the Next button.

7. When the End User License Agreement screen appears, click Accept to continue.

8. Click the Custom button on the screen that appears.

9. Ensure that each of the following items on the screen that appears next is selected. If they are not, click the check box so that a check mark appears in it:

   ■ Common Program Files

   ■ Microsoft Data Access Components

   ■ Microsoft Message Queue

   ■ Transaction Server

10. Because NT Option Pack includes Personal Web Server, you will need to specify the directory for publishing Web pages. Accept the default and click Next.

11. The Microsoft Transaction Server screen allows you to specify where MTS will be installed. If the default directory is acceptable, click Next. Otherwise, enter the new path in the MTS Install Folder field, and then click Next.

12. The screen that appears next allows you to choose between installing Microsoft Message Queue as an Independent Client or as a Dependent Client. The type of client you select here determines how the remainder of the setup will proceed. Independent Clients have their own message store, allowing them to send and receive messages at any time. Dependent Clients use the message store of an MSMQ Server, and must have a connection to it in order to send and receive messages. Select one of the two options, then click Next.

13. If you selected Independent Client, you are required to enter the name of an MSMQ Site Controller, so you can be registered in the MSMQ Information Store database on that computer. If you selected Dependent Client, you must enter the name of a MSMQ Server or Site Controller. Enter the appropriate data, then click Next. The setup program will search for the server, then continue with the installation.

14. You must enter the path of the folder that will store administration tools and the SDK files. If you're unsure of the directory, click the Browse button to look through your hard disk for an appropriate folder. Click Next.

15. The setup program will begin transferring files. You will then be prompted to restart. Click Yes. After restarting, system settings will be modified, thereby completing the installation.

EXERCISE 1-5

Installing NT Option Pack on Windows NT Systems

1. Insert the Visual Studio installation CD-ROM into your CD-ROM drive.

2. With NT Explorer, select the CD-ROM drive and double-click the SETUP.EXE program.

3. Select the Server Applications and Tools (Add only) option, and click Next.

4. From the list of components, select Launch BackOffice Installation Wizard, and then click Install.

5. When prompted, insert the second Visual Studio installation CD-ROM into your CD-ROM drive, then click OK.

6. When the BackOffice Installation Wizard has loaded, a welcome screen will appear. Select the Visual C++ Developer option, then click Next.

7. The screen that follows will tell you what will be installed. The selection you choose will install the NT Option Pack (NT4), SQL Server 6.5 Developer Edition, SQL Server Debugging, Posting Acceptor, and MS Data Access Components.

8. The next screen will enable you to modify components being installed, and check disk space. Click Next to continue.

9. The next screen allows you to assign accounts to SQL Server and MTS. Select SQL Server Developer Edition Executive Logon Account, then click the Assign Account button to bring up a listing of current accounts on your computer. Select your account, enter and confirm your password, then click OK.

10. Select Transaction Server MTS Remote Administrator Account, then click the Assign Account button to bring up a listing of current accounts on your computer. Select your account, enter and confirm your password, then click OK. Click Next to continue.

11. The screen that follows confirms your installation options. Click Next to continue.

12. The installation program will begin installing each of the programs. Once the necessary files have been copied to your hard disk, the final screen will appear. Click the Finish button, and you will be prompted to restart. Click Yes. After restarting, system settings will be modified, thereby completing the installation.

Configuring a Client Computer to Use an MTS Component

As mentioned earlier in this chapter, MTS can be installed on Windows 9*x*, Windows NT Workstation, or Windows NT Server. Once installed, it provides the following features:

- **MTS run-time environment**   Serves as a middle-tier platform for running three-tier components.

- **MTS Explorer**   Is used for managing and deploying components

- **Application Programming Interfaces (APIs) and Resource Dispensers**   APIs are sets of commands used in an application to request services performed by the operating system, whereas Resource Dispensers are used to access shared information.

These features make it easier to build, deploy, and maintain complex applications, and are available when installed on all three platforms.

MTS Explorer allows you to install, delete, and monitor packages on a server computer. In addition to this, you can also create application executables that install to and configure client computers. The executable enables the client computer to access a remote server application. By using the Explorer, you can configure the client computer not only to access applications on the local network, but also to access other computers on the network.

Before delving into configuring client computers to use MTS packages, it is important to understand how to create and modify one. The first step is to decide where the package will be created. You can add computers to MTS Explorer and then administer them. Once a computer has been added to the Computers folder in MTS Explorer, you can create packages that will be installed on that particular computer.

Once you've decided whether you will create a package on the local My Computer or another computer, double-click the computer icon you'll use. You'll then see the Installed Pages folder. Opening this folder reveals all of the packages currently installed on that computer. To create a new package or install an existing one, select Action | New | Package, which will start the Package Wizard. Two buttons appear on the first screen of the Package Wizard:

- Install Pre-Built Packages
- Create an Empty Package

Clicking the first button makes the Package Wizard present you with a screen that allows you to install existing packages. By clicking the Add button, you can select packages on your hard disk, which have the extension .PAK.

The Next button then brings you to a screen that allows you to specify the path where the package will be installed. Creating a new package is equally easy. After clicking the Create an Empty Package button, you are presented with a screen that allows you to enter the name for your new package. Clicking Finish creates the package, which is then displayed in the Installed Packages folder.

After an empty package has been created, you must add components to it. Double-clicking your new package's icon displays a Components folder. After opening the Components folder, you are ready to add components. To do this, select Action | New | Component to start the Component Wizard. The first screen of the Component Wizard has two buttons:

- Install New Component(s)
- Import Component(s) That Are Already Registered

Clicking the first of these buttons brings up the Install Components screen. By clicking the Add Files button, you can select files from your hard disk to add to the package. Clicking Finish adds the files to the package. Selecting Import Component(s) That Are Already Registered makes the Component Wizard build a listing of every component that's been registered with the Windows Registry of the computer. After selecting the components to add from this list, click Finish to add the components to your package. This is the same procedure as adding components to an existing package. To delete components from a package, simply select the component you want to remove and press DELETE on the keyboard.

Source Code Control Using Microsoft Visual SourceSafe

As you or others make changes to source code, there may be times when you'll need to track those changes. You or another programmer may modify the code, only to find that these changes adversely effect your application. You may want to refer to a previous version of your application to see how it was originally written, or to see if you should revert to previously used code. Tracking changes to source code during software development enables you to see what work has been done, who has done the work, and it helps you analyze how those changes have affected the project as a whole. This provides accountability for code that's written for a project. If a question arises about a piece of code, a developer can confer with the programmer who wrote the code. In addition, others won't be able to take credit for the good work you've done, or pass faulty code off on you. If an older version of source code works better, source code control is required to restore those previous versions of code.

If you don't already have a source code control system, you won't need to go out and buy one. Visual SourceSafe (VSS) is a source code control system that comes with Visual C++ and Visual Studio. It allows developers to save copies of their source code to a database. When a file is added to VSS, that file is stored in the VSS database. The database supports many different file types, including binary files, graphics, text files, audio, and video. If the original file becomes corrupt, or modifications that don't work are made to the source code, it doesn't necessarily mean that your previous, functional source code is lost. You can use VSS to restore old versions of files by retrieving them from the database. You can also view information on each version stored in the database. This gives developers the ability to track any changes made to their source code files.

Visual SourceSafe 6.0 is actually comprised of two separate programs:

- Visual SourceSafe Client
- Visual SourceSafe Server

The VSS Client installation is done on machines where users wish to save their source code to the database. Any workstation that will use the VSS database will need to have this client portion installed. The Visual SourceSafe Server installation is used to install a source code control database to store versions of source code. It also installs an administration application that will enable you to control who can access the source code files stored in the database, and who can perform administration tasks.

The client portion works with the server portion of VSS. Through the client portion of VSS, developers can save and retrieve their source code from this database. As all members of the development team can use this database, the server installation only needs to be performed once on a network. The client portion, however, needs to be installed on each and every computer that will access this database. This includes the server itself if it will be used for development work. Even though you have the server portion installed on a server machine, you'll still need to install the client portion on that machine if you're going to develop applications on that machine.

exam
Ⓦatch

Remember that the client portion is used for all developers accessing the source code control database, whereas the server portion provides a centralized database and administration. To use VSS on the computer that's acting as the VSS Server, you'll also need the VSS Client installed.

To facilitate source code control, Visual C++ 6.0 uses the Microsoft Source Code Control Interface. This interface provides a method for source code control systems such as Visual SourceSafe to integrate with the Visual C++ environment. Even though the source code control system is a separate application, you can access aspects of its functionality by using menu items in Visual C++ 6.0. This includes saving your projects and source code files to a Visual SourceSafe database, removing them, examining their history, determining the status, and so on.

Because it is a Microsoft product, VSS conforms to the Microsoft Source Code Control Interface. This means that when the VSS Client is installed, the commands dealing with source code control will be added to the Visual C++ 6.0 environment, as will a new tab under Visual C++ 6.0's Options dialog box. As shown in Figure 1-5, until the VSS Client is installed, menu items dealing with source code control don't appear under Visual C++ 6.0's menu system. Once installed, these items appear, allowing you to interact with VSS.

Installing Visual SourceSafe is a two-part process. The first step is installing the VSS Server, which will provide developers with a centralized, source code control database. This is generally installed by the person who

---

FIGURE 1-1

Source code control commands don't appear in Visual C++ 6.0 until after source code control has been installed

Visual C++ Project menu *before* Source Code Control System is installed

Visual C++ Project menu *after* Source Code Control System is installed

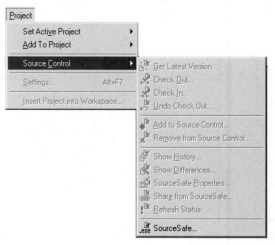

is the designated VSS administrator, and who will be responsible for the administration tasks we'll discuss later in this chapter. The second part of the process is installing the client portion on each workstation that will access this database. As we'll see later in this section, the administrator or individual users may be responsible for installing the VSS Client software.

Regardless of whether you perform a client or server setup of VSS, new folders will be added to your hard disk during the installation. Many of these folders and the files contained within them are similar for each installation. As we'll see in the paragraphs that follow, you are given an opportunity during the installation to specify the name and location of the folder that VSS will install to. However, the subdirectories within this directory will vary, depending on whether a server or client installation is chosen.

on the
Job

It's important that you understand what resides in each of the folders created by VSS during installation. This will allow you to quickly find applications and files needed when administrating VSS.

Only the \Win32 and \Setup folders are installed during the client installation. The \Setup folder contains installation files, which can be used to install additional components or uninstall VSS. The \Win32 folder contains Administration and other 32-bit Intel programs that can be used on Windows 9x or Windows NT machines. We'll discuss these applications in greater detail later in this chapter.

The server installation installs a large number of folders and files. These include a \User folder that stores initialization files for various VSS users, a \Data folder for the database, a \Temp folder to store temporary files, and a \NetSetup folder for the NetSetup installation discussed in this section. A Template folder will also be installed containing templates of initialization files used by VSS. In addition, folders installed in the client installation are also added. These include \Setup and \Win32. The \Setup folder contains installation files, which can be used to install additional components or uninstall VSS. The \Win32 folder contains Administration and other 32-bit Intel programs that can be used on Windows 9x or Windows NT machines.

Remember that of the folders created in the client and server installations of VSS, the \Win32 and \Setup folders are common to each. The \Win32 directory contains tools needed to use VSS effectively, whereas \Setup is used for installing additional components or removing VSS from a system.

Visual SourceSafe Server is installed through the Visual Studio installation CD-ROM, which we used earlier in this chapter. To start the Installation Wizard, you must insert your installation CD-ROM into your CD-ROM drive, and then use Windows Explorer to double-click the SETUP.EXE file on this CD-ROM. Although this is the same procedure mentioned earlier in this chapter to start the Installation Wizard, the first screen that appears will be different. The first screen explains that the wizard recognizes that other Visual Studio products have been installed. It also gives several options of installation types.

The Workstation Tools and Components option is chosen when you want to install additional products that come with Visual Studio. This not only includes Visual C++ 6.0 and other development systems, but, as we'll see later in this section, it is also the option chosen when performing a Visual SourceSafe Client installation. In addition to products, you can also select Other Microsoft Tools to install InstallShield, or MSDN to install the Microsoft Developer Network Library.

The Server Applications and Tools (Add-Only) option is selected when you wish to install various server applications. When installing VSS Server, you would select this option and then click the Next button. This will take you to the Server Setups screen, where you will begin installing VSS Server.

The Server Setups screen provides a listing of server applications to install. Although they're called "server" applications, this doesn't necessarily mean that you can't install them on a workstation. The Visual SourceSafe Server can be installed on any Windows 9x or Windows NT machine. Once installed, other workstations on the network can access the source code database available through this installation.

Select Visual SourceSafe Server from this screen, and then click the Install button. This starts the VSS Server Installation Wizard. You'll be asked to switch the current CD-ROM that is inserted in your CD-ROM drive with the second installation CD-ROM. Clicking the OK button on this message will begin the installation process, and display a welcome screen.

Clicking the Continue button on the welcome screen will cause a second screen to appear. This screen displays a product ID number. This number should be documented, as it may be requested if you need to contact Microsoft for assistance. After installing VSS Server, you'll be able to access this number from the dialog box that appears upon clicking About Administrator from the Help menu of the Visual SourceSafe Admin tool. We'll discuss the Admin tool later in this chapter, but it's important that you document this product ID number during installation. If the Admin tool doesn't run, this will be your only chance to document it. Once you've written this number down, click the OK button to continue.

At this point, a small dialog box will appear. This is your last chance to back out of installing VSS Server by clicking Cancel. By clicking the Server button on this dialog, you're indicating that you want to install VSS Server to your computer.

After you click Server, a small message box will appear. This asks whether all clients will be using this database with version 6.0 client software. This is the client portion of VSS that comes with Visual Studio 6.0 and Visual C++ 6.0. If they are, you click the Yes button on this message box, and a database compatible with version 6.0 will be used. If some users will be using previous versions of the VSS Client, click the No button. This indicates that version 5.0 client software will be used. This may decrease the performance of VSS Server, as the database and components for version 6.0 client software are faster. If this is the first time you'll be using Visual SourceSafe with development systems, then you should click Yes, as we'll be installing the client software next.

After you've answered the yes or no question of this screen, the wizard will begin transferring files to your computer. It will also make the necessary changes to your system settings, and add entries related to VSS Server to your Windows Registry. When this is complete, a small message box will appear stating whether the installation was successful. After clicking OK on this message box, you should be ready to begin installing client software, and configuring Visual SourceSafe. You will likely need to reboot the computer. Upon restarting, VSS Server will be completely installed.

EXERCISE 1-6

Installing Visual SourceSafe Server

1. Insert your Visual Studio installation CD-ROM into your CD-ROM drive. Using Windows Explorer, double-click the SETUP.EXE file on this CD-ROM.

2. Select the Server Applications and Tools (Add Only) option, then click Next.

3. From the listing of Server Components appearing on the Server Setups screen, select Visual SourceSafe Server. Click the Install button.

4. When prompted, insert the second Visual Studio installation CD-ROM, then click OK.

5. When the Visual SourceSafe Server welcome screen appears, click the Continue button.

6. When the Visual Source Safe Server Setup screen appears, showing a product ID number, document the product ID number, then click OK.

7. Click the Server button that appears on the screen that follows.

8. Click the Yes button if everyone using this VSS database will be using version 6.0 client software. If you have previous versions of Visual C++ that use version 5.0 client software, click No.

9. The wizard will then begin transferring files. When it has completed, click OK. When prompted to restart Windows, click Yes.

10. You will return to the Server Setups screen. Click Finish to complete the installation process.

After Visual Studio has been installed, you can still perform a Visual SourceSafe Client installation by using the Visual Studio Installation Wizard. In doing so, Visual C++ 6.0 and other development systems previously installed through Visual Studio will become integrated with the source code control system. As stated previously, this means that you'll be able to access the source code control database of VSS through commands in Visual C++ 6.0.

There are three ways of starting the VSS Client installation once Visual Studio and Visual SourceSafe Server have been installed. These are as follows:

- Using the Add/Remove Programs applet in the Windows Control Panel
- Starting SETUP.EXE from the Visual Studio installation CD-ROM
- Using the NetSetup program that's located in the folder that you installed from Visual SourceSafe Server

In the paragraphs that follow, we'll discuss each of these methods. This will provide you with clear insight of how each of the client installations can be performed.

As we saw when installing Visual SourceSafe Server, you can start installing Visual SourceSafe by inserting your Visual Studio CD-ROM into the CD-ROM drive, and running the SETUP.EXE program. This displays a screen with various installation options. By clicking the Workstation Tools and Components option and clicking Next, you'll be brought to the Maintenance screen. From here, you'll be able to select additional products and tools to install.

This isn't the only way to start the Installation Wizard and get to this screen. After Visual C++ 6.0 has been installed onto a computer, you can add and remove different Visual Studio products with the Add/Remove Programs applet found in the Windows Control Panel. This applet is accessed by selecting Settings from the Windows Start menu, clicking Control Panel, then double-clicking the Add/Remove Programs icon. Add/Remove Programs will then open, and display a listing of previously installed applications. Select Visual Studio from the listing of installed programs, and click the Add/Remove button. This will open the Visual Studio Installation Wizard, and bring you to the Maintenance screen.

The Maintenance screen of the Installation Wizard appears identical to the Custom screen we saw earlier in this chapter. It enables you to add and remove any of the client products and components in Visual Studio. This not only includes development and database applications, but also the client portion of Visual SourceSafe. In the listing of options to add or remove, you simply select the check box beside the Visual SourceSafe entry. If a check mark appears in the check box, then that indicates that the option has either been previously installed, or—if you just checked it—that the option is to be installed after you click the Continue button.

The wizard will check your system, and after it's satisfied there is enough disk space, the files related to this installation will be transferred to your hard disk. Upon completing this, a message box will appear, showing whether installation was successful. If successful, you're ready to configure VSS for use. If not, you may need to re-run the Installation Wizard.

Although installing the Visual SourceSafe Client from a CD-ROM is effective, it is not the only way of performing an installation. There is also the NetSetup method of installing the client portion. This is generally the recommended method of installing the VSS Client software, as it allows users to install NetSetup themselves over the network. Whoever acts as the VSS administrator doesn't need to be present with an installation CD-ROM in hand. No installation CD-ROM is required when performing the installation, because it uses the files in the \Setup folder residing in the folder to which VSS Server was installed. This is a benefit because the VSS administrator doesn't need to spend time installing the client portion on every machine.

on the
() o b

The benefit of installing off of the server applies not only to VSS administrators, but to most developers as well. If the VSS administrator isn't given the task of installing the VSS client to each developer's workstation, individual developers (who have proper permissions to the VSS Server directory on a server) will find it fast and simple to install over the network. Although many development teams allow development tools—and would have access to the VSS installation CD-ROM—they would still require the proper permissions and an account to access the VSS database.

As clients will be using the master database created when VSS Server was installed, NetSetup doesn't install a VSS database or support files. It doesn't install an Admin tool, nor does it install a database, as the client portion is designed to use the services provided by the VSS Server.

Whereas the CD-ROM installation can be installed either before or after Visual SourceSafe Server, NetSetup needs to be run after installing VSS Server. A primary reason for this is because NetSetup is installed into the directory where you installed VSS Server. If you haven't installed VSS Server, then the NetSetup program hasn't been put onto your server's hard disk, and thereby can't be run.

exam
ⓦatch

As NetSetup is the recommended method of installing Visual SourceSafe Client software, you should be especially familiar with this client installation type. The key points to remember are that NetSetup only installs the client portion, it's run from the folder containing VSS Server, no installation CD-ROM is required, and that users themselves can install VSS Client without administrator assistance. However, because it uses the installation files in VSS Server, and NetSetup is installed with VSS Server, this means that you must first install VSS Server before you can run NetSetup.

An exception to using NetSetup is when your network is experiencing heavy traffic. When NetSetup is used, the files transferred to the user's hard disk are sent over the network. If there is significant traffic, and numerous users are installing NetSetup, the network can become seriously bogged down. When this is the case, you would want to perform a CD-ROM installation, or restrict the hours that users can install through NetSetup.

You can begin installing the client portion of Visual SourceSafe over the network by using Windows Explorer (or NT Explorer if you're using a Windows NT machine). By going to the folder in which you installed VSS Server, you'll find a file called NETSETUP.EXE. Double-clicking this file will start the NetSetup Installation Wizard.

As with most setup wizards, the first screen that you'll see welcomes you to the Installation Wizard. Clicking the Continue button on this screen will take you to the Name and Organization screen. Here, you're required to enter your name, and the name of the company you belong to. The two fields on this screen will already have information entered in them, as the Installation Wizard retrieves the name and company name from your Windows Registry. If this information is correct, click OK. Otherwise, correct the information, and then click OK to continue. A message box will appear after this, confirming that the information you entered or accepted is correct. Clicking OK on this message box will take you to the next step in the installation process, whereas clicking Change will take you back to the preceding screen.

The next screen shows the product ID number, which we've discussed when talking about other installations. Document this number, then click OK to continue. This will cause the Installation Wizard to check your system for previous installations of Visual SourceSafe. If it finds a copy, a dialog box will appear. It will state that an "older" copy has been found, but this doesn't mean necessarily that it is a previous version of Visual SourceSafe. This same dialog appears if a current version is found. If you wish to overwrite the currently installed version, you can click OK to continue. If you'd like to keep this previous installation, you can click the Change Folder button, and browse your local or network drives for another folder to install to.

The next screen that appears gives you a final chance to change where Visual SourceSafe will be installed. Again, clicking Change Folder will enable you to browse your local or network drives for another folder to install to. To install the client portion, which allows you to access a remote database, click the button that appears on this screen. Doing so will begin the transfer of files, and install Visual SourceSafe.

<table>
<tr><td>**EXERCISE 1-7**</td></tr>
</table>

Visual SourceSafe Client Installation

1. Open Network Neighborhood on your desktop, and navigate your network to the folder where VSS Server is installed. If it has been installed on the computer you're working on, select Programs from the Windows Start menu, and then click Windows Explorer (if you're using a Windows 9x system) or NT Explorer (if your operating system is Windows NT). When Windows or NT Explorer starts, navigate your local hard disk to the folder where VSS Server has been installed. Double-click NETSETUP.EXE.

2. When the NetSetup welcome screen appears, click Continue.

3. Ensure that your name and company name are correct. If they aren't, enter the correct information. Click OK to continue.

4. Click OK when NetSetup verifies that your name and company name are correct.

5. Document the product ID number, then click OK to continue.

6. If the setup wizard detects that a previous version of Visual SourceSafe has been installed on your machine, and you're certain that this is the VSS Server installation that we did earlier, click the Change Folder button. Enter a new path for the client installation to install to, then click OK to continue.

7. When the screen appears with the licensing agreement, click Agree.

8. Click the Install button that appears on the next screen.

9. Wait as the Installation Wizard checks the availability of hard disk space, begins transferring files, and modifies your system settings. When complete, click OK. This will bring up a prompt to restart Windows. Agree to this to finish the installation.

After you've installed Visual SourceSafe, your work isn't quite over yet. You will still need to configure VSS, and create a list of users who will be able to use the source code control system. This is done through the Admin program, which is formally called Visual SourceSafe Administrator. This program (SSADMIN.EXE) is part of the VSS Server installation, and can be found in the \Win32 folder in the folder containing VSS. In addition to double-clicking this file, you can access it through the Windows Start menu. This is done by clicking Start, and selecting Programs | Microsoft Visual Studio 6.0 | Microsoft Visual SourceSafe, and then clicking Microsoft Visual SourceSafe Admin.

A user list determines who has access to the source code control system's database. Through a user list, an administrator can add and delete user accounts, assign rights, and change passwords. If a user doesn't have an account set up in this way, he or she won't be able to save or retrieve files from the VSS database.

The Users menu of the VSS Administrator program contains various items that allow you to maintain the accounts of users. When you first start this program, you'll notice that two default accounts are already added to the user list. The person acting as VSS administrator uses the Admin account, whereas users who don't have an account currently set up use the

Guest account. When you first start the Admin program, neither of these accounts has passwords associated with it. You will be prompted to enter a password for the Admin account when you first start the VSS Administration program. Although it's not written in stone that you need to set an Admin password, it is wise to do so. The Guest account, however, doesn't have a password associated with it for good reason: because users who don't have an account use it, numerous users may access VSS through this visitor account. As we'll see later, though, you can password-protect this account to limit accessibility. If you'd like, you can also delete this account. The Admin account cannot be deleted.

The first step to setting up a user list is defining which VSS database your user list is for. Some users may have access to one database, but not to another. As such, the Open SourceSafe Database command on the Users menu is used to select and open a specific database. When this item is selected, a dialog box opens that displays a list of current VSS databases. By selecting one of these databases, you can then click the Open button to open that database. If you don't see the database that you wish to use, you can click the Browse button to browse local and network drives for a specific database.

After you've specified which database you want to use, you can use most of the other commands on the Users menu to control the user list associated with that database. The Add User command on this menu adds a new user to the user list. The menu item displays a small dialog box, where you enter a user name and a password. This will be used to identify the user when he or she logs in to VSS to use source code control. If you don't want that user to be able to make changes to files and projects stored in the database, select the Read Only check box. This will only allow the user to read information, but not to change it. Upon clicking OK, the user will be added to the user list.

When a new user is added, Visual SourceSafe creates a folder under \Users with that user's name, containing a new SS.INI file for that new user. This new file is based on the SS.INI file located in the \Users folder where VSS resides. This file is similar to the SRCSAFE.INI that contains global variables that affect the VSS database. Although you can modify these files with any text editor, it's not advised you do so unless you're familiar with what each entry in initialization file represents. User accounts should be modified through the commands available in Visual SourceSafe.

Except for the Exit command (which closes the VSS Admin tool), each of the other commands on the Users menu can be used to modify or remove a user's account. These commands are as follows:

- **Delete User**   Removes the selected user's account from the user list
- **Edit User**   Displays a dialog box enabling you to change the user name of a selected user. It also allows you to toggle the Read Only flag for the user.
- **Change Password**   Displays a dialog box enabling you to change a selected user's password

Each of these commands is used to modify the basic elements of the user's account, which determine whether a user can use a specific database. For more elaborate restrictions and modifications on a user's account, you can use commands found in the Tools menu.

The Tools menu contains a number of commands that control both users and databases. First on this menu are three commands determining rights to data stored in the VSS database. These are as follows:

- **Rights by Project**   Used to set rights on a particular project saved in the database
- **Rights Assignments for User**   Used to set a user's rights
- **Copy User Rights**   Used to copy another user's rights to a selected user's account

By default, these commands are disabled when you first use a new database. They appear shaded, and nothing happens when you click them. This is because project security for the database hasn't been enabled.

Enabling project security is done through the Options dialog box, which appears when you click Options in the Tools menu. This dialog box has a number of tabs, which are used to set the default behavior of VSS Administrator, as well as the databases and users maintained through this tool. The Project Security tab has particular importance, as it determines what rights users have when new accounts are created. Until the Enable Project Security check box has been selected on this tab, security is disabled. When selected, other options on this tab become enabled, as do the three previously mentioned commands on the Tools menu.

When you select Enable Project Security, the check boxes that become enabled on this tab are used to define the default rights of new accounts. These rights consist of the following:

- **Read**   Allows a user to view read-only copies of files

- **Check Out/Check In**   Allows the user to use the Check In and Check Out commands. These are used to store files and projects in the database (check in), or retrieve them to make modifications (check out). Having this permission, however, doesn't enable the user to add, rename, or delete files from a project that's been checked out.

- **Add/Rename/Delete**   Allows the user to add, rename, delete, check in, and check out files. However, the user cannot destroy projects and files.

- **Destroy**   Allows a user to use all commands associated with VSS. This gives the user the ability to permanently delete projects and files from the VSS database. The user's rights are equivalent to the default Read-Write access that is assigned to users before project security is enabled and the default rights of users are modified.

By selecting or clearing these check boxes, you are defining what the default rights of new users are. It's also important to note that these rights are progressive. For example, to have Check Out/Check In as a right, you also need Read. If you want to assign a user Add/Rename/Delete rights, then the previous two rights are automatically assigned as well. Finally, by assigning Destroy, you give the user each of the other previously mentioned rights as well. Also, as we'll see next, these rights can be modified for users on a project-by-project or a user-by-user basis.

After project security has been enabled, the Rights by Project, Rights Assignments for User, and Copy User Rights commands become enabled in the Tools menu. These allow you to control security by determining what rights a user has to specific projects or in general. As we'll see in the paragraphs that follow, each of these commands allows you to control security in different ways.

Clicking Rights by Project from the Tools menu brings up the Project Rights dialog box. The left side of this dialog box displays a tree of projects through which you can navigate. Upon selecting a project, you can then select one of the user accounts associated with this database, and assign user rights to each account. After selecting an account, click a check box beside a particular right to assign or remove that right. If you would like to delete a user from having rights to a project, select the user, and then click the Delete User button. If you would like to add a previously deleted user to the listing, you can click the Add User button.

The Rights Assignments for User command is used to specify project rights to a VSS database. Upon selecting a user from the listing in the VSS Administrator tool, you then click this command to bring up the Rights by User dialog box. The top of this dialog box has a section called User Rights, which lists each of the four rights we've discussed. Beside each right is a check box, which is used to add or remove rights for that user from a project. Below this section is a listing of projects to which you can add or remove assignments. If you'd like to add a project and specify the user's rights to that project, you can click the Add Assignments button. This will display a dialog box with a listing of projects. You can click a project in this tree, and then specify rights for that project by selecting the check boxes for rights on this dialog box. Clicking OK will add a selected project to the listing of projects. Once added to the Assignments for User dialog, you can further modify the user's rights by selecting or clearing the check boxes of specific rights from this screen. Upon clicking OK, those rights are then assigned to the user.

Select a user from the listing in VSS Administrator, and then select the Copy User Rights command to open a small dialog box with a listing of users. Select a user from this list and click the Copy button. The rights of that user are copied to the account that you selected before clicking Copy User Rights. This saves you the time of having to determine which group of rights a user should have. If you know that you want to give a user called Darren the same rights as a user called Julie, you would copy Julie's rights to

Darren's account. Rather than having to determine which rights to give, and then click each right for the user's account, you assign the rights in one easy action.

It's important to note that these rights can only be applied if an account has the default Read-Write rights. If you've selected Edit Account from the File menu, and then selected the Read Only check box, only the Read right is assigned. This disables any additional rights that can be given. The only right that can be effected through the commands on the Tools menu for this user would be the Read right. Although you could remove or add the Read right on this user's account, no other rights could be added.

The Lock SourceSafe Database command in the Tools menu is used to lock users out of an open database. This is used when you're planning to archive or back up the database, or upgrade or run certain executable programs, such as utilities. This command is only available to administrators, and when used, displays a dialog box showing which users are currently logged onto the database. By selecting the Lock all users out of Visual SourceSafe check box and clicking OK, you keep any additional users from logging on and using that database. However, the users who are currently logged onto the database are unaffected by this, and must be notified to logoff.

The way the database is archived after Lock SourceSafe Database has been selected is through the Archive Projects command on the Archive menu. When this is selected, the Archive Wizard appears, and the three-step process of archiving the database begins.

The first screen of the wizard has you select a project to archive. Upon clicking OK, you can either click the Add button to add additional projects to archive, remove the project (by selecting it from the list and clicking Remove), or click Next to continue.

The second screen of the Archive Wizard is where you determine what you want to do with the selected projects. You have three options here:

- Save data to file
- Save data to file, then delete from database to save space
- Delete data permanently

If you select either of the first two options, you need to specify where the data will be archived to, as well as a filename for that archive. The last option purges the data from your database without saving it first.

The last screen of the wizard appears if you've chosen to save data to a file. Here, you can choose to either archive all of the data, or archive the latest version in addition to older versions. If you choose the Archive This Version and Older option, a field becomes enabled in which you specify a version. Any versions between this and the latest version will then be archived. If you'd like to make a comment on what this archive contains, you can enter it in the field below it. Clicking Finish ends the wizard and archives the data.

The Archive Wizard is similar to the Restore Wizard, which is used to restore archived data to the VSS database. Selecting Restore Projects from the Archive menu starts this wizard. The first screen is where you specify which archive file you want to restore. Click Next, and you will see a list of projects stored in the archive. You can select which files you want restored either by clicking a specific file in the tree, or by clicking the Select All button. Just as the Select All button selects all files in the tree, Deselect All clears everything. When you've selected the files to restore, clicking Next will bring you to the final step. Here, you choose whether to restore the files to the project they were archived from, or to restore the files to a new location. If you choose the first option, it will overwrite existing files. Upon selecting one of these options, clicking Finish will restore the files based on the criteria given through the wizard.

In addition to the previously mentioned commands on the Tools menu, there are also the following commands:

- **Clean Up Temp Directory**   Deletes all temporary files in the VSS Temp directory

- **Create Database**   Allows you to create new VSS databases

- **Font**   Allows you to choose a new font with which the VSS Admin tool will use to display information

Whereas the Font command is purely superficial, and the Clean Up Temp Directory command is used for maintenance, the Create Database command is particularly important if you wish to create other databases that developers can save to. When this menu item is selected, a dialog box appears that allows you to enter a location for the new database. You can select the check box on this dialog box to indicate that all users of this database use version 6.0 client software. If they use previous versions of VSS client software, then this check box should be cleared.

EXERCISE 1-8

Creating and Maintaining a User List with VSS Administrator

1. From the Windows Start menu, select Programs | Microsoft Visual Studio 6.0 | Microsoft Visual SourceSafe. Click the Visual SourceSafe 6.0 Admin shortcut in this folder to start the VSS Administrator tool.

2. From the Users menu, click Open SourceSafe Database. Select the COMMON database from the listing of available databases, then click OK.

3. From the Tools menu, click Options. Select the Project Security tab, then click Enable Project Security. This will enable the commands that were previously disabled in the Tools menu.

4. From the Users menu, click Add User. This will display a dialog box. Enter the user name you wish to use, followed by a password. Click OK to save this new account to the list.

5. From the list of users, select the Admin user, and then click the Rights Assignments for User command under Tools. Notice that the Admin user's rights cannot be changed.

6. From the list of users, select the Guest user. Click Edit User in the Files menu, and then select the Read Only check box. Click OK. Notice that the Guest user now has Read-Only access to this database.

7. From the Tools menu, click Rights Assignments for User. Notice when the dialog box appears that no additional rights can be assigned, as the user has Read-Only access.

8. From the list of users, select the account you created in Step 4. Click Rights Assignments for User. Select the check box for the Read right. Notice that all subsequent rights are automatically removed.

9. Select each check box for the rights on this dialog box, so that every check box is selected. This will give your account full rights to VSS commands. Click Close.

Using Visual SourceSafe

As mentioned previously, when a source code control system has been installed, new menu items and dialog boxes will appear in Visual C++ 6.0. A submenu called Source Control will appear in the Project menu, and a new tab will appear in the Options dialog. Through these new additions, you can interact with Visual SourceSafe.

Until you actually open or create a project in Visual C++ 6.0, the only menu item in the Source Control submenu is the one called SourceSafe. Clicking this menu item opens the Visual SourceSafe Explorer. This application is similar to Windows or NT Explorer, except that you use the VSS Explorer to browse and work with projects and files saved to the VSS database. As we'll see, many of the commands found in the Project menu are also available through the VSS Explorer.

When you first open the VSS Explorer, you see an interface with several panes. As this is your first time using the Explorer, most of the panes or windows in this program will appear empty. The left pane lists projects currently stored in the database that you're using. When you click a project in this tree, the right pane displays files contained within the selected project. Below this is the Results pane. The Results pane shows you the results of operations performed through Visual SourceSafe. For example, let's say you tried to check out, or retrieve, a project that you currently have checked out. When you attempt this, the Results pane will inform you, for each file checked out, that a particular file is already checked out by you.

The File menu of Visual SourceSafe Explorer contains a number of commands that affect the database that is being used, the projects in that database, and VSS Explorer itself. The commands in this menu consist of the following:

- **Open SourceSafe Database**   Enables you to open a new VSS database

- ■ **Add Files** Displays a dialog box that enables you to browse your hard disk for files to add to a project that you've selected in the Project pane. These files are added to the VSS database with the currently selected project.

- ■ **Create Project** Allows you to create a new project, to which you can add groups of files

- ■ **Delete** Displays a dialog box that enables you to specify projects and files to delete. When the check box entitled Destroy permanently is selected, these items are permanently deleted and cannot be retrieved again.

- ■ **Rename** Allows you to rename a project or filename

- ■ **Properties** Displays the properties of a selected project or file

- ■ **Set Working Folder** Allows you to change the folder in which your project resides. When you edit or compile projects and files, this is done in the *working folder* to which the project was originally saved. It is not done in the VSS database.

- ■ **Create Shortcut** Adds a shortcut to the currently selected project or file on your Windows desktop

- ■ **Label** Displays a dialog box that enables you to add a label to the currently selected project or file

- ■ **Move** Displays a dialog box that enables you to move a selected project or file to another project that's saved in the VSS database

- ■ **Exit** Closes VSS Explorer

The Edit menu contains fewer commands, all of which are related to selecting and editing files. The View File command displays a dialog box, which allows you to choose whether to view a SourceSafe copy of the file, or to check out the working copy of this file for editing. The Edit File command displays the same dialog box. The first option is selected for View File, whereas the second option of checking out the file for editing is selected for Edit File. *Select* is used to select a specific file, whereas *Select All* selects all files in the File pane. Finally, if you have one file selected, and wish to now select everything but the currently selected file, you can use the Inverse Selection command.

The View menu is used for sorting and searching for files. The Sort submenu is used to specify how files in the File pane are to be sorted (for example, by Name, User, and so on). This results in the same action as if you clicked a column header in the File pane. The Search submenu contains commands for finding and filtering what's displayed in the File pane. You can use this to view files by their checked out status, or find specific files by doing a wildcard search. Finally, you can use Cancel Search to cancel any search you've done, and Refresh File List to refresh the display of information in the File pane.

The SourceSafe menu is where we begin to see menu commands that appear in the Source Control submenu of Visual C++ 6.0's Project menu. The commands common to both menus consist of the following:

- **Get Latest Version**   Used to get the most current read-only version of a file

- **Check Out**   Used to place a copy of a file that you can write to in your working folder

- **Check In**   Used to update the project or file that's been saved to the VSS database

- **Undo Check Out**   Cancels any changes made to a file in your working folder, so that current changes aren't saved to the VSS database

- **Share**   Used to share files from other projects with the one currently in use

In addition to these commands, there are additional commands on the SourceSafe menu in VSS Explorer that don't appear in the Source Control submenu in Visual C++ 6.0. By selecting a shared file and then clicking the Branch menu item, you can branch a file in two directions. From the point where the branch has been set, developers in each project can now modify the file without their work overlapping. Each project has a copy of the shared file. In the Project pane of VSS Explorer, a line will appear between these two projects, showing that they are connected. By selecting Merge Branch from the SourceSafe menu, you can then merge the branched files together.

The Tools menu also contains a number of commands found in the Source Control submenu in Visual C++ 6.0. The Show History command is used to show the history of a project or file. In Visual C++ 6.0, you select a file that you wish to view the history of, and then choose this command from the Source Control submenu. This will show what, if any, changes have been made to the selected file or files. When used through VSS Explorer however, you have the option of viewing the history of files as well as entire projects.

Many of the options are identical on the History Options dialog box, whether you've chosen View History for a file or a project. Common to each of these are the Include Labels and Labels Only check boxes. When Include Labels is selected, the user-defined name that a developer has given to the project or file is shown. If you select the Labels Only check box, then the files and projects with labels are shown in the history. The From, To, and User fields allow you to specify a range of versions to show, or those versions worked on by a specific user. You use the From and To fields together to specify a range, based on the time, date, version, or label of files or projects. When entering dates, they can be in the format of 08.09.65, 08-09-65, or 08/09/65, but not as September 08, 1965. Also, you can't search for file labels when viewing the history of a project. Once you've selected the options that you wish to use, you can then click OK to view the history of versions of a file.

If you've selected View History for a project, there are still two additional check boxes to consider before clicking OK. The Recursive check box is used when you want to include subfolders and the files within those folders. This will allow you to view the history of each subfolder and its contents when viewing history by project. The Include File Histories check box is used to indicate whether you want to include files when viewing the history of a project.

Once you've clicked OK, the History of Project or History of File dialog box will appear. The one that appears depends on whether you've selected to view the history of a project, or selected a specific file before using View

History. This dialog box contains a listing of various files, and by double-clicking one, you can display the history information on that file. You can also do this by selecting a file and clicking Details. By clicking the Next or Previous buttons in the History Details dialog box that appears, you can move up or down the listing of files in the history display. You can also check out and share files, or print or save a report on the various items in the History of Project or History of File dialog box.

In addition to View History, the Show Differences command in VSS Explorer and the Source Control submenu of Visual C++ 6.0 can be used to view information. This command is used to view changes to a file. When selected, it will compare changes made in the working copy to that of the copy in the VSS database. This command is only used to view differences in copies. In addition, it cannot be used to compare two files in a working project, and is only used to compare a file in the working folder to what's been saved in the master copy in the VSS database.

In addition to the commands we've discussed, there are several other menu items appearing in the Tools menu of VSS Explorer that don't appear under the Source Control submenu of Project in Visual C++ 6.0. These include the following:

- **Find in Files**   Enables you to enter part or all of a string used in a specific file or project. Clicking OK then starts a search for that particular line of code.

- **Files Report**   Displays a dialog box that enables you to create a report on files and the people who have modified them

- **Options**   Enables you to change aspects of VSS Explorer

- **Font**   Changes the font used to display files and information through VSS Explorer

- **Customize Toolbar**   Enables you to change buttons on the toolbar

- **Change Password**   Used to change your Visual SourceSafe password

Just as VSS Explorer has some commands that don't appear in Visual C++ 6.0, the reverse also applies. There are some menu items appearing in the Source Control submenu, found in the Project menu of Visual C++ 6.0, which don't appear in VSS Explorer. These consist of the following:

- **Add to Source Control**   Used to add a project's files to the source code control system's database

- **Remove from Source Control**   Removes a project's files from the source code control database

- **SourceSafe Properties**   Displays a specific file or project's source code control properties

- **Refresh Status**   Used to update the status of a file in the source code control system

Multiple User/Multiple Location Development

The default behavior of Visual SourceSafe is that only one user at a time is allowed to check out files. This means that only one developer at a time can work on projects or files that have been saved to the VSS database. However, you can change this setting so that more than one user has the ability to check out a particular file.

To do this, you need to open the VSS Admin tool. Once open, use the Open SourceSafe Database menu item in the Tool menu, and select a database that you want to change. After doing this, select Options from the Tools menu. This brings up the Options dialog box, where you can change settings for VSS. The General tab of Options contains a check box entitled Allow Multiple Check Outs. When this is selected, more than one user can then check out a file.

exam
ⓦatch

Until the Allow Multiple Check Outs check box is selected, only one user at a time can check out a file from the VSS database. Allow Multiple Check Outs is found under the General tab of Options in the VSS Administrator.

When this has been set, and more than one user checks out a particular project, the first time a file is saved to the VSS database, it is updated. After this, each time users check in a file, those subsequent changes are merged. This enables multiple users from multiple locations to work on a single project, using source code control.

Generally, when more than one user is working on a single file, they are modifying different lines of code. There may be times, however, when two users modify the same line of code. As VSS checks changes before merging them into a master file, it can detect when two or more users have made such conflicting changes. When it does detect this, it refuses to allow the check in of that file. It then sends a message to the user checking in the file that the conflicting line of code needs to be changed before the file can be checked in. The user can then change his or her local copy of the file to resolve the problem.

Versioning of the Source Code

As we saw earlier in this chapter, you can view the history of different versions of files and projects that have been saved to the VSS database. This allows us to see changes to files, as Visual SourceSafe maintains multiple versions of a file. This means that each time changes are made to a file, a new version of the source code is stored in the VSS database.

The version control in Visual SourceSafe helps to ensure that only one person at a time is modifying a file. Unless Allow Multiple Check Outs has been selected, only one developer has the ability to check out and modify a file. As we saw in the preceding section, when multiple check outs are allowed, Visual SourceSafe still protects one version of source code from overwriting another.

In previous sections we also saw that you can view the history of a file or a project, and track the different versions of code that have been made. You can then retrieve these previous versions, should you wish to reuse code from older versions in your current project. From this, the versioning of source code also gives you the ability to track which programs use certain object-orientated code, then reuse that code in other projects.

The way that Visual SourceSafe tracks different versions of files and projects is with version numbers, labels, and date/time stamps. In discussing each of these methods, we'll see that these methods are either internally maintained by Visual SourceSafe, or applied by the user. Each method keeps VSS from accidentally overwriting one version of a file with another.

As mentioned, labels are user-defined strings that are applied to a project or a file. They can contain up to 31 characters, and allow the user to give files and projects meaningful names or comments. By using labels, you can provide version information for Visual SourceSafe to use. For example, by giving the label 3.1, 2B or NOT2B, you indicate a version number that is different from other versions of a product. You can even use sentences to indicate what a particular version represents or has achieved in the development process. For example, Bug Fix 3 or Approved by Testing are both valid labels to use.

Date/Time stamps are applied to files, indicating when they were modified or the last time the file was checked into the VSS database. This allows VSS to look at when changes were last made, or when a version was last saved to the database. By looking at this date and time information, VSS can determine which versions came before and after one another.

The version numbers used by Visual SourceSafe are different from the version numbers applied to a project in Visual C++ 6.0. Unlike those in Visual C++ 6.0, you have no control over what version number is applied to a file or project. These are controlled exclusively by the source code control system. Each time a file is updated and saved to the VSS database, Visual SourceSafe automatically increments the version number. This number is always a whole number, and is never decremented.

This is different from the version numbers applied to projects in Visual C++ 6.0. A project in Visual C++ 6.0 includes a resource file that defines the version of a project. There is only one of these files in each project, and it can be accessed by clicking the ResourceView in Visual C++ 6.0, which displays resource files included in the project. ResourceView shows the resources associated with a particular project. Each resource type is contained in its own subfolder, including that of Version. Within the Version resource type is a file called VS_VERSION_INFO, and by clicking it, you can bring up the Version Information Editor.

The Version Information Editor displays a considerable amount of information on a project. This information is added to the compiled program, and much of it is available to an application's user by viewing the program's properties. The FILEVERSION string indicates the version of a file, whereas the PRODUCTVERSION string indicates the version of the project as a whole. You can change the version of a product or a file by respectively double-clicking either the PRODUCTVERSION or FILEVERSION string, which is displayed through the Version Information Editor.

The format of the version information in these strings is read from left to right. Each number indicates a level of change to the application, with the leftmost number indicating a major change. Each number to the right of this first number denotes smaller changes. For example, when Microsoft made major changes to Windows 3.1, it introduced Windows 95. Windows 95 was actually version 4.0. This means the version would have changed from 3, 1, 0, 0 to 4, 0, 0, 0. When Windows 98 was released, the changes to the operating system's code were less drastic, so it was version 4, 1, 0, 0. As patches and updates to the operating system were made, the numbers to the right of 4.1 were incremented. This same type of versioning should be applied when setting version information on applications that you create.

Let's look at some scenario questions and their answers. The questions are common ones that may help you not only with your exam, but also in real world situations that you may encounter.

QUESTIONS AND ANSWERS

I'm trying to install NT Option Pack on a Windows NT Workstation. When I go to the Server Setups screen of the Visual Studio Installation Wizard, the NT Option Pack doesn't appear. Why?	NT Option Pack is installed through the Launch BackOffice Installation Wizard option in Server Setups. In addition to NT Option Pack, a number of other programs are also installed for the development of distributed applications.
What are the four properties of a transaction?	Atomicity, consistency, isolation, and durability.
I tried starting Microsoft Transaction Server (MTS), and received the following message: "Setup library mtssetup.dll could not be loaded or the function MTSSetupProc could not be found." What is the problem?	If you receive this message, you're attempting to run MTS on a Windows 9x computer, or a Windows NT version prior to 4.0. This message appears on these systems when DCOM isn't enabled. Before running MTS, ensure that DCOM is enabled.
What is source code control, and why is it important?	Source code control enables you to track changes in your programming code. This enables you to determine changes that were made to the source code, when, and by whom. This helps to organize the code, and enables you to retrieve previous versions.

FROM THE CLASSROOM

MTS-Based Deviations in the Development Environment

Microsoft Visual Studio allows you to set up an application environment on your development machine, complete with back-end server tools, such as SQL Server and Microsoft Transaction Server. If your development is being done on a Windows 95 or Windows 98 machine, it is important to be aware of the differences between some of the tools provided with the NT Option Pack on Windows 9x platforms versus the Windows NT platform. Microsoft Transaction Server has a slightly different look and feel, and very different security capabilities when running on Windows 9x systems. Failure to recognize these crucial differences can result in occasional hurdles in the development process.

On Windows NT systems, Microsoft Transaction Server capitalizes on the security capabilities of the operating system. Windows NT Security authentication is a powerful means of controlling code access or execution. In conjunction with the Windows NT model of users and groups, server packages in MTS can limit access through declarative security and programmatic security. Both forms of security rely on MTS role-based security being implemented within the MTS environment.

Declarative security explicitly grants access to users and groups through roles defined within the Microsoft Management Console-based MTS administration snap-in. The users and groups are administered through the Widows NT user administration tools, then roles which include these users and groups are defined using the MTS Management Console. Finally, server packages and their components enable security and specify which role(s) have access to available interfaces or objects. Programmatic security utilizes methods of the IObjectContext interface to perform security authorization from within a component's implementation. For example, to implement programmatic security, you can use the IsSecurityEnabled method of the IObjectContext Interface to check whether security is enabled, then call the IsCallerInRole method to see if the client of the component has an assigned role.

Because security in Microsoft Transaction Server is so tightly integrated with Windows NT security, it is not supported in Windows 95 or Windows 98. When you open MTS Explorer on a Windows 9x system, you will notice that the Security tab is missing from your package and component property pages. Likewise, there is no way to add and define new roles to perform declarative security. If your components utilize programmatic

FROM THE CLASSROOM

security, in Windows 9*x* all identities will be mapped to Windows 98 or Windows 95 and checking roles will always return success.

The absence of a security model is the most significant difference between MTS on Windows NT versus Windows 9*x*. Keep this difference in mind so that you may take

advantage of all of the features and functionality of Microsoft Transaction Server, no matter on which platform you are developing your distributed application.

—Michael Lane Thomas,
MCSE+I, MCSD, MCT, MCP+SB, MSS, A+

CERTIFICATION SUMMARY

Visual C++ 6.0 can be acquired on its own or as part of the Visual Studio suite of products. Visual Studio not only includes Visual C++, but also Visual Basic, Visual J++, Visual InterDev, Visual FoxPro, and various tools helpful in creating robust applications rapidly. On its own or as part of Visual Studio, different editions are available. Visual Studio is available in Professional and Enterprise editions, whereas Visual C++ is available in Standard, Professional, and Enterprise editions.

Before attempting to install Visual C++ (or any other software for that matter) onto your computer, you should ensure that the minimum system requirements are met. These are the bare minimum, in terms of RAM, processor, disk space, and so forth, that your computer will need to install and run Visual C++ 6.0. These may vary from edition to edition of Visual C++ 6.0. If your system meets these requirements, then you can be sure that no problems will result from unsatisfied requirements. If these aren't met, Visual C++ 6.0 may not install and run properly.

Installing Visual C++ through Visual Studio is a multipart process. It starts by starting the setup wizard, which gathers information about your computer and asks for input from the installer. It is highly interactive, enabling you to choose the type of installation you wish to do, the products to install, and where to install them. It then moves into installing the MSDN Library and InstallShield, and allows you to install various server tools.

Visual SourceSafe is a source code control system that conforms to the Microsoft Source Code Control Interface. As such, once installed, you can interact with Visual SourceSafe through Visual C++ 6.0, or through the tools included with VSS. Visual SourceSafe Administrator is used to administer VSS databases and users who will use these databases. Visual SourceSafe Explorer allows you to work with projects through an interface similar to that of Windows Explorer. Together, they provide a powerful system of controlling source code.

TWO-MINUTE DRILL

- ❑ Visual C++ 6.0 is available in three different editions: Standard, Professional, and Enterprise.

- ❑ Visual Studio is a suite of products used for developing and managing applications, components, and data access. It provides you with a wider scope of options than Visual C++ alone, because it contains more than just Visual C++ 6.0.

- ❑ Before actually installing Visual C++ 6.0—or any software for that matter—you should determine if the computer meets the minimal system requirements.

- ❑ Windows NT has higher security than Windows 9x, and Windows NT networks use permissions to dictate what applications can be used by users, and which folders on a Windows NT system's hard disk can be accessed.

- ❑ Most of the Distributed Component Object Model (DCOM) utilities that come with Visual C++ 6.0 and Visual Studio will work on Windows 95/98 systems.

- ❑ Service packs can be installed to resolve issues associated with a particular product. These issues may be legal (as was the case with Visual J++), bug fixes, or other problems that weren't realized or couldn't be fixed when the product was initially released.

❑ There are a number of different server services included with Visual Studio and Visual C++ 6.0 that can be set up to assist you in developing distributed applications. What services can be installed, however, depends on the operating system you're using.

❑ Many of the server services available can be installed through the Server Setups screen of the Visual Studio setup program. You can start the Visual Studio setup the same way you did when installing Visual C++ 6.0.

❑ An easy way to remember the order in which server tools should be installed on a Windows 9x system is with the following sentence: "On Fun Days, I Am Awesome." The first letter of each word represents one of the tools: Option pack, FrontPage extensions, Data access, InterDev components, Application performance explorer, and (Visual Studio) Analyzer.

❑ Microsoft Transaction Server (MTS) is a transaction processing system that can be used to simplify your work in developing components. A transaction is a set of actions, or processing steps, that's treated as a single unit of work. Transactions provide protection from system failures or concurrent updates.

❑ An easy way to remember the properties of a transaction is to think of the acronym ACID. Each letter represents a different property of the transaction: Atomicity, Consistency, Isolation, and Durability.

❑ Microsoft SQL Server 6.5, Developer Edition is installed through the BackOffice Installation Wizard on Windows NT. When installed, you can then design, develop, and test Visual C++ programs that work in conjunction with SQL Server.

❑ Microsoft Message Queue (MSMQ) is another program that can aid in the development of distributed applications. The client portion of MSMQ is available for installation on Windows NT Workstation and Windows 9x systems. However, the MSMQ server can only be installed on Windows NT Server, and is included with Windows NT Server 4.0 and later as part of the NT Option Pack.

❏ Remember that asynchronous communication is message queuing whereas synchronous communication is message passing. You should also know what each does. Message queuing and asynchronous communication, and message passing and synchronous communication, are terms that can be used interchangeably, and may appear as such in some questions on the exam.

❏ MTS Explorer allows you to install, delete, and monitor packages on a server computer. In addition to this, you can also create application executables that install to and configure client computers.

❏ Tracking changes to source code during software development enables you to see what work has been done, who has done the work, and it helps you analyze how those changes have affected the project as a whole. This provides accountability for code that's written for a project.

❏ If you don't already have a source code control system, you won't need to go out and buy one. Visual SourceSafe (VSS) is a source code control system that comes with Visual C++ and Visual Studio.

❏ Remember that the client portion is used for all developers accessing the source code control database, whereas the server portion provides a centralized database and administration. To use VSS on the computer that's acting as the VSS Server, you'll also need the VSS Client installed.

❏ It's important that you understand what resides in each of the folders created by VSS during installation. This will allow you to quickly find applications and files needed when administrating VSS.

❏ Remember that of the folders created in the client and server installations of VSS, the \Win32 and \Setup folders are common to each. The \Win32 directory contains tools needed to use VSS effectively, whereas \Setup is used for installing additional components or removing VSS from a system.

❑ As NetSetup is the recommended method of installing Visual SourceSafe Client software, you should be especially familiar with this client installation type. The key points to remember are that NetSetup only installs the client portion, it's run from the folder containing VSS Server, no installation CD-ROM is required, and that users themselves can install VSS Client without administrator assistance.

❑ After you've installed Visual SourceSafe, you will still need to configure VSS, and create a list of users who will be able to use the source code control system. This is done through the Admin program, which is formally called Visual SourceSafe Administrator.

❑ The default behavior of Visual SourceSafe is that only one user at a time is allowed to check out files. However, you can change this setting so that more than one user has the ability to check out a particular file.

❑ The version control in Visual SourceSafe helps to ensure that only one person at a time is modifying a file. The way that Visual SourceSafe tracks different versions of files and projects is with version numbers, labels, and date/time stamps.

SELF TEST

The following questions will help you measure your understanding of the material presented in this chapter. Read all of the choices carefully, as there may be more than one correct answer. Choose all correct answers for each question.

1. Which of the following programs integrates with Visual C++ 6.0, and provides the ability to store and retrieve code to a source code control system database?

   A. Microsoft Transaction Server

   B. SQL Server

   C. Visual SourceSafe Client

   D. Visual SourceSafe Server

2. While installing Visual C++ 6.0 on a Windows 95 machine, you attempt to install the Internet Information Services (IIS) through the NT Option Pack. Unfortunately, you find you cannot do this. Why? (Choose all that apply.)

   A. The NT Option Pack for Windows 95 doesn't include IIS.

   B. You need to download IIS separately from Microsoft's Web site, then install it.

   C. IIS won't run on Windows 9x systems.

   D. These are two separate installations. You need to install NT Option Pack for Windows before installing IIS.

3. Which of the following needs to be enabled for Microsoft Transaction Server to run on a Windows 95/98 computer?

   A. SQL Server

   B. Microsoft Message Queue

   C. DCOM

   D. DNS

4. You are preparing to install SQL Server 6.5 Developer Edition on several computers. Developers will use each installation for creating applications that will work in conjunction with SQL. On which of the following operating systems will you be able to install SQL Server Developer Edition? (Choose all that apply.)

   A. Windows 3.1

   B. Windows 95

   C. Windows NT Workstation

   D. Windows NT Server

5. You are installing Visual C++ Enterprise edition on four computers. Each of the computers has different hardware and operating systems. Which of the following computers are able to install Visual C++ 6.0 on? (Choose all that apply.)

   A. 486/66 MHz computer with 64MB of RAM, running Windows 95

   B. Pentium computer with 32MB of RAM, running Windows NT Workstation

   C. Pentium computer with 24MB of RAM, running Windows NT Workstation

   D. Pentium computer with 16MB of RAM, running Windows 95

6. You are attempting to install the Windows NT Option Pack on two computers. One computer is running Windows NT Workstation, whereas the other is running Windows 95. Each computer has 30MB of free hard disk space. When you attempt to install on the first of these two computers, the installation fails. Based on the information given, why has the installation failed?

   A. The NT Option Pack isn't included with the Professional edition of Visual C++ 6.0.

   B. The NT Option Pack won't install on Windows 95 computers.

   C. The NT Option Pack requires 20MB of free hard disk space on Windows NT computers.

   D. The NT Option Pack requires 200MB of free hard disk space on Windows NT computers.

7. You are preparing to install Visual C++ 6.0 through Visual Studio on three computers over the network. One computer runs Windows 95, another is a Windows NT Workstation, and the third is a Windows NT Server. How will you start the installation process to install on each of these platforms?

   A. Use the NetSetup program, NETSETUP.EXE, to install on each operating system over the network.

   B. You can't install Visual C++ 6.0 over the network.

   C. You would use the SETUP.EXE program to install Visual C++ 6.0 on the Windows 95 computer, and the NTSETUP.EXE to install on each of the computers running Windows NT.

   D. Use the SETUP.EXE program to install Visual C++ 6.0 on each of these operating systems over the network.

8. You are installing Visual C++ 6.0 on your computer, and reach the Product Number and User ID screen. Unfortunately, you don't have the product's ID number (CD-key) handy, and therefore can't enter it at the present time. What will you do?

   A. Either get the product's ID number and enter it, or cancel the installation.

   B. Click the Next button to proceed through the rest of the installation process. You will be able to enter the product's ID number once installation is complete through Visual C++ 6.0's Help menu.

   C. Enter your name and company name, then click the Next button to proceed through the rest of the installation process. Once completed, you will have the opportunity to register online, thereby bypassing the need for the product's ID number.

   D. Enter any number into the product's ID number field, then proceed with the rest of the installation.

9. Which of the following would you install if you wanted to access documentation and samples for Visual C++ 6.0 and other tools used in the development of distributed applications?

   A. MSDN

   B. VSS

   C. InstallShield

   D. MTS

10. Which of the following is Message Orientated Middleware, and uses asynchronous communication so that when you send data to computers on a network, those computers don't have to be online?

   A. MSMQ

   B. MTS

   C. SQL Server

   D. Visual C++ 6.0

11. Transactions have four basic properties associated with them. Which property of a transaction enforces if any of the processing steps in a transaction fail, the transaction is aborted and the data is rolled back to its previous state?

   A. Atomicity

   B. Consistency

   C. Isolation

   D. Durability

12. Which of the following would you use to manage and deploy components? This program will install, delete, and monitor MTS packages on a server computer, and also create application executables that install to and configure client computers.

   A. MTS run-time environment

   B. MTS Explorer

   C. Application Programming Interfaces

   D. Resource Dispensers

13. Before users can access the Visual SourceSafe database, they must be added to a user list. Which of the following would you use to create a listing of users who can access the source code control system, and how would you install it?

   A. User Manager, installed with VSS Server

   B. User Manager, installed with the VSS Client portion

   C. VSS Administrator utility, installed with VSS Server

   D. VSS Administrator utility, installed with the VSS Client portion

14. Which of the following are the minimum rights required for a user to store and retrieve source code to and from the Visual SourceSafe database?

   A. Read

   B. Check Out/Check In

   C. Add/Remove/Delete

   D. Destroy

15. Which of the following rights would you give a user to add, remove, check in, and check out files from the Visual SourceSafe database? This right would also give the user the ability to permanently delete files.

A. Add/Remove/Delete

B. The combination of Read, Check Out/Check In, and Destroy. Add/Remove/Delete would be removed as a right, because this right doesn't allow permanent deletion of files.

C. Destroy

D. Read/Write

16. You have written source code in Visual C++ 6.0 and would now like to store it in the VSS database. When you go to use the commands under the Source Control submenu of the Project menu in Visual C++6.0, you find that the submenu and its commands aren't there. Why?

A. The user doesn't have the proper permissions to use source code control.

B. The client portion of the source code control system hasn't been installed yet.

C. The server portion of the source code control system hasn't been installed yet.

D. Source code control commands appear under the File menu in Visual C++ 6.0.

17. Which of the following are sets of commands that can be installed with MTS, and are used by an application to request services from the operating system?

A. MTS run-time environment

B. Operating System Programming Interfaces

C. Application Programming Interfaces

D. Resource Dispensers

18. Transactions have four basic properties associated with them. Which property of a transaction keeps transactions from seeing the partial or uncommitted results of the other transactions?

A. Atomicity

B. Consistency

C. Isolation

D. Durability

19. You are attempting to install SQL Server 6.5, Developer Edition on two computers through Visual Studio Enterprise Edition. One computer is running Windows NT Workstation, while the other is running Windows 95. Each computer has 100MB of free hard disk space. When you attempt to install on one of these two computers, the installation fails. Based on the information given, why has the installation failed?

A. The installation on Windows 95 has failed because SQL Server can't be installed on Windows 9x computers.

B. The installation on Windows 95 has failed because there isn't enough free hard disk space.

C. The installation on Windows NT has failed because there isn't enough free hard disk space.

D. The installation has failed because SQL Server doesn't come with Visual Studio or Visual C++ 6.0.

20. You have just installed the Visual SourceSafe (VSS) Server on a server computer that will be used for developing applications. After installing VSS Server, Visual C++ is also installed. When the user of this computer attempts saving code to the VSS database, he finds he cannot. Why?

A. VSS was installed before Visual C++, so the VSS commands haven't been integrated into Visual C++ 6.0's interface. VSS Server will need to be reinstalled on this computer.

B. VSS was installed before Visual C++, so the VSS commands haven't been integrated into Visual C++ 6.0's interface. Visual C++ 6.0 will need to be reinstalled on this computer.

C. VSS doesn't conform to the Microsoft Source Code Control Interface.

D. VSS Client hasn't been installed on the computer.

SELF TEST ANSWERS

1. **C.** The Visual SourceSafe Client installation is used to provide developers with the ability to store and retrieve source code to a source code control database. Once installed, it integrates with Visual C++ 6.0, so that you can store current changes to code or retrieve older versions of code.

   A is incorrect because Microsoft Transaction Server isn't a source code control system, but is used for transactions. Although SQL Server is a database server program, and is used to store and retrieve data, it isn't a source code control system. As such, B is wrong. D is also wrong, because Visual SourceSafe Server doesn't integrate with Visual C++ 6.0. Although it is a source code control system, and provides users running the Visual SourceSafe Client portion with the ability to store and retrieve code to the VSS database, it doesn't integrate with Visual C++ 6.0. The client portion integrates with Visual C++, and works with the server portion. When a user uses the commands in Visual C++ 6.0, which are provided through the installation of the client portion, they are able to store and retrieve data to and from the VSS database on the VSS Server.

2. **A, C.** Internet Information Server is a Web server designed to run on Windows NT systems. It will not run on Windows 9x systems. It is included with the NT Option Pack, which is included with both the Professional and Enterprise editions of VSS. If you're installing this on Windows NT Server, the option pack includes Internet Information Server 4.0. On Windows 9x systems, the options in the NT Option Pack are more limited. Installing the option pack on Windows 95 or Windows 98 will install the Personal Web Server.

   B is wrong, because IIS won't run on Windows 9x systems. It is a Web server for computers running Windows NT. Therefore, if you downloaded a copy from Microsoft's Web site, you wouldn't be able to install and run it from the Windows 95 computer anyway. D is also wrong. Although the NT Option pack for Windows 9x doesn't include IIS, installing the NT Option Pack on a Windows NT computer does include IIS. However, even if you've installed the NT Option Pack for Windows 95, you still wouldn't be able to install and run IIS.

3. **C.** DCOM needs to be enabled on a Windows 95/98 computer before Microsoft Transaction Server will run. If DCOM isn't enabled, then you will receive the following error message when attempting to start MTS: "Setup library mtssetup.dll could not be loaded or the function MTSSetupProc could not be found." Once DCOM is enabled, MTS should run fine, and you'll stop receiving this message.

A is wrong, because SQL Server doesn't need to be installed on your computer for MTS to function properly. B is also wrong, as Microsoft Message Queue doesn't need to be installed for MTS to function. Finally, D is wrong, because DNS (Domain Name System) isn't a requirement for MTS to run. DNS is used to identify computers on a TCP/IP network. Although this may be necessary for your computer to find other computers on such a network, it isn't required to start MTS.

4. **C, D.** Microsoft SQL Server 6.5, Developer Edition will only run on Windows NT systems. It is installed through the BackOffice Installation Wizard on Windows NT. When installed, you can then design, develop, and test Visual C++ programs that work in conjunction with SQL Server.
A is wrong, because Windows 3.1 is a 16-bit operating system, and couldn't handle running the 32-bit SQL Server program. B is wrong, as SQL won't run on a Windows 9x system, and is only used on Windows NT.

5. **B, C.** The requirements for running Visual C++ Enterprise includes a Pentium class processor (with Pentium 90 or higher recommended), 24MB of RAM (with 32 MB or higher recommended), and a Windows 95 or Windows NT 4.0 (or higher) operating system.
A is wrong, because it only has a 486/66 MHz processor. Although you could install the Standard edition of Visual C++ on this computer, you wouldn't be able to install the Enterprise edition. D is also wrong, as this computer doesn't have enough RAM. It only has 16MB of RAM, and Visual C++ 6.0 requires a minimum of 24MB, with 32MB or higher recommended.

6. **D.** The question states that each computer has 30MB of free disk space, but the NT Option Pack for Windows NT systems requires 200MB of free disk space. Considerably more features are installed through the Option Pack for Windows NT systems than Windows 9x systems, so more disk space is required for the installation. A is wrong, because NT Option Pack is included with the Professional and Enterprise editions of Visual C++ 6.0. The only edition that doesn't include the NT Option Pack is the Standard edition. B is wrong, as there are NT Option Packs for both Windows 9x and Windows NT platforms. C is also wrong, as the NT Option Pack for NT computers requires 200MB of free disk space. If the NT Option Pack is being installed on a Windows 9x computer, then a minimum of only 20MB of free disk space is required.

7. **D.** If you're installing over the network, you can start the wizard by opening the SETUP.EXE file. From the Windows Start menu, you select Run and then type the path to the SETUP.EXE file. You can also use NT Explorer (on Windows NT machines) or Windows Explorer (on systems running Windows 9x) to browse your local machine or network for the folder or CD-ROM containing the installation files. After double-clicking this file, the setup wizard will start, the Installation Wizard starts and begins the installation process.

   A is wrong, because there is no NetSetup program used for installing over the network. You can use the SETUP.EXE program to install over the network, just as you would if you were installing from a CD-ROM on a local machine. B is also wrong, because you can install over the network, using the SETUP.EXE program. C is wrong, because the same program is used to install Visual C++ 6.0 on Windows 95 and Windows NT systems.

8. **A.** The Product Number and User ID screen is used to prove that you have a legal copy of Visual C++ 6.0 (or Visual Studio if that's what you're installing from). If you don't have the product's ID number, which is also called a CD-key, then you won't be able to proceed through the rest of the installation. You will only be able to cancel the installation.

   B and C are both wrong, because you won't be able to continue past the Product Number and User ID screen without entering the product's ID number. Until this number is correctly entered, the Next button will be disabled. It will appear grayed out and you won't be able to proceed through the rest of the installation process. D is also wrong, as the number must be entered exactly, or installation will fail. The ID number entered on this screen is found on the back of your installation CD-ROM's jewel case (the case the CD-ROM came in), or in your product documentation.

9. **A.** MSDN is the Microsoft Developer Network Library. This is a collection of documentation and samples for the Visual Studio suite of products. If you're installing from Visual Studio, MSDN is included. Although this was the most recent version of MSDN when Visual Studio was released, you can also order a subscription to MSDN through Microsoft's Web site (msdn.microsoft.com).

   B is wrong, because VSS is Visual SourceSafe, which is a source code control system. C is wrong, because InstallShield is used for creating installation programs for applications you create with Visual C++ 6.0. D is wrong, because MTS is Microsoft Transaction Server, which is a transaction processing system.

10. **A.** MSMQ (Microsoft Message Queue) uses asynchronous communications, or message queuing. It is Message Orientated Middleware. When a computer sends a message to another computer, the receiving computer doesn't have to be online. The data is stored in a message queue, until the receiving computer is online.
B is wrong, because MTS is Microsoft Transaction Server, and is a transaction processing system. C is also incorrect, as SQL Server is a database server. D is wrong, as Visual C++ 6.0 is used for development. Visual C++ 6.0 can be used to create applications that work with MSMQ, but doesn't provide message queuing on its own.

11. **A.** Atomicity is an "all or nothing" feature of transactions. Either all of the steps in a transaction succeed or nothing happens. If any of the processing steps in a transaction fail, the transaction is aborted and the data is rolled back to its previous state.
B is wrong, because consistency means that when the data is modified, it matches the state that is expected. When business rules in your application modify data, it is important that the data is correctly modified. C is also wrong, because isolation keeps transactions from seeing the partial or uncommitted results of the other transactions. In other words, when two or more transactions are occurring on the same data, isolation makes it appear that only one transaction is running at a time. Finally, D is wrong, because durability refers to a transactions ability to survive failures. When an update is committed to data, it must be able to survive such things as communication failures, process failures, and server failures.

12. **B.** MTS Explorer is a program that's installed when you install Microsoft Transaction Server on your computer. It is used for managing and deploying components. MTS Explorer allows you to install, delete, and monitor packages on a server computer. It is also used to create application executables that install to and configure client computers.
A is wrong, because MTS run-time environment provides the environment to run components used for transactions. It serves as a middle-tier platform for running three-tier components. C is also wrong, as Application Programming Interfaces (APIs) are sets of commands used in an application to request services performed by the operating system. D is wrong, because Resource Dispensers are used to access shared information.

13. **C.** The VSS Administrator utility is installed with VSS Server. Once installed, you can use this utility to add users of the source code control system to a user list. A user list is a listing of users who have permissions to access the source code control system.

A and B are wrong, as User Manager is an NT Workstation utility, which can be used to control access to resources on an NT Workstation computer. It is installed with the operating system, not with Visual SourceSafe Server or Client portions. D is also wrong, as the VSS Administrator utility is installed with VSS Server. It isn't installed as part of the VSS Client portion.

14. **B.** The minimum rights required for a user to store and retrieve source code to and from the Visual SourceSafe database is Check Out/Check In. With this right, a user can store files and projects in the database (check in), or retrieve them to make modifications (check out). Having this permission, however, doesn't enable the user to add, rename, or delete files from a project that's been checked out.
    A is wrong, because Read allows a user to view read-only copies of files. C is also wrong, as Add/Rename/Delete provides more powerful rights than Check Out/Check In. This right allows the user to add, rename, delete, check in, and check out files. However, the user cannot destroy projects and files. For this, the user would need the Destroy right. Destroy allows a user to use all commands associated with VSS. This gives the user the ability to permanently delete projects and files from the VSS database. As this is the most powerful right, this makes D also wrong.

15. **C.** The Destroy right gives users the ability to add, remove, check in, and check out files, and is the only right that allows users to permanently delete files. Destroy allows a user to use all commands associated with VSS. This gives the user the ability to permanently delete projects and files from the VSS database.
    A is wrong, because Add/Remove/Delete doesn't give a user the right to permanently delete files. B is wrong, as rights are progressive. If you gave a user the Destroy right, all other rights would automatically be given to that user. That means if a user has the Destroy right, then he or she would also have the Add/Remove/Delete right. D is wrong, as users of Visual SourceSafe can't be given the Read/Write right, as this right doesn't exist in VSS. The equivalent to Read/Write is Destroy.

16. **B.** Until the VSS Client is installed, menu items dealing with source code control don't appear under Visual C++ 6.0's menu system. Once installed, these items appear, allowing you to interact with VSS. When the VSS Client is installed, the commands dealing with source code control will be added to the Visual C++ 6.0 environment, as will a new tab under Visual C++ 6.0's Options dialog box. A is wrong, because

commands dealing with source code control will appear under the Source Control submenu of the Projects menu even if the user doesn't have permissions to use source code control. Once the client portion is installed, these commands appear. The user will be unable to use them properly if he or she doesn't have an account set up through VSS Administrator, but the commands will still be there. C is wrong, as the client portion of VSS is what adds commands dealing with source code control to Visual C++ 6.0. Even if the VSS Server is set up on that computer, the user will still need VSS Client installed on that computer, or he or she won't be able to use source code control. D is also incorrect, because the Source Control submenu appears under the Projects menu in Visual C++ 6.0.

17. **C.** Application Programming Interfaces (APIs) are sets of commands installed with MTS. You can use APIs in applications you create with Visual C++ 6.0 to request services performed by the operating system. A is wrong, because MTS run-time environment provides the environment to run components used for transactions. It serves as a middle-tier platform for running three-tier components. B is wrong, because there is no such thing as Operating System Programming Interfaces. APIs are what provide the ability to use services provided by the operating system. D is wrong, because Resource Dispensers are used to access shared information.

18. **C.** Isolation keeps transactions from seeing the partial or uncommitted results of the other transactions. In other words, when two or more transactions are occurring on the same data, isolation makes it appear that only one transaction is running at a time. A is wrong, because atomicity enforces that if any of the processing steps in a transaction fail, the transaction is aborted and the data is rolled back to its previous state. B is wrong, because consistency means that when the data is modified, it matches the state that is expected. D is wrong, because durability enforces that when an update is committed to data, it must be able to survive such things as communication failures, process failures, and server failures.

19. **A.** SQL Server 6.5 Developer Edition can only be installed on computers running Windows NT. This includes NT Server and NT Workstation. It cannot be installed on Windows 95/98 computers.
B and C are wrong, because free hard disk space isn't the issue here. There is more than enough hard disk space on each computer.

To install SQL Server 6.5 Developer Edition you need 80MB of free disk space for a Typical installation, and 95MB for a Full installation. D is wrong, because SQL Server 6.5 Developer Edition comes with the Enterprise Editions of Visual Studio and Visual C++ 6.0.

20. **D.** VSS Client hasn't been installed on the computer. Although VSS Server has been installed on this computer, VSS Client hasn't. For the developer to use the source code control system, both the VSS Client and Server programs need to be installed. The VSS Server has the administration capabilities and database used for source code control, whereas the VSS Client allows the user to store and retrieve source code files to and from the database.

A is wrong, because you can install Visual SourceSafe before or after installing Visual C++ 6.0. If you install the VSS Client before installing Visual C++, the commands for source code control will be integrated with Visual C++. B is wrong, because reinstalling Visual C++ won't make a difference. The missing component to use the source code control system is the Visual SourceSafe Client. C is also incorrect. Visual SourceSafe is a Microsoft product, and conforms to the Microsoft Source Code Control Interface. This allows the source code control system to integrate with Visual C++, so commands appear under the Visual C++ menu system. These commands allow the developer to store and retrieve source code from the VSS database.

MICROSOFT CERTIFIED SOLUTION DEVELOPER

2

The Physical Design

P rior to the introduction of the Microsoft Foundation Class (MFC) Library, all Windows-based applications were created using the Windows Application Programming Interface (API) (Win 16 API). The Windows API is a set of functions and data structures written in C that was used to interact with the Windows operating system. Programming applications in Windows API was extremely complex. The easiest tasks required several hundred lines of code. With MFC, the same tasks can be written in a few lines.

Since the introduction of the Microsoft Foundation Class (MFC) Library, developers have learned that using MFC makes Windows-based application development much easier. MFC functions as a thin layer over the Win32 API so developers can access the Windows API with easy-to-use objects instead of calling the complex API functions. In order to be successful in Windows-based programming with Visual C++, you must be familiar with every aspect of MFC, including the physical design, which we talk about in this chapter.

CERTIFICATION OBJECTIVE 2.01

Elements of an Application Based on the MFC Framework

MFC is a set of pre-built C++ components that are interfaces to Microsoft Windows. These reusable components encapsulate all the common functions so that developers do not have to redevelop them every time. By using MFC, developers can greatly speed up their development time. Another benefit of using MFC is that its included optional architecture simplifies development. Developers will have a common location to add application-specific code in their application. Regardless of how an application is designed and structured, all MFC applications have the same common elements: the documents, the views, the frame windows, the document templates, the application object, and the thread objects. Please note that architecture included in MFC, such as the document/view architecture, does not have to be used.

Try to use MFC as much as possible. It greatly simplifies the coding process.

Documents

The document, specified by the document class, manages your application's data. The document is derived from the CDocument class. The document object provides functions that other objects can use to access the data. The important functions within the document object are as follows:

- **GetFirstViewPosition**   Returns the position of the first view to allow GetNextView to enumerate the views of the document
- **GetNextView**   Returns a CView pointer to the next view in the view list of this document object
- **GetPathName**   Returns path and filename of the document
- **GetTitle**   Returns the document's title
- **IsModified**   Returns nonzero if document has unsaved data and zero if it doesn't
- **SetModifiedFlag**   Can set or reset document's modified flag
- **UpdateAllViews**   Updates all the views associated with this document

Views

The view object determines how the user sees and interacts with the document's data. MFC allows you to open multiple views of the same data with a multiple-document interface (MDI) application, which we will talk about later in this chapter. An easy way to think about views is that the view is just a specific representation of the document. Each document can have multiple views.

The view object is derived from the view class. The view class shows the data on the document and it relies on the surrounding frame windows for the basic windows functionalities, such as moving and resizing. The view class is derived from the CView class or a CView-derived class, and it handles the user interaction that affects the view.

Document Templates

The document template is in charge of linking your application's documents, views, and frame windows, which allows them to function as one entity. You can create single-document or multiple-document templates, which can be used to create single-document interface (SDI) and MDI applications.

Frame Windows

The frame windows host the application's view windows. The application's main frame window specifies the characteristics of the frame windows that contain these views.

Thread Objects

A thread is the most basic unit of execution in a Windows-based application. If your application is multithreaded, you can create multiple threads with the classes derived from CWinThread.

Application Object

The application object, derived from CWinApp, is the backbone of all MFC applications. It manages the start, the execution, and the termination of an application by encapsulating the Win32 WinMain( ) function. The application object is also responsible for creating the main frame window, which is where the user interfaces with the application. This object provides access to the following crucial member functions of the CWinApp class function that dictate the execution of the application:

- InitInstance( )
- Run( )
- OnIdle( )
- ExitInstance( )

InitInstance( ) Member Function

The InitInstance( ) is the most important member function in the application object. This function initializes every instance of the application that is executed. It is very common to override the InitInstance( ) member function in the classes of your application. Many developers do it but are not required to do so.

Run( ) Member Function

The Run( ) function is responsible for sitting in a message loop waiting for and processing incoming messages. Once it receives messages, it will send them to the main frame window of the application. When no messages are available to process, Run( ) will call the OnIdle( ) member function to idle. When termination of the program is requested, the Run( ) member function will run the ExitInstance( ) member function.

OnIdle( ) Member Function

The OnIdle( ) member function is used by the application object for idle processing. You are able to override the OnIdle( ) function to perform other background tasks. The default version updates the user interface element states.

ExitInstance( ) Member Function

The ExitInstance( ) member function is called when an instance of an application is terminated. This function is called by Run( ), usually when the user has requested that the instance of the application be closed. You usually would override the ExitInstance( ) member function to clean up standard objects such as frame windows or views.

Developing an MFC Application

Windows 95, Windows 98, and Windows NT are Microsoft's 32-bit operating systems. Because these operating systems all use the Win32 API and have similar shells, most applications should work the same. However, there are always some applications that developers find that work fine on

Windows 95/98, but encounter problems when running Windows NT. Some of these problems may be caused by not following the proper API calling rules and conventions, misinterpreting the operating system platform, replacing system dynamic link libraries (DLLs) with versions for the wrong platform, or simply bad coding.

However, not all malfunctioning applications are the fault of the developer. Windows 95/98 and Windows NT are different operating systems. Windows NT enforces permissions and rights. Windows NT is also a Unicode operating system. In order for you to successfully develop cross-platform Windows-based applications, you need to follow a few guidelines to minimize problems when developing programs that are going to run on Windows 95/98 and Windows NT. These guidelines cover versioning, DLLs, security, drive size, hard-coded paths, and ANSI versus Unicode.

Versioning

Applications use either GetVersion or GetVersionEx to get the operating system platform, version, and build information. Some applications encounter problems over their incorrect use of GetVersion. GetVersion returns two platform bits as well as the version number. Because many applications only check for the operating system version number, and because Windows 95/98/NT all return 4 as the version number, the application ends up calling Windows 95-specific calls to the KERNEL32.DLL. The same calls are not available on Windows NT, so the Windows NT application ends up failing. Other times, applications only check for the two platform bits but will end up misinterpreting the version of the operating system. In order for you to avoid these problems when using GetVersion, you should get the two return bits as well as the version number or use GetVersionEx. GetVersionEx is the new version of GetVersion and is the preferred method of acquiring version information from the operating system. GetVersionEx returns versioning information in an OSVERSION structure that is less cryptic than the DWORD bits in GetVersion.

DLLs

Not all required DLLs exist on the user's computer. An application should check to see if they are available. If they are not, it should be prepared to install them. If the application detects an older version of a required DLL, users should be prompted to decide whether they want to overwrite it or leave it as is. This is good practice because the user might not want his or her current version of the DLL to be overwritten.

The application should check the operating system version. It is possible that the application will install a DLL from the incorrect platform and this can cause many applications that access DLL to function incorrectly. Applications must use Refcount to maintain the count on the DLLs that exist on the system. MFC and system DLLs should never be removed.

Security

Windows NT is a secure operating system and all applications that are being installed inherit the rights of the current user. Because the application has the same rights as the user, some problems many arise when the current user does not have enough privileges for the application to install critical files or write to the Registry. To avoid problems like this, inform the user that he or she must have sufficient privileges in order to install the application.

exam
ⓦatch

The main difference between Windows 95/98 and Windows NT is security. Developers must keep this in mind when they are designing programs that run on both platforms.

Large Drives

The creation of the FAT32 file system has caused some applications to display incorrect drive size information during installation with drives larger than 2GB. The GetDiskFreeSpace API function, which returns the free space of the drive, caused many applications to fail because it doesn't return the correct free space on a 2+ GB drive. If this is a big issue, you can use the updated API function GetDiskFreeSpaceEx instead of the older GetDiskFreeSpace.

Hard-Coded Paths

API functions are available to start the operating system's executable files. Some developers choose to hard-code the path of the executable rather than to use the API calls. Applications that have hard-coded paths can run into problems because executables are stored in different paths on different operating systems. Sometimes the executables will change their implementation so that calling them explicitly will not work.

Another problem with hard-coded paths is with the Registry. Keys are not necessarily in the same location on all platforms. In order to ensure that your application will work in all platforms, substitute all hard-coded operating system executable calls and Registry keys with API calls.

ANSI versus Unicode

Because Windows NT is a Unicode operating system, all internal routines use Unicode character handling. Windows 95/98 uses American National Standards Institute (ANSI) standards for internal routine character handling. In ensuring that an application is Unicode-ready, it must be able to identify the operating system and use the ANSI or wide function calls (for Unicode) when necessary.

Exercise 2-1 presents a checklist that will help you review the things to watch for when you develop on Windows 95/98/NT.

EXERCISE 2-1

Windows 95/98/NT Applications Development Differences Checklist

1. Ensure that you are retrieving the correct version of your Windows-based application by ensuring that you are returning the correct variables, such as platform, build, and version with GetVersion and GetVersionEx.

2. Check to see if necessary DLLs are available.

3. If Windows NT is detected, be sure to tell users that when applications are installed they must have sufficient rights and privileges to install the program.

4. The most accurate method to return the computer's free disk space is to use GetDiskFreeSpaceEx.

5. Use API calls instead of hard-coding calls to an executable or to access keys within the Registry.

Using the Platform SDK for an MFC Application

With all the advantages surrounding using the MFC and its application framework, why would anybody want to use the Platform software development kit (SDK), when it's more difficult to use and it does not offer the abstractions that the MFC offers? MFC is a C++ class library that is a wrapper around the Win32 API. The newest version, MFC 6.0, has about 200 classes available to it. Although MFC could provide all of what you need, it also might not. Not everything available in the Win32 API is encapsulated in MFC—one example is the list control. Sometimes, with extremely complex applications, you may need to mix your MFC application with some raw Win32 API code. The only way to find out what you need is to gain some experience with MFC so that you understand its strengths and weaknesses. Only then are you able to know when to use MFC by itself, or an MFC/Win32 API hybrid. Exercise 2-2 is a checklist that allows you to review what you should have in mind when choosing between the Platform SDK and the MFC.

<table><tr><td>EXERCISE 2-2</td></tr></table>

Checklist for Choosing between the Platform SDK and the MFC Application Framework

Company X is designing an MFC application. Here are the steps that a consultant will use to decide whether to choose the Platform SDK or the MFC application framework.

1. If the functionality completely exists in MFC, then use MFC.

2. If the functionality is somewhat supported in MFC, then use MFC and the Platform SDK. Remember, MFC should always be your primary choice to develop a Windows-based application as long as the functionality exists and is complete. If not, use as much of

MFC as possible and use the Platform SDK for the features that are not complete.

3. If the functionality is not supported in MFC, then use Platform SDK.

Using the Functionality Provided by the MFC Framework

MFC is more than a class library. The MFC is also an application framework that defines the structure of the application. The framework encapsulates and handles many routine tasks for you. These abstractions are much more convenient and shield many of the nuances that Win32 API programmers face. An example of this is the document/view architecture. If the desired class or function is available in MFC and it is sufficient, you should use the MFC framework.

Choosing an MFC Regular DLL or an MFC Extension DLL

Libraries are sets of compiled code that are included within an application at compile time. With DLL, or dynamic link libraries, the libraries are linked at run-time, hence the name *dynamic link libraries*. DLLs are very flexible, because you can update the libraries without recompiling the entire application. AppWizard lets you create two types of DLLs that support the MFC library: MFC regular DLLs and MFC extension DLLs. DLLs are similar to the static libraries that you encountered when you were dealing with C++. By being able to link to the MFC library, your application is able to access the MFC methods and classes without having to duplicate the object code within the API. With DLLs, code can be shared, which saves memory and space requirements.

An MFC regular DLL can use C++ classes, but it can only export C functions. If you need a DLL that can be loaded in any Win32 programming environment, you should use a regular DLL. With the MFC regular DLLs, you can choose to either dynamically or statically link to the MFC library. With the statically linked library, a copy of the MFC library is included so that the DLL is independently contained. With the dynamically linked library, the DLL is much smaller.

The MFC extension DLL can export entire MFC classes, MFC-derived classes, C++ classes, member functions, and overloaded functions. The client can create objects based on or derived from these classes and functions. The extension DLL can dynamically link to the code in the MFC library's DLL. Thus, the client program must be dynamically linked to the MFC library and the client program and the extension DLL must be synchronized to the same version of the MFC DLLs. Because the client program is dynamically linked to the MFC library, the DLLs are much smaller than the regular, statically linked DLLs. The MFC extension DLL can only be used with C++ compilers, such as Microsoft Visual C++ or Borland C++. Exercise 2-3 helps you to choose between the MFC extension and regular DLL.

| EXERCISE 2-3 | **Match the Platform to the Correct Usage of the MFC Extension DLL and the MFC Regular DLL** |

Identify whether the platforms in the left column use the MFC extension DLL or the MFC regular DLL. (The answers to this exercise appear just before the Self Test at the end of this chapter.)

Platform	MFC extension or regular DLL?
Visual Basic	
Visual C++	
Visual J++	
Borland C++	
Symantec C++	
Symantec Café	

Routing Command Messages Between a User Interface Object and a Handler Function

Messages play a great role in Windows-based applications. Messages are created from a variety of actions, such as a mouse-click on a menu item or by accelerator keystrokes. Command messages are messages that can be handled by many different objects, such as the application, the documents, and the windows. Every object which is capable of receiving command messages has its own message map. Each command message is identified by a constant that is assigned by a resource editor. When the object receives the command message, it looks at its own message maps for a match. If it can't find the handler, it will route the command to the next object.

The handling order for SDI is as follows:

- View
- Document
- Main Frame
- Application

The handling order for MDI is as follows:

- View
- Document
- Child Frame
- Main Frame
- Application

The application will go first to the class to which the message belongs. If it does not find a match, it will go down the list until it finds the proper handlers. If there are multiple handlers, the handler at the higher level will be called.

The Document/View Architecture

The document/view architecture is the core of the MFC application framework. In a document/view application, the data, also known as the document, is managed separately from the application through which the users interact with the data. This allows the data to be encapsulated by the way that the data is shown and the way that the user inputs it. The data and the code are separated. There are two application types that have the document/view architecture: single-document interface and multiple-document interface.

SDI

The simplest application type that has the document/view architecture is the single-document interface (SDI). In an SDI application, only one document is open at a time. An example of this is Notepad, as shown in Figure 2-1.

Four classes make up SDI:

- CWinApp
- CFrameView
- CDocument
- CView

CWinApp creates all the application's components. Another main task is to receive all the event messages and to pass them to the CFrameView and the CView.

FIGURE 2-1

There can be only one document open at a time in an SDI application

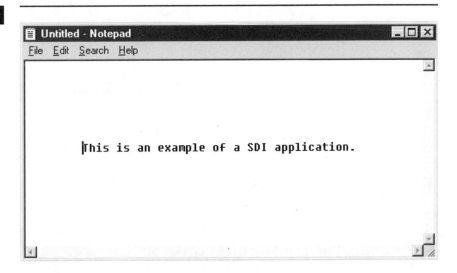

CFrameView is the window frame that holds all the components that you see on the frame, such as the toolbar, the menu, and the scrollbar.

The CDocument class stores and manages your document's data, such as saving and retrieving information.

CView gets information from the CDocument class and it outputs the desired information for the user. This enables the user to interact with the data that is managed by the CDocument-derived class.

MDI

The multiple-document interface (MDI) is similar to the SDI application except that it allows the user to have multiple documents open at the same time. Each document could consist of a different file, or of the same file but of a different view, such as a Microsoft Excel spreadsheet and a chart based on the data from the Microsoft Excel spreadsheet, as shown in Figure 2-2.

Five classes make up an MDI application:

- CWinApp
- CMDIFrameWnd
- CMDIChildWnd
- CDocument
- CView

MDI contains all the same classes as an SDI application, except for CFrameView. Instead, MDI has CMDIFrameWnd and CMDIChildWnd. CMDIFrameWnd is the main frame of the application, where all interactions with the user take place. The CMDIChildWnd class holds the CView class and it passes all messages and events to the CView class. This class makes the access to multiple documents possible and this is where all the multi-document files are defined.

The MFC Drawing Architecture

The drawing capabilities of Windows center on the Graphical Device Interface (GDI). The GDI provides all the services needed to draw in Windows. Prior to the GDI, programmers had to write program graphics to

FIGURE 2-2   MDI applications allow the user to have multiple documents open at the same time

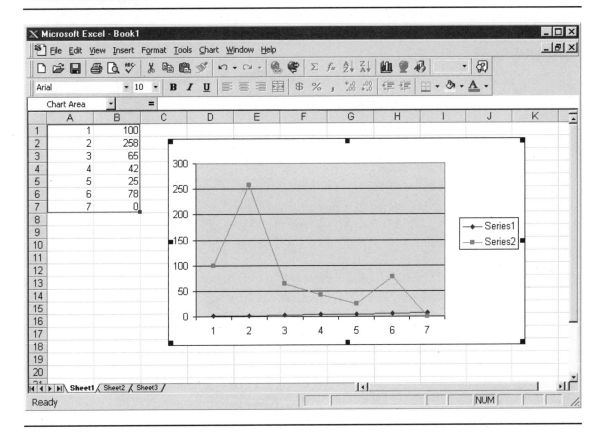

the video hardware and video standard. Programming graphics was extremely frustrating because every new hardware device or standard had programmers scrambling to support it. This all changed with the introduction of the GDI, which is a part of the hardware-independent graphics output model. The programmers write to the GDI and the GDI worries about interpreting the code to the hardware. This model frees up the programmer so he or she can worry about graphics programming.

Whenever the Windows-based application needs to draw to a device, it accesses it through the device context. The device context (DC) is a virtual desktop service that represents the device drawing surface. When you use

MFC, you create a device context object and call its member functions to do the drawing for you.

Components

The graphic components that MFC supports are as follows:

- **Pens**   Used to draw lines and curves
- **Brushes**   Used to paint the interior of polygons and ellipses
- **Palettes**   Set of colors used by GDI to render an image
- **Bitmaps**   Graphical image
- **Fonts**   Defines the style of text being displayed

Drawing

The MFC CDC class encapsulates the device context as well as the GDI function. The CDC functions for drawing lines, curves, and closed figures are as follows:

- **MoveTo**   Sets the current position
- **LineTo**   Draws a line from the current position to the defined position
- **Polyline**   Connects a set of defined points
- **PolylineTo**   Connects a set of points from the current position to a set of defined points
- **Arc**   Draws an arc
- **ArcTo**   Draws an arc and updates the current position to the end of the arc
- **PolyBezier**   Draws Bezier splines
- **PolyBezierTo**   Draws Bezier splines and updates the current position to the end of the Bezier spline

- **PolyDraw** Draws lines and Bezier splines and updates the current position to the last line or Beizer spline
- **Chord** Draws a chord, an intersection of an ellipse, and a line
- **Ellipse** Draws an ellipse
- **Pie** Draws a pie wedge
- **Polygon** Connects a set of points to form a polygon
- **Rectangle** Connects a set of points to form a rectangle
- **RoundRect** Draws a rectangle with rounded corners

Colors

You can set and manipulate colors by using the COLORREF value. COLORREF uses the red-green-blue (RGB) system, which uses the intensity of three colors: red, green, and blue, to specify each color. To set the COLORREF value, you use the RGB macro. The RGB macro takes three parameters: the intensities of red, green, and blue. You can set the colors with numbers in the range of 0 to 255. Table 2-1 shows the RGB values for the most common colors.

TABLE 2-1

RGB Values for Common Colors

Color	Red Value	Green Value	Blue Value
Black	0	0	0
Blue	0	0	255
Green	0	255	0
Cyan	0	255	255
Red	255	0	0
Magenta	255	0	255
Yellow	255	255	0
White	255	255	255
Dark gray	128	128	128
Light gray	192	192	192

Text Drawing

Unlike drawing lines, to draw text you must first set the attributes to the text and then write it out to the device. The following is a list of the main functions that control text-display attributes:

- **SetTextColor** and **GetTextColor**   Control the color of the text displayed.

- **SetBkMode** and **GetBkMode**   Control whether or not the cells that surround each letter are filled before the corresponding characters are displayed. In Opaque mode, the cells are filled with the current background color. In Transparent mode, no fill takes place.

- **SetBkColor** and **GetBkColor**   Control the color of the cells that contain the displayed text. The background mode must be Opaque before this attribute is used in a fill.

- **SetTextAlign** and **GetTextAlign**   Control the alignment of text relative to the window position specified in one of the text-output functions.

The following is a list of functions that control text output:

- **TextOut**   Displays a text string at the given location by using the currently selected font, colors, and alignment

- **TabbedTextOut**   Similar to TextOut, but supports expansion of tab stops

- **DrawText**   Displays formatted text within a bounding rectangle

- **ExtTextOut**   Similar to TextOut, but allows specification of clipping options

Mapping

In Windows, the GDI translates logical coordinates to physical coordinates using the different mapping modes. You can set the mapping modes with the SetMapMode device context function. By setting the different mapping modes, you control how the objects and the coordinates are translated to the screen. Windows supports eight mapping modes.

- **MM_ISOTROPIC**   Logical units are converted into random units with equally scaled axes.

- **MM_ANISOTROPIC**   Logical units are converted into random units with random axes.

- **MM_HIENGLISH**   Each logical unit is converted to 0.001 inch. Positive X is on the right, positive Y is up.

- **MM_LOENGLISH**   Each logical unit is converted to 0.01 inch. Positive X is on the right, positive Y is up.

- **MM_HIMETRIC**   Each logical unit is converted to 0.01 mm. Positive X is on the right, positive Y is up.

- **MM_LOMETRIC**   Each logical unit is converted to 0.1 mm. Positive X is on the right, positive Y is up.

- **MM_TEXT**   Each logical unit is converted to 1 pixel. Positive X is on the right, positive Y is down.

- **MM_TWIPS**   Each logical unit is converted to 1/20 of a point. Positive X is on the right, positive Y is up.

MFC Printing and Print Preview Architecture

Like drawing, printing was a headache prior to Windows. The application had to be coded to deal with the many different print drivers. With Windows, this process was streamlined in that the application printed to the GDI. To print without MFC, the application had to get a device context to the printer and then call the StartDoc Win32 API function, which would start the print job. At every start in a page in a document, the StartPage function would be run. At every end in the page, the EndPage would run.

This would loop until there were no more pages to be printed. Then, the EndDoc function would be called. This process is greatly simplified with MFC. With MFC, the printer device context is automatically created and destroyed and the StartDoc, StartPage, EndPage, and EndDoc functions are called automatically for you by using member functions in the CView class. The necessary MFC functions that you should be familiar with are as follows:

■ **OnPreparePrinting**   Called prior to any printing or previewing.

■ **DoPreparePrinting**   Displays the Print dialog box and creates the printer device context. You set the maximum page count here.

■ **OnBeginPrinting**   Called when the print job starts. You can overwrite this function to create resources that you need for printing, such as fonts. You set the maximum page count here also.

■ **OnPrepareDC**   Called before any drawing starts to prepare the device context. Override this function to modify the device context, such as pagination.

■ **OnDraw**   This function displays the images you see in the Print Preview window as well as how it would appear on the printer.

■ **OnPrint**   Called for printing or print preview. Override this function to provide additional printing features, such as headers and footers.

■ **OneEndPrintPreview**   Called when print preview mode is exited.

■ **OnEndPrinting**   Called when the print job is finished. You must override this function to release any resources that you created.

exam
ⓦatch

The most common print function to override is the OnPrint function. You must override this function to print more standard features such as footers and headers.

Print preview is much different than printing. With print preview, the application simulates the printing of a document onto the screen. This is done with the CDC-derived class, CPreviewDC. When print preview is selected, the CPreviewDC object is created. You can modify print preview so you can get a scrollbar, to maintain the user's original position, and you can make print preview output specially formatted page numbers. Exercise 2-4 will help you become more familiar with the print and print preview architecture in MFC.

MFC Print and Print Preview Architecture

Based on the following scenarios, choose the MFC function that you need to override. (The answers to this exercise appear just before the Self Test at the end of this chapter.)

1. You would like to have customized headers and footers.

2. You want to modify the device context.

3. You want to set the maximum page count.

4. After creating objects, you need to overload this function to release the resources created by your objects.

Multithreading Support with the MFC Architecture

MFC supports multitasking through its threading model. Thread-based multitasking allows users to run more than one instance of a program as well as to run different tasks in a single application. This is similar to running subapplications within a single application. An example of this is running a spell checker while you are typing a document. A thread is the basic unit of execution. With thread-based multitasking, the developer can fully control the way the application executes. MFC has two types of threads: the interface thread and the worker thread. An interface thread can receive and process messages. A worker thread does not receive or process messages, it just provides additional paths of execution for the main thread. The user interface can create windows and process messages sent to those windows. MFC supports multithreading with the CWinThread. The main thread of an executable is always an interface thread. The main thread can spawn additional worker threads that will facilitate multithreading. You create a worker thread with the function AfxBeginThread. You terminate the thread with AfxEndThread. You suspend a thread or pause the

FROM THE CLASSROOM

MFC Printing Support

As discussed in this section, MFC adds printing support through member functions in the CView class. The most important of these member functions are OnPreparePrinting, DoPreparePrinting, OnBeginPrinting, OnPrepareDC, OnDraw, OnPrint, OnEndPrintPreview, and OnEndPrinting. With these functions you can perform all of the tasks necessary to include print and print preview capabilities in your application. There are, however, a couple of other handy printing features built into the CView and CWnd classes that make dealing with printers and print jobs very simple. Specifically, let's look at how to obtain information about the default printer, and how to obtain information about the current print job.

There are two methods to find out default printer settings. You choose the method to use based on when the information needs to be known by your application. If your application needs to know about the default printer on startup, you will need to override the InitInstance member function of the application object derived from CWinApp. In InitInstance, call GetPrinterDeviceDefaults, which gives you a reference to a PRINTDLG object, then call CreatePrinterDC, which gives you a reference to an object containing default printer characteristics. This could be accomplished with code such as the following:

```
PRINTDLG pdialog;
GetPrinterDeviceDefaults(&pdialog);
CDCdefaultCharacteristics;
if (CreatePrinterDC(dc) != 0)
{
```

```
//get default characteristics
}
```

If you need to get the default printer setting some time following application startup, or to monitor any changes made to the default printer, you need to implement the OnWinIniChange member function of the main window class in your application. This method is a member function of the CWnd class that provides the base functionality of all window classes in the Microsoft Foundation Class Library.

You may also want to find out information about the printer's current print job. You can do this by using the pInfo parameter that is passed to the CView member functions. The pInfo parameter of the CView:OnXxxx functions contains a pointer to an object named CPrintInfo. Information about the print job is contained in the CPrintInfo object and accessed using its class members.

The MFC is a valuable tool for building Windows applications, and it has made one of the messiest tasks of application development—printing—seem almost trivial. We have only pointed out some of the major printing features in the MFC, but by no means have we shown all of the printing support built into the Microsoft Foundation Classes. To find out more about these features, try searching on the classes, objects, and member functions we have looked at in this section using MSDN, either on-line, through your subscription, or on the MSDN CD provided with Microsoft Visual Studio.

—Michael Lane Thomas,
MCSE+I, MCSD, MCT, MCP+SB, MSS, A+

execution of a thread with CWinThread::SuspendThread( ). You can resume a suspended thread with CWinThread::ResumeThread.

Priorities

Every process has a priority class assigned to it. The priority is used to help determine how much central processing unit (CPU) time the process has access to. Processes that are crucial have higher priority than lower priority ones. The different priority classes are as follows:

- REALTIME_PRIORITY_CLASS
- HIGH_PRIORITY_CLASS
- NORMAL_PRIORITY_CLASS
- IDLE_PRIORITY_CLASS

By default, programs are given the normal priority class. You need to be cautious with assigning the correct priority class. Assigning an application's priority class to real time can hog the entire CPU and slow down or halt execution of other threads. High priority class is set when you need a priority higher than normal but the program is not crucial to the system. Set applications to the idle priority class when you need the application to run only when no other applications are waiting for the CPU. You can set the priority with the function SetPriorityClass( ). You can return the current priority with GetPriorityClass( ).

You can also set the priority of the individual threads within a process. You use GetThreadPriority( ) and SetThreadPriority to do this. The different priority settings are:

- THREAD_PRIORITY_TIME_CRITICAL
- THREAD_PRIORITY_TIME_HIGHEST
- THREAD_PRIORITY_ABOVE_NORMAL
- THREAD_PRIORITY_NORMAL
- THREAD_PRIORITY_BELOW_NORMAL
- THREAD_PRIORITY_LOWEST
- THREAD_PRIORITY_IDLE

Exercise 2-5 will help you choose the thread priority class when you are developing your application.

Choosing the Thread Priority Class

Based on the following scenarios, choose the thread priority class that you should use. (The answers to this exercise appear just before the Self Test at the end of this chapter.)

1. You want to do a background spell checker.

2. You want to defragment your hard drive when the computer is idle.

3. You want to run a service critical to system operation.

4. You are creating a standard application.

Synchronization

With multithreading, synchronization becomes a necessity when two or more threads need access to a shared resource that has a limit on how many threads can access it. The prevention of one thread from accessing a resource that another thread currently is accessing is called synchronization. The following classes encapsulate synchronization objects:

- **CCriticalSection**   Allows only a section of code to be accessed at one time. This encapsulates the simplest type of thread object. This is done with the CCriticalSection::Lock member function to lock the resource before it is used. CCriticalSection::Unlock unlocks the resource after it is used.

- **CEvent**   Events can block a process from accessing a resource until another thread allows it. CEvent supports two types of events: autoreset and manual reset. An autoreset event will automatically reset itself after the resource is released. Manual reset forces the developer to write code to release the resource. Autoreset events use SetEvent to trigger the event if it is one thread and they use PulseEvent for two or more threads. ResetEvent is run automatically.

With manual reset, the developer can check for the state of the event with the m_hObject data member.

■ **CMutex**   Mutex is a combination of the words *mutually* and *exclusive*. It is used to gain exclusive access to a resource shared by multiple threads, as well as to synchronize the threads running in the same process or in different processes. Like the CCriticalSection, it uses the Lock and Unlock member functions to lock and free resources.

■ **CSemaphore**   A semaphore signals that a limited number of threads can access a resource. This is unlike the other synchronization object classes. A semaphore uses a resource count to determine how many threads are accessing the resource simultaneously. Every time the Lock member function is run, the resource count is incremented. When Unlock is run, the resource count is decremented. When the count hits the resource maximum, Lock will lock the resource until the resource count goes below the threshold.

■ **CSingleLock**   Controls access to one synchronization object. You can use this to control a critical section, a mutex, an event, or a semaphore.

■ **CMultiLock**   Controls access to multiple synchronization objects. This can control a critical section, a mutex, an event, or a semaphore. The advantage of using CMultiLock is that it can block up to 64 synchronization objects at once, and it can block all of them until one of them is free or until all of them are free.

CERTIFICATION OBJECTIVE 2.03

Accessing a Database

As corporations depend more and more on databases, more applications are needed to access a database. Visual C++ provides many technologies to allow access to databases in your applications. It supports Data Access

Objects (DAO), Open Database Connectivity (ODBC), OLE DB, and ActiveX Data Objects (ADO).

Incorporating a Database into the Application

In order for a database to be incorporated into the application, you will need to be able to access the database from your application. Visual C++ contains all the components needed to create a database application. This can be done with the available libraries and database objects included in Visual C++.

Types of Libraries

You can access database objects through libraries included in Visual C++, such as MFC, the Active Template Library (ATL), and the Platform SDK.

MFC

In order to use the MFC library for databases, you must use ODBC or DAO. With the MFC library for ODBC, you can access any database that has an ODBC driver. With MFC ODBC, you can use objects instead of using connection handles and statement handles. MFC DAO is a set of Component Object Model (COM) interfaces. However, DAO only allows access to flat file databases, such as Access. MFC DAO is the fastest way to access the flat file database.

ATL

The Active Template Library (ATL) is used to create lightweight controls based on COM. These controls are much smaller than MFC and are extremely suitable for client/server applications. ATL is the way to develop applications if the functionality is to be used in several applications. ATL will build controls that can be plugged into an application that will extend its functionality. However, ATL can support OLE DB, which allows access to everything ODBC offers as well as access to other data sources, such as an Excel spreadsheet. It must be noted that ATL does not support ODBC. Access to data must go through the OLE DB interface. Because OLE DB is based on COM, data access is encapsulated and made into separate components. This is more efficient compared to traditional database access because access is split into two components: the consumer and the provider. The consumer is the code that uses the OLE DB interface. A provider exposes that interface. By splitting the access to the data, client-side resource overhead is reduced. ATL provides templates to make creating the two components much easier. For client/server applications, ATL is the ideal choice for accessing databases.

The SDK

Using the Platform SDK to access the database is the most powerful way to use databases, but also the most complex. You should use the Platform SDK only if MFC's database classes and ATL's OLE DB are not sufficient to provide what you need.

Types of Objects

You access databases through different objects. There are pros and cons to each object.

ADO

Of all the different data objects available in Visual C++, ActiveX Data Objects (ADO) represents the future of database connectivity for database developers. ADO is a wrapper around OLE DB, which was created to replace ODBC. Microsoft introduced OLE DB in an effort to eliminate any bias to any data storage format. OLE DB allows a direct COM interface to the destination data source.

ODBC

Open Database Connectivity (ODBC) has been the most popular way for database developers to access any relational database. It's a database interface standard that allows access with an ODBC driver. Though ODBC is currently very popular, Microsoft is pushing developers to focus on ADO/OLE DB and wants it to be known that it is the proper way to access data stores.

RDO

Because using the ODBC API can be quite unwieldy, Microsoft introduced Remote Data Objects (RDO). RDO is a thin wrapper around the ODBC API. RDO translates the manipulation of the data objects, as well as their properties and methods, and sends the appropriate calls to the ODBC API. Because RDO has an object-type interface, it takes away a lot of the guesswork involved in connecting to an ODBC data source. However, RDO is not available in Visual C++. Exercise 2-6 will help you choose the correct database object and library.

EXERCISE 2-6

Choosing Database Objects and Libraries

Based on the following scenarios, choose the database object or library that you should use. (The answers to this exercise appear just before the Self Test at the end of this chapter.)

1. You want to do a client/server application. What library should you use?

2. You want to be able to access an Excel spreadsheet. What database object should you use?

3. You want to manipulate data in Access. What library should you use?

4. You are creating a standard database application. The database uses a standard ODBC driver. What database object should you use?

CERTIFICATION OBJECTIVE 2.04

Designing Properties, Methods, and Events of Components

ActiveX controls are software components that can be attached to different programs, providing additional functionality. ActiveX brings this type of "plug and play" interoperability to Windows-based applications. Software components allowed only certain parts of an application to be upgraded or replaced. ActiveX components are based on newer OLE (Object Link Embedding) and use the Component Object Model. COM defines how components can interact seamlessly between each other.

Properties

A main feature of ActiveX controls is their ability to expose their properties using a primary dispatch interface. Through this dispatch interface, an ActiveX control container can access the control as a resource. The properties of the control expose the attributes of the control container to the container. There are two types of properties: stock and custom.

The stock properties are properties already implemented in the COleControl-based class and cannot be altered. This is the common functionality of the ActiveX control. There are nine stock properties:

- **Appearance**   Sets the control as flat or 3-d
- **BackColor**   Sets the control's background color
- **BorderStyle**   Sets the control's border style
- **Caption**   Sets the control's title
- **Enabled**   Determines if the control is enabled
- **Font**   Sets the control's current font
- **ForeColor**   Sets the control's foreground color
- **hWnd**   Sets the control's window object's handle
- **Text**   Sets the control's title

Sometimes the stock properties do not provide enough functionality. You may wish to introduce custom properties. For a custom property, you must provide the declaration and the implementation. There are four types of implementation for a custom property:

- **Member Variable**   Implementation in which the member variable is exposed to a container

- **Member Variable with Notification**   Implementation in which the member variable is exposed to a container and the control is notified when there is a change in the property
- **Get/Set Methods**   Implementation that calls a method that gets the current property value and a method that sets the property value
- **Parameterized**   Same as the Get/Set methods implementation except it allows access to a group of values through a single property

Methods

ActiveX methods allow the client to perform functions on the control. Like properties, the methods are implemented by the primary dispatch interface. There are two types of methods: stock and custom.

Stock methods are methods already implemented by the COleControl base class. There are two stock method implementations.

- **DoClick**   This event is fired when the control is clicked.
- **Refresh**   This event refreshes the control.

Custom methods are methods that you create. The COleControl class does not support custom methods. MFC implements custom methods using the DISP_FUNCTION( ) macro. The macro, which refers to the handler function, must be declared in the control class and implemented in the project's program file. You must also insert the ID statement in the primary dispatch interface of the .ODL file.

Events

Events in ActiveX are a way for the ActiveX control to notify the container about the control. An event is usually activated by mouse actions or keystroke actions. Like properties and methods, MFC supports two types of events: stock and custom.

The COleControl base class implements stock events. They are the most common events for an ActiveX control. The stock events are:

- **Click**   Fired when the control is clicked
- **DblClick**   Fired when the control is double-clicked
- **Error**   Fired when an error has occurred within the control
- **KeyDown**   Fired when the key is pressed down
- **KeyPress**   Fired when the key is pressed and released
- **KeyUp**   Fired when the key is released
- **MouseDown**   Fired when the mouse button is pressed
- **MouseMove**   Fired when the mouse cursor is moving within the control
- **MouseUp**   Fired when the mouse button is released within the control
- **ReadyStateChange**   Fired when the state of the control changes

Custom events are events that are not supported by the COleControl class. Custom events are implemented with the EVENT_CUSTOM macro by MFC. The syntax is: EVENT_CUSTOM(ExtName, FiringFunc,Params)

ExtName is the external name of the event. FiringFunc is the control class's event firing function. Params is the list of parameter types passed to the FiringFunc.

The macro, which refers to the handler function, must be declared in the control class and implemented in the project's program file. You must also insert the ID statement in the primary dispatch interface of the .ODL file. Exercise 2-7 will help you review components.

EXERCISE 2-7

Checklist for Evaluating Components

- If it has to do with the appearance of the component, then set the properties of the component.
- If you need to run a type of macro, then set the methods of the component.

■ If you need to notify the component based on an action, then set the events of the component.

CERTIFICATION SUMMARY

Since the introduction of the Microsoft Foundation Class (MFC) Library, developers have learned that using MFC makes Windows-based application development much easier. MFC functions as a thin layer over the Win32 API so developers can access the Windows application programming interface (API) with easy-to-use objects instead of calling the complex API functions.

MFC applications have the same common elements: -documents, -views, -frame windows, -document templates, -application objects, and thread objects. When developing MFC applications, problems may arise in developing for the Windows 95/98/NT platform. Problems are often caused by not following the proper API calling rules and conventions, misinterpreting the operating system platform, replacing system DLLs with versions for the wrong platform, or simply bad coding.

Prior to MFC, the main way to write a Windows-based application was to do it with the Windows API and the Platform SDK (Platform software development kit). By using the SDK, you are essentially writing programs with the Win32 API. Although MFC makes Windows-based programming much easier, it is not always the best way to create your applications.

Libraries allow you to share code in different applications. DLLs are dynamically linked at run time. There are two different types of DLLs supported in MFC: MFC regular DLL and MFC extension DLL. MFC regular DLL can use C++ classes. However, unlike the MFC Extension DLL, the MFC regular DLL can only export C functions.

The drawing and printing capabilities of Windows center on the Windows GDI in MFC. MFC supports multitasking through its threading model. Thread-based multitasking allows users to run more than one instance of a program and to run different tasks in a single application.

Visual C++ provides many technologies to allow access to databases in your applications. It supports Data Access Objects (DAO), ODBC, OLE DB, and ActiveX Data Objects (ADO). In addition to databases, components such as ActiveX controls can be created, allowing database functionality to be broken into separate components. ActiveX brings this type of "plug and play" interoperability to Windows-based applications.

TWO-MINUTE DRILL

- ❑ MFC functions as a thin layer over the Win32 API so developers can access the Windows API with easy-to-use objects instead of calling the complex API functions.

- ❑ Regardless of how an application is designed and structured, all MFC applications have the same common elements: the documents, the views, the frame windows, the document templates, the application object, and the thread objects.

- ❑ The document is derived from the CDocument class. The document object provides functions that other objects can use to access the data.

- ❑ MFC allows you to open multiple views of the same data with a multiple-document interface (MDI) application.

- ❑ An easy way to think about views is that the view is just a specific representation of the document. Each document can have multiple views.

- ❑ You can create single-document or multiple-document templates, which can be used to create single-document interface (SDI) and MDI applications.

- ❑ The frame windows host the application's view windows. The application's main frame window specifies the characteristics of the frame windows that contain these views.

- ❑ A thread is the most basic unit of execution in a Windows-based application. If your application is multithreaded, you can create multiple threads with the classes derived from CWinThread.

- ❑ The application object, derived from CWinApp, is the backbone of all MFC applications. It manages the start, the execution, and the termination of an application by encapsulating the Win32 WinMain( ) function.

❏ In order for you to successfully develop cross-platform Windows-based applications, you need to follow a few guidelines to minimize problems when developing programs that are going to run on Windows 95/98 and Windows NT. These guidelines cover versioning, DLLs, security, drive size, hard-coded paths, and ANSI versus Unicode.

❏ The main difference between Windows 95/98 and Windows NT is security. Developers must keep this in mind when they are designing programs that run on both platforms.

❏ MFC is a C++ class library that is a wrapper around the Win32 API. The newest version, MFC 6.0, has about 200 classes available to it.

❏ MFC is more than a class library. MFC is also an application framework that defines the structure of the application.

❏ Libraries are sets of compiled code that are included within an application at compile time. With DLL, or dynamic link libraries, the libraries are linked at runtime, hence the name *dynamic link libraries*.

❏ An MFC regular DLL can use C++ classes, but it can only export C functions. If you need a DLL that can be loaded in any Win32 programming environment, you should use a regular DLL.

❏ Command messages are messages that can be handled by many different objects, such as the application, the documents, and the windows.

❏ In a document/view application, the data, also known as the document, is managed separately from the application through which the users interact with the data.

❏ The simplest application type that has the document/view architecture is the single-document interface (SDI). In an SDI application, only one document is open at a time.

❏ The multiple-document interface (MDI) is similar to the SDI application except that it allows the user to have multiple documents open at the same time.

❏ Whenever the Windows-based application needs to draw to a device, it accesses it through the device context. The device context (DC) is a virtual desktop service that represents the device drawing surface.

❑ You can set and manipulate colors by using the COLORREF value. COLORREF uses the red-green-blue (RGB) system.

❑ Unlike drawing lines, to draw text you must first set the attributes to the text and then write it out to the device.

❑ In Windows, the GDI translates logical coordinates to physical coordinates using the different mapping modes. You can set the mapping modes with the SetMapMode device context function.

❑ With MFC, the printer device context is automatically created and destroyed and the StartDoc, StartPage, EndPage, and EndDoc functions are called automatically for you by using member functions in the CView class.

❑ The most common print function to override is the OnPrint function. You must override this function to print more standard features such as footers and headers.

❑ Thread-based multitasking allows users to run more than one instance of a program as well as to run different tasks in a single application. This is similar to running subapplications within a single application.

❑ Every process has a priority class assigned to it. The priority is used to help determine how much central processing unit (CPU) time that the process has access to.

❑ With multithreading, synchronization becomes a necessity when two or more threads need access to a shared resource that has a limit on how many threads can access it.

❑ Visual C++ provides many technologies to allow access to databases in your applications. It supports Data Access Objects (DAO), Open Database Connectivity (ODBC), OLE DB, and ActiveX Data Objects (ADO).

❑ You can access database objects through libraries included in Visual C++, such as MFC, the Active Template Library (ATL), and the Platform SDK.

❑ ActiveX components are based on newer OLE (Object Link Embedding) and use the Component Object Model. COM defines how components can interact seamlessly between each other.

❑ A main feature of ActiveX controls is their ability to expose their properties using a primary dispatch interface.

❑ ActiveX methods allow the client to perform functions on the control. Like properties, the methods are implemented by the primary dispatch interface.

❑ Events in ActiveX are a way for the ActiveX control to notify the container about the control. An event is usually activated by mouse actions or keystroke actions.

Answers to Exercise 2-3

Platform	MFC extension or regular DLL?
Visual Basic	MFC regular DLL
Visual C++	MFC extension DLL
Visual J++	MFC regular DLL
Borland C++	MFC extension DLL
Symantec C++	MFC extension DLL
Symantec Café	MFC regular DLL

Answers to Exercise 2-4

1. You would like to have customized headers and footers. OnPrint

2. You want to modify the device context. OnPrepareDC

3. You want to set the maximum page count. DoPreparePrinting and OnBeginPrinting

4. After creating objects, you need to overload this function to release the resources created by your objects. OnEndPrinting

Answers to Exercise 2-5

1. You want to do a background spell checker.
   THREAD_PRIORITY_LOWEST

2. You want to defragment your hard drive when the computer is idle.
   THREAD_PRIORITY_IDLE

3. You want to run a service critical to system operation.
   THREAD_PRIORITY_TIME_CRITICAL

4. You are creating a standard application.
   THREAD_PRIORITY_NORMAL

Answers to Exercise 2-6

1. You want to do a client/server application. What library should you use? ATL

2. You want to be able to access an Excel spreadsheet. What database object should you use? OLE DB

3. You want to manipulate data in Access. What library should you use? MFC

4. You are creating a standard database application. The database uses a standard ODBC driver. What database object should you use? ODBC

SELF TEST

The following questions will help you measure your understanding of the material presented in this chapter. Read all of the choices carefully, as there may be more than one correct answer. Choose all correct answers for each question.

1. Lucille is developing an application based on the MFC framework. The application's document object has a view list. What function must she utilize to go to the next view?

    A. GetFirstViewPosition

    B. GetNextView

    C. GetPathName

    D. GetTitle

2. Ian at Simple Apps is developing an MFC application, but wants to be able to design everything so that it functions as one entity. How should he go about doing this?

    A. Create the standard MFC application and save all the source code.

    B. Create the application using a template.

    C. Scrap the MFC idea and use the SDK.

    D. You can't. You must do the application from scratch every time.

3. Jason needs to have a function run every time an instance of the application is run. What function must he override?

    A. Run( )

    B. OnIdle( )

    C. ExitInstance( )

    D. InitInstance( )

4. Because DLLs are shared libraries, how can the application tell when the library must be loaded or unloaded from memory?

    A. An application does not need to worry about whether the library must be loaded or not.

    B. DLLs are always loaded in memory, regardless of whether or not they are being used.

    C. The application uses Refcount to ensure proper handling of the DLL.

    D. When an application starts, it automatically loads the correct libraries. When the application closes, all libraries are automatically unloaded.

5. After working long and hard on his application, Howard installs his application on Windows 98. It fails to install. The error being returned says there is not enough disk space even though the computer has sufficient space for the application. What should Howard do?

    A. Run Scandisk

    B. Have the application not check for free space

    C. Use GetFreeSpaceEx instead of GetFreeSpace

    D. Use GetFreeSpace instead of GetFreeSpaceEx

6. Identify the differences between the Windows 95/98 and the Windows NT operating systems. (Choose all that apply.)

   A. Security

   B. Location of Registry keys

   C. Win32 API

   D. MFC

7. Justin's boss is demanding that he create an MFC DLL. Justin knows this DLL must be able to work in many different types of applications: Java, Visual Basic, as well as Visual C++. What kind of DLL must he create?

   A. Extension DLLs

   B. Regular DLLs

   C. Both DLLs

   D. Neither DLL

8. What messages can be handled by the application, the documents, and the windows objects?

   A. Default messages

   B. Response messages

   C. Execution messages

   D. Command messages

9. Andrew is creating an application in which he needs to open multiple documents simultaneously. Each document should also be able to facilitate multiple views of the same document. How should Andrew implement this while using the document/view architecture?

A. Use the single document interface

B. Use the multiple document interface

C. Use the non-document/view architecture

D. Use both the single document interface and the multiple access interface

10. What are the two application types that have the document/view architecture? (Choose all that apply.)

    A. Dialog based

    B. Single document interface

    C. Dual document interface

    D. Multiple document interface

11. What components does the MFC drawing architecture contain? (Choose all that apply.)

    A. Brushes

    B. Palettes

    C. Bitmaps

    D. Fonts

12. What function must you use to control the color of the text being displayed?

    A. SetTextColor

    B. GetTextColor

    C. SetBkMode

    D. GetBkMode

13. Randall is creating an application and he is using the MFC Print Architecture. He wants to be able to add additional features to the print architecture, such as adding

footers to documents. How should he go about accomplishing this?

A. Nothing. It is done automatically

B. Override the OnEndPrinting function

C. Enable the MFC print logics

D. Override the OnPrint function

14. An application is able to run in different priority classes. What function can you use to return the priority class in which it is running currently?

A. GetPriorityClass

B. GetPriority

C. SetPriorityClass

D. SetPriority

15. What MFC synchronization class can a developer use to block a process from accessing a resource until another thread allows it?

A. CCriticalSection

B. CEvent

C. CMutex

D. CSemaphore

16. What technologies should you consider when using Visual C++ to access a database? (Choose all that apply.)

A. Data Access Objects (DAO)

B. Remote Data Objects (RDO)

C. ODBC

D. OLE DB

17. What types of properties are available on an ActiveX component? (Choose all that apply.)

A. Default

B. Stock

C. Custom

D. Changed

18. Isaac is developing an ActiveX Control. The stock properties do not provide enough functionality for what he wants. What are the different ways he can implement a custom property for the component? (Choose all that apply.)

A. Member Variable

B. Member Variable with Notification

C. Get/Set Methods

D. Parameterized

19. What are the stock methods for a component? (Choose all that apply.)

A. DoClick

B. GetColor

C. SetColor

D. Refresh

20. A developer wants to be able to have a control respond whenever the control is clicked. How should he implement this?

A. Set the Click Event

B. Set the MouseDown Event

C. Set the MouseClick Event

D. Set the Down Event

SELF TEST ANSWERS

1. **B.** MFC includes the various view functions that cycle through the different views within a specified list. Lucille can use the GetNextView function. The GetNextView function returns CView pointer to the next view in the view list of the document object. The GetFirstViewPosition returns the pointer to the first view in the view list. GetPathName returns the path and file name of the document. GetTitle returns the document's title.

2. **B.** Ian should create the application using a template because the template allows the application's frame windows, documents, and views to function as one entity. If the user wanted to create other applications with the same interface and structure, he or she can use the Custom AppWizard. It allows one to reuse the same look and feel of the application.

3. **D.** Jason should override the InitInstance( ) function because it is run when every instance of an application is started. The Run function is responsible for sitting in a message loop waiting for and processing incoming messages. The OnIdle member function is used by the application object for idle processing. This ExitInstance member function is called when an instance of an application is terminated.

4. **C.** Before a library is used, the library is not loaded. Once an application is run that uses the library, it is loaded and Refcount is incremented. The application uses Refcount to count the occurrences when the library is being used. When the Refcount reaches 0, the library is automatically unloaded.

5. **C.** By using GetFreeSpaceEx, the application is able to report the correct amount of free space on a FAT32 drive. Scandisk checks the physical hard drive media and is not related to the amount of free space on the disk. GetFreeSpace is the older version of GetFreeSpaceEx and does not return the correct free space on a disk formatted with Fat32.

6. **A, B, C.** There are a few differences in the Windows 95/98 and the Windows NT operating systems. Because Windows NT is Microsoft's corporate desktop and Windows 95/98 is more aimed at the home users, security is one of the major differences. Though the Registry is very similar in both operating systems, they are different. Keys that exist in one operating system might be located elsewhere in another operating system or not exist at all. The Win32 API is also different on both

operating systems. For example, there might be API calls for the NTFS file system in Windows NT but it will not exist for Windows 95/98.

7. **B.** Justin should develop a regular DLL. Regular DLLs are able to be used in a Win32 programming environment. Extension DLLs are only able to be used in the Visual C++ environment.

8. **D.** Command messages are messages that can be handled by many different objects, such as the application, the documents, and the windows. Every object which is capable of receiving command messages, has its own message map. Each command message is identified by a constant that is assigned by a resource editor. When the object receives the command message, it looks at its own message maps for a match. If it can't find the handler, it will route the command to the next object.

9. **B.** If one wishes to develop a multiple document application using the document/view architecture, you must use the multiple document interface. The single document interface is used only when the user needs one view of the document. The non-document architecture is used when no document is being accessed.

10. **B, D.** The two application types that have the document/view architecture are the single document interface and the multiple document interface. Remember to note that you do not have to use the document/view architecture to do the SDI and MDI applications.

11. **A, B, C, D.** The MFC drawing architecture contains many components to simplify drawing in Windows-based applications. This includes brushes, palettes, bitmaps, and fonts. Brushes are used to paint the interior of polygons and ellipses. Palettes are a set of colors used by GDI to render an image. Bitmaps are graphical images that can be placed within the application. Fonts help define the style of text being displayed.

12. **A.** SetTextColor controls the color of the text being displayed. GetTextColor returns the color of the text being displayed. SetBkColor sets the color of the cells that contain the displayed text. GetBkColor returns the color of the cells that contain the displayed text.

13. **D.** Randall must override the OnPrint function. By overriding the OnPrint function, you are able to add additional features to the document right before the document is printed. OnEndPrinting is called when the print job is finished. You must override this function to release any resources you created.

14. **A.** GetPriorityClass is used to return the current priority class. SetPriorityClass allows you to set the current priority class of the application.

15. **B.** CEvent is the MFC synchronization class that can block a process from accessing a resource until another thread allows it. CCriticalSection allows a section of code to be accessed at one time. CMutex is used to gain exclusive access to a resource shared by multiple threads, as well as to synchronize the threads running in the same and different processes. CSemaphore is used when a limited number of threads can access a resource.

16. **A, C, D.** Visual C++ provides many technologies to allow access to databases, such as Data Access Objects (DAO), ODBC, and OLE DB.

17. **B, C.** An ActiveX component has two types of properties: stock and custom. The stock properties are the included properties. Custom properties allow the developer to change the property to how he or she sees fit.

18. **A, B, C, D.** Member Variable, Member Variable with Notification, Get/Set Methods, and Parameterized are the four types of implementation for a custom property for a component. Member Variable is the implementation when the member variable is exposed to a container. Member Variable with Notification is the implementation when the member variable is exposed to a container and the control is notified when there is a change in the property. Get/Set Methods is implemented by a method that gets the current property value and a method that sets the current property value. Parameterized is the implementation that allows access to a group of values through a single property.

19. **A, D.** DoClick and Refresh are the two stock methods for a component. The DoClick event is fired when the control is clicked. The Refresh method refreshes the control.

20. **A.** The developer should set the Click event. The click event is fired when the control is clicked. The MouseDown event is fired when the mousebutton is pressed, not clicked. The mouseclick and down events do not exist.

3

The User Interface

M icrosoft Developer Studio and Visual C++ include a rich set of tools and wizards for handling many of the everyday programming tasks that are a part of almost every distributed application development project. This chapter focuses on the tools that aid the developer in creating the visual elements of an application as well as two of Developer Studio's most important wizards, AppWizard and ClassWizard.

We'll discuss the typical issues you may encounter when creating your application's user interface, including guidelines and principles to follow to ensure your user interface is simple and easy to navigate. We'll describe how to use and enhance the Microsoft Foundation Classes (MFC) toolbars and status bars that are generated by the MFC AppWizard. We'll also look at the capabilities of all the Visual C++ resource editors, which allow you to create and edit various types of Windows resources such as icons, menus, accelerator tables, dialog boxes, and strings.

In our discussion of AppWizard, we'll look at the options and steps involved in creating a new MFC project. Then after seeing how you can enhance your application's user interface with the Visual C++ resource editors, we'll use ClassWizard to "hook-up" events to code when the user interacts with your application's visual elements.

At various stages in the chapter we'll create and build upon a simple sample application to provide a practical demonstration of the concepts discussed in the chapter.

CERTIFICATION OBJECTIVE 3.01

Navigation of the User Interface

Throughout the process of designing and implementing distributed applications using Visual C++, a large amount of time is spent creating and refining the application's user interface. This process involves designing and creating the interactive elements of the application such as toolbars, status bars, menus, dialog boxes, and icons.

One of the biggest challenges in designing and implementing a distributed application comes in the creation of an effective user interface. The design of your application's interface can affect how a user perceives your software more than any other factor. Visual C++ and MFC provide the framework on which to build a visually appealing and conventional user interface.

Careful planning is required to ensure that the user interface exposes all the functionality of your application while being intuitive and simple enough to allow the end user to quickly learn the application. When considering your application's user interface, it is important to maintain the visual and functional consistency that can already be found across the majority of applications running on the Windows platform. This enables the users of your application to apply their experience of using other applications when they are learning to use your application. With this in mind, developers are encouraged to follow the Windows user interface design guidelines, which promote good interface design as well as visual and functional consistency within and across Windows-based applications.

Close compliance to the Windows user interface design guidelines is especially important when you consider the role of the user interface in modern distributed applications. Increasingly, the focus of application development is to separate the user interface from the core functionality of the program. This often takes the form of a distributed architecture with clear separation of user services, business services, and data services. In such a model, the user interface should serve only as a tool for the user to concentrate on the task of interacting with the application data without being distracted or hindered by an overly complex front end. Fortunately, Visual C++ and MFC provide all of the resources necessary to create a conventional and consistent user interface.

Using the Menu Editor

Windows Menu resources allow you to arrange commands in a logical, easy-to-find fashion while using a small amount of screen area. Menus are presented to the user in several different styles. The most common styles are the pull-down and cascading menus. These are the menus that appear at the top of an application window. When the user clicks a menu from the menu bar, a pull-down menu appears with a list of menu items from which to choose. These menu items can spawn cascading menus that appear to the right of the initial menu. There isn't any limit on the number of levels that cascading menus can go down to; however, in practice it isn't practical to go beyond two or three levels. A third style of menu, called the pop-up menu (also known as a context menu or a shortcut menu), can be displayed independently over the application client area, usually in response to the user right-clicking on a visual element of the application.

The Windows Interface Design Guidelines recommend the following conventions when designing menus.

- Items in the top menu bar should use a single word. Two-word menu items in the top menu bar could easily be mistaken for two separate, one-word menu items.

- The File menu should be located as the first menu from the left of the top menu bar. The File menu is the appropriate place to put file-specific commands such as New, Open, Save, and Print. Additionally, the Exit command should be placed at the bottom of the File pull-down menu and it should be preceded by a command separator.

- The Edit menu should be positioned to the immediate right of the File menu and it should contain commands such as Copy, Cut, and Paste.

- If a View menu is required for the application, then it should be positioned to the immediate right of the Edit menu and it should contain commands that affect the appearance of the application.

- The Help menu should be positioned at the rightmost end of the menu bar. It should contain menu entries that give the user access to the application's Help files. Most applications also have an About menu item at the bottom of the Help pull-down menu from which an About dialog box can be displayed.

- In a multiple-document interface (MDI) application, the Window menu should be positioned to the immediate left of the Help menu. The Window menu should contain functions for arranging and switching to child windows.

With the Menu editor, shown in Figure 3-1, you can create and edit menus by working directly with a menu bar that closely mimics the behavior of the menu as it would appear in the finished application.

With the Menu editor, you can perform the following tasks:

- Create standard menus and commands.
- Move menus or commands from one place to another.
- Edit the properties of several menu items at the same time.

Double-clicking a menu item displays the Menu Item Properties dialog box. From there you can change many properties of the menu item such as whether it is checked, inactive, or grayed out. You can also set the caption of the menu item from the Caption field in the Properties dialog box. Following the menu caption text, you can type the tab escape character (\t) followed by text representing the menu's accelerator keys. At runtime, this will show the menu's caption in the format familiar to users, whereby the menu caption text is left-aligned and the text describing the accelerator keys for the menu is right-aligned.

FIGURE 3-1

The Menu editor creates and edits menu items while emulating the runtime behavior of your application's menu bar

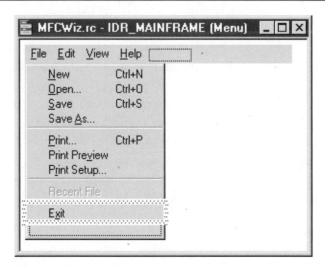

Adding new menu items is simple using the Menu editor. All you have to do is select the new item box (the empty rectangle) on the menu bar, or use your mouse to move the new item box to the appropriate position and type the menu item's caption. Note that when you are typing the caption, you can define a mnemonic key that allows the user to select the menu with the keyboard. To do this, type an ampersand (&) in front of a letter to specify it as the mnemonic, then at runtime that letter will appear underlined. You should take care to ensure that all the mnemonics on a menu bar are unique.

Creating and Integrating Toolbars in an MFC Application

A toolbar is a special organizational visual element that can manage sets of other controls such as buttons, button separators, and combo boxes. The primary role of toolbars in an application is to provide quick access to commonly used functions.

There are various toolbar styles commonly in use; however, the pervasive style at the moment is the Internet Explorer flat toolbar shown in Figure 3-2. This style of toolbar is sometimes referred to as a ReBar. These toolbars provide the user with the additional feedback of seeing the toolbar buttons raise up as the mouse passes over them.

Toolbars are usually positioned at the top of the client area of a main application window. Often, however, toolbars are designed to be *dockable*, whereby the user can drag and place them on any border of the application's top-level window or leave them in their own modeless window at any location on the screen. An application isn't required to expose all of its functionality through toolbars because it may take up far too much screen space. If your application has a lot of functionality that you would like to have exposed through toolbars, then it might be a good idea to dedicate a separate, dockable toolbar to each logical group of commands. You can then allow the user to configure your application so that only the toolbars they frequently use are on the screen. MFC allows you to easily create many conventional styles of toolbars, depending on your choices in the MFC AppWizard.

FIGURE 3-2   Internet Explorer's toolbars are an example of the ReBar style of toolbar

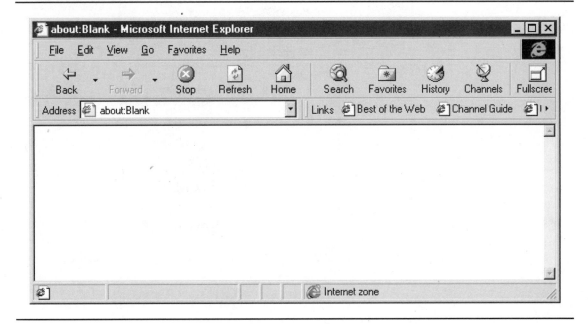

With Visual C++'s Toolbar resource editor, you can perform the following tasks:

- Create new toolbars, toolbar buttons, and separators.
- Convert bitmaps into toolbar resources.
- Create, move, and edit toolbar buttons and separators.

All of the buttons of a toolbar resource are actually stored in a single bitmap. In an MFC project, the bitmap for the initial AppWizard-generated toolbar is stored in the project's *res* subdirectory with the name TOOLBAR.BMP. The Toolbar editor provides a special view of the underlying bitmap, which closely resembles how the toolbar should look when your application is running. Figure 3-3 shows the various display elements of the Toolbar editor.

FIGURE 3-3

Visual C++'s Toolbar editor is used to edit toolbar resources

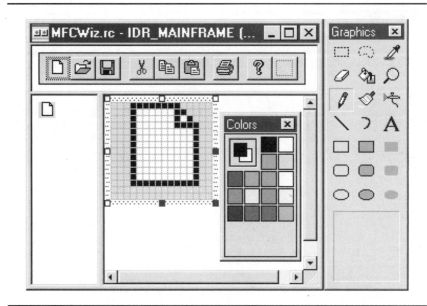

The Toolbar Editor window shows two views of the selected button image separated into two panes. The left pane is editable, but in practice is only used to preview the button at its runtime size; the right pane is where you would normally edit the toolbar button. The functionality provided by the Toolbar editor is reasonably straightforward. You can select from several different types of pens and tools on the Graphics toolbar and select from a range of basic colors from the Color toolbar. Above the two views of the image is the preview display of your toolbar. The button that currently is being edited is indicated by the fuzzy border.

There are two ways to view the properties of a toolbar button:

- Double-click it from the preview display

- Select it in the Toolbar editor preview display, and from the View menu select Properties

The Toolbar Button Properties dialog box, shown next, allows you to change the toolbar button's ID, width, height, and prompt.

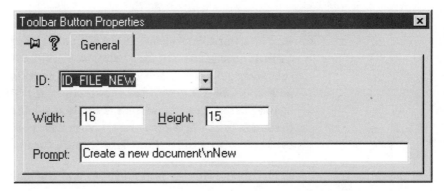

The ID is used by the application to identify the toolbar button resource. The *prompt* contains text that will appear in the status bar when the mouse hovers over this toolbar button; this text is placed in a string table and given the same identifier as the toolbar button. Note that by design, the MFC AppWizard sets up a convenient association between the initial set of toolbar buttons and their corresponding menu items whereby they share the same identifier and string resource. This means you don't have to maintain separate copies of the string for the prompt property of a toolbar button and a menu item that perform the same function. Also in the prompt field of the Properties dialog box shown previously, you'll notice the *new line character* \n followed by the word *New*. Any text to the right of the new line character becomes the ToolTip for the toolbar button.

You might have noticed the blank button that is displayed at the right end of the toolbar in the upper preview display of the Toolbar editor. This button is used to create a new button or a separator. Separators on a toolbar group similar functions into logical sets. For example, the Cut, Copy, and Paste buttons are invariably grouped together.

When you create a new button, another blank button appears to the right of the edited button, but note that when you save your toolbar, the blank button is not saved to the underlying bitmap. Saving the toolbar also updates the application's resource file script with the various resource IDs of the toolbar buttons.

exam
ⓦatch

Often you'll want to add text to your toolbar buttons in the same way Internet Explorer has text captions for its toolbar buttons. Unfortunately, the Toolbar editor doesn't provide any support for this, so you'll need to use the SetButtonText function from within your code. This function takes two arguments: the first is the index of the button, and the second is the text for the button identified by the index in the first parameter. Note that you'll also have to resize the toolbar to ensure that there is room for the text.

Here is a list of common functions that you may have to perform when using the Toolbar editor.

How do you create a toolbar button?	Assign an ID to the blank button at the right end of the toolbar by opening its property page and editing its ID field. Alternatively, you can select the blank button at the right end of the toolbar, and begin drawing in the image editor. A default button command ID will be assigned to the new button using the convention ID_BUTTON<n> where *n* is a sequential number representing how many new buttons have been added this way.
How do you move a toolbar button?	Drag the button that you want to move to its new location on the toolbar.
How do you copy buttons from a toolbar to another toolbar?	Hold down the CTRL key and drag the button to its new location on the toolbar or to a location on another toolbar.
How do you delete a toolbar button?	Select the toolbar button and drag it off the toolbar.
How do you insert a separator before a button that isn't followed by a space?	Drag the button to the right or down until it overlaps the next button by about halfway.
How do you insert a separator before a button that is followed by a space and then retain the following space?	Drag the button until the right or bottom edge is just touching the next button or just overlapping it.
How do you insert a separator before a button that is followed by a space and not retain the following space?	Drag the button to the right or down until it overlaps the next button about halfway.
How do you remove a separator from between two buttons?	Drag a button from one side of the separator toward the button on the other side until it overlaps it about halfway.

Creating a New Toolbar

To insert a new toolbar in your application, you can select Insert Toolbar from the context menu of the Toolbar folder in the ResourceView tab. This creates a new toolbar with a single blank button. For each new button you start to draw, a new blank button is added on to the end of the toolbar.

Once you draw the pictures on your toolbar, you can change the properties for each individual button by double-clicking the button and adjusting the values in the button's properties dialog box. If the button will be used to execute the same operation as an existing menu item, then you assign the menu item's ID to the toolbar button. If you entered an ID that corresponds to an existing menu item, then you'll notice that the Prompt field is automatically populated with the same description that was applied to the corresponding menu item. The description in this Prompt field will appear in the application's status bar when the mouse hovers over the toolbar button. At the end of the prompt, you can add a new line character \n and a short description, which will be used as the ToolTip for the toolbar button.

Having finished designing your new toolbar, you should change the toolbar ID. To change the toolbar ID, right-click the toolbar from the ResourceView and select Properties from the context menu. You will then be able to change the toolbar ID in the toolbar Properties dialog box. By default, it probably would have been called IDR_TOOLBAR1, but you may want to give it a more appropriate name that has some relationship to the context in which it will be used.

A toolbar in an MFC application is actually a CToolBar object declared as a member of your application's CMainFrame class. Therefore, to add your new toolbar to your application, simply add a member variable to the protected section of your CMainFrame class definition, as in the following example:

```
class CMainFrame : public CframeWnd
{
// ...
protected:
    CtoolBar    m_wndToolBar1;
};
```

The toolbar is actually created in the CMainFrame::OnCreate function. OnCreate is called by the MFC framework just after the window has been created but just before it is shown. You can add your code to create the new toolbar in this function as follows:

```
int CMainFrame::OnCreate(LPCREATESTRUCT lpCreateStruct)
{
//...
if (!m_wndToolBar1.CreateEx(this, TBSTYLE_FLAT, WS_CHILD |
        WS_VISIBLE | CBRS_TOP |
        CBRS_GRIPPER | CBRS_TOOLTIPS |
        CBRS_FLYBY | CBRS_SIZE_DYNAMIC)||
        !m_wndToolBar1.LoadToolBar(IDR_TOOLBAR1))
{
    TRACE0("Failed to create toolbar\n");
    return -1;        // fail to create
}
EnableDocking(CBRS_ALIGN_ANY);
m_wndToolBar1.EnableDocking(CBRS_ALIGN_ANY);
DockControlBar(&m_wndToolBar1);
//...
}
```

The first part of this code that you add contains two functions that are required to create the toolbar. The first function, CToolBar::CreateEx, actually creates the toolbar. The first parameter to this function is the only required parameter and it specifies a pointer to the window that will be the toolbar's parent. In this case it is the CMainFrame object itself. The second argument specifies additional styles for the toolbar, most notable of which is the CBRS_TOOLTIPS flag that activates ToolTips for the toolbar.

The second function, CToolBar::LoadToolBar, associates the toolbar object with the toolbar resource that you created in the Toolbar resource editor. This function takes a single argument that specifies the ID of the toolbar resource.

The remaining functions in this OnCreate implementation are used to make the toolbar a dockable toolbar. In order for toolbar docking to be enabled, the first thing you must do is enable docking on the main frame window with the CFrameWnd::EnableDocking function. Then, docking must be enabled on the toolbar itself with the CControlBar::EnableDocking function. Finally, you can specify that the initial position of the toolbar should be docked with a call to CFrameWnd::DockControlBar. Conversely, you can specify that you would like the toolbar to be undocked or *floating* by calling CFrameWnd::FloatControlBar.

Implementing ToolTips for Toolbar Buttons

Toolbars also include ToolTips, which are small modeless windows that are briefly displayed when the mouse lingers over a button for a certain interval. ToolTips are used to proactively give the user some feedback about the purpose of a button.

In order to activate ToolTip support for your toolbar, you need to add the CBRS_TOOLTIPS style to the dwStyle parameter passed into the CToolBar::Create (or CreateEx) function or the CControlBar::SetBarStyle function. Then, use the following procedure to specify the ToolTip text for each individual button on your toolbar.

To create a ToolTip for a toolbar button:

1. Open the Toolbar editor for your toolbar by double-clicking the toolbar in the ResourceView tab.

2. Double-click the button for which you want to define a ToolTip. The Toolbar Button Properties dialog box will be displayed.

3. In the Prompt field, add a description of the button, followed by a new line character (\n) followed by the text of the ToolTip.

Implementing and Writing to the Status Bar in an MFC Application

Status bars give your application a place to display messages and useful information to the user without interrupting the user. They are normally displayed at the bottom of a window and they consist of several *panes*, which can include indicators and a message line. The indicators give the status of such things as Caps Lock, Scroll Lock, and Num Lock. The message panel on the status bar is usually used to display information about the program status or about a toolbar button or menu item that the user is pointing to with the mouse. The following shows a status bar in action. Notice how a description is displayed on the status bar for the toolbar button over which the mouse is hovering.

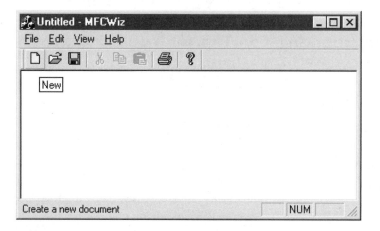

Adding a New Status Bar Pane

You've already seen how simple it is to display text in the status bar when the mouse is over a menu item or a toolbar button. All that was required was to change the value of the Prompt property for the button or menu item resource. However, sometimes you will want to customize a status bar by adding panes that will be used to give the user more detailed feedback regarding the status of your application or about a particular operation that the user is performing.

Use the following procedure to add a new pane to a status bar.

Add a command ID for the new pane. Display the Resource Symbols dialog box, shown in Figure 3-4, by selecting Resource Symbols from the View menu. This dialog box can display all of the currently defined symbols for your application's resources.

Add a new symbol by clicking the New button to display the New Symbol dialog box, shown next. Call the new status bar pane **ID_STATUSPANE1** (in practice you would give a more descriptive name to the new status pane)

FIGURE 3-4

The Resource Symbols
dialog box shows all of
your application's currently
defined symbols

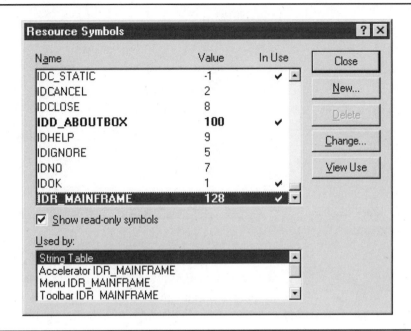

and accept the default value for the ID. Click OK and then Close to add
the new symbol.

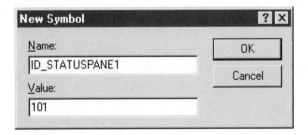

Next, you must assign a default caption for the new status bar pane. The
length of this default string will determine the initial width of the status pane.
To define the string, open the String Table resource editor by double-clicking
the string table in the ResourceView tab of your project's workspace. Then,
display the String Properties dialog box, shown next, for a new string by

selecting New String from the context menu which appears when you right-click inside the String Table resource editor.

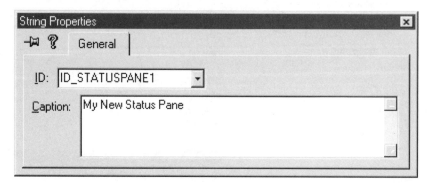

In the ID field of the String Properties dialog box, type the same ID that you assigned to the new pane in the Resource Symbols dialog box. In this case, type **ID_STATUSPANE1**. Then in the caption field, enter the default caption that you would like to appear in the status pane. Close the String Properties dialog and close the String Table resource editor.

Next, you need to add your new pane to your application's status bar's indicators array. A status bar in an MFC application is usually initialized in the CMainFrame::OnCreate function. During the initialization of the status bar, a call is made to CStatusBar::SetIndicators passing in an array of IDs that determine the order and the type of panes to display in the status bar. In a normal MFC AppWizard-generated project, this array is defined near the top of the file called MAINFRM.CPP. You can use the FileView tab of your project workspace to open MAINFRM.CPP. All you have to do to activate your new status pane is add its ID to the array in the position that you would like it to appear, so that the array should now look something like this:

```
static UINT indicators[] =
{
    ID_SEPARATOR,          // status line indicator
    ID_STATUSPANE1,        // our new status pane
    ID_INDICATOR_CAPS,
    ID_INDICATOR_NUM,
    ID_INDICATOR_SCRL,
};
```

Now when you recompile and execute your application, you will see the new status bar pane with your default text. However, it isn't much good if you aren't able to dynamically change the text that is displayed in it. So to make the status bar pane fully functional, you create an UPDATE_COMMAND_UI event handler that you will subsequently be able to use to set the text in the pane.

You would normally use ClassWizard to set up the mechanism for messages to be caught, but ClassWizard doesn't allow you to catch status bar messages. Therefore, you must manually add the event handler entries to the MFC message maps and create the code for the message handler. Note that any code between the AFX_MSG_MAP and the AFX_MSG comments is used by ClassWizard and generally shouldn't be modified. We will be adding our event handler entries outside the ClassWizard blocks.

First, we'll change the message map entries in the header file for your CMainFrame class. You can open this file by double-clicking the CMainFrame class in the ClassView tab of the project workspace. The message map appears near the end of the file. Modify this message map by adding in the **OnUpdateStatusPane1** entry so that it looks like the following listing:

```
//{{AFX_MSG(CMainFrame)
afx_msg int OnCreate(LPCREATESTRUCT lpCreateStruct);
        // NOTE - the ClassWizard will add and remove member functions here.
        //    DO NOT EDIT what you see in these blocks of generated code!
//}}AFX_MSG
afx_msg void OnUpdateStatusPane1(CCmdUI *pCmdUI);
DECLARE_MESSAGE_MAP()
```

Next, you need to add the handler to the message map in the class implementation file in order to associate the status pane's resource symbol with your handler function. This message map is located in the MAINFRM.CPP file. Open this file by double-clicking it from the FileView tab in your project workspace. The message map will be located somewhere near the top of the file. Once you've found it, add the **ON_UPDATE_COMMAND_UI** entry so that it looks like the following listing:

```
BEGIN_MESSAGE_MAP(CMainFrame, CFrameWnd)
    //{{AFX_MSG_MAP(CMainFrame)
            // NOTE - the ClassWizard will add and remove mapping macros here.
            //    DO NOT EDIT what you see in these blocks of generated code !
    ON_WM_CREATE()
    //}}AFX_MSG_MAP
    ON_UPDATE_COMMAND_UI(ID_STATUSPANE1, OnUpdateStatusPane1)
END_MESSAGE_MAP()
```

The mechanism is now in place for a function called OnUpdateStatusPane1 to be called whenever the status bar pane called ID_STATUSPANE1 needs to be updated. All that remains is to add the actual handler function itself. To do this, copy the code from the following listing into the very bottom of the MAINFRM.CPP file.

```
void CMainFrame::OnUpdateStatusPane1(CCmdUI *pCmdUI)
{
    CTime theTime = CTime::GetCurrentTime();
    CString sStatusText = theTime.Format("%H:%M:%S");
    CClientDC dc(this);
    SIZE size = dc.GetTextExtent(sStatusText);
    int index = m_wndStatusBar.CommandToIndex(ID_STATUSPANE1);
    m_wndStatusBar.SetPaneInfo(index,ID_STATUSPANE1, SBPS_POPOUT, size.cx);
    pCmdUI->Enable();
    pCmdUI->SetText(sStatusText);
}
```

The parameter to this message handler function is a pointer to a CCmdUI object. The CCmdUI class is always used within the handler of the ON_UPDATE_COMMAND_UI message. The handler can call member functions of the CCmdUI object to update the status bar pane. The following list describes the purpose of the CCmdUI member functions as they apply to the updating of a status bar pane:

- **CCmdUI::Enable**   Makes text in the status bar pane visible or invisible.

- **CCmdUI::SetCheck**   Changes the border of the status bar pane to be a *pop-out* (raised) border or a normal border.

- **CCmdUI::SetRadio**   Same as SetCheck.

- **CCmdUI::SetText**   Sets the text to display in the status bar pane.

You should now be able to recompile and run your application. You'll notice that the updating of the time in the pane is relatively irregular. This is because the triggering of the message depends on when the application enters an idle state, and that is dependent on many factors. In fact, this method of implementing a clock in the status bar may not be entirely practical in a real application and only serves as an example of how to change the text in a status bar pane.

In the handler function, we are simply formatting and displaying the current time in our new status bar pane. Generally speaking, these types of user interface update handlers should do as little as possible because they can tend to be called very often. This particular handler will be triggered whenever the application is idle.

The first thing we do in the handler is obtain and format the current time, which is then saved in the sStatusText variable. Then, we determine how wide the pane will need to be in order to draw the text. This is done with the call to GetTextExtent, using a device context from the main frame window. Next, we obtain the index of our pane through a call to the CommandToIndex function of the status bar member. The index is then used to set the width of our pane in a call to SetPaneInfo. Notice also in this call that we set a flag which gives the status bar pane a raised bevel effect. Finally, we ensure that the status bar pane is in fact enabled and we set its text value with a call to SetText, passing in the formatted string containing the current time.

CERTIFICATION OBJECTIVE 3.02

Using the MFC AppWizard

The starting point of many Microsoft Visual C++ projects is the AppWizard. The MFC AppWizard gives developers a great head start when beginning a new Windows-based program using MFC. AppWizard helps you generate the basic source files for a variety of different types of Windows-based programs, allowing you to get down to the task of creating your application. The extensive amount of AppWizard-generated code handles many routine programming tasks, freeing the developer to concentrate on implementing program functionality. It is possible to use Visual C++ to create a Windows-based program without using AppWizard, but the range of project types available in AppWizard makes it the sensible choice for any Visual C++ project.

Creating an Application with the MFC AppWizard

We'll now walk through the steps involved in creating a new Visual C++ project using the MFC AppWizard. In this exercise, you'll create a simple MFC executable application to demonstrate the features of the MFC AppWizard. On completion of this exercise you will know about the following items:

- Identification of the different MFC project types supported by AppWizard.

- How to create a new Visual C++ project and project workspace.

- The optional features that can be added to an MFC application through AppWizard.

- The initial source files that AppWizard generates.

- How to compile and run the newly created MFC AppWizard project.

To use the MFC AppWizard to create a new Visual C++ project, select File | New and select the Projects tab from the New dialog box as shown in Figure 3-5. Choose MFC AppWizard (exe) from the list of project types on the left, give the project the name **MFCWiz**, and click OK.

Step 1 of the MFC AppWizard is shown in Figure 3-6. This step requires you to decide upon the basic characteristics of your application, such as whether it will be a single-document interface (SDI), a multiple-document interface (MDI), or a dialog-based application.

There are three main types of application architecture supported by the MFC AppWizard:

- A single-document interface application can only present one document to the user at any given time. A simple example of an SDI is Windows Notepad. Choosing this option will create an application with a view class based on CView.

- A multiple-document interface application can present the user with several documents at once, each in its own child window. An example of an MDI application is Microsoft Word. MDI applications are also based by default on the CView class.

■ A dialog-based application such as Windows Character Map is based on the CDialog class and typically displays a single dialog box to the user.

Beneath the choice of application type is a check box that allows you to indicate whether you want support for the document/view architecture using the CDocument and the CView base classes. You would probably clear this check box if you were porting an application from another development environment. However, an application without the document/view architecture won't have MFC support for opening a file from a disk.

Further down on the screen is a drop-down list box that allows you to select the language for your application's resources. The drop-down list displays the languages available on your system. If you wish to use a

The MFC AppWizard
project type in the Projects
tab of the New dialog box

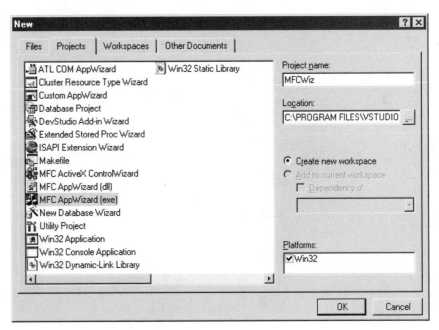

FIGURE 3-6

Step 1 of the MFC
AppWizard requires
you to choose the type
of application you wish
to build

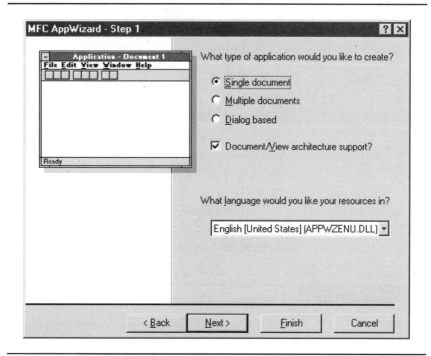

language other than English, the appropriate DLL for that language must
be installed on your system. The DLLs follow a naming convention of
APPWZXXX.DLL, where *xxx* is a three-letter language identifier.

For the purposes of this demonstration, we are going to create an SDI
application with document/view architecture and English (United States)
resources. Select the appropriate options and click Next.

Step 2 of the MFC AppWizard is to select the desired level of database
support for your application. There are four levels of database support for
MFC applications:

■ The default option is None, which specifies that you do not wish
AppWizard to include support for database access in your application.

■ The next level of support, Header Files Only, gives your application
a basic level of database support whereby a header file, AFXDB.H,
and link libraries are created but no database-specific classes are
generated. This allows you to create recordsets and use them to view
and update records from a database.

- The third level of support, Database View without File Support, includes the header and link libraries as well as a record view and a recordset class. Choosing this option will give your program a CRecordView-derived view class. AppWizard will also create a CRecordset-derived class that will be associated with your view class. This option includes document support but no serialization support. A form-based application will be created in which the record view is used to view and update records through its recordset.

- The final level of database support is Database View with File Support. This option will create an application similar to an application created with the previous level of support, except that this application will also support document serialization. If you choose either of the levels of database support that include a database view, you will also have to specify a data source for the application.

The purpose of this exercise isn't to create a database application, so we will select None as our level of database support and click Next.

Step 3 of the MFC AppWizard is concerned with selecting the amount of ActiveX and compound document support for your application. There are five choices for compound document support:

- The default option is to not include support for compound documents in your application.

- The next option, Container, allows your application to contain embedded or linked ActiveX objects, such as Word documents.

- The next option, Mini Server, specifies an application that has the ability to create and manage compound document objects that can be embedded in other applications, but it can't run as a standalone application.

- To have an application that can create and manage compound document objects such as the Mini Server, but also run as a standalone application, choose Full Server.

- Choosing Both Container and Server creates an application that can contain embedded or linked objects from other applications as well as create and manage its own document objects for other applications to use.

If you choose to support compound documents, you can also support compound files. Files saved in the compound file format can contain several automation objects, and those objects are stored in such a way that objects can be changed without rewriting the whole file. This can greatly improve the efficiency of your application. You can use the option buttons in the middle of the Step 3 dialog box to say Yes, Please, or No, Thank You to compound files.

If you want your application to surrender control to other applications through automation, or if you would like your application to control other applications through automation, select the Automation check box. In addition, if you intend to use ActiveX controls in your application, select the ActiveX Controls check box.

In our exercise we will accept all the defaults for this step and move on to Step 4.

Step 4 of the MFC AppWizard, shown in Figure 3-7, is concerned with selecting some of the common features of Windows-based applications such as toolbars, status bars, and print preview support.

FIGURE 3-7

Step 4 of the MFC AppWizard allows you to specify which common features your application will support

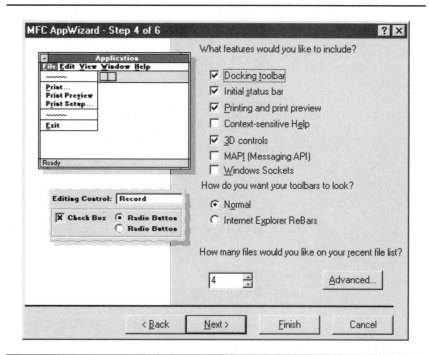

The various options for Step 4 of the MFC AppWizard are described in the following list:

■ Select the Docking Toolbar check box to include a toolbar in your application. The toolbar that is created for you will include buttons for various common operations such as Cut, Copy, and Paste. A couple of menu items will also be created for you to allow the user to choose whether to hide or show the toolbar. Notice that a dockable toolbar will be created by default.

■ Select the Initial Status Bar check box to include a status bar in your application. The default status bar will include panels that display the status of the CAPS LOCK, NUM LOCK, and SCROLL LOCK keys, as well as a panel that displays information when the mouse is passed over menu items. Just like the toolbar, some menu commands will be added to allow the user to choose whether to hide or show the status bar.

■ For applications using the document/view architecture, the Printing and Print Preview check box enables the AppWizard to generate code that will handle the Print, Print Setup, and Print Preview commands. Menu items will be created for these operations.

■ Selecting the Context-Sensitive Help check box will generate a set of Help files that you can compile with the Help compiler.

■ The 3D Controls check box is selected by default and allows the controls that appear in your application to have 3D shading.

■ Selecting the MAPI check box will include support for the Messaging Application Programming Interface in your application.

■ Selecting Windows Sockets will include Winsock support in your application. Winsock support will enable your application to take part in inter-process communication (IPC) through Transmission Control Protocol/Internet Protocol (TCP/IP).

■ If you chose to include a toolbar in your application, you will be able to specify the style of toolbar you prefer. The Normal option button will produce a traditional style of toolbar with a simple list of buttons. The Internet Explorer ReBars option button will create toolbars like those in Internet Explorer, which are capable of containing standard Windows controls such as combo boxes.

- The edit box at the base of the Step 4 wizard form allows you to select the number of files to show in the recently used file list of your application's File menu.

- The Advanced button displays another dialog box that allows you to specify options for document template strings and frame characteristics.

The first tab of the Advanced Options dialog box, Document Template Strings, is shown in Figure 3-8. This tab allows you to specify a file extension for your document type as well as various strings that identify your application's document type and may require localization. These strings are kept in the resource script of the application where they are associated with the resource ID of the main frame window of the application.

The second tab of the Advanced Options dialog box, Window Styles, is shown in Figure 3-9.

FIGURE 3-8

The Document Template Strings tab of the Advanced Options dialog box

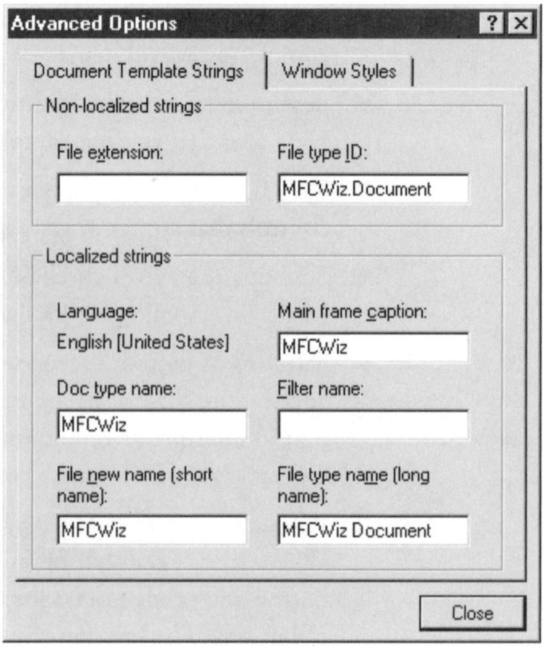

FIGURE 3-9

The Window Styles tab of the Advanced Options dialog box allows you to specify various flags that affect the appearance of your application's window

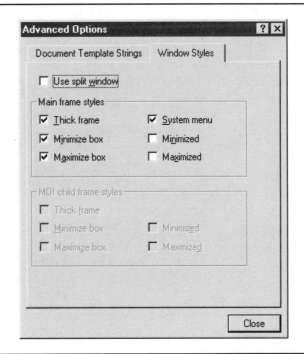

This tab allows you to choose to use a split window in your application. Selecting this option will insert a split bar in your application's main views. In an MDI application, the client area of the child windows will contain the split bar, whereas in an SDI application, the client area of the main application window will contain the split bar. Recall that we chose to build an SDI application back in Step 1 of the AppWizard and so the MDI section of Figure 3-9 is disabled.

The other options on the Window Styles tab are explained here:

■ Selecting the Thick Frame check box will give your application window a thick edge and the user will be able to resize the window. Clearing this option prevents resizing.

■ The Minimize Box check box determines whether your application window will have a minimize button in the top-right corner.

■ The Maximize Box check box determines whether your application window will have a maximize button in the top-right corner.

■ The System Menu check box determines whether or not your application window will have a System menu in the top-left corner of the main window. The System menu is a special pop-up menu that is located at the leftmost end of an application's title bar. It typically includes the Close, Restore, Move, Size, Minimize, and Maximize commands.

■ Selecting the Minimized check box causes your application to be minimized when the application starts.

■ Selecting the Maximized check box causes your application to be maximized when the application starts.

Once again we will stay with the defaults for all the options in Step 4 of the MFC AppWizard and click Next to move on to Step 5.

The items in Step 5 of the MFC AppWizard aren't logically grouped together; they are more of a miscellaneous collection of the remaining information that AppWizard collects.

The first choice that you are required to make concerns the style of application that will be created. The default is to create a standard MFC application using the normal MFC architecture. The alternative is to create an Explorer-like application using a split window, where the left pane is a CTreeView and the right pane is a CListView.

The next set of option buttons is concerned with choosing whether you would like the MFC AppWizard to generate source code comments for your application. These comments include prompts telling you where to add your code and a README.TXT file will be generated in your project directory. This README.TXT file contains comprehensive information regarding all of the files generated by AppWizard.

The next question asks if you would like the MFC libraries installed as a shared DLL or statically linked to your application. Using MFC as a shared DLL will reduce the size of your application's executable, but may introduce complex distribution issues. Choosing to statically link your application to the MFC libraries at build time will produce a much larger executable, but it may be simpler to distribute.

The final step of the MFC AppWizard involves reviewing and confirming the names, filenames, and base classes of the classes that AppWizard will generate. Step 6 is shown in Figure 3-10.

FIGURE 3-10

Step 6 of AppWizard
allows you to change
filenames, class names,
and base classes

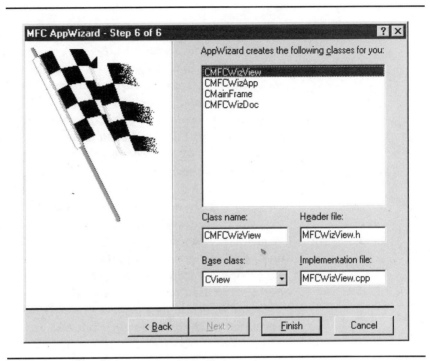

By default, AppWizard creates names for your application classes and
files based around an abbreviation of your project name. The majority of
the time, you won't want to change the default names. If the Base Class
combo box is enabled, you will be able to select a different class from
which to derive your new class. This option usually only applies to your
application's view class. The default is CView, but depending on the type
of application that you are building, you may wish to use another view
class, such as CFormView, CScrollView, or CEditView.

Accept the defaults on the final step and click Finish. You will be shown
a summary of all the options that you have selected for your application.
When you are happy with the selected options, click OK and the project
workspace will be created. You can build and run your application
immediately by selecting Build and then Execute from the Build menu.

on the **!** o b

Sometimes you'll want AppWizard to generate code with different options after you have run AppWizard. AppWizard is a one-time process that you perform at the start of a project. This doesn't give you the opportunity to go back and change options if a new requirement arises at some later stage in the development process. Say, for example, your client suddenly requires that you include Winsock support in your application in order to talk to an external system through TCP/IP. We'll look now at a technique that allows you to still use AppWizard to generate the code that you require. AppWizard works by piecing together bits of code according to the options you select. So if you know exactly what code AppWizard adds into a project to support the feature that you require, you will be able to paste the feature in yourself. Visual C++ includes a tool called WinDiff that can help you do exactly that. Follow these steps to add an AppWizard-generated feature to your existing MFC application:
1. Use AppWizard to create a new project with exactly the same options you used to create the existing project.
2. Create a second new project in a different folder with the same name and all the same settings but also specify the option that you wish to add in (for example, Winsock support).
3. Compare the two directories of the new projects using WinDiff. You'll be able to use the results of WinDiff to discover which parts of the code from the second new project need to be copied into your original project to implement the feature that you want to add.

CERTIFICATION OBJECTIVE 3.03

Resource Editors

An application running under Windows makes use of resources defined in a resource file, which is simply a text file with the extension .RC. A Windows resource file contains a script with various statements that define resources. For resources that exist in separate files, such as icons and cursors, the script specifies the resource and the file that contains it. For certain resources, such as string tables and menus, the entire definition of the resource exists within the script. Visual C++ provides a rich set of tools to simplify the task of editing resource files and visual elements, allowing the developer to easily use and enhance the initial user interface produced by AppWizard.

Although Visual C++ provides many tools to edit resource files visually, there may be times when you want to view the contents of your project resource file as text. For example, you may want to perform a multiple find and replace of a string, or perhaps you are curious to see how much resource script the Visual C++ editors automatically generate for you. You could, of course, open the .RC file in a simple editor such as Notepad, but the file can also be opened as text within Developer Studio. Developer Studio will display it with full-color coding and give you all the benefits of the Developer Studio environment, such as the Find and Replace dialog box.

To open a resource file (.RC) as text, follow these steps:

1. From the File menu choose Open, and use the Open dialog box to navigate to the resource file (.RC) that you wish to view.

2. From the Open As drop-down list, select Text and click the Open button.

It is understood that any manual modification of Visual C++–generated resource scripts should be performed with great care.

The ResourceView Tab

Now that you've taken a look at the underlying content of an AppWizard-generated resource file, the next logical step is to review the tools available within Visual C++ to make editing your application's resources as painless as possible. To see all of your application's resources represented in the Visual C++ ResourceView tab, use the MFC AppWizard to create a new project, and click the ResourceView tab at the base of the Project Workspace window. You will see a list of the project resources, as Figure 3-11 shows.

Expanding the folder for each resource type shows the individual resources of that type in your project. You can right-click this window to bring up a shortcut menu of commands. You can double-click any resource to invoke its resource editor. Right-clicking a resource displays a context

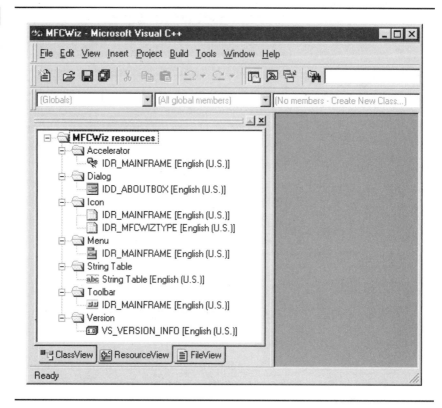

menu that allows you to insert new resources. When you select Insert from
this context menu you are presented with the Insert Resource dialog box
shown here:

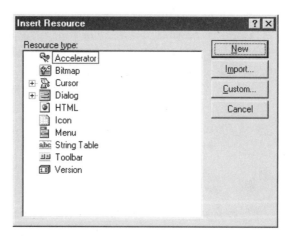

This dialog box is also available by selecting Resource from the Insert menu. Alternatively, the context menu will always have a command that allows you to immediately create a new resource of the type on which you right-clicked.

When a new resource is added to your project, it is automatically given a unique name. For example, a new dialog box resource may be given the name IDD_DIALOG1, then the next dialog box resource added to the project will be called IDD_DIALOG2. It is common convention, however, to change the generated name to one that more accurately reflects the purpose of the particular resource in the context of your application. To view the names of all the resources in the project, select Resource Symbols from the View menu to bring up the Resource Symbols dialog box:

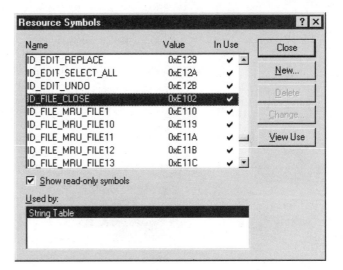

On occasion, you may find it convenient to use the Resource Symbols dialog box to locate a particular resource from its symbolic name. When you have located a resource in the Resource Symbols dialog box, you can go to it by selecting the name in the list and clicking the View Use button.

In the following sections we will briefly describe each of the types of resources that can be created and look at their respective resource editors.

Accelerator Editor

An accelerator table contains a list of accelerator keys (or shortcut keys) and the command identifiers that are associated with them. A program can have more than one accelerator table. Accelerators are usually used as keyboard shortcuts for program commands that appear on your application's menu or toolbar. However, they can also be used to define key combinations for commands that don't have a corresponding user-interface object. Figure 3-12 shows the Accelerator editor.

You can perform the following actions with the Accelerator editor:

■ View, add, edit, and delete accelerator key assignments on individual or multiple accelerator keys.

■ View and change the resource identifier associated with each entry in the accelerator table. The identifier is used to reference each accelerator table entry in your code.

■ Associate an accelerator key with a menu item.

The Accelerator editor is used to edit accelerator table resources

ID	Key	Type
ID_EDIT_COPY	Ctrl + C	VIRTKEY
ID_FILE_NEW	Ctrl + N	VIRTKEY
ID_FILE_OPEN	Ctrl + O	VIRTKEY
ID_FILE_PRINT	Ctrl + P	VIRTKEY
ID_FILE_SAVE	Ctrl + S	VIRTKEY
ID_EDIT_PASTE	Ctrl + V	VIRTKEY
ID_EDIT_UNDO	Alt + VK_BACK	VIRTKEY
ID_EDIT_CUT	Shift + VK_DELETE	VIRTKEY
ID_NEXT_PANE	VK_F6	VIRTKEY
ID_PREV_PANE	Shift + VK_F6	VIRTKEY
ID_EDIT_COPY	Ctrl + VK_INSERT	VIRTKEY
ID_EDIT_PASTE	Shift + VK_INSERT	VIRTKEY
ID_EDIT_CUT	Ctrl + X	VIRTKEY
ID_EDIT_UNDO	Ctrl + Z	VIRTKEY

MFCWiz.rc - IDR_MAINFRAME (Accelerator)

You can display the Accel Properties dialog box, shown next, from its context menu or by double-clicking an accelerator key. This property page allows you to control the values associated with each accelerator key.

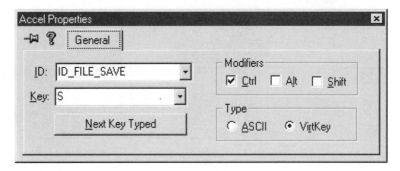

To associate a menu item with a keyboard combination, simply assign the same resource identifier to both the menu item and the relevant entry in the accelerator table. It's often appropriate to edit the menu item's caption to show the name of the accelerator, as this isn't done automatically. Refer to the section on the Menu editor to see how to do this.

Binary Editor

The Binary editor, shown in Figure 3-13, allows you to edit resources at the binary level in either hexadecimal format or ASCII format. It also can be used with the Find command to search for either ASCII strings or hexadecimal bytes with the binary resource. Binary resources are usually custom resources, such as WAV files, for which native editing support isn't provided by the Visual C++ environment. For this reason, it may not always be the most appropriate tool to use for such resources, and incorrect editing of the resource at the binary level could cause the resource to be corrupted.

You can bring a new custom resource into your project by placing the resource in a separate .RC file using normal resource script file syntax, and then including that file by using the Resource Includes command from the View menu. When the Resource Includes dialog box, shown in Figure 3-14, is displayed, you can type an #include statement in the Compile Time

FIGURE 3-13

The Binary editor lets you edit custom resources

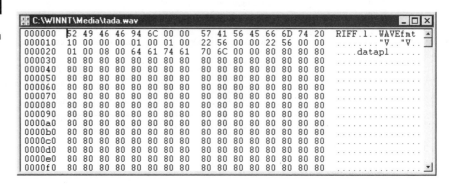

Directives edit box that gives the name of the file containing your custom resource. For example, you can type **#include myres.rc**.

Take care to ensure that the spelling and the syntax of all entries in the Compile Time Directives edit box are accurate because this text is copied directly into your project's resource script.

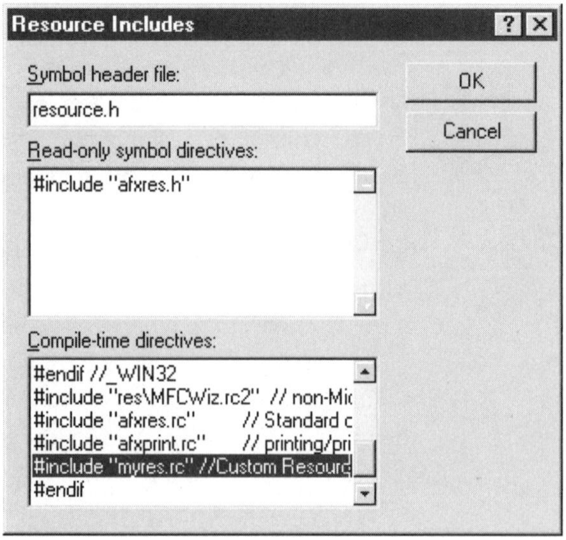

FIGURE 3-14

The Resource Includes dialog box allows you to insert custom resources into your project

Dialog Editor

The Dialog editor, shown in Figure 3-15, can be used to create or edit dialog boxes. Dialog boxes that you create can be stored as templates so that you can reuse them.

The Dialog editor allows you to perform the following tasks:

- Add, arrange, or edit controls on a dialog box.

- Change the tab order of controls on a dialog box.

- Use guides in the dialog box layout to position controls precisely.

- Preview the dialog box as it will appear when your application is running.

- Create message handlers for the dialog box and its controls.

- Jump to the code that implements the dialog box and its controls.

You can add controls to a dialog box by using the Controls toolbar, which enables you to choose the control that you want and drag it to the dialog box. You can also add additional ActiveX controls to the Controls toolbox by using the Insert ActiveX Controls command from the context menu of the Dialog editor. You can change the properties of controls that are in your dialog box by using the control's property page. The property page for a control can be displayed by selecting Properties from the context

FIGURE 3-15

The Dialog editor is used to create and edit dialog boxes

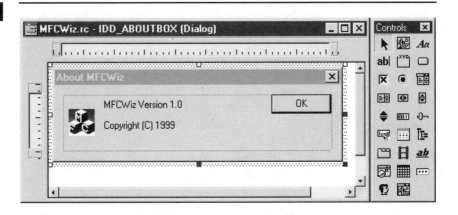

menu of the control. You can also select multiple controls and change their common properties all at the same time.

Double-clicking a dialog box control will take you to the handler code for that control. If a handler function didn't already exist, then a stub handler function will be created. In addition, you can double-click the dialog box itself to jump to its class definition. Windows controls usually have a range of events and messages available to them; you can create and edit handler functions for these events by selecting the Events item from the context menu for the control.

To preview some of the runtime behavior of your dialog box, select Test from the Layout menu. This can speed up the process of building a dialog box by giving you immediate feedback on how the dialog box will look and feel to the end user.

Graphics Editor

The Graphics editor, shown in Figure 3-16, has an extensive set of tools for creating and editing bitmaps, icons, and cursors, as well as integrated features to support the creation of toolbar bitmaps. In addition to creating and editing images in bitmap format, you can edit bitmap images and save them in GIF or JPEG format. You can also convert images in GIF or JPEG format to bitmap format.

Within the Graphics editor workspace, the Image Editor window shows two views of your image resource. The size of the two panes can be adjusted by the split bar that separates them. Also within the Graphics editor is the Graphics toolbar, which consists of the following two sections:

- A toolbar, which contains various tools, shapes, and brushes for drawing, painting, entering text, erasing, and manipulating views.

- An option selector, which can be used to select brush widths and other drawing options.

In addition, the Graphics editor provides the Colors palette, which consists of an indicator showing the current foreground and background colors and selectors for screen and inverse colors. It also has a range of colors from which to select the foreground and background colors. The foreground color is selected by clicking a color in the Colors palette. A background color is selected by right-clicking a color in the Colors palette.

FIGURE 3-16

The Graphics editor
shown here editing an
icon resource

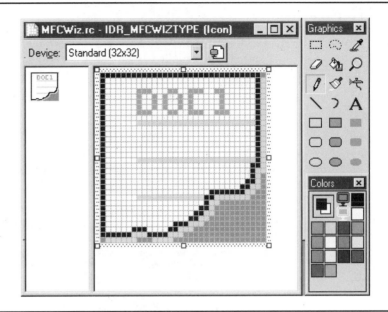

on the
job

When creating images for an application that you plan to distribute internationally, it is important to take into account various localization issues. It can be challenging to design bitmaps that are simple and specific enough to identify a command and at the same time ensure that they avoid cultural references and stereotypes that could offend international users. You could keep separate versions of bitmaps for different language editions of your application; however, this can be very time consuming. A better approach may be to take advantage of the common toolbar buttons defined for Windows or to use internationally recognized symbols, such as those used on road signs or in airports.

Another internationalization issue to keep in mind when using image resources is that it is generally best to keep images free of letters that represent the first letters of commands, such as B for Bold. You certainly should not include text in images unless the text is not intended to be translated (for example, a company name). An alternative might be to retrieve the text from a locale-specific string table and use Win32 API calls to draw the text onto the image.

HTML Resources

A Hypertext Markup Language (HTML) resource is an HTML file that is stored and compiled as part of your resource script. When you create a new HTML resource, Visual C++ includes it in the resource script of the active project, providing you with easy access to the HTML page.

HTML resources were introduced to support the CHtmlView class; however, you can insert them into any project and use them as you would any other resource. With the HTML resource editor, you can create an HTML page using the Text editor's native support for syntax coloring of HTML tags. The following shows an example of an HTML page being edited in the Text editor. You can easily preview the page as you develop it by selecting Preview from the context menu that appears within the Text editor.

```
MFCWiz.rc - IDR_HTML1 (HTML)
<HTML>

<TITLE>
    HTML Resource
</TITLE>

<BODY>

This is my HTML Resource

</BODY>
</HTML>
```

When you create a new HTML page or import an existing one, if your page contains bitmaps or other such graphics, you should be sure to import the relevant images into your project's resource script. This ensures the availability of the images when the application is run on the end user's PC. You should use the *res://* protocol to display such graphic images in your page. The res:// protocol supports the retrieving and displaying of a resource that resides in a compiled .DLL or .EXE module.

String Editor

A string table is a Windows resource that contains a list of IDs, values, and captions for all the strings of your application. For example, the status bar prompts that appear as your mouse moves over menu items are located in the string table. String tables make it easy to localize your application into different languages. If all text that could be displayed in your application is kept in a string table, you can localize the application by translating the strings and still maintain common source code for international editions of the application.

With the String editor, shown in Figure 3-17, you can edit your application's string table resource. In a string table, strings are grouped into segments, or blocks, of 16 strings each. The segment that a string belongs to is determined by the value of its identifier. For example, strings with identifiers of 0 to 15 are in one segment, strings with identifiers of 16 to 31 are in a second segment, and so on. Thus, to move a string from one segment to another you only need to change its identifier.

Segments of the string table are loaded into memory on demand. For this reason, it is a good idea to try and organize your application's string resources

ID	Value	Caption
IDR_MAINFRAME	128	MFCWiz\n\nMFCWiz\nMFCWiz File
AFX_IDS_APP_TITLE	57344	MFCWiz
AFX_IDS_IDLEMESSAGE	57345	Ready
ID_FILE_NEW	57600	Create a new document\nNew
ID_FILE_OPEN	57601	Open an existing document\nOpen
ID_FILE_CLOSE	57602	Close the active document\nClose
ID_FILE_SAVE	57603	Save the active document\nSave
ID_FILE_SAVE_AS	57604	Save the active document with a nev
ID_FILE_PAGE_SETUP	57605	Change the printing options\nPage S
ID_FILE_PRINT_SETUP	57606	Change the printer and printing optior
ID_FILE_PRINT	57607	Print the active document\nPrint
ID_FILE_PRINT_PREVIEW	57609	Display full pages\nPrint Preview
ID_FILE_MRU_FILE1	57616	Open this document

MFCWiz.rc - String Table (String Table)

into logical groups within 16-string segments that are likely to be required at the same time. This ensures that memory is used as efficiently as possible by not keeping the entire string table in memory when only a few strings may be required at any given time.

Double-clicking a string in the String editor will display its property page, which allows you to edit the string's ID or caption. You can also select multiple strings and change their properties all at the same time.

Version Information Editor

A version resource consists of company and product identification such as a product version number, and copyright and trademark information. The Version Information editor, shown in Figure 3-18, is a tool for creating and maintaining this data.

FIGURE 3-18

The Version Information editor allows you to embed information such as your company name into your application

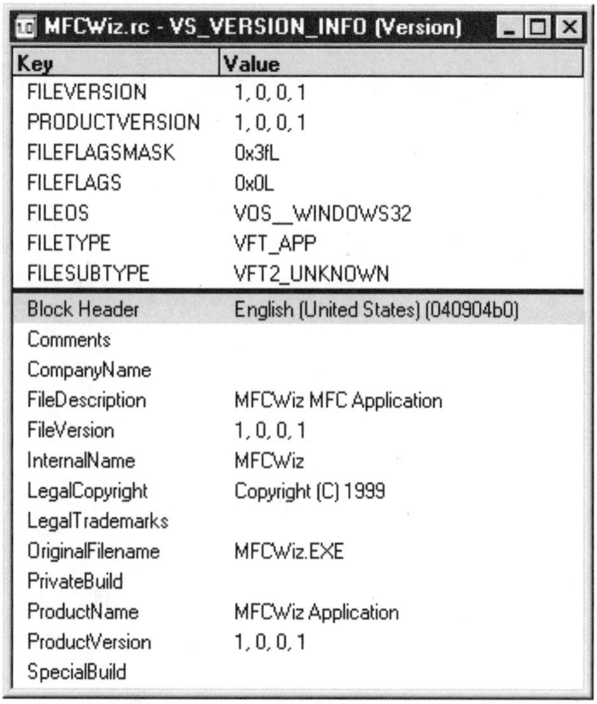
MFCWiz.rc - VS_VERSION_INFO (Version)
Key
Value
FILEVERSION
1, 0, 0, 1
PRODUCTVERSION
1, 0, 0, 1
FILEFLAGSMASK
0x3fL
FILEFLAGS
0x0L
FILEOS
VOS__WINDOWS32
FILETYPE
VFT_APP
FILESUBTYPE
VFT2_UNKNOWN
Block Header
English (United States) (040904b0)
Comments
CompanyName
FileDescription
MFCWiz MFC Application
FileVersion
1, 0, 0, 1
InternalName
MFCWiz
LegalCopyright
Copyright (C) 1999
LegalTrademarks
OriginalFilename
MFCWiz.EXE
PrivateBuild
ProductName
MFCWiz Application
ProductVersion
1, 0, 0, 1
SpecialBuild

A Windows-based application isn't required to contain version information to run, but it would be unconventional not to have a version resource. Note that the Windows standard name for an application version resource is VS_VERSION_INFO. The known formatting of version resources allows the version information to be accessed from other applications. In order to access your application's version information programmatically, you should make use of the GetFileVersionInfo and VerQueryValue Win32 APIs.

CERTIFICATION OBJECTIVE 3.04

Using ClassWizard

Most developers spend a significant amount of time in the early stages of a project working exclusively on the visual elements of their application before moving on to the application-specific functionality. At some stage in the development process it is necessary to hook up the user interface objects to the core functionality of the application. Visual C++ provides a reliable framework within which to achieve this. The principle tool that Visual C++ provides to you to perform these tasks is ClassWizard.

Some of the operations that ClassWizard assists you with include creating new classes, defining message handlers, creating virtual function overrides, and mapping data from dialog box controls to class members. ClassWizard works only with MFC applications.

The user interface of ClassWizard is a tabbed dialog box, as shown in Figure 3-19. You can access ClassWizard by selecting ClassWizard from the View menu.

The following list describes the use of each tab:

- **Message Maps** Use the Message Maps tab to browse the messages that a class can handle and to create, edit, and delete the member functions mapped to the messages. You can also use the Edit Code button to jump straight to a message handler function's code.

■ **Member Variables**   Use the Member Variables tab to bind member variables to dialog, form view, or record view controls. You can also bind record view member variables to both record view controls and the columns of a table in your data source.

■ **Automation**   Use the Automation tab to create and edit the Automation aspects of your application. For example, you can create Automation properties and methods that allow other applications to control your application.

■ **ActiveX Events**   If your project includes a class that implements an ActiveX control, you can use the ActiveX Events tab to specify which actions will cause events to fire in your ActiveX control. For example, you can specify that an event will be raised in the control's container in response to a user's mouse-click.

■ **Class Info**   Use the Class Info tab to browse and set general class options. You can set the message filter to determine what messages ClassWizard offers to map to handlers. You can also view or set a *foreign object* associated with your dialog form view or record view class.

FIGURE 3-19

The MFC ClassWizard

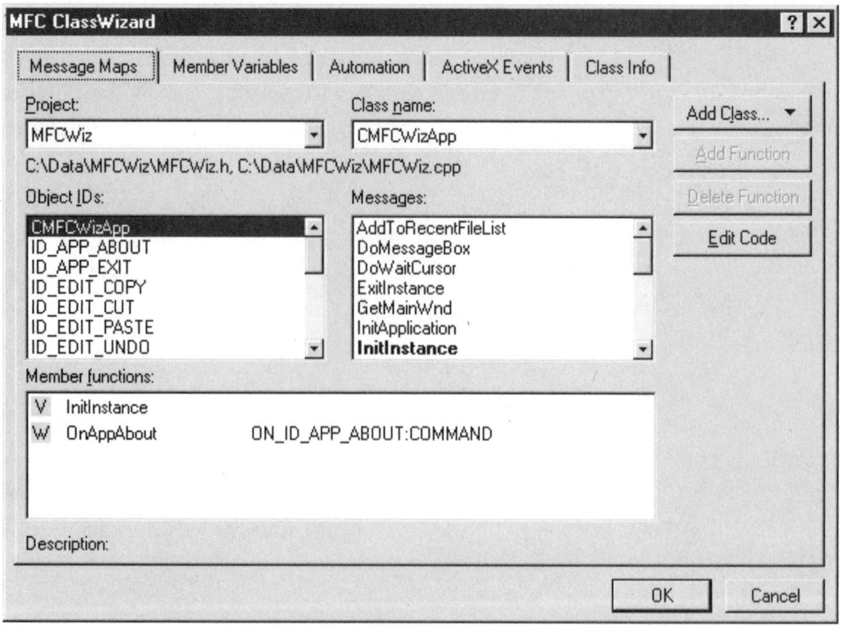

In addition, on every tab of the ClassWizard is the Add Class button that allows you to create a class, import a class from a file, or import a class from an ActiveX type library.

Adding Member Variables

You can use ClassWizard to add member variables to dialog classes to represent the dialog box's controls. The mechanism of mapping a dialog control to a dialog class member variable is called dialog data exchange (DDX). DDX eliminates the need for you to transfer data between the control and its corresponding member variable yourself.

We will do an exercise now that demonstrates creating a simple dialog resource and associating it with a dialog class based on CDialog that includes member variables that map to each of the controls in the dialog resource through DDX.

For each dialog box in your application you need to have a dialog box resource and a dialog box class. The resource script commands making up the dialog box resource are interpreted to determine how the dialog box should be drawn on the screen when your application is running. The dialog box class contains member variables that hold the values of the controls in your dialog box and it also contains member functions that create and show your dialog box. The dialog box resource is built with the Dialog Resource editor. ClassWizard is used to create and manage the dialog box class.

To start the exercise, use AppWizard to create a new SDI MFC executable application. Select the ResourceView tab from the project workspace and choose Insert from the context menu that appears when you right-click inside the ResourceView tab. The Insert Resource dialog box will appear. From this dialog box, select Dialog and click New or double-click Dialog. A simple dialog box with an ID of IDD_DIALOG1 should appear in the Dialog Resource editor, as shown in Figure 3-20.

Now display the Properties dialog box by right-clicking somewhere inside the dialog and selecting Properties from the context menu. The Dialog

FIGURE 3-20

The Dialog Resource editor lets you add user interface elements to a dialog resource

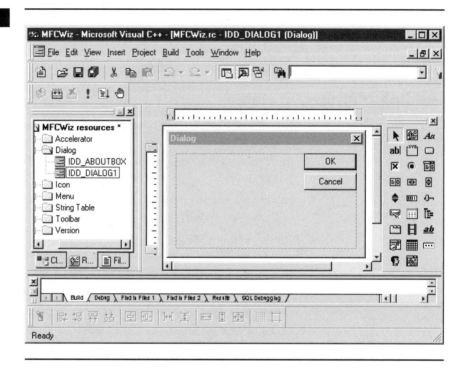

Properties dialog box, shown next, is used frequently when modifying a dialog box resource.

Because of this, you might find it useful to click the Pushpin button in the top-left corner, which will cause the Properties dialog box to become a modeless dialog box that will float on the screen while the Dialog Resource editor is open. Using the Properties dialog box, change the ID of the dialog box resource to **IDD_TESTDIALOG** and change the Caption to **Test Dialog**.

You can add controls to your dialog box resource by dragging and dropping them from the control palette, which is pictured on the right side of the resource editor workspace in Figure 3-20. Because the purpose of this exercise is to demonstrate ClassWizard functionality rather than how to use all of the common user interface elements, we'll keep this dialog box simple by just adding a single Static Text control and a single Edit Box control. Use your mouse to drag each of those controls to somewhere in the middle of your dialog box. Select Static Text and use the Properties dialog box to change its caption to say **Enter some text:**. Now select Test from the Layout menu and you'll be presented with a preview of the dialog box, which should look something like what's shown next. You can close the preview dialog box by clicking either of its command buttons.

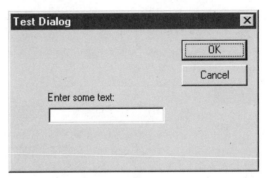

Now that the dialog resource is complete, it's time to create the dialog class. Bring up ClassWizard by choosing ClassWizard from the View menu or by double-clicking somewhere within the dialog box in the resource editor. ClassWizard knows that you haven't yet defined a dialog class for this resource and so it offers to create one for you, as shown here:

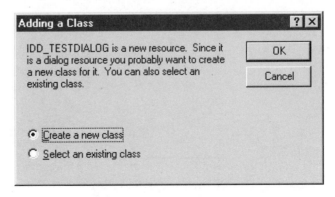

Accept the default option of creating a new class and click OK. The New Class dialog box will appear as shown in Figure 3-21. Give your class a class name of **CTestDialog**. Notice that the base class for this dialog will be the MFC CDialog class and that ClassWizard has already associated your dialog's resource symbol with the new class. When you click OK to create the class, two new files will be created in the directory in which your project resides, TESTDIALOG.CPP and TESTDIALOG.H.

Now you can use the Member Variables tab of ClassWizard to connect the dialog box controls to member variables in your class. The Member Variables tab of ClassWizard, in Figure 3-22, shows a list of the control IDs for the dialog resource associated with the dialog class displayed in the Class Name combo box.

We'll now connect a member variable to the Edit Box on our dialog box by highlighting IDC_EDIT1 in the Control IDs list and clicking the Add

---

The New Class dialog lets you create a new class based on CDialog

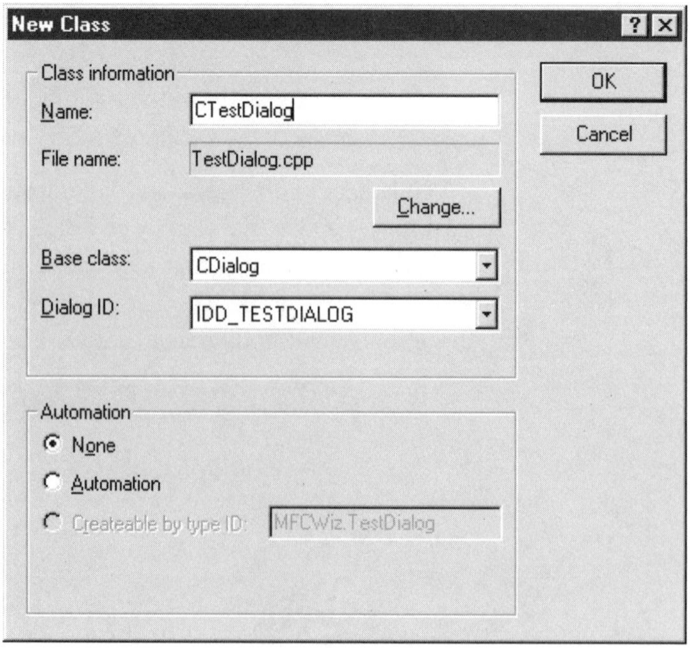

FIGURE 3-22

The Member Variables tab of ClassWizard lets you connect dialog controls to member variables

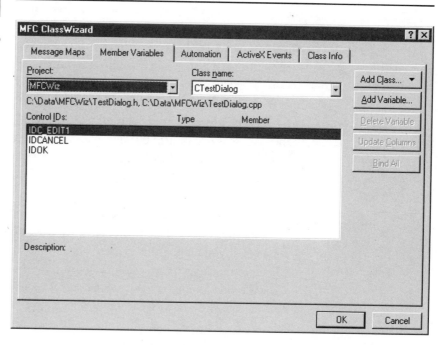

Variable button. The Add Member Variable dialog box, shown here, will be displayed.

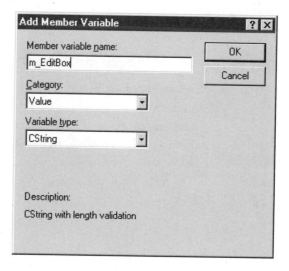

In the Member Variable Name field, give the variable the name **m_EditBox**. You'll notice that ClassWizard suggests a prefix of *m_* for the variable; this is the convention that is used to identify member variables in MFC applications. The Category combo box lets you specify whether this is a value variable or a control variable. For standard Windows controls such as the Edit Box, you should choose Value to create a variable that will contain the text or status of the control as entered by the user. The type of the variable is determined by your selection in the Variable Type combo box. If you choose Control from the Category combo box, the Variable Type will be a class such as CEdit that wraps the functionality of the control. For this exercise, choose Value from the Category combo box and CString from the Variable Type combo box. Click OK to create the variable.

Once the variable m_EditBox is associated with the IDC_EDIT1 resource, if you highlight it in the Control IDs list, you'll see a field labeled Maximum Characters appear at the bottom of the Member Variables tab of ClassWizard. This allows you some control over the validation of the data entered into the control by limiting the length of the text that a user is able to enter into the text box when the application is running. Enter a value of **20** into this field and then click OK to close ClassWizard.

Now that the dialog resource and corresponding dialog class have been created, all that remains is to use the dialog box in the application. In the next section, we'll see how to show the dialog box in response to a menu item being selected.

Adding a Message Handler for an Event

Windows-based applications are *message driven*. This means that for every event such as a mouse-click or a keystroke, Windows sends messages to the appropriate windows. The MFC framework processes Windows messages and in doing so provides some enhancements that make processing messages easier, more maintainable, and better encapsulated.

The main application object of an MFC application is an instance of CWinApp. This class contains a member function called Run, which is responsible for retrieving queued messages. The message loop in the Run member function of class CWinApp retrieves queued messages generated by various events and dispatches them to the appropriate window. In an MFC application, a dedicated handler function processes each separate message. Such message handler functions are member functions of a class.

Each class in the MFC framework that is able to receive messages has a *message map*. Message maps are used to connect messages and commands to their appropriate handler functions. All classes derived from the CCmdTarget base class can have message maps. When such a class receives a message, it searches its message map for an appropriate handler. If it finds one, it calls it; otherwise, it will probably route the message to another command target.

After generating a new application using the MFC AppWizard, you'll find some message maps already defined for you in the command target classes that may look something like the following listing:

```
BEGIN_MESSAGE_MAP(CMFCWizApp, CWinApp)
    //{{AFX_MSG_MAP(CMFCWizApp)
    ON_COMMAND(ID_APP_ABOUT, OnAppAbout)
        // NOTE - the ClassWizard will add and remove mapping macros here.
        //    DO NOT EDIT what you see in these blocks of generated code!
    //}}AFX_MSG_MAP
    // Standard file based document commands
    ON_COMMAND(ID_FILE_NEW, CWinApp::OnFileNew)
    ON_COMMAND(ID_FILE_OPEN, CWinApp::OnFileOpen)
    // Standard print setup command
    ON_COMMAND(ID_FILE_PRINT_SETUP, CWinApp::OnFilePrintSetup)
END_MESSAGE_MAP()
```

The message map consists of several macros. Two macros in particular, BEGIN_MESSAGE_MAP and END_MESSAGE_MAP, define where the message map starts and ends. There are many other macros such as ON_COMMAND that make up the content of the message map. You'll also notice comments in the message map that include tags such as AFX_MSG_MAP. These comments are used by ClassWizard to determine which message map entries it is managing.

on the **Job**

You'll rarely, if ever, need to edit the message map entries between the ClassWizard AFX_MSG_MAP tags. In fact, doing so could prevent ClassWizard from being able to read the message map at all. Many a developer has experienced grief while attempting to bypass ClassWizard and edit these entries directly.

Your implementation of a message handler function is your opportunity to respond to the message in whatever way is appropriate for your application. ClassWizard assists by creating the stubs of the message handler functions for you. It also allows you to logically navigate within your source code by jumping straight to the appropriate handler for various user interface elements such as menu items.

In working with the MFC framework, you'll find that ClassWizard greatly simplifies the task of managing numerous handlers for Windows messages. Changes you make in ClassWizard affect your source files in the following ways:

- Message map entries are written to connect the handler function to the message.

- A message handler function is declared as a member of the class.

- A stub is created for the handler function where you can write your code to handle the message.

Continuing with the dialog box exercise that we created in the previous section on adding member variables, we'll create a menu item that, when selected, will show the dialog box. To start off, open the project workspace from the previous exercise. The first thing we need to do is to add a menu item that will be used to show the dialog box. To display the Menu resource editor, go to the ResourceView tab of the project workspace and expand the Menu folder. Double-click the IDR_MAINFRAME resource. When the Menu editor is open, use your mouse to click the View menu item and then double-click the blank menu item in your View menu's drop-down menu. When the Menu Item Properties dialog box is displayed for the new menu item, assign it an ID of **ID_VIEW_TEST_DIALOG**. Enter the caption as **Test &Dialog**, and in the prompt field type **Display the TestDialog**. When you are done, the Menu Item Properties dialog box should resemble what's shown here:

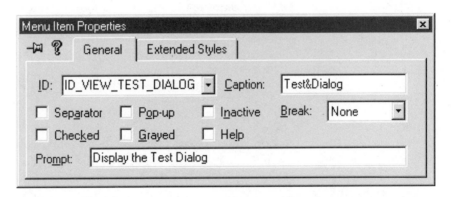

After closing the Properties dialog box for this new menu item, you will see it displayed in the Menu editor. Right-click it in the Menu editor and select ClassWizard from the context menu. When ClassWizard is displayed, go to the Message Maps tab and in the Class Name combo box, select the class that is derived from CWinApp in your application (if you selected the AppWizard defaults when creating your project this will be the class with a name ending in *App*). Now select ID_VIEW_TEST_DIALOG from the Object IDs list box. This list box shows all of the objects in the current class that are able to generate messages. The list box labeled Messages shows the messages that the selected object can handle and any MFC virtual functions that can be overridden. If a message in this list already has a handler function associated with it, the message will be displayed in bold. For the ID_VIEW_TEST_DIALOG menu item, select the message called COMMAND. The ClassWizard should look like Figure 3-23.

Now click the Add Function button to display the Add Member Function dialog box, as shown next. Accept the default function name of OnViewTestDialog and click OK.

When you click the Edit Code button, ClassWizard will close and you'll be taken to the source code editor in the function stub that has been created for you. Complete the implementation of the function so that it is the same as the following listing:

```
void CMFCWizApp::OnViewTestDialog()
{
    CTestDialog testDlg;
    testDlg.DoModal();
}
```

Now, in order for the compiler to recognize an object of type CTestDialog, you must include the header file for the dialog class in the header file of the class to which this handler function belongs. Go to your CWinApp-derived classes header file by selecting the ClassView tab in the project workspace and double-clicking the name of the appropriate class (as previously explained, it will probably be the class with a name ending in *App*). When

FIGURE 3-23

The Message Maps tab of ClassWizard is where handler functions can be created

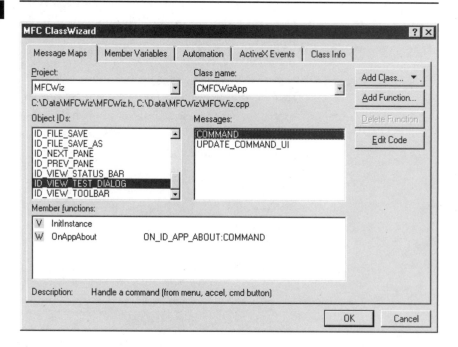

the appropriate header file is displayed, go to the top of the file and type the following line of code after any other #include statements that appear there:

```
#include "TestDialog.h"
```

You'll now be able to recompile and run the application by selecting Build and then Execute from the Build menu. When the application runs, you'll be able to go to the View menu of your application and select Test Dialog and you should see the dialog box modally displayed as shown here:

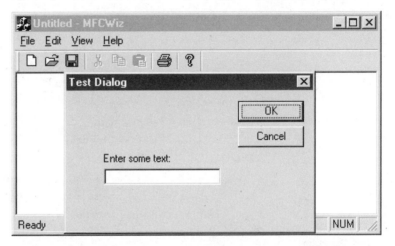

The Test Dialog doesn't do anything at the moment, so to finish the exercise we'll add a message handler member function to the CTestDialog class. This message handler function responds to the user clicking OK in the dialog box and displays any text that the user may have entered in the Edit Box. Perform the following steps to add a message handler function for the OK button in the CTestDialog class:

1. Open ClassWizard and go to the Message Maps tab.

2. Select CTestDialog from the Class Name combo box.

3. Select IDOK from the Object IDs list.

4. Select BN_CLICKED from the Messages list.

5. Click the Add Function button and accept the default function name, OnOK, in the Add Member Function dialog box by clicking OK.

6. Back in the Message Maps tab of ClassWizard, click the Edit Code button. You'll be taken to the message handler function stub in the TESTDIALOG.CPP file.

7. Edit the implementation of the function so that it resembles the following listing:

```
void CTestDialog::OnOK()
{
    // TODO: Add extra validation here
    CDialog::OnOK();
    AfxMessageBox(m_EditBox);
}
```

Notice that this function calls the base class's implementation of OnOK which in turn calls DoDataExchange. The DoDataExchange function performs the DDX for this CDialog-derived class so that when AfxMessageBox is called, the m_EditBox member variable will contain the value that had been entered in our dialog box's Edit Box with the resource ID IDC_EDIT1.

You should now be able to recompile and execute your application again. This time when you display Test Dialog and enter something in its edit box, if you click OK to dismiss the dialog box you'll see a message box containing the text that you entered, just like this:

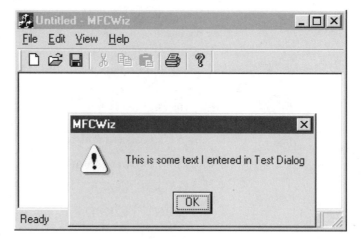

FROM THE CLASSROOM

Enhancing User Interface Navigation Coding Through Dynamic Menus

In this chapter, you were introduced to menus and you learned how to define menus at design-time using the resource editor. When developing an intuitive, user-friendly interface it is sometimes desirable to change the menu items that the user sees based on the activity that the user is currently performing within the application. In order to make your menus context-sensitive, it may be necessary to implement dynamic menus. We will discuss the first step in creating a dynamic menu: consolidating handlers into a command range.

When adding and removing menu items while your application is running, you will benefit from learning how to consolidate handlers into a command range. When implementing command handlers for your menu items, you may find that many command handlers are performing the same, or very similar, functions. Instead of writing individual command handlers for each menu item, a command range can be used to map several menu items to a range of messages.

To consolidate command handlers, first determine the maximum number of new message entries, and add symbolic constants in the resource table for each message entry. To do this, open the Resource Symbols dialog box from the View menu, and select New. In the New Symbol dialog box, specify a name and a value for the menu item. Repeat this for each item that you want to include in the range. Be sure to use consecutive numbers greater than 33,000 for the resource symbol values. Using numbers greater than 33,000 avoids conflicts with any predefined or existing messages.

Next, add an ON_COMMAND_RANGE entry, an option not available through the ClassWizard, to the message map of the class that you want to receive the commands from the dynamic menu. Specify the first and last numbers of the range that you entered in the resource symbols table as the first and second arguments of the ON_COMMAND_RANGE macro, for example:

```
ON_COMMAND_RANGE( ID_VIEW_ITEM1,
ID_VIEW_ITEM4, OnNewItems)
```

You will need to add an entry to the class's header file in the DECLARE_MESSAGE_MAP section, such as the following example:

```
afx_msg void OnNewItems( UINT nID );
```

FROM THE CLASSROOM

To complete the process of adding menu items dynamically, you will need to add entries to the string table to store your menu captions, write the code that adds your menu items, write the code to accept the commands generated by the added menus, and add an entry to the header file for the class. When designing your application's user interface, start by utilizing the code generated by the MFC AppWizard and the ClassWizard, then add some "bells and whistles," such as context-sensitive menus, to make your interface professional and polished.

—Michael Lane Thomas,
MCSE+I, MCSD, MCT, MCP+SB, MSS, A+

CERTIFICATION SUMMARY

This chapter has demonstrated the tools available in Visual C++ that aid the developer in creating the visual elements of an application. We looked at how two of Developer Studio's most significant wizards, AppWizard and ClassWizard, can make it easier to develop Windows-based applications.

You've learned how to create and use MFC toolbars and status bars in your applications, as well as how to use the various resource editors available in the Visual C++ environment and how they assist you in creating common Windows user interface elements.

We used AppWizard to create a new MFC application and then learned how to map messages to member functions through ClassWizard. We also examined how ClassWizard is used to create member variables in a dialog class that are connected to controls in a dialog resource.

TWO-MINUTE DRILL

❑ Visual C++ and MFC provide the framework on which to build a visually appealing and conventional user interface.

❑ A toolbar is a special organizational visual element that can manage sets of other controls such as buttons, button separators, and combo boxes. The primary role of toolbars in an application is to provide quick access to commonly used functions.

❑ MFC allows you to easily create many conventional styles of toolbars, depending on your choices in the MFC AppWizard.

❑ A toolbar in an MFC application is actually a CToolBar object declared as a member of your application's CMainFrame class.

❑ Status bars give your application a place to display messages and useful information to the user without interrupting the user.

❑ The starting point of many Microsoft Visual C++ projects is the AppWizard. The MFC AppWizard gives developers a great head start when beginning a new Windows-based program using MFC. AppWizard helps you generate the basic source files for a variety of different types of Windows-based programs, allowing you to get down to the task of creating your application.

❑ An accelerator table contains a list of accelerator keys (or shortcut keys) and the command identifiers that are associated with them. A program can have more than one accelerator table. Accelerators are usually used as keyboard shortcuts for program commands that appear on your application's menu or toolbar.

❑ To associate a menu item with a keyboard combination, simply assign the same resource identifier to both the menu item and the relevant entry in the accelerator table.

❑ The Binary editor, shown in Figure 3-13, allows you to edit resources at the binary level in either hexadecimal format or ASCII format.

❏ The Dialog editor, shown in Figure 3-15, can be used to create or edit dialog boxes. Dialog boxes that you create can be stored as templates so that you can reuse them.

❏ The Graphics editor, shown in Figure 3-16, has an extensive set of tools for creating and editing bitmaps, icons, and cursors, as well as integrated features to support the creation of toolbar bitmaps.

❏ A Hypertext Markup Language (HTML) resource is an HTML file that is stored and compiled as part of your resource script. When you create a new HTML resource, Visual C++ includes it in the resource script of the active project, providing you with easy access to the HTML page.

❏ A string table is a Windows resource that contains a list of IDs, values, and captions for all the strings of your application.

❏ The mechanism of mapping a dialog control to a dialog class member variable is called dialog data exchange (DDX).

❏ Windows-based applications are *message driven*. This means that for every event such as a mouse-click or a keystroke, Windows sends messages to the appropriate windows. The MFC framework processes Windows messages and in doing so provides some enhancements that make processing messages easier, more maintainable, and better encapsulated.

SELF TEST

The following questions will help you measure your understanding of the material presented in this chapter. Read all of the choices carefully, as there may be more than one correct answer. Choose all correct answers for each question.

1. Your development team is starting a project which involves the creation of an application in which there will be many different dialog boxes. Responsibility for creation of these dialog boxes will be spread across all members of the team. You decide to ensure that all members of the team adhere to the Windows User Interface Guidelines. What benefits will you gain from this decision? (Choose all that apply.)

    A. Your application will maintain the visual and functional consistency that is found in the majority of Windows-based applications.

    B. Users will be able to apply their knowledge of other applications in learning to use your application.

    C. Your application will be able to use lots of bright colors and original fonts.

    D. Members of the development team can focus on the creation of the business logic and core functionality of the application without wasting too much time ensuring everyone's dialog boxes look and behave the same.

2. You have been asked to create an application that must have a toolbar. A graphic artist has been brought into the project to design the images for the toolbar buttons. Which one of the following would be the best way to work with the graphic artist to incorporate the images?

    A. Ask the graphic artist to create each image in a separate 16x16-pixel bitmap which can be brought into Visual C++ as separate bitmap resources.

    B. Ask the graphic artist to create all the button images in a single bitmap lined up side by side, then convert that bitmap into a toolbar resource.

    C. The graphic artist has no choice but to edit the toolbar bitmaps in the Visual C++ Toolbar editor.

    D. The graphic artist can create the images in JPEG format to reduce the file size and you will be able to import them directly into the Toolbar editor.

3. A user group who is beta testing your MFC application would like to change the status bar text that is displayed when the mouse hovers over a certain button on the toolbar of your application. How would you go about doing this?

A. Write functions to intercept the message that is sent when the mouse passes over the button and call an API to change the status bar text.

B. Enter the text in the Prompt field of the Toolbar Button Properties dialog box, ensuring that the text is preceded by a new line character (\n).

C. Enter the text in the Prompt field of the Toolbar Button Properties dialog box. If there is a new line character (\n) followed by some other text, then make sure that the desired status bar text appears before the new line character.

D. Enter the text in the Prompt field of the Status Bar Pane Properties dialog box for the appropriate status bar pane, then make the pane visible when the mouse-over message is received for the toolbar button.

4. You have just decided to include a toolbar in your MFC application. You don't want the toolbar to have text captions because it will take up too much space on the screen, but you would still like to give the user a brief one- or two-word explanation of the purpose of each button. How do you specify ToolTips for the toolbar buttons?

A. Specify the CBRS_TOOLTIPS style flag in the call to CControlBar::SetBarStyle, then enter the ToolTip text in the ToolTip field of the Toolbar Button Properties dialog box.

B. Specify the CBRS_TOOLTIPS style flag in the call to CToolBar::Create, then enter the ToolTip text after the new line character (\n) in the Prompt field of the Toolbar Button Properties dialog box.

C. Specify the TBSTYLE_TOOLTIPS style flag in the call to CToolBar::CreateEx, then enter the ToolTip text after the new line character (\n) in the Prompt field of the Toolbar Button Properties dialog box.

D. Enter the ToolTip text in the ToolTip field of the Toolbar Button Properties dialog box.

5. In an MFC application that you are developing, you are asked to include a status bar pane that will indicate whether or not the database server is active. Which of the following is the appropriate action to take to add the new pane to the status bar?

A. Call CStatusBar::SetIndicators, passing in an array of resource IDs that includes the resource symbol for the new status bar pane.

B. Call CStatusBar::AddPane, passing in the resource symbol for the new status bar pane.

C. Call CStatusBar::LoadIndicator, passing in the resource symbol for the new status bar pane.

D. Call CStatusBar::SetPane, passing in the resource symbol for the new status bar pane.

6. If you are asked to create an ActiveX control using Visual C++, which one of the following project types would you use?

   A. MFC AppWizard (dll)

   B. MFC AppWizard (exe)

   C. MFC AppWizard (ocx)

   D. MFC ActiveX ControlWizard

7. Which of the following methods should you use to create a new MFC application?

   A. From the File menu select New, then choose Win32 Application from the Project tab of the New dialog box.

   B. Use the MFC AppWizard (exe).

   C. Use the ClassWizard.

   D. Use the ATL/COM AppWizard.

8. If you wish to create an application that has a single top-level window that can contain multiple child windows, which of the following application architectures should you choose when running the MFC AppWizard?

   A. single-document interface (SDI) application.

   B. multiple-document interface (MDI) application.

   C. Property Page-based application.

   D. Dialog-based application.

9. If you wish to use the MFC AppWizard to create a form-based database application containing a CRecordView-derived class, which one of the following is the minimum level of database support you should select?

   A. Database view without file support.

   B. Database view with file support.

   C. Header files only.

   D. Data environment with ADO support.

10. When distributing your MFC application, you encounter problems installing it on a user's machine where there are several applications using different versions of the same runtime libraries. What should you do to minimize the impact on your application of this shared environment?

    A. Use the MFC libraries as a shared DLL because it will reduce the size of your application's executable therefore reducing its dependencies on runtime libraries.

    B. Statically link to the MFC libraries to reduce dependencies on runtime libraries.

    C. Statically link to the MFC libraries to reduce the size of your application's executable.

    D. Make your application easier to distribute by using the shared MFC libraries.

11. After using the MFC AppWizard to create a project, you add code to various files in the project until you realize that you forgot to include Winsock support in the initial AppWizard-generated project. Which is the best course of action to allow you to

continue your project without wasting the work that you have done so far?

A. You have no choice but to start again from scratch because running the MFC AppWizard is a one-time process.

B. You run AppWizard two more times to create two additional projects, the first with the original choices and the second with the addition of the Winsock option. Then, use WinDiff to detect the differences between the projects so you can incorporate the changes into your original project.

C. You run the MFC AppWizard again using the same project name and location, but this time specifying the Winsock option.

D. You use the MFC Project Wizard to include the additional code, header files, and libraries required to support Winsock in your project.

12. A developer is sending you a resource file from an MFC application that he attempted to edit directly from Notepad, only to find that it has become out of sync with the Visual C++ resource editors. What is likely to be the file extension of the file that he sends to you?

A. .RC

B. .RES

C. .RSC

D. .SCP

13. To create a multimedia application using Visual C++, you need to order all of the relevant software that will be used to make the application's resources. Which of the following file formats will require third party software because they aren't natively supported by Visual C++? (Choose all that apply.)

A. Bitmap (.BMP) files.

B. Wave (.WAV) files.

C. Windows menus.

D. AVI files.

14. When might you want to use the Visual C++ Accelerator editor?

A. If your application runs slowly, you can use the Accelerator editor to determine the optimum compiler switches to make your application's code execute as fast as possible.

B. You can use the Accelerator editor to enable IntelliSense when you're editing source code so that you can use shortcut keys and automatic statement complete to write code more quickly.

C. You use the Accelerator editor to associate shortcut keys with command identifiers in the application you are creating.

D. You use the Accelerator editor to associate shortcut keys with the menu commands and macros that you use most frequently in Developer Studio.

15. Having created a dialog-based MFC application, you begin to modify the default dialog box to make the user interface for the application. Which one of the following tasks cannot be performed in the Dialog resource editor?

   A. Add, arrange, and edit controls on a dialog box.

   B. Change the tab order of controls on a dialog box.

   C. Add and edit a menu resource for a dialog box.

   D. Preview the dialog box as it will appear when the application is running.

16. After an initial domestic release of your application, some interest has been generated in the application from users in Japan who have seen screen shots of it on your company's web site. The decision is made to sell to this potential new market; however, you need to do some redevelopment of the application. Which of the following issues should be taken into account when creating images to be used in the Japanese version of the application? (Choose all that apply.)

   A. Images should avoid cultural stereotypes.

   B. Images should generally not include letters that represent the first letter of a language-specific command such as *B* for *B*old.

   C. Any words that need to be displayed in an image should be kept in a locale-specific resource file and drawn on the image using API calls.

   D. Internationally recognized symbols such as road signs should never be used in an international application.

17. An application that you have developed includes your company logo in the top right of the main window. It is suggested to you that it would be a good feature to direct users to your company Web site when they click the logo. Which tool should you use to define a message handler to intercept the user's mouse-click?

   A. The resource editor.

   B. The MFC AppWizard.

   C. ClassWizard.

   D. The MessageMap Wizard.

18. After adding a textbox to a dialog box, you go to the Member Variables tab of Class Wizard to create a member variable that will contain the value entered into the textbox by the user. Is the Member Variables tab of ClassWizard the appropriate place to do this?

   A. Yes, because this tab is used to add all types of member variables to classes.

   B. Yes, because this tab allows you to bind member variables to dialog controls.

   C. No, because this tab is used to map property procedures to member variables within ActiveX control projects.

   D. No, because this tab is only used to change the scope of member variables in classes.

19. Which of the following does *not* occur when you use the Message Maps tab of ClassWizard to create a message handler function?

    A. Message map entries are written to connect the message handler function to the message.

    B. The message handler function is declared as a member of the class.

    C. A stub implementation of the message handler function is created.

    D. A dedicated message loop is set up to route the message to the message handler function.

20. Which tab of the ClassWizard dialog box should you use if you need to create a function that is executed when the user clicks a button in a dialog box that you have created?

    A. Member Variables.

    B. Message Maps.

    C. Automation.

    D. ActiveX Events.

SELF TEST ANSWERS

1. **A,B,D.** Adherence to the Windows User Interface Guidelines ensures that your application will maintain a look and feel that is consistent with most other Windows-based applications and so users will intuitively know how to use your application, therefore A and B are correct. D is also correct because the guidelines enable you to use tools such as MFC class libraries to quickly create a conventional user interface. This frees you to concentrate on implementing the core functionality of the application, which should meet the business needs of the user. If all members of the development team adhere to the guidelines, then the user interface elements created by separate developers will still look and behave similarly. Answer C is incorrect because bright colors and nonstandard fonts aren't encouraged by the Windows User Interface Guidelines.

2. **B.** The Toolbar resource editor allows you to create a toolbar based on a single bitmap containing all the button images, therefore B is the correct answer. A is a workable solution but it isn't as easy to implement as B, so it is incorrect. C is incorrect because the graphic artist is able to use other tools to create the images. D is incorrect because there really isn't any need to try and reduce the size of toolbar images by using a graphics format like JPEG.

3. **C.** The text in the Prompt field of the Toolbar Button Properties dialog box that appears to the left of a new line character is displayed in the application's status bar when the mouse passes over the button. If a new line character isn't present, then all the text in the Prompt field is displayed in the status bar. Answer A provides a possible solution but in an MFC application it would be an unconventional method, so it is incorrect. Answer B is wrong because it says the status bar text should appear after the new line character, whereas it should actually appear before it. Answer D is incorrect because there is no Status Bar Pane Properties dialog box in the Visual C++ development environment.

4. **B.** In order to enable a ToolTip for a toolbar button, you must specify the CBRS_TOOLTIPS style flag in a call to CToolBar::Create (or CreateEx), then enter the ToolTip text to the right of the new line character in the Prompt field of the Toolbar Button Properties dialog box. The other answers either refer to nonexistent style flags or property fields that don't exist.

5. **A.** A status bar in an MFC application is usually initialized in the CMainFrame::OnCreate function. During the initialization of the status bar, a call is made to CStatusBar::SetIndicators passing in an array of IDs that determine the order and type of panes to display in the status bar. The other answers refer to nonexistent functions.

6. **D.** Answers A and B are valid project types but A is used to make an MFC-based dynamic link library and B is used to make an MFC executable application. Answer C, MFC AppWizard (ocx) isn't a valid project type. If you wish to create an .OCX or ActiveX control using MFC, then the MFC ActiveX ControlWizard is the appropriate one to use, therefore D is the correct answer.

7. **B.** The MFC AppWizard (exe) should be used to create an MFC application. Answer A specifies using the Win32 Application project type; however, that won't necessarily include support for MFC and the same goes for the ATL/COM AppWizard specified in answer D. Answer C is incorrect because ClassWizard isn't even used to create projects.

8. **B.** Step 1 of the MFC AppWizard allows you to specify the type of application that you wish to create. The choices are single-document interface (SDI), multiple-document interface (MDI), or dialog-based application. An MDI style application is one which has a single main window that can contain multiple child windows, therefore answer B is correct. Answer C is incorrect because the MFC AppWizard doesn't actually present you with the choice of creating a Property Page-based application.

9. **A.** Step 2 of the MFC AppWizard allows you to select the desired level of database support for your application. Choosing answer A will give your program a CRecordView-derived view class and a CRecordset-derived class that will be associated with the view class. This is the minimum level that satisfies the question, so A is the correct answer. Answer B is the next level of support, it includes everything that answer A supports but it also allows document serialization. Answer C is a valid option but it doesn't produce an application with a CRecordView-derived class and so it is incorrect. Answer D, Data environment with ADO support, doesn't exist in Visual C++ and so it is incorrect.

10. **B.** When you choose to use the MFC libraries as a shared DLL, it will reduce the size of your application's executable because its runtime libraries will be shipped in a separate binary that is loaded as required. In this shared environment where there is an incompatible version on the user's machine, the application may not work, so answers A and D are incorrect. Statically linking will link your application to the MFC libraries

at build time and will therefore produce a much larger executable, so answer C is incorrect. Answer B is correct because the application will benefit from static linking by avoiding the reliance on the shared runtime libraries that may be incompatible.

11. **B.** Although AppWizard is a one-time process that you perform at the start of a project, it works by piecing together bits of code according to the options you select. So if you know exactly what code AppWizard adds into a project to support the feature you require, you will be able to paste the feature in yourself. The easiest way to do that is to use a tool called WinDiff that is included with Visual C++ and to follow the steps outlined in answer B.

12. **A.** MFC applications make use of resources defined in a script which is simply a text file with the extension .RC; therefore answer A is correct. A resource script consists of various statements that define the application's resources. This script is usually compiled into a binary file with an .RES extension (answer B).

13. **B, D.** The Visual C++ resource editors offer native support for many different types of Windows resources including bitmaps, cursors, dialogs, accelerators, icons, menus, strings, toolbars, and HTML, but it doesn't offer native support for many other file types including Wave files and AVI files. In such cases, these resources can still be included in your Visual C++ project by including them as binary resources, however you should edit them in a separate editor which natively supports the particular file type.

14. **C.** An accelerator table contains a list of accelerator keys (or shortcut keys) and the command identifiers that are associated with them. The Accelerator editor is used to edit your application's accelerator table.

15. **C.** The Dialog resource editor allows you to add, arrange, or edit controls on a dialog box; change the tab order of controls on a dialog box; use guides in the dialog box layout to position controls; preview the dialog box as it will appear when your application is running; and jump to the code that implements the dialog box and its controls. However, it doesn't allow you to add and edit a menu resource for a dialog box. Menu resources must be edited using the Menu editor.

16. **A, B, C.** When creating images for an application that you plan to distribute internationally, it is important to take into account various localization issues such as avoiding cultural references and stereotypes that could offend international users. One safe approach may be to take advantage of the common toolbar buttons defined for

Windows or to use internationally recognized symbols such as those used on road signs or in airports, therefore answer D is incorrect. It is also best to keep images free of letters that represent the first letters of commands, such as B for bold and certainly don't include text in images unless the text is not intended to be translated.

17. **C.** You should use the Message Maps tab of ClassWizard to browse the messages that a class can handle and to create, edit, and delete the member functions mapped to the messages such as a user's mouse-click, therefore answer C is correct. Answer A doesn't mention a specific resource editor, so it isn't correct. Answer B, the MFC AppWizard, is only used to create the initial project, and answer D, the MessageMap Wizard is a nonexistent tool.

18. **B.** You can use the Member Variables tab of ClassWizard to add member variables to dialog classes to represent the dialog box's controls, therefore answer B is correct. The mechanism of mapping a dialog control to a dialog class member variable is called dialog data exchange (DDX).

19. **D.** Each class in the MFC framework that is able to receive messages has a message map. The contents of the message maps are maintained by ClassWizard. There is a message loop in the Run member function of class CWinApp that retrieves queued messages generated by various events. The message loop dispatches them to the appropriate window where a dedicated handler function processes each separate message as they arrive, but a dedicated message loop isn't set up for each message, so answer D is wrong and therefore is the correct choice.

20. **B.** You should use the Message Maps tab of ClassWizard to create a function called a message handler function that will be executed in response to the message that is generated when a user clicks a button in a dialog box that you have created, therefore answer B is correct. Answer A, the Member Variables tab, is used to bind member variables to dialog box controls. Answer C, the Automation tab, is used to create and edit the Automation aspects of your application. Answer D, the ActiveX Events tab, is used if your project includes a class that implements an ActiveX control, in which case you can specify which actions will cause events to fire in your ActiveX control.

4

Creating the
User Interface

I n this chapter we will discuss the factors involved in creating the user interface, including how to create data input forms and dialog boxes with the Dialog editor. We will also discuss the use of ClassWizard for configuring data dialog validation (DDV) and dialog data transfer (DDX). The process of storing and retrieving personal user settings will also be covered, as well as the implemenatation of online user assistance in its various forms. Finally, we will discuss the appropriate methods of handling errors.

CERTIFICATION OBJECTIVE 4.01

Creating Data Input Forms and Dialog Boxes

Most desktop programs written in Visual C++ provide for user input through some kind of form or dialog box. Using Visual C++ with Microsoft Foundation Classes (MFC), you have several options for creating these data input windows: you can create a form that adheres to the document/view architecture by deriving a class from CFormView; you can create a modal or modeless dialog box from a class derived from CDialog; or you can create a tabbed dialog box, known as a property sheet, from a class derived from CPropertySheet.

Creating a Dialog Box

The steps to creating a dialog box are as follows:

1. Insert a new dialog template.

2. Edit the dialog template using the Dialog editor.

3. Use ClassWizard to associate the dialog template with a C++ class derived from one of the MFC classes.

4. Use the class within the application.

Using the Dialog Editor

The Visual C++ integrated development environment (IDE) provides a Dialog editor for editing dialog templates. You will use the Dialog editor to create and modify the resource templates that describe how dialog boxes will appear and how controls will be laid out on those dialog boxes. In the following section you will see how to add a new dialog template to your project and the role of the Dialog editor in creating your user input form resource templates.

Inserting a New Dialog Template

In order to insert a new dialog template into a project, follow these steps:

1. Select the Resource View.

2. Right-click *Project Name* Resources, select Insert…, select Dialog, and click New; a new template will appear in the tree under the Dialog folder with an ID similar to IDD_DIALOG1.

3. Right-click the new dialog ID and select Properties; you can modify the ID to something more meaningful, such as IDD_CONTACT_DETAILS.

Editing a Dialog Template Using the Dialog Editor

Each of the types of user interface forms and dialog boxes is based upon one or more dialog templates. A dialog template specifies which controls (such as list boxes or option buttons) will be contained on the dialog box, and how they will be laid out. The dialog template also contains a number of different styles that determine how a dialog box should be displayed on the screen.

It is possible to create dialog templates manually using a text editor; however, this would be an extremely tedious operation involving a great deal of trial and error. To make the Visual C++ developer's job easier, the Dialog editor has been provided to allow drag and drop creation of dialog templates. It provides for WYSIWYG, or what you see is what you get editing of the template, along with property sheets for setting the general properties, such as dialog box size and the font to be used, as well as all of the associated styles, such as border type.

The Dialog editor is displayed when a Visual C++ workspace is in Resource View, and a dialog template has been selected. Figure 4-1 shows the Visual C++ IDE when the dialog template with the ID of IDD_DIALOGTEST_DIALOG has been selected in the Resource View. You can see the WYSIWYG view of the dialog template in the rightmost pane, and to the right of that is the Controls toolbar. At the bottom of the IDE you can see the Dialog toolbar. Remember that many windows and toolbars in the Visual C++ IDE can be moved around, docked or undocked, hidden or displayed, and that your own setup may appear different from the figure. Note that toolbars are selected and cleared from the Toolbars tab of the Tools | Customize property sheet.

The Controls toolbar provides a selection of controls that may be dragged onto the dialog template. Simply click a control, such as a button, and drag it onto the template. The control will initially appear with a default size and

---

FIGURE 4-1   The Visual C++ IDE showing the Dialog editor, the Controls toolbar, and the Dialog toolbar

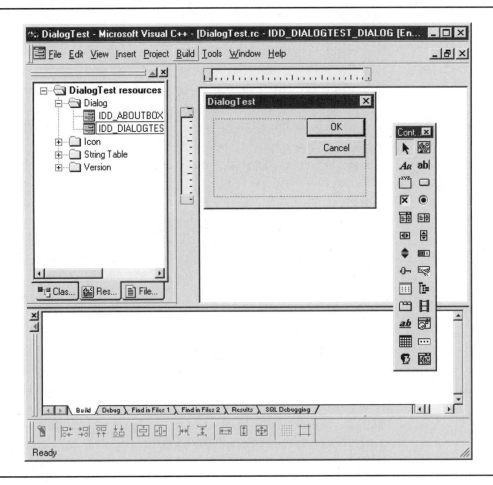

with a number of default properties; you can then resize the control and set its properties. Alternatively, you can select a control from the Controls toolbar by a single click and then place and size it in a single step. Click the dialog template where one corner of the control will appear and then while holding down the mouse button, drag the mouse to where the diagonally opposite corner of the control is to be positioned. By default, the Controls toolbar provides the set of controls shown in Table 4-1.

TABLE 4-1 Controls Provided by the Controls Toolbar

Control	Function
Picture	May contain various types of images including bitmaps and icons
Static text	Places read-only text as a label
Edit box	Input field for alphanumeric text
Group box	Provides a heading and grouped outline to contain other controls
Button	Standard pushbutton-type control
Check box	Allows on and off selection
Option button	Option buttons, also called radio buttons, are buttons that are usually grouped together; when one button is selected, the others in the group are cleared.
Combo box	A combination of a list box and an edit box
List box	Provides for selection of one or more items in a list
Horizontal scroll bar	A narrow bar with a button at each end and a 'thumb' or slider in between for manual scrolling of an associated window
Vertical scroll bar	A vertical version of the horizontal scroll bar
Spin	A pair of up and down arrow buttons; usually used to increment or decrement values in an associated control
Progress indicator	A control used to provide feedback of progress over time
Slider	Similar to slider-type controls found on electronic equipment
Hot key	Used for enabling user-configured hot key functionality in an application
List control	Similar to the rightmost pane of Windows Explorer; allows for different views of information including multiple columns
Tree control	Similar to the leftmost pane of Windows Explorer; presents information in an hierarchical format

TABLE 4-1 Controls Provided by the Controls Toolbar *(continued)*

Control	Function
Tab control	Provides a row of tabs for selection between multiple forms
Animate	Houses Audio-Video Interleaved (AVI) files to display animations without audio
Rich Edit	Enables the display and editing of Rich Text Format (RTF) text
Date Time Picker	Used to allow user input of dates and times
Month Calendar	Calendar control
IP address	Allows user input of Internet Protocol (IP) addresses in dotted decimal notation
Custom control	Allows the use of custom-built controls; it is now recommended to use ActiveX controls instead
Extended Combo box	Combo box control with support for image lists
Additional ActiveX Controls	As ActiveX controls are added to a project, the Controls toolbar will be extended with icons for the additional controls. As covered in a previous chapter, you can add an ActiveX control to a project by right-clicking a dialog template and selecting Insert ActiveX Control... from the context menu.

The Dialog toolbar, which defaults to being displayed at the bottom of the IDE when a dialog template is being edited, provides some very useful functionality for testing your dialog box and for sizing and positioning your controls. There is a Test tool that displays a test version of the dialog box just as it will appear when it is used in your application. The tools for alignment and resizing of controls work on a group of controls; press the SHIFT key and progressively click each control—the last control selected becomes the *Dominant control* and the other controls selected will be resized or aligned to that control's size or position.

Creating Dialog Box Classes and Members Using ClassWizard

Once you have created a dialog template you must create an appropriate C++ class and associate the template with the class before it can be used in your application. In this section we will cover how to use ClassWizard to perform these steps.

Associating the Dialog Template with a C++ Class

A dialog template is purely a resource template; in order for it to be used in your application, it must be associated with, or bound to, a C++ class. ClassWizard manages the creation of these classes and allows you to select the appropriate MFC class to use as a base class.

e x a m
ⓦatch

Be sure that you understand the distinction between dialog templates and the C++ classes that they are associated with. A dialog template purely describes how the dialog box will look, how controls will be laid out on the dialog box, and so on, whereas a C++ class provides the actual code that gives the dialog box functionality to be displayed, respond to messages, validate user input, and the like.

ClassWizard can be used to create new classes that are derived from a wide selection of base classes. Many of these base classes, for example *CAsyncSocket*, are not designed for creating user input forms and cannot be associated with dialog templates; those that can are *CDialog*, *CFormView*, *CPropertyPage*, and *CRecordView*.

When creating dialog boxes, you will derive your classes from CDialog, which is the MFC-provided base class for dialog boxes. When you create a new class using ClassWizard you need to specify a class name; when you type a class name ClassWizard will autogenerate a filename for the C++ class—you should generally accept this name although you may override it. ClassWizard also provides some options for *Automation*, which is the facility for exposing control of the dialog box to external applications; automation is beyond the scope of this chapter.

EXERCISE 4-1

Associating a New Class with a Dialog Template

1. Create a dialog template as described previously.

2. In the rightmost pane of Resource View, right-click the dialog template and select ClassWizard.

3. For a new template, a message box will appear titled Adding a class; select Create a new class and press OK. A dialog box will be displayed similar to Figure 4-2.

FIGURE 4-2

Options for creating a new
class associated with a
dialog template

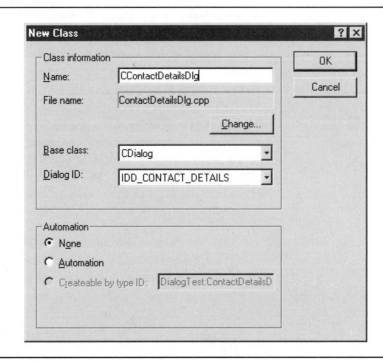

4. Assign a meaningful name to the class, for example,
   CContactDetailsDlg, and select a base class from the list. Dialog
   templates are usually associated with classes derived from CDialog,
   CPropertySheet, or CFormView.

*It has become customary for C++ programmers to name classes using
a capital C as the first letter. If you follow conventions such as these,
your code will be much easier for other people to comprehend and
maintain.*

5. Click OK on the main ClassWizard form.

Using a Dialog Class in an Application

A dialog box can be displayed in one of two ways, either *modal* or *modeless*.
If a dialog box is modal, it must be responded to and dismissed before the
user can interact with any other part of the application. Modeless dialog
boxes, on the other hand, do not cause the rest of the application to be

disabled, and any number of modeless dialog boxes may be displayed by an application at the same time.

For an example of a modal dialog box, take a look at the Options property sheet for Microsoft Visual C++, found under Tools | Options. While this property sheet is being displayed, the rest of the Visual C++ IDE user interface is disabled; you cannot perform any mouse or keyboard interaction with it until you have dismissed the Options property sheet. The Options property sheet is shown in Figure 4-3.

The floating toolbars in Visual C++ are an example of modeless windows; more than one of them can be present at any one time, and they do not cause the application to be disabled while they are displayed. Figure 4-4 shows the Visual C++ IDE with several floating toolbars.

The life cycles of modal and modeless dialog boxes are slightly different. To create and display a modal dialog box, you should perform the following steps:

1. Construct an instance of the dialog box class in your code, for instance:

```
CMyModalDlg  dlgModal;
```

FIGURE 4-3

The Visual C++ Options property sheet as an example of a modal dialog box

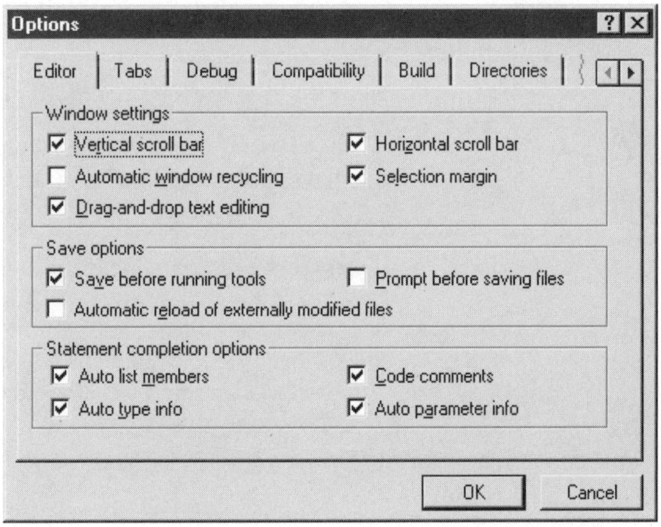

FIGURE 4-4

Floating toolbars
are an example of
modeless windows

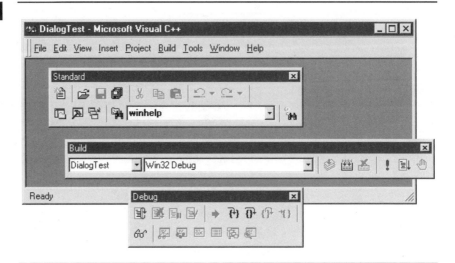

2. Call CDialog::DoModal( ). This will not return until the dialog box
   is dismissed, when it will return the code passed to EndDialog( ).
   The default implementation of CDialog::OnOK( ) actually calls
   EndDialog( ) automatically, passing in a value of IDOK, and
   similarly for OnCancel (which passes a value of IDCANCEL). So,
   unless you add other buttons you do not have to add any additional
   code to the dialog class for EndDialog( ) to be called:

```
int iResult;
iResult = dlgModal.DoModal();
```

3. When a button on the dialog box, such as the OK button, is pressed,
   the dialog box should call EndDialog( ), and pass the ID of the
   button as a parameter.

4. Interpret the return value from DoModal( ) to determine which
   button was pressed to dismiss the dialog box:

```
if (iResult == IDOK) {
    // OK button was pressed
  // Process the dialog's data
}
else {
    // Dialog was canceled
    // Ignore the data
}
```

5. Processing the data collected by the dialog box will be covered in the section on DDX, the dialog data exchange.

To create, display, and dismiss a modeless dialog box, you should perform the following steps:

1. Make sure your dialog class exposes a public constructor which includes a call to the CDialog::Create( ) method, passing in the ID of the associated dialog template. As an example:

```
CMyModelessDlg::CMyModelessDlg(CWnd* pParent /*=NULL*/)
  : CDialog(CMyModelessDlg::IDD, pParent)
{
  //{{AFX_DATA_INIT(CModelessDlg)
    // NOTE: the ClassWizard will add member initialization here
  //}}AFX_DATA_INIT
  Create(IDD_DIALOG1); /* Add this line to the ClassWizard-generated constructor
*/
}
```

2. Instantiate your dialog object, and if the Visible style was not set on the dialog template include a call to ShowWindow( ):

```
CMyModelessDlg*  pDlgModeless;
pDlgModeless = new CMyModelessDlg; // Constructor should call Create()
pDlgModeless->ShowWindow(SW_SHOW); // Make visible
```

3. Add methods to handle events from controls on the dialog box. A common control on a modeless dialog box would be an Apply button; the button needs to perform some kind of action but the dialog box should remain visible. To implement this you would add a button to the dialog template, say with an ID of IDC_APPLY, and then use ClassWizard to implement a message map for the BN_CLICKED event to be mapped to a new member function:

```
void CModelessDlg::OnApply()
{
  // TODO: Add your control notification handler code here
  UpdateData(); /* this will read the contents of controls into mapped variables—see
the section on DDX */
  /* At this point you may wish to make calls back to the parent window object to
save the data */
}
```

4. Ensure that when the dialog box is no longer required, the object is deleted. Believe it or not, the recommended method is for a modeless dialog object to delete itself; override the *PostNcDestroy( )* method and call *delete this* from within it. You should also ensure that *OnOK( )* and *OnCancel( )* are overridden to call *DestroyWindow( )* otherwise the dialog object will disappear but persist in memory if the user presses ENTER or ESC.

Property Sheets Using ClassWizard

A property sheet is a tabbed dialog box, which is really a collection of dialog boxes laid over the top of each other with each one being selectable by a tab. For an example of a property sheet, take a look at ClassWizard itself.

You implement a property sheet by creating a number of objects. One object is instantiated from a class derived from CPropertySheet; this class is not associated with any dialog template. Then for each dialog box that is to be included in the property sheet, a class should be derived from CPropertyPage, and an object of that class added to the property sheet. You will find some of the steps in creating a property sheet are similar to those involved in creating a dialog box:

1. In Resource View, insert one new dialog box for each page required in the property sheet.

2. Edit each of the dialog templates using Dialog editor. Note that each page of the property sheet does not have to be the same size; the property sheet will size itself to accommodate the largest dialog template it contains. It is also important that you set certain styles for the dialog templates, as described in the following table:

Caption	Set to the text that is to appear on the tab for that page
Style	Set to Child
Border	Set to Thin
Title bar	Should be selected
Disabled	Should be selected

3. For each dialog template that you have created, right-click the template and select ClassWizard and then create a new class with a base class of CPropertyPage to be associated with that particular dialog template.

4. Use ClassWizard to create a new class derived from CPropertySheet; this class will not be associated with any dialog templates.

5. Construct a property sheet object in your code, for example:

```
CMyPropertySheet*  pPropSheet;
pPropSheet = new CMyPropertySheet;
```

6. Construct objects for each of the property pages, for example:

```
CMyAddressDetailsPage  pageAddrDetails;
CMyBillingDetailsPage  pageBillingDetails;
CMyFinalPage  pageFinal;
```

7. Add each of the property page objects to the property sheet:

```
pPropSheet->AddPage(&pageAddrDetails);
pPropSheet->AddPage(&pageBillingDetails);
pPropSheet->AddPage(&pageFinal);
```

8. The property sheet can now be displayed; either call DoModal( ) to display it as a modal property sheet, or Create( ) to display it as a modeless property sheet.

9. Data is exchanged and validated using the normal DDX and dialog data validation (DDV) mechanisms as described elsewhere in this chapter; just treat each property page object in the same way as you would one of a CDialog-derived class.

Using the CFormView Class

Sometimes when you are developing a desktop application in Visual C++, you may want to allow for user input through a form that adheres to the document/view architecture rather than through a dialog box. The CFormView class provides the functionality for associating a dialog template with a view class, and allows you to produce an application that combines dialog-style user input with standard application user interface elements such as menus, toolbars, and status bars. An example of an application which employs a CFormView-derived class is shown in Figure 4-5.

FIGURE 4-5

A simple example using a
CFormView-derived class

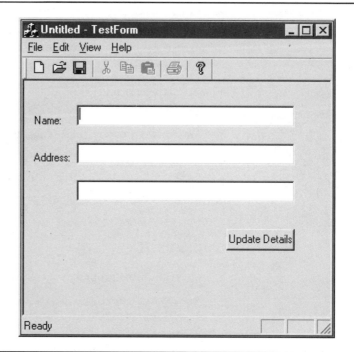

The MFC document/view architecture was covered in Chapter 2. The CFormView base class takes advantage of this architecture and extends CView to provide dialog-style functionality within either single-document interface (SDI) or multiple-document interface (MDI) applications.

There are a few major differences between implementing a form view and implementing a dialog box; the most obvious ones being that form views cannot be modal, and the code to create and display a form view is very different from that used to create and display a dialog box. Objects of the types derived from CdocTemplate, CSingleDocTemplate for SDI applications, and CMultiDocTemplate for MDI applications are used to manage the relationships between documents, views, and frame windows. It is through the use of these objects and the document/view architecture framework that form views are created and displayed at runtime.

Using the CFormView Class

1. Create a single-document interface (or multiple-document interface) application using the MFC AppWizard. You may not wish to include MFC support for the Print and Print preview commands, unless you are willing to write custom printing code. MFC does not provide functionality for printing CFormView views.

2. Create a new dialog template using the Dialog editor. It is *essential* that the following properties are set for the dialog template:

Style	Child
Border	None
Visible	False

3. Right-click the dialog template, select ClassWizard, and select Create a new class.

4. In the Base class list box, select CFormView and assign the class a meaningful name.

5. Use the class within the application. The most straightforward way to do this in an SDI application is to modify the InitInstance( ) method of the application class. This method constructs a new CSingleDocTemplate object; modify the third parameter to your new CFormView-derived class name. Remember that in an MDI application you will be dealing with one or more CMultiDocTemplate objects. The following example demonstrates this for an SDI application:

```
#include "DetailsForm.h"  // Don't forget this!
...
CSingleDocTemplate* pDocTemplate;
pDocTemplate = new CSingleDocTemplate(
  IDR_MAINFRAME,
  RUNTIME_CLASS(CTestFormDoc),
  RUNTIME_CLASS(CMainFrame),
  RUNTIME_CLASS(CDetailsForm)); // This is the new view class
```

6. Build and run the application.

CERTIFICATION OBJECTIVE 4.02

Validating User Input

Visual C++ desktop applications, and any applications that allow some form of user input, must provide some form of validation of the data. Visual C++ provides a mechanism known as *dialog data validation*, or *DDV*, which is configured through the ClassWizard.

DDV

DDV, or *dialog data validation*, provides some fairly basic validation for controls that are mapped to either CString or various numeric variable types. The validation works slightly differently for CString members than it does for the numeric types.

When a control, such as an edit box, is mapped to a CString variable and that variable is selected in the list on the Member variables tab of ClassWizard, an edit box labeled *Maximum characters* will be displayed. If an integer value is typed in this field, DDV will be applied to the control. The control will limit the number of characters that may be typed into it; this applies as the user is typing, and the user will be unable to exceed the maximum number of characters.

When a control, such as an edit box, is mapped to a numeric type, such as int, and that variable is selected in the list on the Member variables tab of ClassWizard, two edit boxes will be displayed: one labeled Minimum value, and the other labeled Maximum value. If values are typed in these fields, DDV will be applied to the control. However, in this case the validation is not performed as a user is typing, but when the UpdateData( ) member of the dialog class is called. This is most commonly called when a user has completed all data input to a dialog box and a button such as OK has been clicked. If UpdateData( ) returns TRUE, the data has been validated correctly and it is safe to dismiss the dialog box. However, if a value has been entered in a control which is below the minimum or exceeds the maximum, a message box will be displayed and focus will be set to the offending control prior to UpdateData( ) returning FALSE. In this case, it is not safe to dismiss the dialog box.

ClassWizard creates DDV mappings within the source code of your dialog class. When you make changes to the DDV configuration in ClassWizard these mappings are maintained within your source code; you should *never* make changes to ClassWizard mappings directly in the code. An example of a ClassWizard data map that validates an edit box to a number between 10 and 250 and another edit box to a string of maximum five characters looks like this:

```
void CDDVDlg::DoDataExchange(CDataExchange* pDX)
{
  CDialog::DoDataExchange(pDX);
  //{{AFX_DATA_MAP(CDDVDlg)
  DDX_Text(pDX, IDC_EDIT_NUMERIC, m_iNumeric);
  DDV_MinMaxInt(pDX, m_iNumeric, 10, 250);
  DDX_Text(pDX, IDC_EDIT_STRING, m_sString);
  DDV_MaxChars(pDX, m_sString, 5);
  //}}AFX_DATA_MAP
}
```

It should also be noted that the implementation of CDialog::OnOK( ) calls UpdateData( ); therefore, if your dialog class makes use of the base class implementation of OnOK( ), it is not necessary to make any additional calls to take advantage of DDV. The implementation of CDialog::OnOK( ) looks similar to this (with some additional debugging code):

```
void CDialog::OnOK()
{
    if (!UpdateData(TRUE))
    {
        return;
    }
    EndDialog(IDOK);
}
```

Adding Numeric and String DDV to a Dialog

In this exercise you will:

- Create a dialog template using the Dialog editor
- Create member variables associated with controls on the dialog box using ClassWizard
- Validate both string and numeric input using DDV

Creating a Dialog Template Using the Dialog Editor

1. In the Visual C++ IDE, select File | New, and select MFC AppWizard (exe) from the Projects tab to invoke the MFC AppWizard.

2. Enter **DDV** as the project name, and click OK.

3. Select Dialog based as the application type, and click Next.

4. Clear the About box option, and click Next.

5. Click Finished, and the new project files will be created.

6. Select the Resource View, and select the dialog ID, IDD_DDV_DIALOG.

7. Resize the dialog template as desired, and add an edit box control. Right-click the edit box control, select Properties, and change the control ID to **IDC_EDIT_NUMERIC**, as shown in Figure 4-6.

8. Add a second edit box and change its control ID to **IDC_EDIT_STRING**.

FIGURE 4-6

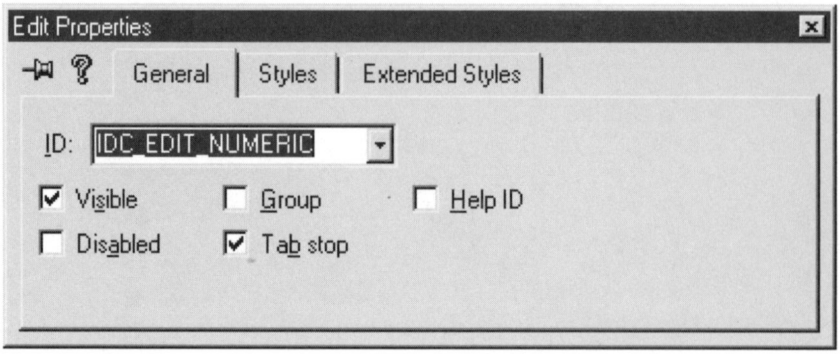

Modifying the control ID from the General tab of the control properties

9. Resize the edit box controls as desired, and add some static text controls. Your dialog template should now look something like the one shown in Figure 4-7.

Creating Member Variables Using ClassWizard

10. Right-click the dialog template, and select ClassWizard.

11. Because the dialog box was already created by the AppWizard, the class CDDVDlg should appear in the Class name field on the Message maps tab of the ClassWizard.

12. Select the Member variables tab; you should see a list of controls: IDC_EDIT_NUMERIC, IDC_EDIT_STRING, IDCANCEL, IDOK.

13. Double-click IDC_EDIT_NUMERIC; the Add member variable dialog box will appear.

14. Type **m_iNumeric** for the Member variable name, select *Value* for the Category and *int* for the Variable type, and press OK.

15. Double-click IDC_EDIT_STRING; the Add member variable dialog box will appear.

16. Type **m_sString** for the Member variable name, select *Value* for the Category and *CString* for the Variable type, and press OK.

FIGURE 4-7

Use the Dialog editor to create this dialog template

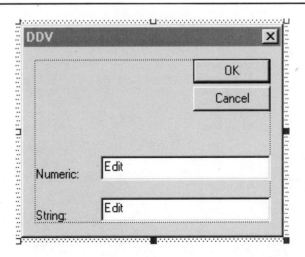

Validating String and Numeric Input Using DDV

17. Select IDC_EDIT_NUMERIC; the DDV parameter fields will appear at the bottom of the ClassWizard. Enter a Minimum value and Maximum value as per Figure 4-8.

18. Select IDC_EDIT_STRING; the DDV parameter fields will appear at the bottom of the ClassWizard. Enter **5** for the Maximum characters.

19. Press OK to dismiss the ClassWizard dialog box.

20. Build and run the application.

21. Observe that you cannot type more than five characters in the string edit box, and that upon pressing OK the numeric edit box is validated for minimum and maximum values.

FIGURE 4-8   Set the DDV parameters using the ClassWizard

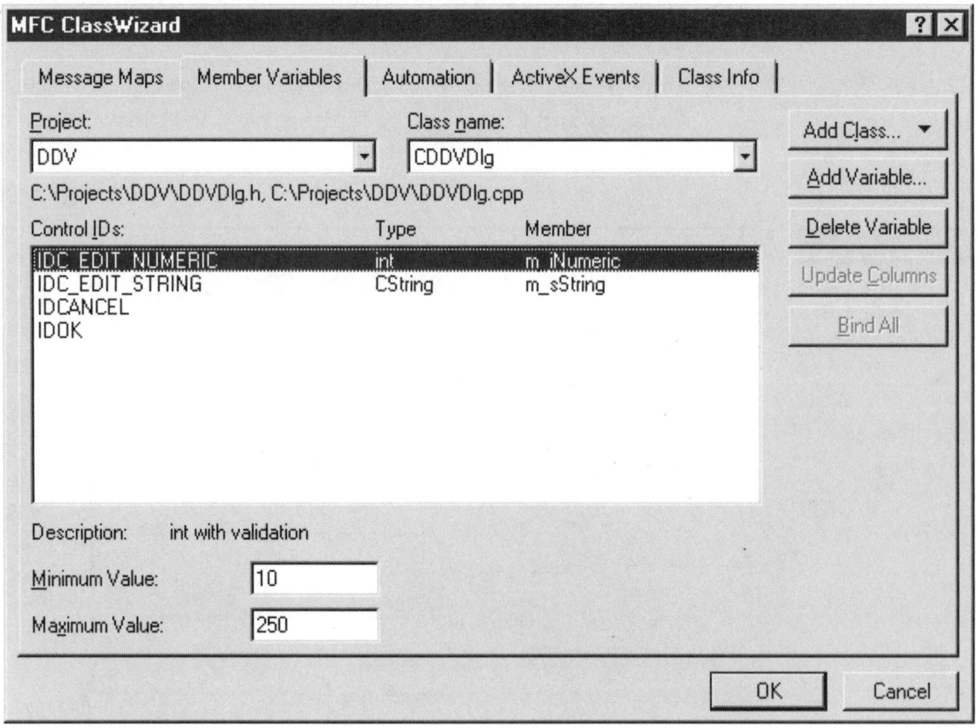

CERTIFICATION OBJECTIVE 4.03

Process User Input Using Dialog Data Exchange (DDX)

MFC provides a very useful method of both initializing data and processing user input on dialog boxes; it is known as dialog data exchange, or DDX. This is a mechanism that maps member variables to controls on dialog boxes. For example, I may map an edit box on my dialog box to a CString variable in my code. I want the initial value of the variable to contain the text *Not Applicable* so I set my variable to contain that text, and DDX transfers it to the edit box control when the dialog box is initialized. Then when the dialog box is dismissed, the new text typed by the user is transferred back to my variable and I can access it from code elsewhere in the application.

The mappings between controls and variables are created and maintained by ClassWizard.

EXERCISE 4-4

Mapping an Edit Box to a CString Variable

The following steps are involved in mapping an edit box to a CString variable:

1. As described previously, create an MFC application containing a dialog template and a class derived from CDialog that is associated with the dialog template.

2. Ensure that the dialog template contains an edit box, with an ID such as IDC_EDIT_DDX.

3. Right-click the dialog template and select ClassWizard; you should be viewing the properties of your existing dialog class. Figure 4-9 shows the ClassWizard Member variables tab.

4. Double-click the Control ID for the edit box. You should see the Add member variable dialog box. Add a meaningful variable name and select the CString type, as shown in Figure 4-10.

FIGURE 4-9 Use the ClassWizard Member variables tab to view the properties of your existing dialog class

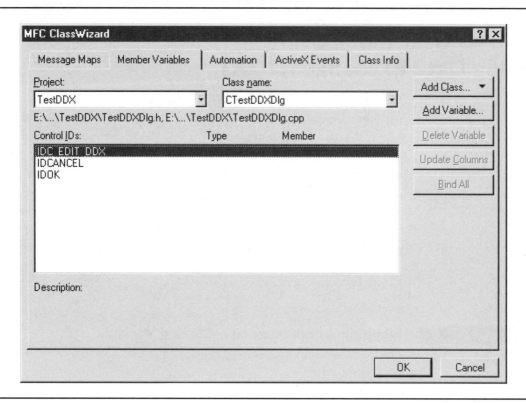

5. Click OK on the Add member variable dialog box, and click OK to dismiss ClassWizard.

6. The actual DDX exchange of data is initiated by the CDialog::UpdateData( ) method; calling UpdateData(FALSE) causes data to be transferred from member variables to controls, whereas calling UpdateData(TRUE) causes data to be transferred from controls to member variables and performs any DDV validation. Note that if no parameter is passed to UpdateData( ), it will default to TRUE.

FIGURE 4-10

Adding a member variable
using ClassWizard

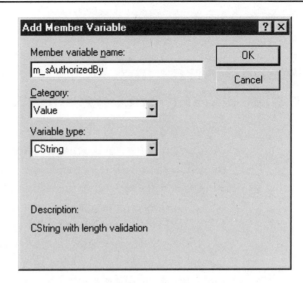

7. Edit the OnInitDialog( ) method of your dialog class to set the member variable to a default value:

```
BOOL CTestDDXDlg::OnInitDialog()
{
    m_sAuthorizedBy = "Not Applicable";
    CDialog::OnInitDialog();   /* This will call UpdateData() */

...

    return TRUE;
}
```

8. Create and display a dialog object. Once the dialog box has been dismissed, read the value from the member variable before the object has been destroyed:

```
CTestDDXDlg  dlg;
int iRes;
CString sQuant;
iRes = dlg.DoModal();
if (iRes == IDOK) {
    sAuth = dlg.m_sAuthorizedBy;
}
else {
    // Dialog was canceled
    sAuth = "Not Applicable"// Set a default value
}
```

Storing and Retrieving Personalized User Settings from the Registry

Often it is desirable to store application settings on a per-user basis; when a particular user logs onto a machine and runs an application, they will find the settings restored to the same state as when they last used the application. This is achieved by storing the settings in the HKEY_CURRENT_USER hive of the Registry, usually as values under the key HKEY_CURRENT_USER\Software*CompanyName**ApplicationName**SectionName*\.

MFC provides a very simple mechanism for reading and writing personalized user settings to and from the registry; several member functions of the CWinApp class are provided to do just that. The steps to achieving this are as follows:

1. Create your MFC application using the MFC AppWizard.

2. Your application will contain a class derived from CWinApp, for example CMyProgramApp. In the InitInstance( ) member of this class, there will be an AppWizard-generated line of code that calls SetRegistryKey( ) and passes in some default text. Modify this line to set the name of your company:

```
SetRegistryKey(_T("ACME Software Company"));
```

3. Integer values can be read from the registry using CWinApp::GetProfileInt( ), and string values can be read from the registry using CWinApp::GetProfileString( ). The following code could be placed in the InitInstance( ) method of your CWinApp-derived application class, after the call to SetRegistryKey( ): The following code could be applied when a user selected some new settings, such as in the handler for an Apply button on a property sheet:

```
// Restore the user's settings from the registry
int nHeight;
CString sMessage
nHeight = pMyApp->GetPRofileInt("Window Settings", "Height", 500); /* 500 is a
default */
sMessage = pMyApp->GetPRofileString(("Window Settings", "Startup Message", "Hi");
/* "Hi" is a default */
```

Integer values can be written to the registry using CWinApp::WriteProfileInt( ), and string values can be written to the registry using CWinApp:: WriteProfileString( ). The following code could be applied when a user selected some new settings, such as in the handler for an Apply button on a property sheet:

```
int nHeight;
CString sMessage
...
// User selects a value of 600 for window height,
// and "Good Morning" for startup message
// Store these settings in the registry
pMyApp->WriteProfileInt("Window Settings", "Height", nHeight);
pMyApp->WriteProfileString("Window Settings", "Startup Message", sMessage);
```

CERTIFICATION OBJECTIVE 4.05

Implementing Online User Assistance in an Application

In developing desktop applications, you will generally want to provide one or more forms of user assistance; Visual C++ provides several mechanisms for you to do this. Status bars can be used to provide feedback to users, tool-tips can be employed to pop up a concise piece of text explaining the function of a tool (a control or child window), and full-blown help systems can be provided that use either WinHelp or Hypertext Markup Language (HTML) Help. It is also possible to link from a WinHelp help system to a Web site that contains help files.

Status Bars

As covered in Chapter 3, status bars comprise a set of panes, each of which may display certain text that may be updated at any time. An example of a status bar giving dynamic feedback to a user is shown in Figure 4-11; Internet Explorer provides useful information in its status bar.

In order to change the text in a pane of a status bar, you use the SetText( ) method, passing in the text to be displayed, the integer index of the pane to display it in, and a type. An example is:

```
myStatusBar.SetText("You may click Finish at any time", 0, SBT_NOBORDERS);
```

FIGURE 4-11   You can create status bars that provide dynamic feedback for user assistance

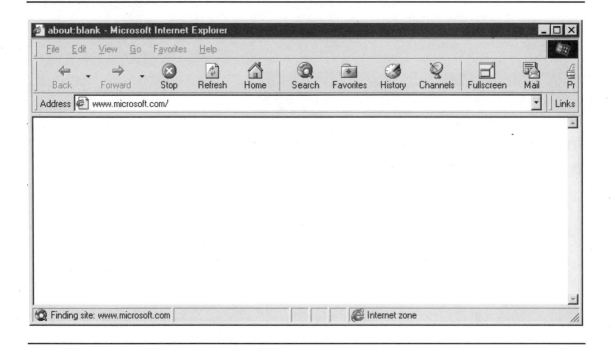

The following types are valid for the third parameter:

0	The text is drawn with a sunken look.
SBT_NOBORDERS	The text is drawn without borders.
SBT_OWNERDRAW	The text is drawn by the parent window.
SBT_POPOUT	The text is drawn with a raised look.

ToolTips

ToolTips are small boxes containing help text specific to a control or child window. As the mouse cursor pauses over the tool the ToolTip is displayed, giving the user potentially valuable information about the usage of the tool. As buttons with only icons and without any textual description have become more popular, ToolTips have become an essential device for a user to learn how to use an application.

In Chapter 3 you saw how support for ToolTips is included with MFC toolbar buttons. However, it is also possible to provide ToolTips for any other tools in your application. This is achieved by following these steps:

1. Construct an instance of a CToolTipCtrl object and call Create( ), passing the parent window as a parameter:

```
CToolTipCtrl*  pMyToolTipCtrl;
pMyToolTipCtrl->Create(pMyDialog);
```

2. Call AddTool( ) to register a tool with the ToolTip control, so that the information stored in the ToolTip is displayed when the cursor is on the tool:

```
pMyToolTipCtrl->AddTool(pMyControl, "This is my control!");
```

Context-Sensitive Help

Context-sensitive help comprises a set of hyperlinked help topics. Many of these topics can relate to a certain *context* within an application; the context may be the top level of the application itself, the dialog box that the user is currently working with, or maybe a particular control. The context-sensitivity comes into play when the help for the particular part of the application that the user is currently working with is displayed.

There are several ways for the user to access help from within your application:

- F1 **Help** The user can press the F1 key from an active window, dialog box, or message box, or with a menu item or toolbar button selected. This will invoke the appropriate Help topic relevant to the selected item. For menu items, help is summoned for the item currently highlighted.

- SHIFT-F1 **Help or Help mode** Help mode can be activated by pressing SHIFT-F1, or clicking the Help toolbar button. In Help mode, the mouse cursor changes to an arrow with a question mark and the user can click any window, dialog box, message box, menu item, or toolbar button to activate specific help for that item. Help mode ends when either ESC is pressed, Help is displayed, or the user switches to another application and back again.

- **Using the Help menu** By selecting a Help menu item, the user can activate the application's Help file. Figure 4-12 shows the result of selecting the Help topics menu item in an MFC application.

When you use the MFC AppWizard to create either an SDI or MDI application, you will be given the opportunity to add context-sensitive help. In Step 4 of the AppWizard, select the check box labeled Context-sensitive Help. When you enable this option, the AppWizard adds the following features to your application:

- The main menu now includes a Help menu with several commands. Note that for an MDI application there will be multiple copies of this menu: one for an application with no documents open, and one for each type of document that uses its own menu structure.

- Your CFrameWnd-derived class will contain several additional message-map entries which bind the F1 and SHIFT-F1 commands to their respective command handlers. These are created by AppWizard

FIGURE 4-12

You can create
context-sensitive Help in
MFC applications

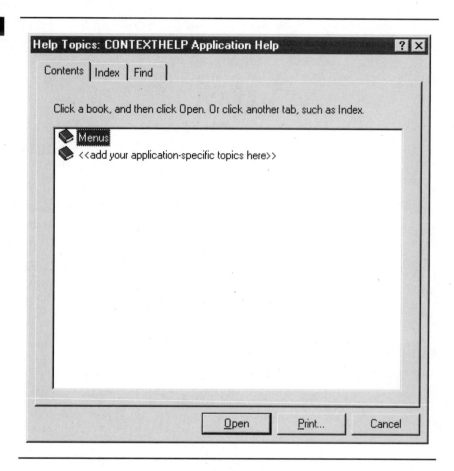

and should not be modified. In a simple SDI application these look
as follows:

```
BEGIN_MESSAGE_MAP(CMainFrame, CFrameWnd)
  //{{AFX_MSG_MAP(CMainFrame)
  // NOTE-the ClassWizard will add and remove mapping macros here.
  //    Do not edit what you see in these blocks of generated code !
  ON_WM_CREATE()
  //}}AFX_MSG_MAP
  // Global help commands
  ON_COMMAND(ID_HELP_FINDER, CFrameWnd::OnHelpFinder)
  ON_COMMAND(ID_HELP, CFrameWnd::OnHelp)
  ON_COMMAND(ID_CONTEXT_HELP, CFrameWnd::OnContextHelp)
  ON_COMMAND(ID_DEFAULT_HELP, CFrameWnd::OnHelpFinder)
END_MESSAGE_MAP()
```

■ The base class CWinApp provides the WinHelp( ) method, which is responsible for invoking the Windows Help program, WINHELP.EXE.

■ AppWizard also adds several skeleton .RTF files that contain Help entries for the common elements of the Windows user interface, such as the File and Edit menus. You can edit these files to revise the supplied text and add your own application-specific Help information. RTF files must be edited by an application that can edit the Rich Text Format; Microsoft Word is such an application.

■ A mechanism and tool for mapping resource and command IDs in your application to *Help contexts* in Windows Help. When you build your application, a tool called MakeHm is run to perform this mapping.

■ An .HPJ file is created by AppWizard, which serves as a Help project. This file will need to be recompiled whenever you add new Help topics to your application.

Linking to a Web Page Containing Help Files

The emerging method of providing Help is HTML Help, which uses Internet Explorer functionality to display the Help. HTML Help applications are compiled into a .CHM file. It is possible to link from a WinHelp topic to an HTML Help topic, and it is also possible for the WinHelp topic to link to a .CHM file located on a Web site. To do this, you add a call to the !execfile WinHelp macro to the link in the appropriate WinHelp topic:

```
!execfile(hh.exe, ms-its:http://www.mysite.com/MyHelpFile.chm::/MyTopic.htm)
```

CERTIFICATION OBJECTIVE 4.06

Error Handling

No matter how much a programmer may believe otherwise, error conditions are to be expected in the use of any desktop application, and the usefulness of an application will depend to a certain extent on how errors are handled. There are a couple of methods of both raising and handling errors in a Visual C++ application; the most common methods are function return values and C++ exceptions.

Exception Handling

Exceptions are error condition objects which are *thrown* by a function when an error condition is encountered. They are then passed progressively back up the call stack until they are *caught* by some code that then handles the error, or else the application will abort.

MFC provides two versions of exception handling: the MFC exception macros, which are provided for backward-compatibility, and C++ exceptions, which are now the recommended mechanism. For the exam, you should understand the C++ exception mechanism.

The base class for all MFC exceptions is CException; a number of other exception classes are derived from this, including CMemoryException, COleException, and CInternetException. All of these classes include the following two methods:

GetErrorMessage( )	Retrieves the message describing an exception. This method takes as minimum parameters a string buffer pointer and the size of the buffer.
ReportError( )	Reports an error message in a message box to the user; does not require any parameters.

The steps for handling exceptions are as follows:

■ Any code that makes calls that may throw exceptions should be wrapped in a *try* block. As an example, the MFC file class CFile constructor throws exceptions of type CFileException when error conditions are encountered:

```
CFile* pMyFile;
try
{
    pMyFile = new CFile("C:\\Nonexistant File.txt", CFile::modeRead);
    // This will throw an exception if the file does not exist
}
```

- Follow the try block with one or more catch blocks for the appropriate exception types, or for CException to catch all exceptions. The following code will display the message box as shown in Figure 4-13:

```
catch(CException* e)
{
    e->ReportError(); // Displays a message box
 e->Delete(); // Delete the exception when we've done with it
}
```

- If you wish to handle different kinds of exceptions selectively, use multiple catch blocks. Control will be passed to the first catch block that matches the type of the exception.

```
catch(CFileException* fileException)
{
    // Handle a file exception
    fileException->Delete();
}
catch(CDaoException* daoException)
{
    // Handle a DAO exception
    daoException->Delete();
}
catch(CException* e)
{
    // 'Default' catch for all other exceptions
    e->Delete();
}
```

exam
ⓦatch

Make sure you are confident with multiple catch blocks for the exam. You should understand that a catch block will catch any exceptions of the specified type, or of any type derived from that class. So catching exceptions of type CFileException will catch any exception class derived from CFileException, and catching exceptions of type CException will catch all exceptions, as CException is at the top of the exception class hierarchy.

■ Handle the exception appropriately. In this example, you would consider prompting the user for a new filename to load, or ask the user if they would like to create the file.

Appropriate Deletion of Exception Objects

It is always safer to use the Delete( ) member of the CException class and its derived classes rather than the C++ *delete* statement, as the exception object may not always have been created using *new* and so may not be on the heap—in this case the *delete* would fail. Also note that if your *catch* block re-throws the same exception object, you should not delete that object; it should be deleted by the *catch* block that catches it further up the chain.

Determining How to Handle an Error

Whether errors have been thrown and caught as exceptions or passed back to the caller as return values, they need to be handled in a fashion appropriate to the situation. There is no point in detecting that an error has occurred in the opening of a file, only to go on and attempt to write to a file. Likewise, your application's users will not be very impressed if the application aborts due to a trivial and noncritical error.

It is impossible to speculate about all of the different error scenarios that may arise in the applications you will build; however, there are some basic rules to keep in mind:

■ Determine which error conditions users should be notified about.

■ Ensure the application cannot get into an inconsistent state.

■ Fatal errors, or errors from which you cannot recover, should cause the program to abort gracefully. A message box should be displayed to inform users, and if possible any data should be saved prior to exit.

These rules on error handling are illustrated by some scenarios.

QUESTIONS AND ANSWERS

A user wishes to save a file to a pre-existing filename.	Inform the user that the file exists and prompt them as to whether they wish to overwrite the file.
A CFile object throws an exception during construction.	Ensure that the program cannot go on to attempt to use that object.
A fatal CMemoryException exception occurs.	Inform the user of the reason that the application must terminate and attempt to save data before exiting.

FROM THE CLASSROOM

Exploring Exception Handling Strategy

With all of the time and effort you put into programming software's desired functionality, it is hard to swallow the fact that about 30 percent of your final code will exist to handle undesired functionality, or error conditions. Considering the large portion of code involved, the need for a planned approach to error handling is evident. There are several factors to consider when constructing your error handling/recovery strategy.

Since exceptions do not have to be handled by the function in which they originate, one factor is simply deciding where the exception will be handled. When an exception is thrown, the call stack is searched for the first handler with an argument that matches the type of the

exception. Let's walk through the steps that occur when a block of code within a try block executes, so we can understand the stack unwinding process better.

The try block is entered as a part of the normal flow of execution in the application. Many functions can be called within a try block, and these functions may throw the same or different types of exceptions. However, only one exception at a time can be handled. If every function within the try block executes normally, the program will skip over the catch block(s) following the try block, and continue executing.

If one of the function calls within the try block throws an exception, the exception will

FROM THE CLASSROOM

then search through the call stack for a catch block that can handle it. First, the catch blocks following the try block will be searched, in order, for one with an argument that matches the type of exception thrown. If no match is found, the exception will be thrown to the try block encompassing the try block where the error occurred. That try block will then search through its catch blocks for a suitable handler, and if a match is not found, the exception will be thrown to the try block encompassing it. This process continues until the exception is either handled, or there are no more encompassing try blocks to which the exception can be thrown. If the exception reaches this level, the process where the exception occurred will be aborted.

Once you decide where to handle an exception, the next consideration is deciding what code to put in the exception handler. Besides sending error messages to the user, or reporting the error to an error tracking system, you need to look carefully at what is skipped after an exception is thrown. It is very important to free allocated memory and close any open files. Using the built-in features of the C++ language, the MFC Exception Classes, and a well thought-out error handling strategy, you will be able to build a robust application that gracefully handles the majority of exceptions that can, and will, occur.

—*Michael Lane Thomas,*
MCSE+I, MCSD, MCT, MCP+SB, MSS, A+

CERTIFICATION SUMMARY

Data input forms and dialog boxes are created by editing dialog templates with the Dialog editor, and then using ClassWizard to create classes derived from CDialog, CFormView, and CPropertySheet or CPropertyPage. ClassWizard can then be used to configure dialog data validation, or DDV, as well as dialog data transfer, or DDX.

Personalized user settings for an application should be stored in the Registry under the HKEY_CURRENT_USER hive. MFC provides facilities for reading and writing string and integer values to the Registry using member functions of the CWinApp class.

Online user assistance can take a number of forms, including status bars, ToolTips, context-sensitive WinHelp Help, and HTML Help. Context-sensitive Help can be added to an application by choosing a setting in the MFC AppWizard. It is also possible to link from a WinHelp topic to compiled HTML Help stored on a Web site.

Error handling is of great importance in a desktop application. There are several methods of passing errors back to calling functions, including C++ exception handling. Depending upon the type of error, the application developer must decide the appropriate method of handling it.

 TWO-MINUTE DRILL

❑ Using Visual C++ with Microsoft Foundation Classes (MFC), you have several options for creating these data input windows: you can create a form that adheres to the document/view architecture by deriving a class from CFormView; you can create a modal or modeless dialog box from a class derived from CDialog; or you can create a tabbed dialog box, known as a property sheet, from a class derived from CPropertySheet.

❑ The Visual C++ integrated development environment (IDE) provides a Dialog editor for editing dialog templates.

❑ To make the Visual C++ developer's job easier, the Dialog editor has been provided to allow drag and drop creation of dialog templates. It provides for WYSIWYG, or what you see is what you get editing of the template, along with property sheets for setting the general properties, such as dialog box size and the font to be used, as well as all of the associated styles, such as border type.

❑ Once you have created a dialog template you must create an appropriate C++ class and associate the template with the class before it can be used in your application.

❑ Be sure that you understand the distinction between dialog templates and the C++ classes that they are associated with. A dialog template purely describes how the dialog box will look, how controls will be laid out on the dialog box, and so on, whereas a C++ class provides the actual code that gives the dialog box functionality to be displayed, respond to messages, validate user input, and the like.

❑ It has become customary for C++ programmers to name classes using a capital C as the first letter. If you follow conventions such as these, your code will be much easier for other people to comprehend and maintain.

❑ A property sheet is a tabbed dialog box, which is really a collection of dialog boxes laid over the top of each other with each one being selectable by a tab.

❑ The CFormView class provides the functionality for associating a dialog template with a view class, and allows you to produce an application that combines dialog-style user input with standard application user interface elements such as menus, toolbars, and status bars.

❑ Visual C++ provides a mechanism known as *dialog data validation*, or *DDV*, which is configured through the ClassWizard.

❑ DDV, or *dialog data validation*, provides some fairly basic validation for controls that are mapped to either CString or various numeric variable types.

❑ Status bars comprise a set of panes, each of which may display certain text that may be updated at any time. In order to change the text in a pane of a status bar, you use the SetText( ) method, passing in the text to be displayed, the integer index of the pane to display it in, and a type.

❑ ToolTips are small boxes containing help text specific to a control or child window.

❑ The context-sensitivity comes into play when the help for the particular part of the application that the user is currently working with is displayed.

❑ The emerging method of providing Help is HTML Help, which uses Internet Explorer functionality to display the Help.

❑ *Exceptions* are error condition objects which are *thrown* by a function when an error condition is encountered. They are then passed progressively back up the call stack until they are *caught* by some code that then handles the error, or else the application will abort.

❑ Make sure you are confident with multiple catch blocks for the exam. You should understand that a *catch* block will catch any exceptions of the specified type, or of any type derived from that class. So catching exceptions of type CFileException will catch any exception class derived from CFileException, and catching exceptions of type CException will catch all exceptions, as CException is at the top of the exception class hierarchy.

❑ Whether errors have been thrown and caught as exceptions or passed back to the caller as return values, they need to be handled in a fashion appropriate to the situation. There is no point in detecting that an error has occurred in the opening of a file, only to go on and attempt to write to a file.

❑ Data input forms and dialog boxes are created by editing dialog templates with the Dialog editor, and then using ClassWizard to create classes derived from CDialog, CFormView, and CPropertySheet or CPropertyPage. ClassWizard can then be used to configure dialog data validation, or DDV, as well as dialog data transfer, or DDX.

SELF TEST

The following questions will help you measure your understanding of the material presented in this chapter. Read all of the choices carefully, as there may be more than one correct answer. Choose all correct answers for each question.

1. Holly needs to build a dialog-based application to display an address book. Which of the following is the best method for her to follow?

   A. Edit the dialog templates using a text editor, and associate the templates with C++ classes.

   B. Edit the dialog templates using the Dialog Editor, and associate the templates with C++ classes.

   C. Create an object of type CDialog and edit it using the Dialog Editor.

   D. Use the Dialog Editor to create a C++ class derived from CDialog.

2. As part of an application Peter is writing, the user is required to enter an IP address in dotted decimal notation. Which of the following is the most appropriate way of achieving this?

   A. Create a custom control which accepts the input of IP addresses.

   B. Create an ActiveX control which accepts the input of IP addresses, and inserts the control into the project.

   C. Use the standard Windows edit box found on the Controls toolbar and provide validation for IP address formats.

   D. Use the IP address control found on the Controls toolbar.

3. During the development process, dialog templates are associated with C++ classes. Which of the following most closely describes the mechanism by which this is done?

   A. Using Class Wizard, a new class is created with a base class chosen from a list of MFC base classes and a dialog resource ID is selected.

   B. Using Class Wizard, a new class is automatically created with a base class of CDialog and a dialog resource ID is selected.

   C. Using Class Wizard, a new class is created with one or more base classes and a dialog resource ID is selected.

   D. Using Class Wizard, an appropriate MFC class is associated with a dialog resource ID.

4. In order to retrieve certain user address details, Liz implements a modal dialog box. Which of the following is a consequence of her design decision?

A. The dialog box will be topmost, being displayed over the top of all other windows.

B. The dialog box will be able to be displayed in one of two modes: interactive and non-interactive.

C. While the dialog box is being displayed, the main window in Liz's application does not receive mouse or keyboard messages.

D. The dialog box will always maintain focus until it is dismissed.

5. Current Situation: Your application logs certain events to a disk-based file. It has become apparent that the log file may become full and that certain actions should be taken if this occurs.
Required Result: Inform the network administrator immediately via e-mail when a full log file is detected.
Optional Desired Results: Inform the application user that the log file is full; prevent the user from interacting with the application until they acknowledge that the file is full.
Proposed Solution: Create an object of a CDialog-derived class and display it with a call to DoModal( ). Then use some previously tested code to send an e-mail to the network administrator.
Which of the following results does the proposed solution produce?

A. The proposed solution produces the required result and both of the optional results.

B. The proposed solution produces the required result and only one of the optional results.

C. The proposed solution produces the required result but does not produce any of the optional results.

D. The proposed solution does not produce the required result.

6. Tony is building an application which allows users to set a number of preferences which may be categorized in three different groups: 'connection', 'display', and 'format'. Which of the following is the most appropriate type of user interface for Tony to implement for this purpose?

A. A set of three modeless dialog boxes, one for each category of preferences.

B. A set of three modal dialog boxes displayed in succession, one for each category of preferences.

C. A property sheet comprising three pages, one for each category of preferences.

D. A single modal dialog, with preferences grouped into three categories within group boxes.

7. In order to create a property sheet, Angela creates three dialog templates and associates them with classes CPage1,

CPage2, and CPage3, each of which is derived from CPropertyPage. She also uses Class Wizard to derive a class, CPropSheet, from CPropertySheet. Which of the following sets of source code should Angela use to display a modal property sheet using the classes she has created?

A.
```
CPropSheet prop;
CPage1 page1;
CPage2 page2;
CPage3 page3;
prop.AddPage(&page1);
prop.AddPage(&page2);
prop.AddPage(&page3);
int iRes = prop.DoModal();
```

B.
```
CPage1 page1;
CPage2 page2;
CPage3 page3;
CPropSheet prop(page1, page2,
    page3);
int iRes = prop.DoModal();
```

C.
```
CPropSheet prop(CPage1, CPage2,
    CPage3);
int iRes = prop.DoModal();
```

D.
```
CPropSheet prop;
CPage1 page1;
CPage2 page2;
CPage3 page3;
int iRes = prop.DoModal(page1,
    page2, page3);
```

8. As the primary client interface for a distributed application, Lucy has chosen to implement a user interface form using a class derived from CFormView. Which two of the following are true about Lucy's choice?

A. The class can be readily used in either an SDI or MDI application.

B. The class can be used to display either a modal or a modeless dialog.

C. As a class derived from CView, it cannot be associated with a dialog template.

D. The framework does not automatically provide functionality for printing the form.

9. You have been given a specification for an application which includes a requirement for the user to input a four-digit number. The requirement specifies that as the user types, they must not be allowed to enter more than four characters. It is considered that the user should know that they are supposed to enter numeric data; if they enter any non-numeric characters they should be prompted to re-enter the data. Which of the following is the best way for you to implement this requirement?

A. Use ClassWizard to map an edit box to an int variable and use DDV to validate the data.

B. Use ClassWizard to map an edit box to a CString variable, use DDV to validate the data, and then attempt to convert the CString data to an int.

C. Use ClassWizard to map an edit box to a control member variable, and override UpdateData( ) to include code to read the data from the control and to validate the data.

D. Use ClassWizard to map an edit box to a control member variable, and use a handler for the WM_CHAR message to validate user keystrokes as they are typed.

10. Once ClassWizard has been used to map controls to member variables, how should a developer configure validation using DDV?

A. DDV is automatically applied when the mappings between member variables and controls are configured.

B. By setting properties in ClassWizard for the member/control mappings.

C. By using ClassWizard to override UpdateData( ) within the dialog class.

D. By modifying the mapping that ClassWizard inserts into the source code.

11. Joe has created a simple dialog box with several controls mapped to integer variables, and two buttons, OK and Cancel, each mapped to the default handling functions. Joe has configured minimum and maximum values for each of the integer variable mappings. What action within the source code must Joe take in order for the DDV to be invoked when a user presses OK?

A. None; the default implementation of OnOK( ) will call UpdateData( ) and the DDV will be applied.

B. Override OnOK( ) to include a call to UpdateData(FALSE).

C. Override OnOK( ) to include a call to UpdateData(TRUE).

D. Override OnOK( ) to include a call to UpdateData( ).

12. Which of the following most closely describes the MFC DDX mechanism?

A. A facility for transferring data from member variables to controls at initialization and from controls to member variables based on mappings configured using ClassWizard.

B. A facility for transferring data between controls that have been mapped using ClassWizard.

C. A facility for dynamically configuring the transfer of data between member variables and controls at runtime.

D. A facility for dynamically exchanging data between applications that may even be running on different computers.

13. Current Situation: Peter is developing an application which includes a dialog for the entry of a user's e-mail address. He has created an edit box control on the dialog and mapped it using ClassWizard to a CString variable named strEmail. He has also placed an OK button on the dialog. Required Result: Once the OK button has been pressed the application must be able

to process the e-mail address that the user typed in.

Optional Desired Result: The application should be able to restrict the number of characters the user types in; if the e-mail address does not contain the '@' symbol the user should be prompted to re-enter it without the dialog box having been dismissed.

Proposed Solution: Override the OnOK( ) function to include the following code:

```
UpdateData( );
EndDialog(IDOK);
```

Which of the following results does the proposed solution produce?

A. The proposed solution produces the required result and both of the optional results.

B. The proposed solution produces the required result and only one of the optional results.

C. The proposed solution produces the required result but does not produce any of the optional results.

D. The proposed solution does not produce the required result.

14. Natasha is developing a distributed application in Visual C++, and she needs to store a database connection string so that it does not have to be re-entered each time the application is run. She decides to store the string in the registry using CWinApp:WriteProfileString( ). Which of the following is true about her decision?

A. It will not work; the data will not be persisted beyond a single instance of the application.

B. It will work only if the user of the application does not have a roaming profile configured.

C. The data will be stored, but can only be retrieved if the application is executed by the same user.

D. It will work as intended; the data will be stored and can always be retrieved by instances of the same application.

15. You are creating a distributed application using the document/view architecture which allows users to download images from a location on the Web and save them to disk. As each download completes, you want to inform the user of the progress. Which of the following is the most appropriate method for you to provide this feedback to the users?

A. Create a dialog template which includes a progress indicator control and associate the dialog template with a class derived from CFormView.

B. Display a modal dialog box as each download completes.

C. Display a modeless dialog box as each download completes.

D. Update the text in the first pane of the application's status bar each time a download completes.

16. As a feature of the application he is building, Gavin has decided to provide context-sensitive help. Which three of the following are true about Gavin's decision?

A. When the user invokes the help, Gavin's application will launch WINHELP.EXE.

B. AppWizard will add skeleton help text for all of the dialogs and menu items in Gavin's application.

C. Whenever Gavin's application is compiled, a tool called MakeHm will be executed.

D. Whenever Gavin adds new Help topics to his application, the file with the extension .HPJ will have to be recompiled.

17. Susan is building a distributed application which includes client software written in Visual C++ which will run on the desktop machines on her company's LAN. Susan wishes to include context-sensitive help, including a link to some help text which will be updated from time to time to reflect current company procedures. What is the most appropriate way for Susan to implement this?

A. Produce an HTML file containing the text for the section which will be updated. Include a button within the client application that makes a call to ShellExecute( ) in order to display the HTML file in the default browser installed on the client machine.

B. Maintain versions of the application within Visual SourceSafe, and redistribute the application whenever the help text is updated.

C. Isolate the text that will require updating into a single .RTF file and only redistribute this .RTF file whenever there is a change.

D. Compile HTML help text for the section which will be updated, and place the compiled .CHM file at a location accessible by all client machines. Link to the .CHM file using the !execfile macro from within the application's context-sensitive help.

18. You have been asked to develop a class CTransferMechanism which will be used within a distributed application being developed by your company. You have identified that the CTransferMechanism constructor will attempt to establish a network connection which may fail. How should you notify the calling code that the constructor has failed?

A. Throw an exception using the MFC exception macro facility.

B. Throw an exception using the C++ exception facility.

C. Return a special value such as -1.

D. Create a member variable which will be initalized with 0 for OK and −1 for error.

19. Jason is writing some code which must catch exceptions of both type CFileException and CXferException, a class derived from CException. Jason's code must display the exception's error message. Which of the following code samples most closely fulfills Jason's requirements?

A.
```
catch(CFileException* e)
{
  e->ReportError();
  e->Delete();
}
catch(CXferException* e)
{
  e->ReportError();
  e->Delete();
}
```

B.
```
catch(CFileException* e)
{
  e->ReportError();
  e->Delete();
}
catch(CException* e)
{
  e->ReportError();
  e->Delete();
}
```

C.
```
catch(CFileException* e1,
      CXferException* e2)
{
  e1->ReportError();
  e1->Delete();
  e2->ReportError();
  e2->Delete();
}
```

D.
```
catch(CException* e)
{
  e->ReportError();
  e->Delete();
}
```

20. You have been provided with a class CWidget, which contains a member function IsComplete( ), which may throw an exception of type CWidgetException. If the error contains message text you should display the message, otherwise re-throw the exception. You are not aware of the details of any of the CWidget code; what is the safest way to fulfill these requirements?

A.
```
catch(CWidgetException* e)
{
  e->GetErrorMessage(szBuf,
    SIZEOF(szBuf));
  if (strlen(szBuf) == 0)
  {
    throw(e);
  }
  else
  {
    MessageBox(szBuf);
  }
  delete e;
}
```

B.
```
catch(CWidgetException* e)
{
  e->GetErrorMessage(szBuf,
    SIZEOF(szBuf));
  if (strlen(szBuf) == 0)
  {
    throw(e);
  }
  else
  {
    MessageBox(szBuf);
    delete e;
  }
}
```

C.
```
catch(CWidgetException* e)
{
    e->GetErrorMessage(szBuf,
      SIZEOF(szBuf));
    if (strlen(szBuf) == 0)
    {
      throw(e);
    }
    else
    {
      MessageBox(szBuf);
    }
    e->delete();
}
```

D.
```
catch(CWidgetException* e)
{
    e->GetErrorMessage(szBuf,
      SIZEOF(szBuf));
    if (strlen(szBuf) == 0)
    {
      throw(e);
    }
    else
    {
      MessageBox(szBuf);
      e->Delete();
    }
}
```

SELF TEST ANSWERS

1. **B.** The Dialog Editor is used to edit dialog templates, which are then associated with C++ classes. A text editor could be used, but is not the best method. The Dialog Editor cannot be used to edit C++ classes or objects.

2. **D.** There is an IP address control on the Controls toolbar. It is no longer recommended to create custom controls instead of ActiveX controls. However, an ActiveX control is not warranted in this case. An edit box is not as good a solution as the IP address control.

3. **A.** Class Wizard will allow you to associate a class derived from an appropriate MFC base class with a dialog resource ID. Dialog templates must be associated with a derived class, not directly with an MFC class.

4. **C.** While a modal dialog box is being displayed, the user cannot interact by mouse or keyboard with the rest of the application. A modal dialog is not necessarily topmost, however, and it will not prevent other applications from receiving the focus. There is no such thing as the concept of interactive and non-interactive modes.

5. **D.** The proposed solution does not produce the required result. Because DoModal( ) does not return until the dialog has been dismissed by a call to EndDialog( ), the e-mail will not be sent until after the user has acknowledged the dialog. The proposed solution does, however, produce both of the optional results.

6. **C.** Property sheets, also known as tabbed dialog boxes, allow a set of dialogs to be displayed and the user to move between them by selecting tabs. All of these solutions could probably be used in this instance, but the property sheet is the most appropriate.

7. **A.** A property sheet is implemented by calling AddPage to add property page objects which represent the individual dialog tabs. DoModal( ) is then called to display a modal property sheet.

8. **A, D.** A CFormView-derived class can be used within an SDI or MDI document/view architecture application, although the MFC framework will not provide the functionality for printing the form. The form is not used to display dialog boxes, either modal or modeless, although it must be associated with a dialog template.

9. **B.** Using DDV for a string variable will fulfill this requirement; it will ensure that the maximum number of characters are not exceeded as the user is typing. DDV for numeric variable mappings is not applied until a call to UpdateData( ). It would be possible to implement your own custom validation method, but in this instance DDV is the best way to implement the requirement.

10. **B.** DDV is configured within ClassWizard through properties for the mappings between member variables and controls. There is no need to override UpdateData( ); the default implementation will invoke the DDV, and the developer should generally avoid modifying the mappings that ClassWizard inserts into the source code.

11. **A.** The default implementation of CDialog::OnOK( ) calls UpdateData(TRUE), which invokes DDV for numeric mappings. There is therefore no need to override OnOK( ) in this situation.

12. **A.** DDX provides a mechanism for transferring data both from member variables that have been mapped to controls using ClassWizard, and from controls to those member variables. It does not allow for exchanging data between controls or between applications, and is not configured at runtime.

13. **C.** The proposed solution produces the required result but does not produce any of the optional results. Calling UpdateData( ), where the parameter defaults to TRUE, causes the contents of the control to be passed to the mapped variable. Calling EndDialog( ) causes the dialog to be dismissed and DoModal( ) to return. However, the calling application can still access the contents of the member variable. There is no way in the proposed solution to limit the number of characters typed in by the user, and if the user did not type in the '@' symbol the dialog will have to be re-displayed in order for the user to type in a valid e-mail address.

14. **C.** Because CWinApp::WriteProfileString( ) stores data under the HKEY_CURRENT_USER hive, the data is only retrievable by applications executed by the same user. This mechanism is intended for storing data that applies to a single user, such as personalization options.

15. **D.** Updating the status bar text is the most appropriate method of user feedback in this instance. A CFormView-based interface is probably not appropriate here, and a progress indicator is more suited to displaying progress over time rather than discreet events such as the completion of a download. Invoking any kind of dialog box is probably not appropriate in this instance either.

16. **A, C, D.** Context-sensitive help is actually displayed by the Windows executable WINHELP.EXE. AppWizard adds skeleton .RTF files for the common elements of the Windows user interface, but not for all of the dialogs and menu items in an application. MakeHm is executed when an application is compiled, and the help project file must be recompiled when new topics are added.

17. **D.** The most appropriate approach here is to link from the Winhelp context-sensitive help to compiled HTML help on the server using the !execfile macro. Launching a browser from the application is not the most appropriate solution, and redistributing the entire application is a very bad approach. Redistributing the .RTF files is not practical, as the users would have to recompile the project themselves.

18. **B.** The C++ exception facility should be used instead of the MFC macros, which are retained for backward compatibility. A constructor cannot return a value, and it is better to not create the object under an error condition such as this than to create the object with a member specifying that an error occurred.

19. **A.** This code fulfills the requirements exactly. Catching exceptions of type CException will also catch any other kinds of exceptions such as CMemoryException, which was not specified as a requirement. Answer C uses an incorrect syntax to attempt to catch exceptions of two different classes.

20. **D.** It is always safer to use the CException::Delete( ) member function, especially if you don't know if the exception object was created on the stack or on the heap. Also, if an exception is re-thrown it should not be deleted by the catch block that throws it.

MCSD
MICROSOFT CERTIFIED SOLUTION DEVELOPER

5

Implementing ActiveX Controls

I n this chapter, we'll discuss Microsoft's ActiveX technology. ActiveX is a set of technologies that enables software components to interact with each other in a networked environment, regardless of the language in which they were created. Using it, you can build real business applications for the Internet and intranets that run across multiple platforms.

An ActiveX *component* is a unit of executable code, such as an .EXE, a .DLL, or an .OCX file, that follows the ActiveX specification for providing objects. ActiveX technology allows programmers to assemble these reusable software components into applications and services. Using ActiveX, you can create controls, documents, and components that run on desktops or the Internet. The functionality packaged within these building blocks can then be easily reused in other Windows-based applications.

A number of vendors offer ActiveX components that you can purchase and use in your applications. These components provide a wide variety of generic services, including numerical analysis, user interface elements, and data management. You can also create your own components and combine these with generic components. Reusing tested, standardized code in this way is called *component software development*.

ActiveX allows you to create compelling, interactive Web sites using a variety of tools. Most importantly, ActiveX provides interoperability between development tools, authoring tools, database products, and networking technologies.

We'll begin our exploration of ActiveX with a discussion of ActiveX controls and how you can utilize them in your applications. We'll also learn about the Internet Server Application Programming Interface (ISAPI). Finally, we'll learn how to implement and use Active documents.

CERTIFICATION OBJECTIVE 5.01

Using an ActiveX User Interface Control

ActiveX controls are reusable objects that include visual elements and code. They are used in some type of container, such as a form, an application, or a Web page, to enable or enhance a user's interaction with an application. These controls have an .OCX file name extension.

ActiveX controls were originally called OLE controls. The first version of the OLE control specification appeared in 1994 and was intended to provide a generic, COM-based architecture for building reusable Microsoft Windows controls. The specification was revised in 1996 and OLE controls were renamed ActiveX controls. At the same time, Microsoft Internet Explorer gained the ability to host ActiveX controls in Web pages. Thus, the primary purposes of ActiveX controls are:

- To provide developers with a way to easily incorporate existing software components into their applications
- To provide Web authors with a way to implement interactive Web pages by providing a standard for components that run on the client computer

You can easily utilize functionality provided by an ActiveX control in your Windows-based applications. In the following section, we'll create a calendar application that uses Microsoft's MonthView Control.

Inserting a Control Using Component Gallery

In this section we'll learn how to use an ActiveX control in a Microsoft Foundation Classes (MFC) application. In order to do this, we must first create a new project which includes support for ActiveX controls.

Creating the Calendar Project

1. Select the File | New menu entry. This opens the New dialog box, as shown next. Click the Projects tab and select MFC AppWizard (exe) as the project type. Type **Calendar** for the project name.

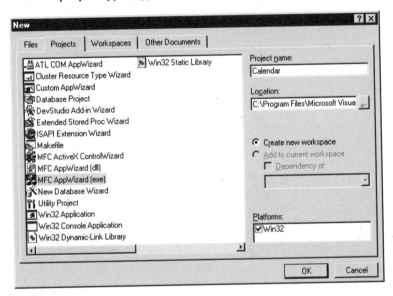

2. Click the OK button in the New dialog box. This runs the MFC AppWizard, which asks a series of questions before generating the project.

3. In the Step 1 dialog box, select Dialog Based for the type of application you want to create, then click Next to proceed to Step 2.

4. In the Step 2 dialog box, make sure that the check box for ActiveX Controls is selected. At this point, click Finish and AppWizard creates and opens the new project.

Now that we have a project that supports ActiveX Controls, we can add to the project the control we wish to use. We will do this using the Components and Controls Gallery, as illustrated in the following exercise.

Inserting an ActiveX Control into the Project

1. Open the Calendar project (if it's not already open).

2. Select the Project | Add to Project | Components and Controls menu entry to open the Components and Controls Gallery dialog box.

3. Open the Registered ActiveX Controls folder. This lists all of the ActiveX components that are registered on your computer.

4. Select the Microsoft MonthView Control, version 6.0 as shown next.

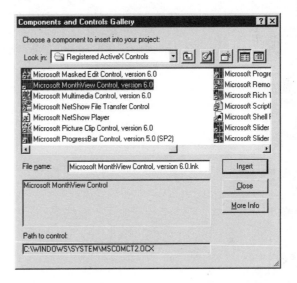

5. Click Insert to insert the control into your project.

6. When the message box appears, confirm that you wish to insert the control into the project by clicking the OK button.

7. When the Confirm Classes dialog box appears, accept the default class and file names by clicking the OK button.

8. Close the Components and Controls Gallery dialog box by clicking the Close button.

Now that we've inserted the MonthView control into our project, we can use the Dialog editor to place it on a dialog box as we would a standard control item.

Adding the ActiveX Control to a Dialog

1. Open the Calendar project (if it's not already open).

2. Switch to ResourceView and expand the Dialog folder.

3. Double-click the IDD_CALENDAR_DIALOG dialog box. This opens the application dialog for editing in the Dialog editor.

4. Delete the static text control created by AppWizard. This contains a note reminding you to place controls on the dialog.

5. Because we have inserted the MonthView control into our project, an icon for it will appear on the Dialog editor's Controls toolbar. Select this icon, as shown in Figure 5-1.

6. Click in the dialog box at the location where you wish to place the control. Once you've placed it, you can move and resize it as you would with any control.

FIGURE 5-1

The dialog editor's Controls toolbar after adding the MonthView control to the project

MonthView control ⟶

7. Using the Dialog editor, resize the dialog and arrange the controls as shown next (the actual date shown in the finished dialog box will vary depending on your system's date setting).

8. Test the dialog box. It should show the current month with today's date circled in red. Try clicking some different dates and using the buttons at the top of the MonthView control to view different months. You can return to the current month at any time by clicking the Today text at the bottom of the control.

That's all there is to using an ActiveX control in an MFC application!

This is very powerful, but what if you want to alter the default appearance or behavior of the control? Fortunately, most ActiveX controls allow a great deal of flexibility by providing customizable properties.

ActiveX Control Properties

In the previous exercise, we placed the MonthView control in a dialog and then tested the dialog box. Because we didn't manipulate any of the control properties, we saw the default appearance and behavior.

Obviously, it would be difficult to write a control that was generic enough to be widely useful without allowing for customization. Yet, that is the driving philosophy behind ActiveX controls. A well-designed ActiveX control provides a great deal of flexibility by providing methods, properties, and events. An ActiveX control fires events to communicate with its control container. The container, in return, uses methods and properties to communicate with the control. In this section, we'll learn about control properties and how to manipulate them. In the next section, we'll talk about methods and events.

Simply put, *properties* are data members of the ActiveX control that are exposed to any container. Properties provide an interface for applications that contain ActiveX controls, such as Automation clients and ActiveX control containers. By manipulating the properties of a control, we can customize its default appearance and behavior.

EXERCISE 5-4

Setting ActiveX Control Properties

Suppose the application we are writing requires that weeks begin on Monday, rather than Sunday. We can easily modify the MonthView control to meet this requirement, as illustrated in the following steps:

1. Open the Calendar project (if it's not already open).

2. Switch to ResourceView and expand the Dialog folder.

3. Double-click the IDD_CALENDAR_DIALOG dialog box. This opens the application dialog for editing in the Dialog editor.

4. Right-click the MonthView control and select Properties MonthView Object from the pop-up menu. This opens the MonthView Properties dialog box.

5. Click the Control tab.

6. Using the drop-down list, change the value of the StartOfWeek item from mvwSunday to mvwMonday.

7. Close the MonthView Control Properties dialog box.

8. Select the File | Save menu entry to save the modifications.

Notice that the MonthView control now displays weeks that run from Monday through Sunday, rather than Sunday through Saturday, as shown next.

The MonthView control provides a number of properties that you can modify through the Properties dialog box. Spend some time experimenting with different properties and determine how they affect the appearance and behavior of the control. When you're finished, close the Dialog editor without saving your changes. We'll be using this project in the next lesson and we want to have the properties set the way we saved them at the end of the exercise.

In the previous example we learned how to set the properties of an ActiveX control and spent some time experimenting with the options available. This is fine for simple controls, but what if you need more information about the properties, methods, and events that a control supports?

Fortunately, most controls provide a Help file that contains this kind of information. The following exercise demonstrates how you can access this information.

EXERCISE 5-5

Getting More Information about an ActiveX Control

1. Open the Calendar project (if it's not already open).

2. Select the Project | Add to Project | Components and Controls menu entry to open the Components and Controls Gallery dialog box.

3. Open the Registered ActiveX Controls folder. This lists all of the ActiveX components that are registered on your computer.

4. Select the Microsoft MonthView Control, version 6.0.

5. Click the More Info button. This opens a Help file, as shown in Figure 5-2.

6. Close the Components and Controls Gallery dialog box by clicking the Close button.

As you can see, the Help file provides extensive information about the MonthView control and the properties, methods, and events it supports. Leave this Help file open because we'll be referring to it in the next lesson, where we'll learn how to use methods and events to interact with the MonthView control within our MFC application.

FIGURE 5-2

Use the Help file to obtain information on using the MonthView control

Handling an Event from an ActiveX User Interface Control

In the previous section, we learned how to add an instance of the MonthView control to a dialog box and manipulate its properties to customize the default appearance and behavior. So far, all of our interaction with the control has been at design time. As we saw, ActiveX controls provide a great deal of power and flexibility that we can use in our applications.

But, suppose that you want to extend the default functionality provided by the control. Perhaps you would like to change the appearance of the control dynamically at runtime based on user input. Or, you might want to customize the control's response to a particular user action.

Fortunately, most ActiveX controls provide methods and events that allow you to accomplish these goals. In this section, we'll learn about methods and events and how to utilize them to interact with a control from its containing MFC application.

Methods are similar in usage and purpose to the member functions of a C++ class. Control methods can be called from a containing application to do useful work, such as dynamically changing control properties or accessing some functionality provided by the control.

ActiveX controls use events to notify a container that something has happened to the control. An example might be a user-input event, such as a mouse-click or a keyboard event. Such an event would cause the control to fire an event to alert the container. By responding to these events, our application can customize the default behavior of the control.

Suppose that you were writing an application to schedule hard disk backups, and wanted to allow the user to select the backup date using a MonthView control. Your application would need to respond to the MonthView control's SelChange event so that it could respond appropriately when the date was changed.

We'll emulate this by adding a couple of controls to our Calendar application's dialog box to display the currently selected backup date. Then we'll learn how to add code to update these controls when the user changes the date using the MonthView control.

Using Methods and Events to Interact with an ActiveX Control

1. Open the Calendar project (if it's not already open).

2. Switch to ResourceView and expand the Dialog folder.

3. Double-click the IDD_CALENDAR_DIALOG dialog box. This opens the application dialog for editing in the Dialog editor.

4. Select the Static Text tool on the Controls toolbar and place a static text control in the dialog box. Right-click the control and click Properties in the shortcut menu to open the Text Properties dialog box. In this dialog box, change the static text control caption to **Backup Date:**.

5. Select the Edit Box tool on the Controls toolbar and place an edit box control next to the static text control in the dialog box. Right-click the control and click Properties in the shortcut menu to open the Edit Properties dialog box. On the General tab, change the edit control's ID to **IDC_BACKUPDATE**. On the Styles tab, click Read-Only.

6. Using the Dialog editor, arrange the controls as shown next.

At this point, we're ready to add code to allow our program to interact with the MonthView control at runtime.

When we add an ActiveX control to our project, the Component and Controls Gallery automatically adds the appropriate wrapper class implementation file (.CPP) and header file (.H) to the project. To get and set properties and invoke methods for the MonthView control, the CMonthView wrapper class provides a declaration of all exposed methods and properties. These functions can then be called from other application procedures using normal C++ syntax. In this example, these declarations are found in MONTHVIEW.H.

After the ActiveX control has been added to the project and embedded in the dialog box container, it can be accessed by other parts of the project. The easiest way to access the control is to create a member variable of the dialog class, CCalendarDlg, that is of the same type as the wrapper class added to the project by the Component and Controls Gallery. You can then use the member variable to access the embedded control at any time.

EXERCISE 5-7

Adding a Member Variable for a Control to a Dialog Box

The following steps illustrate adding a member variable for the MonthView control to our CCalendarDlg dialog box.

1. From the View menu, click ClassWizard.

2. Choose the Member Variables tab.

3. In the Class Name list box, select the main dialog class CCalendarDlg.

4. In the Control IDs list box, select the control ID of the MonthView control, IDC_MONTHVIEW1. Your settings should now match those shown in Figure 5-3.

5. Click the Add Variable button to open the Add Member Variable dialog box.

6. In the Member Variable Name box, type the name **m_monthViewCtl**.

7. In the Category box, select Control.

FIGURE 5-3

Using ClassWizard to add a member variable for the MonthView control to the main dialog box

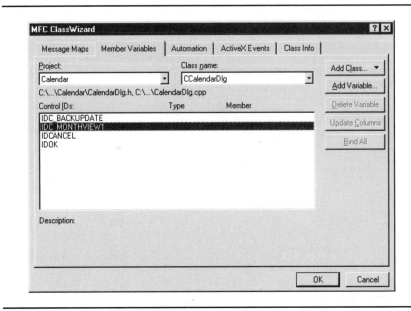

8. Verify that the Variable Type edit box contains the name of the control wrapper class, CMonthView. Your settings should now match those shown next.

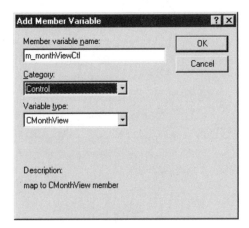

9. Click OK to close the Add Member Variables dialog box.

10. Click OK to accept these changes and exit ClassWizard.

That's all there is to adding a member variable for the MonthView control to our main application dialog box. Now we can use common C++ syntax to access the properties and methods of the embedded control.

A common place to modify the properties of a control is in the OnInitDialog member function of the main dialog class. This function is called just before the dialog box appears and is used to initialize its contents.

The following code example uses the m_monthViewCtl member variable to access the currently selected date within the MonthView control. It then converts this value to a string and uses the string to initialize the Backup Date edit control.

We'll add the following line of code to call a member function to set the value of the IDC_BACKUPDATE edit control. We'll be adding this member function next.

```
SetBackupDateEditCtl(m_monthViewCtl.GetValue());
```

This line should be added near the end of the CCalendarDlg::OnInitDialog function, after the TODO comment line. The finished function should look like this:

```
BOOL CCalendarDlg::OnInitDialog()
{
    CDialog::OnInitDialog();

    // Add "About..." menu item to system menu.

    // IDM_ABOUTBOX must be in the system command range.
    ASSERT((IDM_ABOUTBOX & 0xFFF0) == IDM_ABOUTBOX);
    ASSERT(IDM_ABOUTBOX < 0xF000);

    CMenu* pSysMenu = GetSystemMenu(FALSE);
    if (pSysMenu != NULL)
    {
        CString strAboutMenu;
        strAboutMenu.LoadString(IDS_ABOUTBOX);
        if (!strAboutMenu.IsEmpty())
        {
            pSysMenu->AppendMenu(MF_SEPARATOR);
            pSysMenu->AppendMenu(MF_STRING, IDM_ABOUTBOX, strAboutMenu);
        }
```

```
}

    // Set the icon for this dialog. The framework does this
    //automatically when the application's main window is not
    //a dialog
    SetIcon(m_hIcon, TRUE);                   // Set big icon
    SetIcon(m_hIcon, FALSE);          // Set small icon

    // TODO: Add extra initialization here
    SetBackupDateEditCtl(m_monthViewCtl.GetValue());

    return TRUE;   // return TRUE  unless you set the focus to a control
}
```

We added a call to a member function that sets the contents of the Backup Date edit control, IDC_BACKUPDATE, based on the value of an input variable of type DATE. Notice that in the argument to this function, we use the member variable that we created, m_monthViewCtl, to access the GetValue member function of the MonthView control. The GetValue function returns the current setting of the Value property. Most ActiveX controls supply member functions that allow you to get and set their internal properties in this way.

EXERCISE 5-8

Adding a Member Function to the CCalendarDlg Class

In the previous code sample, we added a call to this member function. Now we need to add this member function to the CCalendarDlg class, as illustrated in the following steps.

1. Switch to ClassView.

2. Right-click the CCalendarDlg class and select Add Member Function from the shortcut menu to open the Add Member Function dialog box.

3. In the Function Type box, type **void**.

4. In the Function Declaration box, type **SetBackupDateEditCtl(DATE currentDate)**.

5. In the Access box, select Protected. Your entries should now match those shown next.

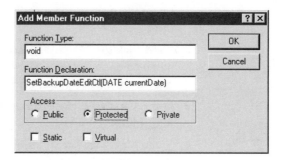

6. Click OK to add the member function. A skeleton of the new member function, SetBackupDateEditCtl, is added to the CCalendarDlg class, as shown:

```
void CCalendarDlg::SetBackupDateEditCtl(DATE currentDate)
{

}
```

7. Add the following lines of code to the function body:

```
COleDateTime date(currentDate);
CWnd* pWnd = GetDlgItem(IDC_BACKUPDATE);
pWnd->SetWindowText(date.Format(VAR_DATEVALUEONLY));
```

The first line of code creates a variable called *date* of the type COleDateTime. The value of this variable is initialized using the input currentDate variable. The second line of code gets a pointer to the Backup Date edit control, IDC_BACKUPDATE. In the third line of code, this pointer is used to call its SetWindowText member function. The Format member function of the COleDateTime class is called to convert the date value to a formatted string.

If we test our program at this point, we'll see that when the main dialog box opens, the Backup Date edit control is correctly initialized to the currently selected date within the MonthView control. However, if we select a different date in the MonthView control, the Backup Date is not updated.

In the following steps, we'll learn how to add an event handler to remedy this problem.

1. Open the main dialog box, IDD_CALENDAR_DIALOG, in the Dialog editor.

2. Right-click the MonthView control and click Events in the shortcut menu to open the New Windows Message and Event Handlers for class CCalendarDlg dialog box.

3. In the Class or Object to Handle list box, select IDC_MONTHVIEW1.

4. In the New Windows Messages/Events list box, select SelChange. Your settings should now match those shown next.

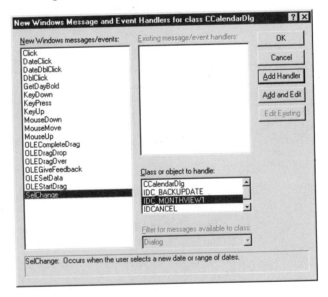

5. Click the Add and Edit button. This will open the Add Member Function dialog box.

6. When the Add Member Function dialog box appears, confirm that the Message is SelChange and the Object ID is IDC_MONTHVIEW1, then accept the default function name of OnSelChangeMonthview1 by clicking the OK button. A skeleton of the new event handler member function, OnSelChangeMonthview1, is added to the CCalendarDlg class, as shown:

```
void CCalendarDlg::OnSelChangeMonthview1(DATE StartDate,
DATE EndDate, BOOL Far* Cancel)
{
    // TODO: Add your control notification handler code here

}.
```

7. Replace the TODO comment line in the function body with the following line of code:

```
SetBackupDateEditCtl(StartDate);
```

Now that we've added an event handler for the SelChange event, it will be called whenever the user selects a new date in the MonthView control. The parameters to this function include the StartDate and EndDate variables of type DATE. Both of these dates are included because, by changing a property of the MonthView control, you can configure it to allow a selection range. Because we're using the default properties that allow the selection of a single date, we'll be interested only in the value of the StartDate variable. The value of StartDate represents the newly selected date.

The line of code that we added to the function body sets the value of the Backup Date edit control, IDC_BACKUPDATE, to the date passed to the function in the StartDate variable.

Test the program now that we've added the event handler. You'll see that the Backup Date edit control is correctly updated when the user selects a new date in the MonthView control. You have successfully added an event handler to an ActiveX control!

Dynamically Creating an ActiveX User Interface Control

Using these features of Visual C++ allows us to create very user friendly and useful applications. Properly designing dialog boxes to help users interact with our applications will help them to be more productive when using these programs. Using the Dialog editor, we are able to design these dialogs with ease. There are times, however, when we are not able to use the Dialog editor to place these controls onto the dialogs and windows in our applications. When needed, Visual C++ allows us to dynamically add these to our projects. In this section we will be discussing how this is done.

Adding controls dynamically at runtime can be as simple as creating a new instance of an existing control onto a defined dialog or as complex as having the user specify the type of control to be added to a window. We will use an example that falls somewhere between these two extremes. This example shows you how to add a control and allows you to respond to the events that are raised by the control. Adding controls that we do not know about in advance is an advanced concept and beyond the scope of the tests or this book.

Dynamically Adding an ActiveX Control at Runtime

In this example we duplicate some of the functionality that we created in the last exercise, but this time we will do it by adding a MonthView control to the view in a single-document interface (SDI) application. By now you should be very familiar with using the AppWizard, so we will not detail those steps in this exercise.

1. Select File | New from the menu and create a new MFC AppWizard (exe) project type.

2. Name the project **DynamicControl** and ensure that the Create New Workspace option button is selected.

3. In Step 1 of the wizard, select Single Document as the type of application to create. Accept the defaults in Step 2. In Step 3, be sure the ActiveX Controls check box is selected. Select Finish and create the application.

4. Again, we will be using the MonthView control from Microsoft, so we will need to add it to this project as we did before. To do this, select Project | Add to Project | Components and Controls. Open the Registered ActiveX Controls folder and select the Microsoft MonthView Control, Version 6.0 control. Click the Insert button. When prompted, click OK to insert the component into the project. Click OK to accept the default class names. Finally, click Close to close the Components and Controls Gallery dialog box. We have now created the necessary wrapper classes for the MonthView control.

5. The next step is to add a Resource Symbol for the control that we will add at runtime. To do this, select View | Resource Symbols. Select New and type **IDC_SELECTDATE**. Accept the default value as shown next, then click OK to create the symbol. Click Close to close the Resource Symbol dialog.

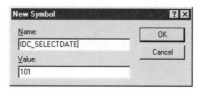

6. As stated earlier, the goal of this exercise is to add a MonthView control to the View window of our SDI application. In Step 4 we created the wrapper classes that define the behaviors of the MonthView control. To allow the View class to interact with this control, we now need to add the MONTHVIEW.H header file to the DYNAMICCONTROLVIEW.H header file. Place this include statement before the class definition in the file as shown.

```
#include "MonthView.h
class CDynamicControlView : public CView
{
```

7. The next step is to add a member variable to our CDynamicControlView class. To do this, right-click the CDynamicControlView class on the Class View tab and select Add Member Variable. Specify **CMonthView** as the variable type and **m_monthSelectDate** as the variable name. Set the Access mode to Protected, and it should look like the dialog shown next, then click OK to create the variable.

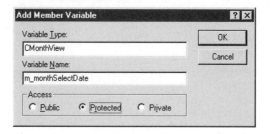

8. The next step is to actually create the control. In our example we will need to add a message handler to our View class. To do this, open

ClassWizard and select as the class name, CDynamicControlView. Next, be sure that the Object ID that is selected is also CDynamicControlView. In the Messages list, select WM_CREATE and click the Add Function button. At this point the ClassWizard's Message Maps tab should look like Figure 5-4.

9. From the ClassWizard, click Edit Code. This will take us to the new message handler that we created and allow us to add code to create our control.

10. Now that we are editing the code, we need to call the Create method of our m_monthSelectDate object from the OnCreate method of the CDynamicControlView class. The code is shown here:

```
int CDynamicControlView::OnCreate(LPCREATESTRUCT lpCreateStruct)
{
    if (CView::OnCreate(lpCreateStruct) == -1)
        return -1;

    // TODO: Add your specialized creation code here
    m_monthSelectDate.Create(NULL, WS_VISIBLE,
        CRect(20,20, 100, 100), this, IDC_SELECTDATE);

    return 0;
}
```

FIGURE 5-4

Adding the OnCreate function to the view class, CDynamicControlView

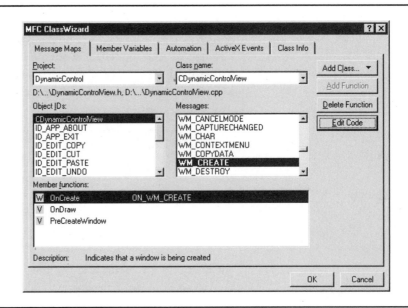

The only call that we have added to the stub code provided by Visual C++ is the call to the Create method of the m_monthSelectDate object. We have provided five parameters to this method. The following table identifies each parameter and indicates the reason why we have supplied each value. Note that the words *control* and *window* seem to be used synonymously in the descriptions in the table. Remember that the MonthView class is derived from the CWnd class and that the control is a special case of a window. I used the terms as I felt they would make the most sense.

Parameter	Value	Description
lpszWindowName	NULL	String containing the name of the window we are creating. In our case, this is NULL.
dwStyle	WS_VISIBLE	Specifies the style or styles that are desired for the created window. In our case, we simply are going to ensure that it is visible.
rect	Crect(20, 20, 100, 100)	This is intended to specify both the size and the position of the control based on the parent. In the case of the MonthView control, the size is predetermined, so the only parameters that matter are those that specify the position.
pParentWnd	this	The parent window of the window that we are creating. In our case we are passing the this pointer, which is actually the CDynamicControlView object.
nID	IDC_SELECTDATE	This is the ID of the window that is being created. This can be left as a NULL, but in our case we will need the control to have an ID so that we can respond to events that it raises.

11. With this code added, we are now ready to build and test our application. We have now completed all of the steps required to dynamically add a control to our application at runtime. Select Build | Execute DynamicControl.EXE and confirm that you want to build the application.

12. Take a moment to exercise the functionality of the control on the view. You will see that it acts just like it did in our earlier example when a dialog box hosted it. Yet it is not yet very useful to us. In the following steps, we will add the required features that will allow us to respond to the events that this control can raise, again acting as it did in our previous example. You can see an image of how this application looks in Figure 5-5.

    Now that we have added the control, and the application is functioning properly, it is time to do something useful with it. In the next few steps we will add the capability to have our View class respond to events that are raised by this instance of the MonthView control.

13. The first step is to add the Event Sync and function mappings. This can be a tedious process, unless you know a good trick. Luckily we

---

FIGURE 5-5

An SDI application running
with a control that was
added at runtime

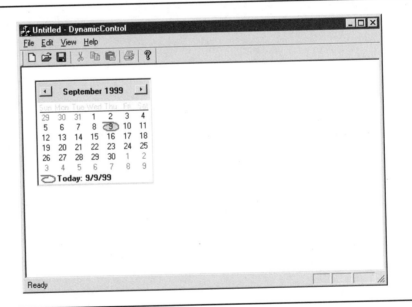

know a trick and have prepared ourselves to make this an easy step. Open a second copy of Visual C++ and load the Calendar project from our earlier exercise. We will be borrowing some code from a Dialog-based application to use in our new SDI application.

14. Using the File View tab, locate and open the header file CCALENDARDLG.H. Move to near the bottom of the file and copy the following lines to the clipboard.

```
afx_msg void OnSelChangeMonthview1(DATE StartDate, DATE EndDate,
    BOOL FAR* Cancel);
DECLARE_EVENTSYNC_MAP()
```

15. I have purposefully changed the ID of our control so that we will better understand all of the steps that must be completed for the piracy of code to work. Now return to our DynamicControl application. Using the File View tab, locate and open the header file CDYNAMICCONTROLVIEW.H.

16. Move towards the bottom of the file and locate the message map. Paste the code from the clipboard into the message map and change OnSelChangeMonthView1 to **OnSelChangeSelectDate**. Although this change is not really required, it will make the code easier to read. This new name is more like the name that ClassWizard would assign if this control were not being created dynamically. Now your message map should look like the following:

```
afx_msg void OnSelChangeSelectDate(DATE StartDate, DATE EndDate,
    BOOL FAR* Cancel);
DECLARE_EVENTSYNC_MAP()
```

17. Return to the Calendar project and open the file named CCalendarDlg.cpp. Again, move towards the bottom of the file and find the code that implements the Event Sync map and the OnSelChangeMonthView1 event handler. Copy this code to the clipboard. The code that you should copy is listed here:

```
BEGIN_EVENTSYNC_MAP(CCalendarDlg, CDialog)
    //{{AFX_EVENTSYNC_MAP(CCalendarDlg)
```

```
    ON_EVENT(CCalendarDlg, IDC_MONTHVIEW1, 4 /* SelChange */,
        OnSelChangeMonthview1, VTS_DATE VTS_DATE VTS_PBOOL)
    //}}AFX_EVENTSYNC_MAP
END_EVENTSYNC_MAP()

void CCalendarDlg::OnSelChangeMonthview1(DATE StartDate,
DATE EndDate, BOOL FAR* Cancel)
{
    // TODO: Add your control notification handler code here
    SetBackupDateEditCtl(StartDate);
}
```

18. You can now close the Calendar project and return to our DynamicControl project. Using the File View tab, open the file named CDYNAMICCONTROLVIEW.CPP. Move to the bottom of the file and paste the code from the clipboard. Now we will have to make some changes to this code.

19. The first change will be replacing each reference to CCalendarDlg with a reference to **CDynamicControlView** (you might want to use Edit | Replace to do this). Associated with this is to change the second parameter of the BEGIN_EVENTSYNC_MAP macro from CDialog to **CView**. This is because we are now using a CView-derived class rather than a CDialog-derived class.

20. Change IDC_MONTHVIEW1 to **IDC_SELECTDATE** in the EventSync map. Here you can see that if we had created the new symbol with the same name as in our Calendar project, we would not have to edit so much. Remember this when working in the real world, but be sure to learn what is really happening.

21. Next we need to replace the method name in all of the code we copied. In our Calendar project, our method was named OnSelChangeMonthView1. In our new project we have decided to call this **OnSelChangeSelectDate**. Make the changes now; it will have to be done in two places.

22. The final step is to add the functionality that we desire to the new method. In the Calendar project we made a call to SetBackupDateEditCtl. In this project we will display the date below

the MonthView control on the view. To do this, place the following code into the OnSelChangeSelectDate method and remove the call to SetBackupDateEditCtl. (Notice that we are doing something very similar to what the SetBackupDateEditCtl method did.)

```
COleDateTime date(StartDate);
CClientDC DrawDC(this);

DrawDC.TextOut(30, 200, date.Format(VAR_DATEVALUEONLY));
```

23. The code at the bottom of the CDYNAMICCONTROLVIEW.CPP file should now look like the following:

```
BEGIN_EVENTSYNC_MAP(CDynamicControlView, CView)
    //{{AFX_EVENTSYNC_MAP(CDynamicControlView)
    ON_EVENT(CDynamicControlView, IDC_SELECTDATE, 4 /* SelChange */,
            OnSelChangeSelectDate, VTS_DATE VTS_DATE VTS_PBOOL)
    //}}AFX_EVENTSYNC_MAP
END_EVENTSYNC_MAP()

void CDynamicControlView::OnSelChangeSelectDate(DATE StartDate, DATE
EndDate,
        BOOL FAR* Cancel)
{
    // TODO: Add your control notification handler code here
    COleDateTime date(StartDate);
    CClientDC DrawDC(this);

    DrawDC.TextOut(30, 200, date.Format(VAR_DATEVALUEONLY));
}
```

24. Run the application by selecting Build | Execute DynamicControl.EXE and allowing Visual C++ to build the new executable. Exercise the functionality of the MonthView control and you should see the selected date appearing below the control for each date selected. Figure 5-6 is a screen image of this exercise running.

In this section you learned how to add a control to an MFC application at runtime. It is important to understand this functionality, and it can be very helpful as you are creating applications for your customers.

FIGURE 5-6

The SDI application now handles an event raised by the control

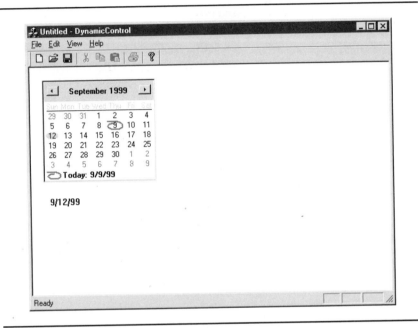

CERTIFICATION OBJECTIVE 5.02

Using the Internet Server API

In this section, we'll be talking about the Internet Server Application Programming Interface (ISAPI). The ISAPI provides a simple and efficient way to extend any ISAPI-compliant Web server. Using it, you can write ISAPI dynamic link libraries (DLLs) that can be loaded and called by a Hypertext Transfer Protocol (HTTP) server.

There are two types of ISAPI DLLs that you can create. They are:

- ISAPI server extensions
- ISAPI filters

ISAPI Server Extensions

An ISAPI server extension, sometimes called an Internet server application (ISA), is a DLL that can be loaded and called by an ISAPI-compliant server to enhance its capabilities. An ISA is invoked from a browser application and provides functionality similar to that of a Common Gateway Interface (CGI) application. An ISA is only executed when the browser navigates to the URL that identifies the server extension. This will be seen in the exercise that we will do shortly. Using an ISA, you can develop an application that processes data collected in a Web page and, based on that data, dynamically creates and sends customized Hypertext Markup Language (HTML) data to the client for display to the user.

Later in this section, we'll work through an example that creates an ISAPI server extension.

ISAPI Filters

ISAPI filters provide the capability of preprocessing and postprocessing all data sent between the client and the server. Filters have no CGI equivalent. Whereas an ISAPI server extension DLL is loaded when first requested, an ISAPI filter is loaded when the Web server is started. This filter can then be used for all interactions with the Web server. When you choose to create an ISAPI filter, you have seven notifications that you can filter. The following is the list of these.

- Incoming raw data and headers
- Outgoing raw data and headers
- Post- and preprocessing of the request headers
- Client authentication requests
- URL mapping requests
- Server log writes
- End of connection notification

Filters are not as common as extensions. The most important thing to know for the test is that extensions process when requested, and filters process all of the time. We will not look at an example of a filter in this chapter.

Advantages of Using ISAPI DLLs

There are several advantages to using ISAPI server extensions as an alternative to traditional CGI applications.

- ISAs run in the same address space as the server and have access to all of its resources.

- ISAs do not require the creation of additional processes and do not perform communications across process boundaries. As a result, ISAs have lower overhead than CGI applications.

- The server may unload both extension and filter DLLs if the memory is needed by another process.

Using the MFC AppWizard to Create an ISAPI DLL

Visual C++ gives us tools to help create ISAPI DLLs. As with many of the other types of applications that we can build with VC++, there is a wizard to help us build these extensions. In the following exercise we will create an ISAPI extension DLL that will return a customized message to the user.

| EXERCISE 5-10 | ### Creating the ISAPI DLL Project

1. Select the File | New menu entry. This opens the New dialog box.

2. Click the Projects tab and select ISAPI Extension Wizard as the project type. Type **Message** for the project name. Click OK.

3. In Step 1 of 1 of the ISAPI Extension Wizard, select the Generate a Server Extension Object check box. Accept the defaults for the class name and description. Choose to have the MFC DLL used as a shared DLL.

   VC++ has now generated an ISAPI extension DLL with a class that it has derived from CHTTPServer. This class has no functionality in it, but it does have a method name default, which is often used with server extensions.

To help us learn more about ISAPI DLLs, we will not use the default method, but rather we will create a new one called GetMessage. This method will be called by the browser when the user wants to run our server extension. To do this, perform the following steps.

4. Adding a new method to the CMessageExtension class involves multiple steps. First we must add the method to the Parse Map. To do this, open the file named CMESSAGEEXTENSION.CPP and move to the top of the file. Locate the Parse Map and add the following lines.

```
ON_PARSE_COMMAND(GetMessage, CMessageExtension, ITS_PSTR)
ON_PARSE_COMMAND_PARAMS("Name")
```

5. Next we must add the actual method to the class. Right-click the CMessageExtension class in the Class View and select Add Member Function. Set the function type to **void** and the function declaration to **GetMessage(CHttpServerContext* pCtxt, LPCTSTR pstrName)**. Your Add Member Function dialog box should look like this:

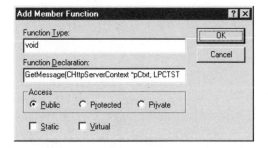

The pCtxt parameter is an object that provides the context for each transaction between the browser and the server. The pstrName parameter will read the name from the user that will be used when creating our message.

6. Next we will add one more method to our CMessageExtension class. This method will be used to set the title for the browser when the results from our DLL are displayed. Right-click the CMessageExtension class in the Class View and select Add Member

Function. Set the function type to **LPCTSTR** and the function declaration to **GetTitle( ) const**, as shown in next.

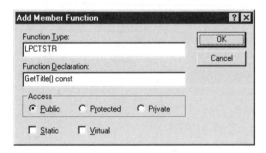

7. Now we will implement the GetTitle method. Locate the code stub and add the following code to it.

```
return "A Special Message";
```

8. Finally, we will add the code for the GetMessage method. This method will accept the name of the user as a parameter and generate a message for the user. Add the following code to the stub created for this method.

```
// setup the Html to be returned
StartContent(pCtxt);
WriteTitle(pCtxt);

// add the custom content
*pCtxt << "Hello, ";
*pCtxt << pstrName;
*pCtxt << " I hope you are having a good day!";

// close the html
EndContent(pCtxt);
```

9. The final step, as far as VC++ is concerned, is to create our DLL. Select Build | Build Message.DLL from the menu. This will create the ISAPI extension DLL for you. Because we are not trying to cover the details of Internet Information Server (IIS), we will skip the steps required to publish this to your Web server—these are not required for the test—and move on to show you the outcome of the process.

10. After you have published this DLL to your Web server, you will most likely build a form from which this will be executed. Again, your focus is to understand the DLL and not HTML, so simply type the request into the Address line of your browser. Type the following address into your browser and replace the server name with the name of your development IIS server:

    http://qss3/ISAPIExt/Message.dll?GetMessage?Name=Phred

11. Doing this will result in the page shown in Figure 5-7 being displayed in your browser.

Notice that the title has been changed, as we requested, to A Special Message. Also, the message that we created has been displayed.

It is worthwhile to remember the three classes with which we have interacted in creating this ISAPI extension. We have worked with two of them directly, and the third has served us without actually showing itself. The following are the three MFC classes that we have used.

Output from our ISAPI extension server

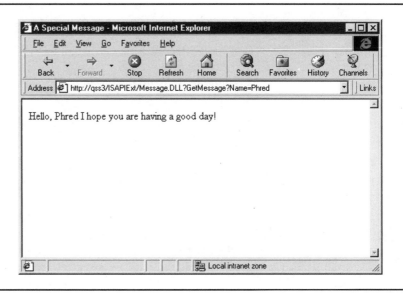

CHttpServer is the class from which our CMessageExtension was derived. This is the main focus of our DLL, and without it we would not be able to create the extension DLL. When the wizard created our class for us, it gave us a method for our derived class called Default. If the request to our DLL does not specify the method to be called, the Default method will be called.

CHttpServerContext is the first parameter that is passed into our GetMessage method. This class represents the information that is required for each interaction between the browser and the server. We used this object to allow the CMessageExtension, StartContent, WriteTitle, and EndContent methods to build the framework of our HTML page that was returned to the browser. A new object is created for each interaction between the browser and the server.

The *CHtmlStream* class was hidden from us in this example. Nonetheless, it is a very important class. The CHttpServerContext class has a member variable called m_pStream which is of this class. This is the class that actually manages the creation of the stream that is returned to the browser. The overloaded << operator of the CHttpServer class actually calls the Write method of this class to place the data that we desire into the stream.

To give you a fully rounded view of ISAPI extensions, we will also introduce the classes that are pertinent when creating an ISAPI filter. In this case there are only two classes and they are described in the following paragraphs.

CHttpFilter is the main class for an ISAPI filter. It is somewhat analogous to the CHttpServer class in the extension arena. This class has virtual functions for each of the notifications that we discussed earlier. It is important that you override only the functions for those notifications that you desire to filter. This will cause only those functions to be called, giving better performance.

CHttpFilterContext is somewhat like the CHttpServerContext we discussed earlier. An object is created for each interaction between the browser and the server. This object is available to you from each of the virtual functions that are provided by the CHttpFilter class.

CERTIFICATION OBJECTIVE 5.03

Incorporating Existing Code into an Application Using Wizards and Scriptlets

One of the things that we have been searching for as an industry is the key to unlocking code reuse. Microsoft and Visual C++ have been helping us along this path. One way that we can begin to get reuse is through Custom AppWizards. In this section we will explore one way in which you can create a Custom AppWizard.

The most common use of the Custom AppWizard functionality is to build an AppWizard that will create a new project that is based on an existing project. This is helpful for situations in which you desire many aspects of an application to be similar and would like to reuse existing code that implements those parts of the application. With this description, it should be obvious that the first step in the process will be to create a project that you want to have as the basis for your new wizard. Once you have created this project, continue on with the following steps.

1. Select File | New.

2. Select the Projects tab.

3. Type a name for the new AppWizard; this will be the default name that you will select from the Project tab in the future.

4. Select Custom AppWizard as the template from which to create this application.

5. Click OK to start the Custom AppWizard.

6. In Step 1 of the Custom AppWizard, select An Existing Project and verify that the name of the new AppWizard is what you want.

7. Click Next to move to Step 2 of the wizard.

8. In Step 2, you need to identify the project on which this AppWizard will be based. To do this, use the Browse button to locate the .DSP file of the project on which you will base the new AppWizard.

9. Click Finish to indicate that you are ready to have the project created.

10. Review the information on the New Project Information dialog box and click OK.

11. Once the new project is open you can select Build | Build *PROJECT*.AWX to generate the new AppWizard.

12. Now that you have built the AppWizard we can test it by selecting File | New and choosing the Projects tab.

13. Select the new AppWizard from the list and type the name of a new project.

14. Be sure that you have selected Create New Workspace.

15. Click OK.

16. On the New Project Information dialog box, click OK. Here you can see that we can customize our AppWizard. We choose not to for this simple example.

17. You should now have a new project that is based on the project from which you created the AppWizard.

The ability to create a new AppWizard is just one of the many features of Visual C++ that allows us to reuse code.

Another way in which we can reuse code is through scriptlets. There has been some misunderstanding as to what a scriptlet is. To understand this technology, we should start with a definition. A *scriptlet* is a Component Object Model (COM) component built using a scripting language. Yes, it really is that simple. Scriptlets can be created using VBScript, JScript, or other scripting languages. Typically, Web developers build scriptlets as part of a Web application. Because these scriptlets are COM components, we are able to use them in our VC++ applications. Scriptlets can have properties and methods. When we use a scriptlet in a VC++ application, we use it as an ActiveX control.

Displaying Data from a Data Source

Most applications that we create manipulate data in one way or another. As VC++ programmers, we have several sources from which to retrieve the data that our users interact with. In this section we will review some of these sources and briefly discuss how we can interact with them to manage the data that is important to our applications.

Implementing Remote Data Sources Using CSocket

When programming Windows, there are many layers of abstraction on top of the low-level network protocols. Sockets are the lowest level to which a VC++ programmer can go for programming interactions between computers using Transmission Control Protocol/Internet Protocol (TCP/IP). WinSock is the term used in the Windows environment. WinSock is based on the concept of sockets that was originally developed in the UNIX environment.

MFC gives us two classes for developing programs using WinSock. They are CAsyncSocket and CSocket. CAsyncSocket is much harder to work with than CSocket. CSocket allows the developer to create two applications, a client and a server, that communicate with each other. Through the use of sockets, these applications pass information back and forth.

The important information for learning socket programming, and for having the knowledge required to understand all of the questions that you might face on the exam, is that the CSocket class can use a CArchive class to manage this communication process. We will discuss the CArchive object shortly. To receive data, you must create a CArchive object that loads data. To send data, you must create a CArchive object that saves data.

Implementing Standard Serialization Using Serialize

If you are new to VC++ you might wonder what the term serialization means. VC++ programmers throw around this term rather freely and it can take some time to get used to it. *Serialization* is the term used to indicate that an object should be able to be persisted, or in other words, it should allow itself to be saved and loaded from some persistent storage like a hard disk.

MFC has several classes that implement a method called Serialize. This is the method through which the given objects are able to serialize themselves. The Serialize method makes use of a CArchive object that in turn uses a CFile object. We will cover these shortly.

To allow an object to implement the Serialize method, there are a few rules which must be followed. The first is that the class must be derived from CObject. As was stated previously, there are several MFC classes that implement the Serialize method, but it is possible for your own classes to implement the same functionality by deriving them from CObject. The second requirement is that the class must include the DECLARE_SERIAL macro in the class definition. Finally, the class must also include the IMPLEMENT_SERIAL macro in the implementation.

If your class has met the requirements, you are now able to implement your Serialize method. The Serialize method receives a single parameter of type CArchive. It is the CArchive object that knows if the data is to be saved or loaded. This object also knows how to utilize a CFile object to interact with the file system. We will now move on to discuss these other classes.

Implementing Persistence Using CFile

MFC supports many different classes for working with files. The base class for all of these is CFile. The CFile class wraps the Windows API calls that interact with the file system. By using the CFile class, you are able to read and write files to and from the hard disk of the computer. It is not too common to use the CFile class itself. Most often the data that is accessed in our applications actually resides in a database. In other chapters, we have covered the topics that help us to understand databases and the ways in which we can manipulate the data stored in them. If we really do need to work with a file on the disk, we often interact with CFile through the CArchive class. This has already been described and we will talk about CArchive next. Because CFile does not buffer any of its function calls prior to passing them on to the Windows API, it can be rather inefficient when reading and writing data. For this reason you would be more likely to use the CStdioFile class when working with disk files.

Displaying Data Using CArchive

The CArchive class is the middleman between the Serialize function and the CFile derived object where our objects are persisted. In the preceding sections we have described how the Serialize method works and given you the basic information needed to understand the CFile class. When serializing your objects you do not use the CFile object directly; rather, you access it through the CArchive object. A CArchive object is created each time that you need to serialize your object. A CArchive object, once created, is only capable of moving data in one direction. To determine the direction in which the CArchive is moving the data, you can evaluate the response from calling the IsStoring function. If the CArchive object is storing the data, this will evaluate to *true*, otherwise it will be *false*. Once you have determined the direction in which the data is moving, you are able to use the CArchive extraction and insertion operators (<< and >>) to move both basic data types as well as your own objects that are derived from CObject to and from the persistent storage.

Connecting a Recordset to Dialog Box Controls

So far in this section we have focused on interacting with data that exists outside of a database management system. In other chapters of this guide we will talk about some of the deeper details that you must understand to work effectively with databases. In this section we will briefly introduce how you can cause the data that you retrieve from a database to be visible to your users in a window.

To understand the functionality of the Recordset object and how it interacts with a dialog box, it is best to start out with a simple example. You can create a new project including database support, either with or without file support. When stepping through the AppWizard you will be required to select a database with which you are going to work. Creating a project in this manner will provide some help for you. First, you will have a class created for you that is derived from the CRecordset class. This class will provide the required interaction with the selected database. Your View class will also have two special features. It will have access to the CRecordset-derived class through a member variable named m_pSet. Additionally, the View class will be derived from the CRecordView class. This will provide a dialog template that you can use to set up the edit boxes and other controls that will allow you to view your data.

Once the project has been created, go to the Resource editor and create the dialog box with the controls that you wish to use to view your data. This is the dialog box that will be displayed inside the view window. After you have drawn the proper controls on the dialog box and given the appropriate Ids, you will map the controls to the members of the m_pSet variable that points to the recordset. To do this, open ClassWizard and move to the Member Variables tab. Be sure that your project and your view class are selected. You should see the list of control IDs that you just created. Select one of them and click the Add Variable button. This will bring up the dialog that allows you to create new member variables to be associated with your control. In this case we will open the combo box and find the member of the m_pSet object that we wish to show in the given control. Select this member variable from the list provided by opening the combo box and clicking OK. If you build your application, you will be able to use the buttons on the toolbar to navigate through the records in the table and see the data in your controls. It is that simple to map our recordset to a dialog box.

CERTIFICATION OBJECTIVE 5.05

Invoking a COM Component

So much of the current talk in the software development world now focuses on components and component development. Of course, as we well know when we are talking about a Microsoft tool, these are obviously COM components. These days, the benefits of component development are well known and most would argue that this is the way to develop software. In other parts of this book, we have talked about how to build various COM components. In this section we will learn how to invoke and use these components in a regular executable.

In the following exercise we will create an instance of a COM component. This component is a simple one that I have created for this exercise. Because a component is a black box of sorts, we do not really need to see the code for it. This component simply exposes one method. If you wish, you may change this example to work with a component that already exists on your system, or you may choose to use the information from some of the other chapters to build your own component. The method exposed by my component is GetAge, which takes the ID of an employee and returns the age of that employee.

EXERCISE 5-11

Invoking a COM Component

1. Select the File | New menu entry to create a new project.

2. Click the Projects tab and select MFC AppWizard (exe) as the project type. Type **MyCOMClient** as the project name and click OK.

3. For this exercise, we will change only two of the default settings for the AppWizard. The first is in Step 1 where we will choose to create a Single Document rather than a Multiple Documents type of application. The second change to the defaults is in Step 3, where we will select Container as the type of compound document support to include in the application.

4. Click Finish to build the application.

5. Add the following line near the bottom of the STDAFX.H header file:

```
#import "D:\MyCOMSvr1\Debug\MyCOMSvr1.dll" no_namespace
```

This line really does most of the work for us. I have imported the DLL that I am using. You will need to modify the #import for the DLL of your choice. The #import directive causes VC++ to do all of the detail work for us. You will soon see just how easy it is to use a COM component. The no_namespace allows us to refer to the component without using namespaces.

6. Navigate to the OnDraw message handler of the CMyCOMClientView class. This is where we will create and use our

component. Of course this is a very simple exercise, but the techniques are the same when working with real life components.

7. Under the //TODO comment, add the following lines of code:

```
CString msg;
IPersonPtr pPer(_uuidof(Person));

msg.Format("The age of employee number 3 is %d.\n", pPer->GetAge(3));
AfxMessageBox(msg);
```

The first and third lines of code are used to create and fill a CString object that will show the results of our method call. We are displaying a message box that tells the age of the selected employee.

The real work happens in the second line. Here we are creating our object. We have declared it to be of type IPersonPtr (our component exposes an IPerson interface). This type is created by our #import statement. (Look at the .TLH file in the Debug directory of your project.)

With this magic known as smart pointers, we are able to create our object with that much ease. As a bonus, we also do not have to manage the reference counting on our object because the smart pointer does this for us.

8. Now go ahead and build your client. Once it is built you can test it. You will see the output from your method call.

As you can see, it can be very easy to create and use components in our applications. If you have worked with components in the past you will quickly recognize that using these technologies, we no longer need to manage the lifetime of our components by explicitly calling AddRef and Release. The smart pointers take care of this for us. This is most certainly the easy way to approach it, and to really get the best understanding of it you spend some time and use some components by coding them longhand. It is also a good idea to have some knowledge of this for the test. As a quick guide, here are the steps that you must complete to do this.

1. Create a standard MFC AppWizard (exe) application.

2. Include a header file describing your component in the class where it will be used or in STDAFX.H.

3. #include <afxole.h> in StdAfx.h.

4. Call AfxOleInit( ); from the InitInstance method of the CWinApp-derived class.

5. Declare your variables. This includes CLSID, LPCLASSFACTORY, LPUNKNOWN, and a pointer to your interface.

6. Identify the CLSID by calling ::CLSIDFromProgID, passing in the program ID of your component.

7. Create the ClassFactory by calling ::CoGetClassObject.

8. Create an instance of your object by calling the CreateInstance method of the ClassFactory. Have this give you an IUnknown pointer.

9. Get a pointer to your desired interface by calling the QueryInterface method of IUnknown.

10. Now you are ready to use your component. You can see now why smart pointers and the #import are so much better. Once you have finished with your object you still have work left to do. Follow the next step to finish; this is important.

11. Call the Release method of the ClassFactory, the IUnknown interface pointer, and your desired interface pointer.

CERTIFICATION OBJECTIVE 5.06

Adding Asynchronous Processing

Many of the tasks that our applications must do are secondary to the actual work that the user is required to interact with. There are many examples of cases in which we want a task to occur, but we do not want the user to have to wait for it to complete before they continue on with other work. There are also cases in which we simply need to be sure that a task will happen, but it does not need to be completed now.

The general nature of a program is to have a single thread of work occurring at one time. If we want to have several things happening at the same time, we can start other threads. For the purposes of this book and for the certification exam, these threads are commonly called *worker threads.* The programmer creates these threads for a specific task. Then in the course of running the application, when the user desires the functionality, the program can create a secondary, or worker thread, to perform the task. There are many issues that must be considered when creating these threads. Refer to the section on thread synchronization in this book for more details.

Creating Secondary Threads

A secondary thread is created to perform a specific task. The program causes a thread to be created when the task is to be accomplished, and the thread goes away on its own once it has finished the work. The following steps are required to create a thread and start it executing within an application.

1. Create a new procedure. Often this procedure is added within the same file as the class that will utilize it, but it is not a method of that class. The prototype for the function is shown here:

   ```
   UINT ThreadProcedure(LPVOID lpVoid)
   ```

2. An example of a true thread procedure is shown here:

   ```
   UINT SpellCheck(LPVOID DocToCheck)
   {
       CClientDoc* pDoc = (CClientDoc*)DocToCheck;
       AfxMessageBox (pDoc->GetTitle());
       return 0;
   }
   ```

   This thread procedure will display a message box when it is run that will show the title of the document that is passed into it. As you can see, the parameter to the function is of type LPVOID. This allows us to pass a pointer to whatever information that we need in the thread procedure. The thread procedure will cast the pointer to the type that it is expecting, as we have done in the first line of code. Although we are showing a message box in this example, that is probably not the best thing to do in a worker thread. But, it does allow us to see when the thread is started. As for killing the thread, it will die once the thread procedure exits.

3. The next step is to actually create the thread. This is accomplished by calling the AfxBeginThread function. The following is the prototype for this function:

```
CWinThread* AfxBeginThread( AFX_THREADPROC pfnThreadProc,
LPVOID pParam, int nPriority = THREAD_PRIORITY_NORMAL,
UINT nStackSize = 0, DWORD dwCreateFlags = 0,
LPSECURITY_ATTRIBUTES lpSecurityAttrs = NULL );
```

The first parameter is the Thread Procedure. Here you can pass the name of the procedure.

The second parameter is the pointer that you wish to pass in. Remember that you must pass an LPVOID and then cast it back to the desired type within the procedure.

All of the other parameters are optional. The thread priority can be set by passing the nPriority parameter. This defaults to *normal* priority but can range from *idle* to *time_critical*. The stack size for the thread can be set using the nStackSize parameter. This defaults to zero, which sets it to the same size as the parent stack. By setting dwCreateFlags to CREATE_SUSPENDED you can cause the thread to be created but not actually executed until a call to ResumeThread. Finally, you can use the lpSecurityAttrs parameter to set the security attributes of the thread. Leaving this as the default value of NULL causes the thread to be created with the same security attributes as the parent.

4. To create the thread you must call AfxBeginThread, as shown in this example code:

```
CWinThread* pThread=AfxBeginThread(SpellCheck, (LPVOID) pDoc);
```

In this example I have placed the call to AfxBeginThread in the OnDraw message handler of my CView-derived class. I am passing in the pointer to the CDocument-derived object that is associated with this view.

It is as simple as that to create a worker thread. This is a powerful feature of VC++, but one that must be used with caution. When used correctly, it can provide a performance increase to your applications.

Downloading ActiveX User Interface Controls

An exciting feature of ActiveX controls is that they are able to exist on a Web page. To do this, we must ensure that the control and all of the required files are on the computer on which the browser is running. We will often create a .CAB file that can be referenced from the HTML.

Because the control must actually exist on the browser's computer, it is important to consider all that might be required to have it run there. If we know that the user has all of the required files, we could simply refer to the .OCX file itself from the HTML page. If this Web page is to be viewed in a very controlled environment, such as an intranet, this might be possible, but it is safest to provide the HTML page with information about all of the files that might be required.

Before we go too much deeper, let's take a look at how the HTML page refers to the control. The following code is a sample of what an <Object> tag in an HTML page might look like.

```
<OBJECT ID="MyControl1" WIDTH=75 HEIGHT=40 CLASSID="CLSID:09189208
-B8D3-301B-5141-0400C8E3D523" CODEBASE="http:// MyWebServer
/MyCoolControl.cab#Version=1,0,0,001"> </OBJECT>
```

The most important things for us to look at here are the CODEBASE and the Version information. The CODEBASE tells the browser where to go to get the control. Here we have told the browser to search for a file called MYCOOLCONTROL.CAB on a server named MyWebServer. Although this is fictitious, it is how a basic object would appear on a normal Web page.

The Version information is the first way in which we can help to minimize the impact of placing a control on our Web page. Remember that this control must exist on the machine on which the browser is running. This means that if the control is not already on the machine, it will be downloaded from the location specified in the CODEBASE tag. By supplying this information, the browser can check to see if this version of this control already exists on this machine. If it does exist, nothing will have to be downloaded.

Next we need to identify what to include in the .CAB file. We need to be sure that this .CAB file can identify all of the supporting files that will be required by the control. We also don't necessarily want to place all of them in it. For example, if our control uses the MFC library, we will need to be sure that this is on the machine, but it is very possible that it is already there, so we do not want the impact of downloading it again. To do this, we will create an .INF file that identifies those supporting files and indicates from where they can be downloaded. When we create our .CAB file we will only include the .OCX and the .INF files. If required, the browser will then follow the information contained in the .INF file to gather all of the supporting files that it needs.

CERTIFICATION OBJECTIVE 5.07

Using an Active Document

We have just reviewed some of the details that allow a developer to place an ActiveX control onto a Web page and provide a more appealing interface for the user. There are other means by which this can be accomplished. In this section we will talk about one more technology that can give us an edge when developing Web applications.

Active documents are actually standalone applications that can be hosted within a Web browser. Using VC++ to create an Active document server is really quite simple and straightforward. We will create a basic MFC AppWizard (exe) application and provide it the means to run in a Web browser.

EXERCISE 5-12

Building an Active Document Server

1. Select the File | New menu entry to create a new project.

2. Click the Projects tab and select MFC AppWizard (exe) as the project type. Type **MyActiveXDoc** as the project name and click OK.

3. Again, this is a pretty generic AppWizard application. Accept the defaults with the following exceptions. In Step 1, select a Single Document application type. In Step 3, select Full-Server and Active Document Server. In Step 4, click the Advanced button and select a File Extension for your application. We will use **MYD**, for My Document. In Step 6, change the base class for the view to **CFormView**.

4. Select Finish and allow the AppWizard to generate your project.

5. Open the Dialog Resource named IDD_MYACTIVEXDOC_FORM and add two labels, two edit boxes, and two command buttons, as shown next.

6. Behind the buttons on this form we would add code to interact with the Web server. In particular, we would have the Submit button generate a POST request that the Web server could then process with an ISAPI DLL. Because this is beyond the scope of this section we will not actually add the code here, but for a true Active document you would need to do this.

7. Build the application. Before we can see our document in the Web browser, we will need to execute the program and save a file. This file will have the extension of .MYD as we requested in the AppWizard.

8. Run your application and save a file. Save the file to C:\MyDoc.myd. Close the application.

9. Open Internet Explorer and select File | Open. Click Browse and browse to the file C:\MyDoc.myd. Open the file. When prompted to Save the File or Open it from the Current Location, choose to Open it from the Current Location. You should see something that looks similar to the screen shown next.

There you have it. You have created an Active document server and hosted it within Internet Explorer. The possibilities seem limitless. By using an Active document, you are not limited by the standard form items that you are allowed to use in HTML. You can also create a standalone application, which is not possible when using ActiveX controls on a Web page. It seems that there are so many possibilities to choose from when creating Web applications that it can be hard to determine which is the proper technology to use. One word of advice is to use the tools that you are comfortable with, but it can also be rewarding to spread your wings and learn some new tricks.

The following table contains some possible scenario questions regarding the use of ActiveX Controls and the appropriate answers.

QUESTIONS AND ANSWERS

What should I do if I want to have a visual element to display and edit data unique to my organization and I want to be able to have a consistent "look and feel" between many different user interfaces?	Create an ActiveX control to interact with the data. This will be available to many different development environments including VC++ and the Internet.
How do I add an ActiveX control to my VC++ project so that I can use it in a dialog box?	Use the Components and Controls Gallery to identify the control and create a wrapper class for it.
What should I do when I don't know if a control should be shown on a dialog box at runtime?	Add code to the project to allow the control to be added dynamically when required. This also works to add multiple instances of the control at runtime.
How can I filter the content of a Web page that is being delivered by my installation of Internet Information Server 4.0?	Create an ISAPI filter to process the desired interactions with the server.
A co-worker has created an ActiveX component as a DLL built with Visual Basic. How can I use this component in my project?	The easiest way is to use the #import and smart pointer functionality in VC++.
How do I cause a task to be performed in the background without the user having to wait for the task to complete?	Create a worker thread by calling AfxBeginThread.
If I want to use an ActiveX control on a Web page, how do I specify where to download the control from?	Use the CODEBASE tag in the <OBJECT> tag of the HTML page.

CERTIFICATION SUMMARY

In this chapter we have covered quite a bit of ground. We have discussed some of the general concepts that originated the idea of using components. We have seen how to identify and use an ActiveX control from within our VC++ projects. We not only reviewed the steps for using a control that was specified at design time, but we also revealed the secrets behind creating controls at runtime.

We saw an example of how to create an instance of a component and how to use it from the VC++ code. In reviewing the steps to use one of these components, we identified both the use of the #import directive and the explicit steps required if we don't use the smart pointers provided by #import.

We worked through an example that allowed us to create worker threads that can complete tasks that do not require the user to wait until they have completed. Finally, we learned how we can create Active document servers to give us a rich user interface when working in a Web environment. The skills that we have covered in this chapter are very useful, both for the exam and for life on the job in the real world.

✓ TWO-MINUTE DRILL

- ❑ ActiveX is a set of technologies that enables software components to interact with each other in a networked environment, regardless of the language in which they were created.

- ❑ An ActiveX *component* is a unit of executable code, such as an .EXE, a .DLL, or an .OCX file, that follows the ActiveX specification for providing objects.

- ❑ Using ActiveX, you can create controls, documents, and components that run on desktops or the Internet.

- ❑ ActiveX provides interoperability between development tools, authoring tools, database products, and networking technologies.

- ❑ ActiveX controls are reusable objects that include visual elements and code. They are used in some type of container, such as a form, an application, or a Web page, to enable or enhance a user's interaction with an application. These controls have an .OCX file name extension. ActiveX controls were originally called OLE controls.

- ❑ *Properties* are data members of the ActiveX control that are exposed to any container. Properties provide an interface for applications that contain ActiveX controls, such as Automation clients and ActiveX control containers.

- ❑ ActiveX controls use events to notify a container that something has happened to the control.

- ❑ An ISAPI server extension, sometimes called an Internet server application (ISA), is a DLL that can be loaded and called by an ISAPI-compliant server to enhance its capabilities.

❑ ISAPI filters provide the capability of preprocessing and postprocessing all data sent between the client and the server. Filters have no CGI equivalent.

❑ *Serialization* is the term used to indicate that an object should be able to be persisted, or in other words, it should allow itself to be saved and loaded from some persistent storage like a hard disk.

❑ Active documents are actually standalone applications that can be hosted within a Web browser.

SELF TEST

The following questions will help you measure your understanding of the material presented in this chapter. Read all of the choices carefully, as there may be more than one correct answer. Choose all correct answers for each question.

1. How can you obtain ActiveX controls that you are able to use in your applications? (Choose all that apply.)

   A. They ship with the Visual C++ product.

   B. You can create your own using Microsoft development tools.

   C. You must submit a special request to Microsoft to have one created.

   D. You can obtain them from many third party vendors.

2. What is the file extension that you will find on a file that implements an ActiveX control?

   A. .COM

   B. .OCX

   C. .EXE

   D. .DLL

3. After adding a new ActiveX control to your project, where can you find the control to place it on a dialog box?

   A. An instance of the control is placed on the dialog that is currently being edited. You must copy this control and paste it to other locations.

   B. The control is added to the Insert | Resource dialog box and from here you can insert the control onto the dialog.

   C. It is added to the Dialog editor's toolbar.

   D. The control must be added to each dialog directly. You do not access the control from within the VC++ environment.

4. What is the process that a developer must follow to modify the default behavior of an ActiveX control on a dialog resource?

   A. They create events for the control.

   B. They set the properties of the control to conform to the desired functionality.

   C. The functionality of a control is completely predefined when the control is created. Thus, the developer that uses the control cannot alter the basic behavior of the control.

   D. All controls have a standard property called BasicBehaviors. This property lists all of the behaviors that the control has. The developer is able to modify this list to cause the control to act as desired.

5. How is a developer able to get information about a control to determine the properties, methods, and events supported by the control? (Choose all that apply.)

   A. From the Web site of the vendor of the control.

   B. By experimenting with the control and observing how it behaves.

   C. By reverse engineering the control and reviewing the code used to create the control.

   D. By reviewing the Help file associated with the control.

6. What is the technology used by a control to inform its container that something has happened?

   A. The control raises an event that the container can handle.

   B. The control sets the value of the UserInteraction property that the container application must check on a regular basis.

   C. The control calls a method of the container application.

   D. Controls are unable to communicate with their container applications.

7. When adding controls dynamically to a dialog, what macro must we add to our application to allow it to handle the events raised by the dynamically created instance of the control?

   A. MAP_EVENTSYNC

   B. MAP_DYNAMIC_CONTROLS

   C. DECLARE_DYNAMIC_CONTROLS_MAP

   D. DECLARE_EVENTSYNC_MAP

8. Which type of ISAPI extension is run continuously while the IIS server is running?

   A. ISAPI filter

   B. ISAPI script

   C. ISAPI server extension

   D. ISAPI component

9. Which type of ISAPI extension is run only when a given URL is requested?

   A. ISAPI filter

   B. ISAPI script

   C. ISAPI server extension

   D. ISAPI component

10. Which of the following URLs would execute the GetMessage function of the MESSAGE.DLL passing in a parameter named Name with a value of Joe?

    A. http://server/ISAPIExt/ GetMessage?Message.dll?Name=Joe

    B. http://server/ISAPIExt/Message.dll/ GetMessage?Name=Joe

    C. http://server/ISAPIExt/ Message.dll?GetMessage?Name=Joe

    D. http://server/ISAPIExt/ GetMessage?Name=Joe?Message.dll

11. Which of the following are MFC classes that support an ISAPI server extension? (Choose all that apply.)

A. CHttpServer

B. CHttpServerStream

C. CHtmlStream

D. CHttpServerContext

12. What is the best way to set up Visual C++ to help you build projects that all contain a set of dialog resources that your company has determined should be included in all applications?

   A. Use Windows NT Explorer to copy the project from one directory structure to another.

   B. Build a basic project using the MFC AppWizard (exe) and then open the base project and copy all of the code over.

   C. Build a custom AppWizard based on a project that has been built that includes the base dialog resources.

   D. There is no easy way to achieve this in Visual C++.

13. What is a Scriptlet?

   A. A COM component built using Visual J++ that we can use in our VC++ projects.

   B. A Web page that Microsoft creates to inform developers about upcoming events in their area.

   C. A type of a macro that we can use when editing code in VC++.

   D. A COM component built using a scripting language that we can use in our VC++ projects.

14. What is a socket and where did the term originate?

   A. A socket is a way to allow applications to communicate across a network. They were originally developed in the UNIX environment.

   B. A socket is the standard way to transfer data to and from an NTFS partition. They were developed by Microsoft.

   C. A socket is a way in which an ActiveX control is able to communicate with its container. They were developed by the VC++ development team.

   D. A socket is a way to allow an application to dynamically add controls to dialogs at runtime. It was originally developed in the UNIX environment.

15. What are the two base classes provided by MFC to work with sockets? (Choose all that apply.)

   A. CSocket

   B. CSyncSocket

   C. CAsyncSocket

   D. CSocketSend

16. To have a class that you define be able to use the Serialize method provided by MFC, from which base class must your class be derived?

   A. CWnd

   B. CCmdTarget

   C. CObject

   D. CFile

17. What can cause the CFile class to be less efficient when working with data contained in a disk file?

    A. CFile does not use the Windows API to access the data file it is working with.

    B. CFile does not buffer its calls to the Windows API.

    C. CFile works with an in memory version of all files and so it is prone to losing data if the application terminates.

    D. CFile only works with removable media such as a floppy disk, so access is somewhat slower than if it were using the hard disk.

18. When using the MFC architecture to serialize an object derived from CObject, how is the CFile object accessed?

    A. Serialize uses a CSocket object that in turn accesses a CFile object.

    B. Serialize uses a CStdio object, not a CFile object.

    C. Serialize uses a CArchive object that in turn accesses a CFile object.

    D. All serialization is done to a database and it does not use a CFile object.

19. Which VC++ tool is used to map a field from a recordset object to a control on a dialog resource?

    A. AppWizard

    B. ClassWizard

    C. Component Manager

    D. Visual SourceSafe

20. What is the proper prototype for a thread procedure?

    A. UINT ThreadProcedure(LPVOID lpVoid)

    B. BOOL ThreadProcedure(LPVOID lpVoid)

    C. LPVOID ThreadProcedure(UINT nID)

    D. LPVOID ThreadProcedure(void)

SELF TEST ANSWERS

1. **A, B, D.** The selling of ActiveX controls has become a big market. To add these controls to your applications, there are many sources from which you can acquire them. Many of them ship with VC++. If these do not serve your needs you can look to the many other companies that develop and market the controls. If all else fails, you can use VC++ or other Microsoft development tools to create a control that you need. There is no need to go to Microsoft to have a control built for you.

2. **B.** ActiveX controls have the extension of .OCX. This is a carry over from when the controls where named OLE Controls.

3. **C.** After adding a control to the VC++ environment using the Component Gallery, the control is added to the Dialog editor's toolbar. From here the developer can select the control, as any other control, and draw it onto a dialog resource.

4. **B.** Controls have three basic means by which a developer is able to work with them. These three things are properties, methods, and events. Properties are the characteristics of the control that the developer is able to set to cause the control to act in a specified manner.

5. **A, B, D.** Controls can be very complex and expose many properties, methods, and events. To understand how these affect the control, the developer has several options. The developer should review the Help file associated with the control. Most controls that have been purchased will have a Help file associated with them. The developer can search the Web site of the vendor. This is useful to find new controls that the vendor might have as well. Finally, one of the best ways to learn about a control is to experiment with it. Don't be afraid to start a test project and see what the control is capable of.

6. **A.** Controls have events that they are able to fire so that the container application can respond if desired. There is no such thing as a UserInteraction property that is standard for ActiveX controls. Methods are called on the control by the container application, not the other way around.

7. **D.** To enable our application to handle the events raised by a dynamically added control, we must add the DECLARE_EVENTSYNC_MAP macro to our code. This task is made easier if we create a new application and copy the code from there into our existing application.

8. **A.** There are only two types of ISAPI extensions: the ISAPI filter and the ISAPI server extension. The ISAPI server extension is run when a particular URL is requested. The ISAPI filter is started when the Web server starts and runs continuously.

9. **C.** There are only two types of ISAPI extensions: the ISAPI filter and the ISAPI server extension. The ISAPI server extension is run when a particular URL is requested. The ISAPI filter is started when the Web server starts and runs continuously.

10. **C.** When you want to execute an ISAPI extension DLL, you must reference the name of the DLL, after the server, followed by the question mark. After the first question mark, you must reference the function that you want to have executed. Finally, you place another question mark, followed by the parameter name and its value separated by an equal sign.

11. **A, C, D.** MFC provides three base classes for creating ISAPI server extensions. These are CHttpServer, CHttpServerContext, and CHtmlStream. For many ISAPI server extensions, the developer does not need to deal directly with the CHtmlStream-derived class.

12. **C.** By creating a custom AppWizard, you will be able to build new projects that are based on a project that includes the dialog resources. This AppWizard could then be installed on all of the developer's machines in your company.

13. **D.** A Scriptlet is a COM component built using HTML and a scripting language. Scriptlets were originally developed for use in Web applications, but we can use scriptlets in our VC++ applications as if they were an ActiveX control.

14. **A.** Sockets are a way in which applications can communicate over a network. Sockets were originally developed in the UNIX environment and work with the TCP/IP network protocol. Sockets are a very low level of API programming in Windows.

15. **A, C.** MFC provides two classes that implement the Socket API. These two classes are CSocket and CAsyncSocket. Of these two, CSocket is the easier class to program.

16. **C.** The basic functionality to implement the Serialize method is included in the CObject class. Because of this, if you wish to have your own objects implement this functionality they must be derived from CObject.

17. **B.** CFile does work with disk files and it is not limited to removable media, therefore choices C and D are incorrect. CFile wraps the Windows API calls that work with disk files, therefore choice A is incorrect. The possible disadvantage to using a CFile object is that it will not buffer the calls that you make. This means that every method you execute on the object will cause the physical file to be accessed. Some of the classes derived from CFile do provided for buffered access.

18. **C.** The Serialize method of a CObject-derived object receives a CArchive object as a parameter. When using the Serialize method, developers do not have to concern themselves with the CFile object; the CArchive object provides that service as well as some buffering that is not directly supported by CFile.

19. **B.** When creating a project that supports database access, AppWizard creates an object that is derived from CRecordset. The view class holds a member variable named m_pSet that references this Recordset object. Through ClassWizard, the developer is able to map a property of m_pSet to a control on a dialog resource causing the value of the current record to be displayed within the control.

20. **A.** UINT ThreadProcedure(LPVOID lpVoid) is the proper prototype for a thread procedure.

MICROSOFT CERTIFIED SOLUTION DEVELOPER

6

Creating and Managing COM Components

T he Component Object Model (COM) is the brave new world of the programming future. The days of writing an isolated application that does everything it needs to do by itself are being left to the history books. The primary motivation for using COM is the ability to write some *Thing* once and use it many times in different applications. Re-use. Leveraging your investments.

You won't read any code written in COM. COM is, as its name states, a model. It is a model to create objects that have qualities or properties and that will do tasks for you. A rubber ball has properties; it is rubber, round, and may be red or blue. That same ball can accomplish tasks such as bounce off a wall or roll on the floor or rise and fall in the air. These tasks that the ball can do are called its *methods*.

COM addresses a group of major problems connected with sharing code between applications.

COM makes it possible to use something that was written in one language with an application written in a different language. For example, I could write a component in Visual C++ and use it in Visual Basic (VB), Delphi, FoxPro, or any other COM-enabled development tool. This is because the component is already compiled and ready to execute. The user of the component does not need the source code, they only need to know what the component is capable of. You will see how to get this information later using a base interface, IUnknown.

Components that conform to the COM standard are reusable because they posses an interface. The component's implementation is purposely separated from the interface. The user of the component does not need to know how the component does what it does.

One component can be used simultaneously by more than one application. The "life" of that component is managed by the operating system. The component is removed from memory when it is no longer in use by any application and not before. These same applications do not need to know how to find the component and they do not need to worry about whether the component is already loaded into memory.

COM components may be upgraded, enhanced, and changed without destroying the applications that depended on an older version of the component. Not only can they be modified, but they are also easy to distribute.

The COM specification is available for free from Microsoft. If you have Internet access you may download it (http://www.microsoft.com/com/). It may also be found on the CDs distributed with many of the books about COM or Distributed Component Object Model (DCOM) on the market.

CERTIFICATION OBJECTIVE 6.01

Creating a COM Component

The evolution of COM has an interesting history, beginning with Dynamic Data Exchange (DDE) and progressing to Object Linking and Embedding (OLE). DDE had a steep learning curve associated with it. Applications using DDE were difficult to develop and to maintain. OLE was an attempt to allow users to include a product of one software application with another application's product. For example, if a user wrote a letter to his boss using Microsoft Word, he may want to include a visual chart representing some data from Microsoft Excel. Both of these applications are COM-enabled and both were instrumental in the evolution of the existing implementation of Active documents.

What does ActiveX have to do with this? ActiveX is a marketing term or an umbrella term for a collection of technologies. Two technologies in this collection are OLE documents and OLE servers, or Automation servers. Microsoft is aware of the confusion caused by using the term *server* because this term is also used extensively in the hardware-networking arena for a LAN server or a database server or an Internet Information server. A name change was in order. Microsoft now encourages the use of the term *component* to be synonymous with *Automation server.*

Another confusing term is client/server. In the networking arena, the meaning of this term may land anywhere along the continuum from a workstation connected through a network interface card to a network server, a database application providing data to a workstation, or an Internet application that is used to get database information. When using this term, one almost has to provide a definition to ensure that the term is correctly understood.

In the COM world there is a precisely ambiguous definition for the term client/server. An application, whether it is written as an executable (.EXE) or as a dynamic link library (.DLL), that may provide services is a *server*. Any executable application that requests services is a *client*. And yes, an executable application may be both a client and a server at the same time.

Appropriate analysis and design techniques are required before you attempt to develop a COM component. In particular, the interfaces between your component and the client must be well defined and generalized enough to enable reuse of your component in other applications, if necessary. Remember that the ability to reuse your component will result in the greatest cost benefits.

Using the SDK

COM component development in Visual C++, with the aid of the Win32 software development kit (SDK), is an exercise in patience and persistence. I am convinced that this activity builds character. The developer then understands why COM works no matter what language the component is coded in—C++, VB, or FoxPro. The effort to achieve this understanding may be greater than the effort needed to understand how to create components using the Microsoft Foundation Classes (MFC) and the Active Template Library (ATL) combined. But when you are done, you will thank yourself. We will explore the MFC and the ATL later in this chapter.

In and Out of Process

You know that every application that you run under Windows 9x or Windows NT runs in its own address space. This protects your application from the oddities of other programs and it protects the rest of your computer from the oddities of your application. If your application blows up mid-stream, it will not hang up your computer or bring down any other applications. Windows gives each program 4GB of virtual address space. This is known as the program's *process space*. You can write a component to run either in the same process space, known as *in-process*, or the component may be written to run in its own process space, known as *out-of-process,* which also means that the component may run as a standalone application. A great example of an out-of-process component is Microsoft Word or Microsoft Excel. Both of these applications may be called by another application to provide their unique functionality, that of word-processing or number crunching. The functionality of Word or Excel may be provided within the other application. Out-of-process components are also called *local servers,* meaning that they run on the same computer as the application that requested its services.

Component Communications

When an out-of-process server needs to respond to the requests of a client application, it uses a tool termed *lightweight remote procedure calls* (LRPCs). RPC is a familiar term to most programmers and LRPC is a smaller version specifically developed for COM. COM is implemented by a runtime library that contains this functionality. Every time a client needs something from the server, COM catches the request from the client and serves it up to the server in another process space by using LRPC and another concept called *marshaling.*

Marshaling is the process of gaining access to another process' address space. Marshaling creates a proxy in the client to connect to a stub in the server. This is how information is passed between processes on the same computer. Marshaling enables location transparency. The client doesn't have to worry about how to find the component, whether the component is loaded into its own process space or on another computer altogether. The proxy contains a copy of the interface pointers of the server. The stub, residing in the server, accepts the call through LRPC, and sorts out the pointers from the parameters and makes the call to the method. Once the method is finished, it then repackages everything and sends it back to the proxy in the client application. COM will supply the proxy and stubs if you use the standard interfaces. If you want custom interfaces then you need to use a specialized language called Microsoft Interface Definition Language (MIDL). Using MIDL, you can optimize local and remote components.

The Windows Registry

The Registry on any computer is unique to that computer. You cannot take the Registry off of one computer and copy it over the Registry of another computer. The Registry contains the identification and other information about all the components located on that machine. Every component is identified by a unique identification number. This number is called a globally unique identifier (GUID), pronounced goo-id. This is a 26-byte series of numbers that includes the network card node identifier of that computer as well as the current date and time and a combination of counters. The class identifier and the interface identifier, which will be discussed later, are specialized GUIDs.

Lucky for us, we don't have to create our own GUIDs. Microsoft ships a GUID generator named GUIDGEN. GUIDGEN has a visual interface, and its DOS counterpart, UUIDGEN, has a command-line interface. GUIDGEN calls a COM application programming interface (API) function CoCreateGuid( ). If you accepted the default installation directories when you installed Visual Studio, you can find GUIDGEN in the C:\program files\microsoft visual studio\common\tools directory. If you installed only Visual C++, just change Visual Studio to Visual C++ in the directory path.

To find a server the COM runtime functions, check out a hive in the Registry named HKEY_CLASSES_ROOT\CLSID. This is also the location from which the COM Viewer gets its information. When you write your component, you will be responsible for registering your component and for providing a mechanism to unregister the same component. You may do this manually, by using REGEDIT, or you may make your component self-registering. If you make the component self-registering, you use a command-line argument to register— /RegServer—or unregister—/UnRegServer—the component.

exam
🐶 *atch*   *Make sure you know how to register your Automation server by using all the different methods. Also, make sure you understand how to register a new version of your server and your custom ActiveX control.*

Interfaces

In COM, the declarations of functions are separated from the implementation of those functions. The implementation is contained in the class but the

declaration is contained in the interfaces. An *interface* is nothing but a
pointer to a pointer to a class. The one interface that all COM components
must have is IUnknown. IUnknown is the base class for the new component's
interface. The IUnknown interface provides three methods, QueryInterface,
AddRef, and Release. QueryInterface returns the information about
whether a particular function exists. AddRef and Release manage the
lifetime of the component in memory. Several client applications may
need to use a component at the same time. When application A first
invokes the component, it is loaded into memory, and *one* is added to
the reference count of the component. When application B invokes the
component, Windows knows that the component is already loaded into
memory so it adds one to the reference count to make the reference count
two. Adding to the reference count is completed using the AddRef function.
When application A is finished with the component, Windows cannot
unload the component from memory because application B still needs it.
Instead, Windows decrements the reference count by one and waits until
the reference count reaches zero before unloading the component. This
activity is managed by the Release method of IUnknown.

The application that I am using as an example is simple to the extreme. All
it does is return the name of a food that is randomly selected from a list of
foods. It doesn't even have a fancy interface; it simply opens a DOS window
and spits out the name of a food. What you see in Figure 6-1 is what you get. I
have kept this simple because the focus is only on a component example.

The header module for my Food component interface, IFOOD.H, is
as follows:

```
#ifndef IFOOD_H
#define IFOOD_H
#include "FoodGuids.h"
DECLARE_INTERFACE_(IFood, IUnknown)
{
    STDMETHOD(GetFood)(PBSTR) PURE;
};
typedef IFood* pIFood;
#endif
```

You can see, next to the DECLARE_INTERFACE macro, that the
component inherits the IUnknown interface. In the next line, you can see
that my component has only one of its own functions, GetFood.

FIGURE 6-1

The Foods application returns a randomly selected food name

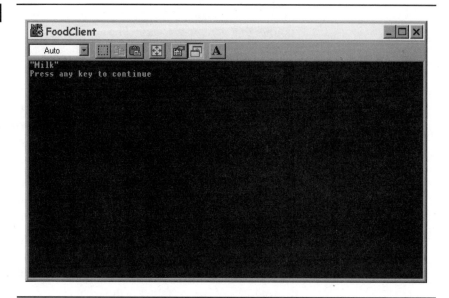

The header module to my component, FOOD.H, then includes the IFOOD.H file:

```
#ifndef FOOD_H
#define FOOD_H
#include "IFood.h"
class ComFood : public IFood
{
public:
    ComFood();
    STDMETHODIMP            QueryInterface(REFIID, PPVOID);
    STDMETHODIMP_(ULONG)    AddRef();
    STDMETHODIMP_(ULONG)    Release();
    STDMETHOD(GetFood)(BSTR*);
protected:
    ULONG m_cRef;
};
typedef ComFood* PComFood;
#endif
```

In this header, the three functions belonging to IUnknown are listed as the first three, and then my component's only function follows.

The implementation module, FOOD.CPP is as follows:

```cpp
#include <string>
#include "Food.h"
#include "FoodFactory.h"
using namespace std;
static string g_strFoods[] =
{
"Apple",
"Lemon",
"Bread",
"Meat",
"Milk",
"Cheese",
"Popcorn",
"Carrots",
"Broccoli",
"Artichokes"
};
static const ULONG g_ulNumberofFoods = sizeof(g_strFoods)/sizeof(string);
ComFood::ComFood()
: m_cRef(0)
{
g_strFoods[rand() % g_ulNumberofFoods].c_str();
}
STDMETHODIMP ComFood::QueryInterface(REFIID rIID, PPVOID ppInterface)
{
if (rIID == IID_IUnknown)
{
*ppInterface = this;
}
else if (rIID== IID_IFood)
{
*ppInterface = this;
}
else
{
*ppInterface = NULL;
return E_NOINTERFACE;
}
((LPUNKNOWN) *ppInterface) -> AddRef();
return NOERROR;
}
STDMETHODIMP_(ULONG) ComFood::AddRef()
{
m_cRef++;
return m_cRef;
}
STDMETHODIMP_(ULONG) ComFood::Release()
{
m_cRef--;
if (m_cRef)
{
```

```
return m_cRef;
}
delete this;
return 0;
}
STDMETHODIMP ComFood::GetFood(PBSTR pbstrFood)
{
g_strFoods[rand() % g_ulNumberofFoods].c_str();
return NOERROR;
}
```

Class Factory

A class factory is the way that COM creates and destroys specific instances of components. In other words, if your application needs to use a component, the application must first call the component's class factory to create an instance of that component. When you no longer need the component, then you call the class factory to get rid of the component for you. Although a class factory is often called a *class object*, it would make more sense if a class factory were called an object factory because it does not create the template, the recipe, or the cookie-cutter, but rather the actual object to be used.

Following is the class factory header module, FOODFACTORY.H:

```
#ifndef FoodFactory_H
#define FoodFactory_H
#include "IFood.h"
class ComFoodFactory : public IClassFactory
{
public:
    ComFoodFactory();
    STDMETHODIMP QueryInterface(REFIID, PPVOID);
    STDMETHODIMP_(ULONG) AddRef();
    STDMETHODIMP_(ULONG) Release();
    STDMETHODIMP CreateInstance(LPUNKNOWN, REFIID, PPVOID);
    STDMETHODIMP        LockServer(BOOL);
protected:
    ULONG m_cRef;
    ULONG m_cLocks;
    ULONG m_cNumObjects;
};
typedef ComFoodFactory* ptrComFoodFactory;
#endif
```

Following is the class factory implementation module, FOODFACTORY.CPP:

```cpp
#include <iostream>
#define INITGUID
#include "Utilities.h"
#include "FoodFactory.h"
#include "Food.h"
ULONG m_cLocks = 0UL;
ULONG m_cNumObjects = 0UL;
ComFoodFactory::ComFoodFactory()
        : m_cRef(0)
{
    VerboseMsg("HI!\n");
}
STDMETHODIMP ComFoodFactory::QueryInterface(REFIID rIID, PPVOID ppvInterface)
{
    *ppvInterface = NULL;
    if (rIID == IID_IUnknown)
    {
         *ppvInterface = this;
    }
    else if (rIID == IID_IClassFactory)
    {
         *ppvInterface = this;
    }
    else
    {
         *ppvInterface = NULL;
         return E_NOINTERFACE;
    }
         ((LPUNKNOWN) *ppvInterface)->AddRef();
         return NOERROR;
    }
STDMETHODIMP_(ULONG) ComFoodFactory::AddRef()
{
    m_cRef++;
    return m_cRef;
}
STDMETHODIMP_(ULONG) ComFoodFactory::Release()
{
    m_cRef--;
    if (m_cRef)
        return m_cRef;
    /* Counters::DecObjectCount(); */
    delete this;
    return 0;
}
```

```
STDMETHODIMP ComFoodFactory::CreateInstance (LPUNKNOWN pUnkOuter,
                                             REFIID rIID,
                                             PPVOID ppvInterface)
{
    PComFood      ptrObj;
    HRESULT           hResult;
    *ppvInterface = NULL;
    if (pUnkOuter && rIID !=IID_IUnknown)
          return CLASS_E_NOAGGREGATION;
    ptrObj = new ComFood;
    hResult = ptrObj -> QueryInterface(rIID, ppvInterface);
    if (FAILED(hResult))
    {
          delete ptrObj;
          return hResult;
    }
    return NOERROR;
}
STDMETHODIMP ComFoodFactory::LockServer(BOOL fLock)
{
    // Are we locking or unlocking?
    if (fLock) {
      // Locking
      m_cLocks++;
    }
    else {
      // Unlocking
      m_cLocks--;
    }
    return NOERROR;
}
```

Using the MFC

The MFC is commonly thought of as the tool of choice for creating
the user-interface oriented Windows-based application. But so much of
COM support is embedded within the MFC that it can greatly decrease
the lines of code. There are MFC macros that replace chunks of COM-
specific code. During my discussion, I will refer back to the Food component
and attempt to specify which lines in which modules the MFC will eliminate
or replace.

The MFC was originally named the Application Framework, which is
why you run into the acronym AFX quite often. Distributed with Visual

Studio or Visual C++ is the source code to the MFC. This is located at C:\program files\microsoft visual studio\vc98\mfc\src.

The MFC class CCmdTarget is the source of the IUnknown functionality. This class implements QueryInterface, AddRef, and Release. This is a small portion of what this valuable class can do for you. It also contains support for critical message handling, automation, and basic Windows graphical user interface (GUI) elements. This class is in the AFXWIN.H header file in the C:\program files\microsoft visual studio\vc98\mfc*include subdirectory*, assuming that when you installed Visual Studio, you accepted the default installation directories. The exact names of the methods to call are ExternalQueryInterface( ), ExternalAddRef( ), and ExternalRelease( ). The one small caveat here is that because every class must implement IUnknown, you must redirect any class' calls to these three methods into the CCmdTarget external methods.

The MFC implements multiple interface inheritance through the use of nested classes. The MFC macros BEGIN_INTERFACE_PART and END_INTERFACE_PART are actually class declarations. The BEGIN_INTERFACE_PART needs the name of the class and the name of the interface class as parameters. These macros are contained in the AFXDISP.H header file in the C:\program files\microsoft visual studio\vc98\mfc*include subdirectory*. What the END_INTERFACE_PART does for you is make the class you want to nest a friend of the wrapper class so that the nested class can access all data and methods of the outer class.

One of the major benefits of using the MFC is that it implements a class factory, the module responsible for the creation and destruction of your component, for you. You won't need to write the module FOODFACTORY.H.

The DECLARE/IMPLEMENT_DYNCREATE and DECLARE/IMPLEMENT_OLECREATE macros actually create the implementation of the class factory. These are macro pairs that must work together. The header file of your class needs the DECLARE_DYNCREATE and DECLARE OLECREATE declarations, and the code file of your class needs the IMPLEMENT_DYNCREATE and IMPLEMENT_OLECREATE calls.

The class header module would include the following statements:

- // Enable dynamic creation of the Class Factory
- DECLARE_DYNCREATE(ComFood)

- ■ // Actually declare the Class Factory
- ■ DECLARE_OLECREATE(ComFood)

An *interface map* is a table that has pointers to every interface implemented by a class. The Declare macro is the declaration of this map and the Begin/End pair of macros are the wrappers for the actual table. The DECLARE_INTERFACE_MAP MFC macro is needed in the header module and its corresponding macros BEGIN_INTERFACE_MAP and END_MESSAGE_MAP are needed in your .CPP module.

Using the ATL

The Active Template Library (ATL) is a collection of prefabricated code for writing COM objects. Many of its features are similar to the MFC and it has some additional advantages, but the basic concept of the ATL, that of enabling accelerated C++ development, is the same as the MFC. When you are considering writing components or controls that may be downloaded over the Internet, the size of the resulting file becomes important. The ATL was created to specifically address not only the size issue but also the speed of the resulting control or component.

Dual interface is a term that refers to the two ways that any component may be located once it is loaded into memory. The Registry takes care of locating the executable for the operating system to load but, once loaded, how does your client application find it in memory? One method is a *virtual function table* (vtable). This is a series of pointers that specify the address of the object's method. For example, my Food object had one method, GetFood, in addition to the three methods of IUnknown. The vtable could be graphically modeled as in Figure 6-2.

FIGURE 6-2

Vtable mapping

| QueryInterface |
| AddRef |
| Release |
| GetFood |

TABLE 6-1	Method Name	Method Description
IDispatch's Methods	Invoke	Invokes a component's method
	GetIDsOfNames	Returns the dispatch ID
	GetTypeInfo	Returns the pointer to ITypeInfo for the component's type information
	GetTypeInfoCount	If the component has type information, this method returns a one

IDispatch is the other way to find a component in memory. IDispatch, like IUnknown, is a standard interface that the component author grows to know and love. Four methods are implemented by IDispatch and are shown in Table 6-1. The *dispatch identifier* (dispid) is an integer that identifies the sequence in the list of method addresses of the pointer to the corresponding method. So to use IDispatch, one would first call GetIDsOfNames to get the dispid and then call Invoke, which would use the dispid to find the method and start it.

Vtable interfaces are faster, but automation interfaces are nice to have for those environments that can't access the vtable interface.

The creation of low-level COM objects with dual interfaces is greatly simplified by the ATL because it also manages the proxy and stubs required for marshaling. Marshaling, you may recall from our previous discussion, is the way COM enables cross-process communication through LRPC.

Whereas the MFC supports only apartment-model threading, ATL servers may use apartment-model threading, free threading models, or both. Threading models are discussed later in this chapter.

Creating an ATL COM In-Process COM Component

CWinApp is the base class for every MFC application. You may decide to create an in-process ATL COM server that has MFC support. Because of this decision, you will get a larger application than if you simply used the ATL without support for MFC.

The ATL has CComModule, which is similar to CWinApp. If you want an in-process server though, you have to take care of your own messaging. The message loop is not provided for you in CComModule as it is in CWinApp. This can be a good thing because you don't have to provide all the messaging code, just the portions that your server can't serve without. The following are some of the tasks that CComModule does provide for you:

- Registers class factories
- Registers the server
- Unregisters the server
- Manages server locks

Another class that is mandatory for an ATL component is CComObjectRoot. This is to ATL what CCmdTarget is to the MFC. It controls reference counting. But, if you were to look for IUnknown in the CComObjectRoot class declaration, you would not find it. IUnknown is in the CComObject class. CComObject is a trick class. Unlike other classes, it is derived from the class that you create. Because it is derived from your class, CComObject will provide the implementation of IUnknown and you get to ignore it. Macros declare the aggregation of your component and define the implementation of the CComObject class. These macros expand into a typedef. This typedef is for the constructor, which is used to create instances of your class when the client calls CoCreateInstance( ) or IClassFactory::CreateInstance( ). There are four different macros for four different purposes, but they all basically work the same way:

- DECLARE_AGGREGATABLE (default)
- DECLARE_NOT_AGGREGATABLE
- DECLARE_ONLY_AGGREGATABLE
- DECLARE_POLY_AGGREGATABLE

These macros all use the IUnknown methods contained in CComObjectRoot.

CComCoClass magically binds your class to the default class factory. No explicit coding is required from you so long as this is one of the classes on which your component is based. Here again are macros that expand into a typedef.

- DECLARE_CLASSFACTORY (default)
- DECLARE_CLASSFACTORY2
- DECLARE_CLASSFACTORY_AUTO_THREAD
- DECLARE_CLASSFACTORY_SINGLETON

After all of the base classes, the MIDL compiler will create interface classes based on your customer interfaces. This is achieved by writing implementation code for each function declared in each interface class.

Creating an ATL COM Out-of-Process COM Component

Remember, an out-of-process COM component is an .EXE. As such, you may run it without a client to activate it. However, if you do intend to allow other applications to create an instance of an object based on your component, you would be wise to test your component's behavior with a client. A local, out-of-process server must worry about one thing that an in-process server may ignore. The local server must concern itself with whether its internal object count is zero. If it is zero, the local server must bring itself down. This requires a CComModule subclass.

CERTIFICATION OBJECTIVE 6.02

Creating ActiveX User Interface Controls

An ActiveX control must interact with its container using COM, specifically the IUnknown interface, and it must be able to register itself in the system Registry. Controls are similar to components in that they may send and receive data from their container applications and do things for their container applications. Therefore, controls have properties and methods just as components do. But programmers also use the controls in their development environment and must be able to dictate how the control will react in the application. Therefore, controls must also have events.

TABLE 6-2	Type of Property	Type Definition
Properties and Their Definitions	Ambient	Items that affect the environment of the control's container.
	Control	Values that define the control. These may be altered by the control.
	Extended	Values that define the control. These may be altered by the control's container.

There are three different kinds of properties, as shown in Table 6-2.

on the **Job**

Remember that you must test your custom ActiveX control's behavior in two environments. The first environment is the most obvious: the runtime environment after you have used your control in a sample application. The second is the design-time environment. Other programmers who will be using your control in their development efforts must be able to rely on its correct behavior.

A control's base class, COleControl, provides two methods, and the control may provide custom methods that may be used by the container. The two methods that COleControl provides are Refresh( ), which redraws the control, and DoClick( ), which activates the event invoked in response to a click from the mouse.

COleControl also supports a handful of standard events, Click, DblClick, KeyDown, KeyUp, KeyPress, MouseDown, MouseUp, MouseMove, and Error. *Events* are messages sent by the control to the container. The container may need to provide functionality for these events when they happen.

All properties, methods, and events of a control have an identification number called a dispatch identifier (dispid). The dispid makes it possible for the control to use the properties, methods, and events. When programmers use a control in a container application, they need to know what is available to them to use. The dispids are referred to in a type library file (.TLB). The type library enables other languages to do early binding to an object because the compiler knows what functionality is offered by the control and the syntax of that functionality.

IDispatch is the interface that permits runtime binding of an OLE object. See Table 6-1 for the names and definitions of the methods for IDispatch.

IDispatch::Invoke is the magician that permits your container application to start up any method of the object, get a property of the object, or set a property of the object. This is done by passing the identifying number, dispid, to IDispatch::Invoke. Please understand that the dispid of Object A's Save method may be five, but the dispid of Object B's Save method may be nine. Additionally, the object that is not concerned with persistent data doesn't have a Save method. One of the major challenges in Automation is finding out the exposed methods and properties of the object.

Using ATL

e x a m

Ⓦa t c h   *Make sure you know the benefits of using the ATL for your ActiveX controls. Because the ATL was designed to address the issues of a small size and fast execution, you may expect to see a scenario question about whether to base a control on the MFC or the ATL.*

Create a new project using the ATL COM AppWizard. Decide on a name for your project and specify the directory to locate the project workspace. Make sure that you specify a .DLL for this project. Then, insert an ATL object by dropping down the Insert menu and choosing New ATL Object. In the dialog box that is then displayed, Figure 6-3, select Full

FIGURE 6-3

Select the category and the type of object that you want to create

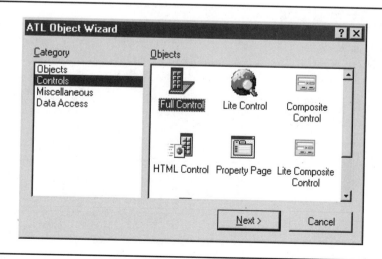

FIGURE 6-4

After you complete the Short Name field, the ATL Object Wizard fills in the rest of the text boxes

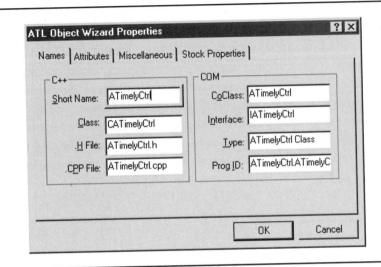

Control. A second dialog box, the control's properties dialog, is then displayed, as shown in Figure 6-4.

This dialog box is interesting because as you enter the Short Name for your ATL control, the other text boxes fill in automatically.

Click the Attributes tab to set the COM options for your control. Figure 6-5 shows the options set for the ATimelyCrtl control. The Apartment

FIGURE 6-5

Select your ActiveX control's attributes

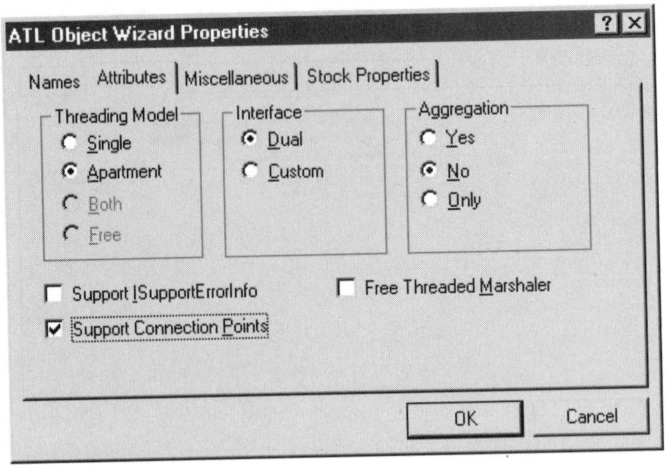

threading model is the default threading model for a full control and is the better choice for this control, which uses in-place activation.

You do want to specify a Dual interface because the IDispatch interface is used by the container. The Dual interface option button is the default. The Yes option button for the Aggregation group is the default and for my control, unnecessary. I changed this to No Aggregation. I also selected the Support Connection Points check box because my control will activate events for the container.

Stock properties, shown in Figure 6-6, are those properties that most controls need to be concerned about. When creating a control using the MFC, you can invoke the properties wizard, at any time as you are developing your control. This is not so with the ATL. This wizard is only shown while originally defining the control.

Using the SDK

Controls written without the MFC or the ATL may be highly focused, fast, and without any overhead. The downside is that without the MFC or ATL-enabling tools, you must worry about communication from your control to the container. Three interfaces that you can use specifically for this task are IOleControl, IOleControlSite, and ISimpleFrameSite.

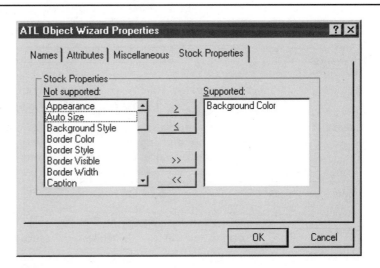

FIGURE 6-6

Select the stock properties that your ActiveX control will support

The user interface at design time must support access to properties and provide specific support for OLEIVERB_PROPERTIES (which displays the properties item on the container's menu), manipulating through the list of properties, and property change notification messages. The two types of properties available to ActiveX controls are ambient properties and extended properties. *Ambient properties* provide environment values that apply to all controls of that type. It is IOleControl::OnAmbientPropertyChange that is called whenever an ambient property is changed.

Extended properties are those properties that the container provides for the control. These properties look like native control properties. The method IOleControlSite::Get ExtendedControl allows the control access to the extended property.

Refresh, DoClick, and AboutBox are the standard methods of controls.

A control must notify its container of the control's events, and the container must be able to respond to these events, if needed. The four types of events that a control may support are listed in Table 6-3.

| TABLE 6-3 | Control Event Types |

Type of Event	Description
Request events	A control requests permission from its client to do something by calling a method in the outgoing interface, thus triggering a Request event. The client signals the control through a Boolean, out-parameter in the method that the control called. The client can thus prevent the control from performing the action.
Before events	A control notifies its client that it is going to do something by calling a method in the outgoing interface, thus triggering a Before event. The client does not have the opportunity to prevent the action, but it can take any necessary steps given the action that is about to occur.
After events	A control notifies its client that it has just done something by calling a method in the outgoing interface, thus triggering an After event. Again, the client cannot cancel this action, but it can take necessary steps given the action that has occurred.
Do events	A control triggers a Do event to allow its client to override the control's action and provide some alternative or supplementary actions. Usually, the method that a control calls for a Do event has a number of parameters for negotiating with the client about the actions that will occur.

Standard events that controls can support are Click, DblClick, KeyDown, KeyPress, KeyUp, MouseMove, MouseUp, and Error.

Be aware that the control has the responsibility of drawing itself, and the control's container has the responsibility to position and size the control.

Using the MFC

To create the control, use the MFC ActiveX ControlWizard, as shown in Figure 6-7. Because most of us are familiar with text boxes, I will base the control on the CEditBox class and give our text box some custom functionality. Figure 6-8 shows how to base your custom class on another class. In the second drop-down list box in Figure 6-8, you can see a selection of standard controls. In this example, you would select Edit.

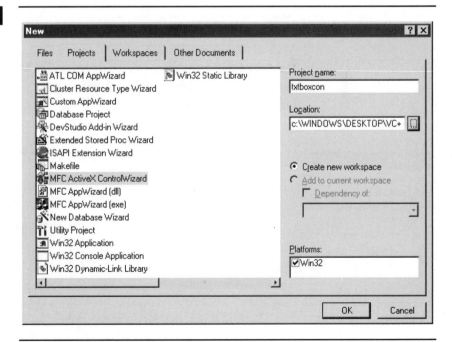

FIGURE 6-8

Use the ControlWizard to
select the features that you
want your control to have

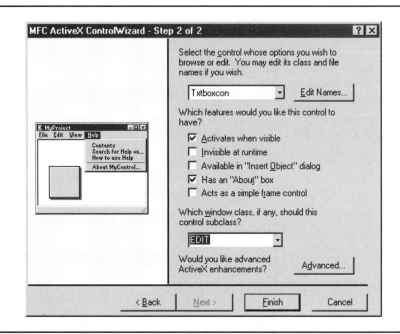

Even though the custom component is based on a standard control
class, the EDIT control is, in turn, based on COleControl, which is based
on COleControlModule, which is itself based on CWinApp. A hierarchy
model is provided in Figure 6-9.

FIGURE 6-9

The TxtBoxCon
inheritance hierarchy

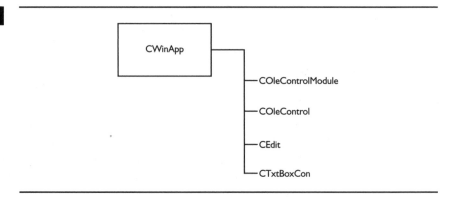

Creating a COM Component Reusing Existing Components

Components were devised to be reused. The ability to reuse what has already been written can result in a massive savings of development dollars. By using functionality that has already been tested, you only need to focus on testing the use of the component.

Aggregation versus Containment

Inheritance can be a wonderful thing, but it can also be taxing. Microsoft needed a concept that could exploit the ability to write components that are extensible without the need for invasive maintenance. Aggregation and containment both are similar to inheritance in that you can retain the original functionality of a component, then add new functionality without trashing the original functionality. The crucial difference is that with aggregation and containment only the interfaces are maintained, not the functionality itself.

Objects already exist that have functionality defined. You create an object that needs the capabilities of the existing objects. The existing objects can be bound together and placed inside your new object. The new object can also have capabilities that are unique to it. This is *containment*.

For example, my Food component has a useful method, GetFood. I could create a different component, PackagedFood, that has a method called PercentOfMDR, which returns the calculated percentage of the Minimum Daily Requirements of each vitamin and mineral that a packaged food contains. A packaged food is a combination of foods that have been prepared and perhaps enhanced, such as Strong-Person Bread.

The interface module for Food is as follows:

```
#ifndef FOOD_H
#define FOOD_H
#include "IFood.h"
class ComFood : public IFood
```

```
{
public:
    ComFood();
    STDMETHODIMP                QueryInterface(REFIID, PPVOID);
    STDMETHODIMP_(ULONG)    AddRef();
    STDMETHODIMP_(ULONG)    Release();
    STDMETHOD(GetFood)(BSTR*);
protected:
    ULONG m_cRef;
};
typedef ComFood* PComFood;
#endif
```

The interface module for PackagedFood is as follows:

```
#ifndef PACKFOOD_H
#define PACKFOOD_H
#include "IPackFood.h"
class ComPackFood : public IPackFood
{
public:
    ComPackFood();
    STDMETHODIMP                QueryInterface(REFIID, PPVOID);
    STDMETHODIMP_(ULONG)    AddRef();
    STDMETHODIMP_(ULONG)    Release();
    STDMETHOD(PercentOfMDR)(BSTR*);
protected:
    ULONG m_cRef;
};
typedef ComPackFood* pComPackFood;
#endif
```

A client may use either of these components separately or a client may need both. Both of these components implement IUnknown. When the methods of IUnknown are called, which IUnknown is used? One solution is to create a wrapper component that implements both Food and PackagedFood.

A picture of the relationship between MenuItems, Food, and PackagedFood using containment is shown in Figure 6-10. When MenuItems needs to use the Food method, GetFood, it forwards the method to the contained Food. Likewise, if it needs to use the PercentOfMBR, then the method is forwarded to the contained component.

Aggregation is slightly different. Whereas containment forwards the calls to the internal objects, aggregation directly exposes the interfaces to the internal objects as though the capabilities were its own. Look at Figure 6-11.

FIGURE 6-10

The MenuItems, Food, and PackagedFood components are using containment

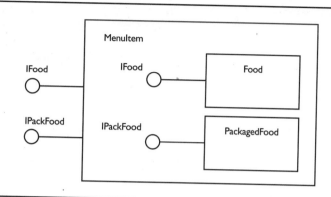

Aggregation makes the inner contained components look like they are actually part of the outer component, MenuItems. No forwarding of methods is done, the pointer returned is the true pointer of the inner methods.

FIGURE 6-11

The aggregation of Food and PackagedFood

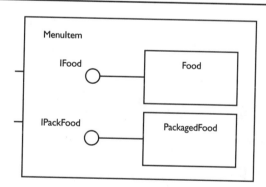

CERTIFICATION OBJECTIVE 6.04

Adding Error Handling to a COM Component

The three interfaces used for error handling are shown in Table 6-4. Be very clear that with an Automation server you need to report errors, using ISupportErrorInfo, back to the container application.

	Interface	Description
TABLE 6-4 Error Handling Interfaces	IErrorInfo	Supplied with the error object by the operating system.
	ICreateErrorInfo	Supplied with the error object by the operating system.
	ISupportErrorInfo	Used by the Automation server to manage errors and report errors back to the container application.

The operating system creates an error object that supplies IErrorInfo and ICreateErrorInfo.

The Windows API CreateErrorInfo is the function that returns an error object to your server. It is the server's responsibility to fill in the blanks with descriptive information about the error. Using ICreateErrorInfo you can insert a description, specify the path and context of the Help file, and state the GUID and the ProgID for the interface that contains the error definition. Once all of this information is set, call SetErrorInfo by using QueryInterface to get the IErrorInfo interface. You have to pass IErrorInfo's pointer to SetErrorInfo.

CERTIFICATION OBJECTIVE 6.05

Logging Errors into an Error Log

The system error log under the Windows NT 4.0 operating system is the place for logging errors. Not only is it already created for you but it is managed for you as well. The Service Control Manager (SCM) is the Windows NT service that accomplishes this task. Three types of errors are logged into the Windows NT Event Log. The Event Viewer, a utility program provided with Windows NT, can be used to look at the information that was logged. The three types of errors are application errors, system errors, and security errors. Our applications can use this error log for our own purposes. It may be used as an aid in debugging and then

TABLE 6-5	
Error Log Data	

Data Name	Data Description
Date	Date error happened
Time	Time error happened
User	User ID that was logged on when error happened
Computer	Workstation ID on which the error happened
Event Type	Informational, Warning, Severe, or Security
Source	Name of the application that generated the error
Category	User defined
Event ID	The sequence number of the event that was added to the event log
Description	User supplied textual explanation. May be localized
Event Data	Any raw data to be used in problem resolution

used by the released application for other error logging. Table 6-5 contains a list of the standard information kept in the error log.

CERTIFICATION OBJECTIVE 6.06

Creating and Using an Active Document

Active documents are the remaining vestiges of OLE. The theory behind this is the reuse advocate's dream. You write applications that do one thing very well and then use that same application in other applications that need that functionality. For example, spreadsheet tasks are aptly implemented by Excel, but you are working in a Word document that needs background data and a line chart based on that data. Although Word does have simple spreadsheet and graphing capabilities, you already have the data entered into an Excel worksheet. Your choices, without OLE, are to re-enter the data into Word, or copy and paste the Word text into Excel. With OLE, you can simply insert an OLE object into your Word document, tell the application in what form the linked data should be used, and then tell the file name. You then have a Word document with an Excel worksheet as part of the document. To modify the Excel worksheet, all you have to do is click in the worksheet to gain access to all of Excel's functionality. That is the process in a nutshell. Yes, there is more to it than that and we will explore the nuances in a moment. My point is that in the applications that you write, you can do the very same thing: get all the functionality of an existing application simply by embedding an OLE object.

There are two ways that one application's product may appear in another application. In the preceding example, where you have an Excel spreadsheet inside a Word document, the spreadsheet may be linked or embedded. If the spreadsheet is *linked*, then all that is contained in the Word document is a reference to the spreadsheet. The upside to this approach is that the size of the Word document is smaller and, if you make a change to the worksheet outside of the Word document, the change is immediately reflected. The downside is that if you move the Excel worksheet to another directory, the Word document will not be able to find it. You will have broken the link.

With *embedded* objects, the entire Excel worksheet would be copied into the Word document, enlarging the final size and creating a copy of the Excel worksheet that can only be modified from within the Word document. Any change made to the original worksheet is not reflected in the copy in the Word document.

There are also two different ways to make the Excel application do its thing. You may use *in-place activation*. What this means is that when the Word document is being edited and you double-click the Excel worksheet, Excel's menus merge with Word's menu and it appears as one application. The fact that the object has in-place activation is denoted by the hatched border around the object. Without in-place activation, when you double-click the Excel worksheet, Excel starts up in a second window and you can clearly see that there are two distinct applications running. This is the only way an embedded object can run. A linked object may run in-place or in its own window.

The two interfaces, IOleObject and IOleClientSite, make in-place activation possible.

Using AppWizard to create an OLE component creates an application class, a main frame class, and a view class. The menu for your component, IDR_SRVR_INPLACE, is the menu that may be merged with the container's menu at runtime when it is using in-place activation. If it is running as an embedded component, it will create a class named IDR_SRVR_EMBEDDED. If the container can also execute as a standalone application, the menu will be IDR_MAINFRAME.

Replacing CDocument is the COleServerDoc which supports OLE's connection to the container and interacts with the COleServerDoc class. These two classes implement IOleObject, IDataObject, IPersistStorage, and IOleInPlaceActiveObject. The container hands off the interface pointers to these classes.

To demonstrate a compound document we will create a simple application. The following exercise is intended to give you a brief introduction to an Active document. If you start the Visual C++ IDE, you may follow these steps to create the server. The screen shots show how you should complete the screens that require information. For other screens that you encounter, just accept the default selections.

EXERCISE 6-1

Creating an Active Document

1. Start the AppWizard.

2. In the Step 1 screen of the wizard, select Multiple Documents for the type of application you'd like to create; check the Document/View Architecture Support box; and choose English (United States) for the language you would like your resources in.

3. When the AppWizard's Step 2 of 6 asks for the type of database support, make sure that None is selected. This is the default.

4. In Step 3 of 6 you must click the Mini-Server option button for the type of compound document support you want to include, because the mini-server contains just enough support for what we want the Active document to accomplish.

5. In the next steps, Steps 4 and 5, simply accept the default. In Step 6, shown in the following screen, you see what files are generated for you.

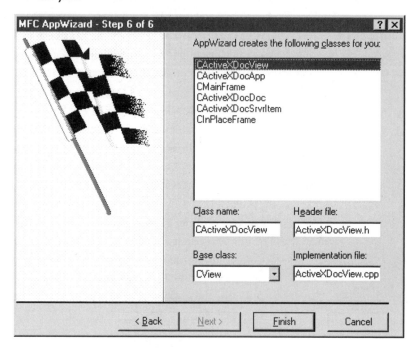

Creating a COM Component That Can Participate in a Transaction

The Microsoft Transaction Server (MTS) is an object request broker (ORB) and can also manage transactions. Using the MTS can simplify the development of components because MTS manages resources, threading, and allows the developer to concentrate on the business objective of the component rather than worrying about technical details. You need to be aware of a few COM options to write a component that is able to participate in transactions. First, MTS components must support the IClassFactory interface. Second, they must support single threaded apartments (STA), discussed in depth in the next few pages. Third, they must be a .DLL, and they must use dual interfaces. However, STA is the default threading model, a dual interface is the default interface, and .DLLs are much simpler to write. Class factories were covered in a previous section and we saw an example of an interface based on the IClassFactory interface.

The other issue is that, although MTS manages resources, it does need some help from the participating components.

Transactions

ACID enters into the game in the world of transactions. ACID is an acronym that stands for atomicity, consistency, isolation, and durability.

Atomicity refers to the rule that either all of the transaction is valid or everything is rolled back. The most common example is the banking example in which you request a transfer of $100 from savings to checking. If the debit from savings occurs but for some reason the credit to checking does not, you want to cancel everything and not allow the debit to your savings to go through. Either everything happens or nothing happens.

The concept of *consistency* protects the integrity constraints of the underlying database. If you attempt to charge a $5000 vacation on a credit card with a $2000 limit, the transaction will be stopped because a constraint on the data has been violated.

Isolation protects simultaneous transactions from getting confused. If my spouse uses his bankcard to withdraw cash at the same time I use my bankcard to withdraw cash from the same account, it is as if each transaction was conducted on its own.

The ability to survive failures, whether they are hardware, network, or application failures, is the earmark of *durability*. Once the transaction is successful, it has been committed and will not simply slide off into the proverbial bit bucket.

MTS uses the interface IObjectContext to manage transactions. Components must call the CreateInstance method of ObjectContext, which creates a subordinate object. After a new transaction finishes, the root object identifies the end by calling either IObjectContext.SetComplete if successful, or IObjectContext.SetAbort if not successful. These two methods will be discussed shortly. MTS at this point either commits the transaction or aborts the transaction. It does this through the two-phase commit protocol. Then it discards all objects used for the transaction, thereby freeing the resources.

SetComplete

As we explained earlier, SetComplete is a method of IObjectContext that is used by subordinate objects to signal MTS that it can be deactivated. The subordinate object is wrapped in a context that MTS uses to activate and deactivate the objects. The client holds a pointer to this object context to enable MTS to perform its resource management duties. An object may be one of several objects involved in a complete transaction. SetComplete is how a single object casts its vote for committing the transaction. SetAbort is how the object votes to abort the transaction.

Security

Role-based security, declarative security, and automatic security all refer to the same concept. Under Windows NT, the access control list (ACL) indicates whether an object can use a resource. Components are managed based on a user. The component has permissions and rights to some resources and not to others. Component developers declare the type of security needed and the MTS handles resource access. The MTS administrative tools provide the security administrator a way to assign users to roles when the application is deployed.

Interface Pointers

In our discussion of context wrappers for objects, we mentioned that clients have a pointer to object contexts to help MTS determine when transactions are complete and resources can be freed. This pointer is an interface pointer, and getting the initial interface pointer is an expensive step. Once the client has the pointer, it should hold it as long as needed. Because the client and server are normally on different machines, the client must find the correct machine, use DCOM, and then make the connection. This is one reason for the slower response of distributed processing.

Using and Releasing Resources

Because the greatest expense is incurred by first acquiring a resource it would make sense to hold onto the resource, but resources are limited. If the client uses the resource then releases it right away, MTS can place this resource into a connection pool. The next time a resource request comes in, MTS first checks the pool. If a resource connection already exists, MTS assigns that connection to the server, which makes the connection time very quick. This is particularly useful with database connections. If the database connections were held as long as possible by a server, connection licenses would quickly be depleted. But having a connection in the pool allows the next request to have the available database connection.

CERTIFICATION OBJECTIVE 6.08

Signing a COM Component

Code signing accomplishes two major tasks. It ensures authenticity and integrity. It assures users that they know where the code came from and it verifies that the code hasn't been tampered with. Digital signatures are created using an algorithm such as the RSA public-key cipher. A public-key algorithm uses two different keys: a public key and a private key.

Only the owner knows the private key, which is needed for encryption, and the public key, which is needed for decryption. The decryption key cannot be calculated from the encryption key. In digital signatures, the private key generates the signature and the corresponding public key validates it.

Debugging a COM Component

There are several steps in the debugging process for an ActiveX component and the client that uses the component. First, you must build both the client and the component with the debug compiler option turned on to create the symbolic debugging information, set a breakpoint in the component, then start the client under debug mode in the integrated development environment (IDE). Once the component has been instantiated by the client, the load event has executed. If your breakpoint was set in the load event, then this is when you would hit the breakpoint. When you call the component, the IDE spawns a second debug session for the component. You have to be aware of what component methods are being called and set the breakpoint in those methods. An alternative is to set a breakpoint in the client right before the component is called and then single-step into the component. You are able to step into and out of as many components as you need to and you can step across remote procedure calls as well. One advantage of this approach to debugging a COM component is that you can investigate problems if the component does not start or load properly. After you have built the component with the debug parameter on, don't forget to register the component by running it.

Apartment-Model Threading

A process may have one thread or multiple threads. These threads are managed by the operating system. It may look like multiple threads are running simultaneously but the process is implemented by swapping threads at small intervals. A *thread* is a path of executing machine-level code. To achieve high levels of performance, you may write your code so that multiple paths of code are executing at what appears to be the same time. Within a single 4GB virtual address space of an application, there are areas of memory named *apartments* and it is inside these apartments that COM objects' code executes.

Single-Threaded Apartment

The single-threaded apartment (STA) model may provide one apartment in which all of the threads of all the objects run. This makes life easy because no marshaling or cross-process communication is needed. COM method calls are placed on the window's message queue. This is done so that the operating system can attend to the calls one at a time. Legacy code often ignores threading altogether and, by default, uses a single STA.

More sophisticated coding tactics use multiple STAs within a single process space. This can make the application run faster.

An STA is started by CoInitializeEx(NULL, COINIT_APARTMENTTHREADED) and then shut down by CoUninitialize( ). COINIT_APARTMENTTHREADED is the default. If you omit this parameter, you automatically use the STA model.

Multithreaded Apartment

The multithreaded apartment model does not synchronize COM calls on the window's message queue. In fact this model calls COM components' methods without placing the request on the message queue. Only one MTA is allowed per process space, but all threads in each apartment are allowed to communicate with each other without using marshalling. The MTA model runs faster than the STA model because it does not have to toy with the window's message queue. The MTA simply uses the vtable addresses to call a component's methods. All serialization must be managed by the programmer using mutexes or events to protect shared memory or vmember data.

An MTA is started by CoInitializeEx(NULL, COINIT_MULTITHREADED) and shut down by CoUninitialize( ).

TABLE 6-6	Function Name	Description
Thread Functions	CreateThread( )	Creates a new thread
	SuspendThread( )	Pauses a running thread
	ResumeThread( )	Restarts a suspended thread
	TerminateThread( )	Kills a thread
	GetExitCodeThread( )	Queries the exit code
	ExitThread( )	Does not complete the thread function. Simply gets out of the thread
	_beginthreadex( )	Creates a new thread but also starts up and shuts down the C runtime library

Both Single-Threaded and Multithreaded

The Windows API functions that are used to manipulate threads are shown in Table 6-6. The Microsoft Developer Network (MSDN) section for Visual C++ documentation has excellent sample applications (these may be found under the MSDN directory \samples\vc98\sdk\com\tutsamp).

CERTIFICATION OBJECTIVE 6.11

Creating a Package Using the MTS Explorer

A package is a collection of related COM classes. More specifically, a package is a collection of DLLs and MTS catalog entries. They are related by the types of business functionality that they provide to the application. If I have an address object, a client object, an orderheader object, and an orderitem object, I would package the two order objects together and the client and address objects together because their business functionality is related. Both of these are examples of *server packages*. A server package executes as an MTS managed process. A library package, on the other hand, is a standard in-process Automation server in that it runs in the same process space as the client.

Each component must use DllRegisterServer which enters all IDs, CLSID, ProgID, IID, and type libraries. MTS uses this function to register all of the components in the package. Before you can add components to a package you must first create a package. To do this, you must first start the MTS Explorer. There are two sections to the Explorer window. The left section contains the computers on which you can create packages. You select a computer and select the Packages Installed folder. Right-click this folder and select New and then Package. The Package Wizard starts. Click the Create an Empty Package button. You must enter a name and click the Next button.

At this point you must indicate the identity of the package. The default is Interactive User and is usually sufficient during development. The identity refers to the Windows NT security model, which we will discuss later. Click the Finish button and the package will appear in the Packages Installed folder.

Adding Components to the MTS Package

After you have created your package, you may then add components to the package. Make sure your package is selected and then select the Components folder. Right-click the Components folder, select New, then select Component, and the Component Wizard will start. Click the Install New Component button and the next step presents your components. Select the DLLs to be installed along with any type library or proxy/stub DLL and then click the Finish button. If you can't see a component that you know should be there, make sure you have a type library for every component. If MTS cannot find the type library, it won't include that component in the list.

Using Role-Based Security to Limit Use of an MTS Package

After you have added components to your package you may define the security for the package. Because you have to define roles to be used by the entire package, you may need to set up authorization checking for specific components. This will allow you to assign roles to specific components in the package. You may do the same for interfaces. If any component uses authorization checking then the package must use authorization checks as

FROM THE CLASSROOM

The Invaluable Variant Data Type

Through the experience of developing general use COM components, I have become very familiar with the VARIANT data type and its COM wrapper, _variant_t. In order to perform its magic, the Invoke method of the IDispatch interface relies on the use of the VARIANT data type. Because using the VARIANT data type is invaluable and unavoidable when doing any development of COM components, let's take a close look at it and its usage.

To put it simply, the VARIANT data type is a union of many different data types. A VARIANT contains a data value and a value indicating the actual data type of the data. A VARIANT is 16 bytes in size and is generally used to pass around arbitrary automation data. VARIANTs can contain most primitive data types, strings, and arrays. However, it cannot contain fixed-length strings or user-defined types. Here is what the declaration of the VARIANT data type looks like:

```
struct tagVARIANT
{
        VARTYPE vt;
        union
        {
                LONG            lVal;           //VT_I4
                SHORT           iVAl;           //VT_I2
                FLOAT           fltVal;         //VT_R4
                DOUBLE          dblVal;         //VT_R8
                VARIANT_BOOL    boolVal;        //VT_BOOL
                SCODE           scode;          //VT_ERROR
                CY              cyVal;          //VT_CY
                DATE            date;           //VT_DATE
                BSTR            bstrVal;        //VT_BSTR
                IUnknown        *punkVal;       //VT_UNKNOWN
                IDispatch       *pdispVal;      //VT_DISPATCH
                SAFEARRAY       *parray;        //VT_ARRAY
                SHORT           *piVal;         //VT_I2  | VT_BYREF
                LONG            *plVal;         //VT_I4  | VT_BYREF
```

FROM THE CLASSROOM

```
        FLOAT        *pfltVal;     //VT_R4 | VT_BYREF
        DOUBLE       *pdblVal;     //VT_R8 | VT_BYREF
        SAFEARRAY    **pparray;    //VT_ARRAY | VT_BYREF
        VARIANT      *pvarVal;     //VT_VARIANT | VT_BYREF
    }
};
typedef tagVARIANT VARIANT;
```

The vt member of a VARIANT contains a constant (see the comments to the side of each member's declaration) which indicates the data type contained by the VARIANT. So, a method that receives a VARIANT parameter is able to parse the vt member to determine the actual type of the parameter. Likewise, when creating a VARIANT, the data value, as well as a constant indicating the vt value, must be set. The value of a VARIANT containing no data and no data type is indicated by the VT_EMPTY constant.

Several API calls are available that help us deal with variant types. These API calls are: VariantInit, which initializes a variant to VT_EMPTY; VariantClear, which initializes a variant by freeing the memory used within the variant; VariantChangeType, which can convert the vt property containing the data type of the variant variable to another data type (this can throw an exception if the coercion is not possible); and VariantCopy, which makes a copy of the variant and frees any existing memory in the destination before making the copy—it basically makes a call to VariantClear before changing the vt value.

The last useful construct to look at when utilizing the VARIANT type in your COM components is _variant_t. This construct encapsulates COM variant types and provides useful methods and operations that make dealing with variants within your components much easier by handling resource allocation and deallocation by calling VariantInit and VariantClear when required. Take a good look at the VARIANT data type, and its COM encapsulation _variant_t, and use these constructs when calling methods through the IDispatch interface.

—Michael Lane Thomas, MCSE+I, MCSD, MCT, MCP+SB, MCDBA, MSS, A+

well. If not, you may disable it for the package. To disable authorization checking for the package, select the package, pull down the Action menu, and choose Properties to display the package's Properties dialog box. Select the Security tab and clear the Enable Authorization Checking check box.

If you have authorization checking enabled, you must list the roles used by all the components in the package. This is for the authorization checking of the package as a whole, not for the individual components. Double-click the package and select the Roles folder. In the Action menu select New and then select Role. A dialog box will appear with a place to enter the role name and description.

The same process is used for components. If authorization checking is enabled for the package then it is enabled for all the components. If you want to disable authorization checking for a component, then select that component, display its Properties, select the Security tab, and clear the Enable Authorization Checking check box. If you want to retain the authorization checking and add roles to the component, select the Role Membership folder of that component, then select New | Role under the Action menu. A dialog box is then displayed that contains all roles available to the package. You may then select all roles that you want to have permission to use the component.

CERTIFICATION SUMMARY

The topic of COM is of profound importance and you can be sure the exam will include extensive coverage of the topic. Because ActiveX is an umbrella term there appears to be a mish-mash of different concepts, but after studying ActiveX components, Active documents, and ActiveX controls, you begin to understand that the underlying enabler for all these concepts is one model and that is COM.

For components, the major issues are whether they are in- or out-of-process, how they are registered, and how the versioning is controlled. For Active documents, the concept of in-place activation versus a separate window is important, as is understanding the difference between linked and embedded. ActiveX controls typically are downloaded and the distribution issues are extremely important.

Microsoft Transaction Server is used to wrap your COM servers and manage their resources during transactions. MTS is also used as an object request broker to initialize and destroy objects.

The best study aid is to write code using the concepts that have been covered in this chapter.

TWO-MINUTE DRILL

- ❏ ActiveX is a marketing term or an umbrella term for a collection of technologies. Two technologies in this collection are OLE documents and OLE servers, or Automation servers.

- ❏ Windows gives each program 4GB of virtual address space. This is known as the program's *process space*.

- ❏ When an out-of-process server needs to respond to the requests of a client application, it uses a tool termed *lightweight remote procedure calls* (LRPCs).

- ❏ Make sure you know how to register your Automation server by using all the different methods. Also, make sure you understand how to register a new version of your server and your custom ActiveX control.

- ❏ The MFC was originally named the Application Framework, which is why you run into the acronym AFX quite often. Distributed with Visual Studio or Visual C++ is the source code to the MFC.

- ❏ One of the major benefits of using the MFC is that it implements a class factory, the module responsible for the creation and destruction of your component, for you.

- ❏ The Active Template Library (ATL) is a collection of prefabricated code for writing COM objects.

- ❏ CWinApp is the base class for every MFC application.

- ❏ An ActiveX control must interact with its container using COM, specifically the IUnknown interface, and it must be able to register itself in the system Registry.

- ❏ *Stock* properties are those properties that most controls need to be concerned about.

❑ Without the MFC or ATL-enabling tools, you must worry about communication from your control to the container. Three interfaces that you can use specifically for this task are IOleControl, IOleControlSite, and ISimpleFrameSite.

❑ The system error log under the Windows NT 4.0 operating system is the place for logging errors. Not only is it already created for you but it is managed for you as well.

❑ With OLE, you can simply insert an OLE object into your Word document, tell the application in what form the linked data should be used, and then tell the file name.

❑ There are several steps in the debugging process for an ActiveX component and the client that uses the component. First, you must build both the client and the component with the debug compiler option turned on to create the symbolic debugging information, set a breakpoint in the component, then start the client under debug mode in the integrated development environment (IDE).

❑ A process may have one thread or multiple threads. These threads are managed by the operating system.

❑ The single-threaded apartment (STA) model may provide one apartment in which all of the threads of all the objects run.

❑ The multithreaded apartment model does not synchronize COM calls on the window's message queue.

❑ A package is a collection of related COM classes, more specifically, a collection of DLLs and MTS catalog entries.

❑ If MTS cannot find the type library, it won't include that component in the list.

❑ After you have added components to your package you may define the security for the package.

SELF TEST

The following questions will help you measure your understanding of the material presented in this chapter. Read all of the choices carefully, as there may be more than one correct answer. Choose all correct answers for each question.

1. What are the activities of an object called?

    A. Tasks

    B. Functions

    C. Methods

    D. None of the above

2. Why can a COM object written in Visual Basic be used with a client written in Visual C++?

    A. The source code from the client may be copied and pasted into the COM object.

    B. A COM object is binary.

    C. It can't be done.

    D. It can be done only if the COM object is a .DLL.

3. ActiveX is a specific term identifying what?

    A. Internet controls

    B. Compound documents

    C. Automation storage

    D. ActiveX data objects

    E. All of the above

    F. None of the above

4. What is a component called that loads into the same process space as the client?

    A. An in-region server

    B. A remote server

    C. A local server

    D. An in-process server

5. An out-of-process server and the client communicate using what protocol?

    A. TCP/IP

    B. Ethernet

    C. The Clipboard

    D. LRPC

6. What is the name of the activity that creates a proxy in the client and a stub in the server to take care of inter-process communication?

    A. ComManager

    B. Process Procedure Call

    C. Marshaling

    D. Remoting

7. The CLSID and IID are acronyms for what?

    A. Clear Screen Indirectly and Internet Indirector

    B. Class ID and Interface ID

    C. COM Lightweight Server ID and Intersection ID

    D. Common Last Screen ID and Internationalization ID

8. An interface is...?

   A. The declaration of functionality for a COM component

   B. An area of memory set up by the stub to copy the client's parameters

   C. Only needed if there is not a type library

   D. Functionality to provide inter-process communication

9. The base interface that provides QueryInterface, AddRef, and Release is named what?

   A. ICoBaseInterface

   B. IDispatch

   C. IClassContext

   D. IUnknown

10. If two different clients are using the same server, when is the server unloaded from memory?

   A. After the last client calls the UnloadNow( ) method of the server

   B. Only when the server calls the CoCanUnload method of IDispatch

   C. When the reference count is decremented to zero

   D. After AddRef adds one to the Reference Count

11. COM creates and destroys instantiations of components using what?

   A. IUnknown::AddRef and IUnknown::Release

   B. The class factory

   C. CComModule

   D. END_INTERFACE_PART

12. What is the name of the MFC class that implements IUnknown?

   A. CComObjectRoot

   B. DECLARE_INTERFACE

   C. CCmdTarget

   D. CWinApp

13. What is the name of the ATL class that implements IUnknown?

   A. Refresh

   B. CComObjectRoot

   C. AFXWIN.H

   D. CCmdTarget

14. What is the method of IDispatch that allows the container to start an ActiveX control method or get/set property method?

   A. DECLARE_DYNCREATE

   B. AFXDISP.H

   C. Invoke

   D. DECLARE_INTERFACE

15. If an Active ActiveX control uses in-place activation, which is the best threading model to use?

   A. Apartment-threading

   B. Single-threaded

   C. Free threaded

   D. It is best not to use threading at all.

16. What are the two ways to implement a dual interface?

    A. IUnknown::QueryInterface and IClassContext::InitInterface

    B. IDispatch and z-order

    C. Virtual table and the Registry

    D. Vtable and IDispatch

17. ACID stands for what?

    A. Atomicity, Consistency, Isolation, and Durability

    B. The concept that a transaction may be responsible for corrupting the database

    C. Arithmetic, Calculated, Integral, and Divisive

    D. Absolute, Central, Integer, and Decimal

18. To what must a component conform to participate in a MTS transaction? (Choose all that apply.)

    A. MTS components must support the IClassFactory interface.

    B. They must support single-threaded apartments.

    C. They must be a .DLL.

    D. They must use dual interfaces.

19. What method must a COM component participating in a MTS transaction use when it has completed its tasks?

    A. SetComplete

    B. IUnknown::Release

    C. END_INTERFACE_PART

    D. IDispatch::GetTypeInfo

20. Security for a package is based on authorization checking. Where are the roles defined for components that are also based on authorization checking?

    A. Within the User Administration in Windows NT.

    B. In the MTS Explorer, the Roles folder for the package.

    C. In the MTS Explorer, the Roles folder for the component.

    D. In the MTS Explorer, pull down Action and then click New.

SELF TEST ANSWERS

1. **C.** Methods. Method is the best term for the activities of an object. The term *tasks* is not applied to the behaviors of an object. Although methods are implemented as functions, the word *function* is used for a section of code which may return a result.

2. **B.** A COM object is binary. A COM object has been compiled and linked and therefore transformed into binary code. Any binary code module can invoke a COM object. A is incorrect because if you cut and paste C++ source code into a Visual Basic module, the module would not compile. C is not correct because this capability is a major advantage of COM. D is incorrect because the COM object may be either a .DLL or an .EXE.

3. **E.** All of the above. Answers A, B, C, and D are all terms for technologies based on COM and are part of the ActiveX group. F is incorrect because the term ActiveX is an umbrella term applied to all of these technologies.

4. **D.** An in-process server. Answer A is not correct because there is no such thing as an in-region server. A remote server cannot load into the same process space as the client because it is running on a physically separate computer. A local server runs on the same computer as the client but, because it is an .EXE, it is loaded into its own process space, not the client's process space. An in-process server is loaded into the same process space as the client that invoked it.

5. **D.** LRPC. Lightweight remote procedure calls is the correct answer. TCP/IP is a communications protocol that is a physical networking communications protocol. Ethernet is a network interface protocol. The Clipboard, although instrumental in the development of inter-process communication, is no longer used for this task.

6. **C.** Marshaling. ComManager is not correct because there is no such activity. Process Procedure Call does not exist either, although remote procedure call does and it does create proxies and stubs. Remoting is a generalized term used for any communications across a wire. Marshaling is the concept in COM that establishes the proxy in the client, packs up the information for the server, and then unpacks it in the stub of the server.

7. **B.** Class ID and Interface ID. Class ID and Interface ID are the correct answers and they are both specialized GUIDs. Clear Screen Indirectly and Internet Indirector, COM Lightweight Server ID and Intersection ID, and Common Last Screen ID and Internationalization ID are fictitious choices and do not exist.

8. **A.** The declaration of functionality for a COM component. The correct answer, the declaration of functionality for a COM component, indicates that there is no functionality at all in the interface of a component. Although the marshaling process does copy client information into the stub in the server, that area of memory does not have a name. An interface is needed along with a type library for a component. Interfaces, as a construct, do not have anything to do with inter-process communication.

9. **D.** IUnknown. IUnknown is the interface for the base COM class that every component must implement. ICoBaseInterface is a fictitious interface name. IDispatch is a way to find a component that has already been loaded into memory. IClassContext is the interface for object participation in an MTS transaction.

10. **C.** When the reference count is decremented to zero. The COM runtime will unload a component from memory only when its reference count is zero. There is no standard UnloadNow( ) function requirement for a server. IDispatch, a way to find a component in memory, does not have a method named CoCanUnload. AddRef does add one to the reference count of the component but does not unload the component from memory.

11. **B.** The class factory. The class factory is used by COM through IClassFactory to create and destroy objects, which are instantiations of a component. AddRef and Release are methods of IUnknown but they manage loading and unloading components from memory. CComModule is an ATL class that implements IUnknown. END_INTERFACE_PART is an MFC macro that enables a nested class to be a friend of the superclass.

12. **C.** CCmdTarget. CCmdTarget is the correct answer and is the MFC implementation of the IUnknown interface. DECLARE_INTERFACE is an MFC macro that specifies the IUnknown interface but it does not implement the interface. CComObjectRoot is the ATL implementation of IUnknown, not the MFC. CWinApp is the base class for window functionality in the ATL.

13. **B.** CComObjectRoot. CComObjectRoot is the correct answer and is the ATL implementation of the IUnknown interface. CCmdTarget is the MFC implementation of IUnknown, not the ATL. Refresh is an event of the base control class, COleControl. AFXWIN.H is the header file for the module that contains the CCmdTarget class.

14. **C.** Invoke. Invoke is the method of IDispatch that manages the initialization of a control's method. DECLARE_DYNCREATE and DECLARE_INTERFACE are both MFC macros. AFXDISP.H is a header file for the module that contains the BEGIN/END_INTERFACE_PART macros.

15. **A.** Apartment threading.

16. **D.** Vtable and IDispatch. IUnknown::QueryInterface is used to determine the functionality that a component implements and IClassContext::InitInterface is a fictitious method. Z-order refers to the layering of windows on top of one another on the desktop. The Registry takes care of locating the executable for the operating system to load. Vtable and IDispatch are the two techniques used to locate a component in memory.

17. **A.** Atomicity, Consistency, Isolation, and Durability. A transaction must be complete, be the same every time, be separated from all other transactions, and remain intact after a failure. The last three choices are fictitious.

18. **A, B, C, D.** All choices are required.

19. **A.** SetComplete. When a component is finished with resources, it must call SetComplete to let MTS know that it can release resources back into the pool. IUnknown::Release is not correct because this is the base interface that all components must implement and it decrements the component's reference count. END_INTERFACE_PART is an MFC macro that enables a nested class to be a friend of the superclass. IDispatch::GetTypeInfo returns the pointer to ITypeInfo for the component's type information.

20. **B.** In the MTS Explorer, the Roles folder for the package. Answer A is not correct because, although this may be where Windows NT roles are initially defined, they also must be defined to MTS. C is not correct because roles are chosen from the list of roles initially defined in the Roles folder for the package. D is not a complete answer because the package must be expanded and then the roles folder must be selected.

7

Data Services

I n this chapter we will discuss some of the services that are performed to access data in a database using ActiveX Data Objects (ADO). We will discuss what cursors are and how to use the different options available for cursors. Some of these options include where the cursor should be located (client-side or server-side) and the different types of cursors. We will discuss how to handle errors that occur while performing database operations. This chapter also covers how to use transactions to preserve the integrity of the data in case of failures or errors. You will learn how locking is done on records in a database to prevent concurrent access. You can use the Supports method of a Recordset object to determine which options are available for a recordset.

Manipulating Data Using Different Cursor Locations

You can query a database to return a set of records that match the criteria for your query. This result set is called a *cursor*. The reason it is called a cursor is because it will track which record is current in the recordset. The result set is stored in a Recordset object. Using the Recordset object, you can navigate through the records to view or manipulate the fields in the current record. There are some options available for using a cursor in ADO. In this section we will discuss the different locations at which a cursor can run and how to choose which location to use. The cursor can be built on either the client or the server. There are different capabilities associated with each.

To specify where you want the cursor to be built, you can set the CursorLocation property. This property is available in the Connection and Recordset objects. When you open a connection to a data source, you need to set the CursorLocation property before opening the connection. Changing the property after the connection is open has no effect on the existing connection. This can also be set on a Recordset object before it is opened. This will cause the recordset to be built on the specified location. To specify that a cursor should be built on the server, set the CursorLocation to *adUseServer*. To specify that a cursor should be built on the client, set the CursorLocation to *adUseClient*.

Server-Side Cursors

When using ADO, the cursor will be built on the server by default. This means that the records will be physically stored on the server. If the data provider that you are accessing doesn't support server-side cursors, then a client-side cursor will be built. Server-side cursors can improve the performance of an application because there is less overhead on the client and the amount of network traffic is reduced. You might be wondering how the network traffic can be reduced. This is because the entire rowset isn't passed across the network. Only a portion is sent across the network at a time. This way, if you are not parsing the entire recordset, less data is sent across the network. How much data is sent across at a time is determined by the caching properties. Following is an example of opening a connection and a recordset using a server-side cursor.

```
//open a connection to a data source
_bstr_t strCnn("Provider=sqloledb;Data Source=SRV;"
              "Initial Catalog=pubs;User Id=sa;Password=;");
hr = pCnn1.CreateInstance(__uuidof(Connection)));
hr = pCnn1->Open(strCnn,"","",NULL);

//open a recordset
hr = pRst.CreateInstance(__uuidof(Recordset)));
pRst->CursorLocation = adUseServer;
//the other options will be discussed later in the chapter
pRst->Open("table",_variant_t((IDispatch *) pCnn1, true),
          adOpenForwardOnly, adLockReadOnly, adCmdTable);
```

Client-Side Cursors

You can specify that the cursor should be built on the client. This means that the records will be physically stored on the client. If the data provider that you are accessing doesn't support server-side cursors, then a client-side cursor will be built. One of the main features of the client-side cursor is that it allows you to use a disconnected recordset. This also offloads some of the overhead from the server. The entire recordset will be stored and processed on the client. You can also create recordsets in code without connecting to a data source. Currently, ADO supports only the static cursor type for client-side cursors. We will discuss the different cursor types in the next section. There are some disadvantages to using client-side cursors. If the client has limited resources and the recordset is large, it can decrease the performance of the application. If you are not using the disconnected recordset, then the client-side cursor should generally be limited to small recordsets.

One of the benefits of a client-side cursor is the ability to use a disconnected recordset. A recordset becomes disconnected when you disable the active connection. This allows you to use a recordset without being connected to the data source. As an example, say a salesman wants to retrieve a recordset each morning to his laptop that contains the data for the customers he is meeting with that day. He can connect to the data source, retrieve the data, and then disconnect from the data source. He can then have all the data with him and update the data for new orders or any changes that are necessary. He can even add new customers to the recordset. Then, at the end of the day, he can connect back to the data source and update the data source with the changes that are made and any new records that have been added. As the example shows, this can be a powerful feature. In addition, you can save the disconnected recordset to a file and then retrieve the recordset from a file for persistent storage. To do this, use the Open and Save methods of the Recordset object. The data can be saved in two formats: the Microsoft Advanced Data Table Gram (ADTG) format using the adPersistADTG parameter or the Extensible Markup Language (XML) format using the adPersistXML parameter. When you wish to use a disconnected recordset, the *lock type* must also be set to *batch optimistic*. We will cover lock types later in the chapter. See the following code for an example of disconnecting a recordset and saving and retrieving the data using a disconnected recordset.

```
//open a connection
_bstr_t strCnn("Provider=sqloledb;Data Source=SRV;"
               "Initial Catalog=pubs;User Id=sa;Password=;");
hr = pCnn1.CreateInstance(__uuidof(Connection)));
hr = pCnn1->Open(strCnn,"","",NULL);

//open a recordset using the connection object
hr = pRst.CreateInstance(__uuidof(Recordset)));
pRst->Open("table",_variant_t((IDispatch *) pCnn1, true),
           adOpenStatic, adLockBatchOptimistic, adCmdTable);

//now let's disconnect the recordset
pRstAuthors->ActiveConnection = NULL;
```

```
//save to a file
 pRstAuthors->Save("C:\\records.dat",adPersistADTG);
//now let's retrieve the data from the file
pRstAuthors->Open("C:\\records.dat", "Provider=MSPersist;", adOpenStatic,
               adLockBatchOptimistic, adCmdFile);
//now let's reconnect to the data source and update
//because we didn't close the connection, we can just set the active
//connection back to the object, or if needed, you could open a new connection
//and set the active connection to that object
pRstAuthors->ActiveConection = pCnn1;
//now let's update the data source with changes to all records
pRstAuthors->UpdateBatch(adAffectAll);
```

There are ways to solve data conflicts for the disconnected recordset. Say for example, you update a record while disconnected and someone who was connected to the data source updated the record after you retrieved it, but before you updated it. ADO will not update that record, but will give you the means to determine if there was a conflict and the opportunity to resolve it. How the conflict is resolved is up to you. You may wish to simply overwrite the existing data, discard your changes, or merge them. When you have a client-side cursor, each field in a record has multiple values stored. There is an original value that contains the value that was retrieved from the data source. There is an underlying value that you can use to re-query the data source to see what existing values are currently in the data source. Additionally, there is the current value for the field. If any records could not be updated, a warning will be returned in the Errors collection of the Connection object. The Errors collection will be covered later in the chapter. Each record also has a Status property that can be checked to determine if the update was completed for each record. Instead of iterating through each record in the recordset, you can use the Filter property of the Recordset object by setting it to adFilterConflictingRecords to limit the records available to the records that failed the batch update. When you are finished, set the Filter property back to adFilterNone to make all of the records available.

Another benefit is the ability to create recordsets through code without connecting to a data source. This allows you to collect data from multiple data sources and return it as a single recordset, or if you have a proprietary data source that you want to expose as a standard recordset, you can create the recordset in code and return the recordset. A common example of this is creating a Component Object Model (COM) object in the business tier that reads data from a nonstandard data source and returns a standard ADO recordset to the client. This way, the client doesn't have to know anything about the underlying data source. The COM object becomes a data source. In Exercise 7-1, we will see how to set the cursor location when connecting to a data source.

<table>
<tr><td>**EXERCISE 7-1**</td></tr>
</table>

Setting the Cursor Location

1. Start Visual C++ 6.0 and from the File menu, select New.

2. Select the Projects tab and select Win32 Console Application.

3. In the Project name field, type **Chap7_1** and click the OK button.

4. Select An Application That Supports MFC and click the Finish button.

5. When the New Project Information dialog box appears, verify the information and click the OK button to create the project.

   The first thing we need to do is import the DLL functionality into the project. We will do this using the #import command. This will import type library information into the project. It will create two header files (with extensions .TLH and .TLI) that contain the type library information so that it can be used in the project. It will also create smart pointers for interfaces as discussed in earlier chapters, declarations for typedefs, and enumerated constants.

6. Open the STDAFX.H file and go to the bottom of the file.

7. Type the following code after the comment. You might want to verify that this is the correct path to your ADO library. If not, edit the path as necessary. The EOF property is renamed because of a conflict with the file I/O EOF property.

```
#import "C:\Program Files\Common Files\System\ADO\msado15.dll" \
        no_namespace rename("EOF", "EndOfFile")
```

8. Open the Chap7_1.CPP source file.

9. At the top of the _tmain function add the following lines of code to initialize the COM library. If you do not add this code, you will not be able to use ADO.

```
int _tmain(int argc, TCHAR* argv[], TCHAR* envp[])
{
    int nRetCode = 0;

    //Add code here
    ::CoInitialize(NULL);
```

10. In the else block of the _tmain function you will see a comment and code similar to the following code. Delete the code below the comment inside the else block. There should be three lines of code that prints the Hello string. We will be inserting some code here.

```
// TODO: code your application's behavior here.
CString strHello;
strHello.LoadString(IDS_HELLO);
cout << (LPCTSTR)strHello << endl;
```

11. We will be using an Access database that comes with the Visual Studio applications. It is called NWIND.MDB. You need to know where yours is located on your computer, so we will search for it. From the Start menu, click Find, and then Files or Folders. This will bring up the Find dialog box. Make sure the Name & Location tab is selected. In the Named field, type **NWind.MDB**. In the Look In field, select Local Hard Drives. The dialog box should look similar to the one shown next.

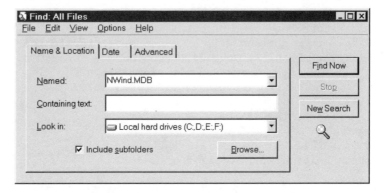

12. Click the Find Now button and wait for it to search your hard drives. When it finds the file, write down the path to where it is located.

It is probably similar to c:\program files\visual studio\vc98. If you don't have this file, you can either reinstall Visual C++ 6.0 and add installation of the samples, or select any other Access database. Search on *.MDB to find other Access databases. From here on out, we will refer to this as the DB path.

13. Replace the code deleted earlier with the following code.

```
HRESULT hr = S_OK;
_RecordsetPtr pRst = NULL;
//create the connection string
//NOTE: if you have a version of ADO that is later than 2.0,
//      replace 3.51 with version 4.0
//Also, replace the following path with your DB path
_bstr_t strCnn("Provider=Microsoft.Jet.OLEDB.3.51;
    Data Source=e:\\Program Files\\Microsoft Visual
        Studio\\VB98\\nwind.mdb;"
    "Persist Security Info=False;");
//open a recordset
hr = pRst.CreateInstance(__uuidof(Recordset));
//see if successful
if (hr < 0)
{
    printf("Error# %d when creating the recordset\n", hr);
    getchar();
    return -1;
}
//or could set to adUseClient
pRst->CursorLocation = adUseServer;
//the other options will be discussed later in the chapter
if (pRst->Open("Employees",strCnn, adOpenForwardOnly,
            adLockReadOnly, adCmdTable)  < 0)
    printf("Error opening the database\n");
else
    printf("The database was opened successfully\n");
getchar();
pRst->Close();
pRst->Release();
```

14. Run the project. The console should display that the database was opened.

15. Save this project. We will be using it in later exercises.

Manipulating Data Using Different Cursor Types

With ADO, there are four types of cursors; forward-only, static, dynamic, and keyset. The different types of cursors each have their own advantages, and you need to understand when each one should be used for a given scenario. You must select the cursor type before opening the recordset. You cannot change the cursor type of a recordset after opening it. In order to change a recordset type after opening it, you would have to close the recordset and then reopen the recordset with the new cursor type. This is also true of the cursor location and the lock type. To set the cursor type, either set the property before opening the recordset, or pass it in as a parameter to the Open method of the Recordset object. When a recordset is closed, the CursorType property is read/write. When a recordset is open, the property is read-only. If you set the type of cursor to a type that is not supported, it will return a type that is closest to the requested type.

Forward-Only Cursors

By default when you open a recordset, the cursor type is forward-only. This cursor type allows you to navigate through the recordset from the first record to the last. You cannot navigate backwards through the recordset. You can only use the MoveNext method of the recordset. If you try another navigation method such as MovePrevious, it will generate an exception. Even though the forward-only cursor is the default type, it is good practice to specify it. To specify the cursor to be of the forward-only type, set the Recordset object's CursorType property to adOpenForwardOnly.

The forward-only cursor type may seem very limited in functionality, but it has the least amount of overhead of the cursor types and is therefore the fastest and most efficient. This cursor type is useful for filling list boxes, for example. Because you do not need to navigate back and forth through the recordset, but just need one pass through, this is the preferred cursor type for recordsets that are created for this type of use. If you set a property for a recordset, and then pass in a different value for that property in the Open method, the value in the Open method will override the previous setting of the property, so you need to be careful. Generally, if you need to pass in a property to the Open method, there is no reason to explicitly set it. I have been explicitly setting some properties to show how to use them.

```
pRst->CursorType = adOpenForwardOnly;
//or
hr = pRst->Open("table", strCnn, adOpenForwardOnly,
                            adLockReadOnly, adCmdTable));
```

Static Cursors

You can think of a static cursor as a snapshot of the result set. Any updates, additions, or deletions to the result set that are made after the recordset is opened will not be reflected in the recordset. If a change is made to the underlying data source, you will not be able to see the change in your recordset. In order to see changes made by other users, you have to close the recordset, and then reopen it. This can cause conflicts to occur if you made changes to records that were also changed by another user after you opened the recordset. As discussed earlier, you would have to resolve the conflict. A static cursor does give you more flexibility than a forward-only cursor. You can navigate back and forth through the recordset. This type of cursor is good for data that never or seldom changes, and you need to be able to navigate throughout the recordset. Also, this type of cursor must be used for a client-side cursor and disconnected recordsets. A static cursor has more overhead than the forward-only type, but less than the dynamic and keyset cursor types. To set the cursor type to *static*, set the Recordset object's CursorType to adOpenStatic.

```
pRst->CursorType = adOpenStatic;
//or
hr = pRst->Open("table", strCnn, adOpenStatic,
                          adLockReadOnly, adCmdTable));
```

Dynamic Cursors

When you need to have access to the most up-to-date data for a recordset, then you use a dynamic cursor. Of all the cursor types, dynamic provides the most functionality. Any changes that are made to the underlying data source are detected by the cursor and these changes are available in your recordset. This includes updates to records, records being deleted, records that are added, and any changes to the order of the recordset. For example, say you opened a recordset, and another user updated some of the fields in a record that you opened, deleted one of the records, and added another record. Your recordset would be updated to reflect the changed fields, the record that was deleted from your recordset, and the new record would be made available in your recordset. Thus, you have access to live data. As the data changes, so does your recordset data. This cursor type has the most functionality and therefore the most overhead of all the cursor types. To open a recordset with a dynamic cursor type, set the Recordset object's CursorType property to adOpenDynamic.

```
pRst->CursorType = adOpenDynamic;
//or
hr = pRst->Open("table", strCnn, adOpenDynamic,
                         adLockReadOnly, adCmdTable));
```

Keyset Cursors

If you need more functionality than you get from a static cursor, but you don't need all of the functionality of a dynamic cursor, then a keyset cursor might be your choice. You can see some of the changes in the underlying data source, but not all of them. You can see changes to the values of records in your recordset, but you cannot see records that are added and your recordset will not reflect any changes to the order of your recordset. However, records that are deleted by other users will no longer be available in your recordset. So, if you want to see changes to the data in records, but not additions of records, then keyset is a good choice. To specify a recordset to be a keyset cursor type, set the Recordset object's CursorType property to adOpenKeyset.

```
pRst->CursorType = adOpenKeyset;
//or
hr = pRst->Open("table", strCnn, adOpenKeyset,
                           adLockReadOnly, adCmdTable));
```

In Exercise 7-2, we will add code to set the cursor types.

EXERCISE 7-2

Setting the Cursor Type

1. Open project Chap7_1.

2. In the else block of the _tmain function, we will add code to set the cursor type.

3. The following code is how your code should look now. We will add code, as shown, after the comment that says *Added code here*. In the Open method, we will change the CursorType parameter.

```
HRESULT hr = S_OK;
_RecordsetPtr  pRst = NULL;
//create the connection string
//NOTE: if you have a version of ADO that is later than 2.0,
//      replace 3.51 with version 4.0
_bstr_t strCnn("Provider=Microsoft.Jet.OLEDB.3.51;
     Data Source=e:\\Program Files\\Microsoft Visual
          Studio\\VB98\\nwind.mdb;"
     "Persist Security Info=False;");
//open a recordset
hr = pRst.CreateInstance(__uuidof(Recordset));
//see if successful
if (hr < 0)
{
    printf("Error# %d when creating the recordset\n", hr);
    getchar();
    return -1;
}
//or could set to adUseClient
pRst->CursorLocation = adUseServer;

// Added code here
pRst->CursorType = adOpenStatic;
```

```
//the other options will be discussed later in the chapter
if (pRst->Open("Employees",strCnn, adOpenStatic,
                adLockReadOnly, adCmdTable)  < 0)

    printf("Error opening the database\n");
else
    printf("The database was opened successfully\n");
getchar();
pRst->Close();
pRst->Release();
```

Even if you set the property as we did earlier, the Microsoft Foundation Classes (MFC) wrapper to the Open method of the Recordset object still requires the CursorType to be passed in as a parameter. Normally, you wouldn't set the property and then pass it in to the Open method. It is being shown here only to demonstrate the property.

4. Run the project. The console should display that the database was opened.

5. Save this project. We will be using it in later exercises.

CERTIFICATION OBJECTIVE 7.03

Handling Database Errors

The Connection object contains an Errors collection. This collection contains Error objects, which are errors returned by the data source provider. These are the errors that are specific to the provider, not ADO. Errors that occur in ADO will cause an exception. The provider can also return warnings that will not cause an exception. You can check the Errors collection after each operation to look for warnings, if desired. The Errors collection has the following properties and methods:

- **Count** A property that can be used to determine how many Error objects are in the collection. The collection is zero-based.

- **Clear**   A method that is used to remove all of the Error objects in the collection. You should call this method after you have viewed the errors. When an error occurs, all of the existing errors are removed from the collection before populating it with the new errors. If you are periodically checking the collection for errors, you should clear the collection whenever it is checked and there are errors in the collection.

- **Item**   A property used to retrieve the Error objects from the collection.

The Errors collection can contain one or more Error objects. Each Error object represents a separate error. Each Error object contains the following properties:

- **Description**   Contains a textual description of the error.

- **Number**   Contains a unique long value indicating the error that occurred.

- **HelpFile**   Contains a string that identifies the path and a file name that can be used to display additional information about a particular error.

- **HelpContext**   Contains a long value that is a context ID for where in the Help file, specified by HelpFile, the information is located.

- **Source**   Contains a string that identifies the object that raised the error.

- **SQLState**   Contains a five-character string identifying an American National Standards Institute (ANSI) Structured Query Language (SQL) error code.

- **NativeError**   Contains a provider-specific error code.

An important point about using ADO object properties is that you can either use the property directly as shown throughout the chapter or you can use a MFC wrapper function that prefixes the property name with *Get* or *Put*. The main difference is that when using the MFC wrapper, if the operation is not successful it will throw a COM error (_com_error) exception, whereas using the property directly will not cause an exception.

For example, to retrieve the Error objects from the collection, instead of using the Item property directly, you can use the GetItem method. If there is an error retrieving the object, it will throw a _com_error exception. Also, most operations return a HRESULT return code that can be checked to see if the operation failed. If it fails, it will be a value that is less than zero. The following is a code example of using the Errors collection to view errors.

```
try
{
  //Intentionally trigger an error.
  // open an invalid connection
  hr = pCnn1->Open("nothing","","",NULL));
}
catch(_com_error)
{
  //find out how many errors there are
  nCount = pCnn1->Errors->Count;
  if (nCount > 0)
  {
    // Collection ranges from 0 to nCount - 1
    for(i = 0; i < nCount; i++)
    {
      //get the ith error
      pErr = pCnn1->Errors->GetItem(i);
      //display the properties of the error
      printf("Error #%d\n", pErr->Number);
      printf("%s\n",(LPCSTR)pErr->Description);
      printf("Source: %s\n",(LPCSTR)pErr->Source);
      printf("SQL State: %s\n",(LPCSTR)pErr->SQLState);
      printf("NativeError: %d\n",(LPCSTR)pErr->NativeError);
      //use the Get wrapper in case of error
      if ((LPCSTR)pErr->GetHelpFile() != NULL)
      {
        printf("HelpFile: %s\n" ,pErr->HelpFile);
        printf("HelpContext: %s\n" , pErr->HelpContext);
      }
    }
  }
  else
    //handle other error types
}
```

| EXERCISE 7-3 | **Handling ADO Errors** |

1. Open project Chap7_1.

2. In the else block of the _tmain function, we will add code to handle errors.

3. The following code is how your code should look now. We will add code, as shown, after the comment that says *Added code here*. To use the Errors collection, you must open a connection. We will remove the checks for the return results because we are enabling exception handling.

```
else
{
    HRESULT hr = S_OK;
    _RecordsetPtr  pRst = NULL;

    //Added code here
    _ConnectionPtr pCnn = NULL;

    //create the connection string
    _bstr_t strCnn("Provider=Microsoft.Jet.OLEDB.4.0;
        Data Source=e:\\Program Files\\Microsoft Visual
            Studio\\VB98\\nwind.mdb;"
        "Persist Security Info=False;");

    //Added code here
    try
    {
        //Added code here
        // open connection
        hr = pCnn.CreateInstance(__uuidof(Connection));
        pCnn->Open(strCnn,"","",NULL);

        //open a recordset
        hr = pRst.CreateInstance(__uuidof(Recordset));
        pRst->CursorLocation = adUseServer;
        pRst->CursorType = adOpenStatic;
        //the other options will be discussed later in the chapter
```

```
    hr = pRst->Open("Employees",_variant_t((IDispatch *)pCnn,true),
                    adOpenStatic, adLockReadOnly, adCmdTable);

    printf("The database was opened successfully\n");
    getchar();
    pRst->Close();
    pRst->Release();
}
//Added code here
catch(_com_error &e)
{
    // pErr is a record object in the Connection's Errors collection.
    ErrorPtr pErr    = NULL;
    long     nCount = 0;
    long     i      = 0;
    if( (pCnn->Errors->Count) > 0)
    {
        nCount = pCnn->Errors->Count;
        //the Errors collection ranges from 0 to nCount -1.
        for(i = 0; i < nCount; i++)
        {
            pErr = pCnn->Errors->GetItem(i);
            printf("Error number: %x\t%s", pErr->Number, pErr->Description);
        }
    }
    getchar();
    }
}
```

4. Now let's cause an error and see how the error is caught. In the line of code where we open the recordset, change the table name from Employees to **Nothing**, as follows:

```
hr = pRst->Open("Nothing",_variant_t((IDispatch *)pCnn,true),
                adOpenStatic, adLockReadOnly, adCmdTable);
```

5. Rebuild the project and run the program.

6. Your console should display an error message similar to Figure 7-1.

7. Save your project. We will be using this for another exercise.

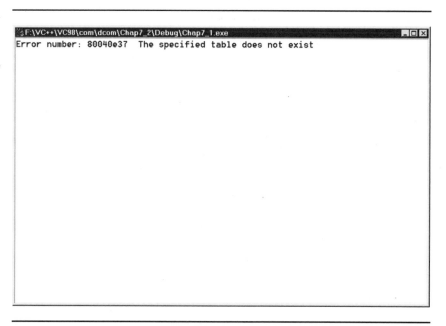

CERTIFICATION OBJECTIVE 7.04

Managing Transactions to Ensure Data Consistency and Recoverability

Transactions group SQL statements as if they are one logical operation. Either all of the statements are successful or all of them fail. If they are all successful, then the transaction is committed (the SQL statements are run against the data source and made permanent). If any of the SQL statements fail, the entire group can be rolled back (none of the SQL statements are run against the data source).

The common example is an ATM machine. If you were transferring money from one account to another, the operations would be to withdraw money from one account and then deposit it into the other account. What if there was a power failure after the money was withdrawn but before it was deposited into the other account? You would be very upset if your money was lost. With transactions, your operation would either fail and the money withdrawn from the first account would be put back, or when power was restored, the transaction would finish and deposit the money into the other account. Transactions fulfill the ACID properties. ACID is an acronym for the four main properties of transactions:

- **Atomicity** Ensures that all of the operations in the transaction occur or none of them do. If the transaction is aborted, the data will be restored to its original state.

- **Consistency** A transaction leaves the data in a state that is expected. This means the transaction should not violate any business rules.

- **Isolation** If multiple transactions are operating on the same data, the transactions will not be aware of any partial results from other transactions. This prevents one transaction from performing operations on some partial result of another transaction, and then that transaction being rolled back. This could cause the first transaction to be invalid.

- **Durability** A transaction can survive a failure such as a computer crash. This means that if there is some type of failure, even if the computer crashes, the transaction can be rolled back or committed.

To manage transactions using the Connection object, there are three methods for transactions:

- **BeginTrans** Begins a transaction.
- **CommitTrans** Saves the changes and ends the transaction. The changes are now made permanent.
- **RollbackTrans** Aborts the changes made in the current transaction, restoring the data to its original state, and ends the transaction.

Once a transaction is started using the BeginTrans method, any recordset or command objects created will become part of the transaction. This means that any operations performed by these objects will automatically become part of the transaction and will either be committed or rolled back. For an example of using a transaction, see the following code.

```
pCnn->BeginTrans();
//perform operations on recordset
if (Successful)
  pCnn->CommitTrans();
else
  pCnn->RollbackTrans();
```

In Exercise 7-4, we will see how to use transactions.

EXERCISE 7-4

Using Transactions in ADO

1. Open project Chap7_1.

2. In the else block of the _tmain function, we will add code to use transactions.

3. The following code is how your code should look now. We will add code, as shown, after the comment that says *Added code here*. We will use the Products table and count all of the units in stock. If any of the record reads fail, the transaction will abort. This isn't something you would normally use transactions for, but I didn't want to edit any databases and this will show you how to use the transactions. We will add some code to perform transactions.

```
else
{
    HRESULT hr = S_OK;
    _RecordsetPtr  pRst = NULL;

    //Added code here
    _ConnectionPtr pCnn = NULL;
    _variant_t vUnitsInStock;

    //create the connection string
    _bstr_t strCnn("Provider=Microsoft.Jet.OLEDB.4.0;
        Data Source=e:\\Program Files\\Microsoft Visual
            Studio\\VB98\\nwind.mdb;"
        "Persist Security Info=False;");
```

```
//Added code here
try
{
    //Added code here
    // open connection
    hr = pCnn.CreateInstance(__uuidof(Connection));
    pCnn->Open(strCnn,"","",NULL);
    //start the transaction
    pCnn->BeginTrans();

    //open a recordset
    hr = pRst.CreateInstance(__uuidof(Recordset));
    pRst->CursorLocation = adUseServer;
    pRst->CursorType = adOpenStatic;
    //the other options will be discussed later in the chapter
    //Added code here - changed to Products table
    hr = pRst->Open("Products",_variant_t((IDispatch *)pCnn,true),
                    adOpenStatic, adLockReadOnly, adCmdTable);
    printf("The database was opened successfully\n");

    //added code here
    vUnitsInStock.iVal = 0;
    while (!(pRst->EndOfFile))
    {
        _variant_t Temp;
        Temp = pRst->Fields->Item["UnitsInStock"]->Value;
        vUnitsInStock.iVal += Temp.iVal;
        pRst->MoveNext();
    }
    //Added code here
    printf("There are a total of %d Units in stock\n", vUnitsInStock.iVal);
    //successful, so let's commit the transaction
    pCnn->CommitTrans();

    getchar();
    pRst->Close();
    pRst->Release();
}
//Added code here
catch(_com_error &e)
{
    // pErr is a record object in the Connection's Errors collection.
    ErrorPtr pErr  = NULL;
    long      nCount = 0;
    long      i      = 0;
```

```
if( (pCnn->Errors->Count) > 0)
{
    nCount = pCnn->Errors->Count;
    //the Errors collection ranges from 0 to nCount -1.
    for(i = 0; i < nCount; i++)
    {
        pErr = pCnn->Errors->GetItem(i);
        printf("Error number: %x\t%s", pErr->Number, pErr->Description);
    }
}

//Added code here
//had an error, so let's abort the transaction
pCnn->RollbackTrans();

getchar();
    }
}
```

4. Now recompile and run the project. Your console should look similar to Figure 7-2.

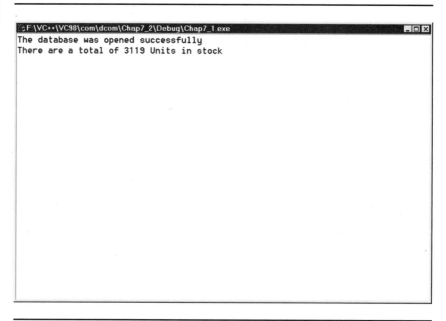

CERTIFICATION OBJECTIVE 7.05

Using Appropriate Locking Strategies

With the development of enterprise-wide applications, applications have to take into account that multiple users may try to access the same data in a data source at the same time. ADO provides different locking options so the programmer can determine the appropriate locking strategy for their application. Locking involves managing access to records so that multiple users cannot access the same record at the same time. This helps prevents inconsistent data due to users overwriting each other's data. For example, two users retrieve the same record and one user changes one field in that record, then the second user changes a different field in that record. The second user changed that record based on the original value, not the changed value. This could cause an invalid result. How a record can be updated is a combination of the cursor location, cursor type, and lock type chosen for the recordset. It is important to understand the effects of using different combinations of these properties. There are two basic locking strategies: pessimistic and optimistic.

Implementing Pessimistic Locking

Pessimistic locking is used to prevent conflicts between users accessing the same record. Pessimistic locking means that concurrent access to the same record is a high possibility and you don't want to allow data in a record to be accessed while another user is editing it. When you use pessimistic locking, it locks access to the record as soon as any field in the record is edited. The lock is then released when the record is updated. This ensures that the data cannot be accessed at any time when the record is being edited. This lock type should be used when there is a high possibility of concurrent access to records and you don't want to rely on transaction rollbacks to prevent inconsistent data, which is more expensive resource-wise. This method is the most secure, but it can slow down performance for other users if they have to wait for the record to be updated. If you are using this method, try to perform the editing as quickly as possible.

Implementing Optimistic Locking

Optimistic locking is used when concurrent access to records is not expected. Access to the record isn't restricted while it is being edited. The record isn't locked until the actual update occurs. This means that the data must be checked to see if it was changed since it was read. If so, an exception will occur and steps must be taken to resolve the conflict. If you are in a transaction, you can just roll back the transaction. It is more expensive to do the roll back, but because contention is not expected, it is better than locking access to the record for a longer time period.

To set the locking type of a recordset, you set the LockType property of a Recordset object. ADO provides the following lock types: *read-only*, *pessimistic*, *optimistic*, and *batch optimistic*.

Read-Only

A read-only lock type is just what it sounds like, the data can be read, but it cannot be changed. This is the default lock type for a Recordset object. This is a good choice for retrieving data for generating reports or filling list choices from a data source. To set the locking type to read-only, set the Recordset object's LockType property to adLockReadOnly.

```
pRst->LockType = adLockReadOnly;
//or parameter to Open method
hr = pRst->Open("table", strCnn, adOpenForwardOnly,
                           adLockReadOnly, adCmdTable);
```

Pessimistic

A pessimistic lock type performs pessimistic locking. The record is locked as soon as editing starts and is not unlocked until the record is updated. To use the pessimistic lock type, set the Recordset object's LockType property to adLockPessimistic.

```
pRst->LockType = adLockPessimistic;
//or parameter to Open method
hr = pRst->Open("table", strCnn, adOpenForwardOnly,
                   adLockPessimistic, adCmdTable);
```

Optimistic

An optimistic lock type performs optimistic locking. The record is only locked while it is being updated using the Update method of the Recordset object. To use the optimistic lock type, set the Recordset object's LockType property to adLockOptimistic.

```
pRst->LockType = adLockOptimistic;
//or parameter to Open method
hr = pRst->Open("table", strCnn, adOpenForwardOnly,
                adLockOptimistic, adCmdTable);
```

Batch Optimistic

A batch optimistic lock type performs optimistic locking in batch mode. The record is only locked while it is being updated using the UpdateBatch method of the Recordset object. To use the batch optimistic lock type, set the Recordset object's LockType property to adLockBatchOptimistic.

```
pRst->LockType = adLockBatchOptimistic;
//or parameter to Open method
hr = pRst->Open("table", strCnn, adOpenForwardOnly,
                adLockBatchOptimistic, adCmdTable);
```

QUESTIONS AND ANSWERS

Now that you know more about cursors and transactions, here are some possible scenario questions and their answers. There are different types of cursors. Which one is the most efficient?	The most efficient is a forward-only cursor with read-only locking.
I want to update my database by moving some records from one table to another. How can I be sure that none of my data is lost?	By using transactions, you can make sure that when the data is removed from one table and inserted into another, either both operations will succeed or both will be rolled back.
I have to dial up long distance to access a database. I don't want to stay connected all day. What should I do?	Use a client-side cursor with batch update locking to create a disconnected recordset. That way, you only have to connect when you want to retrieve the data and when you want to update data.
Server-side cursors are generally faster; when would I want to use a client-side cursor?	Some recordset operations can only be performed with a client side cursor. These include disconnected recordsets, batch updates, and creating your own recordsets.

CERTIFICATION SUMMARY

In this chapter, we discussed some of the important services available in ADO. ADO allows you to specify where the cursor should be located. It can be located on the server or on the client. The server generally gives you better performance, but having the cursor on the client allows the use of disconnected recordsets and can take some of the load off the server if needed. There are different types of cursors that you can use. Each type has different characteristics and should be used in different situations. The options range from a simple forward-only cursor to a full-blown dynamic cursor for live data.

ADO extended the errors that can be handled. The Connection object contains an Errors collection, which contains Error objects. These objects are returned by the provider and can contain an error or warning. If you are performing inline error handling, then you need to clear the collection; otherwise, you might think you received another error the next time you check it.

We discussed transactions. Transactions allow you to perform multiple operations on a data source as if they were one operation. That way, if one operation failed, you could roll back the previous operations performed in the transaction and return the data source to its previous state. A transaction fulfills the ACID properties to ensure your data is consistent.

Finally, we covered the different locking strategies for updating data. The optimistic locking strategy does not lock the recordset until the update actually occurs. You should use this strategy when you don't expect any conflicts. The pessimistic locking strategy locks the recordset as soon as you start editing the data. You should use this strategy when you expect to have conflicts. Remember, you need to understand how the cursor location, cursor type, and lock type can affect performance and functionality and be able to determine the best combination for a given scenario.

TWO-MINUTE DRILL

- ❑ You can query a database to return a set of records that match the criteria for your query. This result set is called a *cursor*.

- ❑ With ADO, there are four types of cursors; forward-only, static, dynamic, and keyset.

❑ ACID is an acronym for the four main properties of transactions: **Atomicity:** Ensures that all of the operations in the transaction occur or none of them do. If the transaction is aborted, the data will be restored to its original state. **Consistency:** A transaction leaves the data in a state that is expected. This means the transaction should not violate any business rules. **Isolation:** If multiple transactions are operating on the same data, the transactions will not be aware of any partial results from other transactions. This prevents one transaction from performing operations on some partial result of another transaction, and then that transaction being rolled back. This could cause the first transaction to be invalid. **Durability:** A transaction can survive a failure such as a computer crash. This means that if there is some type of failure, even if the computer crashes, the transaction can be rolled back or committed.

❑ Locking involves managing access to records so that multiple users cannot access the same record at the same time.

❑ Pessimistic locking is used to prevent conflicts between users accessing the same record. Pessimistic locking means that concurrent access to the same record is a high possibility and you don't want to allow data in a record to be accessed while another user is editing it.

❑ Optimistic locking is used when concurrent access to records is not expected. Access to the record isn't restricted while it is being edited. The record isn't locked until the actual update occurs.

❑ A read-only lock type is just what it sounds like, the data can be read, but it cannot be changed. This is the default lock type for a Recordset object.

❑ ADO allows you to specify where the cursor should be located. It can be located on the server or on the client. The server generally gives you better performance, but having the cursor on the client allows the use of disconnected recordsets and can take some of the load off the server if needed.

SELF TEST

The following questions will help you measure your understanding of the material presented in this chapter. Read all of the choices carefully, as there may be more than one correct answer. Choose all correct answers for each question.

1. You are developing a function that will be searching in a very large customer database. You will only be retrieving one record at a time. Which cursor location type should you use?

   A. SQL

   B. Client-side

   C. Server-side

   D. None

2. You have a sales force that is on the road during the week. On Monday morning, they want to retrieve data for the customers for the week. They need to be able to edit the data throughout the week and update the database with the changes at the end of the week. You decide to implement disconnected recordsets. Which of the following is the correct code to set the cursor location, cursor type, and lock type that you must use for a disconnected recordset?

   A. pRst->LockType = adLockBatchOptimistic;
      pRst->CursorLocation = adUseServer;
      pRst->CursorType = adOpenStatic;

   B. pRst->LockType = adLockReadOnly;
      pRst->CursorLocation = adUseClient;
      pRst->CursorType = adOpenDisconnect;

   C. pRst->LockType = adLockOptimistic;
      pRst->CursorLocation = adUseServer;
      pRst->CursorType = adOpenDynamic;

   D. pRst->LockType = adLockBatchOptimistic;
      pRst->CursorLocation = adUseClient;
      pRst->CursorType = adOpenStatic;

3. You are implementing disconnected recordsets in an application. You will be saving these recordsets to disk periodically. Which of the following formats can be used for saving recordsets to a file? (Choose two.)

   A. ADTG

   B. FAT

   C. XML

   D. NTFS

4. You have written an application that allows users to select a tab-delimited text file containing rows of data. You would like to place it in a recordset so you can process the data as if it came from a database. Which of the following should you do?

A. Use the import function of your database to import the file into a table. Then you can open a recordset on that table. When you are finished, delete the table from the database.

B. Open a recordset that has the same fields as the file, delete all the records, and then populate the recordset with the data from the file.

C. Create a recordset using a client-side cursor. Then, add the fields needed for the recordset and populate it with the data from the file.

D. Create a recordset using a server-side cursor. Then, add the fields needed for the recordset and populate it with the data from the file.

5. You have an application that will retrieve data from a table that will be used to fill a combo box with the selections for the user to choose from. Which cursor type should you use?

A. Forward-only

B. Static

C. Keyset

D. Dynamic

6. You are writing a function in an application that allows you to update all of the prices in a database for certain products by a percentage specified by the user. You want the code to be as efficient as possible. Which cursor type should you use?

A. Forward-only

B. Static

C. Keyset

D. Dynamic

7. You are developing an application that has a form that displays catalog information. You want the user to be able to navigate back and forth and be able to perform searches. The users will not be editing the data and the database gets updated only on the first of the month at midnight. Which cursor type should you use?

A. Forward-only

B. Static

C. Keyset

D. Dynamic

8. You are developing an application that allows customer service personnel to update customer information. They need to be able to navigate through the database to search for customers. They can also add and delete customers and need to be able to see changes made by other customer service personnel. Which cursor type should you use?

A. Forward-only

B. Static

C. Keyset

D. Dynamic

9. You are accessing a database to which you have an unreliable connection. You want to check for errors after certain ADO database operations. Which of the following should be used to check for errors? (Choose the best answer.)

    A. The Error object

    B. The Recordset object's Error property

    C. The Connection object's Errors collection

    D. The Connection object's Error property

10. You are developing a method for a class that performs some database operations. After each operation, you check for errors in the Error collection. What should you do if there is an error or a warning in the collection, before performing the next operation?

    A. Release each of the Error objects in the collection

    B. When you retrieve each Error object, it is automatically removed, so you should do nothing

    C. Call the clear method of the Errors collection

    D. Release the Errors collection

11. You are creating a COM component that returns an ADO recordset. Sometimes this COM component returns errors in the Errors collection. The error number and description are kind of cryptic and you would like some more detailed information. Which properties of the Error object that you retrieved from the Errors collection should you check for more information? (Choose two.)

    A. Count

    B. HelpFile

    C. HelpFileName

    D. HelpContext

12. You are developing an application that connects to a proprietary database. You are receiving errors during development, but the error number and description retrieved from the Errors collection doesn't help. What property can you check for an error code that will be specific to the database?

    A. ProprietaryCode

    B. OtherCode

    C. NativeError

    D. SQLState

13. When accessing properties of the ADO objects, you don't want to check the Errors collection for errors after each access. How can you use the properties so that an exception is thrown when a provider error occurs?

    A. Use them normally and an exception will be thrown if the provider has an error.

B. Use the Get and Put methods that MFC creates for the properties.

C. Use the Get and Set methods that MFC creates for the properties.

D. You cannot accomplish this. You must check the Errors collection after each property is accessed.

14. You are developing an application for the financial community. It is critical that when certain sets of operations are performed, either they all are successful, or they all fail. Which of the following properties of transactions satisfies this requirement?

A. Atomicity

B. Consistency

C. Isolation

D. Durability

15. You are writing an application for a bank that transfers money from one account to another. It is critical that if there is any kind of failure, including the computer crashing, the operations are either completed later or rolled back. Which of the following transaction properties will fulfill this requirement?

A. Atomicity

B. Consistency

C. Isolation

D. Durability

16. You are writing a program that accesses a database and performs several operations on it. You want either all of the operations to be completed or none of them. Which line of code should you use in the case where one of the operations fails?

A. pCnn->RollbackTrans( );

B. pRst->RollbackTrans( );

C. pCnn->AbortTrans( );

D. pRst->AbortTrans( );

17. You are developing a COM component that retrieves product information from a recordset to be displayed on a Web page. The data will be displayed in static HTML and will not be able to be edited. Which lock type should you use?

A. Read-only

B. Pessimistic

C. Optimistic

D. Batch optimistic

18. You are developing a COM component that accesses data that can be viewed, edited, deleted, and added from a Web page. Multiple users can access the same record at the same time. Which lock type should you use?

A. Read-only

B. Pessimistic

C. Optimistic

D. Batch optimistic

19. You are developing a COM component that allows users access to their personal information on a Web page. The users will be able to edit their information. Which lock type should you use?

    A. Read-only

    B. Pessimistic

    C. Optimistic

    D. Batch optimistic

20. You have created an application that connects to a database at corporate headquarters and retrieves data needed for the day. It is a long distance call to connect, so you don't want to stay connected all day. At the end of the day, it will connect to the corporate headquarters database again to update any changes. Which lock type should you use?

    A. Read-only

    B. Pessimistic

    C. Optimistic

    D. Batch optimistic

SELF TEST ANSWERS

1. **C.** You should use a server-side cursor in this case. Only the records that are requested will be sent to the client. With client-side cursors, all of the records that fulfill the select statement or all of the records in the table (depending on how you request the data) will be sent across the network to the client and the records will be searched on the client. This creates a lot of unnecessary traffic across the network and is inefficient.

2. **D.** In order to use a disconnect recordset, you must use a client-side cursor location, a static cursor type, and a batch optimistic lock type.

3. **A, C.** Recordsets can be saved to files in the Advanced Data Table Gram (ADTG) format or the Extensible Markup Language (XML) format.

4. **C.** To create a recordset without connecting to a data source, you need to use a client-side cursor. Then, you add the fields needed for the recordset and populate the recordset with the data from the file.

5. **A.** When choosing the cursor type for a recordset, you want to choose the type that is the most efficient and that fulfills the functionality you require. You only want to scroll through the recordset once to fill a combo box, so choose the forward-only cursor type. The forward-only cursor is the most efficient cursor type.

6. **A.** When choosing the cursor type and lock type for a recordset, you want to choose the types that are the most efficient and that fulfill the functionality you require. You only want to scroll through the recordset once to add a percentage to the prices, so choose the forward-only cursor type.

7. **B.** When choosing the cursor type for a recordset, you want to choose the type that is the most efficient and that fulfills the functionality you require. You want to be able to navigate through the recordset in any direction and you don't expect the data to change, so choose the static cursor type. A static cursor allows you to navigate through the recordset in any direction, but it will not detect records that were changed, inserted, or deleted.

8. **D.** When choosing the cursor type for a recordset, you want to choose the type that is the most efficient and that fulfills the functionality you require. You want to be able

to navigate through the recordset in any direction, you expect the data to change, including insertions and deletions, so choose the dynamic cursor type. The dynamic cursor type allows you to see the data that has been changed, deleted, and inserted. The keyset type does not detect records that are added to the recordset.

9. **C.** The Connection object contains an Errors collection. This is a collection of Error objects that describes errors and warnings returned from the provider.

10. **C.** Errors are removed from the Errors collection only when a new error occurs. So if you are checking for errors inline, you need to clear the collection, otherwise the error will still be there the next time it is checked. This would cause the application to think the error occurred again.

11. **B, D.** When an error is thrown, it can include a Help file name and the context ID for the error. To access these, use the HelpFile and HelpContext properties. There isn't a HelpFileName property.

12. **C.** The NativeError property of an Error object contains an error code that is specific to the provider. The SQLState is incorrect because this is for ANSI SQL error codes. The question stated a proprietary database, not ANSI SQL compliant.

13. **B.** The MFC creates wrapper methods for the ADO properties by prefixing the property name with Get and Put. By using the MFC wrapper, if the operation fails, it will throw a COM error (_com_error) exception, whereas using the property directly will not cause an exception.

14. **A.** Atomicity guarantees that all operations within a transaction occur, or none of them do.

15. **D.** Durability guarantees that all transactions will survive any kind of failure, including computer crashes. If there is a failure, the transaction will either be rolled back or committed.

16. **A.** In the case where an operation fails and you want to abort the transaction, use the connection object's RollbackTrans method. This method will roll back any changes made and the database will be restored to its original state.

17. **A.** When choosing the lock type for a recordset, you want to choose the type that is the most efficient and that fulfills the functionality you require. You are only retrieving the data to be displayed, it will not be edited, so choose the read-only lock type. The read-only lock type is the most efficient lock type. You should also use the forward-only cursor type for this scenario.

18. **B.** When choosing the lock type for a recordset, you want to choose the type that is the most efficient and that fulfills the functionality you require. Because multiple users can access the data simultaneously, there is a higher probability of conflicts. In this case, you should use the pessimistic lock type, which will lock the record the entire time it is being edited.

19. **C.** When choosing the lock type for a recordset, you want to choose the type that is the most efficient and that fulfills the functionality you require. You want to enable the data to be edited, so you can't use the read-only lock type. Because the customers are updating their own data, it is very unlikely there will be a conflict with other users, so choose the optimistic lock type. The optimistic lock type locks the record only when the update occurs. You should also use the static cursor type because the data is unlikely to be changed by another user.

20. **D.** When choosing the lock type for a recordset, you want to choose the type that is the most efficient and that fulfills the functionality you require. When using a disconnected recordset, you must use the batch optimistic lock type. This allows you to update multiple records at once and to see the status of each record's update.

MICROSOFT CERTIFIED SOLUTION DEVELOPER

8

Invoking Data Services

I nvoking data services is a necessity for developing distributed applications. Visual C++ contains all the components you'll need to write distributed database applications for Windows. In a typical distributed application, sometimes referred to as an *n-tier application*, data services constitute the Data tier. This allows for more efficient data access, as we will discover in this chapter. You want to make sure your distributed application uses the appropriate data services to ensure peak performance and reliability. This is also an important part of the exam.

We will cover the different database programming models and their related concepts. Visual C++ comes with four separate database access systems: ODBC (Open Database Connectivity), ADO (ActiveX Data Objects), DAO (Data Access Objects), and RDO (Remote Data Objects). We will cover these different database programming models and their related concepts. Visual C++ also includes tools and Microsoft Foundation Classes (MFC) for ODBC and DAO. In this chapter we will cover some common concepts on invoking data services in a distributed application. The ability to access and manipulate data using ad hoc queries, accessing data using the stored procedure model, Structured Query Language (SQL) statements, creating a stored procedure that returns information, creating triggers that implement rules, creating reports that use summary data, displaying data in a customized sorted format, and creating stored procedures to enforce business rules are applicable to the exam as well as on the job.

CERTIFICATION OBJECTIVE 8.01

Accessing and Manipulating Data Using Ad Hoc Queries

Database access and manipulation involves querying and updating the data stored in the database. Examples of queries are "retrieve the address of Smith"; "list the names of people who reside in Houston, Texas"; and "what are the home phone numbers of all contractors?" Examples of updates are "change the address of Smith to Philadelphia, Pennsylvania"; "create a new salary for Jones"; and "enter the zip code for Galax, Virginia." These query and update statements must be specified more precisely in the programming model understood by the database before they can be processed. There are many techniques available for database access and manipulation. In this chapter, we will only cover the techniques relevant to the Microsoft Certification Exam. We will cover the programming models and techniques available in Visual C++ and when to use each of the models and techniques.

ODBC

The Microsoft Open Database Connectivity (ODBC) standard defines not only the programming interface to a SQL database but also the rules of SQL grammar. We will discuss SQL later in this chapter. It is possible to use Visual C++ to access and manipulate any database management system (DBMS) that has an ODBC driver. Some programmers dislike ODBC because it doesn't allow programmers to take advantage of certain features of some particular DBMSs and is too low-level when compared to ADO, DAO, and RDO. We will cover ADO, DAO, and RDO in the following sections, so you can be the judge as to which you prefer. The advantage of ODBC is that it allows programmers to learn one application programming interface (API) when accessing and manipulating data. There is no need to learn the specific features of any specific DBMS. Your application written in Visual C++ using ODBC can access any ODBC-compliant DBMS, allowing you to choose the DBMS that best suites your organization's needs.

ODBC Architecture

ODBC employs a DLL-based architecture that makes the system fully modular (see Figure 8-1). Each application communicates with the ODBC driver manager. The driver manager in turn loads the appropriate driver for the database. Once the specific database driver is loaded, it translates the ODBC API and SQL commands into the commands required by the given

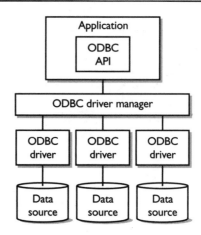

database. The database-specific DLLs that are available to your application are tracked in the Registry.

MFC ODBC Classes: CRecordset and CDatabase

MFC provides two basic classes for working with ODBC. These two classes are CRecordset and CDatabase. Using these two classes makes it easier to develop database applications based on ODBC. Of the two, it is most common to derive a class from CRecordset. This derived class provides the functionality to access data retrieved from the database. The CRecordset class allows the application to interact with rows returned from the database based on a query or table identified when the application is created.

When accessing a single recordset from the database, it is not necessary to declare an instance of the CDatabase class. If multiple recordsets are used then it is common to declare a member variable of type CDatabase in the applications document and use it for each recordset. The CDatabase class contains the information needed to attach to and communicate with the database.

ADO

ADO is Microsoft's premier data access and manipulation technology. The ADO object model defines a collection of programmable objects that support the Component Object Model (COM) and OLE Automation to use the partner technology called OLE DB. OLE DB is a system-level programming interface that provides a standard set of COM interfaces for exposing database management system functionality. With ADO's object model you can easily access these interfaces using Visual C++ to add database functionality to your distributed application. In addition, you can also use ADO to access ODBC-compliant databases. The ADO object model—when compared to other data access technologies such as ODBC, RDO, or DAO—is flatter (has fewer objects) and easier to use.

When building applications that use ADO there are two primary methods that can help the developer to implement the data access technologies. The first is to include a #import statement to import the ADO type library and allow the use of smart pointers. The second is through the use of the Active Template Library (ATL) to create data providers and data consumers. The next section includes information about the ADO architecture and object model.

on the
j o b

Although Microsoft has had its share of data access technologies, ADO is the latest and has been created by pulling together the best parts of the earlier technologies. For these reasons you should use ADO for all new application development.

ADO Architecture

There are three different kinds of components that make up the ADO architecture. These are data consumers, data providers, and service providers. Data consumers are the applications that use the data. These include the user interfaces that we create using VC++. Data providers are the source for the data. This actually consists of a data provider component and the data source itself. The actual data provider exposes the requisite COM interfaces that can be used by the data consumer. This is only functional as far as there is a data source to supply the data. Typically this data source is a relational database, but with OLE DB and ADO it can be any source of data. The final piece that makes up the OLE DB/ADO architecture is the service provider. The service provider allows for added functionality for any data providers. The common example of this is a query engine, serving as a service provider, for a non-relational data source.

ADO Objects

There are seven objects in the ADO object model (see Figure 8-2), as described in the following list:

- **Connection object** Maintains connection information such as cursor type, connect string, query time-out, connection time-out, and default database. The connection object is also responsible for managing database transactions.

- **Error object** Contains extended error information about error conditions encountered by the data provider. Because a single statement can generate two or more errors, the Errors collection can contain more than one Error object at a time.

- **Command object** Maintains information about a command, such as a query string, parameter definitions, and so on. You can execute a command string on a Connection object of a query string as part of opening a Recordset object, without defining a Command object. The Command object is useful where you want to define query parameters or execute a stored procedure that returns output parameters. The Command object supports a number of properties to describe the type and purpose of the query and help ADO optimize the operation.

- **Parameter object** A single parameter associated with a command. The Command object uses the Parameters collection to contain all of its Parameter objects. ADO Parameter objects can be created automatically by sending queries to the database. However, you can also build this collection programmatically to improve performance at runtime.

ADO object model

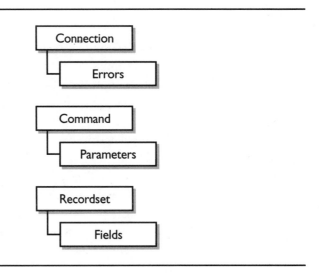

- **Recordset object** A set of rows returned from a query, including a cursor into those rows. You can open a Recordset object (that is, execute a query) without explicitly opening a Connection object. However, if you do first create a Connection object, you can open multiple Recordset objects on the same connection.

- **Field object** Contains information about a single column of data within a recordset. The Recordset object uses the Fields collection to contain all of its Field objects. This field information includes data type, precision, and numeric scale.

In addition, there is also a:

- **Property object** A provider-defined characteristic of an ADO object. ADO objects have two types of properties: built-in and dynamic. Built-in properties are those properties implemented in ADO and available to any new ADO object. Dynamic properties are defined by the underlying data provider and appear in the Properties collection for the appropriate ADO object. For example, a property may indicate if a Recordset object supports transactions or updating. This is one of the greatest features of ADO, in that it lets the ADO service provider present special interfaces.

DAO

Data Access Objects (DAO) is a data access technology that was developed to help applications interact with a Jet database engine. The first thing to understand is the difference between Microsoft Access and the Jet engine. Microsoft Access is a complete development environment that utilizes a Jet database. The Jet database engine is the technology that actually stores and manipulates the data.

Using DAO, it is not only possible to access a Jet database, but it is also possible to efficiently access any indexed sequential access method (ISAM) type of database. You will typically choose to use DAO when working with a database that is local to the machine where your application will run. It is possible to use this technology to access any ODBC-compliant database, but it works most efficiently with local databases.

DAO Architecture

DAO is a set of COM objects that wrap the functionality of the of the Jet database engine. Through the use of these objects it is possible to control the Jet engine and manipulate the data in several databases. The Jet engine has the functionality to work with many ISAM and ODBC databases. The key point to remember when using the Jet engine to work with a non-Jet database is that the Jet engine intervenes in all of the database transactions. Because of this, you must also work with each data source using the commands and SQL syntax that are recognized by the Jet engine.

DAO Objects

There are several objects that make up the DAO library (see Figure 8-3). MFC implements classes to support these. Of these, the two most common are CDaoDatabase and CDaoRecordset. These work similarly to the ODBC classes described earlier. The following list shows all of the MFC classes that represent the object identified in the DAO object model.

- **CDaoDatabase**   Maintains the connection to the database
- **CDaoWorkspace**   Defines a session for the user and includes the ability to maintain transactions

DAO object hierarchy
viewed with MFC classes

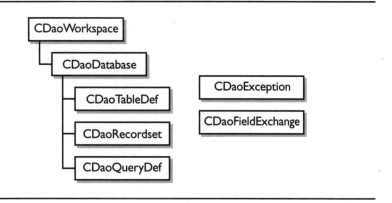

- **CDaoException**   Manages exceptions created in the MFC DAO classes
- **CDaoQueryDef**   Manages the creation and use of queries
- **CDaoTableDef**   Represents tables as defined in the database
- **CDaoRecordset**   Contains and controls the data retrieved from the database
- **CDaoFieldExchange**   Exchanges the data from the fields in the recordset with the member variables of the CDaoRecordset derived class

exam
ⓦatch

Be sure to remember which MFC objects implement the DAO objects and which implement the ODBC library. CRecordset and CDatabase are used to implement the ODBC library, whereas CDaoRecordset and CDaoDatabase are used to implement the DAO object model. Also remember that you do not use CRecordset or CDaoRecordset directly; rather you always use a class derived from these.

RDO

Remote Data Objects (RDO) is a technology that was created after ODBC and DAO. Its purpose is to provide an easy-to-work-with object model that wraps the ODBC library and allows programmers to work quickly and easily with remote databases. Although VC++ programmers have never heavily used RDO, it is important to have some understanding of it for the exam.

RDO Architecture

RDO was created as a tool to help programmers easily utilize the ODBC library. For VC++ programmers, the MFC classes that were discussed in the ODBC section already accomplished this. The RDO object model closely resembles that of the DAO object model. The main differences lie in additional functionality that increases performance when working across a network. This includes such things as asynchronous queries.

RDO Objects

It is possible to use RDO by either of two methods: you can create a wrapper class using ClassWizard and specifying MARDO20.DLL as the type library from which to create the new class; or you can use the #include directive in one of your class modules. Either way you will have access to the various objects exposed by this COM library (see Figure 8-4). These objects are as follows:

- **rdoEngine**   Base object in the object model.
- **rdoError**   Contains errors generated while working with RDO.
- **rdoEnvironment**   Manages connections to the data store and controls transactions.
- **rdoConnection**   An actual connection to the data source.
- **rdoQuery**   A query to run against the data store; this can include parameters.
- **rdoParameter**   A parameter used for a query.
- **rdoPreparedStatement**   Maintained for backwards compatibility; this has been replaced by rdoQuery.
- **rdoTable**   A view of the entire contents of either a table or a view defined in the database.
- **rdoResultset**   Contains and controls the data returned when processing records from the database.
- **rdoColumn**   Contains information about a column in a resultset, including the value.

FIGURE 8-4

RDO object hierarchy
viewed with MFC

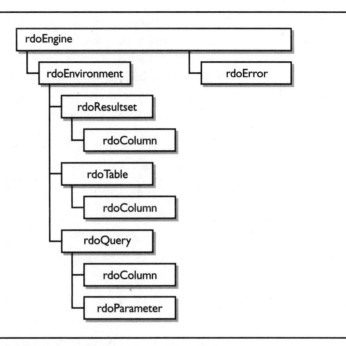

CERTIFICATION OBJECTIVE 8.02

Accessing Data Using the Stored Procedure Model

Many databases now include functionality known as stored procedures.
Microsoft SQL Server has provided this feature for a long time and most
users of SQL Server have found it to be very beneficial. In this section we
will review some of the features of stored procedures and note why they are
useful. Later in the chapter we will look at how to create them.

Stored procedures are SQL commands that are stored inside of
the database. In this discussion we will focus our review on their
implementation in Microsoft SQL Server, but it is important to realize
that many other databases support them, although with slightly different
implementations. If you are not using SQL Server, review your database
documentation for the details.

Stored procedures not only allow for the use of the basic SQL syntax, which we will learn in the following sections, but they also allow for the extensions known as Transact SQL or T-SQL for short. This allows stored procedures to include actual programming logic rather than simply providing a way to store basic SQL statements. Some of the advantages of stored procedures are as follows:

- The SQL and programming logic are precompiled and stored in the database for faster execution.

- All syntax is checked when the procedure is first compiled.

- Once it is run on the server, the procedure remains cached and provides an increase in performance for future calls.

- Complex processing can be handled at the database server without requiring excess network traffic.

- Stored procedures can be used to encapsulate business logic to maintain a consistent handling of data between different applications.

- Stored procedures allow for greater security of the database.

These are just a few of the advantages of using stored procedures. Learning about stored procedures is important for both the exam and for building scalable distributed applications in the real world.

To successfully use stored procedures you must be comfortable with the SQL language. We will look at this next.

Be prepared to identify situations in which stored procedures would provide an advantage over passing SQL strings to the database to be processed. One situation to be aware of is the case where several SQL statements must be processed and programming logic is used to identify the flow of execution. Of these, it is even more likely that a stored procedure will be advantageous when only the final results are needed by the client application.

SQL Statements

There are many different database systems that exist, and each has advantages and disadvantages. Several factors are involved in choosing the DBMS that is used for a project. One of the factors that differs very little between different DBMSs is the language that is used to query the database. The standard language, used by nearly all DBMSs, is the Structured Query Language. This is a language that has gained widespread acceptance and also has an ANSI standard that is followed by most database vendors. In the following sections we will be reviewing some of these standards and how they are implemented in Microsoft SQL Server.

Writing SQL Statements That Retrieve and Modify Data

As developers, we are most concerned with creating SQL statements that work with the data in the database. When working with data, there are two different types of actions that we typically perform. We retrieve data from the database to use in our applications and we modify the data that is in the database as per the requests of the users of our applications. In this section we will review the SQL syntax for performing both of these tasks.

Retrieving Data

The first way in which we interact with a database is to retrieve data to be used in our application. The SQL command to do this is the Select statement. The basic structure of the Select statement is as follows:

```
SELECT select list
FROM table list
WHERE criteria
```

Although it may look rather simple, be prepared because it can get rather complex as you delve deep into SQL. Let's look a little deeper into the various clauses that are available in the Select statement. First let's review what the *select list* provides. This is where we identify the columns that we want returned from the database. Here we have two options, we can use an * (asterisk) to indicate that we desire all columns from the specified table, or we can list the names of the columns individually as in the following example:

```
SELECT au_id, au_lname, au_fname, phone
```

Here we have indicated that we want the author's ID, first name, last name, and phone number returned (we are building this example using the Authors table of the Pubs example database that ships with SQL Server). Once we have identified the columns that we desire, we need to identify from where we want this data to be retrieved. To do this we use the From clause. The following example tells the database that we want this information retrieved from the Authors table:

```
FROM authors
```

The final step is to state the criteria that each row must meet to have that data returned to us. To do this we use the Where clause. The following example will give us the requested information for all authors that live in Utah:

```
WHERE state = 'UT'
```

This is a simple example of a database query. There are other clauses that can be used and each of the clauses that we have reviewed could become more complex. To successfully build distributed applications you must master SQL, and it goes beyond what we have covered so far. To help you prepare for your certification exams we will continue to review this syntax in the following sections.

Updating Data

There are three ways in which we can update the data stored in the database. In this section we will cover each of these and show a simple example of them. The three ways to update a database are to change the values stored in an existing row; add a new row to a table; and remove a row from a table.

To update the value of one or more columns in an existing row you will use the Update statement. The following is the syntax for updating a record:

```
UPDATE table name
SET column1 = new value [, column2 = new value, …columnx = new value]
WHERE criteria
```

Again, we will review the various clauses. First we identify the table that we wish to update. To do this we use the Update keyword and give the name of the table, as follows:

```
UPDATE authors
```

Next we identify the column or columns that we wish to change by giving the name of the column and the new value to set for the column. In the following example we indicate that we wish to change the value of the state column to CA:

```
SET state = 'CA'
```

Here we could list other columns if we so desire. Finally, we will identify the rows that we wish to have changed. To do this we must supply criteria in the Where clause. The structure of the Where clause is the same as for the Select statement outlined earlier. In this example we are asking SQL Server to change the values for authors whose last name starts with RI:

```
WHERE au_lname like 'RI%'
```

This is a very simple example, but it shows the basics of the Update statement. Let's move on to talk about how we can add new rows to the table.

To add rows to a table in the database, we use the Insert statement. This allows us to add new data to the database to be tracked. The following is the syntax of the Insert statement:

```
INSERT INTO table name
(column1 [, column2, … columnx])
VALUES
(value1 [, value2, … valuex])
```

You should start to see a pattern here. Many of the SQL commands look very similar and as you become familiar with one you will be able to use the others quickly and easily. To insert a row into a table we must first identify the table to insert the data into. In the following example we are asking SQL Server to add a row to the Authors table:

```
INSERT INTO authors
```

We will give a list of the columns for which we will supply values. When inserting data into a table we must be sure that we supply data for all columns that have been created with the NOT NULL constraint. These values can be supplied in one of three different ways: first, a default constraint can be assigned to the column; second, the column may be an Identity column; and third, we supply the value in our list. For this example we will provide all of the data in our column list. We declare that we will give values for the ID, the author's name, the phone number, and the contract information.

```
(au_id, au_fname, au_lname, phone, contract)
```

After declaring the columns that we will give new values to, we need to list the new values. To do this we use the Values keyword and then supply a list, in the same order as the columns, of the new values. In this example we are adding the following values to the Authors table:

```
VALUES
('123-12-1234', 'John', 'Doe', '123-123-1234', 1)
```

By following this example you will be able to add new data to the database as required for your applications. Finally, we will see how to remove records from the database. As our example we will remove the row that we just inserted. The following shows the syntax of the Delete statement:

```
DELETE table name
WHERE criteria
```

Things should look familiar to you. To delete a row from a table in the database, we begin by using the Delete keyword and identifying the table from which the rows will be deleted. In this example we will delete the row we just inserted into the Authors table:

```
DELETE authors
```

Once we have identified the table, we must then identify the criteria used to select the rows to be deleted. If we fail to supply any criteria here, all the rows in the table will be removed. We will delete the row whose author ID is 123-12-1234, as shown here:

```
WHERE au_id = '123-12-1234'
```

This will cause the specified row to be deleted from the table.

Writing SQL Statements That Use Joins to Combine Data from Multiple Tables

The previous examples are very simple. They serve to introduce us to the SQL syntax. In this section we will see how we can get more data from the database. Most of the databases that we work with today are known as relational databases, and SQL is the language used to interact with these relational databases. As the name implies, a relational database contains relationships between the tables that comprise the database. There are many sources, including other chapters in this book, that cover the theory of relational databases. In this section we will learn to retrieve data from multiple tables with a single Select statement.

There are two methods that we can use to join two or more tables together to retrieve related data. For the certification exam you should be able to recognize either method. The first method that we will introduce is the method that has been used in the past. Next we will cover the new method of joining tables. The original method used to join tables was to supply the information required to connect the tables as part of the Where clause. To do this you would set criteria that would only return rows where the primary key from the first table matched the foreign key from the second table. The following example shows how this technique can be used to join the Publishers table to the Titles table:

```
WHERE publishers.pub_id = titles.pub_id
```

This would allow us to retrieve any information that we desired from the combination of the two tables. For instance, we could select the publisher's name and the title of all books that they have published, as in this example:

```
SELECT p.pub_name, t.title
FROM publishers p, titles t
WHERE p.pub_id = t.pub_id
```

Here we have also introduced the ability to alias a table in the From clause. When we refer to a column in the select list or the criteria, we must be sure that SQL can identify which table we are referring to. If the column names are unique in each table, we can simply use the name of the column. If, however, the column name appears in both tables, we must identify the table we are referring to. We can do this by typing either the name of the table, or its alias as defined in the From clause. Then we use a . (period) and give the name of the column. Using aliases will keep us from typing so much.

Another topic to consider when talking about joining two tables is how to deal with the rows where there is not a match in the second table. There are several kinds of joins; an *equijoin* is the type that we have just seen. This will return all rows from both tables where the criteria match. Another type of join to consider is the *cross join*. This join is not very useful because it ignores the relationship between the tables and returns all possible combinations of rows. This is also known as a Cartesian product. You create a cross join when you do not supply any criteria in the Where clause. The final type of join that we should consider is an outer join. Using an outer join, we are able to retrieve all the rows from one of the tables, and for those rows where matches exist we can retrieve the correlating data from the second table. Where there is not a match, we will be passed a NULL value for the second table's columns. An outer join can be created as either a left outer join or a right outer join. The syntax for creating a left outer join is as follows:

```
SELECT p.pub_name, t.title
FROM publishers p, titles t
WHERE p.pub_id *= t.pub_id
```

This will cause all rows from the Publishers table to be returned, regardless of the number of titles that the publisher has published. When we run this query against the Pubs database, we will see that several of the publishers do not have titles in the Titles table. To create a right outer join, we would move the * to the right side of the equal sign.

Now we will cover the new style of defining joins in your Select statements. This is the preferred method to use now, but many "old" SQL programmers are much more comfortable with the style shown previously, so expect to see it often.

The new style of defining a join moves the join into the From clause. Most often you will use one of two new phrases in the From clause: either the INNER JOIN or LEFT OUTER JOIN (or RIGHT OUTER JOIN). To demonstrate these we will rewrite the queries introduced earlier. First we will retrieve all of the publisher names and titles for all of the publishers that have titles in the Titles table.

```
SELECT p.pub_name, t.title
FROM publishers p INNER JOIN titles t ON p.pub_id = t.pub_id
```

Here we have used the keywords INNER JOIN…ON to identify the tables that we wish to join and to provide the criteria by which they will be connected. We can also do an outer join to retrieve all of the publishers regardless of the number of titles they have in the Titles table.

```
SELECT p.pub_name, t.title
FROM publishers p LEFT OUTER JOIN titles t ON p.pub_id = t.pub_id
```

Using these techniques, you will be able to slice and dice your way through all of the data and relationships in your database.

Writing SQL Statements That Create Views or Queries

When accessing data from a relational database such as SQL Server you are able to retrieve data directly from the tables or from views that are defined by the database administrator. These views, known as queries in some databases, are simple SQL statements that identify the columns and rows to be returned. They are named and can be used in the From clause of a Select statement as if they were a table. Views are often used to implement security. Through the use of views, the database administrator is able to grant access to select groupings of data for different users of the database. For example, we might define a view in the Pubs database that we could grant to a single publisher that would allow them to see only the titles that they have in the database. By creating this type of view, we could implement security that would prevent one publisher from seeing the new titles that another publisher is working on.

To create a view you use the Create View statement. The syntax for this statement is as follows:

```
CREATE VIEW NewMoonTitles AS
SELECT *
FROM titles
WHERE pub_id = '0736'
```

This will create a view that will show all of the information in the Titles table for titles published by the New Moon Books publisher. This view will provide security by returning a subset of the rows in the actual table. We can then grant select privileges on the view rather than the actual table. The users will not see the difference. It is also possible to return a subset of the columns to implement another type of security. This may be used when giving all employees access to the Employee table in our company's database so that they are able to find another employee's phone number or office number. Imagine if this table also held the employees' salary. This is something that we would not want all employees to have access to. To provide this type of security, we might create a view that returned all of the rows in the Employee table, but returned only the Name, Phone, and Office Number.

Another reason that views are created is to reduce the complexity of ad-hoc queries for users of our database. Often we want to allow administrative users to query the database to create custom reports. Many of these users are not very knowledgeable in the SQL syntax. To help these users, we may want to create views that expose the information retrieved from a join as a single 'table'. We might create a view called TitleInformation that includes the name of the publisher rather than just the publisher's ID. This will help our less sophisticated users to get the data they require. To create such a view we would use the following command:

```
CREATE VIEW TitleInformation AS
SELECT t.title_id, t.title, t.type, p.pub_name, t.price
FROM titles t INNER JOIN publishers p ON t.pub_id = t.pub_id
```

This view does not return all of the columns from the Titles table, but it serves as an example of how we can create a view to help users query our database.

CERTIFICATION OBJECTIVE 8.04

Creating a Stored Procedure That Returns Information

In an earlier section we described the benefits of using stored procedures. Here we will introduce how to create a simple stored procedure that returns information in the form of a resultset.

Stored procedures are very flexible. We can create stored procedures that accept parameters, return parameters, return a result code, and return records. When we create the procedure, we identify any parameters and whether they are input or output parameters. We are also able to return a value from within the procedure. This value is often used to identify any errors that are encountered while processing the procedure. Zero is, by convention, a successful return value. Negative numbers indicate errors raised from SQL Server, and positive numbers are, by convention, used to identify business logic errors.

Whenever we write a Select statement inside of a stored procedure it will create a resultset that will be returned to the caller. Stored procedures allow multiple resultsets to be returned from a single call.

The syntax for creating a stored procedure is shown here:

```
CREATE PROCEDURE procedure name [@param1 datatype [= default] [output],
...@paramn ...] AS
SQL Statement [...SQL Statement n]
```

Using this format, we can create stored procedures that provide all of the benefits that we have cited earlier. We are not limited to SQL statements; rather, we can also include T-SQL syntax that gives us standard programming constructs. Although we won't go into any details about these, the following list outlines some of the constructs that are available:

- IF…Else
- Begin…End
- Case
- While
- Goto

As VC++ programmers, these constructs should be somewhat familiar and knowing that we are able to use these features in our stored procedures should give you an idea of the power they hold.

The following statement creates a stored procedure that returns the titles of all books published by a specified publisher. The procedure has an input parameter that is the ID of the desired publisher.

```
CREATE PROCEDURE GetPublisherTitles (@PublisherID char(4)) AS
SELECT title, price
FROM titles
WHERE pub_id = @PublisherID
```

This stored procedure, named GetPublisherTitles, will return all of the titles and prices for titles published by the publisher whose ID is sent in as the parameter. To call this procedure you would execute a statement like the following:

```
GetPublisherTitles '0736'
```

Although this is a very simple example, it provides the knowledge required to begin utilizing stored procedures in your development work. Additionally, it shows you the basics required for passing the certification exam. One final note to remember about stored procedures is that they are not invoked directly by SQL Server. These procedures will only be executed when called from code that you have written. In the next section we will introduce triggers, which are invoked automatically by the database.

CERTIFICATION OBJECTIVE 8.05

Creating Triggers That Implement Rules

Triggers are very similar to stored procedures. They are like stored procedures that are sets of SQL statements that are precompiled and stored in the database. Unlike stored procedures, triggers are invoked automatically by SQL Server when certain conditions arise. In this section we will discover how to create these triggers and when SQL Server will automatically execute them for us.

The syntax for creating a trigger is shown here:

```
CREATE TRIGGER trigger name
ON table
FOR { [DELETE] [,] [INSERT] [,] [UPDATE] }
AS SQL Statement
```

You might notice there are three major differences between how we define a trigger and how we define a stored procedure. First, notice that triggers do not allow any parameters. Because triggers are called directly from SQL Server we never have the opportunity to call them passing in parameters as we do with stored procedures. Second, a trigger is associated with a single table when it is created. The trigger will always be associated with this table. Finally, a trigger is defined so that it will be triggered on certain events that occur on the specified table. A trigger can be created to fire when rows are inserted into the table, when rows are deleted from the table, or when the values in an existing row are changed. This is how SQL Server knows when to execute the trigger.

When writing the SQL statement for a trigger, there are two new tables that we have to be aware of. These are the Inserted and Deleted tables. These tables only exist in memory and are available only while the trigger is executing. When a row is inserted into the table, a duplicate row is inserted into the Inserted table. When a row is deleted from the table, the values of the deleted row are available in the Deleted table. When a row is updated, the pre-update values are available in the Deleted table and the new values are available in the Inserted table. Using these tables in the trigger, we can check the work that has been done and verify that it is okay. We can also use these values to maintain audit trails and logs of the changes that have occurred. Triggers are also useful for ensuring database integrity by *cascading* changes to other tables. If we find that the changes that have occurred should be rolled back, we can call the T-SQL command ROLLBACK TRANSACTION that will cause all of the changes to be discarded.

The following statement creates a trigger that checks the price of a new title that has been inserted into the Titles table. If the price is less than 10.00 dollars, the insert is rolled back.

```
CREATE TRIGGER TitlesInsTrg
ON titles
FOR INSERT
AS
IF (SELECT price FROM INSERTED) < 10
BEGIN
    ROLLBACK TRANSACTION
END
```

Here we have selected the price from the row that has just been inserted into the Titles table. If we find that the price is less than ten, we will cause the transaction to be rolled back, undoing the insert into the Titles table. This trigger will be executed once for each row that is inserted into the Titles table. Also worth noting is the name of the trigger. Although this can be any name that meets the standard SQL Server object naming conventions, it is wise to adopt a naming convention for triggers, as well as other database objects. Here I have named the trigger using the table name, the type of trigger that is defined, and placed *trg* at the end to signify that it is a trigger.

Triggers are commonly used to help enforce data integrity, provide audit information, and duplicate data to other tables.

Creating Reports That Use Summary Data

SQL provides more features that can assist us when we want to summarize data from the database. The typical way to accomplish this is to use aggregate functions. The following list outlines the most common aggregate functions:

- **AVG**   Returns the average of the selected column.
- **COUNT**   Returns the count of non-null records.
- **MIN**   Returns the lowest value from the selected column.
- **MAX**   Returns the highest value from the selected column.
- **SUM**   Returns the sum of all the selected columns.
- **DISTINCT**   Returns a single row for each unique value from the selected column.

Using these aggregate functions, we are able to have the database do some of the work required for creating summary reports. Many of these functions require the use of two new clauses that we add to the Select statement. These clauses are the Group By clause and the Having clause. The Group By clause is required when we want to select some columns using an aggregate function and other columns that do not use an aggregate. For example, look at the following Select statement:

```
Select p.pub_name, COUNT(t.title)
FROM publishers p INNER JOIN titles t ON p.pub_id = t.pub_id
GROUP BY p.pub_name
```

This Select statement will return the publisher name and a count of the number of titles for that publisher in the Titles table. To have this query function properly, we must use the Group By clause to cause all of the records to be grouped by the publisher's name. This allows SQL to group the records together to produce the count that we have requested in the select list.

We can limit the information that is returned by requiring the aggregate function to meet certain criteria. Normal criteria are checked in the Where clause, but to check the value of an aggregate function we must use the Having clause. The syntax for the Having clause is similar to the Where clause. For example, look at the new line added to the query that we reviewed earlier:

```
Select p.pub_name, COUNT(t.title)
FROM publishers p INNER JOIN titles t ON p.pub_id = t.pub_id
GROUP BY p.pub_name
HAVING COUNT(t.title) > 5
```

This will return only the rows where the count of titles for the publisher is greater than five. Using these additions to the Select statement, we can have the database server do much of the computation that may be required for many of the summary reports that we need to produce in our applications.

CERTIFICATION OBJECTIVE 8.07

Displaying Data in a Customized Sorted Format

By definition, the data in a relational database system is unordered. Because of the way that databases are implemented, we can often find an order to the records in the various tables. SQL Server provides a clustered index that allows us to define the order. Nonetheless, we will often want to ensure that the data we retrieve from our Select statements is in a known order. To do this we can add an Order By clause to the Select statement. This will be the final clause in any Select statement and will have the following syntax:

```
ORDER BY column1 [ASC | DESC] [, ...column n [ASC | DESC]]
```

The Order By clause can contain one or more columns. The results returned from the Select statement will be sorted in the order of the columns in the list. For each column that we include in the list, we are able to specify that the sort be done in ascending (the default) or descending order. Each column can be sorted in a different order.

The following Select statement retrieves all of the information about each title, sorted by the type of book and the price. The type is sorted in the default (ascending) order and the price is sorted with the highest price first and the lowest price last.

```
SELECT *
FROM titles
ORDER BY type, price DESC
```

Using the various techniques that we have learned throughout this chapter, you can now create very sophisticated SQL statements that can push much of the work that our applications must do onto the database server. Remember that the database server has been optimized to perform these functions and we will often see a great increase in the speed at which our applications perform by ensuring the database does this work. Additionally, it will increase the speed at which we can create new custom solutions because it is very easy to build the SQL statements that perform these complex functions.

CERTIFICATION OBJECTIVE 8.08

Creating Stored Procedures to Enforce Business Rules

One of the benefits of using a stored procedure is the ability to encapsulate business logic into the procedure. Doing this allows the database administrator to lock down access to the underlying tables and force all users and applications to modify the database through the stored procedures. To execute a stored procedure, the users needs to have rights to the stored procedure, but not to the underlying objects that are modified by the stored procedure. When many different users using many different applications can access a single database, using stored procedures to enforce business logic guarantees that all users and applications will behave in the same manner with regards to any table. This helps to maintain the integrity of the data that is so important in ensuring the success of our businesses.

As an example of a stored procedure that could be used to enforce business rules, look at the following procedure:

```
CREATE PROCEDURE AddTitle
(
@TitleID   varchar(6),
@Title          varchar(80),
@Type           char(12),
@Price          money,
@PubID          char(4),
@PubDate   datetime
)
AS
Insert into Titles
(title_id, title, type, price, pub_id, royalty, pubdate)
VALUES
(@TitleID, @Title, @Type, @Price, @PubID, 10, @PubDate)
```

Using a stored procedure like this, we can force certain criteria to be met when inserting data into our tables. This procedure requires that certain data be set when inserting the row. This goes beyond the NOT NULL constraints identified when the table was created. It also enforces a standard 10 percent royalty for all new titles. Admittedly, this is a simple example, but the fact remains that this technique can be used to enforce business rules inside the database. Using stored procedures to enforce these rules also assures us that all applications that access the database will use the same business logic, thereby increasing the integrity and consistency of our data.

Creating User-Defined Procedures and System Stored Procedures

To complete our coverage of the various database features, we will change our focus to system stored procedures. *System stored procedures* are procedures that are accessible from any database on the server. Most often these procedures are predefined and installed when SQL Server is installed. Often these procedures return information about the systems tables. When they are executed outside of the master database, they reflect the information from the system tables for the database in which they were run. The following list identifies some of the most common and useful system stored procedures:

- **sp_columns**   Returns information about the columns in the specified table or tables.

- **sp_configure**   Displays or changes settings for the current server.

- **sp_databases**   Lists the databases that are accessible from the current server.

- **sp_datatype_info**   Returns information about the data types that are supported in the current environment.

- **sp_dboption**   Displays or changes options on the current database.

- **sp_depends**   Displays the database objects on which a particular object is dependent.

- **sp_help**   Displays information about a particular database object.

- **sp_helpdb**   Displays information about the specified database.

- **sp_helptext**   Prints the SQL used to create a stored procedure, a trigger, or a view.

- ■ **sp_lock**   Displays information about current locks on the database.

- ■ **sp_recompile**   Causes all stored procedures and triggers to be recompiled the next time they are executed.

- ■ **sp_rename**   Allows the name of a user-defined object in the database to be changed.

- ■ **sp_who**   Displays information about the current users and processes running on the server.

Although these are only a small portion of the system stored procedures that exist, they are some of the ones most commonly used by developers. It is wise to know these and understand their uses, not only for your development work, but also as preparation for the exam.

Predefined system stored procedures are important and very helpful, but SQL Server also allows us to create our own user-defined system procedures. These procedures are created in the master database and are then available to all databases on the server. These procedures must be named using the standard naming convention of sp_*descriptive_name*. Once these procedures have been created in the master database they are then available for all databases. The following example creates a user-defined system procedure:

```
CREATE PROCEDURE sp_count_user_tables
As
select count(*) from sysobjects where type = 'U'
```

This procedure, named sp_count_user_tables, will be available from all databases on my server. The purpose of this procedure is to return the count of all rows in the sysobjects table whose type is *U*. For those who have worked with SQL Server very much, you know that this will return the count of user-defined tables in the current database. User-defined system procedures allow you to create common procedures that can be used on all databases on your server.

QUESTIONS AND ANSWERS

I am creating a new VC++ distributed application that works with a database. Which data access technology should I use?	ADO. For most new projects, ActiveX Data Objects should be the data access technology of choice.
What SQL statement should I use to add records to my database?	The Insert statement allows new records to be added to the database.
How can I force the records that I return from my Select statement to be in the order that I want?	Add an Order By clause to the end of the Select statement. This allows the returned rows to be sorted in the order that you desire.
I have a command that I often run that queries the system tables for the current database. How can I save this command to be used in all databases on my server?	You can create a user-defined system procedure that is available to all databases on the server by naming a procedure sp_procedure_name and creating it in the master database.

CERTIFICATION SUMMARY

We have covered quite a bit of material in this chapter. The process of creating distributed applications not only requires us to understand Visual C++ and its environment, but it also means that we must have a strong understanding of the databases that we will use. Much of the focus of this chapter has been on SQL Server. SQL Server is a very good choice for many database applications, but most of the concepts we have covered will be applicable even if you are using another database.

We introduced the various technologies that we can use to communicate between VC++ and the database. These included older technologies such as ODBC and DAO, and we also talked about ADO, the newest member of the Microsoft data access technologies. We discussed when each method should be considered for use.

The rest of the chapter focused on SQL, the language used to communicate with the database. We were introduced to the four major

SQL commands: Select, Insert, Update, and Delete. As we progressed through the chapter, we learned more about the various clauses that we can add to our SQL statements to improve their performance. We reviewed the aggregate functions that provide summary data when selecting information from the database.

We also looked at how we can store SQL statements in the database. We learned how and why to use stored procedures, when and why to use database triggers, and the advantages of using and creating system stored procedures.

TWO-MINUTE DRILL

- ❏ In a typical distributed application, sometimes referred to as an *n-tier application*, data services constitute the Data tier.

- ❏ Visual C++ comes with four separate database access systems: ODBC (Open Database Connectivity), ADO (ActiveX Data Objects), DAO (Data Access Objects), and RDO (Remote Data Objects).

- ❏ The Microsoft Open Database Connectivity (ODBC) standard defines not only the programming interface to a SQL database but also the rules of SQL grammar.

- ❏ ODBC employs a DLL-based architecture that makes the system fully modular.

- ❏ MFC provides two basic classes for working with ODBC. These two classes are CRecordset and CDatabase.

- ❏ The CRecordset class allows the application to interact with rows returned from the database based on a query or table identified when the application is created.

- ❏ The CDatabase class contains the information needed to attach to and communicate with the database.

- ❏ ADO is Microsoft's premier data access and manipulation technology. The ADO object model defines a collection of programmable objects that support the Component Object Model (COM) and OLE Automation to use the partner technology called OLE DB.

- ❏ OLE DB is a system-level programming interface that provides a standard set of COM interfaces for exposing database management system functionality.

❑ Data consumers are the applications that use the data.

❑ Data providers are the source for the data.

❑ The service provider allows for added functionality for any data providers.

❑ Data Access Objects (DAO) is a data access technology that was developed to help applications interact with a Jet database engine.

❑ The Jet database engine is the technology that actually stores and manipulates the data.

❑ Be sure to remember which MFC objects implement the DAO objects and which implement the ODBC library. CRecordset and CDatabase are used to implement the ODBC library, whereas CDaoRecordset and CDaoDatabase are used to implement the DAO object model. Also remember that you do not use CRecordset or CDaoRecordset directly; rather, you always use a class derived from these.

❑ Remote Data Objects (RDO) is a technology that was created after ODBC and DAO. Its purpose is to provide an easy-to-work-with object model that wraps the ODBC library and allows programmers to work quickly and easily with remote databases.

❑ *Stored procedures* are SQL commands that are stored inside of the database.

❑ Be prepared to identify situations in which stored procedures would provide an advantage over passing SQL strings to the database to be processed. One situation to be aware of is the case where several SQL statements must be processed and programming logic is used to identify the flow of execution. Of these, it is even more likely that a stored procedure will be advantageous when only the final results are needed by the client application.

❑ A relational database contains relationships between the tables that comprise the database.

❑ Triggers are invoked automatically by SQL Server when certain conditions arise.

❑ *System stored procedures* are procedures that are accessible from any database on the server.

SELF TEST

The following questions will help you measure your understanding of the material presented in this chapter. Read all of the choices carefully, as there may be more than one correct answer. Choose all correct answers for each question.

1. What is the standard language used to interact with a relational database?

    A. ODBC

    B. SQL

    C. DAO

    D. SELECT statements

2. Which data access technologies are supported by classes in the MFC framework? (Choose all that apply.)

    A. ODBC

    B. ADO

    C. RDO

    D. DAO

3. Which two of the following are advantages of using ODBC as the data access method for your application? (Choose all that apply.)

    A. It provides a common interface for all relational databases.

    B. It causes all databases to behave like SQL Server.

    C. It is widely accepted and drivers are available for many relational databases.

    D. It is the only data access technology supported by Visual C++.

4. On which technology is ADO based?

    A. ODBC

    B. DAO

    C. OLE DB

    D. RDO

5. Which object in the ADO hierarchy manages transactions in the database?

    A. Connection

    B. Command

    C. Recordset

    D. Properties

6. Which of the following is not an advantage of using stored procedures?

    A. The SQL is precompiled and stored in the database.

    B. They provide consistent logic between applications accessing the same data.

    C. They are most efficient when the procedure will be called only one time.

    D. They reduce network traffic.

7. What is the SQL statement that is used to retrieve data from the database to be used by a VC++ project?

    A. Select

    B. Update

    C. Delete

    D. Insert

8. What is the SQL statement that is used to change the contents of data that exists in the database?

   A. Select
   B. Update
   C. Delete
   D. Insert

9. What is the SQL statement that is used to add data to the database?

   A. Select
   B. Update
   C. Delete
   D. Insert

10. What is the SQL statement that is used to remove data from the database?

    A. Select
    B. Update
    C. Delete
    D. Insert

11. What is the result of executing the following SQL statement?

```
Select p.pub_name, t.title
From publishers p, titles t
  Where p.pub_id = t.pub_id
```

    A. This is an invalid SQL statement.
    B. This will return all records from both tables where the pub_ids match.
    C. This will return all records from the Publishers table and the matching records from the Titles table.
    D. This will return all records from the Titles table and the matching records from the Publishers table.

12. What is the result of executing the following SQL statement?

```
Select p.pub_name, t.title
From publishers p, titles t
Where p.pub_id *= t.pub_id
```

    A. This is an invalid SQL statement.
    B. This will return all records from both tables where the pub_ids match.
    C. This will return all records from the Publishers table and the matching records from the Titles table.
    D. This will return all records from the Titles table and the matching records from the Publishers table.

13. What is the result of executing the following SQL statement?

```
Select p.pub_name, t.title
From publishers p Inner Join
   titles t On p.pub_id = t.pub_id
```

    A. This is an invalid SQL statement.
    B. This will return all records from both tables where the pub_ids match.
    C. This will return all records from the Publishers table and the matching records from the Titles table.
    D. This will return all records from the Titles table and the matching records from the Publishers table.

14. What is the result of executing the following SQL statement?

```
Select p.pub_name, t.title
From publishers p Left Outer Join
   titles t On p.pub_id = t.pub_id
```

A. This is an invalid SQL statement.

B. This will return all records from both tables where the pub_ids match.

C. This will return all records from the Publishers table and the matching records from the Titles table.

D. This will return all records from the Titles table and the matching records from the Publishers table.

15. Which of the following are reasons for creating views in a database? (Choose all that apply.)

A. Views are the only way to access data from VC++.

B. Views allow for creating a level of security that defines who can see what data.

C. Views allow easier ad-hoc querying of the database.

D. Views increase performance when selecting data.

16. On which of the following events can a trigger be defined? (Choose all that apply.)

A. Insert

B. Create Table

C. Drop Procedure

D. Delete

17. Which tables are available only during the time that a trigger is being executed and allow the trigger to view the data that has changed? (Choose all that apply.)

A. Inserted

B. Updated

C. Modified

D. Deleted

18. Which of the following are aggregate functions that can be used to create SQL select statements that return summary data? (Choose all that apply.)

A. Count

B. Min

C. Avg

D. Sum

19. Which clause must be added to a Select statement that returns columns that contain aggregate functions and columns that do not?

A. Order By

B. Having

C. Group By

D. Aggregate On

20. In which database must a user-defined system procedure be created?

A. Model

B. Tempdb

C. Master

D. The database used by the current project

SELF TEST ANSWERS

1. **B.** All relational databases support a common language known as Structured Query Language (SQL). ODBC and DAO are Microsoft-defined data access technologies; they are not the language used to communicate with the database. The Select statement is part of the SQL language.

2. **A, D.** Although all of the answers are data access technologies supported by VC++, only ODBC and DAO have classes built into the MFC framework that support their use. The other two technologies must be supported by using #import, creating a wrapper class, or using ATL.

3. **A, C.** ODBC is a data access technology that has been available for many years and has gained wide-spread acceptance. Because of this, most databases have ODBC drivers which allow a common interface to interact with the various databases. Although it does not cause all databases to behave like SQL Server, it does cause all databases to support common functions. This is an advantage, but it is also a disadvantage in that to be truly compatible with all databases, you are not able to use functionality that is specific to the database for which you are developing. VC++ allows several options when choosing the database access technology, not just ODBC.

4. **C.** ADO is based on OLE DB, Microsoft's newest data access technology. This is part of Microsoft's Universal Data Access strategy that allows all data sources to be accessed in a common fashion. This includes not only relational data stores, but any storage of data that is available on our systems. All of the other options are technologies which can be used in place of ADO.

5. **A.** The Connection object is responsible for establishing a connection to the database. It is also the object that is responsible for managing database transactions. Typically an application will try to use a single connection to the database, but when multiple concurrent transactions are required then there will need to be multiple Connection objects instantiated.

6. **C.** Stored procedures provide many benefits when implemented properly. These include having the SQL statements precompiled and stored within the database. They provide a common function to be called by any application accessing the database and reduce network traffic. Stored procedures also provide even more efficient processing when they are called many times. This is because the procedure is loaded into the cache when it is run the first time and then can be executed even faster on subsequent calls.

7. **A.** All of the choices presented are proper SQL statements. Only answer A, Select, is the one used to return data to the VC++ project. Update allows the contents of an existing record in the database to be modified. Delete causes one or more records to be removed from the database. Insert allows new records to be added to the database.

8. **B.** All of the choices presented are proper SQL statements. Only answer B, Update, is the one used to modify data that exists in the database. Select returns the contents of existing records to the application. Delete causes one or more records to be removed from the database. Insert allows new records to be added to the database.

9. **D.** All of the choices presented are proper SQL statements. Only answer D, Insert, is the one used to add data to the database. Select returns the contents of existing records to the application. Update allows the contents of an existing record in the database to be modified. Delete causes one or more records to be removed from the database.

10. **C.** All of the choices presented are proper SQL statements. Only answer C, Delete, is the one used to remove data from the database. Select returns the contents of existing records to the application. Update allows the contents of an existing record in the database to be modified. Insert allows new records to be added to the database.

11. **B.** This SQL statement joins the Publishers table and the Titles table in an equijoin. That causes only those records that have matching values in each table to be returned.

12. **C.** This SQL statement joins the Publishers table and the Titles tables using a left outer join. That causes all of the records from the Publishers table to be returned as part of the resultset. For those publishers that have matching records in the Titles table, the title of each book will also be returned. For those publishers that do not have matching records in the Titles table, a single record will be returned with a null value for the title.

13. **B.** This SQL statement joins the Publishers table and the Titles table in an equijoin, which is also known as an inner join. This is the proper way to identify a join. Executing this join causes only those records that have matching values in each table to be returned.

14. **C.** This SQL statement joins the Publishers table and the Titles table using a left outer join. This is the proper way to identify a join. Executing this join causes all of the records from the Publishers table to be returned as part of the resultset. For those publishers that have matching records in the Titles table, the title of each book will also be returned. For those publishers that do not have matching records in the Titles table, a single record will be returned with a null value for the title.

15. **B, C.** Views are commonly used to create a level of security allowing certain users to only see portions of the data stored in the database. Views provide a simpler interface for producing ad-hoc queries by hiding the joining of tables. Views are not the only way through which we are able to access data from VC++, and when used improperly, views can actually degrade performance when selecting data from the database.

16. **A, D.** Triggers are SQL statements that are stored in the database and are automatically executed by SQL server when a predefined event occurs. Triggers are related to tables. Of the choices listed, only Insert and Delete are correct. Triggers identified as Insert triggers are fired once for each row that is added to the table. Triggers identified as Delete triggers are fired once for each row that is removed from the table. Although it is not listed here, the final event on which a trigger can be defined is on Update.

17. **A, D.** The Inserted and Deleted tables are available only during the execution of a trigger and contain the data that has changed. The Inserted table contains a copy of the record that has been inserted into the database. The Deleted table contains a copy of the row that has been deleted from the table. When a row has been updated, the Deleted table contains a copy of the data as it was prior to the update, whereas the Inserted table contains a copy of the data as it now exists.

18. **A, B, C, D.** All of these are aggregate functions that allow a Select statement to return summary data. Other aggregate functions include Max and Distinct.

19. **C.** When a Select statement returns columns that include an aggregate function and other columns that do not, you must add a Group By clause to the Select statement. This clause must include all columns that do not include an aggregate function. This allows the data that is returned to be grouped together based on the values for the columns that are not aggregated.

20. **C.** When defining a user-defined system procedure, you must follow two rules. The name of the procedure must start with sp_ and the procedure must be created in the master database on the server on which it will be used.

9

Creating a Physical Database

I n this chapter, we will discuss the physical design of a database. It will be kept as general as possible, but some areas will be focused on SQL Server 7.0. We will discuss how databases are physically stored. We will cover how files and filegroups can be used to store data and how transaction log files are used. Next, we will cover how to implement data integrity on a database. Data is very important to a business, and the integrity of that data needs to be preserved. We will discuss indexes and how they help make searching a database more efficient and faster. We will also discuss some of the tools available for importing data into a database.

Implementing a Data Storage Architecture

How the data is physically stored on the hard disk varies from database to database. SQL Server 7.0 stores its data differently than it did in earlier versions. The database is stored directly in files on the hard disk. In earlier versions, the database was stored in devices and segments. A *device* is a logical storage location for a database and transaction logs. When you create a device, you specify a size, and a file will be created of that size to store the database and other data that is needed to manage the database. When the device is full, you must increase the device size in order to hold more data. *Segments* are pointers to a device. A database can be split up and have different tables stored in different devices, so segments allow the database management system to locate where the table is stored. In SQL Server 7.0, the database is stored directly in files. Each database has its own separate set of files. This allows the database to grow and shrink as needed and not worry about competing for space with other databases. You no longer have to administer devices as databases grow and shrink. You can set up databases to automatically increase and decrease the size of files as needed. You can specify how much the file will grow or shrink at a time. If a database grows or shrinks rapidly, you can set it to grow or shrink in larger chunks so it doesn't have to be increased or decreased frequently. You can also specify a maximum size for a file. If there isn't a maximum specified, it will grow until it runs out of disk space. These options decrease the amount of administration needed for the database.

Files

A database is stored in a set of files. Each file belongs to only one database. Transaction logs and data are stored in separate files. There are three different types of files: primary data files, secondary data files, and log files. *Primary data files* contain data and pointers to the location of the other files in the database. There is one primary data file for every database. They have an extension of .MDF. *Secondary data files* contain the data in a database that is not stored in the primary data file. It is not required to have a secondary data file. They have an extension of .NDF. *Log files* are used to store logging information. This information is used to recover a database after a failure. There is at least one log file per database and there can be multiple log files. They have an extension of .LDF.

exam
ⓦatch

Remember that every database in SQL 7.0 contains at least one Primary Data File. Each database can contain one or more Secondary Data Files, but they are not required.

Filegroups

The data in a SQL Server 7.0 database is now stored in one or more data files. These files can be logically grouped into filegroups. You can define which data files are placed in filegroups. It is not required to specify filegroups. If one is not specified, the files are placed in a default filegroup. If you do specify filegroups, you can map tables and indexes to different filegroups. You can place the data files on different physical disks, which allows you to control which tables and indexes are placed on which disks. Placing the tables and indexes on different physical disks can increase the performance of your database because each physical disk has its own controller, allowing the files on different disks to be accessed in parallel. If you have a table that is heavily used, you can place it on a separate disk to increase performance. Another benefit is when performing backups. If the database is too large to back up at one time, you can back up one filegroup at a time on a rotating basis. This way, you can back up one piece of the database at a time.

Log files are not part of filegroups. These files are managed separately from the data files. In general, a single data file in the default filegroup is sufficient. When using multiple filegroups, put the system tables in the primary data file into one filegroup and the data tables in one or more secondary data files into another filegroup. You will then need to make this second filegroup the default because user data is always placed in the default filegroup. You can maximize performance by creating files on all the physical disks on the server and putting the largest tables in different filegroups on the different disks. If possible, place the log files on different disks from the data files.

Transaction Logs

Log files contain data to recover the database after a system failure. This maintains the integrity of a database even in the event of a system failure. The log files contain records of all changes to the database and the transaction that the modification is part of. These records are stored in the order that they occur. The log grows as operations are performed in the database. It also records the committing or rolling back of any transactions. This way, in the event of a system failure, the database server can still complete a commit or a rollback. When aborting a transaction, it can use the records to undo all of the modifications performed so far in the transaction. Log files can also be spanned across multiple physical disks to increase performance. Transactions were covered in Chapter 7.

In earlier versions of SQL Server, the log data was stored in system tables in a device. You had the same problem as with data tables, in that you had to administer the device to ensure there was enough space available in the device for the logs. With log files, the file sizing is handled automatically by SQL Server. Log files are divided into *virtual log files*. These are units of a log file. When there are no records from active transactions left in the virtual log file, the unit can be removed (or truncated) and the space can then be reused for new log records. This means that all of the records' transactions in the virtual log file have either been committed or rolled back. This method prevents the server from having to search through all of the records when a transaction ends and remove each record individually. After a transaction ends, it simply has to check to see if all of the transaction records in a portion of the log file are completed. The size of these virtual log files depends on how fast the log file grows. It prevents having a large number of small virtual log files. If the log file grows slowly, the virtual log file size will be small. If the log file grows rapidly, the virtual log files will be larger. The minimum size of a virtual log file is 256KB, and the minimum size of a transaction's records is 512KB.

Creating Databases and Database Tables That Enforce Data Integrity and Referential Integrity

Data integrity ensures that the data stored in a database is correct and is what you expect to be stored. The data in a database is often critical to a business' operation. You cannot afford to have corrupt data. There are different ways to ensure data integrity. There are three types of data integrity: entity, domain, and referential.

Entity integrity requires uniqueness in rows. That is, each row in a table must be unique in some way. A common way to implement this is with a primary key or a unique constraint. This uses one or more columns in a table to force rows to be unique in a table. We will discuss primary keys and unique constraints later in the chapter.

Domain integrity requires that the data in a column is of a certain data type, within a range of values, uses a specified format, and is allowed to be empty (or null). It checks to see if data being put into a column is valid for that column. Domain integrity can be enforced through validity checks before inserting the data, data types, and check constraints.

Referential integrity makes sure that tables that have columns that are linked through primary and foreign keys do not violate the relationship. This regulates when rows can be deleted, when a primary key can be changed, or when a row can be inserted that has a primary and foreign key relationship. We will cover primary and foreign keys next.

Primary Keys

Primary keys have several functions. A primary key ensures that each row in a table is unique. It uses one or more columns in a table as the key, and there can only be one primary key per table. A common way to implement this is to use an ID column that contains a number that is automatically incremented for each new row added to the table. If you attempt to add a row that is not unique, you will receive an error and the row will not be added to the table. Also, every row must have a primary key value; it cannot be left blank. Any violations to these rules will cause an error. The primary key can be referenced from another table as a foreign key to prevent data duplication. We will see how this works shortly.

Foreign Keys

Foreign keys contain the value of a primary key in another table. They allow you to link (or create a relationship) with another table. A foreign key can be one or more columns. It does not have to be unique. If it was unique, we could make it part of the primary key or combine the two tables into one. The value placed in the foreign key must match a primary key value in the linked table. If there isn't a match, an error will occur. The one exception is that you can allow empty (or NULL) values for the foreign key. However, if the key encompasses multiple columns, if one of these columns is empty then they must all be empty. See Figure 9-1 for an example of the primary key to foreign key relationship. The table on the right contains customer information. This table has a primary key on the CustID column. The table on the left contains a primary key on the OrderID column and a foreign key on the CustID column. The value placed in this foreign key column must have a matching value in the primary key column of the table referenced. This foreign key can be used to retrieve information about the customer who placed the order. This helps minimize the amount of space used to store the customer information. Otherwise you would have to store

The primary key to foreign key relationship

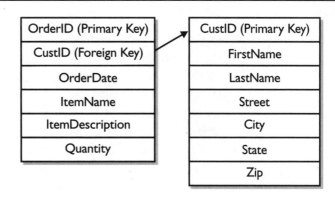

OrderID (Primary Key)
CustID (Foreign Key)
OrderDate
ItemName
ItemDescription
Quantity

CustID (Primary Key)
FirstName
LastName
Street
City
State
Zip

all of the customer information with every record. If the same customer made several orders, the customer's data would be duplicated. Also, if the customer's data changed, you would have to change it in every record where it was stored.

Remember that a foreign key is related to a primary key in another table. The value in the foreign key field must have a corresponding primary key field value in the related table.

Even though you might not be involved with the creation and maintenance of a database, you still should be familiar with the database and understand what integrity checks are implemented in the database that you are accessing. This allows you to perform some data validation in your application. It can save time because if you didn't check it first, the data would be sent across the network and checked at the database. If there is an error, you would have to determine what the error was, fix the error, and then re-send the data from your application. Also, by understanding data integrity, if you receive an error from the database, you will be able to understand why the error occurred. If you don't understand it, it will be difficult for you to correct the error. There are many ways to implement data integrity. We will discuss some of the main concepts for implementing data integrity. You can normalize the data, use business rules to verify correct data, and use referential integrity to implement data integrity.

Normalization

Normalization of data means organizing the data in a database by protecting the data, removing all duplication of data, and making the retrieval of data from the database more efficient and faster. Duplication of data wastes disk space and makes maintaining the database more difficult because if you edit data, you have to make sure that it is updated everyplace that it is duplicated. If there is any data duplicated between tables, that data should be broken up and put in a new table. There are different levels of normalization and the higher the level, the more complex it becomes to implement. The rules for normalization break up tables so that all of the columns in a row are of one basic group or entity (person, address, order, and so on). Normalization is broken down into rules. Each rule is called a normal form. For instance, the first rule is called the first normal form.

The first normal form specifies that every row in a table must be unique and each column cannot be decomposable. Uniqueness is usually implemented with a primary key. Not being decomposable means that a column cannot be broken down into separate columns. A common example of this is using one column for a name. This should be broken down into first, middle, and last name columns as necessary. Decomposable also means that you don't have multiple fields with the same basic data. For example, if you had a table that contains items ordered by a customer, you shouldn't use columns such as Item1, Item2, and Item 3 in a row. You should break it down so that each item is in a separate row. Exercise 9-1 gives an example of the first normal rule.

EXERCISE 9-1	**Using the First Normal Form**

1. Look at the Order table shown here:

CustName
CustAddress
OrderDate
Item1
Item2
Item3

2. Let's look at using the first normal form on this table. First of all, none of the fields can guarantee that all rows have a unique identifier. Let's add a primary key and call it OrderID.

3. Not all of the fields are of one entity. Let's put Item1, Item2, and Item 3 in separate rows with one item per row.

4. We now have this table:

OrderID (Primary Key)
CustName
CustAddress
OrderDate
Item

5. Now let's look at the columns in the Order table. CustName should be decomposed. We will break it up into two columns, FirstName and LastName. CustAddress should also be broken up. Break it up into Street, City, State, and Zip. Our new Customer table, with the customer information decomposed, is shown here:

OrderID (Primary Key)
FirstName
LastName
Street
City
State
Zip
OrderDate
Item

6. We will decompose the Item column. Break it up into the ItemName and ItemDescription fields. Our first normal form table is shown next.

OrderID (Primary Key)
FirstName
LastName
Street
City
State
Zip
OrderDate
ItemName
ItemDescription

The second normal form specifies that all data that can apply to multiple columns should be stored in a separate table, and the tables that need the data must reference the data with a foreign key. All of the requirements of the first normal form must also be met to be considered the second normal form. Each column in the row should be directly related to the primary key. Any data that is not directly related to the primary key should be placed in a separate table. For example, if you had a table that included the item ordered and customer information, the customer information is not directly related to the primary key, which would normally be some ID for each order. Exercise 9-2 gives you an example of implementing the second normal form.

EXERCISE 9-2 **Implementing the Second Normal Form**

1. The following illustration shows the table after we finished the first normal form and then added a Quantity field for the number of the item ordered.

OrderID (Primary Key)
FirstName
LastName
Street
City
State
Zip
ItemName
ItemDescription
Quantity

2. The customer information is not directly related to the order. Also, if the same customer made multiple orders, the information would be duplicated. So, we will place the customer information in a separate table called Customer and reference the primary key in that table. The two tables will look like the ones shown here:

OrderID (Primary Key)
CustID (Foreign Key)
OrderDate
ItemName
ItemDescription
Quantity

CustID (Primary Key)
FirstName
LastName
Street
City
State
Zip

3. Let's look at the Order table. We need to decompose the Item columns. We will have one item per row and break up the item into easier-to-use columns. Instead of using the name of an item to

describe it, we will assign an identifier to all items. This will cause us to add another table called Item. The Order table will now have the following columns: the OrderID, which is the primary key; an ItemID that is a foreign key to the new Item table and lets us know which item was ordered; a CustID that is a foreign key to the Customer table so we know which customer placed the order; and a Quantity column that lets us know the amount of this item that was ordered. The Item table contains an ItemID that is the primary key, a Name column, and a Description column. This will prevent problems that can occur with the Item name, such as misspelling it. By using the ItemID, you are required to choose a valid item. If a customer places multiple orders, we don't have to enter their data again. We only have to find out the customer's ID and place it in the Order table. Also, we don't have to re-enter item names. We simply look up the ID in the Item table and enter it in the Order table. We can also look up the description for an item without having to place it in every row where it was ordered. See the new tables illustrated here:

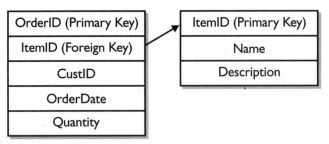

4. Notice now that the Order table is still not done. If a customer placed an order with multiple items, then there would be duplication of data. We will place the ItemID and Quantity in another table called OrderDetails. The new table is illustrated next. The OrderDetails primary key will be a combination of the OrderID and ItemID columns. The OrderID column itself will not be unique because there could be multiple items per order.

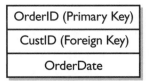

OrderID (Primary Key)
CustID (Foreign Key)
OrderDate

OrderID (Primary Key)
ItemID (Primary key)
Quantity

5. We now have four tables from our original Order table.

The third normal form requires all columns in a row to be directly related to the primary key. It must also meet the second normal form to be considered the third normal form. If a column is not part of the primary key then it does not belong in the table. This normally is not practical. In our Customer table, this would require putting the city, state, and zip code into separate tables. If this data doesn't change often, then leave it in the table. The fourth and fifth normal forms are seldom used and are not required for the exam.

In reality, you will not implement complete normalization through the fifth rule. It is common to only implement partially through the third normal form. The third normal form is not always practical. You will need to perform some benchmark testing and use your experience to determine what level you need to implement.

Declarative Data Integrity

There are other ways of enforcing data integrity. *Declarative data integrity* defines the criteria that the data must meet and is performed by the database management system. Integrity checks are defined in the database itself, normally in the tables and columns. By defining different checks during the creation of a table, you don't have to worry about the implementation. Because it is done by the database, it is less likely to have errors. There are three types of declarative data integrity: identities, constraints, and defaults or rules.

Identities allow you to create special columns that identify the rows in the table. These contain values that are generated by the database. It is a value that is automatically incremented by the database for each row. You don't have to worry about what value to assign or whether it is unique or not, because it is handled by the database. You can specify the increment value. When a new row is added, it will see what the previous row value was and increment that value by the increment value specified. Generally, the increment value defaults to one. There can only be one identity column per table, but it can be in any column in the table.

Constraints determine what values can be placed in a column. Constraints are actually stored as part of the table itself. If the table is deleted, so are the constraints associated with it. There are different types of constraints. The primary key and the foreign key are types of constraints. For the primary key, the data placed in the columns has to be unique. For the foreign key, the value has to have a corresponding primary key value in the referenced table. The foreign key is used to enforce referential integrity. There is also a *unique constraint*. It requires the column to have a unique value for each row, but it is not a primary key. The unique constraint cannot be referenced as a foreign key in another table. However, unlike a primary key, it does allow null values. If the value is null, then it is not verified for uniqueness. You can have multiple rows with null values. The primary key and the unique constraint are used for enforcing entity integrity. A *default constraint* defines a value that will automatically be placed in the column if no value is specified when the row is added to the table. For example, say you were adding a customer to a database and a table had a column containing the amount overdue by the customer. Generally, this value would always be zero, so you create a default to set the column to zero unless there was an extenuating circumstance, in which case you could insert a value for the column. Make sure you specify a default value that is valid for the column. The *check constraint* allows you to specify what values are allowed to be placed in a column. A check constraint can be set against multiple columns and multiple check constraints can be set against one column. You can create simple or complex check constraints. You can check for several conditions within the same constraint. The default and check constraints are used to enforce domain integrity. The check constraint can also be used to enforce referential integrity. For example, in our previous exercises we had a Quantity column for the quantity ordered for an item. You would not want this value to be less than or equal to zero, so you could create a check constraint to verify that each value placed in the column was greater than zero. You could also verify that a value was in a list. For example, say you accepted credit cards, you could verify that the credit card type was only VISA or MasterCard.

Defaults and *rules* are database-wide objects similar to constraints. They are stored as part of a database and can be bound to columns and even user-defined data types in different tables. A default has the same functionality as the default constraint. If no value is given for the column when a row is added, it places a value in the column automatically. A rule allows you to specify the data that can be put in a column. Constraints provide the same functionality as defaults and rules. If they are only going to be used in one table, you should use constraints whenever possible. The defaults and rules are still available for backwards compatibility.

Procedural Data Integrity

Another way to ensure data integrity is through *procedural data integrity.* This allows you to check for more than just data placed in a column. You can also enforce business rules here. Although it is recommended to implement business rules in the business services, it is sometimes more appropriate to implement them in the data services. When the business rule directly affects the database, it is more efficient and practical to enforce it in the database. For example, you might want to create a procedure that is part of the database so that when you delete a customer, you delete all the related data. Implementing this in the database would be better than doing it from within the business services. Procedural data integrity uses stored procedures and triggers.

Stored procedures are sequences of Transact-SQL statements that can be called from applications to be executed and run in the database. The first time a stored procedure is run, the Transact-SQL statements are checked for syntax and then compiled and stored on the server in a cache. This makes it more efficient than performing the Transact-SQL statements one at a time. This way, the database doesn't have to check the Transact-SQL statements for errors and they are already compiled and optimized. Stored procedures can be invoked by applications outside the database. If multiple applications were going to perform the same functions, a stored procedure would be an ideal way to enforce a business rule. If all applications use a stored procedure that has been tested, then you don't have to worry about how each developer implements that business rule. Also, if the business rule changes, you only have to change the stored procedure. You don't have to change each application and then redistribute that application hoping each developer implemented the change correctly.

Triggers are stored procedures, but how they are invoked is different. A stored procedure can be called from an application, but a trigger is automatically invoked by the database when you try to modify a column that a trigger is protecting. Triggers are commonly invoked when you add, delete, or edit rows. The most common use for a trigger is performing cascading deletes and updates. If you wanted to delete a row with a primary key, a cascading delete would delete the rows in other tables that had a foreign key with the same value as the row you were deleting. This makes sure you don't have any foreign keys without a corresponding primary key. The trigger can be set up to perform this automatically whenever a row is deleted in a table. This could also be used for cascading updates. An example would be when you changed the primary key for a row. All corresponding foreign keys would be updated to reflect the change. You always want to ensure that a foreign key has a corresponding primary key. This enforces the data integrity of the database. Triggers enforce data integrity because they are run automatically when an operation on the database is performed. Stored procedures have to be called to run, so they play a lesser role in enforcing data integrity. The two can be used in conjunction with each other. You can have a trigger run a stored procedure and that same stored procedure can also be called from an application if the functionality is needed for a manual operation.

There are times when a constraint cannot support all of the required functionality. In these cases, you should use a trigger. A check constraint can validate data in a column in a row in a table, but if you need to validate data against multiple tables, then you need to use a trigger. For example, a foreign key requires a corresponding primary key, but a constraint cannot perform a cascading delete because the operation would span multiple tables, so you use a trigger to perform one. A constraint can only notify you of errors through standard system messages. If you need added notifications or some database-level error handling, then you need to use a trigger.

CERTIFICATION OBJECTIVE 9.03

Creating and Maintaining Indexes

One of the most common operations on a database is to retrieve data. The number of rows in a table can be very large, and therefore you want to optimize the retrieval of data and make it as fast as possible. One of the optimization methods that can be used is implementing indexes. An *index* is a structure that contains keys from one or more columns in a table. The keys are pointers to the data in a table. The keys are stored in a way to speed up the process of finding a particular row in a table and make the retrieval of data more efficient. When a particular row is being searched for, the search can be performed against the index instead of the table itself. A common example of the use of an index is a telephone book. When you want to find the phone number for someone, imagine if you had to search the entire phone book because there wasn't any order to the numbers. Instead, they are stored in alphabetical order based on last name, then first name. This makes finding a particular person's number much faster. There are two common ways to implement indexes. These are called clustered indexes and nonclustered indexes.

In a *clustered index*, the order of the index is the same as the order in the table. Basically, the data is stored as the index. This follows the example of the phone book. The index is based on the last name and the data itself is stored in order based on the last name. The index determines the order in which the rows are stored in the table. This also means that there can only be one clustered index per table. You couldn't physically store the data based on two different indexes. A clustered index can span multiple columns though. Following our telephone book example, you could have an index based on the last name and the first name columns so that the data will also be sorted on the first name for the rows that have the same last names.

In a *nonclustered index*, the data is physically stored differently from the index. The index is stored separately from the table. It contains keys that point to where the data is physically stored. When the table is searched, the index will be used to find the desired row. It will search the index for the desired column value, and when it finds the value, it will use the pointer to retrieve the data from the row. Even with the extra step of using the index, which is separate from the data, it is still more efficient than searching the entire table row by row. You can think of this like an index in a book. The word you want to search on could be anywhere in the book, but by looking in the index, you can find the locations of that word in the book fairly quickly. Because the data is not physically stored in the same way as the index, you can have multiple nonclustered indexes. For example, if you had a customer table, you might want one index for the name and another for the city or state that they live in.

When creating a table, you need to decide which columns need an index and what type of index to use. For a nonclustered index, the data contained in the column in the table is also stored in the index. This means that you only want to create an index when necessary because this uses more disk space and as data is changed, the index must also be changed. Each time the index columns are changed, or rows are added, the table will have to be rearranged to maintain the index. This can slow down operations that insert data into tables. Also, if your index will store a large amount of duplicated data, the index will not provide much benefit. You don't necessarily want to create one for every column. The columns that will be searched on frequently are the ones for which you should create indexes. From our customer example, the name and city or state might be searched for frequently, but the street address probably won't be. So, create an index for the name, city, and state columns, but not the street address column. In general, you should also consider creating a clustered index comprised of the primary key and the foreign key if they are going to be searched. Some databases automatically optimize searching on the primary key. In Exercise 9-3, we will look at choosing columns for which we will create indexes.

Choosing the Columns for Which We Should Create Indexes

1. In this exercise, we will use the Customer table from Exercise 9-2. We will look at each column and decide whether or not it needs an index. Remember that this discussion is a general discussion and there may be instances where you would decide differently. It all depends on how you will be using the data. First, we will look at the Customer table. The Customer table is illustrated here:

CustID (Primary Key)
FirstName
LastName
Street
City
State
Zip

2. The CustID column is the primary key. Whether or not this needs an index depends on the database. Generally, this will be an auto increment column and will already be in ascending order. Also, some databases automatically optimize searching the primary key. In this case, it would not need an index.

3. The FirstName column generally would not be searched for exclusively and therefore wouldn't need an index.

4. The LastName column probably would be searched frequently and would need an index. You might consider the FirstName column as a secondary column in the index.

5. The Street column probably won't be searched on very often, so don't create an index for this column.

6. The City, State, and Zip depend on the use of the table. If you want to search for all the customers in the respective area, create an index for the columns on which you plan on searching.

Populating the Database with Data from an External Data Source

There are many methods of populating a database with data from external data sources. You might be converting from one database management system to another or maybe you receive your data in a format such as a comma-delimited text file. SQL Server comes with two main ways to populate a database from external data sources. These methods are the bulk copy program (BCP) and the Data Transformation Services (DTS).

The bulk copy feature of SQL Server allows you to import or export large amounts of data from a table. Bulk copy can import data from a file. The format of the data in the data file is defined in a format file. This is faster and more efficient than creating an application that parses the data in the file and inserting it into a database with SQL statements. However, you can create applications that can use the bulk copy operations using the SQL Server 7.0 ODBC driver. This is an extension to Open Database Connectivity (ODBC) that is specific to SQL Server 7.0. It is not a standard ODBC operation. To use the bulk copy operations in Visual C++, you need to use the following ODBC files: ODBCSS.H, ODBCBCP.LIB, and ODBCBCP.DLL. The ODBCSS.H is a header file that contains the function prototypes and constant definitions for the functions used in bulk copy operations. The ODBCBCP.LIB file is a library file that can be statically linked to the application. It contains the implementation of the bulk operations. The ODBCBCP.DLL is a dynamically linked file that contains the implementation of the bulk copy operations. The bulk copy operations can copy the data from a file into a table. You can also use a format file to determine the structure of the data in the file. You can also load the data into variables in the application and then bulk copy the data into a table one row at a time. See the following code for an example of the SQL statement. It imports data from the DATA.DAT data file using the ASCII format, a tab character as the column delimiter, and carriage return as the row delimiter.

```
BULK INSERT SomeDatabase.dbo.[SomeTable]
FROM 'C:\data.dat'
WITH
(
DATAFILETYPE='char',
FIELDTERMINATOR = '\t',
ROWTERMINATOR = '\n'
)
```

You can also use the bulk copy program. It is a command-line utility that can perform bulk copy operations for inserting large amounts of data into SQL Server. This utility was actually written using the ODBC bulk copy API. When using BCP from the command line, if there are any spaces or other special characters in any object names such as a database or table name, you need to enclose the name in either double quotes (" ") or square brackets ([ ]). When using the quotes or brackets, you must use the –q option. You can also use the BCP utility to create a format file. Following is the basic syntax for using the BCP utility.

```
bcp {[[database_name.][owner].]{table_name}}
{in | out | format} data_file
[-f format_file] [-n] [-c] [-q]
[-t field_term] [-r row_term]
```

Arguments

- *database_name*   The name of the database in which the table resides. If not specified, then it uses the default database.

- *owner*   The name of the owner of the table. If you are the owner of the table, you do not have to include this parameter.

- *table_name*   The name of the destination table when copying data into SQL Server (**in**), and the source table when copying data from SQL Server (**out**).

- *in | out | queryout | format*   Specifies the direction of the bulk copy. **in** copies from a file into the database table or view. **out** copies from the database table or view to a file. **format** creates a format file based on the option specified (**-n**, **-c**, **-w**, **-6**, or **-N**) and the table or view delimiters. If **format** is used, the -f option must be specified as well.

■ *data_file* The full path of the data file used when bulk copying a table or view to or from a disk. When bulk copying data into SQL Server, the data file contains the data to be copied into the specified table or view. When bulk copying data from SQL Server, the data file contains the data copied from the table or view. The path can have from 1 through 255 characters.

■ **-f** *format_file* Specifies the full path of the format file that contains stored responses from a previous use of **bcp** on the same table or view. Use this option when using a format file created with the **format** option to bulk copy data in or out. Creation of the format file is optional. After prompting you with format questions, **bcp** prompts whether to save the answers in a format file. The default file name is Bcp.fmt. **bcp** can refer to a format file when bulk copying data; therefore, re-entering previous format responses interactively is not necessary. If this option is not used and **-n**, **-c**, **-w**, **-6**, or **-N** is not specified, **bcp** prompts for format information.

■ **-n** Performs the bulk copy operation using the native (database) data types of the data. This option does not prompt for each field; it uses the native values.

■ **-c** Performs the bulk copy operation using a character data type. This option does not prompt for each field; it uses **char** as the storage type, no prefixes, \t (tab character) as the field separator, and \n (newline character) as the row terminator.

■ **-q** Specifies that quoted identifiers are required, for example, when the table or view name contains characters that are not ANSI characters. Enclose the entire three-part table or view name (which may contain embedded special characters, such as spaces) in double quotation marks (" ").

■ **-t** *field_term* Specifies the field terminator. The default is \t (tab character). Use this parameter to override the default field terminator.

■ **-r** *row_term* Specifies the row terminator. The default is \n (newline character). Use this parameter to override the default row terminator.

The data file can be created in any fashion. It doesn't have to be created by another bulk copy program. The data file and the format file just have to follow the bulk copy definitions. A common example is to export an Excel spreadsheet into a comma-delimited file and then create a format file defining the structure of the data. These files can then be used to import the data into SQL Server.

Data can be stored in data files in either ASCII format or native format. When the data is stored using the ASCII format, the data is stored as ASCII characters. This allows you to import data from other data sources. Each piece of data will then have to be converted into the SQL Server data type. The native format means that each piece of data is stored in the SQL Server-defined data type. This is useful for moving data from one SQL Server to another. The native format is more efficient because the data doesn't have to be converted.

See the following example for using the bulk copy program from the command line. The example will bulk copy the data in the DATA.DAT file to the Some Table table using the ASCII format. The –q option is included because our table name has a space in it. It uses the default field and row terminators.

```
bcp SomeDatabase..[Some Table] in data.dat -c -q
```

Data Transformation Services (DTS) enables you to import and export data between data sources that use OLE DB. It allows you to transfer databases between SQL Server 7.0 servers. It is also used for building data warehouses and data marts. DTS contains wizards to step you through the process. Using the wizards, you can import, export, and transform data by creating DTS packages that use OLE DB and ODBC. You can also copy data and the structure of the data between databases.

DTS contains an import wizard and an export wizard. You can import data from the following sources: ASCII text files with fixed-length fields; ODBC data sources; SQL Server databases; Excel spreadsheets; Access databases; FoxPro databases; dBase databases; Paradox databases; and OLE DB data sources.

Commonly, desktop databases are converted to a client-server database. There are many reasons for doing this. A client-server database generally provides better performance, is more reliable, and has better security. One example would be converting a Microsoft Access database to SQL Server. Microsoft Access databases are a good choice for desktop applications or small network applications. There are even a good number of Access databases used for Web applications. An Access database's efficiency starts to degrade after about 50,000 records. If business is good and your application's database is growing, you need to upsize your database to SQL Server or another higher-end database server. To convert an Access database to SQL Server, you can use the Microsoft Upsizing Tool to do most of the work for you.

QUESTIONS AND ANSWERS

You have a database that you want to improve the performance of. There is a table that is queried frequently. What should you do?	Implement filegroups. Create a secondary data file on an unused disk drive and put it in a separate filegroup. Then assign the frequently used table to the new filegroup.
You have normalized a database to the fourth normal form. It seems to be running very slowly. What should you do?	At some point, there is a tradeoff between the level of normalization and performance. There aren't any defined rules describing when performance will start to suffer. You must perform benchmark testing in order to determine what is best for your database.
You have a table that already contains a primary key. You have a field in the table that cannot have duplicates. However, the field can be left empty. How can this be enforced by the database?	Use a unique constraint. It will ensure all the rows have a unique value for the field, but also allow NULL values.

CERTIFICATION SUMMARY

In this chapter, we discussed the physical design of a database. We covered how the data is physically stored. SQL Server 7.0 changed drastically from earlier versions by saving databases directly to files on the physical disk. There are one or more data files with one primary data file and the optional secondary data files. These files can be logically grouped into filegroups. This allows you to assign files to filegroups on different physical disks and span your data across the different disks to increase performance. Transaction log files keep records of every change that is made to the database. This allows the database to be recovered in the event of a system failure. The log file is broken down into virtual log files. When every record's transaction in the virtual log file is complete, the virtual log file is cleared to be used for new records.

The integrity of a database is critical. You will lose customers fast with bad data. Data integrity can broken down into three basic types. Entity integrity requires each row to be unique. Domain integrity specifies the valid data for a column. Referential integrity links tables together through primary and foreign keys. Normalization of your database can also improve the performance of your database, depending on the amount of normalization. At some point, it will degrade performance. That is why you should perform testing to determine what is best for your application. The integrity of your data can be enforced through identities, constraints, defaults, rules, stored procedures, and triggers. For more complex processing, use stored procedures. Stored procedures can also be used to enforce simple business rules.

Indexes allow you to increase the performance of your database. They allow you to order the data in the columns so that it is easier and quicker to search. There are two basic types of indexes: clustered and nonclustered.

Clustered indexes order how the data is physically stored in the table. Nonclustered indexes store the column data separately from the table. The data is then arranged in the index to optimize searches. When the column in the index is found, the row pointer is used to retrieve the data in the row.

When you need to import data from external data sources, there are many tools available. We discussed using the bulk copy program and API. This is useful for copying large amounts of data into SQL Server. SQL Server 7.0 also includes Data Transformation Services wizards to import and export data. An Access database can be upgraded to SQL Server using the Microsoft Upsizing Tool. It steps you through the conversion process.

TWO-MINUTE DRILL

- ❑ A *device* is a logical storage location for a database and transaction logs.

- ❑ *Segments* are pointers to a device. A database can be split up and have different tables stored in different devices, so segments allow the database management system to locate where the table is stored.

- ❑ *Primary data files* contain data and pointers to the location of the other files in the database. There is one primary data file for every database. They have an extension of .MDF.

- ❑ *Secondary data files* contain the data in a database that is not stored in the primary data file. It is not required to have a secondary data file. They have an extension of .NDF.

- ❑ *Log files* are used to store logging information. This information is used to recover a database after a failure. There is at least one log file per database and there can be multiple log files. They have an extension of .LDF.

- ❑ Log files are divided into *virtual log files*. These are units of a log file.

- ❑ A primary key ensures that each row in a table is unique. It uses one or more columns in a table as the key, and there can only be one primary key per table.

❑ Foreign keys contain the value of a primary key in another table. They allow you to link (or create a relationship) with another table.

❑ Normalization of data means organizing the data in a database by protecting the data, removing all duplication of data, and making the retrieval of data from the database more efficient and faster.

❑ *Data integrity* ensures that the data stored in a database is correct and is what you expect to be stored.

❑ *Entity integrity* requires uniqueness in rows. That is, each row in a table must be unique in some way.

❑ *Domain integrity* requires that the data in a column is of a certain data type, within a range of values, uses a specified format, and is allowed to be empty (or null).

❑ *Referential integrity* makes sure that tables that have columns that are linked through primary and foreign keys do not violate the relationship.

❑ *Declarative data integrity* defines the criteria that the data must meet and is performed by the database management system.

❑ *Identities* allow you to create special columns that identify the rows in the table.

❑ *Constraints* determine what values can be placed in a column.

❑ Data Transformation Services (DTS) enables you to import and export data between data sources that use OLE DB.

❑ Indexes allow you to increase the performance of your database. They allow you to order the data in the columns so that it is easier and quicker to search. There are two basic types of indexes: clustered and nonclustered. Clustered indexes order how the data is physically stored in the table. Nonclustered indexes store the column data separately from the table.

SELF TEST

The following questions will help you measure your understanding of the material presented in this chapter. Read all of the choices carefully, as there may be more than one correct answer. Choose all correct answers for each question.

1. You are designing a database. You have decided to use SQL Server 7.0, which now uses files for database storage. Which of the following files is required for every database? (Choose all that apply.)

   A. Primary data file

   B. Secondary data file

   C. Index file

   D. Log file

2. You are trying to find the files for a database on your hard disk. You are not sure what the filename is. You decide to look for all of the files on your hard disk by the filename extensions. Which of the following file types has the incorrect filename extension?

   A. .MDF primary data file

   B. .SDF secondary data file

   C. .NDF secondary data file

   D. .LDF log file

3. You are designing a database. You have decided to implement filegroups. Which of the following is not a benefit of using filegroups?

   A. Allows tables and indexes to be placed on different physical disks to increase performance

   B. Allows backing up the database in pieces

   C. Allows transaction logs to be placed on different physical disks to increase performance

   D. Allows a heavily used table to be placed in a filegroup on an isolated physical disk

4. Your customer is concerned about how their database will handle the integrity of data in the event of a system failure. You tell them that the database management system has fault tolerance built in. Which of the following is used for this?

   A. Fault tolerance logs

   B. Secondary data files

   C. System failure logs

   D. Transaction logs

5. You are designing a database. You are trying to maximize performance and ensure the integrity of the data. You decide to create a primary key for a table. Which of the following types of data integrity will this fulfill?

   A. Entity integrity

   B. Domain integrity

   C. Referential integrity

   D. Declarative integrity

6. You are designing a database. You are working on the design to ensure the integrity of the data. You are assigning data types to the columns and adding constraints to the columns. What kind of data integrity are you implementing?

   A. Entity integrity
   B. Domain integrity
   C. Referential integrity
   D. Declarative integrity

7. You have designed a database with a Customer table and an Order table. The Customer table has a primary key and the Order table has a foreign key with a relationship to the Customer table. What kind of data integrity does this enforce?

   A. Entity integrity
   B. Domain integrity
   C. Referential integrity
   D. Declarative integrity

8. You have created a table in a database. You have verified that all the rows will be unique and none of the columns can be broken down into more columns. Which normal form is this?

   A. First
   B. Second
   C. Third
   D. None of the above

9. You have designed a table in a database. You would like to optimize the database and you decide to normalize the table. In the following table, what normal form is met?

OrderID (Primary Key)
FirstName
LastName
Street
City
State
Zip
OrderDate
ItemName
ItemDescription

   A. First normal form
   B. Second normal form
   C. Third normal form
   D. It doesn't meet any of the normal forms.

10. You have created a table in a database. All of the columns are directly related to the primary keys and for data not directly related to the primary key, a foreign key is used to access that data. Which normal form is this?

    A. First
    B. Second
    C. Third
    D. None of the above

11. You have decided to implement constraints in your database to enforce data integrity. Which of the following is not a constraint?

    A. Default
    B. Unique
    C. Validate
    D. Check

12. You have designed a table with a column that stores a value that has to be between 1 and 10. You decide to enforce this on the column in the table. Which of the following should you use to implement this?

   A. Stored procedure

   B. Check constraint

   C. Trigger

   D. Rule

13. You need to validate some data being inserted into a column in a table. In order to validate the data, you have to use a factor that is stored in another table. Which data integrity method should you use to implement this?

   A. Foreign key

   B. Stored procedure

   C. Check constraint

   D. Default

14. You have a database with a Customer table that contains a primary key and is referenced by a foreign key in an Order table. When you delete a row from the Customer table, you want the rows that reference the primary key in the Order table to be automatically deleted also. How should you implement this?

   A. Check constraint

   B. Rule

   C. Stored procedure

   D. Trigger

15. You are designing a database and you have a large table that will be searched frequently. You want to make sure the searches are performed as fast as possible. Which of the following should you implement to fulfill this need?

   A. Stored procedure

   B. Index

   C. Transaction

   D. Primary key

16. You have created a table with a primary key and a clustered index on the primary key column. You have also placed a nonclustered index on another column. You decide to create a clustered index on a foreign key column. Why do you receive an error when you try to do this?

   A. Because there already is a nonclustered index

   B. Because a foreign key cannot have a clustered index

   C. Because there already is a clustered index

   D. None of the above

17. You have designed the following table. You are trying to decide which columns to create indexes for. Which of the following columns is not a good choice for creating an index on?

| OrderID (Primary Key) |
| CustID (Foreign Key) |
| OrderDate |
| Quantity |
| Notes |

A. OrderID

B. CustID

C. OrderDate

D. Notes

18. You have just created a SQL Server database and you want to import data from a very large Excel spreadsheet. You have exported the data in the spreadsheet to a tab-delimited text file. You want to import this data into the database without writing an application. Which of the following will allow you to do this?

A. The Excel Importer program

B. The bulk copy program

C. You have to import it into an Access database and then use the Microsoft Upsizing Tool to import the data into SQL Server

D. It cannot be done

19. You want to import the data from an ASCII data file named DATA.DAT. The format of the data is in a file called DATA.FMT. The field delimiter is the | character and the carriage return is the row delimiter. The data will be imported into the Some Table table in the SomeDatabase database. Which of the following will do this?

A. bcp SomeDatabase..[Some Table] in data.dat -c

B. bcp SomeDatabase..[Some Table] in data.dat -c -f data.fmt

C. bcp SomeDatabase..[Some Table] in data.dat -n -f data.fmt -t '|' -r '\n'

D. bcp SomeDatabase..[Some Table] in data.dat -c -f data.fmt -t |

20. You have a Web site that retrieves data from an Access database. Your data has grown considerably and the Web site has increased usage. You would like to convert the Access database into SQL Server. You don't want to manually import the data into SQL Server. Which of the following should you use?

A. The bulk copy program

B. The Data Transformation Services

C. The Microsoft Upsizing Tool

D. The Access Conversion Tool

SELF TEST ANSWERS

1. **A, D.** Every database must have at least a primary data file and a log file. The secondary data file is optional and an index file is not applicable.

2. **B.** A secondary data file has an extension of .NDF, not .SDF. A primary data file has an extension of .MDF, and a log file has an extension of .LDF.

3. **C.** Transaction logs are not part of filegroups. They are managed separately from data files. Filegroups allow you to place tables and indexes in different filegroups, which allows you to put different tables and indexes on different physical disks. Filegroups can be backed up separately, allowing you to back up a database in pieces.

4. **D.** Transaction log files are used to recover from system failures. They store records for every modification made to the database. Secondary data files are used to store user data. Fault tolerance and system failure logs do not exist.

5. **A.** Entity integrity requires that all of the rows in a table be unique. Creating a primary key enforces uniqueness between the rows.

6. **B.** Domain integrity ensures that the data being put in a column meets some requirements such as data type, a range of values, and whether or not it can be null. This is enforced through data types and constraints.

7. **C.** Referential integrity is enforced by using foreign keys that are linked to the primary key in another table. The foreign key value must have a corresponding value in the primary key of the referenced table.

8. **A.** The first normal form requires that all rows in a table be unique and all columns are not decomposable.

9. **A** The first normal form is met. The first normal form requires that all of the rows are unique and all of the columns cannot be broken down into more columns. The primary key meets the uniqueness requirement. All of the columns are broken down as far as they can be. It doesn't meet the second normal form. The second normal form requires that all of the columns be directly related to the primary key. The customer information and the item information are not directly related to the primary key OrderID. The customer information and item information should be put in separate tables and referenced with a foreign key.

10. **B.** The second normal form specifies that all data that can apply to multiple columns be stored in a separate table and the tables that need the data, reference the data with a foreign key.

11. **C.** Validate is not a type of constraint. Default, unique, and check are types of constraints used to enforce data integrity.

12. **B.** A check constraint should be used to specify a range of valid values on a column. A stored procedure is not needed because it is not complex and doesn't span multiple tables. Because this is only being implemented on one table, a constraint should be used rather than a rule.

13. **B.** A stored procedure should be used when performing data integrity checks that span multiple tables. A check constraint cannot access data in another table. A foreign key doesn't allow you to perform custom validation, and a default just inserts a value into a column if no value is supplied.

14. **D.** A trigger can be created that is automatically invoked when a row is deleted. Inside the trigger, you can either call another stored procedure or write Transact-SQL statements to search for all the rows in the Order table that reference the primary key being deleted and delete those rows from the Order table. A stored procedure has to be called to run, so it cannot occur automatically.

15. **B.** An index can be used to increase the efficiency and speed of searching on a column. A primary key enforces uniqueness; it does not help with searching on the table.

16. **C.** There can only be one clustered index per table. A clustered index determines the physical order of the table, so you could not have two indexes that determine the order.

17. **D.** Notes would not be a good choice for creating an index. The Notes field would seldom, if ever, be searched on. Primary and foreign keys should generally have an index created for them, and the OrderDate is a common column to search. You might want to search for all orders placed on a date.

18. **B.** The bulk copy program is a command-line utility that can be used to import data from a formatted ASCII text file into SQL Server.

19. **D.** A does not work because it doesn't specify a format file or the field delimiter. B is not correct because it does not specify the field delimiter. C is not correct because the

-n option specifies the native format and the data file is in the ASCII format, and the field and row delimiters do not use quotation marks. D specifies the ASCII format, the format file, and the field delimiter. The row delimiter is not needed because the default is the carriage return.

20. **C.** The Microsoft Upsizing Tool is the best choice for converting an Access database to SQL Server. That's what the program was developed for. The bulk copy program cannot read data from an Access database.

MCSD
MICROSOFT CERTIFIED SOLUTION DEVELOPER

10

Testing and Debugging the Solution

Testing and debugging are very important areas in application development. You want to make sure your application works properly for your customers. This is also an important area for the exam. There are commonly quite a few questions covering this area and it is critical to passing the exam. We will cover testing and debugging an application and the tools included with Visual C++ to help this process. For debugging applications, Visual C++ comes with run-time library support, tools built into the integrated development environment (IDE), the Depends tool, the Spy++ tool, and Microsoft Foundation Class Library (MFC) macros. For testing applications, we will cover the elements of a test plan including Beta, unit, integration, and stress testing.

CERTIFICATION OBJECTIVE 10.01

Debugging Techniques

Debugging an application allows you to find errors in your application. Errors can be programmatic or logical. There are many techniques and tools available for debugging applications. In this chapter, we will only cover the areas relevant to the Microsoft Certification Exam. We will cover the tools available in Visual C++ and when to use each of the tools.

Using Library Debugging Support

When you create a project, both a debug version and a release version are created. For the debug versions, some extra files are created to hold debugging information. Two .PDB (Program Database) files are created. One is a VC*x*0.PDB file, where *x* is the version number of Visual C++ (for example, VC60.PDB). This file contains debug information about types for the object files and is placed in the same directory as the makefile. This file is created when you compile an .OBJ file. The other file created is the *project*.PDB file, where *project* is the name of the project. It contains all debugging information for the .EXE file. This file is placed in the \Debug directory. This file is created by the linker. The *project*.PDB file is used by the Visual C++ debugger.

Visual C++ includes debugging support in the run-time library. This allows you to step into a run-time function's code and contains functions to help locate memory leaks and other memory problems, and to view the heap. When you build a debug version of your application, the run-time debug libraries are linked by default.

There are three common debug libraries. The library that is linked depends on the project you are building. The LIBCD.LIB library is used for single-threaded, static link projects, the LIBCMTD.LIB library is used for multithreaded, static link projects, and the MSVCRTD.LIB library is used for multithreaded, dynamic link projects.

The debug libraries include debug versions of *malloc, free, calloc, realloc, new,* and *delete.* These can be used for finding memory leaks. A memory leak can be caused by not freeing memory when it is no longer needed or goes out of scope or by changing a pointer without freeing the memory it was pointing to. This memory cannot be used again. You could eventually run out of memory if this occurs enough times. These problems can be difficult to isolate because the results can be intermittent and not apparent until a different part of the code is executed. Also, small leaks might not have any visible side effects until the application has been running for a long time. The following code demonstrates some examples of memory leaks:

```
//memory is allocated, but not freed when the procedure loses scope
void OutOfScope()
{
  int *ptr;
  ptr = new int;
  *ptr = 1;
}
//a pointer is changed without freeing the memory it was pointing to
void ChangePointer()
{
  int *ptr1;
int *ptr2;
  ptr1 = new int;
  ptr2 = new int;
  *ptr1 = 2;
  ptr2 = ptr1;
  free(ptr2);
}
```

Another common memory problem is writing past the allocated memory. An example would be creating an array and writing to an index beyond the size of the array. Another example would be writing to a pointer that hasn't been allocated. See the following code for examples.

```
//writing past the allocated memory
void WriteTooFar()
{
  int i;
  int ptr[3];
  //when the below for loop reaches 3, it is writing to memory that is not
  //allocated to the array
  for (i = 0; i < 5; i++)
    ptr[i] = i;
}
  // would be writing to a pointer that hasn't been allocated
  //when you compile this code, you will receive the following warning:
  // warning C4700: local variable 'str2' used without having been initialized
void WriteToUnallocated()
{
  char str1[20];
  char *str2;

  strcpy(str1, "Copy a string.");
  strcpy(str2, str1);
}
```

In a debug build of a project, the debug versions of the preceding memory heap functions are called by the function. For example, when malloc is called, it would in turn call the malloc_dbg function. Extra memory is allocated for debug information. Part of the extra memory allocation is to put known values in memory before and after the allocated memory. This is checked to see if the memory is being written to in error. This gives you a debug heap that can be checked for integrity. You must make calls to check the integrity of the heap. As an example, call the CrtCheckMemory function to inspect all memory blocks in the heap, verify that the debug information is valid, and confirm that the buffers around the memory allocated have not been written over. You can also control how the debug heap keeps track of allocations using the CrtSetDbgFlag function. You can instruct the debug heap to check for memory leaks when the program exits, and report any leaks that are detected. Table 10-1 displays a listing of other debugging functions.

To set the project build version, you need to set the active project configuration. To accomplish this, from the Build menu, select Set active configuration. This will bring up the Set Active Project Configuration window. From here, you can choose between the Debug and Release versions of your application. This will determine which version is built or

TABLE 10-1   Descriptions of Some Debugging Functions

Function	Description
_CrtDumpMemoryLeaks	Used to dump all of the memory blocks on the debug heap when a memory leak occurs
_CrtIsValidHeapPointer	Used to verify that a pointer is in the local heap
_CrtIsMemoryBlock	Used to verify that a memory block is in the local heap
_CrtIsValidPointer	Used to verify that a specified memory range is valid
_CrtMemCheckpoint	Used to obtain the state of the debug heap and place it in a _CrtMemState structure
_CrtMemDifference	Used to compare two memory states for significant differences
_CrtMemDumpAllObjectsSince	Used to dump information about objects on the heap since a specified checkpoint or start of program execution
_CrtMemDumpStatistics	Used to dump the debug header information for a specified memory state in a user-readable form
_CrtSetAllocHook	Used to install an allocation function you created by hooking it into the C run-time debug memory allocation process
_CrtSetBreakAlloc	Used to set a breakpoint on an object allocation
_CrtSetDumpClient	Used to install a function you created that is called every time a dump function is called for **_CLIENT_BLOCK** type memory blocks
_CrtSetReportFile	Used to set the file that is to be used as a destination for a report made by _CrtDbgReport
_CrtSetReportHook	Used to install a reporting function you created by hooking it into the C run-time debug reporting process
_CrtSetReportMode	Used to set the general destination for a report made by _CrtDbgReport
_RPT[0,1,2,3,4,]	Used to track the application's progress by generating a debug report with a formatted string. It doesn't provide source file and line number information.
_RPTF[0,1,2,3,4]	Same as the _RPTn macros, but adds the source file name and line number where the report request was made

run from the Project Workspace. The Set Active Project Configuration
window is shown in Figure 10-1.

FIGURE 10-1

Use the Set Active Project Configuration window to choose between the release version and the debug version of your application

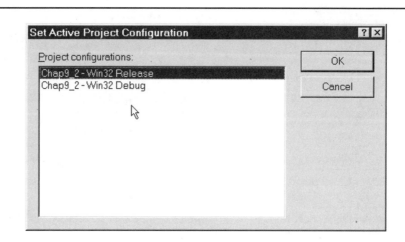

Using the IDE

The IDE has many debugging features available. Many of the features can be accessed from the Debug, Build, View, and Edit menus. The most common of these debugging commands can also be accessed by the Debug toolbar. Table 10-2 describes the debugging commands most likely to be seen on the exam.

Debug Toolbar

Some of the debugging commands can also be accessed by the Debug toolbar. The toolbar contains the most commonly used debugging commands. The Debug toolbar is shown in Figure 10-2. This toolbar contains buttons for the following commands in the order on the toolbar from left to right: Restart, Stop Debugging, Break Execution, Apply Code Changes, Show Next Statement (shows the next statement to be executed in your code), Step Into, Step Over, Step Out, Run To Cursor, Quick Watch, Watch, Variables, Registers, Memory, Call Stack, and Disassembly.

TABLE 10-2	Command	Function
Debugging Commands	Restart	Restarts the execution of the program from the beginning. It reloads the program into memory, and resets all variables.
	Stop Debugging	Stops the execution of the program that is currently being debugged
	Break Execution	Suspends the execution of the program from where it is currently executing. Can be thought of as a pause button
	Apply Code Changes	This applies the changes to code for use with the new Edit and Continue feature.
	Step Into	Single steps through lines of code. When it reaches a function call, it steps into the function allowing you to step through the lines of code inside the function call.
	Step Over	Single steps through lines of code. When it reaches a function call, it steps over the function so you do not have to step through the function code.
	Step Out	Exits the current function to the line of code immediately after the call to the function
	Run To Cursor	Executes the program until it reaches the line of code that the cursor is currently on
	Quick Watch	Displays the Quick watch window
	Watch	Displays the Watch window
	Variables	Displays the Variables window
	Registers	Displays the Registers window
	Memory	Displays the Memory window
	Call Stack	Displays the Call Stack dialog box
	Disassembly	Displays the Disassembly window

FIGURE 10-2

The Debug toolbar
contains commonly used
debugging commands

Even though the debug commands can be executed from the Debug
menu or the Debug toolbar, most of them can also be executed from
function keys on the keyboard. Many programmers, myself included, like to
do as much as possible from the keyboard. It slows you down to have to
reach over and use the mouse. The function keys that can be used instead of
the menu and toolbar can be seen in Figure 10-3. Some additional
commands available are:

Step Into Specific Function	Steps through the code in the program, and step into the specified function call.
Exceptions	Displays the Exceptions dialog box. This can be used to specify how you want the debugger to handle your program exceptions.
Threads	Displays the Threads dialog box. This can be used to control program threads.

FIGURE 10-3

You can use the function
keys shown on the Debug
menu to execute the debug
commands

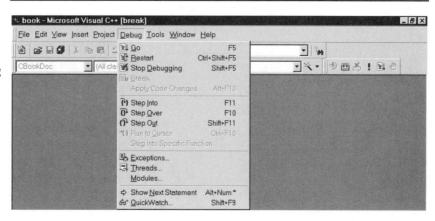

Build Menu

On the Build menu, there is a Start Debug item that contains a submenu. It includes commands to start debugging a project. The command available on this menu that we have not covered yet is Attach to Process. This command can be used to attach the debugger to a process that is running on the system. This way, you can break into a process and perform debugging operations on it. The process does not have to be started from within Visual C++. This can be useful if you have a module you are working on that is part of an application for which you do not have all of the source code. In this scenario, you cannot start the application from within Visual C++, but you can attach to the process and perform debugging on the modules for which you have the source files. The Build menu is shown in Figure 10-4.

View Menu

On the View menu, you can open up the debug windows. This menu is shown in Figure 10-5. You can open the following debug windows: Watch, Call Stack, Memory, Variables, Registers, and Disassembly. These can also be opened using the ALT+*X* keys as seen in the figure.

Watch Window

The Watch window is probably one of the most commonly used debug windows. You can use it to specify local and global variables and expressions

FIGURE 10-4

You can access the Start Debug command from the Build menu

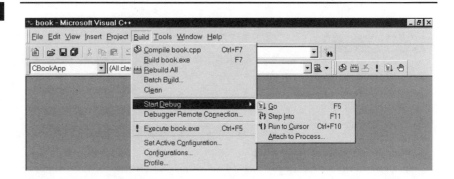

FIGURE 10-5

The Debugging commands
on the View menu help you
to debug your applications
efficiently

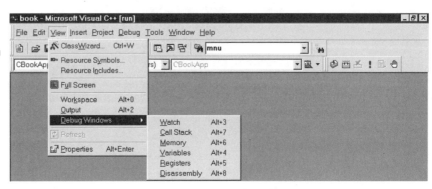

that you want to watch while running your program. You can modify a
local variable's value from this window. The Watch window is shown in
Figure 10-6.

There are four tabs at the bottom of the window. This allows you to
maintain separate sets of watch variables without having to wade through
variables that are not in the current scope. If you have an array, an object,
or a structure variable in the Watch window, a plus (+) or a minus sign (−)
appears in the Name column. You can use these boxes to expand or collapse
the variable data to see the data contained within the variable. There are
several ways to add variables to this window. Type, paste, or click in the
first column of an empty row to enter the variable name. You can also drag
and drop variables onto the Watch window. To accomplish this, highlight
the variable you want to drag, hold the mouse down until a small box

FIGURE 10-6

The Watch window allows
you to watch specific
variables and expressions
while running your program

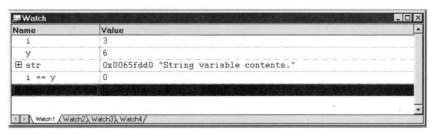

appears below the mouse cursor, and then drag it to the Watch window. This is helpful when you have several nested structures and it saves you from having to type the entire variable. Also, when you have nested structures, the pop-up ToolTip sometimes doesn't show the value. Another way to add a variable is to place the cursor on the variable, press SHIFT-F9 to bring up the Quick Watch dialog box, and click the Add Watch button to add it to the Watch window.

Call Stack Window

The Call Stack window displays the active functions on the stack. The function that is currently executing is at the top of the window. The function that called the currently executing function is below that and so on. The window will also display function parameters along with their values and types. This allows you to see all of the parameters that are passed along down the stack. This can be helpful in looking for an unexpected value or a possible NULL or invalid value for a pointer. You can also move to the code for the different functions by double-clicking the function that you want to view in the Call Stack window. This will bring you to the line of code where the function above it was called. See the code and Figure 10-7 for an example. The call stack that is shown is from stopping inside Func2.

```
int Func2(int Val)
{
  //the call stack is viewed from this line of code.
  return (Val + 2);
}
int Func1(int Val)
{
  return Func2(Val + 1);
}
int main()
{
  int x = 5;
  int Res;

  Res = Func1(x);
  return 0;
}
```

FIGURE 10-7

The Call Stack window
displays the active functions
on the stack

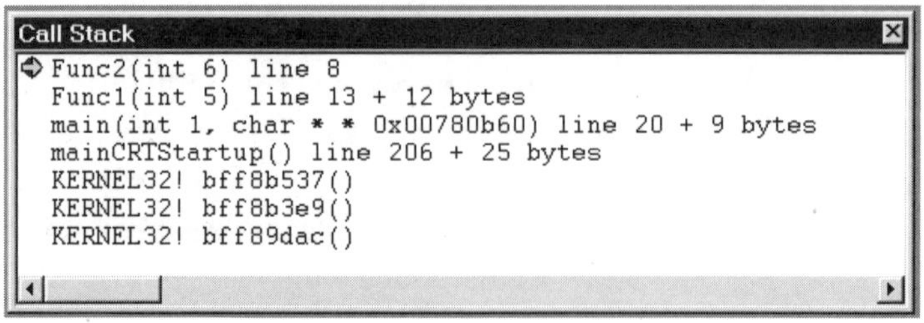

```
Call Stack                                                    ☒
⇨ Func2(int 6) line 8
  Func1(int 5) line 13 + 12 bytes
  main(int 1, char * * 0x00780b60) line 20 + 9 bytes
  mainCRTStartup() line 206 + 25 bytes
  KERNEL32! bff8b537()
  KERNEL32! bff8b3e9()
  KERNEL32! bff89dac()
◄                                                            ►
```

Variables Window

The Variables window displays the variables in a tree that are important in the program's current context. You cannot add variables to this window as you could in the Watch window. As in the Watch window, you can expand and collapse variables with the plus (+) and minus (-) signs. You can modify the value of a variable from the Value column. Also, the call stack can be viewed from the Context box.

There are three tabs on the Variables window. The tab that you select determines which variables are displayed. In a sense, you are determining which variables you deem important. The Auto tab displays variables from the current and previous lines of code. The Locals tab displays all of the local variables in the current function. The This tab displays the object pointed to by the this pointer. See the following code and Figure 10-8 for an example of the Variables window.

```
int main(int argc, char* argv[])
{
  int x = 0;
  int i;
  int Res;

  for (i=0; i < 4; i++)
    x = x + 3;
  //the Variables window is shown from the line of code below.
  Res = Func1(x);
  return 0;
}
```

FIGURE 10-8

You can see all of the variables in the current function by using the Locals tab of the Variables window

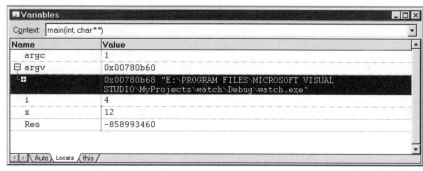

EXERCISE 10-1

Using the Call Stack and Watch Windows

1. Create a new Win32 Console Application project named Chap10_1.

2. When asked "What kind of Console Application?", select A Hello World Application.

3. Open the Chap10_1.CPP file.

4. Add the following functions:

```
int Func2(int Val)
{
  //the call stack is viewed from this line of code.
  return (Val + 2);
}
int Func1(int Val)
{
  //Place a breakpoint on the line of code below.
  return Func2(Val + 1);
}
```

5. Add the following code to the main procedure.

```
int x = 5;
  int Res;

  Res = Func1(x);
```

6. Right-click the line of code in the function Func1 and select Insert/Remove Breakpoint from the pop-up menu or press F9. Notice the red button that appears next to the line. This will stop

the application when it executes this line of code. A breakpoint suspends the execution of the program at the specified line of code. This allows you to view how a program is executing a particular piece of code. We will cover this later in the chapter.

7. From the Build menu, select Start Debug and select Go, or press F5.

8. When the debugger stops at the breakpoint, go to the View menu, select Debug Windows, and select Call Stack. (You can also press ALT-7 or press the Call Stack button on the Debug toolbar.) If the Debug toolbar is not visible, select Customize from the Tools menu. Go to the Toolbars tab and select the Debug box to turn on the Debug toolbar.

9. Notice that the top of the Call Stack window displays Func1(int 5).

10. On the Debug toolbar, click the Step Into button or press F11.

11. Notice that the top of the Call Stack window displays Func2(int 6) and the next line displays Func1(int 5).

12. Double-click the line containing Func1 in the Call Stack window.

13. Notice that a green arrow appears next to it in the Call Stack window. In the source file, a green arrow appears by the line of code that called Func2.

14. Double-click the line that contains *main* in the Call Stack window.

15. Notice that a green arrow appears next to it in the Call Stack window. In the source file, a green arrow appears by the line of code that called Func1.

16. On the Debug menu, select Go or press F5 to let the program finish executing.

17. From the Build menu, select Start Debug and select Go, or press F5.

18. When the debugger stops at the breakpoint, go to the View menu, select Debug Windows and select Watch, press ALT-3, or press the Watch button on the Debug toolbar.

19. On the following line of code, where the breakpoint is set, right-click the Val variable and select Quick Watch from the pop-up menu.

```
return Func2(Val + 1);
```

20. When the Quick Watch window comes up, notice that Val = 5. Press the Add Watch button. This will add Val to the Watch window.

21. In the Watch window, double click the cell below Val to allow editing.

22. Enter Val == 6 and press enter. Notice this expression is 0.

23. Press the Step Into button on the Debug Window or press F11. You are now in function Func2. Notice that Val = 6 in the Watch window, and the expression Val == 6 is now 1.

24. Press the Stop Debugging button on the Debug toolbar, or press SHIFT+F5, to terminate the program.

Using Depends

The Depends tool can assist you in determining the dependencies of .EXEs, .DLLs, .OCXs, .COMs, and other file types. For debugging, it can be used to determine files that are missing, files that are invalid, import and export mismatches, circular dependencies, and when modules being loaded were built for another type of machine. It can also be used for general information about modules in an application. The Depends tool is shown in Figure 10-9.

For troubleshooting purposes, the Depends tool can be used to detect files that are required by a module, but cannot be found. It can find files that aren't Win32 compliant or files that are corrupt. It can find import and export mismatches such as when imported functions are not resolved. It can even find circular dependencies. Another common error is when a DLL cannot be found at a specified path. Depends can find the complete path of all the modules being loaded for an application so you can check to see if the DLL is in the path being searched.

Depends can also be used for general information purposes. It can show all the modules required for an application. This can help you in determining if you have included all required files in your setup program. It can list the functions that are called in each module by other modules. This can help you understand why a module is being linked, and help you to remove modules that are not needed. The following information is included for each module found:

- Full path to the module file
- Time and date of the module file
- Size of the module file

FIGURE 10-9

The Depends tool can assist you in determining the dependencies of file types

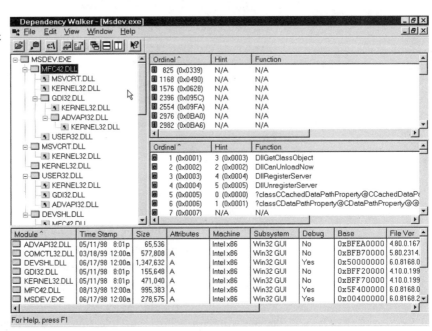

- Attributes of the module file

- Type of machine that the module was built to run on

- Type of subsystem that the module was built to run in

- Whether or not the module contains debugging information

- The preferred base load address of the module

- The file version found in the module's version resource

- The product version found in the module's version resource

- The image version found in the module's file header

- The version of the linker that was used to create the module file

- The version of the operating system (OS) that the module file was built to run on

■ The version of the subsystem that the module file was built to run in

■ A possible error message if any error occurred while processing the file

EXERCISE 10-2

Using the Depends Tool

1. Open the Depends tool. It can be opened from Start | Programs | Microsoft Visual Studio 6.0 | Microsoft Studio 6.0 Tools | Depends. Notice the window title says Dependency Walker.

2. From the File menu, select Open or click the Open button on the toolbar.

3. Find the *install path*\microsoft visual studio\commmon\msdev98\bin\ MSDEV.EXE file and click open. Notice the tree view in the top-left pane. If the tree is not expanded, right-click MSDEV.EXE and select Expand All from the pop-up menu.

4. In the bottom pane, the dependent modules are listed with information for each module. Click each column header. Notice that the list can be sorted by each column.

5. Notice the top-right pane. These are import functions.

6. Notice the bottom-right pane. These are export functions.

7. In the top-left pane, right-click MFC42.DLL, and select Full Path from the pop-up menu. Notice all of the modules are now listed with the full path to where they are located.

8. In the top-left pane, double-click MFC42.DLL. Notice a Quick View window opens up. This will contain technical information about the selected file.

9. From the File menu, select Exit to close the Depends tool.

Using Spy++

Spy++ is a utility that has windows to view the system's processes, threads, windows, and window messages. To start Spy++, go to the Tools menu and select Spy++. When Spy++ starts, a tree view of the windows and controls opens in the system. Spy++ is shown in Figure 10-10. You can also open views for messages, processes, and threads. To open a view, go to the Spy

FIGURE 10-10

Use the Windows view of
the Spy++ tool to find
properties of open windows

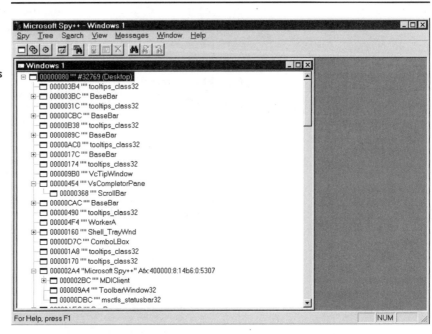

menu and select the view you want to open. The tree views can be expanded
and collapsed by clicking the + or – symbol to find the desired object.

Windows View

The Windows view can be used to find windows that are open in the system
and view the properties of them. The Windows view has the Desktop as the
top window. All other windows are child windows to the Desktop. You can
find windows by scrolling though the view and expanding the tree as
needed. You can see more detailed information for a window by double-
clicking the desired window. You can also use the Window Finder tool to
find windows. The Window Finder tool is shown in Figure 10-11. To use
this tool, arrange your windows so that you can see both the window you
are looking for and Spy++. From the Spy menu, select Find Window. Click
the Finder tool, and drag it to the window for which you want to see the
properties. As you drag the mouse over a window, the properties of that

FIGURE 10-11

FIGURE 10-11

The Spy++ Find Window dialog box displays the properties of a window as you drag the Finder tool over it

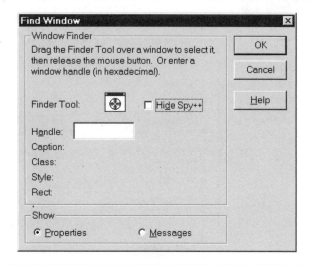

window will be displayed on the Window Finder tool. If you know the handle of a window, you can also use that to find a window. Select the Hide Spy++ check box to help find a window. This will minimize Spy++ to get it out of your way.

The Window Properties dialog box contains five tabs: General, Styles, Windows, Class, and Process. The General tab contains information about the window's caption, the handle, the dimensions of the window, and more. The Styles tab displays the window display codes. The Windows tab shows the handles for the Next, Previous, Parent, First Child, and Owner Window. To see the properties of any of these windows, just click the handle link. The Class tab displays information about the window class, name of the menu, icon handle, cursor handle, and handle for the Background. The Process tab displays information about the Process and Thread ID's.

Processes View

The Processes view is used to display information about what processes are running on the system and view information about those processes. The Processes view is shown in Figure 10-12. Processes are identified by

Use the Processes View in Spy++ to display information about the processes that are running on a system

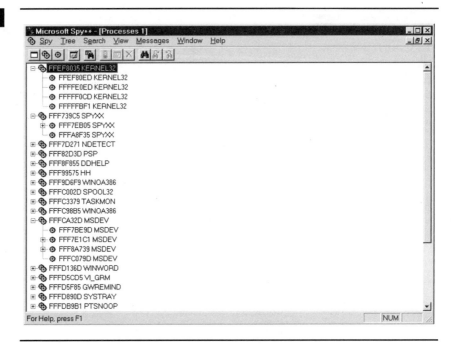

their module names. The Processes view tree can be expanded to see threads that belong to each process. To search for a particular process, with the Processes window in the foreground, go to the Search menu and select Process. When the Process Search dialog box comes up, type the process ID or a module name to search on. Then choose either up or down for the direction of the search.

Threads View

The Threads view displays a tree of all of the active threads associated with windows. The Thread ID and module name are shown for each thread. Processes are displayed in this view. From this view, you can search for threads by the thread's ID or module name. You can view the properties for a particular thread by double-clicking it. This will bring up a dialog box which will display the module name, thread, and process ID, and the thread's current and base priority. The Threads view with a Properties dialog box is shown in Figure 10-13. This can be especially helpful if you suspect that a low priority for your thread is causing it to not run as expected.

FIGURE 10-13

The Threads view in Spy++ allows you to search for active threads and displays their properties

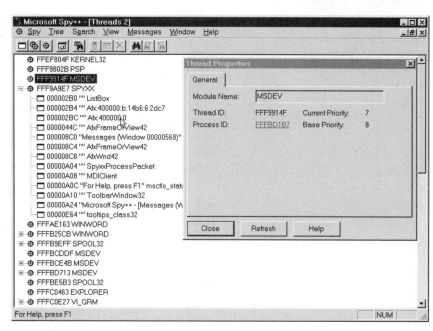

Message View

The Message view allows you to see the messages associated with a thread, process, or window. Messages are what make the graphical user interface (GUI) in Windows work. Everything you do with the mouse, keyboard, or other device is represented by a message. For example, when you move your mouse, WM_MOUSEMOVE messages are created to indicate where the mouse is. Also, when you click a button, a WM_LBUTTONDOWN message is created when the button goes down. The Messages window allows you to see the message stream being used by the selected thread, process, or window. By capturing the messages for a process, you can view the initialization of all windows. The first column contains the window handle, and the second column contains a message code. The third column contains the decoded message parameters and return values. When the Messages view is first opened, an options dialog box opens allowing you to select the window to view, and the types of messages to log. You can also start and stop the logging of messages and format the Messages view. The Messages view is shown in Figure 10-14.

FIGURE 10-14

You can select the types of messages that you want to log from the Messages view in Spy++

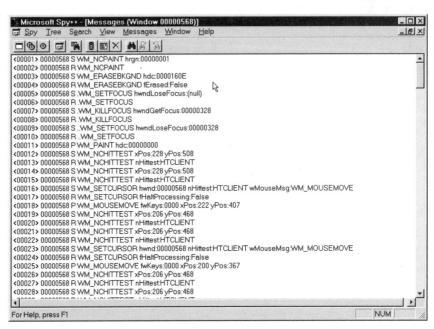

```
Microsoft Spy++ - [Messages (Window 00000568)]
Spy   Tree   Search   View   Messages   Window   Help

<00001> 00000568 S WM_NCPAINT hrgn:00000001
<00002> 00000568 R WM_NCPAINT
<00003> 00000568 S WM_ERASEBKGND hdc:0000160E
<00004> 00000568 R WM_ERASEBKGND fErased:False
<00005> 00000568 S .WM_SETFOCUS hwndLoseFocus:(null)
<00006> 00000568 R .WM_SETFOCUS
<00007> 00000568 S .WM_KILLFOCUS hwndGetFocus:00000328
<00008> 00000568 R .WM_KILLFOCUS
<00009> 00000568 R ..WM_SETFOCUS hwndLoseFocus:00000328
<00010> 00000568 R .WM_SETFOCUS
<00011> 00000568 P WM_PAINT hdc:00000000
<00012> 00000568 S WM_NCHITTEST xPos:228 yPos:508
<00013> 00000568 R WM_NCHITTEST nHittest:HTCLIENT
<00014> 00000568 S WM_NCHITTEST xPos:228 yPos:508
<00015> 00000568 R WM_NCHITTEST nHittest:HTCLIENT
<00016> 00000568 S WM_SETCURSOR hwnd:00000568 nHittest:HTCLIENT wMouseMsg:WM_MOUSEMOVE
<00017> 00000568 R WM_SETCURSOR fHaltProcessing:False
<00018> 00000568 P WM_MOUSEMOVE fwKeys:0000 xPos:222 yPos:407
<00019> 00000568 S WM_NCHITTEST xPos:206 yPos:468
<00020> 00000568 R WM_NCHITTEST nHittest:HTCLIENT
<00021> 00000568 S WM_NCHITTEST xPos:206 yPos:468
<00022> 00000568 R WM_NCHITTEST nHittest:HTCLIENT
<00023> 00000568 S WM_SETCURSOR hwnd:00000568 nHittest:HTCLIENT wMouseMsg:WM_MOUSEMOVE
<00024> 00000568 R WM_SETCURSOR fHaltProcessing:False
<00025> 00000568 P WM_MOUSEMOVE fwKeys:0000 xPos:200 yPos:367
<00026> 00000568 S WM_NCHITTEST xPos:206 yPos:468
<00027> 00000568 R WM_NCHITTEST nHittest:HTCLIENT
<00028> 00000568 S WM_NCHITTEST xPos:206 yPos:468

For Help, press F1                                          NUM
```

EXERCISE 10-3

Using Spy++

1. Open the Chap10_1 project you created in Exercise 10-1.

2. Open the Chap10_1.CPP file.

3. On the Tools menu, select Spy++.

4. Notice the Windows view appears. If the Windows view is not visible, on the Spy menu, select Windows or press CTRL-W.

5. Find the Microsoft Spy++ window and double-click it to see the properties of the window.

6. Click Close to close the window.

7. Click the + symbol next to the Microsoft Spy++ window to expand the tree.

8. Click the + symbol next to the MDI Client window to expand the tree. Notice the Windows window. Keep expanding this tree until you get to the bottom. Notice the window is a list box.

9. Arrange your windows so that you can see Chap10_1.CPP in Visual C++ and the Spy++ tool.

10. On the Spy menu, select Messages. Notice the Message Options dialog box appears.

11. Click the Finder tool and drag it to the Chap10_1.CPP window.

12. Click OK on the Message Options dialog box.

13. Move the mouse over the Chap10_1.CPP window and notice the Messages view displaying the mouse and cursor messages.

14. On the Messages menu, select Stop Logging.

15. Close the Spy++ tool.

Integrated Debugger

The integrated debugger can be used to find bugs in executables, DLLs, and ActiveX controls. One of the ways to check how your code is executing is stepping through your code one line at a time. If you don't want to step through your entire program, you can set a breakpoint on a particular line of code. This will cause the program to stop execution at that line of code. We have used some of these features in earlier exercises in this chapter. We are going to cover how to step through your code and using breakpoints in more detail in this section.

Breakpoints

First, let's talk about setting breakpoints. You can set one or more breakpoints to stop execution at the point where you want to debug your program. You can also set breakpoints when certain conditions exist. After the program has stopped, you can then inspect your code to look for problems. To set and view breakpoints, you can use the Breakpoints dialog box. The Breakpoints dialog box has three tabs: Location, Data, and Messages. To open the Breakpoints dialog box, from the Edit menu, select Breakpoints, or press ALT-F9.

The Location tab of the Breakpoints dialog box allows you to set a breakpoint by source code line number, memory address, register, or function name. This tab is only available in the Enterprise Edition of Visual

C++ 6.0. Enter this information in the Break at text box. The existing breakpoints are displayed at the bottom of the dialog box. If you click the Edit Code button, it will take you to the line of code where the breakpoint is set. The Location tab is shown in Figure 10-15.

If you are not sure how to enter the information in the Break at text box, click the button with the arrow next to it for more options. When you click this button, you will see a pop-up menu with two options. The first is the line number that the cursor is currently at in your project. Select this to add a breakpoint at the current line. The other option is advanced. If you click this, it will bring up the Advanced Breakpoint dialog box. You can enter the location (which is the same information as the Break at text box), or enter information in the Context section. This allows you to set a breakpoint outside of the current scope by selecting a function in a different source or executable file. The Advanced Breakpoint dialog box is shown in Figure 10-16.

You can also set the breakpoint based on a condition. To do this, click the Condition button. This will bring up the Breakpoint Condition dialog box. This will allow you to enter an expression to break on at the location specified. When the expression evaluates to true, the program will break. You might want to check for a variable equal to a certain value. If you enter

---

FIGURE 10-15

The Location tab of the Breakpoints dialog box provides options for setting breakpoints

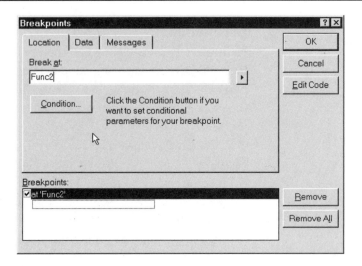

Use the Advanced
Breakpoint dialog box to
set a breakpoint outside of
the current scope

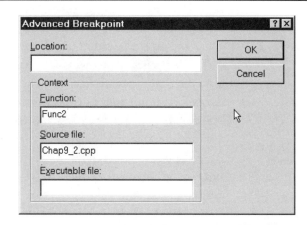

an expression you can also enter how many times to skip this breakpoint
before stopping on the breakpoint. You can also set the breakpoint based on
an array element being changed. Set the expression to an array index (for
example, YourArray[0]), and enter how many elements in the array you
want to watch (one to number of elements in array). The Breakpoint
Condition dialog box is shown in Figure 10-17.

The Data tab in the Breakpoints dialog box allows you to enter an
expression within the current scope. You can set a breakpoint for when a

The Breakpoint Condition
dialog box allows you to
set a breakpoint based on
a condition

variable changes or an expression evaluates to true. You can also set a breakpoint for an array element changing or an expression being true, as you could on the Location tab. The Data tab is shown in Figure 10-18.

The Messages tab allows you to set breakpoints when specified window procedure messages are received. The Break at WndProc list box contains the exported functions in your project. The Set One Breakpoint for Each Message to Watch list box contains messages to break on. You can select multiple messages as desired. The Messages tab is shown in Figure 10-19.

At the bottom of each tab is a list of existing breakpoints. You can edit and remove these breakpoints. To edit them, select one and the properties for that breakpoint will be displayed. Edit the properties as desired. To remove breakpoints, highlight the breakpoint and click the Remove button. Click the Remove All button to remove all of the breakpoints.

You don't always have to use the Breakpoints dialog box to set breakpoints. You can place the cursor on a line of code and press F9, click the Insert/Remove button on the Build toolbar, or right-click a line of code and select Insert/Remove Breakpoint. You can use the Find box on the Standard

---

FIGURE 10-18

You can use the Data tab of the Breakpoints dialog box to stop execution when a specified expression is true

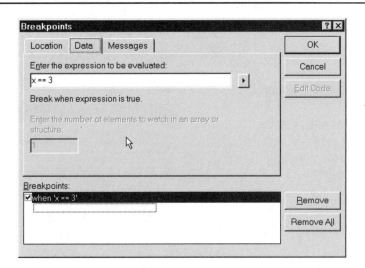

You can set breakpoints
for window procedure
messages with the
Messages tab of the
Breakpoints dialog box

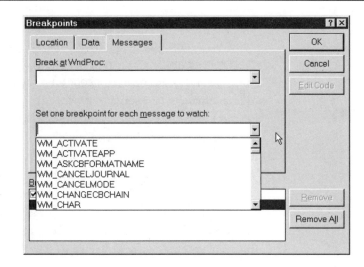

toolbar to search for a function or label and click the Insert/Remove
Breakpoint button to set the breakpoint. You can also use the Call Stack
window to set breakpoints with the Insert/Remove button or by pressing F9.

Stepping Through Code

Now that we can set breakpoints, let's talk about stepping through your
code. Once you have stopped the execution of your application, you can
step through lines of code to determine if your code is doing what you
expect. While you are stepping through your code, you can use the debug
windows to see the values of variables, expressions, the call stack, parameters
passed, and so on. You can modify variable values and view debug output.

To step through your code, use the Debug menu or the Debug toolbar.
To move to the next line of code, use Step Into or Step Over. When you get
to a line of code with a function call, these two commands have different
effects. The Step Into command will go to the first line of code inside the
function being called. Use this command when you want to see how the

function executes. The Step Over command will go to the line of code following the current line of code. Use this command when you know the function is executing correctly. It will not go into the function being called.

If you are inside a function, you can use the Step Out command to exit the function and go to the line of code after the line that called the function. Use this command when you have reached the part of a function that you wanted to check and don't want to step through the rest of the function.

Another command is Run To Cursor. This command will execute the program until it reaches the line of code the cursor is on. This can be helpful for skipping loops so you don't have to step through 1000 iterations.

The Step Into Specific Function command allows you to view the code inside a function that you specify. This is used when there are nested function calls on the same line of code. This allows you to view how a function executes without having to step through all of the functions.

Edit and Continue

A new feature added to Visual C++ 6.0 is Edit and Continue. If you have used Visual Basic, you are already familiar with this feature. This allows you to edit the source code while debugging and apply these changes without having to rebuild the application. The application will be returned to the state that it was in when the bug occurred and you can see if your change fixes the bug. If you have compile errors, the changes are not applied, and your compiler errors are displayed in the Output window. You can change variable values, expressions, and function parameters, and you can even add new functions and call them in the code that you are debugging. When you are finished editing the code, select Apply Code Changes from the Debug menu.

You can configure your project to automatically perform the Apply Code Changes command when a Debug command is executed. This way you don't have to keep running the command every time you edit the code. To set this option, on the Tools menu, select Options. When the Options dialog box comes up, go to the Debug tab and select Debug Commands Invoke Edit and Continue. The Debug tab on the Options dialog box is shown in Figure 10-20.

FIGURE 10-20

The Debug tab on the Options dialog box contains options that allow you to change the code and then continue debugging

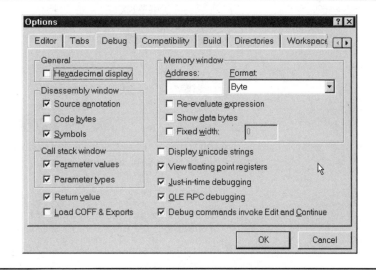

EXERCISE 10-4

Using Breakpoints and Stepping Through Code

1. Create a new Win32 Console Application project named Chap10_4.

2. When asked "What kind of Console Application?", select A Hello World Application.

3. Open the Chap10_4.CPP file.

4. Add the following functions:

```cpp
int Func2(int Val)
{
  int x = 6;

  Val += (x / 2);
  return Val;
}

int Func1(int Val)
{
  int x;

  x = Func2(Val);
  return x;
}
```

5. Add the following code to the main function:

```
int y = 4;
 int res;

res = Func1(y);
printf("Func1 returned %d\n", res);
getchar();
```

6. Place the cursor on the following line of code in the main function and press F9 to set a breakpoint. Notice the red dot that appears next to the line of code.

```
res = Func1(y);
```

7. From the Edit menu, select Breakpoints or press ALT-F9. Notice the breakpoint at the bottom of the dialog box.

8. Place the cursor inside the Func2 function.

9. Go to the Data tab and click the arrow button to bring up the Advanced Breakpoint dialog box.

10. In the Expression text box, enter **Val == 7**.

11. In the Function text box, enter **Func2**.

12. In the Source File text box, enter **CHAP10_4.CPP**.

13. Click OK to close the Advanced Breakpoint dialog box. Notice the breakpoint has been added at the bottom of the Breakpoints dialog box. It should appear similar to: when '{Func2,chap10_4.cpp,} Val == 7'.

14. Click OK to close the Breakpoints dialog box.

15. From the Build menu, select Start Debug, and select Go or press F5 to start the program. Notice the program stopped at the breakpoint in the main function.

16. Click the Step Into button on the Debug toolbar or press F11 twice to step into the Func1 function. This will bring you to the following line of code.

```
x = Func2(Val);
```

17. Click the Step Over button on the Debug toolbar or press F10 to step over the Func2 function call. Notice that you received a message box for the breakpoint that we set when Val == 7.

18. Click OK. Notice it took you inside the Func2 function.

19. Hold the mouse over the variable Val. You should get a ToolTip showing Val = 7.

20. If the Variables window is not visible, from the View menu, select Debug Windows, and select Variables. Notice the variables Val and *x* are displayed.

21. Press F5 to continue the program. Notice the console displays Func1 returned 7.

22. Press the ENTER key to finish the program.

23. From the Build menu, select Start Debug, and select Go or press F5 to start the program.

24. After it stops at the breakpoint, press F5 and click OK when you get to the Breakpoint message box.

25. On the following line of code, change Val to **15**. On the Debug menu, select Apply Code Changes, or make sure that the Debug Commands Invoke Edit and Continue option is selected on the Options dialog box, as described earlier in the chapter. Press F5 to continue the program.

```
return Val;
```

26. Notice the console now displays Func1 returned 15. This is an example of using the new Edit and Continue feature.

27. Press the ENTER key to let the program finish.

MFC Macros Used to Debug Applications

The MFC library contains macros that can be used for debugging applications during run-time. These macros can be used to display debugging information during run-time. This can make the debugging process much less difficult. A couple of the most commonly used macros are ASSERT and TRACE. These macros allow you to check for logic errors and to output diagnostic data. The first step in using these macros is to include the CRTDBG.H file in which they are defined.

ASSERT

The ASSERT macro allows you to check for logic errors during program execution. When the expression is false or 0, it prints a message and aborts the program. The message includes the expression checked for, the source file name that the error occurred in, and the line number in the source file. The error is displayed in a message box with an OK button that will terminate the program. If the application has been linked to the debug versions of the run-time library, the message box will have three buttons, Abort, Retry, and Ignore. If you press Abort, the program is terminated. If you press Retry, the debugger is opened and you can then debug the application. If you press Ignore, the ASSERT is ignored and application execution continues. Be careful though, you could have unexpected results by ignoring the error condition.

When you have finished debugging and testing your application, build a release version of your program. This will use the run-time libraries that do not contain the debug versions of functions, and ASSERT statements will be ignored. This will significantly increase the performance of your application. You don't want your program aborting on an ASSERT statement when your customer is using it; you should have ways of handling errors in the code. Assert checking can also be turned off by defining NDEBUG with a *#define*. It must be defined before the ASSERT.H include statement. ASSERT is used to notify you when there is an unexpected error. As an example, let's say you are programming a linked list and you are deleting a node from the list. You could use an ASSERT to check for the node pointer being NULL. Obviously, you shouldn't be trying to delete a node from a NULL pointer. A word of caution: do not use ASSERT for all of your error checking. Remember that ASSERT is ignored in the release version of your application. Do not put code in the ASSERT statement. For example, if you set a variables value inside the ASSERT statement, when the release version runs, that variable would not be set. See the following code for an example.

```
ASSERT((x = ComputeValue()) == 0);
```

One solution to the preceding problem would be to use the VERIFY macro. It is the same as ASSERT, except the expression is executed without the assert test being performed in the release version. If there is any error checking that should always be performed, use error checking that will handle the error. You would not want the assert functionality in your release version anyway because the unneeded overhead would cause a performance hit. Also, imagine the displeasure of your customers if they received a dialog box informing them of the error and then the application terminated. Your application should handle all errors gracefully. You can also use the ASSERTE macro. It is the same as the ASSERT macro, except it also displays the expression that was evaluated.

One of the new library functions in version 6.0 is the debug report function for logging errors and warnings during application execution. The ASSERT macro calls the _CrtDbgReport function for sending messages for debugging. These messages can be sent to a file, the Visual C++ debugger, or a debug message window. The message can also include the source file name, the line number in the source file, and the .EXE or .DLL filename. The message can be formatted similar to the printf function using a format-control string.

TRACE

The TRACE macro allows you to send formatted strings to a dump device. The formatting of the TRACE string is the same as printf. The strings can be dumped to a file or debug monitor. To turn on tracing, you must define _DEBUG, use the debug version of your application, enable the afxTraceEnabled flag, and set the afxTraceFlags to determine the level of detail output. These flags can be set using the TRACER.EXE tool. This tool modifies the AFX.INI file. You can use TRACE to display variable values or any other logging functionality that you require.

Be careful in the use of TRACE. Don't output too much information or you won't be able to sort through it. Imagine sifting through a file over a megabyte in size looking for the answer to your problem. Try not to put TRACE statements inside loops that iterate a large number of times. When different developers are working on different units, you will have to sift through all of their TRACE statements also. One common solution is to use conditional compilation for each developer. TRACE is useful when you need to see a sequence of events that you cannot create by stepping through the code. Put TRACE statements at the beginning and end of critical functions and where critical events occur.

DEBUG_NEW

The DEBUG_NEW macro is used to help find memory leaks. It is used in place of the *new* operator in the debug version. This macro tracks the filename and line number for each object allocated. When you want to see the memory allocations, call DumpAllObjectsSince to view all objects allocated with the source filename and the line number where they are allocated. You can review this list to check objects allocated and determine which ones should have been freed and to see if any objects are lost in memory. Use the following macro to define the new operator to use the DEBUG_NEW macro. You still use the new operator in your code, but it will then use DEBUG_NEW to allocate the object. This will add debugging information to each allocation. It is only used in the debug version. In the release version, DEBUG_NEW is resolved to a new operator and there isn't any debugging information saved. Therefore, you don't get a performance penalty in the release version.

```
#define new DEBUG_NEW
```

Other Commands

Some less common MFC macros used for debugging are listed in Table 10-3.

TABLE 10-3	Macro	Description
Descriptions of MFC Macros	ASSERT_KINDOF	Checks to see if an object is of a specified class or derived from the specified class
	ASSERT_VALID	Checks the validity of an object by calling its AssertValid member function
	TRACE0	Same as TRACE but the format string has no arguments
	TRACE1	Same as TRACE but the format string has one argument
	TRACE2	Same as TRACE but the format string has two arguments
	TRACE3	Same as TRACE but the format string has three arguments
	VERIFY	Similar to ASSERT but evaluates the expression in the release version of the library as well as in the debug version

Using the ASSERT Macro

1. Create a new Win32 Console Application project named Chap10_5.

2. When asked "What kind of Console Application?", select A Hello World Application.

3. Open the Chap10_5.CPP file.

4. Add the following code:

```
#include "crtdbg.h"
int Func2(int Val)
{
   Val += 3;
   return Val;
}

int Func1(int Val)
{
   _ASSERT((Val = Func2(Val)) != 0);
   return Val;
}
```

5. Add the following code to the main function:

```
int x = 3;
x = Func1(x);
printf("x = %d\n", x);
getchar();
```

6. From the Build menu, select Start Debug, and then select Go or press F5 to run the application. Notice that the application displays x = 6.

7. Press ENTER to let the application finish executing.

8. Now let's set the application to run in release mode. From the Build menu, select Set Active Configuration. Select Chap10_5–Win32 Release and click OK.

9. From the Build menu, select Execute Chap10_5.EXE or press CTRL-F5 to run the application. Notice that the application displays x = 3. This is because the code in the ASSERT macro is not executed and therefore the function Func2 is not executed.

10. Press ENTER, and then press any key to allow the application to finish executing.

Elements of a Test Plan

Testing is different from debugging. Debugging is the process of fixing bugs. Testing is the process of finding those bugs. There aren't too many software engineers who enjoy testing. It is also difficult for developers to do extensive testing because the developer already knows how the application should work. However, testing is crucial to the success of an application. Testing is needed to find bugs in a program. I know, good programmers wouldn't have any bugs to find.

Testing is also commonly cut short due to delivery deadlines. In today's rapid application development (RAD) environment, testing is even more necessary. Two important tools needed for testing are source control, such as Visual Source Safe, and a bug tracking system. Bug tracking tools can be as simple as a spreadsheet or as intricate as some third-party tools. This allows everyone on the team to know what bugs there are, and the status of those bugs. This is a broad area and we will only cover the areas needed for the exam. The areas of testing we will cover are Beta testing, Regression testing, Unit testing, Integration testing, and Stress testing.

All software contains bugs when it is released. You want to ensure that you know what those deficiencies are. If you weren't able to fix the bug before release, make sure you have a work-around in place. This should only be done for what is deemed a rare occurrence. This is not ideal, but it is much better than your customer calling you and you having no idea how to solve the problem. You should include any work-around in your release notes. You cannot account for everything, but the more you do account for, the better.

Beta Testing

Beta testing of an application allows testing by users who are not a part of or do not have any ties to the development process. The testers are completely independent of the development of the application. You can accomplish beta testing with a test team internal to the company or by releasing beta software to the general public as Microsoft does. It allows you to receive unbiased feedback on bugs, features, or any other aspects of your application. This allows a completely independent test environment for your application.

When you beta test your application, choose a group of advanced users who are more competent and knowledgeable. You don't want to be bombarded with simple questions. Choose users who know what you are trying to achieve with your application. This will also allow your application to be tested for those unknown, random configurations. For instance, users will have different computers. There will be different operating systems, processors, motherboards, amounts of memory, hard drives, and so on. You cannot set up a test bed for every possible computer that your application will be run on unless you are in a very controlled environment.

Evaluating the Need for Beta Testing

When do you need to perform beta testing? Beta testing should always be performed whether you are releasing beta versions of your product to some of your advanced customers or to a group of employees who will be using your application internally. There are some instances where beta testing is even more critical. If your application will be used by a wide range of users or different computer configurations, then beta testing can help you work out problems before your release, instead of after. These types of applications would need more extensive beta testing than an internal-use program, although you should perform some level of beta testing on all applications.

Use the following checklist to help determine when to beta test your application. All applications should have some Beta testing.

- Different operating systems (Windows 3.1, Windows 95/98, and Windows NT)

- Different computer configurations (CPU, RAM, hard drive space, CD-ROM, sound, and video)

- Different levels of users (that is, from the beginner to the expert)
- Different languages as necessary

Regression Testing

Regression testing is repeating previous testing to show that a change to the application does not affect other aspects of the application. The results of testing parts of the application that were not changed should be the same as they were in previous tests. Regression testing is also important when you have earlier versions of your product released. You will have to test to ensure that you are completely backwards compatible, as necessary. As an example, if you updated your database structure, you would need to ensure that your new version could still read the old data and convert it to the new database. Also, if you have more than one version of your application and you update a DLL, you have to test to ensure that the DLL will work with all versions. Regression testing is commonly performed by a software test engineer.

Unit Testing

Unit testing is testing the smallest part of an application that can be tested. This involves more than making sure that your unit will compile. It is testing to show functionality that is required has or has not been met. Unit testing is generally performed by the programmer. The testing should validate that the unit completely meets the requirements for which the unit is designed. Another important area to check is how your unit handles invalid data.

Unit testing should start at the same time you start writing your code. This will involve writing test code for your unit. When you start creating your interfaces, you can start testing those interfaces. Then as you add functionality, you can test it along the way. If you wait until you believe you are done, you might have to redesign some areas to solve unexpected problems. If you had tested along the way, chances are, you would have discovered the problem much earlier and wouldn't have to re-write any code.

Use the following checklist for areas to check in unit testing:

- Meets requirements for which it was designed
- Performs the functionality desired
- Handles invalid data (data too large, NULL values, user entry)
- Handles expected steps being out of sequence
- Does not crash

Integration Testing

Integration testing is used to demonstrate that all of the units work together. Just because unit testing is completed, it does not guarantee it will work correctly with other units of an application. This is especially true of large applications where there are many different programmers working on it.

Use the following checklist for areas to check in integration testing:

- Units can interface with each other correctly
- All units meet overall application functionality and requirements
- Handles missing modules gracefully
- Uses different paths for the application and support files

Stress Testing

Stress testing places the highest possible loads with the lowest possible resources available to an application. This could be a high rate of data input on a machine with the minimum required resources. This can also help in determining the minimum requirements for an application.

Incorporating Stress Tests

Microsoft Visual Studio comes with a tool to assist in stress testing. It is called Stress! It uses up system resources for low resource stress testing. It can acquire resources such as the global heap, user heap, GDI heap, disk space, and file handles. You can configure the Stress tool to allocate resources in fixed, random, and message-dependent allocations. It also provides logging options to help locate and reproduce bugs. You can preconfigure it by setting the options that you desire in a STRESS.INI file. The Stress tool is shown in Figure 10-21.

When stress testing applications, you want to see how your application performs under different types of conditions. If your application gets an error due to a stress condition, it should notify the user of the problem and either allow the user to fix the problem if possible, or exit gracefully. Your program should check each memory allocation, check for free disk space before writing to a file, and so forth. This is what the tester will be looking for. Following is a checklist of items that should be tested during the stress test:

- Minimum required CPU

- Minimum required RAM

- Amount of free disk space

- Minimum CD-ROM drive speed

- Maximum data load that the application is required to handle

---

FIGURE 10-21

The Stress tool assists you with stress testing

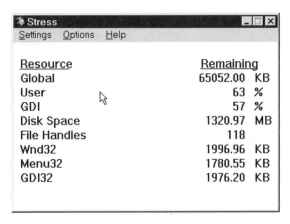

FROM THE CLASSROOM

Don't Undervalue the Process of Debugging Your Application

Throughout this chapter you have learned various debugging techniques and the elements of a test plan. These elements are important to provide you with the tools you need to thoroughly test your C++ applications. In many projects, software testing can account for 30 to 50 percent of software development costs. But why is testing so important? And how can we ensure that our software is properly tested?

The main goal of testing is to ensure that we deliver a quality software product. Quality software must satisfy user and system requirements in areas of reliability, functionality, application performance, and system performance. Because software quality has a variety of measures, it is important to incorporate many different debugging techniques and types of tests into your test plan. Verifying your software's reliability may include using debugging functions during unit testing of a class to ensure that it does not leak any memory. Test cases can be developed for each feature in your application's feature set to ensure that all the necessary functionality is included in the application. Stress testing may be performed at the application and system level to ensure your software performs well under typical and maximum load situations.

Another good reason to test software completely is to reduce the number of errors that you have to fix after the software is deployed. It always costs more to fix a problem after software deployment than it does to fix the problem before the software is released to the users. This is in addition to the decrease in user satisfaction that accompanies software products requiring many post-release fixes.

Ensuring that software is thoroughly tested comes down to one thing: planning. As you define the requirements of your application and create a development plan, you should also be defining your test plan. The first part of the test plan is to perform risk analysis of your system. Use this analysis to define your test objectives. The highest risk elements of your application should be tested, and verified, early on in the development cycle.

A good test plan is also one to which you adhere throughout the software development cycle, not just before your software ships. Coding and testing in incremental fashion will identify defects early, so they can be fixed early, before fixing the error produces a "ripple effect" (you end up breaking multiple features built on top of the faulty code). Finally, develop a plan for tracking and managing defects. Armed with the debugging tools and features of Visual C++ 6.0, and a plan, you can deliver quality C++ applications.

—Michael Lane Thomas, MCSE+I, MCSD, MCT, MCP+SB, MSS, A+

CERTIFICATION SUMMARY

Visual C++ contains many features to assist you in debugging and testing your application. Debugging is fixing errors in your code. Testing is finding those errors in your code.

You can make different versions of your application, a release version and a debug version. For the debug version, Visual C++ comes with debugging libraries which contain debug versions of memory functions to help find memory leaks. There is debugging support in the run-time libraries to allow you to step into run-time functions. It also creates .PDB files to hold debugging information for your application. The debugging overhead is not used in the release version.

Visual C++ provides many debugging features in the IDE. It provides commands for viewing different types of data and controlling the execution of your program. These include windows for viewing variables, expressions, the stack, memory, registers, and assembly code.

Use the Depends tool to assist you in determining the dependencies of .EXEs, .DLLs, .OCXs, .COMs, and other file types. This can be used for debugging or for finding general information about your application.

The Spy++ tool is a utility that has windows to view the system's processes, threads, windows, and window messages. It also comes with a Finder tool so you can use your mouse to choose an application for which you want to view the properties.

The integrated debugger is a very useful tool in the debugging process. It allows you to set breakpoints for stopping program execution at specified points in your code and allows you to step through your code to determine if your program is executing correctly. It also has a new feature called Edit and Continue. This allows you to edit code while your program is stopped and continue execution from where you stopped without having to rebuild your application and restart it from the beginning.

The MFC library contains some macros that can be used for debugging. The ASSERT macro allows you to check for unwanted conditions in your code and stop program execution. The TRACE macro allows you to output messages to aid in debugging your application. You can use it to show program flow and data values.

There are many phases to the testing process. Beta testing allows pre-release testing of your application. Regression testing is used to ensure backward compatibility and verify that you didn't break other aspects of your application. Unit testing is usually performed by the developer to make sure the unit fulfills what it was designed for. Integration testing verifies overall application functionality. Integration testing is normally performed by a tester and it brings all of the units together to see how they operate as a whole. Stress testing sees how your application performs under adverse conditions.

TWO-MINUTE DRILL

- ❑ Debugging an application allows you to find errors in your application. Errors can be programmatic or logical.

- ❑ When you create a project, both a debug version and a release version are created.

- ❑ Visual C++ includes debugging support in the run-time library. This allows you to step into a run-time function's code and contains functions to help locate memory leaks and other memory problems, and to view the heap.

- ❑ The debug libraries include debug versions of *malloc, free, calloc, realloc, new,* and *delete*. These can be used for finding memory leaks.

- ❑ The IDE has many debugging features available. Many of the features can be accessed from the Debug, Build, View, and Edit menus. The most common of these debugging commands can also be accessed by the Debug toolbar.

- ❑ For troubleshooting purposes, the Depends tool can be used to detect files that are required by a module, but cannot be found.

- ❑ Spy++ is a utility that has windows to view the system's processes, threads, windows, and window messages. To start Spy++, go to the Tools menu and select Spy++.

- ❑ The integrated debugger can be used to find bugs in executables, DLLs, and ActiveX controls. One of the ways to check how your code is executing is stepping through your code one line at a time. If you don't want to step through your entire program, you can set a breakpoint on a particular line of code.

❑ The MFC library contains macros that can be used for debugging applications during run-time. These macros can be used to display debugging information during run-time.

❑ Testing is different from debugging. Debugging is the process of fixing bugs. Testing is the process of finding those bugs.

❑ Beta testing of an application allows testing by users who are not a part of or do not have any ties to the development process. The testers are completely independent of the development of the application.

❑ Regression testing is repeating previous testing to show that a change to the application does not affect other aspects of the application. The results of testing parts of the application that were not changed should be the same as they were in previous tests.

❑ Unit testing is testing the smallest part of an application that can be tested. This involves more than making sure that your unit will compile. It is testing to show functionality that is required has or has not been met.

❑ Integration testing is used to demonstrate that all of the units work together. Just because unit testing is completed, it does not guarantee it will work correctly with other units of an application.

❑ Stress testing places the highest possible loads with the lowest possible resources available to an application. This could be a high rate of data input on a machine with the minimum required resources. This can also help in determining the minimum requirements for an application.

SELF TEST

The following questions will help you measure your understanding of the material presented in this chapter. Read all of the choices carefully, as there may be more than one correct answer. Choose all correct answers for each question.

1. You want to include the debugging files in your setup program for the testing team. Your project is named APP1. Which files would you include? (Choose all that apply.)

    A. VC60.PDB file

    B. VCAPP1.PDB

    C. DBUG.PDB

    D. APP1.PDB

2. Which of the following files is not a debug library file?

    A. LIBCD.LIB

    B. DEBUG.LIB

    C. LIBCMTD.LIB

    D. MSVCRTD.LIB

3. What does the Apply Code Changes command do?

    A. Saves your source code to file

    B. Allows your source files to be edited

    C. Rebuilds your application

    D. Applies changes to code for use with the new Edit and Continue feature

4. You have set a breakpoint inside a function that you are trying to debug. You use Quick Watch to see that a variable is not what you expect it to be. Which window would you drag the variable to so that you could modify the variable's value to see if that generates the correct results?

    A. Variables window

    B. Call Stack window

    C. Watch window

    D. Quick Watch window

5. You have created a setup program that does not run when it is executed on a customer's computer. When the program is executed, you get an error saying that some files are missing. Which tool would you use to compare the files in the setup program to the files that are required by the application to run?

    A. Spy++

    B. Depends

    C. Process Viewer

    D. Tracer

6. Which of the following can be viewed using Spy++?

    A. Processes

    B. Threads

    C. Windows

    D. Messages

    E. All of the above

7. When you have a conditional breakpoint, at which line of code will the program break?

    A. The line before the condition is true

    B. The line where the condition is true

    C. The line after the condition is true

    D. It does not break, it just displays a message box indicating the condition is true

8. Which of the following tabs in the Breakpoints dialog box is used to set breakpoints outside of the current scope?

    A. Location

    B. Data

    C. Messages

    D. None of the above

9. Which of the following variables will appear in the Auto tab of the Variables window if you put a breakpoint on the line of code containing the printf statement? (Choose all that apply.)

```
int main()
{
  int x = 3;
  int y = 5;
  int z = 6;
  int i = 3;

  z = i + 5;
  x = Func1(Func2(y));
  printf("Put breakpoint here\n");
  return 0;
}
```

    A. x

    B. y

    C. z

    D. i

10. You put a breakpoint inside the function Func2 at the printf statement. When you execute the program and it stops at the breakpoint, you execute the Step Out command. After it is executed, which function is the current line of code moved to?

```
int Func2(int x)
{
    int y = 5;

    y = x +3;
    x = y - 6;
    printf("Put breakpoint here\n");
    return y;
}
int Func1(int x)
{
  return (x/2);
}
int main(int argc, char* argv[])
{
  int x = 3;
  int y = 5;

  x = Func1(Func2(y));
  return 0;
}
```

    A. Func2

    B. Func1

    C. main

    D. There isn't a Step Out command

11. You have a breakpoint set inside a particular function. The results you are seeing are incorrect. You notice that a

variable is initialized to the wrong value. You want to change the value to which the variable is initialized. The problem is, you had to run the application for half an hour to get to this spot. Which of the following features allow you to change your code and execute those changes without rebuilding and restarting your application?

A. Run-time editing

B. Debug Edit and Run

C. Edit and Continue

D. Change and Run

12. Which of the following macros allows you to check for logic errors during program execution?

A. CrtMemoryDump

B. ASSERT

C. TRACE

D. CHECKERROR

13. Which of the following buttons on the Assert message box will bring you to the source code in debug mode?

A. Abort

B. Retry

C. Ignore

D. Debug

14. You are debugging a function that is called many times. You don't want to step through the code, but you would like to see some interim results of the function after the program is finished executing. Which of the following macros allows you to do this?

A. ASSERT

B. VERIFY

C. TRACE

D. DEBUGREPORT

15. Your application is complete. You believe you are ready to release it, but you would like some additional testing to be done by people who are not part of the development process. You allow some of your more computer savvy customers to try out your application for feedback. What type of testing would this be?

A. Beta testing

B. Unit testing

C. Integration testing

D. Stress testing

16. You have developed an application that has been tested by the developers and the test team. This application will be used on Windows NT and Windows 95/98 on computers with different configurations. You are tasked with deciding what else needs to be done with the application. Required results: The application should be tested by people independent of the development process, on Windows NT and Windows 95/98.

Optional Results: The application should be tested on different computer configurations. The application should be tested on different software configurations. Proposed Solution: Have some independent testers in your company perform Beta testing on your application. They will test your application on Windows NT and Windows 95/98. They all have Microsoft Office 97 and Internet Explorer 4.0 installed on their computers, but they have different computer configurations including processor, memory size, hard drive space, and other peripherals.

A. The proposed solution meets the required result and both optional results.

B. The proposed solution meets the required result and only one optional result.

C. The proposed solution meets the required result and none of the optional results.

D. The proposed solution does not meet the required result.

17. Your testing team found some bugs in your application. You have fixed these bugs and performed some testing to prove the bug is fixed. You now send it to the testing team. They will perform some testing to prove that the bug is fixed, and also verify that the fix did not cause problems in other parts of the application. Which of the following types of testing is this?

A. Beta

B. Unit

C. Regression

D. Stress

18. You have finished developing your module of an application. You want to ensure that the module meets all the requirements and does not have any bugs before sending it to the testing team. Which of the following types of testing is this?

A. Beta

B. Unit

C. Integration

D. Stress

19. You are in charge of the testing team of an application. The development team has performed their testing to ensure their modules all meet the requirements. You are now tasked with pulling all of the modules together to verify they work together and meet the overall system requirements. What kind of testing is this?

A. Beta

B. Unit

C. Stress

D. Integration

20. Which conditions should not be tested for when performing Stress testing?

A. Low amount of memory available

B. Low amount of free disk space

C. Low amount of data to process

D. Minimum CPU speed

21. In the following code, which assert will stop program execution?

```
int Func2(int x)
{
   int y = 5;
      y = x +3;
      x = y - 6;
      _ASSERT(x);
      return y;
}
int Func1(int x)
{
  _ASSERT(x == 6);
  return (x/2);
}
int main(int argc, char* argv[])
{
  int x = 3;
  x = Func1(Func2(x));
  _assert(X == 3);
  return 0;
}
```

    A. The assert in the main function

    B. The assert in Func1

    C. The assert in Func2

    D. No asserts will stop program execution

22. You have written a function that, when executed, produces erratic results. What could cause this in the following code?

```
int main()
{
  int i;
  char str[] = "This is a string.";
  for (i=0; i<20; i++)
      str[i] = '\0';
  return 0;
}
```

    A. The str variable should be initialized as str[18] instead of str[].

    B. The str variable should have been declared as a char pointer, then allocated memory of 18 bytes, and then the string copied to it using strcpy.

    C. The variable str is initialized to less than 20 characters, and the for loop is overwriting memory that is being used.

    D. There is nothing wrong with this code; the error must be somewhere else.

23. To determine how many threads are being spawned by a process, you can use the Spy++ tool. In the following figure, how many threads are there for the KERNEL32 process?

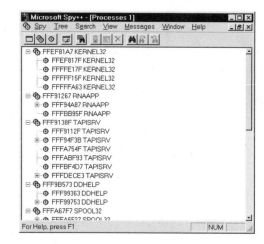

    A. 1

    B. 2

    C. 3

    D. 4

SELF TEST ANSWERS

1. **A, D.** The VC60.PDB file contains debug information about types for the object files and is placed in the same directory as the makefile. The APP1.PDB file contains all debugging information for the .EXE file.

2. **B.** DEBUG.LIB is not a debug library used by Visual C++. LIBCD.LIB, LIBCMTD.LIB, and MSVCRTD.LIB are debug libraries that include debug versions of malloc, free, calloc, realloc, new, and delete. Notice the D at the end of each filename.

3. **D.** It allows you to continue running your application with the changes made without having to rebuild or restart the application. This allows you to test changes without having to restart the application and get to the current state again. The application will be returned to the state that it was in when the bug occurred, and you can see if your change fixes the bug.

4. **C.** Watch window is correct. You cannot add variables to the Variables windows although you can modify them. The Call Stack window displays the stack and cannot be modified. The Quick Watch window can display the value of a variable, but it cannot be modified. You can add the variable to the Watch window and modify it there.

5. **B.** The Depends tool will find all module dependencies needed for your application. It can be used to determine files that are missing, files that are invalid, import and export mismatches, circular dependencies, and when modules being loaded were built for another type of machine. It can also be used for general information about modules in an application.

6. **E.** Spy++ can view a system's processes, threads, windows, and messages. The Processes view is used to display information about what processes are running on the system and view information about those processes. The Threads view displays a tree of all of the active threads associated with windows containing the Thread ID and module name. The Windows view can be used to find windows that are open in the system and view the properties of them. The Messages view allows you to see the messages associated with a thread, a process, or a window.

7. **B.** It breaks on the line of code that made the condition true. The application will stop running at the line of code containing the breakpoint, and the debugger will appear displaying the source code at the breakpoint.

8. **A.** The Location tab is used to set a breakpoint outside of the current scope. Remember, this only available in the Enterprise Edition. This allows you to set a breakpoint by source code line number, memory address, register, or function name. To guide you in entering the breakpoint information, use the Advanced Breakpoint dialog box.

9. **A, B.** Variables from both the current and previous lines of code are displayed in the Auto tab of the Variables window. This allows you to view the variables that are in close proximity to where the program is suspended. The y variable is used in the call to Func2, so it is included.

10. **C.** The Step Out command steps out of the current function to the line of code to where the function was called. Use this command when you have reached the part of a function that you wanted to check out and you don't want to step through the rest of the function.

11. **C.** Edit and Continue is the new feature of Visual C++ 6.0 that allows you to change your code and then run without restarting. This allows you to edit the source code while debugging and apply these changes without having to rebuild the application. The application will be returned to the state that it was in when the bug occurred and you can see if your change fixes the bug.

12. **B.** The ASSERT macro allows you to check for logic errors in your code. For any expression that evaluates to false, it will stop the program and notify the user. The TRACE macro allows you to send formatted strings to a dump device which you can view later for errors, but will not stop the application at the point of the error.

13. **B.** The Retry button will bring up the source code in debug mode if the source code is available. The Abort button will terminate the application. The Ignore button will allow the application to continue execution if possible. There isn't a Debug button.

14. **C.** The TRACE macro allows you to send formatted strings to a dump device such as a file or Debug Monitor. The ASSERT macro allows you to check for logic errors in your code. For any expression that evaluates to false, it will stop the program and notify the user in a pop-up dialog box.

15. **A.** Beta testing allows some advanced users to take your application for a test drive. The users are independent of the development team. Unit testing is done by the developer. Integration and Stress testing are done by people who know the application, they are not independent.

16. **B.** The proposed solution meets the required result because there are independent people performing the testing and the testing is done on Windows NT and Windows 95/98. The first optional result of different computer configurations is met by the proposed solution, but the second one isn't. All of the testers have the same software loaded.

17. **C.** Regression testing is used to verify that changes to the application did not affect other parts of the application. You want to ensure that fixing one problem didn't break another area of the application. This allows you to verify previous testing is still valid.

18. **B.** Unit testing is usually performed by the developer to ensure it meets the functionality for which it was designed. This allows the developer to verify that the unit itself functions correctly before integrating it with other units. This normally entails writing a test program developed specifically to test a unit.

19. **D.** Integration testing verifies that all of the modules can interface with each other and perform the overall functionality required of the application. This test verifies the units can communicate with each other and that the interfaces between modules are being used correctly.

20. **C.** Stress testing is used to test for low amounts of memory, free disk space, and minimum CPU speed. It should test for processing a large amount of data, not a low amount. It should verify that the application can handle extreme conditions and still function correctly. You can use the Stress tool to help with this testing.

21. **C.** The assert in the function Func2 will stop program execution. When x is passed into Func2, it is equal to 3. Then, y is set to x + 3 which equals 6. Then x is set to y – 6 which equals 0. This causes the assert. The assert in Func1 does not stop program execution because x does equal 6 and the assert in the main function does not stop program execution because x does equal 3.

22. **C.** The variable str is automatically initialized to length of 18; 17 for the string and one more for the string delimiter. The for loop writes to 20 bytes when the string is initialized to 18 bytes. A is not correct, because the results would be the same even if you explicitly declared str to size of 18. B also wouldn't solve the problem because the for loop would still write past the end of the string.

23. **D.** There are four threads for the KERNEL32 process. The main branch of the tree view is the process. When you click the + symbol to expand it, the threads are listed below the process. There are four threads below the KERNEL32 process. They are all called KERNEL32. Remember, there is always at least one thread for every process.

MICROSOFT CERTIFIED SOLUTION DEVELOPER

11

Distributing an Application

CERTIFICATION OBJECTIVES

Distributing an application is one of the critical parts for your application's success. Users get their first impression of your application during installation. If users see that the setup program provides everything they need, they are most likely to begin using your application with a good attitude. So, the setup functions for a distributed application must be simple, easy to use, efficient, and effective. Microsoft Visual C++ provides the InstallShield program, which allows you to create a setup program that copies files, registers all required components, and provides the uninstall options for removing the application.

CERTIFICATION OBJECTIVE 11.01

Installing an Application

Now that you have done the grunt work of finally getting your application finished, there is one hurdle that remains. This hurdle is packaging your application and distributing it. Keep in mind that your application has been coded, debugged, and tested.

At this moment, you need make decisions regarding the environment in which you plan to use the application. The in-house developers won't have the same packaging concerns as the ones doing retail or public development. You also need to think about which files are needed by the application and where they should be placed in the user's hard disk. For example, all your Microsoft Foundation Classes (MFC) applications will need MSVCRT.DLL and MFC42.DLL to be located on the user's machine so that your program can link to them. Sometimes these files are not installed on a user's computer. They should be included in the portion of your distribution package that you ship to the users. Normally, you can figure out which dynamic link libraries (DLLs) you need to include in your package by using utilities such as QuickView, DumpBin, and Depends. For example, I use the DumpBin utility to find out the requirements of my application DRAWSERV.EXE in Figure 11-1. All I need to type at a command line to use this program is the following:

```
DumpBin /IMPORTS DrawServ.exe
```

FIGURE 11-1

Use the DumpBin MS-DOS
utility to determine the
dependency files

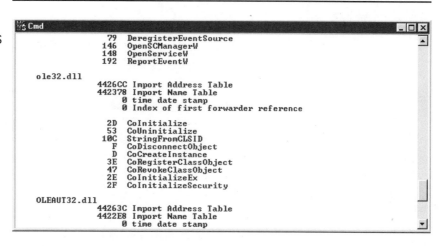

```
Cmd                                                                    _ □ ×
                    79   DeregisterEventSource
                   146   OpenSCManagerW
                   148   OpenServiceW
                   192   ReportEventW

    ole32.dll
                  4426CC  Import Address Table
                  442378  Import Name Table
                       0  time date stamp
                       0  Index of first forwarder reference

                    2D   CoInitialize
                    53   CoUninitialize
                   10C   StringFromCLSID
                     F   CoDisconnectObject
                     D   CoCreateInstance
                    3E   CoRegisterClassObject
                    47   CoRevokeClassObject
                    2E   CoInitializeEx
                    2F   CoInitializeSecurity

    OLEAUT32.dll
                  44263C  Import Address Table
                  4422E8  Import Name Table
                       0  time date stamp
```

DumpBin is the program and /IMPORTS will tell you which files the
DRAWSERV.EXE will import.

Creating a Setup Program

By now, you should know how you want to package your application,
such as whether it is a shrink-wrapped program or perhaps a shareware
CD-ROM-based program, and you should have a complete list of
the files needed to run your application. Additionally, you should have
fully compiled and tested your application and associated files on a
fresh machine.

Visual C++ 6.0 provides the InstallShield Project Wizard to create
an InstallShield setup program, which includes the necessary files and
dependencies to install your application, to register the Component Object
Model (COM) components, and to allow for uninstallation.

If you already have a project handy, you can practice using it. If you
don't, you can practice with a sample project from your Microsoft
Developer Network (MSDN) CDs. Here we use the DRAWCTRL.EXE
project as an example.

Creating a Setup Program

1. Start InstallShield for Microsoft Visual C++ 6.0 from Start | Programs | InstallShield for Microsoft Visual C++ 6.0. The Project Wizard will start and the Welcome dialog box will appear, as shown in Figure 11-2.

   Note: You could also start the InstallShield Wizard from the Tool menu of the Microsoft Visual C++ 6.0 integrated development environment (IDE). We chose to start with the standalone InstallShield program instead of the wizard to fully illustrate the whole packaging and deploying process.

2. Type your application name and your company name in the corresponding fields.

3. Select the development environment; this is always Microsoft Visual C++ 6.0. Select the application type that best suits your application. You can choose Database Application, Finance Application, Internet

FIGURE 11-2

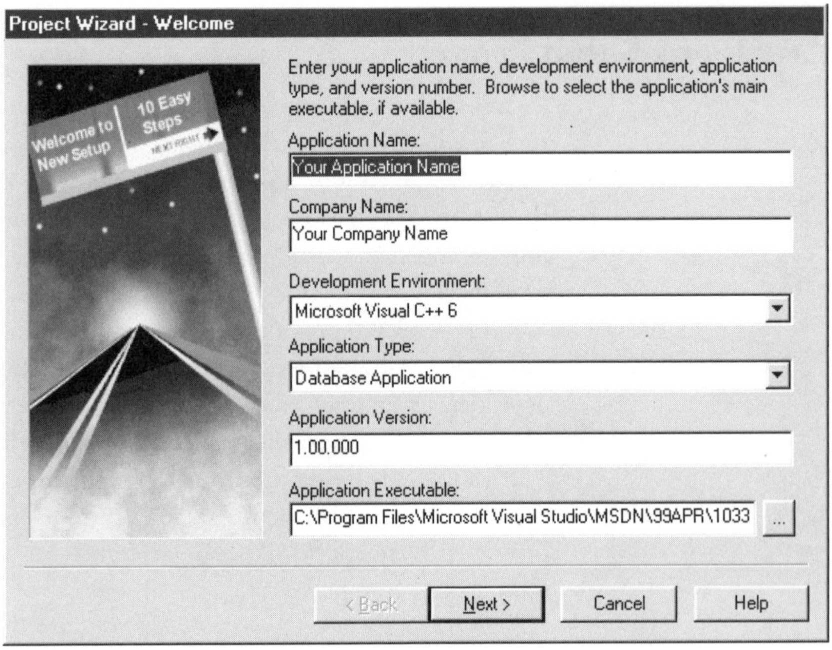

The first step in the InstallShield Project Wizard is to enter information about your application

Application, Software Development Application, and Statistical
Application. For our example, you might choose the Software
Development Application, which is a generic type for purposes
like this.

4. Type the application version number in the Application Version field.
   You should use any versioning scheme that complies with your
   company's version control policies.

5. Click the Ellipsis (...) button next to the Application Executable field
   to browse for the application that you need to distribute on your
   system. Another option is to type your application's full path name
   in the field if you know it exactly. I usually suggest browsing for it,
   because this is less error prone.

6. Click Next. You'll see the Project Wizard - Choose Dialogs screen,
   shown in Figure 11-3.

Choose the dialog boxes
that the user will see
during the installation of
your application

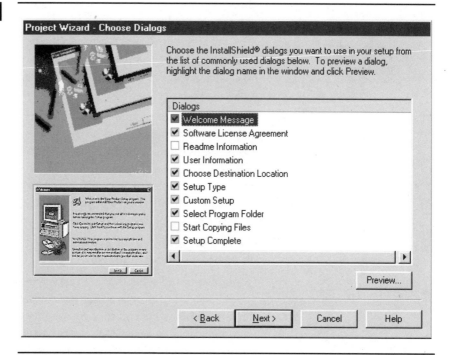

Based on the packaging model on which you decided earlier, you need to choose the series of dialog boxes that users will see when installing your application. If this is an internal project, you may not need a license agreement or custom setup options, nor will you have to choose a destination location. If this is a public application you will want to make it as configurable as possible. When you highlight a dialog name, you will see a thumbnail view of the dialog in question, which makes it easier to determine whether you actually want to use it or not. As you go through the installation steps, you can see that you will be able to modify the context of the dialog later.

7. Check Next. You'll see the Project Wizard - Choose Target Platforms dialog box. In the Operating System window, you can choose one or many operating systems on which your application can be installed. You can check the Show Only Available Platforms box to reduce the available platforms that the InstallShield program supports. Select the platforms that are absolutely necessary to reduce the size of your distributing package and reduce the chance that someone will try to use your program under the wrong platform.

8. Click Next. You'll see the Project Wizard - Specify Languages dialog box, where you can select one or more languages for which you are localizing your setup.

9. Click Next. You'll see the Project Wizard - Specify Setup Types dialog box. The InstallShield program provides a wealth of Setup Types—Compact, Typical, Custom, Network, Administrator, Network (Best Performance), and Network (Efficient Space). In this example, we chose the very common setup types, Compact, Typical, and Custom. Remember that you can change the setup type later on at any point during setup creation.

10. Click Next. You'll see the Project Wizard - Specify Components dialog box like the one shown in Figure 11-4.

    Components and subcomponents give you the flexibility to package your application and related software accessories for setup. You can think of components and subcomponents as your customer's view of your application. If your setup installs a suite of products, you can make each product in the suite a component. You can specify

FIGURE 11-4

Customize your
components

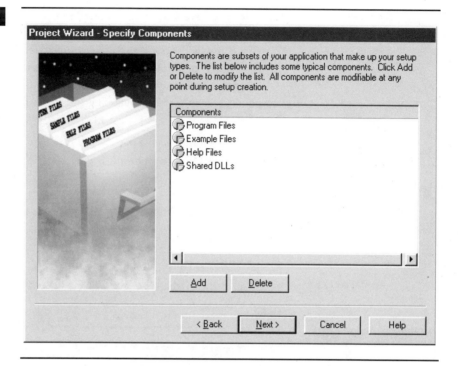

products such as a word processor, a spreadsheet program, a
database program, and a drawing program as components. Each
component (product) could then have subcomponents allowing the
user to install optional pieces of the program such as help files,
tutorials, optional support files such as graphics libraries, and so
on. With InstallShield, you are free to take advantage of the
component-subcomponent relationship to achieve any setup
configuration that you desire.

11. Add or delete component types as needed, and then click Next,
You'll see the Project Wizard - Specify File Groups dialog box. Our
example program uses Program Executable Files, Program DLLs, and
Shared DLLs. Normally you'll create file groups so that all of the files
needed for a specific task are copied at one time. For example, say
you have four COM DLLs, which need self-registration at the time
of installation. You could define a common file group for the DLLs
where you can set the Self_Registration property on the file group.

12. Add or delete file groups as needed and then click Next. You'll see a Project Wizard - Summary dialog box. At this point you should check the list of options to make sure everything is correct. Click the Finish button; InstallShield will create the installation program using the options you've just specified. Then, the InstallShield generates several files including the setup rule (SETUP.RUL) file. Its interface is shown in Figure 11-5.

Finally, you should have a bare bones functional installation program. There's still additional configuration that needs to be done. You need to perform the following tasks:

■ Set up components

■ Set up file groups

■ Define resources

■ Determine media type (we'll discuss this in detail later in this chapter)

FIGURE 11-5

Once you've created a project, InstallShield generates all the frame code for you and displays it

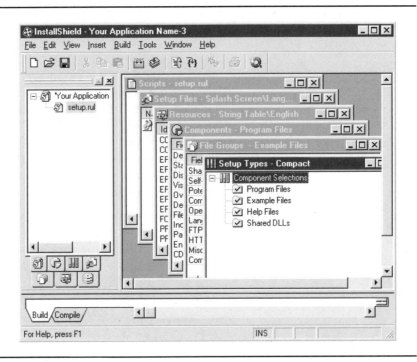

Setting Up Components

Click the Components tab. The window that is shown will be similar to mine, shown here:

You use this Components - Program Files window to view the current properties of the files that will be installed. You should pay close attention to the Overwrite, FTP Location, HTTP location, Required Components, and Included File Groups fields. Following is a brief description of these fields:

- **Overwrite**   Used to tell InstallShield whether you want to check the date/time stamp on the component file first before overwriting it. It's wise to choose *NEWERVERSION/NEWERDATE* or *SAMEORNEWERVERSION/SAMEORNEWERDATE* instead of the default *ALWAYSOVERWRITE*. In essence, these options tell InstallShield to overwrite a file only if the source has both a newer (or same) date and newer (or same) version than the one on the user's computer.

- **Required Components**   Used to set up dependencies between components.

- **FTP Location**   Used to allow a user to start the installation from a Web site link and then copy the needed files from your Web server.

■ **HTTP Location**   The same as FTP Location, except the files are under the control of an HTTP server.

■ **File Groups**   Used to add file groups represented by the component. Here you are making the links between component groups and file groups.

Setting Up File Groups

In this step, you'll assign a set of files to each of the file groups that you defined previously. The first thing you need to do is click the File Groups tab. What you'll see is a list of the file groups and the File Groups dialog box shown in Figure 11-6.

Click the plus sign next to the file group folder that you want to configure in the File Groups window. Click the Links entry under it and you'll see the File Groups - Program Executables\Links dialog box, as shown

---

The File Groups dialog box allows you to add a set of files to each of the file groups

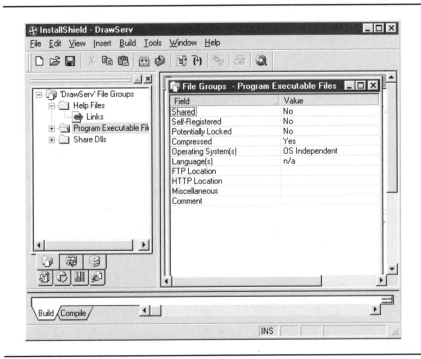

here. This is where you'll define a list of one or more files to include in this file group.

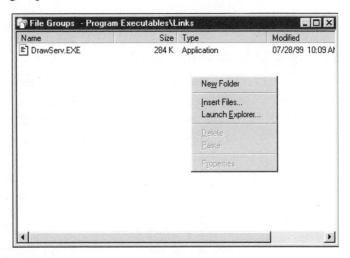

Right-click in this dialog and choose Insert Files from the shortcut menu. You'll see a standard File Open type dialog box. Browse to the file that you want to add. Click OK to add this file. You also need to add files to the other file groups.

Customizing Resources

Click the Resources tab and you'll see the Resources dialog box shown here. Make changes to the string table to provide some identification information for your application.

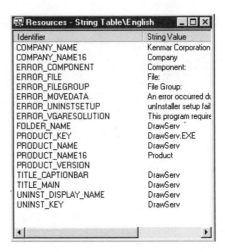

Now you are done with the biggest part of creating the setup program. We'll continue our journey later in this chapter to determine and create media types.

Registering COM Components

When you deploy an application, you must make sure that you include all of the COM components that you use in the application. These COM components include ActiveX controls, COM DLLs, and COM executables.

In order for COM applications to communicate with the COM components, each COM server, control, or container must place certain information in the Windows Registry (32-bit Windows) or registration database (16-bit). Entering this information in the Registry is referred to as registering the file or application. If a COM component is intended to be available to clients at any time, as most applications are, you usually register it through an installation and setup program. This means putting information about the application into the Registry, including how and where its objects are to be instantiated. This information must be registered for all class IDs (CLSID). Other information is optional. The InstallShield setup program makes it very simple to register COM components at installation.

InstallShield calls the necessary functions or passes the necessary command line arguments to self-registering files when you select the Self-Registered option for a file group, or when you call XCopyFile or VerUpdateFile with the SELFREGISTER option in your SETUP.RUL.

Self-registering .DLLs must contain two functions, DllRegisterServer and DllUnregisterServer. When a file's DllRegisterServer function is called, it adds or updates Registry information for all the classes implemented by the .DLL, allowing COM applications to find it. When the .DLL's DllUnregisterServer function is called at uninstallation time, the DLL's information is removed from the Registry.

In order for an .EXE file to be an *automation server*, it must support the command line argument /REGSERVER for registration purposes and /UNREGSERVER for unregistration.

If you are not relying on system defaults, there are two important keys in the Registry: CLSID and AppID. Among the important pieces of information under these keys is how the object is to be instantiated. Objects can be designated as in-process, out-of-process local, or out-of-process remote.

When a class is registered as in-process, a call to CoGetClassObject to create its class object is automatically passed by COM to the DLLGetClassObject function, which the class must implement to give the calling object a pointer to its class object. Classes implemented in executables can specify that COM should execute their process and wait for the process to register their class object's IClassFactory through a call to the CORegisterClassObject function.

Table 11-1 lists the Win32 API registry functions available to the developer. Use these functions to register and unregister a component.

Registering a Component That Implements DCOM

You must register the Distributed Component Object Model (DCOM) components on both server and client machines so that the client is able to

TABLE 11-1	Function	Description
Win32 API Registry Functions	RegCloseKey	Closes a specified key
	RegCreateKeyEx	Creates a specified key
	RegDeleteKey	Deletes a specified key
	RegDeleteValue	Deletes a value associated with a key
	RegEnumKeyEx	Enumerates the subkeys of an open key
	RegEnumValue	Enumerates the values of an open key
	RegOpenKeyEx	Opens a specified key
	RegQueryInfoKey	Returns information about an open key
	RegQueryValueEx	Returns a value of an open key
	RegSetValueEx	Sets the value for an open key

locate the DCOM server. For this reason, you must copy the server to each client and register it on the client.

When registering a DCOM component you need to ensure that the client side can map their program name (ProgID) to an identifier (CLSID) that can be used again. For this reason, the ProgID of the server must be in the client-side Registry and map to the class ID of the server-side DCOM object.

For example, if you expose a DCOM component called MyBObj with a specific class ID—for instance, "{00112233-4455-6677-8899-00AABBCCDDEE}"—you should make sure the following entries are added to the client-side Registry:

```
[HKEY_CLASSES_ROOT]
\MyBObj
   \Clsid
   (Default) "{00112233-4455-6677-8899-00AABBCCDDEE}"
[HKEY_LOCAL_MACHINE]
\SOFTWARE
    \Classes
          \APPID
        {00112233-4455-6677-8899-00AABBCCDDEE} \RemoteServerName = Your
                                                    Server Name
```

The RemoteServerName named value on client machines configures the client to request that the object be run at the *Your Server Name* machine whenever an activation function is called for which a COSERVERINFO structure is not specified.

CERTIFICATION OBJECTIVE 11.02

Configuring DCOM on the Client and Server Computer

After registering the DCOM component, you must configure both client and server computers to enable the component to communicate.

The easiest place to begin configuring the DCOM component is with the DCOM configuration utility (called DCOMCNFG.EXE, which is found in the System folder). The DCOM configuration utility is a powerful tool that is used to configure your computer as a client, a server, or both. In addition, you can use it to view and edit the properties and security settings for DCOM components. Additionally, you can use it to

- Enable DCOM service on a computer
- Activate and specify where DCOM components run
- Specify who can access, launch, and configure DCOM components
- Configure levels of security for a particular application

on the
Job

While running the DCOMCNFG.EXE on Windows 95/98, you must set the access control to User Level using the Network applet in Control Panel. User-level access control determines the security model that will be used by the operating system. The machine should be connected to a network with a Windows NT domain controller that can be used to provide pass-through security, so that COM security can be enabled.

You can launch the DCOM utility by choosing Start | Run and typing **DCOMCNFG**. Figure 11-7 shows the DCOMCNFG utility that is provided with Windows NT 4.0.

System-Wide DCOM Configuration
The Distributed COM Configuration Properties dialog box has four pages: Applications, Default Properties, Default Security, and Default Protocols. They are used to configure the system-wide default settings of DCOM.

APPLICATIONS   You change the settings for a particular object with the Applications page (see Figure 11-7). Simply select the application from the list and click the Properties button. The Properties window has four pages.

Use the Distributed COM
Configuration Properties
window to configure
DCOM components

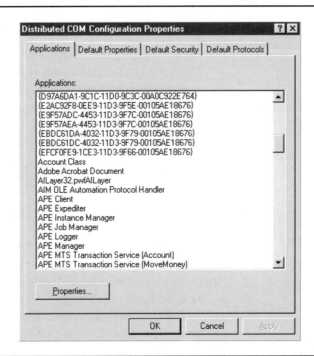

DEFAULT PROPERTIES   This tab is used to enable Distributed
COM and to specify the authentication level and impersonation level used
for communicating between the client and server. You must select the
Enable Distributed COM on This Computer check box, as shown in Figure
11-8, if you want clients on other machines to access COM objects running
on this machine. Selecting this option sets the *HKEY_LOCAL_MACHINE\
Software\Microsoft\OLE\EnableDCOM* value to *Y*.

DEFAULT SECURITY   You can use the Default Security page to
enable Remote Connection, which is used instead of directly modifying
the System Registry. Also, you can specify default permissions for objects
on the system. The Default Security page has three sections: Access,
Launch, and Configuration. To change a section's defaults, click the
corresponding Edit Default button. These settings are stored in the

FIGURE 11-8

Use the Default Properties page to specify the authentication level for communication between the client and the server

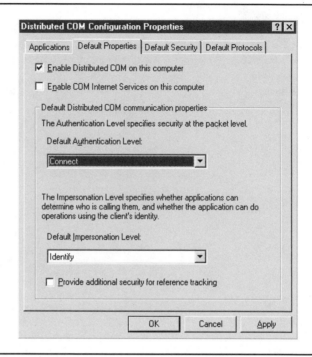

Registry under *HKEY_LOCAL_MACHINE\Software\Microsoft\OLE*. Figure 11-9 shows the Default Security page.

DEFAULT PROTOCOLS   From the Default Protocols tab, you can add, remove, or change properties of a list of network protocols available to the Distributed COM. In addition, you can order the priorities for these protocols.

Setting Process-Wide Security Using DCOMCNFG

You might want to enable security for a particular application if an application has security needs that are different from those required by other applications on the machine. For instance, you might decide to use machine-wide settings for your applications that require a low level of

FIGURE 11-9

Use the Default Security
page in DCOMCNFG.EXE
to specify permissions for
objects on the system

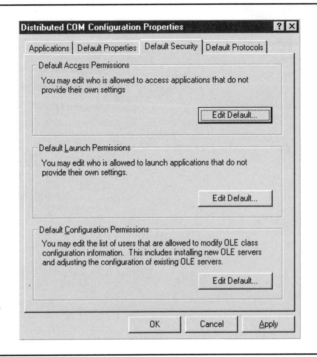

security, but set a higher level of security for a particular application. You
can do it by selecting the object in the Application tab of the main DCOM
dialog box and then clicking Properties to open the Properties dialog box in
Figure 11-10.

The Properties dialog box consists of the General, Location, Security,
Identity, and Endpoints tabs.

GENERAL   The General tab gives a description of the selected
application. This description includes the application's name, type, and its
location on the network.

LOCATION   The Location tab allows you to specify where the
application should run when a client calls *CoCreateInstance* on the relevant
CLSID. If you select the Run Application on the Following Computer
check box and enter a computer name, then a *RemoteServerName* value is

FIGURE 11-10

The DCOMCNFG utility allows your application to have a level of security that is different from that of other applications on a machine

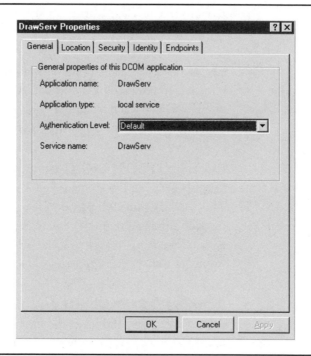

added under the *AppID* for that application. Clearing the Run Application on This Computer check box renames the *LocalService* value to *_LocalService* and thereby disables it.

SECURITY The Security tab is similar to the Default Security page found in the DCOMCNFG window, except that these settings apply only to the current application. Again, the settings are stored under the AppID for that object. However, security settings in the Registry that apply to a particular application are sometimes not used. For example, the application-wide settings that you set in the Registry using DCOMCNFG.EXE will be overridden if a client calls CoSetProxyBlanket to set security for a particular interface proxy. Similarly, if a client or server (or both) calls CoInitializeSecurity to set security for a process, then the settings in the Registry will be ignored and the parameters specified to CoInitializeSecurity will be used instead.

IDENTIFY The Identify tab identifies which user is running the application.

ENDPOINTS The Endpoints tab allows you to identify the endpoint information required by the RPC mechanisms used by DCOM. This is often necessary when wrapping legacy applications with COM components and the need for custom marshalling occurs.

Running DCOMCNFG on the Client Machine

Select your server (by name or by CLSID) and click the Properties button. This will bring up a Properties dialog box. Select the Location tab. Select the Run Application on the Following Computer check box and specify the name of the server machine. Clear the other check boxes, and then click the Apply button.

Running DCOMCNFG on the Server Machine

Select your server, and select the Properties dialog box. Select the Security tab. You can choose to apply the default access and launch permissions to the server or you can choose to apply custom permissions. The default permissions can be changed using the Default Security tab in DCOMCNFG. Make sure that *SYSTEM* is in the Launch and Access permissions, and then add the account of the user on the client machine to the Launch and Access permissions. Click the Apply button. You are now ready to access the server from the client.

on the
job

You bet DCOM is a powerful technology for distributed applications. The nature of its complexity makes it difficult to master the configurations of DCOM components. You may expect various errors to occur when you attempt to call the DCOM server. The best way to make it work is to gain experience with the DCOMCNFG utility; try to understand the concept behind the screen.

CERTIFICATION OBJECTIVE 11.03

Using .CAB Files

A cabinet is a single file, usually with a .CAB extension, that stores compressed files in a file library. The cabinet format is an efficient way to package multiple files because compression is performed across file boundaries, which significantly improves the compression ratio.

If you plan to distribute Microsoft Foundation Class (MFC) library and Active Template Library (ATL) controls using the Internet, you should package them as signed cabinet (.CAB) files. Signed files ensure that a user downloading your control knows where the control comes from and that it hasn't been modified after its creation. A .CAB file contains a compressed version of your control plus information about how your control is to be installed, for example, what .DLLs need to be installed along with the .OCX.

Packaging and Distributing an Application

You can use a cabinet file creation tool such as CABARC.EXE to make cabinet files. This tool writes to the Diamond cabinet structure. Some tools you can use to create and sign .CAB files are available on the Visual Studio 6.0 CD-ROM.

The following are the steps to create and sign a .CAB file. We will cover each objective in its own section.

1. Retrieve a Software Publisher Certificate, which needs to be done only once.

2. Create your .CAB file.

3. Sign the files.

4. If you like, you can embed the .CAB on a Web page.

Getting a Software Publisher Certificate

Prior to signing your files, you will need to get a Software Publisher Certificate (SPC). To obtain one, you must send a request to a Certification Authority. In your application you should provide information about your name, address, and a public key; these will be used as a key pair. In the process, a legally binding pledge is made to not knowingly distribute viruses or other harmful code. The Certification Authority then generates an industry standard Software Publisher Certificate that is an X.509 format with version 3 extensions. This certificate uniquely identifies you and contains the public key you provided. The Certification Authority stores it for reference and a copy is e-mailed to you. When you receive this certificate you should sign it and include a copy with your software.

Creating a .CAB File

To create a .CAB file, you first have to figure out which files need to be included in the application. For example, users will probably have a copy of all the ATL files from using other programs. You don't want them to waste time downloading these files over and over again if they don't need to. In most cases, you'll want to limit yourself to the files that are unique to your Web site. You can provide a location from which the user is able to download the dependency files if these files are missing in the user's company. Then, you need to create an .INF file.

The .INF file is an ASCII text file that lists the files, for example a .DLL, that you will need to download or already have so that your control can run. Using an .INF file lets you add all of the files that you will need to one simple cabinet file. As a default, files on the local machine that are newer than yours are, or that have the same date will not be overwritten.

Creating an .INF file is fairly easy. All you really need to do is to consider what you need to include and where it's located. The following is an example .INF file for the ATL SuperScroll control. You will need ATL.DLL, but there's a good chance it's already installed on the client machine. ATL.DLL will need to be registered before SSCROLL.DLL, so you need to put ATL.DLL first in the .INF.

```
; INF file for SSCROLL.DLL
[Add.Code]
```

```
sscroll.dll=sscroll.dll
atl.dll=atl.dll
[atl.dll]
file-win32-x86= http://www.mysite.com/mydir/ATL.DLL
FileVersion=2,00,0,7024
RegisterServer=yes
[sscroll.dll]
file-win32-x86=mycab
clsid={11111111-2222-3333-4444-000000000000}
FileVersion=1,0,0,1
RegisterServer=yes
; INF file EOF
```

When using *file-win32-x86,* you specify that this implementation is specific to the x86 platform.

A version number for a file can be obtained by right-clicking the file and selecting Properties, or by pressing ALT-ENTER when in Windows Explorer. When this dialog box comes up, you can then select the Version tab to view the version information. Sometimes we have to insert an extra zero in the .INF file, such as in the preceding example where we have the ATL.DLL version as 2,00,0,7024. When you look at this on the Properties page from within Explorer, you will see it listed as 2.00.7024. The DestDir setting specifies the directory in which the file will end up. Using the number 11 uses the system directory WINDOWS/SYSTEM or WINNT/SYSTEM32; the number 10 uses the Windows directory WINDOWS or WINNT. If you don't use this setting, such as in the example, the code is placed in the fixed OCCACHE directory. The *clsid* field is the CLSID of the control that you have installed.

After you have made your .INF file, you can use the CABARC program to create the cabinet file. Typically, the CABARC utility is run where your source files are located. When using the utility on the command line, you should list the source files as they are used in the .INF file, then follow it up with the .INF file. For our .INF file we would make a .CAB file with the following command line.

```
C:\YourBinDir\CABARC -s 6144 n SSCROLL.CAB SSCROLL.DLL SSCROLL.INF
```

CABARC.EXE will create your .CAB file and it will be named SSCROLL.CAB. The *-s* option reserves space in the cabinet for code signing. The *n* command specifies that you want to create a .CAB file. For a list of commands and options, type **cabarc** alone on the command line. This .CAB file contains a compressed version of SSCROLL.DLL along with the information needed to extract it in the SSCROLL.INF file.

Signing a .CAB File

To sign a .CAB file, you can use the code-signing wizard called SIGNCODE.EXE.

EXERCISE 11-2

Signing a Cabinet File Using the Code Signing Wizard

1. Launch the SIGNCODE utility.

2. Click Next on the Welcome screen.

3. On this page, you should type the name of the Software Publisher Certificate in the first dialog; this is an .SPC file. In the next dialog you sign it with your private key, so type the name of a private key file (.PVK).

4. Click Next twice and click Sign to sign your file.

Embedding a Signed .CAB File on a Web Page

HTML uses the <OBJECT> tag to embed an ATL or MFC control onto a Web page. The <OBJECT> tag has a few attributes that need to be addressed. They are as follows:

■ **ID**   The control's name.

■ **CLASSID**   The control's CLSID.

■ **CODEBASE**   Where you can download this control.

The following example Web page will display your control that is stored in the cabinet file that we created earlier.

```
<HTML>
<HEAD>
<TITLE>Page to embed object SuperScroll</TITLE>
</HEAD>
<BODY>
<OBJECT
ID="SScroll"
CLASSID="CLSID: 11111111-2222-3333-4444-000000000000"
```

```
CODEBASE="http://www.mysite.com/mydir/sscroll.cab">
</OBJECT>
<SCRIPT LANGUAGE="VBScript">
<!--
Sub SScroll_ClickUp(x)
ScrollUp()
End Sub
Sub SScroll_ClickDown(x)
ScrollDown()
End Sub
-->
</SCRIPT>
</BODY>
</HTML>
```

Your CODEBASE can point to an .OCX or a .DLL file directly.

If you decide to include a version number with the CODEBASE, you should make sure that it matches your control's version. As an example, because our SSCROLL.DLL is version 1,0,0,1, our CODEBASE is also 1,0,0,1.

```
CODEBASE="http://www.mysite.com/mydir/sscroll.cab#version=1,0,0,1"
```

Including the version number is beneficial. If the user has an earlier version present on his or her machine, the file might be replaced. If the file is older it won't, but if you did not include a version number it never would be replaced.

exam
ⓦatch

Currently everyone, including Microsoft Corporation, embraces Web technology. You should be familiar with how to embed a .CAB file on a Web page and what the CODEBASE and OBJECT tags mean.

CERTIFICATION OBJECTIVE 11.04

Planning Application Distribution

After you have packaged the application, you should copy the files onto the media that you intend to use to distribute the application. Currently, the compact disc is the most popular distribution method. You may decide to use floppy disks as a distribution method if the application is small enough and the overall user base is small-scaled as well. There are other widely used distribution methods such as network-based, Web-based, e-mail attachment, login script, and Systems Management Server (SMS) package distributions.

InstallShield provides the Media Build Wizard to let you build the distributing disk images fairly easily. By default, after you go through the setup procedure using InstallShield, the CD disk image has already been built. If your only distribution method is going to be CD, you're done. Otherwise, choose the Media Build Wizard from the Build menu of the VC++ 6.0 IDE to add another media type to your installation program.

Floppy Disk–Based Distribution

The Media Build Wizard lets you build disk image folders that are appropriate for any distribution medium including floppy disks, and it lets you specify the languages and operating systems for that build. Figure 11-11 shows the Media Build Wizard—the Disk Type dialog box, in which the 3.5" Diskette - 1.44 MBytes disk type is selected.

EXERCISE 11-3

Building Your Disk Image for Floppy Disk-Based Distribution

1. In the project workspace, click the Media pane tab to bring up the Media tree view panel.

2. Double-click the Media Build Wizard icon in the Media panel. The Media Build Wizard dialog appears.

3. Type **Floppy Disk** in the Media Name field of the Media Build Wizard dialog. Click Next.

4. Select 3.5" Diskette - 1.44 MBytes in the Media Build Wizard - Disk Type dialog. Click the Next button.

5. Select Full Build in the Build Type group box of the Media Build Wizard - Build Type dialog. Click Next.

FIGURE 11-11

Select the disk type
for distribution

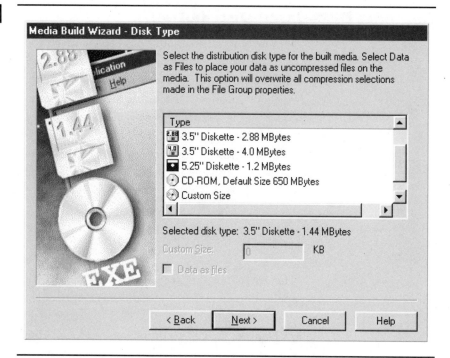

6. In the Media Build Wizard - Tag File dialog, perform the
   following actions:

   ■ Enter your company name in the Company Name text field.

   ■ Enter your application in the Application Name text field.

   ■ Select Development Tool in the Product Category field.

   ■ Leave the Misc field blank. Click Next.

7. In the Media Build Wizard - Platforms dialog, select all platforms.
   Click the Next button.

8. The Media Build Wizard - Summary dialog shows the choices and
   entries you made. Click Finish.

9. When the Media Build Wizard finishes building your disk images,
   the Finish button will come back into focus. Click Finish, and
   InstallShield will add your new disk images to the Media tree view
   in the Media panel.

Compact Disc–Based Distribution

Because of its large amount of available space, the compact disc (CD) is often the medium of choice. Both Windows 95/98 and Windows NT support the AutoRun feature so most application setups are designed to be highly automated, requiring little or no user interaction. Whenever a CD-ROM is inserted, the computer immediately checks to see if the CD-ROM has the AUTORUN.INF file. If the file exists, the computer follows the instructions contained in the file, which usually involves running a setup application of some sort. The following example shows a simple AUTORUN.INF file.

```
[AutoRun]
open=filename.exe
icon=filename.ico
```

The *open* command specifies the path and filename of the startup application. The *icon* command specifies the filename that contains the icon.

To make the CD medium, you need a CD burner (a writeable CD-ROM drive) attached to your deployment computer.

Web-Based Distribution

The Internet is an effective way of distributing an application to the end users. Deploying a package using the Web requires you to have some sort of Internet access and the necessary permissions to a directory on a Web site. You also need to set up your Internet server so that it can perform the user access and security permission check.

If you are releasing software as shareware then Web-based distribution can be seen as a must-do. This is the best way to target many millions of potential users with minimal costs. There are many repositories out on the Web that deal mainly in archiving and distributing software, such as download.com and tucows.com. You may recall that popular games, such as Doom, were released first as shareware, thus exposing them to many millions of users. Utilities that you may know, like WinZip, still are released as shareware. This benefits both the user as well as the company. The user is able to try software out before they decide to purchase it. The company has a low-cost distribution vehicle and can have many people demo (or bug test) an application, which in turn increases probability of purchases.

Network-Based Distribution

The network-based distribution is very similar to the CD-based distribution. In fact, you select the Folder option of the CD media type when you build the disk images using the Media Build Wizard. You should store the media files in a central location on your network's file server. The network administrator may set up the security permission on the folder to eliminate unauthorized installation of the files.

CERTIFICATION OBJECTIVE 11.05

Using Microsoft Systems Management Server to Distribute an Application

With network diagnostic tools and software distribution features, Microsoft Systems Management Server (SMS) allows you to automatically distribute your application. This tool also allows you to assess current client configurations and it helps in the planning and final execution of the deployment to the client's machine. The following are the components with which you need to be familiar:

- **Packages**   This is the basic unit of software distribution in the SMS architecture. A package contains all the information for deploying your applications, including command lines, schedules, configurations, and so on.

- **Programs**   Programs are sets of commands that run on clients to automate the package distribution. One or more programs are contained within the package.

- **Advertisement** A piece of information that displays the package, its programs, the schedule of when the program is available, and the computers that it is targeting for the purpose of notification.

- **Package Source Files** Files that execute the programs within the package.

- **Distribution Folder** The directory on the distribution points where the package source files are placed; these are shares on the network to which the package source files are copied. The distribution folder can be a directory on a drive or the drive itself, including a CD-ROM drive. This directory is created just like any other directory.

Physically, the machines in a network are divided into four roles to be played during the process of distributing an application—the primary site server, the distribution point, the client access point, and the targeted collection.

- **Primary Site Server** Where the System Management Server is located. A special service account is needed to run SMS.

- **Targeted Collection** The machines to which the applications need to be distributed. The Advertised Programs Client Agent must be installed at each client in the targeted collection. The Advertised Program Client Agent enables and performs the process of software distribution to the client.

- **Distribution Point** Where the distribution folder and the package source files are located. It receives the packages sent by the primary site server. At least one distribution point must be available to the targeted collection.

- **Client Access Point** A site system that provides a communication point between the site server and the clients. It receives the advertisement sent by the primary site server and passes the advertisement to the targeted collection. At least one client access point (CAP) must be available to the targeted collection for the advertised programs to run successfully.

Packages are created from the primary site server with the Systems Management Server administrator console or by obtaining a package definition file (.PDF), which automates the process, and using one of the wizards that guides the package creation process. After the package is created, it is distributed to the targeted collection of machines by using a set method. The targeted collection does not receive the package information directly from the site server. Instead, the information is mediated from the server to the clients through two gateways: the *client access point* and the *distribution point.*

In the first step of distribution, the package source files are copied to these distribution points. Next, an *advertisement* of the package is made and copied to the client access point. The target collection of machines contacts the client access point within the same network to see if the advertisement is applicable to them. If they find out that they are targeted by the advertisement, then they contact the distribution point to obtain the program and files associated with the package. Figure 11-12 gives a brief overview of the deployment process.

Systems Management Server uses the Create Package from Definition Wizard, the SMS Installer, and the Distribute Software Wizard to assist you with the deployment process of an application in a familiar, wizard-based manner. These tools are used to deploy your application, from package creation to advertisement execution, in the following steps:

- Creating packages
- Creating programs
- Creating setup programs
- Creating and distributing advertisements
- Setting up package source files and managing distribution points
- Distributing applications to the target collections

Creating Packages

You can create your distribution package either with the Distribution Wizard or manually with the Systems Management Server administrator

FIGURE 11-12

Using SMS to distribute
an application

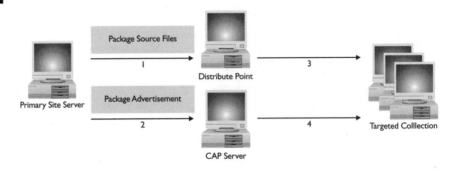

1. Administrator chooses the distribution points and SMS copies the package source files to distribution points.

2. SMS sends the package Advertisement from Primary Site Server to CAP Server.

3. The Advertised Programs Client Agent in the targeted collection recognizes the Advertisement.

4. The client agent receives the package source files and runs the command lines to install the application.

console. The steps are the same with either process. Creating a new package
involves creating a distribution folder for package source files and
determining package properties. A Systems Management Server package
contains all the files and commands that are needed to distribute the
programs in the package, as well as other information such as which
distribution points will provide the package source files to the clients.

Creating Programs

A program is required in each software distribution package. Programs are
created when a package is created. Almost any activity can be assigned to a
program. For example, a program can run batch files, copy data files,
register COM DLLs, and so on.

Creating Setup Scripts

In order to automate the distribution process, you need a setup program
that can be created with the Systems Management Server Installer. Using
the setup scripts, you can schedule your application deployment to occur
late at night so disruption to the network is minimized. For example, your

application distribution can be performed all at one time, or after hours, when the network is relatively at ease. These are useful when the program requires input; they will automatically enter the required input after you configure them.

Creating and Distributing Advertisements

The Systems Management Server advertises the package to make it available to the targeted collection. An advertisement can be created manually in the Systems Management Server administrator console or by using the Distribute Software Wizard.

Each advertisement requires a single collection, but can include members of subcollections. Systems Management Server provides some commonly used collections, but for the best result, you may need to create your own collection based on your organization's own users, user groups, and software packages.

Setting Up Package Source Files and Managing Distribution Points

The targeted collection must have access to at least one distribution point to install distributed packages. When distribution points are specified, Systems Management Server uses the original schedule specified by the administrator to determine when the package should be copied to the distribution point.

Systems Management Server ensures that a distribution point contains all the information that it needs to respond to the advertisement that the client received. If the package source files referred to by the advertisement are not already on the distribution point, then Systems Management Server sends the correspondent package to that distribution point.

Distributing Applications

The targeted collection monitors the client access point in the network to see if there is an advertisement that is applicable to it. If yes, they contact the distribution point within their site to obtain the program and files associated with the package, then automatically run the setup scripts and programs for application installation.

CERTIFICATION OBJECTIVE 11.06

Installing and Uninstalling an Application

Users may need to remove your application to make more disk space or to move the application to another location. To facilitate this, you need to provide an uninstall program with your application that removes its files and settings. Remember to remove Registry entries and shortcuts that your application may have placed in the Start menu hierarchy. You must be careful when removing your application's directory structure not to delete any user files (unless you confirm their removal with the user).

Your application must be accompanied by a setup program that has a graphical user interface (GUI). The setup program must be named SETUP.EXE so it can be identified by the Add/Remove Programs applet in Control Panel. Your application must also add entries to the system Registry specifying the command that is needed to uninstall your application. Again, this allows your uninstall program to be identified by the Add/Remove Programs applet.

When uninstalling an application, decrement the usage count in the Registry for any shared component such as a dynamic link library (DLL). If the result is zero, give the user the option to delete the shared component with the warning that other applications may use this file and will not work if it is missing.

Registering your uninstall program will display your application in the list of the Uninstall page of the Add/Remove Program utility included with Windows. To register your uninstall program, add the entries for your application to the subkey HKEY_LOCAL_MACHINE\SOFTWARE\ Microsoft\CurrentVersion\Uninstall.

Creating a Setup Program

The InstallShield for Visual C++ 6.0 comes with a built-in uninstallation program called UNINST.EXE. During setup, InstallShield automatically records events for uninstallation—the creation of files, folders, program items, and Registry entries. When uninstalling, UNINST.EXE removes any items properly created and logged by InstallShield setup.

As UNINST.EXE performs the uninstallation, a dialog box shows progress by checking off each category of uninstallable items. When uninstallation is complete, a message appears at the bottom of the uninstallation dialog box. If any items could not be removed, the message informs the user that the uninstallation was incomplete and that some items must be removed manually. Click the Details button to see a list of uninstallable items.

What UNINST.EXE Removes and What It Doesn't Remove

The UNINST.EXE program removes files, folders, program items, and Registry entries that were logged for uninstallation. It will remove read-only files, but it cannot remove files with a hidden or system attribute, except .GID, .FTG, and .FTS files created by Windows Help engines that it always removes. Any program folders, menu items, and program groups that are created and logged during setup, and are empty after UNINST.EXE has removed their contents, are also removed. UNINST.EXE cannot remove items added after InstallShield runs or folders that contain new items. The UNINST.EXE program can reverse changes made to .INI files, .BAT files, and .SYS files.

CERTIFICATION OBJECTIVE 11.07

Using Zero Administration for Windows (ZAW) to Distribute an Application

The Zero Administration Initiative for Windows (ZAW) is a key component of the Microsoft Windows Client Strategy. It refers to a set of core technologies that will give IT professionals new levels of control and manageability over their Windows-based environments by automating such tasks as operating system updates and application installation, and providing tools for central administration and desktop system lockdown. Users will be able to easily roam between different PCs without requiring their applications and files to be reinstalled each time. The Zero Administration Initiative for Windows will also enable application software developers to more easily develop and deploy a wide range of applications. All of these benefits will be realized without sacrificing compatibility with existing Windows-based software.

A number of components that support the Zero Administration Initiative for Windows are available today. These include the inventory, distribution, and remote diagnostics capabilities of Systems Management Server. In addition, new components of the Zero Administration Initiative for Windows will be delivered in Windows NT 2000. The Zero Administration Kit for Windows NT is also available for Workstation 4.0 and Windows 95/98.

You may want to ask what is the relationship of the Zero Administration Kit and the Systems Management Server product. Both the Zero Administration Kit and the Systems Management Server are part of the Zero Administration Initiative for Windows. The two products are complementary products in the sense that they are both designed to reduce the cost of desktop management. The Zero Administration Kit uses the system policies and user profiles to do the following:

- Enable administrators to lock down desktops and prevent end user operations that result in help desk calls
- Provide centralized configuration of the desktop
- Eliminate end-user access to system files and features
- Remove the ability to install unapproved applications

Systems Management Server provides distributed management for networked Windows-based PCs by providing the following:

- Hardware and software inventory
- Scheduled software distribution
- Remote diagnostics capabilities (including remote control and network monitoring)

The two technologies are complementary in that the Zero Administration Kit maintains the state of the Windows NT Workstation or Windows 95 desktop, while the Systems Management Server inventories, distributes, and diagnoses the desktop.

Now that you know more about packaging and distributing applications, here are some possible scenario questions and their answers.

QUESTIONS AND ANSWERS

What can I use to package and deploy my MFC application under the VC++ 6.0 IDE?	You can use the InstallShield Wizard for Microsoft VC++ 6.0 that is found in the Tool menu.
Normal software distribution in my company is with SMS. How do I develop a contingency deployment plan in case either SMS is unavailable or the backing SQL Server used by SMS is unavailable?	Because SMS is a network-based facility used to distribute your application, the contingency deployment plan should be to create a central folder to store your application and use a network-based distribution method.
Does the Zero Administration Kit/Zero Administration Initiative for Windows announcement mean that Systems Management Server is dead?	Absolutely not. SMS is an integral part of the Zero Administration Initiative for Windows and an important tool to help customers reduce their desktop management costs.
How can I give a user the ability to fully uninstall my application?	InstallShield comes with a built-in uninstallation program called UNINST.EXE.

CERTIFICATION SUMMARY

The InstallShield for Microsoft Visual C++ 6.0 allows you to bundle an application into an installation package, and then to deploy it to a distribution site or media. When installing your application, an .ISU file is generated for use in uninstallation. Before packaging your application, you should decide what packaging type you want. You need to gather all the files needed for the package; for example, you must include MSVCRT.DLL and MFC42.DLL for your MFC application. COM and DCOM components need to be registered in the System Registry. Two command-line switches are supported for the .EXE file: /REGSERVER and /UNREGSERVER. The .DLL files use the REGSVR32.EXE command-line utility for registration. You can use the DCOMCNFG.EXE utility to configure both clients and server DCOM components. You should package your MFC and ATL controls as signed cabinet (.CAB) files when you plan to distribute them through the Internet. You can also use ZAW and SMS together to distribute your application.

TWO-MINUTE DRILL

- ❑ Microsoft Visual C++ provides the InstallShield program, which allows you to create a setup program that copies files, registers all required components, and provides the uninstall options for removing the application.

- ❑ The InstallShield program provides a wealth of Setup Types—Compact, Typical, Network, Administrator, Network for Best Performance, and Network for Efficient Space.

- ❑ You should pay close attention to the Overwrite, FTP Location, HTTP location, Required Components, and Included File Groups fields.

- ❑ When you deploy an application, you must make sure that you include all of the COM components that you use in the application. These COM components include ActiveX controls, COM DLLs, and COM executables.

- ❑ In order for COM applications to communicate with the COM components, each COM server, control, or container must place certain information in the Windows Registry (32-bit Windows) or registration database (16-bit).

❑ Self-registering .DLLs must contain two functions, DllRegisterServer and DllUnregisterServer. When a file's DllRegisterServer function is called, it adds or updates Registry information for all the classes implemented by the .DLL, allowing COM applications to find it. When the .DLL's DllUnregisterServer function is called at uninstallation time, the DLL's information is removed from the Registry.

❑ You must register the Distributed Component Object Model (DCOM) components on both server and client machines so that the client is able to locate the DCOM server.

❑ When registering a DCOM component you need to ensure that the client side can map their program name (ProgID) to an identifier (CLSID) that can be used again.

❑ While running the DCOMCNFG.EXE on Windows 95/98, you must set the access control to User Level using the Network applet in Control Panel. User-level access control determines the security model that will be used by the operating system. The machine should be connected to a network with a Windows NT domain controller that can be used to provide pass-through security, so that COM security can be enabled.

❑ The Properties dialog box consists of the General, Location, Security, Identity, and Endpoints tabs. The General tab confirms the application that you are working with. The Location tab allows you to specify where the application should run when a client calls *CoCreateInstance* on the relevant *CLSID*. The Security tab is similar to the Default Security page found in the DCOMCNFG window, except that these settings apply only to the current application. The Identify tab identifies which user is used to run the application.

❑ A cabinet is a single file, usually with a .CAB extension, that stores compressed files in a file library.

❑ The .INF file is an ASCII text file that lists the files, for example a .DLL, that you will need to download or already have so that your control can run.

❑ The UNINST.EXE program removes files, folders, program items, and Registry entries that were logged for uninstallation. It will remove read-only files, but it cannot remove files with a hidden or system attribute, except .GID, .FTG, and .FTS files created by Windows Help engines that it always removes.

SELF TEST

The following questions will help you measure your understanding of the material presented in this chapter. Read all of the choices carefully, as there may be more than one correct answer. Choose all correct answers for each question.

1. You have developed an application that is composed of one executable, several COM DLLs, a help system, and a bundle of sample projects. You're using the InstallShield for Microsoft Visual C++ 6.0 utility to create a setup program.
Required results: The setup program ensures that the application is running on the users' machine without further effort after installation, and can be uninstalled using the Add/Remove Programs applet on Control Panel.
Optional Results: The files should be checked before overwriting. Overwrite a file only if the source has both a newer or the same date and a newer or the same version compared to the one on the user's computer. Upon uninstalling, the COM DLL files need be unregistered and removed.
Proposed Solution: Use the InstallShield Wizard from the Tool menu. Choose Windows 95, Windows 98, and Windows NT 4.0 on the Project Wizard - Choose Target Platforms dialog box. Create four components: Program Files, Example Files, Help Files, and Shared DLLs, and

   four file groups with the same names. Link the executable file of the application to the Program File group. Link the Help file to the Help File group. Link the four DLLs in the application into the Share Files group, and the example projects files to the Example Files group. In the Components-Program Files dialog box, modify the Overwrite field to SAMEORNEWERVERSION/SAMEOR NEWERDATE. In the File Groups - Shared DLL dialog box, modify the Self-Registered field to Yes.

   A. The proposed solution meets the required result and both optional results.

   B. The proposed solution meets the required result and only one optional result.

   C. The proposed solution meets the required result and none of the optional results.

   D. The proposed solution does not meet the required result.

2. Which utility enables you to find out all the dependency files for your applications? (Choose all that apply.)

   A. QuickView

   B. DumpBin

   C. Depends

   D. APIViewer

3. Which function(s) must a self-registered DLL component contain? (Choose all that apply.)

   A. DllRegisterServer

   B. DllUnregisterServer

   C. RegServer

   D. UnRegServer

4. Which command line argument(s) must a self-registered .EXE component support? (Choose all that apply.)

   A. /DllRegisterServer

   B. /DllUnregisterServer

   C. /RegServer

   D. /UnRegServer

5. You need to register a DCOM component. Which of the following steps must you perform? (Choose all that apply.)

   A. Install the DCOM component on the server computer

   B. Register the DCOM component on the server computer

   C. Register the DCOM component on the client computer

   D. Configure the DCOM setting using the DCOMCNFG utility

6. You want clients on the other machines in the same domain to access DCOM objects running on the NT server computer DCOMSERVER. How do you do this?

   A. Modify the NT access permission to let everyone run an application

   B. Register the DSCOM object on the clients' System Registry with RemoteServerName value set to DCOMSERVER

   C. Change the HKEY_LOCAL_MACHINE\ Software\Microsoft\DCOM\EnableD COM value to Y in the DCOMSERVER's System Registry

   D. Select the Enable Distributed COM on this Computer check box on DCOMSERVER

7. As administrator, you used DCOMCNFG.EXE to set up a DCOM component called YourApp's Security. You denied access permission to the user called Bruce. You made sure that you set it up right by checking the Registry setting. Later on, you noticed that Bruce is still able to access YourAPP. Why?

   A. You set access permission of the Managers group, to which Bruce belongs, to Allow Access.

   B. YourApp calls the CoInitializeEx to overwrite Bruce's access permission.

   C. YourApp calls the CoInitializeSecurity to overwrite Bruce's access permission.

   D. None of the above.

8. What does the CODEBASE point to? (Choose all that apply.)

   A. .OCX file

   B. .DLL file

   C. .CAB file

   D. .EXE file

9. To create a .CAB file, which file do you need to create first?

   A. .DDF file

   B. .INF file

   C. .DEF file

   D. .OCX file

10. You're embedding your ATL controls on a Web page, so users are able to download if it's new, and running on the user's machine. How can you make sure that upon downloading of your ATL control, your ATL control does register by itself?

    A. Add the SelfRegister tag into the Web page containing your control.

    B. Use the command line argument /SelfRegister of the Cabarc ultity to make a .CAB file.

    C. Create an .INF file with the RegisterServer value set to *yes* under your control's section, and make a .CAB file based on it.

    D. You need do nothing; the control will self-register automatically upon its downloading to the client's machine.

11. During installation, the file called UNINST.ISU is created. Where is this file stored on the user's hard disk and why?

    A. The application directory, for use in uninstalling the application

    B. The system directory, for use in uninstalling the application

    C. The root directory, for logging the success or failure of installation

    D. The system directory, for logging the success or failure of installation

12. You intend to create a .CAB file embedded in a Web page for your control. The control includes two DLLs: First.DLL and Second.DLL. First.DLL goes first. You've created an .INF file, MYCONTROL.INF, indicating the order. What do you type on the command line now?

    A. Cabarc n MyControl.Inf First.DLL Second.DLL

    B. Cabarc n First.DLL Second.DLL MyControl.Inf

    C. Cabarc n Second.DLL First.DLL MyControl.Inf

    D. The order doesn't matter for the Cabarc utility

13. Bruce works on his desktop computer running Windows 98. The company deployed distributed accounting software using the DCOM technology. As administrator in the company, you try to configure and manage the security of the DCOM application on Bruce's computer. What type of security level must be set?

    A. Windows 98 doesn't support DCOM security

    B. Account level

    C. User level

    D. Share level

14. What authentication level for your DCOM server do you set if you want security checking to occur on every call for the duration of the connection?

    A. Default

    B. Connect

C. Call

D. Package

15. What is the default distribution method when you use the InstallShield to distribute your application?

   A. Floppy disk–based.

   B. Compact disc–based

   C. Web-based

   D. Network-based

16. What is the basic unit of software distribution for using the Systems Management Server to deploy your application?

   A. Packages

   B. Programs

   C. Package Source Files

   D. Distribution Folder

17. What is the tool or wizard of the Systems Management Server that is used to create the .PDF (Package Definition File) file?

   A. The Distribute Software Wizard

   B. The Systems Management Server Installer

   C. The Manage Distribution Points Wizard

   D. Advertised Programs Client Agent

18. You deployed a database application called FancyApp using the InstallShield for Visual C++ 6.0 onto a user's desktop under C:\program files\your company\fancyapp. The application is loaded with features of sample projects, Help systems, COM components, and dynamic link libraries. The user has worked on the application for a full year, and has created several useful database projects under C:\program files\your company\fancyapp\my projects. Now you want to uninstall the software in order to use another application.

Required results: The data files in My Projects must not be removed.

Optional Results: All the other files related to FancyApp, including the executables, sample databases, Help files, the DLLs, and the entries in the System Registry should be removed. Also the .GID, .FTG, and .FTS files created by Windows Help engines should be removed.

Proposed Solution: Use the Add/Remove Programs applet in Control Panel, select the FancyApp application, and click Remove.

   A. The proposed solution meets the required result and all optional results.

   B. The proposed solution meets the required result and only one optional result.

   C. The proposed solution meets the required result and none of the optional results.

   D. The proposed solution does not meet the required result.

19. In order to utilize the Add/Remove Programs utility to remove your application called YourApp, which key do you need to register your uninstallation program under?

A. HKEY_LOCAL_MACHINE\
SOFTWARE\Microsoft\
CurrentVersion\Uninstall\YourApp

B. HKEY_LOCAL_MACHINE\
SOFTWARE\YourApp\Uninstall

C. HKEY_CURRENT_USER\
SOFTWARE\Microsoft\
CurrentVersion\Uninstall\YourApp

D. HKEY_CURRENT_USER\
SOFTWARE\YourApp\Uninstall

20. What are the minimum requirements to perform ZAW tasks on your company's Windows NT 4.0 network? (Choose all that apply.)

A. The Zero Administration Kit for Windows NT

B. The Systems Management Server

C. The SQL Server

D. The Exchange Server

SELF TEST ANSWERS

1. **B.** The proposed solution does not meet the second optional result because even if you have modified the Self-Registered variable of the Shared DLL file groups to Yes, the default Shared field is No. The component files can be unregistered only when both the Shared and Self-Registered Fields are set to Yes.

2. **A, B, C.** The QuickView, DumpBin and Depends utilities enable you find out the dependency files for your application. APIView is a utility for viewing Win32 API constants, declarations, and types.

3. **A, B.** Self-registered DLLs must contain two functions, DllRegisterServer and DllUnregisterServer.

4. **C, D.** Self-registered .EXEs must support two command line arguments, /RegServer and /UnregServer.

5. **A, B, C, D.** All the steps are needed in order to allow the client and server to communicate.

6. **D.** If you want the clients to access DCOM objects on your machine, you must select the Enable Distributed COM on this Computer check box, which sets the HKEY_LOCAL_MACHINE\Software\Microsoft\OLE\EnableDCOM value to Y.

7. **C.** The application-wide settings that you set in the Registry using DCOMCNFG.EXE will be overridden if a client calls CoInitializeSecurity to set security for a particular interface proxy.

8. **A, B, C.** When you use the OBJECT tag to embed a control in a Web page, you use CODEBASE to point to the location from which to download the control. CODEBASE can point to .CAB, .OCX, and .DLL file types successfully.

9. **B.** The .INF file is a text file that specifies the files (such as .DLLs or other. OCXs) that need to be present or downloaded for your control to run. An .INF file allows you to bundle all the needed files in one compressed .CAB file.

10. **C.** .INF files allow you to specify your control to be self-registered with the RegisterServer key-value set.

11. **A.** UNINST.ISU is created in the application directory and is used for uninstalling the application.

12. **B.** The order for the Calarc utility does matter, You should order your control .DLL so that the first one called goes first. The .INF file should be placed at the end.

13. **C.** User-level security must be set so that the Windows 98 machine can be connected to a network with a Windows NT domain controller that can be used to provide pass-through security, so that COM security can be enabled.

14. **C.** The Call level. Call level means the security checking occurs on every call for the duration of the connection. Connect levels do the security checking for only the initial connection. Packet security checking means that the sender's identity is encrypted to ensure the authenticity of the sender.

15. **B.** Compact disc-based distribution is the default method for InstallShield.

16. **A.** A package is the basic unit of software distribution when using SMS.

17. **B.** The Systems Management Server Installer is used to create the .PDF file, which is a script and a compressed executable file that is distributed to distribution points, client access points, and the clients.

18. **A.** The proposed solution meets the required result and all the optional results because the unInstallShield program removes files, folders, program items, and Registry entries that were logged for uninstallation, It also removes the .GID, .FTG, and .FTS files created by Windows Help engines. It doesn't remove the files generated after installation.

19. **B.** In order to utilize the Add/Remove Programs utility to remove your application called YourApp, you need to register your uninstallation program under HKEY_LOCAL_MACHINE\SOFTWARE\Microsoft\CurrentVersion\Uninstall\YourApp.

20. **A, B, C.** You need The ZAW Kit for Windows NT, SMS, and SQL Server to perform ZAW tasks.

12

Maintaining and Supporting an Application

I n an Enterprise environment, your system has to be able to handle the load as usage increases. As more resources are required to support your users, you will have to provide the extra resources or your users will not be happy. This can be done using load balancing.

Errors are a fact of life for programmers. Even the best-designed programs will have some errors that have to be fixed. Sometimes errors can take longer to fix than it took to write the original code that you are fixing. This is why testing is a very important part of the development process. Depending on the complexity of your program, errors might not even appear until long after your program has been released. If an error is fixed after your program has been released, then you will need to create an update. It has become a common occurrence to release updates to an application. Microsoft routinely releases service packs to update its products. Updates can fix errors as well as make changes to business rules.

In this chapter, we will discuss static load balancing, some common errors and how to fix them, how to prevent future errors, and how to distribute an update to your application. These concepts are applicable to the exam as well as on the job.

CERTIFICATION OBJECTIVE 12.01

Implementing Static Load Balancing

As the usage of your distributed application increases, you need to provide your users with the extra resources needed to handle the extra load. If you have a great application and you have an increasing demand to use it, you do not want to upset the users by not being able to support them all.

If your application uses Component Object Model (COM) objects that are maintained by Microsoft Transaction Server (MTS), then you can place these objects on multiple servers and have your customers use the COM objects from different servers to help balance the load. There are two different types of load balancing, dynamic and static.

Dynamic load balancing uses an algorithm to determine the load on each server. As each new request comes in, it determines the best server to use to service the request and automatically redirects the request to that server. Currently, MTS does not support dynamic load balancing for COM objects. Microsoft is developing dynamic load balancing as part of the COM+ specification using MTS and Windows NT Clustering Services.

Static load balancing is a manual process. You will make the COM objects available on multiple MTS servers and then manually set up your users to use the different servers. You will have to determine which users will use each server. This will require a judgement on which users will use the COM objects the most and try to determine how to distribute the load. This is not the best method, and it can be tedious work, but it is better than having your users getting timeouts when trying to use the COM objects. To implement static load balancing, you will need to make the COM objects available on the servers that you plan on using to balance the load and then set up each user to use the appropriate server. We will discuss how to use MTS to implement load balancing statically.

To make the COM objects available on multiple servers, you will need to install the package on the other servers. You can do this by exporting the package and installing it on the remote computer. By exporting the package, you can copy a package from the local MTS computer and install it on another server that you are using for load balancing. Packages are exported using MTS Explorer. When packages are exported, a package file is created. This file has the extension of .PAK. It contains information about the components and roles that belong to the package being exported. It also contains information about the component files for the package. These files are copied to the same directory as the package file. Keep in mind that if a component's class ID (CLSID) or interface identifier (IID) is changed after exporting the package, you need to export the package again to reflect the changes. When making the exported package file available for installation on other computers, make sure you copy the package file and all the files in the directory to whatever media you are using. Typically, you would copy it to a shared network folder and install it on all the other servers from there. To import a package on the other servers, use the Package Wizard. The Package Wizard can be started by right-clicking the

Packages Installed folder and selecting New | Package, or from the Action menu, selecting New | Package. In the wizard, choose the Install Pre-Built Packages option. This will allow you to browse for the .PAK file of the package that you want to install. Another way to import a package is from Windows Explorer: drag the .PAK file into the right pane of MTS Explorer when Packages Installed is selected in the left pane.

When you export a package, it generates an MTS executable that will install and configure a user's computer to access the component. The executable is placed in a subfolder called Clients that is automatically created when the package is exported. The user's computer that will be using the component must have Distributed COM (DCOM) support enabled, but it doesn't require any MTS server files other than the executable generated to access the MTS component on the server. To implement the static load balancing, you will create a separate export package for each server that will be used for load balancing. You need to divide up the users between the servers based on your load projections. You can either go to each server and export the package to create the different client executables, or you can create the client executables from the same server, but change the server name to be used by the client. This is done from the Options tab of the Properties dialog for My Computer in MTS Explorer. In the Replication frame, enter the server name to use in the Remote server name field. Be careful not to run the client executable on the MTS server computer because it will overwrite the MTS settings in the Registry and it will not work correctly in MTS. If you do this by mistake, you must delete the package from MTS, uninstall the package from Control Panel, Add/Remove Programs, and then reinstall the package in MTS. In Exercise 12-1, we will walk though exporting and importing a package and creating the client executable to another server.

EXERCISE 12-1

Exporting a Package in MTS

1. Start Microsoft Transaction Server Explorer.

2. If the tree view in the left pane is not expanded, double-click the Console Root folder icon. To expand a node in the tree view display, you can either double-click the folder or click the plus sign. Expand Microsoft Transaction Server, Computers, My Computer, and Packages Installed.

3. First we will create an empty package to use. In the left pane, right-click the Packages Installed folder and select New | Package to bring up the Package Wizard.

4. Click the Create Empty Package button to bring up the Create Empty Package dialog box.

5. Type **Chap12_1** in the Name field.

6. Click the Next button to bring up the Set Package Identity dialog box.

7. We will use the default, Interactive User—the current user logged on. Click the Finish button to create the package. A package named Chap12_1 should now be available in the left and right panes, as shown in Figure 12-1.

8. Before we export the package, let's set it up to configure the client to use a different server. Select the My Computer icon. To set the remote server name, you can either right-click it and select Properties, or from the Action menu select Properties to bring up the My Computer Properties dialog box.

FIGURE 12-1

The MTS Explorer shows a new package that we created with the Package Wizard

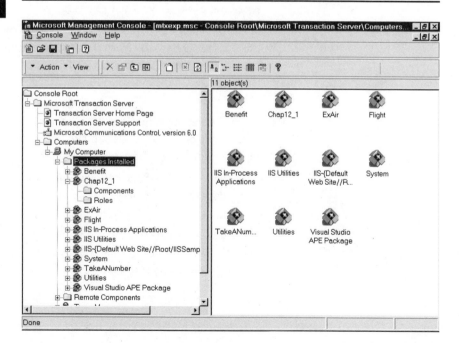

9. Click the Options tab. In the Replication frame, type **LoadBalancingServer** in the Remote Server Name field.

10. Click OK to accept the change.

11. Now we will export the package that we just created. Keep in mind that there are no components in the package, but they are not necessary for the exercise.

12. Select the Chap12_1 package from the left pane of the Explorer. You can either right-click it and select Export, or from the Action menu, select Export to bring up the Export Package dialog box.

13. Type **C:\CHAP_12_1\Chap12_1.PAK** in the Package File field. It will automatically add the extension .PAK to the end of the package file name if you do not enter it. The component files will be copied to the same directory as the package file. If you want to export the roles for the package, select the Save Windows NT User IDs Associated with Roles check box.

14. Click the Export button to create the files to export your package. Now that we have created an export package, we need to import it. For this exercise, we will just delete the package from MTS and then install the package we just exported.

15. Select the Chap12_1 package. To delete it, you can either right-click it and select Delete, or from the Action menu, select Delete. When the Confirm Item Delete message box pops up, click the Yes button. The package Chap12_1 is no longer available in the Packages Installed folder.

16. Select the Packages Installed folder. To install the package, you can either right-click it and select New | Package, or from the Action menu, select New | Package. This will bring up the Package Wizard.

17. Click the Install Pre-Built Packages button. This will bring up the Select Package Files dialog box.

18. Click the Add button. This will bring up a standard File Open dialog box. Browse to the C:\Chap12_1 directory. Select the CHAP12_1.PAK file and click the Open button. The package file is now in the list, as shown in Figure 12-2.

Use the Select Package
Files dialog box to find the
package files to install

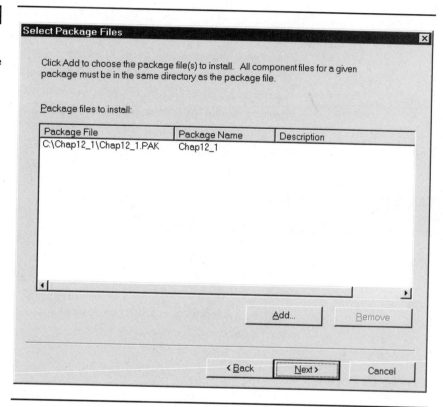

19. Click the Next button. This will bring up the Set Package Identity dialog. We will use the default, Interactive User—the current logged on user.

20. Click the Next button. This will bring up the Installation Options dialog box. The Install directory should default to \program files\mts\packages. We will use the default.

21. Click the Finish button. This will install the package. The Chap12_1 package is now available in the Packages Installed folder.

There are several ways to distribute the client configuration executable. You can share a directory to which your users have access. You can send an e-mail with the executable as an attachment that clients can save on their computers. You can push the executable to the client using Systems Management Server (SMS). Or you can make it available on a Web site. However you distribute the client executable, the clients need to run it on their computers to configure the client computer to use the component from the MTS server.

Fixing Errors

There are three basic types of errors in programming: logic, syntax, and runtime. Each type of error has to be dealt with differently and you need to understand the differences among them.

Logic Errors

Logic errors are often the cause when the results of your program are not what you expected. This situation is commonly referred to as a *bug* in the code. The application will compile and run without any problems, but the code does not perform the expected task. For example, let's say you are trying to delete customers from a database who have not placed an order in one year, but instead, your application deletes all of the customers who have placed an order from you in the past year. This would definitely cause some problems. The code didn't cause your application to generate a runtime error, but it is a more critical error as far as the people using your application are concerned.

So, how do we find logic errors? You can find some through code reviews and walkthroughs, but the best way is to test your program. We discussed the different types of testing and debugging techniques in Chapter 10. You should perform unit testing before integrating the unit with other modules. Then your application should go through beta testing. This allows independent testing of your application. As errors are found, you can use the debugging techniques discussed in Chapter 10 to assist you in determining where the error is. Breakpoints, the TRACE macro, and assertions can help you see intermediate values. Breakpoints allow you to pause program execution at the lines of code that you suspect contain errors and then walk through the code and view data and conditions at intermediate steps. The TRACE macro will write information that you specify to the Debug window. You can use assertions to find logical errors in your code. Assertions are not error handlers, but a debugging tool to check expressions. For example, in the following code, a function returns a value. If the function returns a negative number, it wouldn't cause an error; however, if your logic didn't expect negative values, your results could be inconsistent. By using the ASSERT macro, you can check for logic errors.

```
int x = ReturnValueFunction(y);
ASSERT(x >= 0);
```

Syntax Errors

Syntax errors are the result of using the programming language incorrectly. You might have forgotten a bracket, misspelled a keyword or variable, or didn't include the correct parameters in a function call. There are many different ways to create syntax errors. When you compile your program, you will receive compile errors telling you the line of code on which the error occurred. Of course, this isn't necessarily the actual line where the error occurred, just where the compiler found an error. You will have to find these errors and fix them in order to compile your program.

Visual C++ 6.0 offers some features to help you prevent syntax errors. These options can be selected by clicking the Tools menu and then clicking Options. Click the Editor tab to see the Options dialog box, as shown in Figure 12-3.

The Auto List Members option will display a list of methods and properties when you type a period (.) or an arrow (->) after a valid variable that is a structure or an object. You can select the desired method or property and not have to worry about spelling errors because it will insert the name of the method or property for you. As shown in the following

FIGURE 12-3

Choose syntax features
from the Options
dialog box

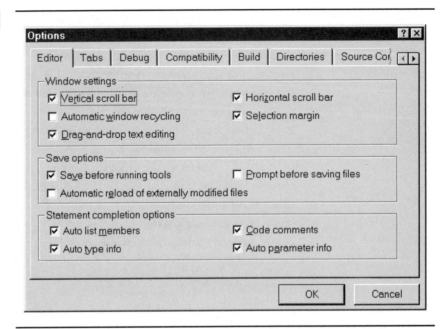

illustration, we are using a structure that contains service status information. When we type the variable name for that structure, **m_status**, and then type . (period), we get a list of the contents of that structure. You no longer have to go and look it up in the header file or in Help.

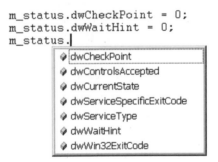

```
m_status.dwCheckPoint = 0;
m_status.dwWaitHint = 0;
m_status.|
```

Auto Type Info allows you to view type information for a variable by placing the pointer over it. Using the m_status structure variable, as shown here, you can see that by placing the pointer over the variable we get information about the variable, including the type of variable and the class that it belongs to.

```
m_status.dwCheckPoint = 0;
m_status.dwWaitHint = 0;
```

```
_SERVICE_STATUS CServiceModule::m_status
```

Auto Parameter Info will display the parameters required for a function. This will assist you in determining which parameters are needed as well as the parameter data types and return data type. Using a class variable, as shown next, you can see that when the open parenthesis is typed, we get the information for the method. It displays the return type as well as the parameters and their types for the method.

```
res = _Module.GetClassObject(
```

```
HRESULT GetClassObject (REFCLSID rclsid, REFIID riid, LPVOID *ppv)
```

Syntax coloring uses different colors for various code elements, such as keywords or comments. This can give you some visual representation of your code. You can even define some custom keywords that you would like to have in color, and what color you want them. If this book were printed in color, you would see in the following listing that the keywords *else, while, if,* and *break* are different colors and the code and the comments are another color. If you type the following code in a source code file in Visual C++ 6.0, you can see the different colors used.

```
else
{
    pTrav = pHead->Next;
    while (pTrav)
    {
        /* insert at end of queue */
        if (pTrav->Next == NULL)
        {
            pTrav->Next = pNewNode;
            pNewNode->Next = NULL;
            break;
        } /* if */
        /* insert in middle of queue */
        else if (pTrav->Data->Priority > pTrav->Next->Data->Priority)
        {
            pPrev->Next = pNewNode;
            pNewNode->Next = pTrav;
        } /* else if */
        /* look at next node */
        else
        {
            pPrev = pTrav;
            pTrav = pTrav->Next;
        } /* else */
    } /* while */
} /*else */
```

Runtime Errors

Runtime errors are errors that occur while the application is running. These can be errors that occur due to an invalid action (using a pointer that you haven't allocated memory for), invalid data (dividing by a variable with a value of zero), or system conditions that prevent an action from occurring (out of memory or out of disk space). There are different methods for fixing runtime errors. Which method you use depends on what kind of error you are fixing.

Another use of assertion statements is to test for error conditions. Assertion statements should not be used to replace error-handling code. You should use assertion statements to check for errors in your code where errors should have been handled by the preceding code. In the following example, a function returns zero if it succeeds and it returns a negative number to indicate an error code if an error occurs. What if the function returned a positive number? The error-checking code does not account for it. Using the ASSERT macro, you can check to see if that is a condition that is occurring. If the function returns a positive value, then the Assertion dialog box will appear. You should use assertions anywhere in your program that an assumption is being made. As an example, use an assertion anywhere that you rely on the data being a certain range of values or non-NULL.

```
res = myFunction(x);
/* Code to handle errors */
if (res < 0)
{
/*handle error*/
}
ASSERT(res <= 0);
```

You can also use breakpoints to assist you in finding errors. Place breakpoints in the code that you suspect and then step through the code to find where an unexpected result is located. The Watch window or Quick Watch can be used to view variable and expression values. These techniques were discussed in more detail in Chapter 10.

CERTIFICATION OBJECTIVE 12.03

Preventing Future Errors

To prevent errors from happening after you distribute your application, you need to implement error trapping and handling. This will require you to write good error checking that anticipates problems or conditions that are not under the control of your application and that will cause your program to execute incorrectly at runtime. This should be accomplished largely during the planning and design phase of your application. It requires a thorough understanding of how your application should work and the anomalies that can pop up at runtime.

For runtime errors that occur because of conditions that are beyond a program's control, you should use exception handling and check for common problems before executing an action. An example of checking for errors would be to make sure there is a floppy disk in the drive before trying to write to it or make sure a file is there before trying to read from it. An example of when to use exception handling would be retrieving a recordset from a database. You might have a valid connection, but something might have happened after your connection to cause the retrieval of a recordset to fail. You could use exception handling to trap this error rather than having a cryptic message appear and then having to quit your application.

Exceptions should be used to prevent your application from quitting. We will cover the exception handling that is provided by the C++ programming language and the Microsoft Foundation Class Library (MFC). They provide support for handling runtime errors, called exceptions, which can occur when your program is running. Using exception handling, your program can take steps to recover from abnormal events outside your program's control rather than crashing your application. These exceptions are handled by code that is not run during normal execution. Exceptions can be handled by throwing and catching exceptions. When an exception is raised, it is called "throwing" it. When you create an exception handler, it will then "catch" the exception.

To enable the C++ programming language exception handling, click the Project menu and then select Settings to bring up the Project Settings dialog box. Go to the C/C++ tab and select C++ Language in the Category box, as seen in Figure 12-4, or you can use the /GX compiler option.

Now that we have enabled exception handling, let's look at how to implement it using the C++ programming language. You use the *try*, *catch*, and *throw* keywords for exception handling. The syntax is as follows:

```
try-block :
try {
    code to handle exceptions for
    (code that is vulnerable to throwing exceptions)
}
catch-block :
catch ( exception-declaration )
{
    code to handle the exception
}
throw-expression :
throw assignment-expressionopt
```

FIGURE 12-4

Enable C++ exception handling from the Project Settings dialog box

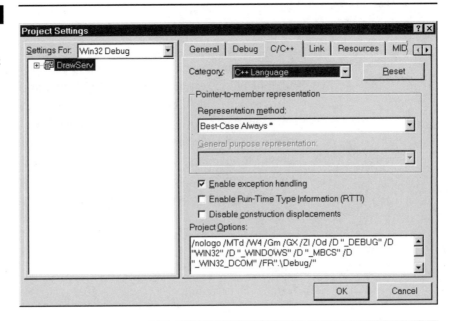

The *try* keyword basically turns the exception handler on. This is code that you believe is susceptible to errors and could cause an exception. The compound statement following the try keyword is the "guarded" section of code. If an exception occurs inside the guarded code, it will throw an exception that can then be caught, allowing your code to handle it appropriately. The catch keyword allows you to handle the exception. You can use multiple catch blocks to handle specific exceptions by placing an argument in the exception-declaration statement that indicates the type of exception the clause handles. The type can be any valid data type, including a C++ class. You can use an ellipsis (…) as the exception-declaration, which will catch all exceptions. The catch handlers are examined in order of their appearance following the try block. This is important to remember for the exam. If the first catch uses the ellipsis, it will always catch the exception, and any handlers after it will never be used. The throw keyword raises the exception. The assignment-expression can be any valid data type, including a C++ class. If the assignment-expression is blank, it throws the current exception. In the following code, we are calling the function SomeFunction. Inside SomeFunction, if the variable x equals zero, then an exception is thrown with a value of 10. If the variable x is a negative number, then it raises an exception with a string to identify the exception.

```
void SomeFunction(int x)
{
  if (x == 0)
    throw (10); //throw a specific error code
  if (x < 0)
    throw ("Negative Number");//throw an error string
}
main(){
  int x;
  try {
    SomeFunction(x);
  }
  catch(int& I){
    //An integer is caught
  }
  catch(…){
    //catch anything that can be thrown. Any primitive type and object
  }
}
```

You can also implement exception handling using the MFC exception macros. Microsoft recommends using the exception handling supported by the C++ language. It is recommended to convert existing code using the MFC exception macros to the C++ language exception handling. Converting to C++ exception handling results in smaller executables and it has more flexibility in the types of exceptions that can be handled. You do need to understand how the MFC macros work though.

The syntax for the MFC exception handling is a little more extensive than the C++ language, but it is similar to the C++ exceptions. The syntax for the MFC exception handling is as follows:

```
Try Block:
TRY
{
   code to handle exceptions for
  (code that is vulnerable to throwing exceptions)
}
Catch Blocks:
CATCH (exception class, exception object pointer name)
{
   code to handle an exception
}
AND_CATCH(exception-declaration)
{
   code to handle another exception
}
END_CATCH

or

Try Block:
TRY
{
   code to handle exceptions for
  (code that is vulnerable to throwing exceptions)
}
Catch Block:
CATCH_ALL(exception object pointer name)
{
   code to handle all other exceptions
}
END_CATCH_ALL
```

```
or
Try Block:
TRY
{
   code to handle exceptions for
  (code that is vulnerable to throwing exceptions)
}
Catch Blocks:
CATCH (exception class, exception object pointer name)
{
   code to handle an exception
}
AND_CATCH(exception-declaration)
{
   code to handle another exception
}
AND_CATCH_ALL(exception object pointer name)
{
   code to handle all other exceptions
}
END_CATCH_ALL

Throw statements:
THROW(exception object pointer)
THROW_LAST()
```

Notice the exception handler is terminated with the END_CATCH_ALL macro. If there wasn't a CATCH_ALL or an AND_CATCH_ALL macro, then the exception handler would end with the macro END_CATCH. Also, if the only catch block is a "catch all" type, the syntax would be CATCH_ALL instead of AND_CATCH_ALL. If there is more than one catch macro after the first catch macro, you add AND_ in front of it. Also notice the syntax is a little different for the catch macro arguments. For the CATCH macros, you pass in two parameters, the exception class type to catch and a name for the pointer to the exception object. The CATCH_ALL macros only have one parameter, the name for the pointer to the exception object. The THROW macro throws a specified exception. The THROW_LAST macro re-throws the locally created exception to an outer exception handler. Another difference is that you have to throw and catch CException objects or objects derived from it. You cannot throw just any data type as you could in the C++ language. Let's look at an example.

The following example attempts to open a file using the CFile class that reads data from the file. If the file did not open correctly, then the CATCH block, using the CFileException type, would handle the error. If any other exception types occurred, then the AND_CATCH_ALL handler would handle them. Of course, it would be better programming practice to check to see if the file is open before attempting to read from it and allow the user to choose another file.

```
CFile f;
char* pFileName = "test.dat";
char buf[100];

TRY
{
  f.Open( pFileName, CFile::modeWrite );
  f.Read( buf, 99 );
}
CATCH(CFileException, e)
{
  AfxMessageBox("Error opening file.");
  f.Abort();
  e->Delete();
}
AND_CATCH_ALL( e )
{
 THROW_LAST();
}
END_CATCH_ALL
```

As stated earlier, a catch block in the C++ programming language can take an argument of just about any data type, but MFC exception handlers can only handle exceptions from the CException class. MFC functions throw exceptions of the class CException, or classes derived from it. You use a variable that is a pointer to a CException object so that you can see more information about the exception. The information available depends on the exception class used. As an example, you can use the CFileException class to determine exceptions caused by file input/output (I/O) operations. The class has an m_cause member that can be used to determine the cause of a file I/O exception. See the following code for an example. The example uses the classes enumerated types of fileNotFound as a possible value in the m_cause member. Notice that the exception is freed in the catch block. You must delete an exception object in a catch block whenever a catch block throws a new exception. If it re-throws the same exception, do not delete it. You also need to delete an exception if the catch block just returns to normal execution. Exceptions are deleted using the Delete method of the exception class as shown in the following example.

```
try
{
  //code for doing File operations
}
catch( CFileException* e)
{
  if( e->m_cause == CFileException::fileNotFound )
    AfxMessageBox("The file could not be found.");
  e->Delete();
}
```

If you use the CATCH_ALL or the catch(...) handler, you can determine what type of exception occurred by using the IsKindOf method, which takes an argument for a pointer to the class structure. You can use the RUNTIME_CLASS macro to return the class structure of a class type. In the following example, instead of a CATCH statement looking for a CFileException type, we determine the exception type using the IsKindOf method of the CException class.

```
try
{
  //code for doing File operations
}
CATCH_ALL( e )
{
  if ( e->IsKindOf(RUNTIME_CLASS( CFileException )))
  {
    f.Abort();
    AfxMessageBox("Error opening file.");
  }
  else
    AfxMessageBox("Other error.");
  e->Delete;
}
```

There are some exception classes derived from the CException class that are provided by the MFC. To throw these specific exception types, use the throw exception functions. Table 12-1 lists the classes and throw functions.

Exception handlers can be nested. Nested exception handlers can be thought of like the call stack. When you return from an inner exception handler, the executing code is now guarded by the handler that is next on the stack. If your handler throws an exception, it will be caught by the next outer-level handler. A catch block can throw a different exception or re-throw the caught exception using the throw keyword with no argument to let an outer-level exception handler handle the exception. If there isn't an exception handler to catch it, your program will quit. Exceptions are also

| **TABLE 12-1** | MFC Exception Classes Derived from the CException Class | |

Exception Class	Throw Function	Use
CMemoryException	AfxThrowMemoryException	Out of memory conditions when using the new operator
CFileException	AfxThrowFileException	File exceptions when using the CFile class
CArchiveException	AfxThrowArchiveException	Serialization exceptions when using the CArchive class
CNotSupportedException	AfxThrowNotSupportedException	Exception from request for unsupported service
CResourceException	AfxThrowResourceException	Exception from a Windows resource request that cannot be allocated or found
CDAOException	AfxThrowDAOException	Exceptions from a DAO class database's operations
CDBException	AfxThrowDBException	Exceptions from an ODBC class database's operations
COleException	AfxThrowOleException	Exceptions from OLE operations
COleDispatchException	AfxThrowOleDispatchException	Exceptions from OLE operations that use the Idispatch interface
CUserException	AfxThrowUserException	Exceptions that are specific to an application

handled in a *calling chain*. If a function calls other functions, and one of the called functions has an exception without an exception handler, then it will be passed up the chain of functions.

The calling chain works as follows: if a procedure has an exception without a handler, it passes the exception up the calling chain to the procedure that called it until it finds one that has an exception handler. For example, in the following code, the only exception handler is in proc1.

```
void proc1()
{
    try
    {
        proc2();
    }
    catch(...)
    {
        //handle exception
    }
    return 0;
}

void proc2()
{
    proc3();
}

void proc3()
{
    throw 1;
}
```

If proc1 calls proc2, which calls proc3, when an exception is thrown in proc3, it checks for an exception handler in proc3. When it doesn't find one, it goes up the calling chain to proc2. When it doesn't find an exception handler there, it goes up the calling chain again to proc1. There is an exception handler here, so the exception can then be handled by the catch blocks. If no exception handler is found, a message box is displayed and the program ends. Also, if an exception occurs inside a catch block, the exception will be passed up the calling chain. Any code in the handler that came after the exception would not be executed. This is also true if you use a throw statement to re-throw an exception. Because exceptions can occur inside a catch block, be sure to keep exception handlers simple. Analyze the code for possible problem areas and be sure to test it thoroughly. You could also call functions within the handler that contains exception handling, and those functions could provide exception handling for your handler, but that isn't good practice. Take extra care when developing your exception handlers. Exercise 12-2 shows how exception handlers work.

EXERCISE 12-2

Using Exception Handlers

1. Create a new Win32 Console Application project named **Chap12_2**.

2. When asked What kind of Console Application?, select A Hello World Application.

3. Open the CHAP12_2.CPP file.

4. Add the following functions:

```
int Func2(int x)
{
  int res = 0;

  try
  {
    res = 1 / x;
  }
  catch (...)
  {
    if (x == 0)
      throw 1;
    else
      throw "Unknown Error";
  }
  return res;
}

int Func1(int x)
{
  int res;

  try
  {
    res = Func2(x);
```

```
      }
      catch (...)
      {
         throw;
      }
      return res;
   }
```

5. Add the following code to the main function.

```
int x, y = 0;

   try
   {
      x = 1 / Func1(y);
   }
   catch (int err)
   {
      if (err == 1)
         x = 0;
      else
         x = -1;
   }
   catch (...)
   {
      x = -1;
   }
   return 0;
```

When you type **Func1(** you will get the Auto Parameter Info, as shown here:

```
   try
   {
       x = 1 / Func1(
   }              ┌─────────────────┐
                  │int Func1 (int x)│
                  └─────────────────┘
```

6. Right-click the lines of code in the Func1, Func2, and main functions in the try and catch blocks and select Insert/Remove Breakpoint from the pop-up menu, or press F9. Notice the red button that appears next to the line. This will stop the application when it executes this line of code. Also notice the coloring used. By default, the keywords, such as try, would be in blue. Add a comment to your code. By default, it will be colored green.

7. From the Build menu, select Start Debug and select Go, or press F5.

8. When the debugger stops at the breakpoint in main where Func1 is called, notice it is inside a try block. Hold the pointer over the variable *y* to verify that the value is zero.

9. From the Debug menu, select Go, or press F5. The debugger will stop at the breakpoint inside Func1 where Func2 is called. Hold the pointer over the variable *x* to verify that the value is zero.

10. Press F5. The debugger will stop at the breakpoint inside Func2 where one is divided by *x*. Hold the pointer over the variable *x* to verify the value is zero.

11. Press F5. The debugger will stop at the breakpoint inside the catch block inside Func2 because the code attempted a division by zero. Press F10 to step to the next line of code. You are now going to throw an exception with a value of one.

12. Press F5. The debugger will stop at the breakpoint inside the catch block inside Func1. The code is now in another exception handler. The throw statement will throw the current exception, which is an integer value of one, to the next exception handler. If there had been a different error, it would have thrown an exception with the string Unknown Error.

13. Press F5. The debugger will stop at the breakpoint inside the catch block inside main. The code is now in another exception handler. Notice it stopped in the catch block that had the integer. Hold the pointer over the variable *err* to verify it is equal to one. Press F10 to step to the next line of code. Here, *x* is set to zero. When execution resumes, the code following the catch blocks will execute.

14. Remove the try and catch blocks in the main function. It should now look like the following code.

```
int x, y = 0;

x = 1 / Func1(y);
return 0;
```

15. Remove all the breakpoints in the project. From the Build menu, select Set Active Configuration, verify that the Debug version is selected, and click the OK button. Press F5 to run the program. A dialog box will pop up notifying you that some files are out of date. Click Yes to build them and then a message box similar to the one shown here:

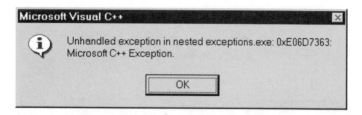

16. From the Build menu, select Set Active Configuration, choose the Release version, and click the OK button.

17. From the Build menu, select execute CHAP12_2.EXE or press CTRL-F5. A message box will appear that is similar to the one shown next. This is what users of the program would see. Make sure you handle exceptions rather than your program displaying this message box.

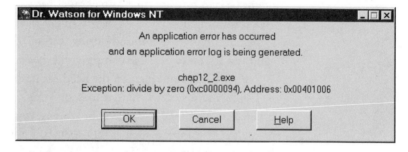

In some situations you can save yourself some coding time and decrease the code in an application. Look through your project for code that is repeated. For example, there may be multiple places where you are opening a file. Consider creating a generic function that can be used instead of writing the code where files are being opened. Then put exception handling within the function and have the function return an error code for success or failure of opening the file. This also helps in preventing logic errors because you are not writing the code over and over. You can test the function and then you don't have to worry about testing the code for each place in which you are opening a file. This also makes your application smaller.

Another way to implement exception handling is to centralize exception handling. You can create a function that is called from all catch blocks. The function would be called and then passed the exception. Inside the function, you would parse for different types of exceptions and handle them appropriately. It is important to remember that this does not preclude you from adding exception handling in your functions. It does minimize the exception handling code in each function.

Distributing Application Updates

Don't plan on releasing version 1.0 of your application and then thinking you are done. At some point in the future, you will more than likely need to make an update to it. There are different reasons for needing updates. It might be that because the business rules for your application have changed you are adding new features, or you might have customers who discover some bugs that weren't found during testing. This is common because you can't test for every possible computer hardware and software configuration. Whatever the reason, plan on the need for updates.

Deploying updates is similar to deploying a full application, which was covered in Chapter 11. You will be placing your update on some type of media for distribution such as CD-ROMs, floppy disks, or a Web site for Internet or intranet downloads. We will be discussing how to deploy an application update.

The first step to deploy your application is to package it. Files will be compressed and packaged into .CAB files. In an update, you don't necessarily need to deploy all the files that were deployed in the full installation. You should deploy only the files that have changed. There are several reasons for this. This will make your update smaller, which is more critical for floppy disk and Web site deployment methods. Another reason is that you can distribute the update freely without worrying about licensing issues because you are only deploying a small (hopefully it's small) subset of your application that cannot be run by itself. The files included in your update will overwrite the files already on the customer's computer. If you made changes to a database file, you have to be careful. You don't want to overwrite the existing database with the new one that doesn't contain the data in the customer's database. This would cause the customer to lose all of their data. If this is the case, you will need to give the customer a way to convert their data to the new database. You can do this through a utility program or handle it in your application when the updated application is first run. Files such as database drivers, the MFC DLLs, and controls do not need to be included unless your update was developed using newer versions of these files.

Visual C++ 6.0 provides the InstallShield Wizard to create an InstallShield setup program which includes the necessary files and dependencies to install your application, register the COM components, and allow for uninstall, as covered in Chapter 11. To start the InstallShield Wizard, from the Tools menu select InstallShield Wizard, or click the Start button on the desktop and select Programs | InstallShield for Microsoft Visual C++ 6.0.

The InstallShield Wizard will walk you through most of the process of creating an installation program for your application. The basic procedure for creating an update is described in the following paragraphs.

The first step is to enter some basic information about your application. Include the name of the application and the name of the company that wrote the application. Choose the development environment. Unless you have the full version of InstallShield, the only option available will be Microsoft Visual C++ 6.0. Choose the type of application that you are deploying. The options available are Database Application, Finance Application, Internet Application, Software Development Application, and Statistical Application. Enter the version of the update. The version should represent the fact that this is an updated version of the application.

Next you will decide which dialog boxes to display during the installation process. Because this is an update, you will generally want to minimize the dialog boxes that are displayed. Which ones you choose will depend on your application and personal preferences. The Welcome Message dialog box displays a welcome message and some information about running the installation program. The Software License Agreement dialog box displays a license agreement for your update. The Readme Information dialog box displays some information such as what is included in the update or warnings about performing the installation. Generally, you will give the user the option to view update information when the setup is complete. The User Information dialog box asks the user to enter a Name, a Company, and a Serial Number. You should have already retrieved this information from the user during the full installation and saved it in the Registry, so it normally wouldn't be used. The Choose Destination Location dialog box allows the user to specify where to install the application files. This information should already be in the Registry from the full installation. Normally, you would put code in the script to first check to see if this information is in the Registry and then automatically install it there. If it is not there, then you could display this dialog box. The Setup Type and Custom Setup dialog boxes normally wouldn't be used because you shouldn't need to ask the users which options to update. If you have a large update that has some files that are only used in certain setup types, you could ask the user. However, this could cause problems if the user didn't remember which option was selected during the full installation and then selected the wrong one during the update. For example, say the user did a Custom setup type during the full installation and then chose compact this time. Your update would only update the compact files. This could cause problems. It would be better to retrieve the setup type from the Registry and use it if needed. The Select Program Folder dialog box allows the user to specify in which Program folder on the Start menu a shortcut to the application will be placed. This should have been done during the full installation and therefore not used during the update. The Start Copying Files dialog box displays the setup options selected, which is not applicable to an update because you would retrieve this information from the Registry. The Setup Complete dialog box notifies the user that the setup has completed and it gives the user the option to view a Readme file and launch the program. This is a better place to put information about your update than the Readme Information dialog box.

Now you need to choose on which operating systems the update can be installed. You will need to decide between Windows 95/98, Windows NT 3.51, and Windows NT 4.0. For the Windows NT platforms, you will also decide between the Intel or Alpha platforms. Select the operating systems that are absolutely necessary to reduce the size of your distributing package and reduce the chance that someone will try to use your program under the wrong operating system. You can also select one or more languages for which you are running your setup.

You will also decide the components that will be included in your update. You can group your files into components. Components and subcomponents give you the flexibility to package your application and related software accessories into logical groups for setup types. These components will be displayed to the user. Generally, you will only need one component, such as the Program Files component, for the executable and DLLs for your application. You will also decide on file groups, which are related to the components. These are the actual file groupings that will be installed.

When you are done, InstallShield will create the installation program using the options that you've specified. InstallShield generates several files including the setup rule (SETUP.RUL) file that is the script for the installation process. The SETUP.RUL file can be modified. It uses a language similar to the C programming language. This file needs to be compiled when changes are made.

In Exercise 12-3, we will step through the Project Wizard to choose the options for an update. We are going to start InstallShield from the Start menu because it has more options available than using the wizards.

EXERCISE 12-3

Choosing Update Options Using the Project Wizard in InstallShield

1. Start the InstallShield for Microsoft Visual C++ 6.0 from Start | Programs | InstallShield for Microsoft Visual C++ 6.0. You'll see the Projects pane in the top window, as shown in Figure 12-5.

2. Double-click the Project Wizard icon to create your update. This will bring up the Project Wizard Welcome window.

3. For the Application name, type **Chapter 12_2 Update**.

4. Type a company name of your choice.

5. Select the development environment. Unless you have the full version of InstallShield, the only option available will be Microsoft Visual C++ 6.0.

FIGURE 12-5

The Project Wizard of InstallShield for Microsoft Visual C++ 6.0 helps you to create an update to your application

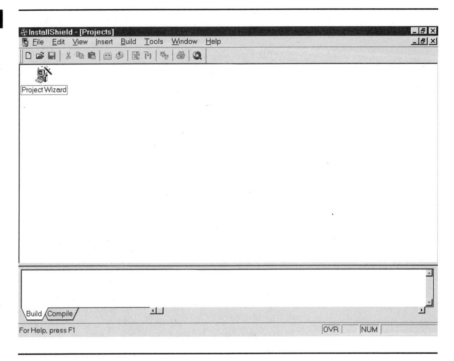

6. In the Application Type field, select Software Development Application.

7. For the Application Version, type **1.1**.

8. Click the ellipsis button next to the Application Executable field to find the CHAP12_2.EXE application that we created in Exercise 12-1. See Figure 12-6 for an example of how your completed Welcome screen should look.

9. Click the Next button. This will bring up the Project Wizard - Choose Dialogs window. Here we need to decide which dialog boxes will be displayed to the user. You can preview each of the dialog boxes by selecting one of the dialog boxes and then clicking the Preview button.

10. Select the Welcome Message dialog box.

11. Select the Software License Agreement dialog box.

12. Clear the check box for the Readme Information dialog box.

FIGURE 12-6

Enter the information about your application on the Welcome screen

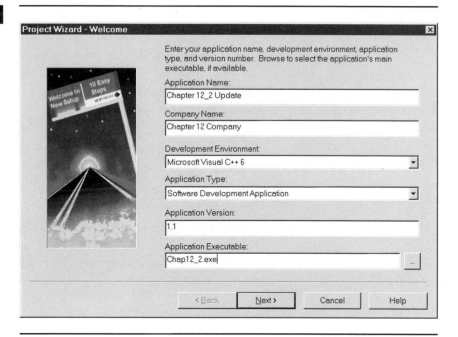

13. Clear the check box for the User Information dialog box.

14. Select the Choose Destination Location dialog box.

15. Clear the check boxes for the Setup Type and Custom Setup dialog boxes. For our exercise, we are only updating a small application, so we don't need these dialog boxes.

16. Clear the check box for the Select Program Folder dialog box.

17. Clear the check box for the Start Copying Files dialog box. For our exercise, it is not applicable.

18. Select the Setup Complete dialog box. Your Choose Dialogs screen should now have four boxes checked: Welcome Message, Software License Agreement, Choose Destination Location, and Setup Complete.

19. Click the Next button. This will bring up the Project Wizard - Choose Target Platforms dialog box. You can select the Show Only Available Platforms option to reduce the available platforms that the InstallShield program supports. We will use these operating systems:

Windows 95, Windows NT 3.51 (Intel), and Windows NT 4.0 (Intel).

20. Click the Next button. This will bring up the Project Wizard - Specify Languages dialog box. Select English.

21. Click the Next button. You'll see a Project Wizard - Specify Setup Types dialog box.

22. Cancel the selection of all of the options. We are not going to use Setup Types for this exercise. Your completed screen should look similar to Figure 12-7.

23. Click the Next button. This will bring up the Project Wizard - Specify Components dialog box.

24. Delete all of the components except the Program Files component. To delete a component, select the component and then click the Delete button. We will only need the Program Files component for this exercise.

FIGURE 12-7

You can select your setup types from the Specify Setup Types screen (we're not using Setup Types for this exercise)

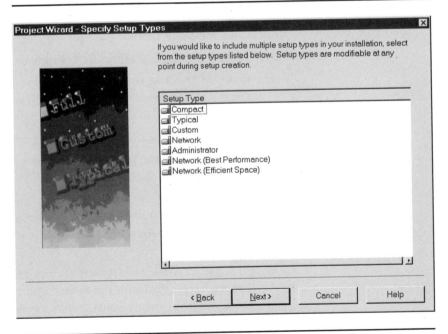

25. Click the Next button. This will bring up the Project Wizard - Specify File Groups dialog box.

26. Delete all of the file groups except the Program Executable Files. To delete file groups, select the file group and then click the Delete button. In this exercise we will only be installing the executable. Your Specify File Groups screen should show only Program Executable Files in the File Groups area.

27. Click the Next button. This will bring up the Project Wizard - Summary dialog box. At this point you should check the list of options to make sure everything is correct.

28. Click the Finish button. InstallShield will create the installation program using the options you've just specified. The InstallShield window should look similar to Figure 12-8.

FIGURE 12-8

The InstallShield window after the frame code has been created for the setup program

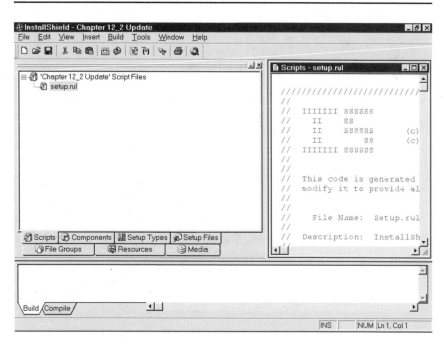

Now that you have chosen the options for the update, you have some properties to set for the files that will be installed. You have to decide on when they should be installed. On the Components tab, components have a property called Overwrite. The Overwrite property lets you specify the conditions under which the files of the component will or will not overwrite existing files on the user's computer. The available options are as follows:

- **ALWAYSOVERWRITE**   Overwrites the file no matter what.
- **NEVEROVERWRITE**   Installs the file only if it doesn't exist.
- **NEWERDATE**   Overwrites the file only if it has a newer date.
- **NEWERVERSION**   Overwrites the file only if it has a newer version number.
- **NEWERVERSION/NEWERDATE**   First checks for a newer version, then if necessary, checks for a newer date.

Because we are creating an update, we want to overwrite existing files. Instead of using the default to always overwrite files, use the Overwrite Files by Version option. This way, if a user has run an update that is newer than the current update, it will not overwrite these files. As an example, if you ran Visual Studio Service Pack 3, then for whatever reason you ran Service Pack 2, you would not want your files updated by the older version. This could cause unpredictable results. In the File Groups tab, you will decide which files to include in the update.

EXERCISE 12-4

Setting Properties for the Files to be Installed

1. Click the Components tab and select the Program Files component. The right pane will display the Components-Program Files window, shown next, which lists the current properties of the files that will be installed in the update.

Field	Value
Description	
Status Text	
Display Name	
Visible	Yes
Overwrite	ALWAYSOVERWRITE
Destination	<TARGETDIR>
File Need	STANDARD
Include in Build	Yes
Password	
Encryption	No
CD-ROM Folder	
FTP Location	
HTTP Location	
Miscellaneous	
Comment	
Required Components	None Selected
Included File Groups	None Selected

2. Double-click the Overwrite field. This will bring up the Overwrite Properties dialog box. Select the Overwrite Files by Version option. The Overwrite Properties dialog box should look similar to Figure 12-9.

3. Click the OK button to use this option.

4. Click the File Groups tab. This will display the File Groups in the right pane. We will accept the defaults. It should look similar to this:

Field	Value
Shared	No
Self-Registered	No
Potentially Locked	No
Compressed	Yes
Operating System(s)	OS Independent
Language(s)	n/a
FTP Location	
HTTP Location	
Miscellaneous	
Comment	

FIGURE 12-9

Use the Overwrite
Properties screen to specify
when the distributed files
will overwrite the user's
existing files

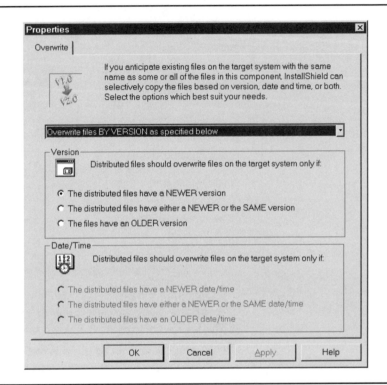

5. Click the plus sign (+) next to the Program Executable Files folder icon. Then click the Links entry under it and you'll see the File Groups - Program Executable Files\Links dialog box. This is where you'll define the executable to include in this file group.

6. Right-click the File Groups - Links dialog box and choose Insert Files from the shell extension menu. This will bring up the Insert File Link(s) into File Group dialog box. This is a standard File Open dialog box.

7. Browse to the CHAP11_2.EXE file, select it, and click OK. This will put the file in the Links window in the right pane, as shown in Figure 12-10.

The last step to deploy our update is to package it and choose the type of media by which our update will be distributed. By default,

The selected program executable file for your update will appear in the Links window

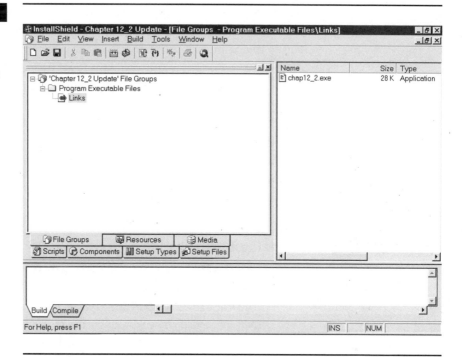

a CD-ROM media package is created because the CD-ROM–based distribution is the most typical type. There are other widely used distribution methods such as floppy disks, network-based, Web-based, and e-mail attachment package distributions.

Because CD-ROMs have a large amount of available space (over 600MB), the CD-ROM is often the medium of choice. To put your update on a CD-ROM, you need a writeable CD-ROM drive attached to your deployment computer. Floppy disks are still a viable option. Some older computers may not have a CD-ROM drive, so it is a good idea to have a floppy disk as an option. Also, if your update is less than 1.44MB, you might want to consider using floppy disks. The network-based distribution is very similar to the CD-ROM deployment method. If you select the Folder option of the CD-ROM media type when you build the disk images, you can select a folder on a network server. This makes deployment easy because you don't have to copy CD-ROMs or floppy disks and then distribute them. The Internet is an effective way of distributing an application to the end users. Deploying a package through the Web requires you to have some sort of Internet access and necessary permissions to a directory on a Web site. You also need to set up your Internet server to perform the user access and security permission check in the directory. This is also a less expensive deployment method because you don't have to create and distribute CD-ROMs or floppy disks. Another option is to attach the setup files to an e-mail message and send it to your users. Be careful about the size of the update. Some Internet Service Providers will not let their customers receive e-mail attachments larger than 1MB. In Exercise 12-5, we will create a package for distributing our update using floppy disk media.

EXERCISE 12-5

Creating Packages for a Floppy Disk Distribution

1. Click the Media tab. We are now ready to choose the deployment options for our update.

2. Right-click the Chapter12_2 Update Media icon and select the Media Build Wizard. This will bring up the Media Build Wizard - Media Name screen. Enter **Floppy** for the Media Name. Notice that the default of CD-ROM is already created. We will create a floppy disk media distribution type for this exercise because our update will be very small. Your screen should look similar to Figure 12-11.

3. Click the Next button. This will bring up the Media Build Wizard - Disk Type screen. This screen allows you to choose the distribution media for this media build. You can choose from different floppy disk sizes, CD-ROMs, custom sizes, and Install From the Web if you have the InstallFromTheWeb Internet Setup Tool. This is another tool available from InstallShield to allow users to install your application over the Internet.

4. Select 3.5" Diskette - 1.44MB and click the Next button. This will bring you to the Media Build Wizard - Build Type screen. Select Full Build.

5. Click the Next button. This will bring up the Media Build Wizard - Tag File screen. The purpose of tag files is to mark each disk of a multidisk distribution. You can place application information in them. In the Tag File panel, the data is filled with the data that we entered earlier. We will accept the defaults.

FIGURE 12-11

Choose the media for your update from the Media Name screen

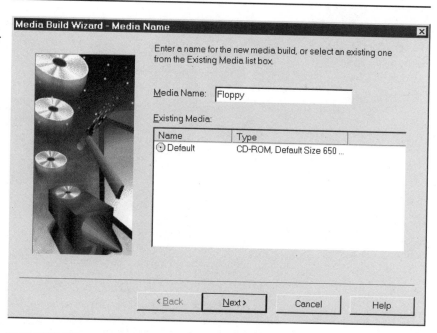

6. Click the Next button. This will bring up the Media Build Wizard - Platforms screen. Select Windows 95 and Windows NT 4.0 (Intel).

7. Click the Next button. This will bring up the Media Build Wizard - Summary screen. This will display the options you have selected. Look it over for errors.

8. Click the Finish button. This will generate the setup files needed for this media image. When it is complete, click the Finish button again. This will bring us back to InstallShield.

9. To see the files that were created, click the plus sign (+) next to the Chapter 12_2 Update media icon. Click the plus sign next to the Floppy icon. Click the plus sign next to the Disk Images icon. Click the Disk1 icon. The files for this image will be displayed in the right pane, as shown in Figure 12-12.

10. To put your setup on a floppy disk, from the Build menu, select Send Media To…. This will bring up the Send Media To - Select Media screen. For the Media Name, choose Floppy.

FIGURE 12-12

The setup files for the
Floppy media image

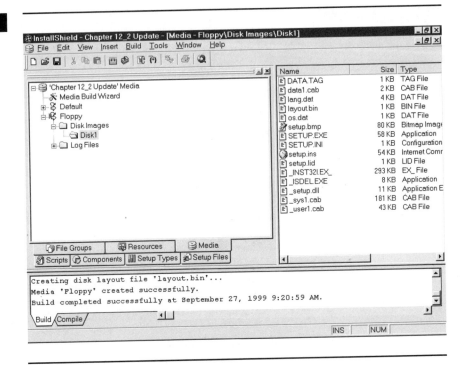

11. Click the Next button. This will bring up the Send Media To - Select Type screen. You can choose to put the media in a folder or on a removable disk. Select Copy Each Disk in the Media to a Removable Disk.

12. Click the Next button. This will bring up the Send Media To - Select Removable Drive screen. This will allow you to choose the removable drive on which the setup program is placed.

13. Select drive A: or the drive of your 3.5-inch floppy disk.

14. Click the Next button. This will bring up the Send Media To - Status screen.

15. Click the Start button. When a floppy disk is in the drive, click OK on the message box that appears. A progress bar will appear that shows the status of copying the files. When it is done, the screen will have a message telling you it was successfully copied.

16. Click the Close button. You have now created a setup program for your update and put it on a floppy disk.

Now that you have a better idea of how to fix errors and deploy updates, here are some possible scenario questions and their answers.

QUESTIONS AND ANSWERS

How do I configure client computers to reference different MTS servers to implement static load balancing?	By default, when you export a package, the client executable that is created references the local computer. To have the client executable reference another MTS server, set the Remote Server Name to the other server in the My Computer properties.
What is the difference between logic, syntax, and runtime errors?	Logic errors occur when the results are not what you expected, but there weren't any syntax or runtime errors. Syntax errors occur due to the incorrect use of the programming language. Runtime errors occur when an application attempts an invalid action.
What happens if an exception occurs within my exception handler?	The exception will be passed up the calling chain to the procedure that called it until it finds an exception handler. If an exception handler is not found, your application will quit.
I have fixed some errors and added exception handling to make my program more robust. How do I get this update to my users?	Use InstallShield to create a setup program and only include files that have changed. Create the appropriate media types and distribute the update.

CERTIFICATION SUMMARY

There are two types of load balancing: dynamic and static. Currently, with MTS, only static load balancing is available. Static load balancing is achieved by installing the package that contains the components that you need to balance on each server and creating client executables that reference the different servers. Then, you distribute the different client executables to your users as appropriate to balance the load.

There are three basic type of errors: logic, syntax, and runtime. Logic errors are incorrect results without a runtime error. Syntax errors result from using the programming language incorrectly. Visual C++ has some tools to help prevent syntax errors. Runtime errors are the result of invalid actions, invalid data, or system conditions that prevent code from executing correctly. Runtime errors can cause your program to quit. Exception handling is used to prevent runtime errors from stopping your application while it is running. It is important to incorporate exception handling throughout your code to make it more robust. Both the MFC and the C++ programming language support exception handling. Both of these methods use the try statement to enable exception handling and catch statements to handle any exceptions that occur within the try statement block. The MFC provides some exception classes that are derived from the CException class. Exception handlers can be nested and you must be able to determine the flow of execution through the calling chain.

Once you have fixed the errors, or updated the business rules, you need to create a setup program and deploy it to make it available to your users. You will be distributing only the files that have changed in your update. You can use InstallShield to step you through the process. You will determine which dialog boxes are displayed during setup, and which files will be included in the update during this process. You can deploy your update using CD-ROMs, floppy disks, a network server, or over the Internet from a Web site or by using e-mail attachments.

TWO-MINUTE DRILL

- ❑ *Dynamic load balancing* uses an algorithm to determine the load on each server. As each new request comes in, it determines the best server to use to service the request and automatically redirects the request to that server.

- ❑ *Static load balancing* is a manual process. You will make the COM objects available on multiple MTS servers and then manually set up your users to use the different servers.

- ❑ There are several ways to distribute the client configuration executable. You can share a directory that your users have access to. You can send an e-mail with the executable as an attachment that clients can save on their computers. You can push the executable to the client using Systems Management Server (SMS). Or you can make it available on a Web site.

- ❑ Logic errors are the cause when the results of your program are not what you expected. This situation is commonly referred to as a *bug* in the code.

- ❑ Syntax errors are the result of using the programming language incorrectly.

- ❑ Runtime errors are errors that occur while the application is running.

- ❑ Auto Type Info allows you to view type information for a variable by placing the pointer over it.

- ❑ A catch block in the C++ programming language can take an argument of just about any data type, but MFC exception handlers can only handle exceptions from the CException class.

- ❑ Visual C++ 6.0 provides the InstallShield Wizard to create an InstallShield setup program which includes the necessary files and dependencies to install your application, register the COM components, and allow for uninstall.

- ❑ The Select Program Folder dialog box allows the user to specify in which Program folder on the Start menu a shortcut to the application will be placed.

❑ Components and subcomponents give you the flexibility to package your application and related software accessories into logical groups for setup types.

❑ The Overwrite property lets you specify the conditions under which the files of the component will or will not overwrite existing files on the user's computer.

❑ There are two types of load balancing: dynamic and static. Currently, with MTS, only static load balancing is available.

SELF TEST

The following questions will help you measure your understanding of the material presented in this chapter. Read all of the choices carefully, as there may be more than one correct answer. Choose all correct answers for each question.

1. You are using the MTS Package Wizard to create a new package. If you want the package identity to be set to the account that you are logged in as, which of the following should you perform?

   A. On the Set Package Identity dialog, choose the This User option, then enter your username, but leave the password blank.

   B. On the Set Package Identity dialog, choose the This User option, then enter a username and password that has the same rights as you.

   C. On the Set Package Identity dialog, choose the Interactive User option.

   D. You cannot do this when creating a new package, only when exporting a package.

2. You have exported a package and now you want to install it on another server that is going to be used to implement load balancing. Which of the following steps will accomplish this?

   A. Right-click the Packages Installed folder and select Import. This will bring up the Import Packages Wizard. Just follow the steps in the wizard.

   B. Right-click the Packages Installed folder and select New, then Package. This will bring up the Package Wizard. Click the Import Package button and follow the instructions.

   C. Right-click the Packages Installed folder and select New, then Package. This will bring up the Package Wizard. Click the Install Pre-Built Packages button, browse to the folder where the .COM file is located, and follow the instructions.

   D. Right-click the Packages Installed folder and select New, then Package. This will bring up the Package Wizard. Click the Install Pre-Built Packages button, browse to the folder where the .PAK file is located, and follow the instructions.

3. You have created a distributed application that allows users to access COM components on a server named MTSServer1. You are getting complaints that the application has gotten too slow. You want to implement static load balancing. Which of the following should you do to make the COM components

available on a server named MTSServer2 and split your users between the two servers?

A. Export the package from MTSServer1. Import the package into MTSServer2. Distribute the executable located in the Clients folder.

B. Export the package from MTSServer1. Import the package into MTSServer2. Export the package from MTSServer2 and distribute the executable located in the Clients folder.

C. Export the package from MTSServer1. Import the package into MTSServer2. Distribute the executable located in the Clients folder to half your users. In MTSServer1's MTS Explorer Options tab of My Computer Properties, set the Remote Server Name to MTSServer1. Export the package again. Distribute the executable in the Clients folder to the remaining users.

D. Export the package from MTSServer1. Import the package into MTSServer2. In MTSServer1's MTS Explorer Options tab of My Computer Properties, set the Remote Server Name to MTSServer2. Export the package. Distribute the executable in the Clients folder to half of the users.

4. While you are developing an application, you sometimes receive errors when you are trying to compile it. What kind of error is this?

A. Syntax

B. Logic

C. Exception

D. Runtime

5. You have developed an application that converts user information from one database type to another. You want to ensure the data is being converted correctly. Which of the following should you perform to check for logic errors?

A. Use the program.

B. Run the Visual C++ Logic Error Checker program.

C. Turn on the Auto Logic Error Checking in the Options settings.

D. Build the application. If there aren't any errors, then there aren't any logic errors.

6. You are new to Visual C++. You are having trouble with writing an application. What features of Visual C++ can assist you in developing the application? (Choose all that apply.)

A. Auto List Members

B. Auto Type Info

C. Auto Code Generation

D. Auto Parameter Info

7. Visual C++ 6.0 comes with some features to help prevent syntax errors. You are using a class named clsSomeClass that was written by someone else. You want to use a method called DoSomething available in the class, but you don't know the parameters and the return type of the method. Which feature of Visual C++ 6.0

will display this information when you enter *clsSomeClassVar->DoSomething*?

A. Auto List Members

B. Auto Type Info

C. Auto Syntax Checker

D. Auto Parameter Info

8. You have developed an application that runs without errors, but it performs some calculations incorrectly. You have narrowed the error down to several functions. Which of the following can you use to assist you in finding these errors? (Choose all that apply.)

A. TRACE

B. Watch window

C. Syntax Coloring

D. Breakpoints

9. You have deployed an application and users have complained about it sometimes quitting in the middle of some operations. You are going to update the application and include exception handling in your application. When you finish adding the exception handling, you compile it and you get a warning that exception handling is not enabled. How do you enable exception handling? (Choose all that apply.)

A. You don't have to do anything; it is always enabled.

B. In Settings C/C++ tab, select the C/C++ category and click Enable Exception Handling.

C. Use the /GX command line compiler option.

D. In Settings Debug tab, click Enable Exception Handling.

10. You have an exception handler that catches an exception of type CFileException. In the catch block, you want to re-throw the exception. Which of the following will do this?

A. throw "Pass up calling chain"

B. throw new CFileException

C. throw

D. re-throw CFileException

11. Procedures proc1 and proc2 have an exception handler. Procedure proc3 does not have an exception handler. Proc1 calls proc2, which then calls proc3. What will happen if proc3 generates an exception?

A. A message will be displayed and the application will exit.

B. proc2 will handle the exception.

C. proc1 will handle the exception.

D. proc3 will handle the exception.

12. Procedures proc2 and proc3 have an exception handler. Procedure proc1 does not have an exception handler. Proc1 calls proc2, which then calls proc3. What will happen if proc3 generates an exception that is caught by proc2, which re-throws this exception?

A. A message will be displayed and the program will exit.

B. The application will exit.

C. The exception handler is still active, and will handle the re-throw.

D. The exception will be handled by the built-in application scope exception handler and then resume execution.

13. You have an exception handler that doesn't work like you expected. You added some TRACE macros to help debug it. If the following code executes, but generates an out of memory exception, what will be output to the Debug window?

```
try
{
  float *fp;
  fp = new float;
}
catch (...)
{
  TRACE("Caught the exception");
}
catch(CMemoryException* e)
{
  TRACE ("Caught
CMemoryException...");
}
```

A. Caught the exception.

B. Caught CMemoryException....

C. Both A and B will be output to the Debug window.

D. Nothing will be output to the Debug window.

14. You have implemented an error handler using the MFC macros. When you

compile the following code, it generates errors. What should you do to fix the compilation error? (Choose all that apply.)

```
TRY
{
  x = 1 / y;
}
CATCH_ALL (...)
{
  THROW;
}
END_CATCH
```

A. Change TRY to try.

B. Change CATCH_ALL(...) to CATCH_ALL(e).

C. Change THROW to THROW_LAST.

D. Remove the END_CATCH statement.

E. Change END_CATCH to END_CATCH_ALL.

15. You are writing a proposal to your boss for how much work is required to maintain an application. You have to explain why updates are needed in the proposal. Which of the following reasons would you include? (Choose all that apply.)

A. The business rules of the application have changed.

B. There was a logic error in the application.

C. There was a syntax error in the application.

D. There was a runtime error found by one of the users.

16. Your application had some bugs in it and you developed an update to fix the bugs in the executable of the program. Your boss only wants to distribute the update on one floppy disk to minimize cost. Which of the following methods should you use to distribute the update to your users?

    A. Create a new setup program including all the files needed to run the application.

    B. Create a new setup program including all the files needed to run the application except the Microsoft support files.

    C. Put the executable onto a floppy disk and distribute it to your users with instructions on how to copy it to their computer.

    D. Create a new setup program including only the files that have changed.

17. You have an application that calculates insurance rates. The underwriters have added some new information that is required to calculate insurance rates. You must now add some fields to the database being used by the application. This required changes to the executable and the database file. You are now ready to deploy the update.
    Required Results: Minimize the size of the update.
    Optional Results: Make the update available on floppy disk and CD-ROM.
    Do not lose any of the user's existing data.

Proposed Solution: Create a setup program using InstallShield and only include the new executable and database files. Create a new media type for floppy disks. Distribute the update to your users. Which of the following results does the proposed solution produce?

    A. The proposed solution meets the required result and all optional results.

    B. The proposed solution meets the required result and only one optional result.

    C. The proposed solution meets the required result and none of the optional results.

    D. The proposed solution does not meet the required result.

18. You have an application that calculates insurance rates. The underwriters have added some new information that is required to calculate insurance rates. You must now add some fields to the database being used by the application. This required changes to the executable and the database file. The executable has a feature that allows the user to convert the existing data to the new database and delete the old database. You are now ready to deploy the update.
    Required Results: Minimize the size of the update.
    Optional Results: Make the update available on floppy disk and CD-ROM.
    Do not lose any of the user's existing data.

Proposed Solution: Create a setup program using InstallShield and only include the new executable and database files. Create a new media type for floppy disks. Distribute the update to your users. Which of the following results does the proposed solution produce?

A. The proposed solution meets the required result and all optional results.

B. The proposed solution meets the required result and only one optional result.

C. The proposed solution meets the required result and none of the optional results.

D. The proposed solution does not meet the required result.

19. You are teaching someone how to create an installation program to deploy an update. You are going to teach them how to use InstallShield to create the installation program. How do you start InstallShield? (Choose all that apply.)

A. From the Tools menu select InstallShield Wizard.

B. From the Tools menu select Application Setup Wizard.

C. Select the Start button on the desktop, select Programs, then InstallShield for Microsoft Visual C++ 6.0.

D. Select the Start button on the desktop, select Programs | Microsoft Visual Studio 6.0 | Microsoft Visual Studio 6.0 Tools | InstallShield for Microsoft Visual C++ 6.0.

20. You have an application that has had two updates. A user calls and says they lost their last update disk and would like a new disk that contains the last update. They couldn't remember if they had installed it or not, so they installed it again. They call back and say that their program is behaving erratically. Some functionality works and some doesn't. You realize you had accidentally sent them the disk for the first update. What Overwrite property setting for the files should you have set in order to prevent this problem?

A. ALWAYSOVERWRITE

B. NEVEROVERWRITE

C. NEWERUPDATE

D. NEWERVERSION

21. You are using the Media Build Wizard to create some different media deployment packages. You notice that one has already been created before you ran the Media Build Wizard. Which type had already been created?

A. Floppy disk-based

B. CD-ROM–based

C. Web-based

D. Network-based

22. You are working on a COM component that is being tested by the Integration and Test department with 20 testers. You want to distribute a new version to them at the end of each day for them to test the next day. You create a setup program to create

an installation program for them to run in the morning. Which method should you use to deploy it? (Choose all that apply.)

A. Copy the update to 20 floppy disks, and leave a floppy on each of the tester's desks.

B. Copy the update to 20 CD-ROMs, and leave a CD-ROM on each of the tester's desks.

C. Put the update on a network server and e-mail the testers the location of the update.

D. Attach the update to an e-mail and send it to all of the testers.

23. You have developed an application that catalogs images. When you distribute the application, you want to include some sample images. These images are very large (over 100MB in size). You have created an update that now catalogs another image type. You want to distribute the same images but in the new type with your update. The images use the same amount of disk space. Which deployment media should you use?

A. Floppy disks

B. CD-ROM

C. Internet download

D. E-mail attachment

SELF TEST ANSWERS

1. **C.** By choosing the Interactive User option, the identity of the package is set to the user who is currently logged on. You could also do this using the This User option by entering your username and password.

2. **D.** To import a package, you start the Package Wizard and then choose the Install Pre-Built Packages option. You need to browse to the folder where the .PAK file is located to import it. All of the component files needed by the package should also be in the same directory.

3. **D.** To implement static load balancing, you need to make the package available on both servers by exporting the package from the server that has the MTS package installed on it and then import it to the remaining servers. When a package is exported, a Clients subfolder contains an executable that can configure the user's computers. To split the users between the servers, half of the users should use the Client executable that points to MTSServer1 and the other half to MTSServer2. Set the My Computer Properties to point to MTSServer2, export the package again, and distribute that executable to half of the users. You could also create another export package from MTSServer2 and use that executable. The other half of the users are already configured to use MTSServer1.

4. **A.** Syntax errors are errors that occur during compilation. Logic errors are errors that don't produce runtime errors, but the application doesn't run as the users expect it to. Runtime errors occur at runtime, not compile time.

5. **A.** The only way to test for logic errors is to use the application. Create some known correct results, then run your application to see if it generates the same results.

6. **A, B, D.** Visual C++ offers Auto List Members, which will display a list of methods and properties when you type a . or a -> after a valid variable. Auto Type Info allows you to view type information for a variable by placing the pointer over it. Auto Parameter Info will display the parameters required for a function. This will assist you in determining which parameters are needed as well as the parameter data types and return data type.

7. **D.** Visual C++ offers Auto Parameter Info to display the parameters and return types of a function or method when you type a . or a -> after a valid variable.

8. **A, B, D.** You can use the TRACE macro and the Watch window to help you locate logic errors. These allow you to view intermediate results of your program execution. Breakpoints allow you to pause program execution and step through your code a line at a time to follow the execution of the program. Syntax coloring assists you in finding *syntax* errors because incorrect sequence can result in the code being a different color than expected. For example, if you forgot to terminate a comment, all the code would be green (the default comments color) even if it wasn't meant to be commented out.

9. **B, C.** You enable exception handling from the Settings dialog, C/C++ tab or by using the /GX compiler option.

10. **C.** To re-throw the same exception just call the throw statement without any parameters. B is incorrect because you would be creating a new exception that wouldn't necessarily be the same as the exception that was caught.

11. **B.** The exception will be passed up the calling chain to proc2, which will handle the exception. When an exception occurs, it is passed up the calling chain until it reaches an exception handler.

12. **A.** When an exception handler passes an exception up the calling chain and there aren't any exception handlers in the chain, a message will be displayed and then the program will exit. If the throw statement is used inside the handler, it exits the handler and goes up the calling chain.

13. **A.** Because the first catch statement is an ellipsis, it will catch all exceptions. Remember, exceptions are processed in the order that they appear.

14. **B, C, E.** Using the MFC macros, the CATCH_ALL macro takes an argument that is the name of a pointer to an exception object. To re-throw an exception, use the THROW_LAST macro. It does need an exception handler terminator, but because it has a CATCH_ALL, the correct syntax is END_CATCH_ALL.

15. **A, B, D.** Common reasons for updates are changes to the business rules or a logic or runtime error was found. A syntax error isn't a reason because the application wouldn't build and be able to be deployed.

16. **D.** You should only include the files that have changed in an update to minimize the size of the update. It also allows you to distribute it without worrying about licensing issues because the update will not run by itself. You should not leave it to the user to copy a file onto their computer.

17. **B.** The proposed solution meets the required result by only including the changed files. This minimizes the update. The first optional result was met because a floppy disk media type was added to the default CD-ROM type. The second optional result was not met because when the new database file was copied, it would overwrite the existing database and the users would lose all of their data.

18. **A.** The proposed solution meets the required result by only including the changed files. This minimizes the update. The first optional result was met because a floppy disk media type was added to the default CD-ROM type. The second optional result was met because the new database file has a different name and the executable can copy in the user's existing data.

19. **A, C.** You can start InstallShield either from the Tools menu | InstallShield Wizard or from Start | Programs | InstallShield for Microsoft Visual C++ 6.0.

20. **D.** NEWERVERSION is correct because it would not have overwritten the files when update 1.2 was run, assuming, of course, that file versions were used. ALWAYSOVERWRITE is what would have caused the problem in the first place because update 1.2 would have overwritten version 1.3. NEVEROVERWRITE is incorrect because the update wouldn't work for files that already existed.

21. **B.** CD-ROM-based distribution is the default method for use of InstallShield and is created automatically.

22. **C, D.** A and B are incorrect because you are doing a lot of unnecessary work as well as wasting floppy disks or CD-ROMs. C and D make the update available to the testers and all you would have to do is deploy it once.

23. **B.** CD-ROM is correct because it can hold over 600MB. Floppy disks would require at least 70 disks, which is unmanageable. Internet download is incorrect because it would take your users too long to download, assuming they even had Internet access. E-mail attachment is incorrect because many ISPs limit e-mail attachments to less than 1 MB.

A

About the CD

This CD-ROM contains a browser-based testing product, the *Personal Testing Center*. The *Personal Testing Center* is easy to install on any Windows 95/98/NT computer.

Installing the Personal Testing Center

Double-clicking on the Setup.html file on the CD will cycle you through an introductory page on the *Test Yourself* software. On the second page, you will have to read and accept the license agreement. Once you have read the agreement, click on the Agree icon and you will be brought to the *Personal Testing Center* main page.

On the main page, you will find links to the *Personal Testing Center*, to the electronic version of the book, and to other resources you may find helpful. Click on the first link to the *Personal Testing Center* and you will be brought to the Quick Start page. Here you can choose to run the Personal Testing Center from the CD or install it to your hard drive.

Installing the *Personal Testing Center* to your hard drive is an easy process. Click on the Install to Hard Drive icon and the procedure will start for you. An instructional box will appear, and walk you through the remainder of the installation. If installed to the hard drive, the "Personal Testing Center" program group will be created in the Start Programs folder.

Should you wish to run the software from the CD-ROM, the steps are the same as above until you reach the point where you would select the Install to Hard Drive icon. Here, select Run from CD icon and the exam will automatically begin.

To uninstall the program from your hard disk, use the add/remove programs feature in your Windows Control Panel. InstallShield will run uninstall.

Test Type Choices

With the *Personal Testing Center*, you have three options in which to run the program: Live, Practice, and Review. Each test type will draw from a pool of over 200 potential questions. Your choice of test type will depend on whether you would like to simulate an actual MCSD exam, receive instant feedback on your answer choices, or review concepts using the testing simulator. Note that selecting the Full Screen icon on Internet Explorer's standard toolbar gives you the best display of the *Personal Testing Center*.

Live

The Live timed test type is meant to reflect the actual exam as closely as possible. You will have 120 minutes in which to complete the exam. You will have the option to skip questions and return to them later, move to the previous question, or end the exam. Once the timer has expired, you will automatically go to the scoring page to review your test results.

Managing Windows

The testing application runs inside an Internet Explorer 4.0 or 5.0 browser window. We recommend that you use the full-screen view to minimize the amount of text scrolling you need to do. However, the application will initiate a second iteration of the browser when you link to an Answer in Depth or a Review Graphic. If you are running in full-screen view, the second iteration of the browser will be covered by the first. You can toggle between the two windows with ALT-TAB, you can click your task bar to maximize the second window, or you can get out of full-screen mode and arrange the two windows so they are both visible on the screen at the same time. The application will not initiate more than two browser windows, so you aren't left with hundreds of open windows for each Answer in Depth or Review Graphic that you view.

Saving Scores as Cookies

Your exam score is stored as a browser cookie. If you've configured your browser to accept cookies, your score will be stored in a cookie named History. If you don't accept cookies, you cannot permanently save your scores. If you delete the History cookie, the scores will be deleted permanently.

Using the Browser Buttons

The test application runs inside the Internet Explorer 4.0 browser. You should navigate from screen to screen by using the application's buttons, not the browser's buttons.

JavaScript Errors

If you encounter a JavaScript error, you should be able to proceed within the application. If you cannot, shut down your Internet Explorer 4.0 browser session and re-launch the testing application.

Practice

When choosing the Practice exam type, you have the option of receiving instant feedback as to whether your selected answer is correct. The questions will be presented to you in numerical order, and you will see every question in the available question pool for each section you chose to be tested on.

As with the Live exam type, you have the option of continuing through the entire exam without seeing the correct answer for each question. The number of questions you answered correctly, along with the percentage of correct answers, will be displayed during the post-exam summary report. Once you have answered a question, click the Answer icon to display the correct answer.

You have the option of ending the Practice exam at any time, but your post-exam summary screen may reflect an incorrect percentage based on the number of questions you failed to answer. Questions that are skipped are counted as incorrect answers on the post-exam summary screen.

Review

During the Review exam type, you will be presented with questions similar to both the Live and Practice exam types. However, the Answer icon is not present, as every question will have the correct answer posted near the bottom of the screen. You have the option of answering the question without looking at the correct answer. In the Review exam type, you can also return to previous questions and skip to the next question, as well as end the exam by clicking the Stop icon.

The Review exam type is recommended when you have already completed the Live exam type once or twice, and would now like to determine which questions you answered correctly.

Questions with Answers

For the Practice and Review exam types, you will have the option of clicking a hyperlink titled Answers in Depth, which will present relevant study material aimed at exposing the logic behind the answer in a separate browser window. By having two browsers open (one for the test engine and one for the review information), you can quickly alternate between the two windows while keeping your place in the exam. You will find that additional windows are not generated as you follow hyperlinks throughout the test engine.

Scoring

The *Personal Testing Center* post-exam summary screen, called Benchmark Yourself, displays the results for each section you chose to be tested on, including a bar graph similar to the real exam, which displays the percentage of correct answers. You can compare your percentage to the actual passing percentage for each section. The percentage displayed on the post-exam summary screen is not the actual percentage required to pass the exam. You'll see the number of questions you answered correctly compared to the total number of questions you were tested on. If you choose to skip a question, it will be marked as incorrect. Ending the exam by clicking the End button with questions still unanswered lowers your percentage, as these questions will be marked as incorrect.

Clicking the End button and then the Home button allows you to choose another exam type, or test yourself on another section.

MICROSOFT CERTIFIED SOLUTION DEVELOPER

B

About the Web Site

A t Access.Globalknowledge, the premier online information source for IT professionals (http://access.globalknowledge.com), you'll enter a Global Knowledge information portal designed to inform, educate, and update visitors on issues regarding IT and IT education.

Get *What* You Want *When* You Want It

At the Access.Globalknowledge site, you can:

- Choose personalized technology articles related to your interests. Access a new article, review, or tutorial regularly throughout the week, customized to what you want to see.

- Continue your education, in between Global courses, by taking advantage of chat sessions with other users or instructors. Get the tips, tricks, and advice that you need today!

- Make your point in the Access.Globalknowledge community with threaded discussion groups related to technologies and certification.

- Get instant course information at your fingertips. Customized course calendars show you the courses you want, when and where you want them.

- Obtain the resources you need with online tools, trivia, skills assessment and more!

All of this is available on the Web at http://access.globalknowledge.com Visit today!

C

Conventions

As with anything that's been around a while, there are conventions that apply to good programming. *Conventions* are a standardized way of doing things, and they often make things much easier in programming. They affect the structure and appearance of code, making it easier to read and maintain. There are naming conventions, coding conventions, and constant- and variable-naming conventions. Together they allow a programmer to look at the work of another, and help him or her to determine what is going on in code.

Coding Conventions

When you're programming, you should follow certain conventions in your code. This includes the placement of variables and the structure of the code itself. The C++ language allows you to declare your variables anywhere before they are used. With this, it has become the convention in C++ to declare variables just prior to their use. While this is not commonly done in other languages, and it was not done when coding in C, it is considered standard now.

Another common convention when coding in C++ is to assign to constants values that either never change, or change very infrequently. An example of this might be an application that needs to use the minimum wage. A developer would likely declare a constant at the top of a file, assigning it to be a value that represents minimum wage. Because the minimum wage changes every few years, this gives the developer a single place to look for the value when it must be changed. In such an example, the code might appear as follows:

```cpp
const double MINIMUM_WAGE = 6.85;
const int HOURS = 40;
double WorkWeek()
{
    return MINIMUM_WAGE * HOURS;
}
int main(int argc, char* argv[])
{
    double dWeeklyIncome = WorkWeek();
    printf("The weekly income is %f.\n", dWeeklyIncome);
    return 0;
}
```

This example shows several things that can help to make a program follow the acceptable conventions. First, notice the use of the constants. As we discussed above it is standard to place these types of values into constants and to place the declaration of the constants at the top of the file. Next, it shows that we are able to declare variables at any point, and to assign them a value when they are declared (although in an example this small, it is hard to show the full extent of this). Finally, it shows the importance of using meaningful names. By looking at dWeeklyIncome you can automatically tell what this variable represents. While you could have used names like x, y, and z for variables, these names don't explain much about their purpose. This also applies to naming procedures. When you see a name like WorkWeek, you can determine that this probably has something to do with a work week.

This example also displays the use of spacing in your code. Visual C++ ignores white space (the spacing in your code where nothing appears). So indenting code and adding blank spaces to separate parts of code (by pressing ENTER) is ignored by VC++. Though the compiler ignores the white space, its presence makes it considerably easier for programmers to read.

on the
Job
Constants are very valuable and should be used in situations like those described above. It has also become quite common to store many of these values in a database, if your application uses one, and then retrieve the values and store them into variables in your application. By approaching the problem in this manner, it is very easy to change the values in the future and it will not require the developer to return to the code and then recompile the application.

While a procedure or function should always deal with one task (such as calculating your paycheck or opening and displaying a dialog), you will always have parts of code that deal with different things. For example, declaring variables and code that deals with those variables are two different parts of code (unless you declare the variables inline as shown in the example above). You should leave a blank line between such items. If your code does different tasks, such as running a loop and displaying a message box, you should separate the code with blank lines. By doing this, your code becomes significantly easier to read.

You should also indent your code to show different tasks in your code. For example, using nested If statements can be confusing if they are bunched together. If parts of the code are indented, it becomes easier to read. Compare the following examples, and you can see the difference:

```
if (x < y)
{
if (z > x)
{
afxMessageBox "z > y";
}
afxMessageBox "x < y";
}
```

```
if (x < y)
{
    if (z > x)
    {
        afxMessageBox "z > y";
    }
    afxMessageBox "x < y";
}
```

When the lines of code are indented, you can easily see which braces (i.e. "{" and "}") apply to which If statement. You can also see what code applies to which If statement. Indenting code organizes it so that you can read it much more easily.

on the Job

I once worked with someone who would come to me to help debug her code. I discovered that the source of many of the bugs that I found was that the developer would not maintain the indentations in her code as changes were made. After a while it became impossible to identify which statements would be executed in which blocks of code without a very careful examination. Ultimately I told her that I would not come and look at her code until she had fixed all of the indentations. This allowed that developer to find the majority of her problems on her own.

If you have lines of code that are particularly long, stretching past the width of your code window, you should split the line of code across two or more lines. This will make your code easier to read, without affecting its performance. VC++ will simply continue reading until it finds the end of the line, which is usually marked by a semicolon (;). The following is an example of a single line of code, split into two lines in the editor.

```
double dWeeklyIncome(dStandardRate, nRegularHours, dOvertimeRate,
    dOvertimeHours);
```

While one statement should appear on each line of code, it should also be mentioned that you can put several lines of related code on the same line. The following example shows how this is done:

```
dStandardRate = 6.85; dRegularHours = 40;
```

This shows two related statements appearing on the same line. When VC++ reads this, it will recognize this as two different statements.

In addition to conventions that affect the appearance of your code, you should also use comments in your code. Comments can be placed in code by using one of several notations that are acceptable in the C++ language. The first and oldest is to place all of your comments between a beginning comment identifier /* and an ending comment identifier */. The second way is to place a // on a line. Following the // everything else on that line is considered to be a comment. Comments can be placed alone on a line, or at the end of a line of code. The following shows examples of comments in action:

```
/* this is a comment that
covers multiple lines */
// this is a comment that runs an entire line
dStandardHours = 40;  // this is a comment for the remainder of the line
```

In addition to knowing how to place comments in your code, it is important to know what to place in your comments. You should avoid commenting code that is obvious (stating that "this starts my program") and commenting on everything occurring in your code. Another bad example is explaining that a variable is being declared. Try to code with other programmers in mind. Ask yourself, "Will this be obvious to another programmer?" If the answer is no, then comment it. In addition, keep in mind that, while a chunk of code makes sense to you now, it may not be so clear to you six months or a year from now. Commenting code avoids such problems.

A colleague of mine experienced a particularly funny example of bad commenting. He was working on some code written by a person who no longer worked for the company. While working on the code, he came across the comment "Don't touch this. It's important!" Since the code was being upgraded, he had to spend extra time determining if the code was still "important" or was now obsolete. Unfortunately, it was a particularly long and elaborate piece of code. I say this example is funny, because it happened to him, not me. It does illustrate the need to come straight to the point and explain things properly when writing comments.

Resource-Naming Conventions

Resource-naming conventions allow you to look at a resource id and easily determine what type of resource it is. This is done by adding a prefix to the resource id to specify the type.

Table C-1 lists prefixes commonly used for resources in VC++ version 6.

TABLE C-1	Resource	Prefix	Example
Standard Prefixes for Resource-Naming Conventions	Menu Item Resources	ID_	ID_FILE_NEW
	Bitmap Resources	IDB_	IDB_BITMAP1
	Cursor Resources	IDC_	IDC_CURSOR1
	Dialog Control Resources	IDC_	IDC_EDIT1
	Dialog Resources	IDD_	IDD_DIALOG1
	Icon Resources	IDI_	IDI_ICON1
	Multiple Resources (Accelerator, HTML, Menu, Toolbar, Version and other resources)	IDR_	IDR_ACCELERATOR1
	String Resources	IDS_	IDS_STRING1

Variable-Naming Conventions

In addition to resources, you should also use naming conventions for variables. VC++ naming conventions also provide for identifying the scope of a variable. This will allow you to identify easily the data type of your variable, and avoid improperly matching data types. An example of such an error would be trying to multiply a Boolean data type called Answer by an integer named Amount. By using the prefixes of variable-naming conventions, you would rename these to nAmount and bAnswer, and avoid such an error. Table C-2 lists the standard prefixes.

TABLE C-2

Variable-Naming
Conventions

Data Type or Scope	Prefix	Example
Member variable for a class	m_	m_bAnswer
Global variable	g	gUserID
Array	a	aTestScores
Function	fn	fnReportFunction
Handle	h	hWnd
Pointer	p	paTestScores
Boolean	b	bAnswer
Character	c	cSelection
Unsigned Long (double word)	dw	dwPageCount
Integer or Short	n	nAge
Long	l	lCustomerID
String	s	sCustomerName
Null terminated string	sz	szCustomerName
Unsigned Integer (word)	w	wAge

on the
!
() o b

Most of the data type prefixes are not as set in stone as the scope prefixes. (That is, the most widely accepted naming conventions are included down through Handle on the list in Table C-2.) While the prefixes listed in the lower part of the table are very common, many corporations or other groups of developers have adopted their own standards for many of these types. The most important thing is that a standard is identified and used—it is not as important what that standard is.

If you are using prefixes, I can't stress enough that you should give your variable a meaningful name. Renaming a variable called x to nx may follow the naming convention, but it hardly gives an accurate indication of what the variable is for. You should always try to name the variable something that indicates what it is being used for.

Using meaningful names is equally important when naming procedures, functions, and objects. You should try to determine what something is being used for, and name it accordingly.

While it may seem difficult to remember the methods and prefixes of conventions, they are well worth learning and using. In the long run, they will save you a substantial amount of time. You (and anyone who reads your code in the future) will certainly prefer taking a moment to look up a prefix rather than spending considerably more time searching through code to figure out the data type of a variable.

MCSD
MICROSOFT CERTIFIED SOLUTION DEVELOPER

D

Making IT Work for You

by Steve McMahan

The Bureau of Labor Statistics expects information technology careers to continue to grow at an average rate of 30 percent annually. Therefore, you've chosen a great time to complete your MCSD certification; these skills are more in demand than ever.

However, being in demand can present a whole spectrum of challenges. It's an employee's market, but only if you know how to make the most of it.

In the next few pages, I'm going to try to help you develop a job-search strategy. As a certified professional and seasoned technical recruiter, I'll try to give you a little insight from both sides of the table.

Each phase of the job search can be likened to a phase of the typical project lifecycle. Say your manager wants you to head up a project to develop and implement a new payroll system at work. You wouldn't attempt this large-scale task without first defining the requirements and the various tools needed. Why should your career planning be any different?

Career Planning

As an information technology professional, the first step you would take after being assigned a project would be to define the basic requirements. Take the time to do the same for your career. Identify issues such as the scope of your responsibilities, potential upward mobility, promotion opportunities, desired salary, and benefits. Having a long-term career goal in mind at all times can help you focus on developing the skills that you need to move to the next level.

To help define your ambitions, you might start by asking yourself a few questions.

- What would happen to me if I got laid off today?

- Am I making the most of my abilities in my current position?

- How does my salary compare to industry standards?

- What position would I like to have in five years? In ten years?

- Am I missing any opportunities?

- What new technologies are emerging that might change my industry?

If you'd like to learn more about industry standards, such as salary ranges and required experience, a number of good resources exist. I suggest that you start with the "Salary Survey and Career Navigator" from Romac International. From there, you might join a professional organization and subscribe to trade journals.

Once you have evaluated your career needs and desires, write them down. Just as you would continue to revisit your requirements document as you proceed with your project, evaluate your plan often so that you keep your long- and short-term goals in mind.

Remember, in today's rapidly changing job market, loyalty is no guarantee that a company will continue to employ you. Keep up with industry advances and new technologies. Look around. Read trade publications to find out what new technologies are hot. Browse the Internet. Talk to co-workers and friends. You'll be better prepared to find a new position—and your current boss will be impressed with your savvy, too.

Think of your career plan as your requirements document. This is the place where you think about short- and long-term career goals and the strategies needed to achieve those objectives. Planning can also help you envision possible pitfalls, such as overstaying a company. While you may become a highly paid expert within the organization, you may find when it comes time to change jobs that you make too much for your current skills.

The All-Important Resume

Your resume probably will be the first contact between you and a recruiter or hiring manager. It represents you and your experiences. So, it follows that you should invest some time to make sure your resume is an accurate and eye-catching summary of your qualifications. Plan to compose your resume over a series of days.

I could easily write a whole book about resumes. If you need more advice, invest in one of the many excellent publications on this subject. In the meantime, here are a few basic tips:

- Avoid being too wordy. Use more facts and fewer adjectives.

- Don't overlook the primary purpose of your resume: to get you in the door for an interview. Save the details for a face-to-face opportunity.

- If necessary, don't be afraid to list early jobs without descriptions. You want to highlight your current skills, not the first stepping stones in your career.

- Ask a colleague to give you feedback. You may have overlooked some accomplishments or talents that should be highlighted.

- Proofread, and then proofread again.

These days, there is a good chance that your printed resume will be scanned and entered into a database. It is also becoming increasingly acceptable to send it by fax or e-mail. To make the most of the technological options available, avoid using graphics and unusual typefaces. Your resume should be clean and clear. If it isn't, no one will take the time to enter it manually or unscramble an electronic file.

Knowing that your resume may end up in a database, write it wisely. Use as many keywords as possible, including all software that you are proficient with, the programming languages that you know, your certifications, and any professional organizations to which you belong. You may also want to list your years of experience with each language or tool.

Once you've created a resume, keep it up-to-date. Even if you are satisfied with your current position, you never know when opportunity may knock.

In a technical project, the next phase after the requirements definition might include selecting the best programming language, such as C, Microsoft Visual Basic, or Java. As you construct a resume, you must speak the language of your profession.

The Job Re-Search

Many people hope that a job will find them. You'll be a step ahead if you take an active, not passive, role in your career advancement.

Time seems to be the biggest factor when it comes to looking for a new job. How long is this going to take? That's a tough question. The answer depends on the market, on the type of job you are looking for, and your personal situation. Luckily for you, your skills are in demand.

If you currently have a job that you enjoy, you can take your time. Think about broadening your search into areas or industries that you might not have otherwise considered. You may want to upgrade other skill sets (in addition to the certification you've just completed) to prepare for a big change. Or, you may simply hold out for the right company, salary, position, and maybe even a signing bonus.

If you are between jobs at the moment, you have a variety of options. There has never been a better time to be out of work with an MCSD or CCIE certification. You may choose to "go contract" and dive into various projects as a consultant. This option can be very lucrative in the long run, provided you have the temperament to handle a fluctuating income stream. Or, you can devote a significant amount of time to your search for a permanent position.

Either way, you need to find resources that will provide job leads and insights into your prospective employer's position in the marketplace. The following sections should give you some basic pointers—use them as a springboard for your own exploration.

For a technical project, you would do research to find the best hardware and software; only after careful planning and study would you begin to code the new system. Your career deserves at least as much attention. You must do your homework if you want to find the perfect job.

Research: Networking

Your colleagues, friends, and neighbors can be an excellent resource in the job search. The more "insiders" that you know at a company, the better your odds are of hearing about openings. But what if you need to cast a wider net?

One way to quickly establish a range of contacts in your industry is to join a professional organization. Pick one that is a well-respected and prestigious group, pay the dues (your current employer may even cover these costs), and then take an active role. Meetings and conferences are more than just learning opportunities. While there, you can meet many people and show off your social skills. Advancement requires communication and people skills, even in the most technical positions.

You'll meet directors, project managers, senior technical leads, and entrepreneurs at these gatherings. All of these people are on the lookout for talent—it's ingrained. Every time they meet someone new, you want them to think, "How can I use this person to advance my company?"

Give them the answer in your conversations and actions. At a minimum, you have gained recognition from an influential person inside the organization. That puts you about a light-year ahead of your competitors who are just answering ads from the Sunday paper.

Be sure to include your association membership on your resume. Staying current and involved in your profession will increase your value in the mind of the recruiter or hiring manager.

You should join any user groups that focus on the tools of your trade. Sharing experience and advice about common issues lets you learn who else has projects and opportunities that interest you. And, if you really get involved, you may even be viewed as an expert—when others seek your advice, you know you have very salable skills.

Research: Working the Internet

I don't have to tell you that you can find a wealth of information on the Internet. This includes company marketing information, securities exchange information, and recruiting information. Almost all companies have Web sites that tout their goods and services and include postings of employment opportunities. You don't have to be a sleuth to learn who's out there.

What else can you do? Explore sites posted by professional organizations and other special interest groups, or join newsgroups. And don't forget the growing number of online job boards. As the Internet expands, many technical professionals are using these cybertools to manage their careers.

Now you really need to have an e-friendly resume. On the Internet, there is no time to mail or fax your career profile. Be sure to pick a common format, such as Rich Text Format (RTF) or Microsoft Word 95, for your resume. And remember that all the rules listed previously apply. It's still your resume; a professional representation of who you are. Avoid high-tech tricks.

When submitting a resume through an online form, you need to modify your strategy a bit. Think keywords. The information you are entering is bound to be stored in a database, especially if you send it through a job board. At some point, someone is going to run a query against that database that goes something like this, "Show me all of the MCSDs with at least two years' work experience and certified on Visual Basic." Include as many keywords as possible without making your resume repetitive or awkward.

Remember to include a cover letter that mentions your desired position, even if it is somewhat generic. A blind resume is a blind resume, regardless of the medium. As for posting your current salary online, I don't think it's wise to put it out there for the world to see.

One final thought: Many Web sites include the names of principals or key executives. You may want to use these contact names if you choose to mail in a paper copy of your resume.

Research: The Headhunters

As someone looking for a job, I loved working with headhunters. As a recruiter, I hate competing with them. So for the purpose of this discussion, I'm going to try to think like someone looking for a job.

The really nice thing about headhunters is that most of them are paid a finder's fee that is a percentage of the salary of the person hired. Consequently, the more money you make, the more money your headhunter makes. This is one of the few situations in life where your agent's best interests are truly your best interests. Also, most headhunters don't get paid at all unless they fill a position. They work fast, and usually with remarkable results.

Headhunters often specialize in a particular type of job, location, or industry. If you are looking for something specific, ask around and find someone with that expertise. Not only will this person know what is going on in his or her specialty, he or she can help tailor your presentation to that area. Think of these consultants as industry insiders for hire—only you don't have to pay the bill! That's a real benefit for a job candidate.

At the first meeting with the headhunter, you both will go over your resume and career goals. The headhunter may make some resume suggestions and let you know if what you are looking for is compatible with your skill set.

If the headhunter does tell you that you're not qualified, you can either find another headhunter or listen to what this one is saying. Because headhunters don't make money unless you find a job, the headhunter is probably giving you good advice. Don't be discouraged; headhunters can give you suggestions for how to become qualified for the job of your dreams.

Many people worry that they will be pushed into inappropriate positions by headhunters who are anxious to get paid. Remember, you are the ultimate decision-maker in this process. In addition, there is a growing trend that postpones paying the headhunter in full until the client has held the job for six months.

A word of caution: There are people out there calling themselves career consultants, or even headhunters, who want you to pay them a few hundred dollars to build a resume and to tell you what your ideal job is.

First of all, you don't need someone to tell you what your ideal job is. Second, if these people even have a placement service, you would be amazed at how many times your ideal job just happens to be the position that they are trying to fill. Third, there are too many good recruiters and headhunters who don't charge you a dime. You should never pay someone to find you a job!

Interviewing for the Perfect Job

If you've been taking my advice, you have already researched the firm where you will interview. You can speak intelligently about the company and its industry. The posted ad or job description should give you some insights into the technology they use, but don't be afraid to ask for details.

Confidence and expertise are important qualities to reveal, but don't be too bold about making recommendations or finding fault with current systems and procedures. You're an outsider. You don't have the big picture. And you don't want to inadvertently insult your interviewer (or future coworkers) with a know-it-all attitude.

Like resume-writing advice, interview tips could fill a complete book. I trust that you will use your common sense. Dress professionally. Be on time. Don't lie about skills or experience. Above all, be yourself. When answering questions, give direct and concise answers. Feel free to take a moment to compose your thoughts before speaking. And if you don't know the answer, admit it. An interviewer will appreciate your honesty more than an obviously phony answer.

You'll find plenty of good resources and workshops to help you enhance your interviewing skills. If you'd prefer to polish them at home, here are a few additional hints.

- With a friend, record a mock interview on video or audiotape. An instant replay can be very enlightening.

- Determine all the points that you want the interviewer to know about you. If he or she skips something, be sure to bring it up at the end.

- Prepare a list of questions that you'd like answered. Remember that you are interviewing the company just as much as they are interviewing you.

When you are asking questions, try to target the correct individuals. For example, a question about bandwidth or programming languages is only appropriate for a technical interviewer. Reserve the business questions for a vice-president or senior manager. Take notes.

Believe it or not, a company often gets the feeling that the candidate is disinterested. Your demeanor may be affected by fatigue or nerves, so don't send out unintentional signals. At the end of the day, reiterate your interest if you sincerely want the job.

Get a business card from each person who interviews you. And be sure to ask about the interviewing and decision-making timeline so you know when you can expect to hear back from them.

The next step in a technical project turns all your hard work into reality. This is the most crucial step in the process. You may have created the best plan, but it won't make a bit of difference if your implementation strategy is flawed. Your interviews are similar. No matter how much research you've done and how great your resume is, you must do well at this essential stage or you won't land the job.

After the Interview

The follow-up note is a polite way to refresh the memory of your interviewer(s), to project a positive impression, and again demonstrate your interest and eagerness to work for this company. Tradition requires a hand-written thank you; however, a thoughtfully composed e-mail has become widely accepted. Either way, your message should be personalized and mention something specific about your discussion. Never send a "group" thank you.

If you haven't heard from your interviewer in a reasonable amount of time, feel free to call to check on the status of your application. Don't worry about looking desperate; you are more likely to come off as confident and professional. In many companies, the people doing the interviewing are also the people doing real work. Interviewing is not their primary responsibility. Consequently, it may be up to you to keep the ball rolling. You might even get hired though persistence alone!

Negotiating the Salary

You've finally been offered the job—congratulations! But before you accept it, take a deep breath and negotiate.

Yet another topic that merits an entire book, these negotiations can involve salary, benefits, responsibilities, perks, or any number of other factors.

If nothing else, make sure you have a salary survey that shows current figures for your profession and geographical location. At Romac, we print ten industry-specific guides annually; you may also find similar information in trade publications such as *MCP Magazine*.

A Last Piece of Advice

Never stop looking for the perfect job. You should test the waters and go out on an interview or talk to a headhunter once every six months. High-tech industries change rapidly, and with that change comes a myriad of new opportunities.

Note: Steve McMahan is a regional vice-president for Romac Information Technology, one of the leading specialty staffing companies.

MICROSOFT CERTIFIED SOLUTION DEVELOPER

Glossary

Active document   A document that contains objects such as ActiveX controls, HTML pages, or Java applets. Active documents are actually standalone applications that can be hosted within a Web browser.

Active Template Library (ATL)   Used to create lightweight controls based on COM. These controls are much smaller than MFC and are extremely suitable for client/server applications.

ActiveX   ActiveX is a set of technologies that enables software components to interact with each other in a networked environment, regardless of the language in which they were created.

ActiveX component   A unit of executable code, such as an .EXE, a .DLL, or an .OCX file, that follows the ActiveX specification for providing objects.

ActiveX controls   Reusable objects that include visual elements and code. They are used in some type of container, such as a form, an application, or a Web page, to enable or enhance a user's interaction with an application. These controls have an .OCX filename extension.

ActiveX Data Objects (ADO)   Programming objects that represent the structure of your database and the data it contains. ADO enables you to write a client application to access and manipulate data in a data source through a provider.

aggregation   A way to implement COM objects. It enables a new object to reuse one or more existing objects. Reuse is accomplished by exposing one or more of the interfaces in the original object. Aggregation directly exposes the interfaces to the internal objects as though the capabilities were its own. *See also* **containment**.

American National Standards Institute (ANSI)   An American organization of business and industry groups that develops communication and trade standards for the United States. These standards are coordinated with corresponding international standards.

American Standard Code for Information Interchange (ASCII)   A character set built into every PC consisting of 96 uppercase and lowercase letters and 32 control characters. Note that ASCII does not include any formatting information such as font variances, bold face, or italics.

apartment   Areas of memory within the virtual address space of an application in which a COM object's code executes.

apartment-model threading   A threading model that can be used only on the thread that created it. *See also* **free threading model**.

application programming interface (API)   The set of routines in an application that are used to request and perform the lower-level services of an operating system. OLE DB, ODBC, and DB-Library are examples of APIs.

beta testing   Testing of an application by users who are not part of or do not have any ties to the development process. It allows the developer to receive unbiased feedback on bugs, features, or any other aspects of an application.

breakpoint   A place in a program where execution is stopped to allow the developer to look at the program's code or variables, and then to make changes, continue execution, or terminate execution.

cabinet file (.CAB)   Cabinet files compress the files that they contain and use an efficient non-file-specific compression algorithm. Additionally, by packing many files into a .CAB file you reduce the total file count.

cache   A buffer that holds data during an input/output (I/O) transfer between a disk and the random access memory (RAM).

call stack   An ordered list of functions that have been called but have not returned. The currently executing function is listed first. During debugging, you can view the functions that have been called but have not returned.

class   A type that defines the interface of a specific kind of object.

class factory   The way that COM creates and destroys specific instances of components.

ClassWizard   A wizard included in the Microsoft Foundation Classes which helps create new classes, define message handlers, and perform other routine tasks.

client   (1) A workstation accessing the resources in a client/server model. *See also* **client/server model**. (2) A program that runs on a computer, such as Microsoft Access, Microsoft Word, and Microsoft Excel.

client/server model   A model in which multiple user workstations connect to one central server or many different servers with the intention of sharing information. The server manages a common resource, such as a database, and responds to client requests for data from this resource.

CLSID (class identifier)   A universally unique identifier that identifies a type of OLE object. Each type of OLE object has its CLSID in the Registry so that it can be used by other applications.

Common Gateway Interface   A device that allows a Web server to run a program on the server and send the output to a Web browser. *See also* **Internet Server Application Programming Interface**.

Component and Controls Gallery   Stores links to all components and controls registered on a user's machine. It is used to add components and controls to a project.

Component Object Model (COM)   An architecture for cross-platform development of client/server applications.

component software development   Software development that cuts programming time and produces more robust applications by allowing developers to assemble applications from tested, standardized components.

container   An object or application that contains other objects.

containment   A composition method for accessing COM objects through a single interface. It enables one object to reuse the interface implementations of other objects. The outer object administers requests to other objects, delegating implementation when it uses the services of one of the contained objects. *See also* **aggregation**.

Data Access Objects (DAO)   A high-level set of objects that insulates developers from the details of reading and writing records.

database (DB)   An organization of alphanumeric information designed so that users may easily access and retrieve the information. Databases are organized into objects known as tables, which are groups of data that all have something in common.

database management system (DBMS)   A container for the collection of computerized data files that allow users to perform operations on the files, including appending, editing, generating reports, retrieving, and updating.

data type   Specifies what type of data can be stored in a column. Some of the data types include int, real, float, datetime, and char.

DB-Library   A group of high-level language libraries that provide the application programming interface (API) for the client in a client/server system.

dialog data exchange (DDX)   The mechanism of mapping a dialog control to a dialog class member variable. DDX is the second of two steps that MFC completes to connect a recordset to dialog box controls.

document/view architecture   The core of the Microsoft Foundation Classes application framework. In a document/view application, the data, also known as the document, is managed separately from the application through which the users interact with the data. The data and the code are separated.

dynamic link library (DLL)   An executable routine that contains a specific set of functions stored in a .DLL file. It can be loaded upon demand by the program that calls it.

event   An action or occurrence to which a program may respond. ActiveX controls use events to notify a container that something has happened to the control. An example might be a user-input event, such as a mouse-click or a keyboard event.

exceptions   Error condition objects which are *thrown* by a function when an error condition is encountered. They are then passed progressively back up the call stack until they are *caught* by some code that then handles the error, or else the application will abort.

filegroups   Collections of files sharing some common thread.

foreign key   The column or columns whose values match the primary key in the same or another table. It does not have to be unique.

free threading model   A model in which an object can be used on any thread at any time. *See also* **apartment-model threading**.

global temporary table   Prefaced by # #, these tables are available to every client and act as a temporary storage area for work tables and store procedures.

GUID (globally unique identifier)   A GUID is a binary number that is guaranteed to be unique.

heaps   Tables that are created without a clustered index.

HTTP (Hypertext Transfer Protocol)   The protocol that you use to connect to the Internet to view Web pages.

in-place activation   The capability to activate an object within the context of its container document, rather than opening it in a separate window.

in-process component   A component that runs in the same process space as its client.

InstallShield   A program used when setting up installation packages for programs created with Visual C++ 6.0.

instantiate   Create an object of a data type, such as a class.

integration testing   Used to demonstrate that all of the units work together.

interface thread   A type of MFC thread that can receive and process messages. The main thread of an executable is always an interface thread.

Internet Information Server (IIS)   Provides FTP, Gopher, and Web services in Windows NT. You can use this server application for publishing Web pages and testing any of the Web applications you create with Visual C++ 6.0.

Internet Server Application Programming Interface (ISAPI)
A set of functions for Internet servers. Using it, you can write ISAPI dynamic link libraries (DLLs) that can be loaded and called by a Hypertext Transfer Protocol (HTTP) server. *See also* **ISAPI server extension** and **ISAPI filter.**

interprocess communication (IPC)   A method of communication between one program and another. Depending on the IPC method being used, this communication can even be across a network. IPC is often used in the client/server environment as a means of communication between the server and the client across the network.

ISAPI filter   A type of DLL that provides the capability of preprocessing and postprocessing of all data sent between the client and the server. An ISAPI filter is loaded when the Web server is started. This filter can then be used for all interactions with the Web server.

ISAPI server extension   An ISAPI server extension, sometimes called an Internet server application (ISA), is a DLL that can be loaded and called by an ISAPI-compliant server to enhance its capabilities. An ISA is invoked from a browser application and provides functionality similar to that of a Common Gateway Interface (CGI) application. An ISA is only executed when the browser navigates to the URL that identifies the server extension. *See also* **Common Gateway Interface.**

Library   A set of compiled code that is included within an application at compile time.

lightweight remote procedure call (LRPC)   A smaller version of the Remote Procedure Call (RPC) that was specifically developed for COM. *See also* **Remote Procedure Call (RPC).**

logic errors   Errors that are the cause when the results of your program are not what you expected. This situation is commonly referred to as a *bug* in the code.

Marshaling   The process of gaining access to another process' address space. Marshaling creates a proxy in the client to create to a stub in the server. This is how information is passed between processes on the same computer. *See also* **Remote Procedure Call (RPC).**

member function   In C++, a function declared inside a class definition. Member functions of a class are used to get and set data members, display information to the user, and manage data to suit the needs of the program.

message map   Used to connect messages and commands to their appropriate handler functions. Each class in the MFC framework that is able to receive messages has a message map.

method   A procedure that provides access to an object's data. In C++, public member functions are the equivalent of methods.

MFC ActiveX ControlWizard   A wizard included in the Microsoft Foundation Classes that is used to create the files necessary to build an ActiveX control.

MFC AppWizard   A wizard included in the Microsoft Foundation Classes which helps create executable and dynamic link library (DLL) programs.

MFC ClassWizard   A wizard that assists the developer with operations such as creating new classes, defining message handlers, creating virtual function overrides, and mapping data from dialog box controls to class members.

Microsoft Access   A database that operates as a development tool, by using Visual Basic for Applications (VBA), and a database.

Microsoft Developer Network (MSDN)   A comprehensive source of information. It includes a knowledge base of information, product and software development kit (SDK) documentation, technical documents, examples, and sample code.

Microsoft Foundation Classes (MFC) Library   The classes, global functions, global variables, and macros used in programming Visual C++ 6.0 applications.

Microsoft Interface Definition Language (MIDL) A specialized language used to create custom interfaces. Using MIDL, you can optimize local and remote components.

Microsoft Systems Management Server (SMS) Part of Microsoft's Zero Administration strategy. SMS allows network engineers to manage software installations, network resource usability, workstation software installations, policies, and profiles. It is designed to exploit the Windows operating systems to their full potential in a network environment.

Microsoft Transaction Server A server used to store and distribute components. These components are developed using Microsoft's Component Object Model (COM).

Microsoft Visual SourceSafe (VSS) A source code control system used for version control of source code. It allows developers to save copies of their source code to a database.

modal dialog A dialog box that must be responded to and dismissed before the user can interact with any other part of the application. A modal dialog box is used to alert the user to serious and potentially damaging errors that need immediate attention.

modeless dialog A modeless dialog box does not cause the rest of the application to be disabled, and any number of modeless dialog boxes may be displayed by an application at the same time.

multiple-document interface (MDI) Allows the user to have multiple documents open at the same time. Each document could consist of a different file, or of the same file but of a different view, such as a Microsoft Excel spreadsheet and a pie chart based on the data from the Microsoft Excel spreadsheet. It is the standard user-interface architecture for Windows-based applications.

multithreading   The capability of an application to start two or more threads of execution, which can then be concurrently processed.

Object Linking and Embedding (OLE)   A technology standard created by Microsoft Corporation, and adopted by Apple Computers, that allows for data to be shared and automatically updated between running applications. An object (picture, document, and so on) created with one client can be then placed within or called from another client.

OLE DB   A set of initialization interfaces required for an OLE DB application to connect to an OLE DB data store. OLE DB is an application programming interface (API) that is based on the Component Object Model (COM).

open database connectivity (ODBC)   An interface that permits an application developer to develop and ship an application without specifying a database management system (DBMS).

out-of-process component   A component that runs in its own process space. An out-of-process component may run as a standalone application.

permissions   Authorization granted to users to access database resources.

primary key   A column or columns that uniquely identify one row from any other row in a table.

process space   Windows gives each program 4GB of virtual address space. This is known as the program's process space. *See also* **in-process component** and **out-of-process component**.

property   The data associated with an object. ActiveX control properties provide an interface for applications that contain ActiveX controls, such as Automation clients and ActiveX control containers.

property sheet A tabbed dialog box, which is really a collection of dialog boxes laid over the top of each other with each one being selectable by a tab.

proxy An interface-specific object that bundles parameters for methods in preparation for a remote method call. A proxy runs in the sender's address space and communicates with a stub in the receiver's address space. *See also* **stub** and **Marshaling**.

query A request for the retrieval, deletion, or modification of specific data.

record field exchange (RFX) Method that MFC uses to bind member variables to fields in the database. RFX is the first of two steps that MFC completes to connect a recordset to dialog box controls. *See also* **dialog data exchange (DDX)**.

Registry A database in Windows 95/98 and Windows NT that is used to store system configuration information as well as user information.

regression testing Testing that repeats previous testing to show that a change to the application does not affect other aspects of the application. The results of testing parts of the application that were not changed should be the same as they were in previous tests.

relational database management system (RDBMS) An organization of databases that share data, often across multiple networks. Data can be entered into one database and another database can access this data and make it available to users or to other databases.

Remote Data Objects (RDO) Provides an information model for accessing remote data sources through ODBC. It offers a set of objects that make it easy to connect to a database, execute queries, and commit changes to the server. *See also* **open database connectivity (ODBC)**.

Remote Procedure Call (RPC)   A standard for distributed computing that enables a process to make calls to functions that are part of another process. The other process can be on a different computer on the network or on the same computer.

resource editor   An interface that allows you to view and modify information contained in resource files of your project. It can be used to create new resources, and modify or delete existing ones. Resource editors in Visual C++ 6.0 include the following: Accelerator editor, Binary editor, Dialog editor, Graphics editor, Toolbar editor, Menu editor, String editor, and Version Information editor.

run-time errors   Errors that occur while the application is running.

scalability   The capability to expand to meet future needs (in other words, to upgrade). It is a characteristic of both software and hardware.

server   A computer that provides shared resources to network users.

single-document interface (SDI)   The simplest application type that has the document/view architecture. In an SDI application, only one document is open at a time. An example of this is Notepad.

software development kit (SDK)   A set of libraries, header files, books, tools, and sample programs that provides help to a developer creating software.

Spy++   A utility that has windows to view the system's processes, threads, windows, and window messages.

stress testing   Testing that places the highest possible loads with the lowest possible resources available to an application. This can help in determining the minimum requirements for an application.

stub   An object that unpackages the parameters for that interface after they are marshaled across the process boundary, and makes the requested method call. *See also* **Marshaling** and **proxy**.

synchronization   The prevention of one thread from accessing a resource that another thread currently is accessing. Synchronization becomes a necessity when two or more threads need access to a shared resource that has a limit on how many threads can access it.

syntax errors   The result of using the programming language incorrectly.

TCP/IP (Transmission Control Protocol/Internet Protocol) An industry standard suite of protocols designed for local and wide area networking. Widely used for Internet communication.

thread   The smallest unit of code in a process.

ToolTips   Small modeless windows that are briefly displayed when the mouse lingers over a button for a certain interval. ToolTips are used to proactively give the user some feedback about the purpose of a button.

transaction   A group of tasks that are executed as a single action.

Unicode   A 16-bit character set that uses two bytes to represent every character regardless of whether it's an ASCII character. It is capable of encoding all known characters and is used as a worldwide character-encoding standard.

unit testing   Testing the smallest part of an application that can be tested. It should validate that the unit completely meets the requirements for which it is designed.

URL (Uniform Resource Locator)   The Internet address for a specific resource or Web site.

virtual table (vtable)   A table that contains the addresses (pointers) for the methods and properties of each object in an Automation server.

worker thread   An MFC thread that provides additional paths of execution for the main thread. It does not receive or process messages.

Zero Administration Initiative for Windows (ZAW)   A new strategy developed by Microsoft to reduce the total cost of ownership when setting up and maintaining employees' machines. It refers to a set of technologies that will give IT professionals expanded control and manageability over their Windows-based environments by automating such tasks as operating system updates and application installation, and providing tools for central administration and desktop system lock down.

INDEX

D

E

F

W

Custom Corporate Network Training

Train on Cutting Edge Technology   We can bring the best in skill-based training to your facility to create a real-world hands-on training experience. Global Knowledge has invested millions of dollars in network hardware and software to train our students on the same equipment they will work with on the job. Our relationships with vendors allow us to incorporate the latest equipment and platforms into your on-site labs.

Maximize Your Training Budget   Global Knowledge provides experienced instructors, comprehensive course materials, and all the networking equipment needed to deliver high quality training. You provide the students; we provide the knowledge.

Avoid Travel Expenses   On-site courses allow you to schedule technical training at your convenience, saving time, expense, and the opportunity cost of travel away from the workplace.

Discuss Confidential Topics   Private on-site training permits the open discussion of sensitive issues such as security, access, and network design. We can work with your existing network's proprietary files while demonstrating the latest technologies.

Customize Course Content   Global Knowledge can tailor your courses to include the technologies and the topics which have the greatest impact on your business. We can complement your internal training efforts or provide a total solution to your training needs.

Corporate Pass   The Corporate Pass Discount Program rewards our best network training customers with preferred pricing on public courses, discounts on multimedia training packages, and an array of career planning services.

Global Knowledge Training Lifecycle   Supporting the Dynamic and Specialized Training Requirements of Information Technology Professionals

- Define Profile
- Assess Skills
- Design Training
- Deliver Training
- Test Knowledge
- Update Profile
- Use New Skills

College Credit Recommendation Program   The American Council on Education's CREDIT program recommends 53 Global Knowledge courses for college credit. Now our network training can help you earn your college degree while you learn the technical skills needed for your job. When you attend an ACE-certified Global Knowledge course and pass the associated exam, you earn college credit recommendations for that course. Global Knowledge can establish a transcript record for you with ACE, which you can use to gain credit at a college or as a written record of your professional training that you can attach to your resume.

Registration Information

COURSE FEE: The fee covers course tuition, refreshments, and all course materials. Any parking expenses that may be incurred are not included. Payment or government training form must be received six business days prior to the course date. We will also accept Visa/MasterCard and American Express. For non-U.S. credit card users, charges will be in U.S. funds and will be converted by your credit card company. Checks drawn on Canadian banks in Canadian funds are acceptable.

COURSE SCHEDULE: Registration is at 8:00 a.m. on the first day. The program begins at 8:30 a.m. and concludes at 4:30 p.m. each day.

CANCELLATION POLICY: Cancellation and full refund will be allowed if written cancellation is received in our office at least six business days prior to the course start date. Registrants who do not attend the course or do not cancel more than six business days in advance are responsible for the full registration fee; you may transfer to a later date provided the course fee has been paid in full. Substitutions may be made at any time. If Global Knowledge must cancel a course for any reason, liability is limited to the registration fee only.

GLOBAL KNOWLEDGE: Global Knowledge programs are developed and presented by industry professionals with "real-world" experience. Designed to help professionals meet today's interconnectivity and interoperability challenges, most of our programs feature hands-on labs that incorporate state-of-the-art communication components and equipment.

ON-SITE TEAM TRAINING: Bring Global Knowledge's powerful training programs to your company. At Global Knowledge, we will custom design courses to meet your specific network requirements. Call 1 (919) 461-8686 for more information.

YOUR GUARANTEE: Global Knowledge believes its courses offer the best possible training in this field. If during the first day you are not satisfied and wish to withdraw from the course, simply notify the instructor, return all course materials, and receive a 100% refund.

In the US:

CALL: 1 (888) 762-4442

FAX: 1 (919) 469-7070

VISIT OUR WEBSITE:

www.globalknowledge.com

MAIL CHECK AND THIS FORM TO:

Global Knowledge

Suite 200

114 Edinburgh South

P.O. Box 1187

Cary, NC 27512

In Canada:

CALL: 1 (800) 465-2226

FAX: 1 (613) 567-3899

VISIT OUR WEBSITE:

www.globalknowledge.com.ca

MAIL CHECK AND THIS FORM TO:

Global Knowledge

Suite 1601

393 University Ave.

Toronto, ON M5G 1E6

REGISTRATION INFORMATION:

Course title _____

Course location _____ Course date _____

Name/title _____ Company _____

Name/title _____ Company _____

Name/title _____ Company _____

Address _____ Telephone _____ Fax _____

City _____ State/Province _____ Zip/Postal Code _____

Credit card _____ Card # _____ Expiration date _____

Signature _____